AMERICA

C A N A D A

ROCKY MOUNTAINS

GREAT PLAINS

WASHINGTON
Puget Sound
Seattle
Olympia ✪
Spokane ●

OREGON
Portland ●
Salem ✪
Eugene ●
Columbia R.

CASCADE RANGE

Helena ✪
MONTANA
Billings ●
Missouri R.

IDAHO
Boise ✪
Snake R.

NORTH DAKOTA
Bismarck ✪
Fargo ●

SOUTH DAKOTA
Pierre ✪
Black Hills
Sioux Falls ●

WYOMING
Casper ●

CALIFORNIA
Sacramento ✪
Reno ●
Carson City ✪
San Francisco ●
SIERRA NEVADA
San Joaquin Valley

NEVADA
Great Salt Lake
Salt Lake City ●
UTAH
Grand Junction ●
Colorado R.

Cheyenne ✪
NEBRASKA
Lincoln ●

Denver ✪
COLORADO
Colorado Springs ●
Arkansas R.

KANSAS
Wichita ●

Las Vegas ●
Lake Mead
Death Valley
Mojave Desert
Grand Canyon

Los Angeles ●
San Diego ●

ARIZONA
Phoenix ●
Tucson ●

Santa Fe ✪
Albuquerque ●
NEW MEXICO

OKLAHOMA
Oklahoma City ✪

El Paso ●
Rio Grande
Pecos R.
Colorado R.
Brazos R.

Dallas ●
Ft. Worth ●
TEXAS
Austin ✪
San Antonio ●
Nueces R.

Corpus Christi ●

Brownsville ●

PACIFIC OCEAN

HAWAII
Kauai
Niihau
Oahu
Honolulu
Molokai
Lanai
Kahoolawe
Maui
PACIFIC OCEAN
Hilo
Hawaii

0 50 100 Miles
0 50 100 Kilometers

RUSSIA
Bering Strait
BEAUFORT SEA
Brooks Range

BERING SEA

Aleutian Islands

ALASKA
Fairbanks ●
Anchorage ●
Juneau ✪
Gulf of Alaska
Kodiak Island

CANADA

MEXICO

0 250 500 Miles
0 250 500 Kilometers

PACIFIC OCEAN

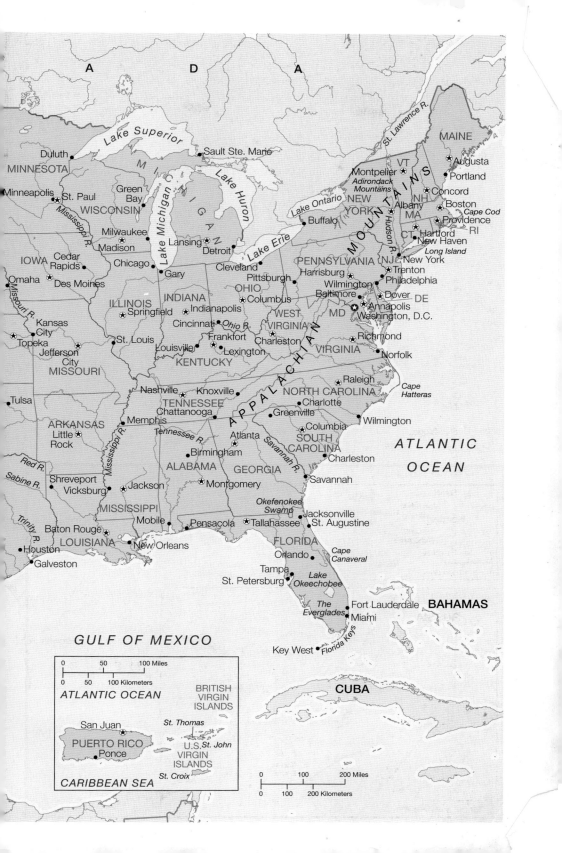

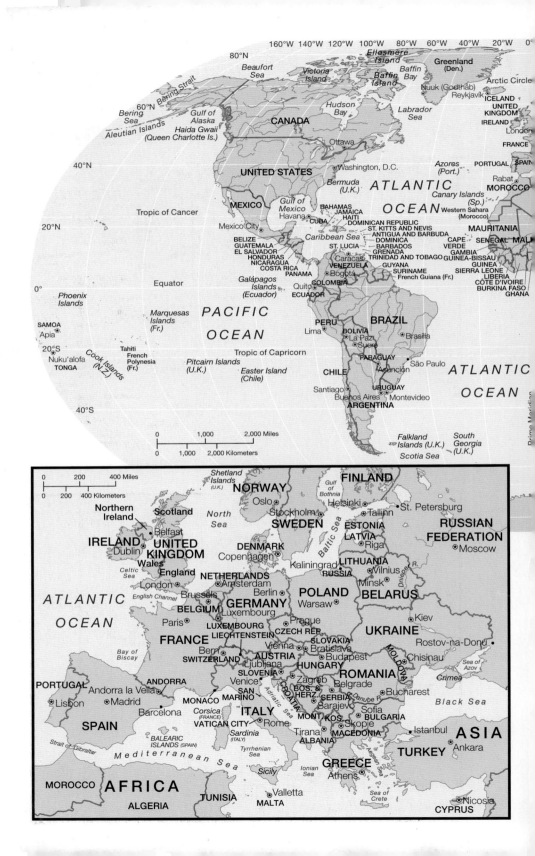

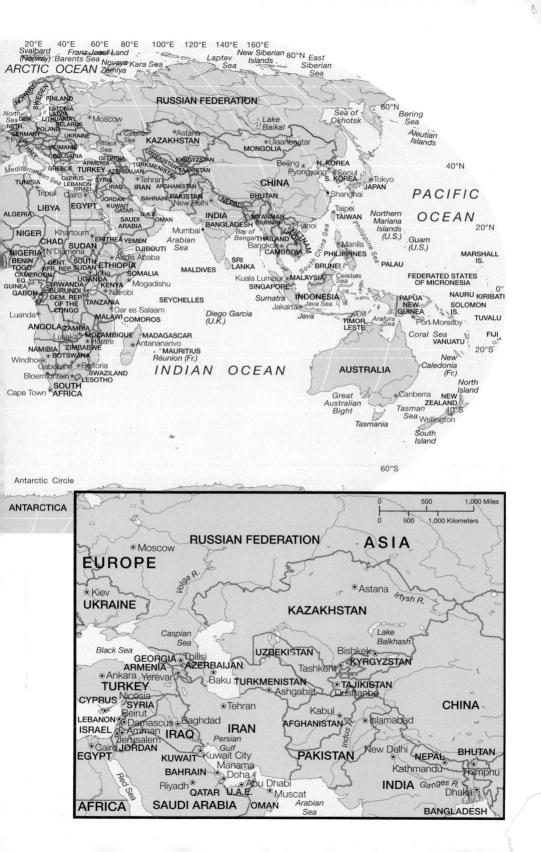

brief eleventh edition
VOLUME 1

AMERICA

A Narrative History

David Emory Shi

W. W. NORTON & COMPANY, INC.
New York • London

Editor: Jon Durbin
Associate Managing Editor: Melissa Atkin
Editorial Assistant: Lily Gellman
Managing Editor, College: Marian Johnson
Managing Editor, College Digital Media: Kim Yi
Production Managers: Ashley Horna and Benjamin Reynolds
Media Editor: Carson Russell
Media Project Editor: Rachel Mayer
Media Associate Editor: Sarah Rose Aquilina
Media Editorial Assistant: Alexandra Malakhoff
Marketing Manager, History: Sarah England Bartley
Design Director: Hope Goodell-Miller
Photo Editor: Travis Carr
Composition: SixRedMarbles / Jouve – Brattleboro, VT
Manufacturing: Transcontinental Interglobe

Permission to use copyrighted material is included on page A151.

The Library of Congress has cataloged the Full, One-Volume, Edition as follows:

Names: Shi, David Emory, author.
Title: America : a narrative history / David Emory Shi.
Description: Eleventh edition. | New York : W. W. Norton & Company, 2019. |
  Includes bibliographical references and index.
Identifiers: LCCN 2018046039 | ISBN 9780393689693 (hardcover : alk. paper)
Subjects: LCSH: United States—History—Textbooks.
Classification: LCC E178.1.T55 2019 | DDC 973—dc23 LC record available at
  https://lccn.loc.gov/2018046039

ISBN this edition: 978-0-393-66896-4

W. W. Norton & Company, Inc., 500 Fifth Avenue, New York, NY 10110-0017
wwnorton.com

W. W. Norton & Company Ltd., 15 Carlisle Street, London W1D 3BS
1 2 3 4 5 6 7 8 9 0

FOR
GEORGE B. TINDALL (1921–2006)
HISTORIAN, COLLEAGUE, FRIEND

CONTENTS

PART ONE A NOT-SO-"NEW" WORLD 1

1 The Collision of Cultures 4

2 England's Colonies 46

3 Colonial Ways of Life 94

MAPS

PREFACE

This Eleventh Edition of *America: A Narrative History* Brief Edition improves upon a textbook celebrated for its compelling narrative history of the American experience. Over the past thirty years, I have sought to write an engaging book centered on political and economic developments animated by colorful characters, informed by balanced analysis and social texture, and guided by the unfolding of key events. Those classic principles, combined with a handy size and low price, have helped make *America: A Narrative History* one of the most popular and well-respected textbooks in the field.

This Eleventh Brief Edition of *America* features important changes designed to make the text more teachable and classroom-friendly. The Eleventh Brief Edition is fifteen percent shorter than the Full Edition, and is a more affordable option for students. The overarching theme of the new edition is the importance of immigration to the American experience. Since 1776, the United States has taken in more people from more nations than any other country in the world. By welcoming newcomers, America has enriched its economy, diversified its people and culture, and testified to the appeal of a democracy committed to equal opportunity and equal treatment. Writer Vivian Gornick, the daughter of Russian Jewish immigrants, cherished the ethnic mosaic of her childhood New York City neighborhood: "The 'otherness' of the Italians or the Irish or the Jews among us lent spice and interest, a sense of definition, an exciting edge to things that was openly feared but secretly welcomed." At times, however, the nation's Open Door policy has also generated tension, criticism, prejudice, and even violence. Those concerned about immigration, past and present, have complained about open borders and called into question the nation's ability to serve as the world's "melting pot." The shifting attitudes and policies regarding immigration have testified to the continuing debate over the merits of newcomers. Immigration remains one of the nation's most cherished yet contested values, and as such it deserves fresh emphasis in textbooks and classrooms. While an introductory textbook must necessarily focus on major political, constitutional, diplomatic, economic, and social changes, it is also essential to convey how ordinary people managed everyday concerns—housing, jobs, food, recreation, religion, and entertainment—and surmounted exceptional challenges—depressions, wars, and racial injustice.

I have continued to enrich the political narrative by incorporating more social and cultural history into this new edition. The text has been updated to include the following key new discussions:

- **Chapter 1** "The Collision of Cultures" highlights President John F. Kennedy's emphasis on the United States as "a nation of immigrants," and revised assessments of Christopher Columbus's roles as colonial governor, ship captain, and slave trader.
- **Chapter 2** "England's Colonies" includes expanded coverage of the various factors that led Europeans to relocate to the American colonies, new discussion of the varied fates of British convicts and others who were sent involuntarily to America, the experience of indentured servants, and expanded focus on Chief Powhatan and his response to English colonists who were determined to "invade my people."
- **Chapter 3** "Colonial Ways of Life" features fresh insights into nativism and xenophobic sentiment toward German immigrants in the American colonies, including anti-immigrant comments from Benjamin Franklin in Pennsylvania; and discussion of the plight of immigrant women who worked in Virginia's textile factories.
- **Chapter 4** "From Colonies to States" includes new assessment of the small, but distinctive French immigration to North America before 1750; new focus on the massive surge in immigration and slave imports after the French and Indian War; and, new treatments of the first Revolutionary battles.
- **Chapter 5** "The American Revolution" features new discussion of the system of enslaved labor during the War of Independence, the discriminatory legal status of African Americans, and British characterizations of American colonies as the "land of the free and the land of the slave." There is also a profile of Thomas Jeremiah, a South Carolina "boatman" whom colonial authorities executed after he alerted enslaved blacks that British soldiers were coming to "help the poor Negroes." The chapter also includes a new photo depicting free black soldiers fighting in the Revolution.
- **Chapter 6** "Strengthening the New Nation" expands discussion of the delegates to the Constitutional Convention and their involvement with slavery, features debates over immigration in the new nation, offers new perspective on Alexander Hamilton's development as an

immigrant to the United States, and includes new photos of naturalization in 1790.

- **Chapter 7** "The Early Republic" includes expanded treatment of the Lewis and Clark expedition, of the strategic significance of the Louisiana Purchase, and the legacy of the War of 1812.
- **Chapter 8** "The Emergence of a Market Economy" includes new discussions on anti-Catholic and anti-Irish sentiments during the first half of the nineteenth century, the changing dynamics among immigrants of different nationalities, and the challenges immigrant workers faced in forming unions. New photos that depict symbols of organized labor have been added.
- **Chapter 9** "Nationalism and Sectionalism" features a revised profile of John Quincy Adams and fresh coverage of Henry Clay.
- **Chapter 10** "The Jacksonian Era" includes expanded coverage of Andrew Jackson's Indian Removal policy, the Deposit and Distribution Act, the Specie Circular, and the Eaton Affair.
- **Chapter 11** "The South, Slavery, and King Cotton" highlights the changing dynamics between slave labor and immigrant labor in the Old South and new coverage of sexual violence upon female slaves in the New Orleans slave trade and other regions.
- **Chapter 12** "Religion, Romanticism, and Reform" includes revised discussions of religious awakenings, Mormonism, and transcendentalism, with expanded focus on transcendentalist Henry David Thoreau and Christian revivalist Peter Cartwright. The chapter also features social developments in women's rights and the transition from gradualism to abolitionism among those opposed to slavery.
- **Chapter 13** "Western Expansion" includes a new biographical sketch of John A. Sutter, the Swiss settler who founded a colony of European emigrants in California and created a wilderness empire centered on the gold rush. There is also expanded content on Irish and German immigrants in the Saint Patrick's Battalion in the Mexican army. The chapter also reveals the development of John C. Calhoun's race-based ideology following the Texas Revolution and includes a new photograph of the Donner party.
- **Chapter 14** "The Gathering Storm" features new discussion of the California gold rush's impact on the Native American population, new biographical material on Presidents James Buchanan and Abraham Lincoln, and expanded coverage of the Lincoln-Douglas debates.
- **Chapter 15** "The War of the Union" discusses the substantial immigrant participation in the Civil War, features a new biographical sketch and

photo of Private Lyons Wakeman—a young woman who disguised herself as a man in order to fight in the Union army.

- **Chapter 16** "The Era of Reconstruction" explains changing immigration policy in the context of the Naturalization Act of 1870 and offers new treatments of Indian policies, Congressional Reconstruction, and the legacies of Reconstruction.
- **Chapter 17** "Business and Labor in the Industrial Era" includes broader discussion of immigrant women, the contributions of inventors like Croatian immigrant Nikola Tesla, the relationship between immigration—especially Chinese immigration—and the railroad boom beginning in the 1860s. There is fuller coverage of immigrants and the settlement house movement, union organizers such as Eugene Debs, and textile mill and factory strikers.
- **Chapter 18** "The New South and the New West" expands explanation of the spread of institutional racial segregation and the emergence of the southern tobacco industry after the Civil War.
- **Chapter 19** "Political Stalemate and Rural Revolt" includes new coverage of the unemployed protesters who marched in Coxey's Army protesting the recession of the late nineteenth century.
- **Chapter 20** "Seizing an American Empire" includes expanded content and a new photo regarding Japanese immigration to the United States.
- **Chapter 21** "The Progressive Era" features increased discussion of the social gospel movement and the women's suffrage movement, new biographical material on Presidents Taft, Roosevelt, and Wilson, and expanded focus on the racial biases of the Wilson administration.
- **Chapter 22** "America and the Great War" includes expanded coverage of immigrants, including Italian American Tony Monanco, who fought in World War I; new coverage of Woodrow Wilson's prosecution of immigrants who spread the poison of disloyalty during the war; nativism's ties to racism and eugenics; and increased discussion of the Palmer raids.
- **Chapter 23** "A Clash of Cultures" includes new discussion of flappers, the sexual revolution, and the new woman; revised treatments of Albert Einstein, scientific developments, and the impact of the radio; and, fresh insights into Ernest Hemingway and the "Lost Generation."
- **Chapter 24** "The Reactionary Twenties" expands discussion of reactionary conservatism and restrictive immigration policies; extends content on the revival of the Ku Klux Klan, prohibition, racial progressivism, and President Herbert Hoover's financial and social policies; and adds new coverage of the Johnson-Reed Act.

- **Chapter 25** "The New Deal" features expanded coverage of the New Deal's impact on women and Native Americans; there is new material on President Franklin Delano Roosevelt's relationship with his wife Eleanor Roosevelt.
- **Chapter 26** "The Second World War" includes expanded coverage of social and racial prejudice against African Americans and Japanese Americans; features a new discussion of army enlistment after the attack on Pearl Harbor; and a new set piece on the Battle of the Bulge.
- **Chapter 27** "The Cold War and the Fair Deal" includes discussion of the Immigration and Nationality (McCarran-Walter) Act of 1952 within the contexts of the Red Scare and McCarthyism.
- **Chapter 28** "America in the Fifties" highlights the emergence of a "car culture," expanded discussion of the communist politics of Cuba, and bolstered coverage regarding Elizabeth Eckford, the student who attempted to enter Little Rock High School in Arkansas after the desegregation of public schools.
- **Chapter 29** "A New Frontier and a Great Society" includes fresh coverage of the Immigration and Nationality Services Act of 1965, of the Logan Act regarding communication with foreign governments, and of U.S. Attorney General Robert Kennedy. It also features new set pieces highlighting the work of organizers Audre Lorde and Angela Davis, both of whom were involved with the Black Panther party.
- **Chapter 30** "Rebellion and Reaction" features new discussions on the founding of the United Farm Workers and the organizing efforts of Dolores Huerta and Cesar Chavez, including Chavez's twenty-five-day hunger strike in 1968 and the pathbreaking worker's rights negotiations with grape growers in the 1970s. It also includes a new set piece spotlighting feminist pioneer and *Ms.* magazine founder Gloria Steinem, and another covering clinical psychology professor Timothy Leary's crusade on behalf of psychedelic drugs.
- **Chapter 31** "Conservative Revival" includes expanded discussion of the Carter administration, new coverage of the Immigration Act of 1990, and revised treatment of George H. W. Bush's presidency.
- **Chapter 32** "Twenty-First-Century America" includes new coverage and photos of the Black Lives Matter movement, the 2016 election, and the Me Too movement. New Trump administration coverage includes the efforts to restrict immigration and movement (travel ban, family separation, and increased border security); the proposed ban of transgender service members; and Supreme Court appointments.

In addition, I have incorporated throughout this edition fresh insights from important new books and articles covering many significant topics. Whether you consider yourself a political, social, cultural, or economic historian, you'll find new material to consider and share with your students.

As part of making the new editions even more teachable and classroom friendly, the new Eleventh Edition of *America: A Narrative History* also makes history an immersive experience through its innovative pedagogy and digital resources. Norton InQuizitive for History—W. W. Norton's groundbreaking, formative, and adaptive new learning program—enables both students and instructors to assess learning progress at the individual and classroom level. The Norton Coursepack provides an array of support materials—free to instructors—who adopt the text for integration into their local learning-management system. The Norton Coursepack includes valuable assessment and skill-building activities like new primary source exercises, review quizzes, and interactive map resources. In addition, we've created new Chapter Overview videos that give students a visual introduction to the key themes and historical developments they will encounter in each chapter (see pages xxiv–xxviii for information about student and instructor resources).

MEDIA RESOURCES FOR INSTRUCTORS AND STUDENTS

America's new student resources are designed to develop more-discriminating readers, guiding students through the narrative while simultaneously developing their critical thinking and history skills.

The comprehensive ancillary package features a groundbreaking new formative and adaptive learning system, as well as innovative interactive resources, including maps and primary sources, all designed to help students master the Focus Questions in each chapter and continue to nurture their work as historians. W. W. Norton is unique in partnering to develop these resources exclusively with subject-matter experts who teach the course. As a result, instructors have all the course materials needed to manage their U.S. history survey class, whether they are teaching face-to-face, online, or in a hybrid setting.

NEW! HISTORY SKILLS TUTORIALS

With the Eleventh Edition we've expanded our digital resources to include a new series of tutorials to build students' critical analysis skills. The History Skills Tutorials combine video and interactive assessments to teach students how to analyze documents, images, and maps. By utilizing a three-step process, students learn a framework for analysis through videos featuring David Shi, and then are challenged to apply what they have learned through a series of interactive assessments. The History Skills Tutorials can be assigned at the beginning of the semester to prepare students for analysis of the sources in the textbook and beyond, or they can be integrated as remediation tools throughout the semester.

New! Chapter Overview Videos

New Chapter Overview Videos, featuring author David Shi, combine images and primary sources to provide visual introduction to the key themes and historical developments students will encounter in each chapter. These are in addition to the Author Videos in which David Shi explains essential developments and difficult concepts, with available closed captioning.

Norton InQuizitive for History

This groundbreaking formative, adaptive learning tool improves student understanding of the Focus Questions in each chapter. Students receive personalized quiz questions on the topics with which they need the most help. Questions range from vocabulary and concepts to interactive maps and primary sources that challenge students to begin developing the skills necessary to do the work of a historian. Engaging game-like elements motivate students as they learn. As a result, students come to class better prepared to participate in discussions and activities.

Student Site

Free and open to all students, the Student Site includes additional resources and tools.

- **Author Videos:** These segments include the NEW! Chapter Overview Videos and feature David Shi discussing essential developments and difficult concepts from the book.
- **Online Reader:** This resource offers a collection of primary source documents and images for use in assignments and activities.
- **iMaps:** Interactive maps allow students to view layers of information on each map with accompanying printable **Map Worksheets** for offline labeling.

NORTON EBOOKS

Norton Ebooks give students and instructors an enhanced reading experience at a fraction of the cost of a print textbook. Students are able to have an active reading experience and can take notes, bookmark, search, highlight, and even read offline. As an instructor, you can add your own notes for students to see as they read the text. Norton ebooks can be viewed on—and synced between—all computers and mobile devices. The ebook for the Eleventh Edition includes imbedded Author Videos, including the new Chapter Overview Videos; pop-up key term definitions; and enlargeable images and maps.

NORTON LMS RESOURCES

Easily add high quality Norton digital media to your online, hybrid, or lecture course—all at no cost. Norton Coursepacks work within your existing learning-management system; there's no new system to learn, and access is free and easy. Content is customizable and includes:

- **Author Videos:** These segments include the NEW! Chapter Overview Videos and illuminate key events, developments, and concepts in each chapter by bringing the narrative to life with additional context and anecdotes.
- **Primary Source Exercises:** These activities feature primary sources with multiple-choice and short-response questions to encourage close reading and analysis.
- **iMaps:** These interactive tools challenge students to better understand the nature of change over time by allowing them to explore the different layers of maps from the book. Follow-up map worksheets help build geography skills by allowing students to test their knowledge by labeling.
- **Review Quizzes:** Multiple-choice and true/false questions allow students to test their knowledge of the chapter content and then identify where they need to focus their attention to better understand difficult concepts.
- **Online Reader:** This resource includes about 1,000 additional primary sources (textual and visual). These are also available grouped by **Research Topic** for further investigation and writing assignments.
- **Flashcards:** This tool aligns key terms and events with brief descriptions and definitions.
- **Forum Prompts:** Three to five suggested topics per chapter offer additional opportunities for class discussion.

INSTRUCTOR'S MANUAL

The Instructor's Manual for *America: A Narrative History*, Eleventh Edition, is designed to help instructors prepare lectures. It contains chapter summaries; chapter outlines; lecture ideas; in-class activities; discussion questions; and a NEW! Quality Matters correlation guide.

TEST BANK

The Test Bank contains over 2,000 multiple-choice, true/false, and essay questions. The questions are aligned with the chapter's Focus Questions and classified according to level of difficulty, and Bloom's Taxonomy, offering multiple avenues for content and skill assessment. All Norton Test Banks are available with ExamView Test Generator software, allowing instructors to easily create, administer, and manage assessments.

CLASSROOM PRESENTATION TOOLS

- **Lecture PowerPoint Slides:** These ready-made presentations feature images and maps from the book as well as bullet points to encourage student comprehension and engagement.
- **Image Files:** All images and maps from the book are available separately in JPEG and PowerPoint format for instructor use.
- **Norton American History Digital Archive:** The archive includes over 1,700 images, audio and video files that are arranged chronologically and by theme.

PRIMARY SOURCE READERS TO ACCOMPANY AMERICA: A NARRATIVE HISTORY

- **NEW!** Seventh Edition of *For the Record: A Documentary History of America*, by David E. Shi and Holly A. Mayer (Duquesne University), is the perfect companion reader for *America: A Narrative History*. *For the Record* now features 268 primary-source readings from diaries, journals, newspaper articles, speeches, government documents, and novels, including several readings that highlight the substantially updated theme of immigration history in this new edition of *America*. If you haven't scanned *For the Record* in a while, now would be a good time to take a look.

- **Norton Mix: American History** enables instructors to build their own custom reader from a database of nearly 300 primary- and secondary-source selections. The custom readings can be packaged as a standalone reader or integrated with chapters from *America* into a custom textbook.

ACKNOWLEDGMENTS

This Eleventh Edition of *America: A Narrative History* has been a team effort. Several professors who have become specialists in teaching the introductory survey course helped create the Test Bank, instructor resources, and interactive media:

David Cameron, Lone Star College–University Park

Brian Cervantez, Tarrant County College–Northwest Campus

Manar Elkhaldi, University of Central Florida

Christina Gold, El Camino College

Maryellen Harman, North Central Missouri College

David Marsich, Germanna Community College

Lise Namikas, Baton Rouge Community College

Matthew Zembo, Hudson Valley Community College

The quality and range of the professorial reviews on this project were truly exceptional. The book and its accompanying media components were greatly influenced by the suggestions provided by the following instructors:

Milan Andrejevich, Ivy Tech College–South Bend

Carol A. Bielke, San Antonio Independent School District

April Birchfield, Asheville-Buncombe Technical Community College

Howard Bodner, Houston Community College

Matt Brent, Rappahannock Community College

Sharon J. Burnham, John Tyler Community College

Michael Collins, Texas State University

Scott Cook, Motlow State Community College

Carrie Coston, Blinn College

Nicholas P. Cox, Houston Community College

Tyler Craddock, J. Sargeant Reynolds Community College

Carl E. Creasman Jr., Valencia College

Stephen K. Davis, Texas State University

Frank De La O, Midland College

Jim Dudlo, Brookhaven College

Robert Glen Findley, Odessa College

Brandon Franke, Blinn College

Chad Garick, Jones County Junior College

Christopher Gerdes, Lone Star College–Kingwood and CyFair

Mark S. Goldman, Tallahassee Community College

Abbie Grubb, San Jacinto College–South Campus

Devethia Guillory, Lone Star College–North Harris

Jennifer Heth, Tarrant County College–South Campus

Justin Hoggard, Three Rivers College

Andrew G. Hollinger, Tarrant County College

David P. Hopkins Jr., Midland College

Justin Horton, Thomas Nelson Community College

Theresa R. Jach, Houston Community College

Robert Jason Kelly, Holmes Community College

Jennifer Lang, Delgado Community College

Nina McCune, Baton Rouge Community College

Richard Randall Moore, Metropolitan Community College–Longview

Ken S. Mueller, Ivy Tech College–Lafayette

Lise Namikas, Colorado State University–Global

Brice E. Olivier, Temple College

Candice Pulkowski, The Art Institutes

Shane Puryear, Lone Star College–Greenspoint and Victory Centers

Carey Roberts, Liberty University

John Schmitz, Northern Virginia Community College–Annandale

Greg Shealy, University of Wisconsin–Madison

Thomas Summerhill, Michigan State University

Christopher Thomas, J. Sargeant Reynolds Community College

Scott M. Williams, Weatherford College

Laura Matysek Wood, Tarrant County College–Northwest

Crystal R. M. Wright, North Central Texas College

As always, my colleagues at W. W. Norton shared with me their dedicated expertise and their poise amid tight deadlines, especially Jon Durbin, Melissa Atkin, Lily Gellman, Carson Russell, Sarah Rose Aquilina, Ben Reynolds, Sarah England Bartley, Hope Goodell Miller, Travis Carr, and Marne Evans. In addition, Jim Stewart, a patient friend and consummate editor, helped winnow my wordiness.

Finally, I have dedicated this Eleventh Edition of *America* to George B. Tindall, my friend and co-author who until his death in 2006 shared his wisdom, knowledge, wit, and humor with me. Although few of his words remain in this book, his spirit continues to animate its pages.

THE NORTON STORY

W. W. Norton & Company has been independent since its founding in 1923, when William Warder Norton and Mary D. Herter Norton first published lectures delivered at the People's Institute, the adult education division of New York City's Cooper Union. The firm soon expanded its program beyond the Institute, publishing books by celebrated academics from America and abroad. By midcentury, the two major pillars of Norton's publishing program—trade books and college texts—were firmly established. In the 1950s, the Norton family transferred control of the company to its employees, and today—with a staff of four hundred and a comparable number of trade, college, and professional titles published each year—W. W. Norton & Company stands as the largest and oldest publishing house owned wholly by its employees.

AMERICA

A NOT-SO- "NEW" WORLD

History is filled with ironies. Luck and accidents—the unexpected happenings of life—often shape events more than intentions do. Long before Christopher Columbus happened upon the Caribbean Sea in search of a westward passage to the Indies (east Asia), the native peoples he mislabeled "Indians" had occupied and transformed the lands of the Western Hemisphere (also called the Americas—North, Central, and South) for thousands of years. The "New World" was thus *new* only to the Europeans who began exploring, conquering, and exploiting the region at the end of the fifteenth century.

1

Over time, indigenous peoples had developed hundreds of strikingly different societies. Some were rooted in agriculture; others focused on trade or conquest. Many Native Americans (also called Amerindians) were healthier, better fed, and lived longer than Europeans, but when the two societies—European and Native American—collided, Amerindians were often exploited, infected, enslaved, displaced, and exterminated.

Yet the conventional story of invasion and occupation oversimplifies the process by which Indians, Europeans, and Africans interacted in the sixteenth and seventeenth centuries. Native Americans were more than passive victims of European power; they were also trading partners and military allies of the transatlantic newcomers. They became neighbors and advisers, religious converts and loving spouses. As such, they participated actively in the creation of the new society known as America.

The European colonists who risked their lives to settle in the Western Hemisphere were a diverse lot. They came from Spain, Portugal, France, the British Isles, the Netherlands (Holland), Scandinavia, Italy, and the German states. (Germany would not become a united nation until the mid–nineteenth century.) What they shared was a presumption that Christianity was superior to all religions and that all other peoples were inferior to them and their culture.

A variety of motives inspired Europeans to undertake the harrowing transatlantic voyage. Some were fortune seekers lusting for gold, silver, and spices. Others were eager to create kingdoms of God in the New World. Still others were adventurers, convicts, debtors, servants, landless peasants, and political or religious exiles. Most were simply seeking opportunities for a better life. A settler in Pennsylvania noted that workers "here get three times the wages for their labor than they can in England."

Yet such wages never attracted enough workers to keep up with the rapidly expanding colonial economies, so Europeans eventually turned to Africa for their labor needs in the New World. Beginning in 1503, European nations—especially Portugal and Spain—transported captive Africans to the Western Hemisphere. Throughout the sixteenth century, slaves were delivered to ports as far south as Chile to as far north as Canada. Thereafter, the English and Dutch joined the effort to exploit enslaved Africans. Few Europeans saw the contradiction between the promise of freedom in America for themselves and the institution of race-based slavery.

The intermingling of people, cultures, plants, animals, microbes, and diseases from the continents of Africa, Europe, and the Western Hemisphere gave colonial American society its distinctive vitality and variety. The shared quest for a better life gave America much of its drama—and conflict.

The Europeans unwittingly brought to the Americas a range of infectious diseases that would prove disastrous for the indigenous peoples—who had no natural immunities to them—and no knowledge of how to cope with them. As many as 90 percent of Native Americans would eventually die from European-borne diseases. Proportionally, it would be the worst human death toll in history.

At the same time, bitter rivalries among the Spanish, French, English, and Dutch triggered costly wars in Europe and around the world. Amid such conflicts, the monarchs of Europe struggled to manage often-unruly colonies, which, as it turned out, played crucial roles in their frequent wars.

Many of the colonists displayed a feisty independence, which led them to resent government interference in their affairs. A British official in North Carolina reported that the colonists were "without any Law or Order. Impudence is so very high, as to be past bearing."

The colonists and their British rulers maintained an uneasy partnership throughout the seventeenth century. As the royal authorities tightened their control during the mid–eighteenth century, however, they met resistance, which exploded into revolution.

1

The Collision of Cultures

De Soto and the Incas This 1596 color engraving shows Spanish conquistador Hernando de Soto's first encounter with King Atahualpa of the Inca Empire. Although artist Theodor de Bry never set foot in North America, his engravings helped shape European perceptions of Native Americans in the sixteenth century.

America was born in melting ice. Tens of thousands of years ago, during a period known as the Ice Age, immense glaciers some two miles thick inched southward from the Arctic Circle at the top of the globe. The advancing ice crushed hills, rerouted rivers, gouged out lakebeds and waterways, and scraped bare all the land in its path.

The glacial ice sheets covered much of North America—Canada, Alaska, the Upper Midwest, New England, Montana, and Washington. Then, as the continent's climate began to warm, the ice slowly started to melt, year after year, century after century. As the ice sheets receded, they opened pathways for the first immigrants to roam the continent.

Debate still rages about when and how humans first arrived in North America. Yet one thing is certain: the ancestors of *every* person living in the United States originally came from somewhere else. America is indeed "a nation of immigrants," a society of striving people attracted by a mythic new world promising new beginnings and a better life in a new place of unlimited space. Geography may be destiny, as the saying goes, but without pioneering people of determination and imagination, geography would have destroyed rather than sustained the first Americans.

Until recently, archaeologists had assumed that ancient peoples from northeast Asia began following herds of large game animals across the Bering Strait, a waterway that now connects the Arctic and Pacific Oceans. During the Ice Age, however, the Bering Strait was dry—a treeless, windswept, frigid tundra that connected eastern Siberia with Alaska.

The place with the oldest traces of human activity in the Bering region is Broken Mammoth, a 14,400-year-old site in central Alaska where the first

focus questions

1. Why were there so many diverse societies in the Americas before Europeans arrived?

2. What major developments in Europe enabled the Age of Exploration?

3. How did the Spanish conquer and colonize the Americas?

4. How did the Columbian Exchange between the "Old" and "New" Worlds affect both societies?

5. In what ways did the Spanish form of colonization shape North American history?

aboriginal peoples, called Paleo-Indians (Ancient Indians), arrived in North America. More recently, archaeologists in central Texas unearthed evidence of people dating back almost 16,000 years.

Over thousands of years, as the climate kept warming and the glaciers and ice sheets continued to melt, small nomadic groups fanned out from Alaska on foot or in boats and eventually spread across the Western Hemisphere, from the Arctic Circle to the southern tip of South America. The Paleo-Indians lived in transportable huts with wooden frames covered by animal skins or grasses ("thatch").

Paleo-Indians were skilled hunters and gatherers in search of game animals, whales, seals, fish, and wild plants, berries, nuts, roots, and seeds. As they moved southward, they trekked across prairies and plains, working in groups to track and kill massive animals unlike any found there today: mammoths, mastodons, giant sloths, camels, lions, saber-toothed tigers, cheetahs, and giant wolves, beavers, and bears.

Recent archaeological discoveries in North and South America, however, suggest that prehistoric humans may have arrived thousands of years earlier from various parts of Asia. Some may even have crossed the Pacific and Atlantic Oceans in boats from Polynesian islands in the southern Pacific or from southwestern Europe.

Regardless of when, where, or how humans first set foot in North America, the continent eventually became a dynamic crossroads for adventurous peoples from around the world, all bringing with them distinctive backgrounds, cultures, technologies, religions, and motivations that helped form the multicultural society known as America.

EARLY CULTURES IN AMERICA

Archaeologists have labeled the earliest humans in North America the *Clovis* peoples, named after a site in New Mexico where ancient hunters killed tusked woolly mammoths using "Clovis" stone spearheads. Over the centuries, as the climate warmed, days grew hotter and many of the largest mammals—mammoths, mastodons, and camels—grew extinct. Hunters then began stalking more-abundant mammals: deer, antelope, elk, moose, and caribou.

Over time, the Ancient Indians adapted to their diverse environments—coastal forests, grassy plains, southwestern deserts, eastern woodlands. Some continued to hunt with spears and, later, bows and arrows; others fished or trapped small game. Some gathered wild plants and herbs and collected acorns and seeds, while others farmed using stone hoes. Most did some of each.

By about 7000 B.C.E. (before the Common Era), Native American societies began transforming into farming cultures, supplemented by seasonal hunting and gathering. Agriculture provided reliable, nutritious food, which accelerated population growth and enabled once nomadic people to settle in villages. Indigenous peoples became expert at growing plants that would become the primary food crops of the hemisphere, chiefly **maize** (corn), beans, and squash, but also chili peppers, avocados, and pumpkins.

Maize-based societies viewed corn as the "gift of the gods" because it provided many essential needs. They made hominy by soaking dried kernels in a mixture of water and ashes and then cooking it. They used corn cobs for fuel and the husks to fashion mats, masks, and dolls. They also ground the kernels into cornmeal, which could be mixed with beans to make protein-rich succotash.

Mayan society A fresco depicting the social divisions of Mayan society. A Mayan high priest, at the center, is ceremonially dressed.

THE MAYANS, INCAS, AND MEXICA

Around 1500 B.C.E., farming towns appeared in what is now Mexico. Agriculture supported the development of sophisticated communities complete with gigantic temple-topped pyramids, palaces, and bridges in Middle America (*Mesoamerica*, what is now Mexico and Central America). The Mayans, who dominated Central America for more than 600 years, developed a written language and elaborate works of art. Mayan civilization featured sprawling cities, hierarchical government, terraced farms, and spectacular pyramids.

Yet in about A.D. 900, the Mayan culture collapsed. Why it disappeared remains a mystery, but a major factor was ecological. The Mayans destroyed much of the rain forest, upon whose fragile ecosystem they depended. As an archaeologist has explained, "Too many farmers grew too many crops on too much of the landscape." Widespread deforestation led to hillside erosion and a catastrophic loss of nutrient-rich farmland.

Overpopulation added to the strain on Mayan society, prompting civil wars. The Mayans eventually succumbed to the Toltecs, a warlike people who conquered most of the region in the tenth century. Around A.D. 1200, however, the Toltecs mysteriously withdrew after a series of droughts, fires, and invasions.

THE INCAS Much farther south, many diverse people speaking at least twenty different languages made up the sprawling Inca Empire. By the fifteenth century, the Incas' vast realm stretched 2,500 miles along the Andes Mountains in the western part of South America. It featured irrigated farms, stone buildings, and interconnected networks of roads made of stone.

THE MEXICA (AZTECS) During the twelfth century, the **Mexica** (Me-SHEE-ka)—whom Europeans later called Aztecs ("People from Aztlán," the place they claimed as their original homeland)—began drifting southward from northwest Mexico. Disciplined, determined, and aggressive, they eventually took control of central Mexico, where in 1325 they built the city of Tenochtitlán ("place of the stone cactus") on an island in Lake Tetzcoco, at the site of present-day Mexico City.

Tenochtitlán would become one of the grandest cities in the world. It served as the capital of a sophisticated **Aztec Empire** ruled by a powerful emperor and divided into two social classes: noble warriors and priests (about 5 percent of the population) and the free commoners—merchants, craftsmen, and farmers.

When the Spanish invaded Mexico in 1519, they found a vast Aztec Empire connected by a network of roads serving 371 city-states organized into

38 provinces. Towering stone temples, broad paved avenues, thriving market-places, and some 70,000 *adobe* (sunbaked mud) huts dominated Tenochtitlán. As the empire expanded across central and southern Mexico, the Aztecs developed elaborate societies supported by detailed legal systems and a complicated political structure. They advanced efficient new farming techniques, including terracing of fields, crop rotation, large-scale irrigation, and other engineering marvels. Their arts flourished, their architecture was magnificent. Their rulers were invested with godlike qualities, and nobles, priests, and warrior-heroes dominated the social order. The emperor's palace had 100 rooms and 100 baths replete with amazing statues, gardens, and a zoo; the aristocracy lived in large stone dwellings, practiced polygamy (multiple wives), and were exempt from manual labor.

Like most agricultural peoples, the Mexica were intensely spiritual and worshipped multiple gods. Their religious beliefs focused on the interconnection between nature and human life and the sacredness of natural elements—the sun, moon, stars, rain, mountains, rivers, and animals. They believed that the gods had sacrificed themselves to create the sun, moon, people, and maize. They were therefore obliged to feed the gods, especially Huitzilopochtli, the Lord of the Sun and War, with the vital energy provided by human hearts and blood. So the Mexica, like most Mesoamerican societies, regularly offered live human sacrifices.

Warfare was a sacred ritual for the Mexica, but it involved a peculiar sort of combat. Warriors fought with wooden swords—to wound rather than kill; they wanted live captives to sacrifice to the gods and to work as slaves. Gradually, the Mexica conquered many neighboring societies, forcing them to make payment of goods and labor as tribute to the empire.

In elaborate weekly rituals, captured warriors or virgin girls would be daubed with paint, given a hallucinatory drug, and marched up many steps to the temple platform, where priests cut out the victims' beating hearts and offered them to the sun god. The constant need for human sacrifices fed the Mexica's relentless warfare against other indigenous groups. A Mexica song celebrated their warrior code: "Proud of itself is the city of Mexico-Tenochtitlán. Here no one fears to die in war. This is our glory."

NORTH AMERICAN CIVILIZATIONS

North of Mexico, in the present-day United States, many indigenous societies blossomed in the early 1500s. Over the centuries, small kinship groups (*clans*) had joined together: first to form larger *bands* involving hundreds of people, which then evolved into much larger regional groups, or *tribes*, whose members spoke the same language. Although few had an alphabet or written language, the different societies developed rich oral traditions that passed on spiritual myths and social beliefs, especially those concerning the sacredness of nature, the necessity of communal living, and a deep respect for elders.

Like the Mexica, most indigenous peoples believed in many "spirits." To the Sioux, God was Wakan Tanka, the Great Spirit, who ruled over all spirits. The Navajo believed in the Holy People: Sky, Earth, Moon, Sun, Thunders, Winds, and Changing Woman. Many Native Americans believed in ghosts, who acted as their bodyguards in battle.

The importance of hunting to many Indian societies helped nurture a warrior ethic in which courage in combat was the highest virtue. War dances the night before a hunt or battle invited the spirits to unleash magical powers. Yet, Native American warfare mostly consisted of small-scale raids intended to enable individual warriors to demonstrate their courage rather than to seize territory or destroy villages. Casualties were minimal. Taking a few captives often signaled victory.

DIVERSE SOCIETIES

For all their similarities, the indigenous peoples of North America developed markedly different ways of life. In North America alone in 1492, when the first Europeans arrived, there were perhaps several million native peoples organized into 240 different societies speaking many different languages.

These Native Americans practiced diverse customs and religions, passed on distinctive cultural myths, and developed varied economies. Some wore clothes they had woven or made using animal skins, and still others wore nothing but colorful paint, tattoos, or jewelry. Some lived in stone houses, others in circular timber wigwams or bark-roofed longhouses. Still others lived in sod-covered or reed-thatched lodges, or in portable tipis made from animal skins. Some cultures built stone pyramids graced by ceremonial plazas, and others constructed huge burial or ritual mounds topped by temples.

Few North American Indians permitted absolute rulers. Tribes had chiefs, but the "power of the chiefs," reported an eighteenth-century British trader, "is an empty sound. They can only persuade or dissuade the people by the force of good-nature and clear reasoning." Likewise, Henry Timberlake, a British soldier, explained that the Cherokee government, "if I may call it a government, which has neither laws nor power to support it, is a mixed aristocracy and democracy, the chiefs being chosen according to their merit in war."

For Native Americans, exile from the group was the most feared punishment. They owned land in common rather than individually as private property, and they had well-defined social roles. Men were hunters, warriors, and leaders. Women tended children; made clothes, blankets, jewelry, and pottery; cured and dried animal skins; wove baskets; built and packed tipis; and grew, harvested, and cooked food. When the men were away hunting or fighting, women took charge of village life. Some Indian nations, like the Cherokee and Iroquois, gave women political power.

THE SOUTHWEST The arid (dry) Southwest (present-day Arizona, New Mexico, Nevada, and Utah) featured a landscape of high mesas, deep canyons, vast deserts, long rivers, and snow-covered mountains that hosted corn-growing societies. The Hopis, Zunis, and others still live in the multistory adobe cliff-side villages (called *pueblos* by the Spanish), which were erected by their ancient ancestors.

About 500 C.E. (Common Era), the Hohokam ("those who have vanished") people migrated from Mexico northward to southern and central Arizona, where they built extensive canals to irrigate crops. They also crafted decorative pottery and turquoise jewelry, and constructed *temple mounds* (earthen pyramids used for sacred ceremonies).

The most widespread and best known of the Southwest pueblo cultures were the Anasazi (Ancient Ones), or Basketmakers. Unlike the Aztecs and Incas, however, Anasazi society did *not* have a rigid class structure. The Anasazi engaged in warfare only as a means of self-defense, and the religious leaders and warriors worked much as the rest of the people did.

THE NORTHWEST Along the narrow coastal strip running up the heavily forested northwest Pacific coast, shellfish, salmon, seals, whales, deer, and edible wild plants were abundant. Here, there was little need to rely on farming. In fact, many of the Pacific Northwest peoples, such as the Haida, Kwakiutl, and Nootka, needed to work only two days to provide enough food for a week.

Such population density enabled the Pacific coast cultures to develop intricate religious rituals and sophisticated woodworking skills. They carved towering totem poles featuring decorative figures of animals and other symbolic characters. For shelter, they built large, earthen-floored, cedar-plank houses up to 500 feet long, where groups of families lived together. They also created sturdy, oceangoing canoes made of hollowed-out red cedar tree trunks—some large enough to carry fifty people. Socially, they were divided into slaves, commoners, and chiefs. Warfare was usually a means to acquire slaves.

THE GREAT PLAINS The many tribal nations living on the Great Plains, a vast, flat land of cold winters and hot summers west of the Mississippi River, included the Arapaho, Blackfeet, Cheyenne, Comanche, Crow,

Apache, and Sioux. As nomadic hunter-gatherers, they tracked herds of buffaloes (technically called bison) across a sea of grassland, collecting seeds, nuts, roots, and berries as they roamed.

At the center of most hunter-gatherer religions is the idea that the hunted animal is a willing sacrifice provided by the gods (spirits). To ensure a successful hunt, these nomadic peoples performed sacred rites of gratitude beforehand. Once a buffalo herd was spotted, the hunters would set fires to drive the stampeding animals over cliffs, often killing far more than they could harvest and consume.

THE MISSISSIPPIANS   East of the Great Plains, in the vast woodlands reaching from the Mississippi River to the Atlantic Ocean, several "mound-building" cultures prospered. Between 700 B.C.E. and 200 C.E., the Adena and later the Hopewell societies developed communities along rivers in the Ohio Valley. The Adena-Hopewell cultures grew corn, squash, beans, and sunflowers, as well as tobacco for smoking. They left behind enormous earthworks and elaborate **burial mounds** shaped like snakes, birds, and other animals, several of which were nearly a quarter mile long.

Like the Adena, the Hopewell developed an extensive trading network with other Indian societies from the Gulf of Mexico to Canada, exchanging

Great Serpent Mound More than 1,300 feet in length and three feet high, this snake-shaped burial mound in Adams County, Ohio, is the largest of its kind in the world.

exquisite carvings, metalwork, pearls, seashells, copper ornaments, bear claws, and jewelry. By the sixth century, however, the Hopewell culture disappeared, giving way to a new phase of development east of the Mississippi River, the *Mississippian* culture.

The Mississippians were corn-growing peoples who built substantial agricultural towns around central plazas and temples. They developed a far-flung trading network that extended to the Rocky Mountains, and their ability to grow large amounts of corn in the fertile flood plains spurred rapid population growth around regional centers.

CAHOKIA The largest of these advanced regional centers, called *chiefdoms*, was **Cahokia** (600–1300 C.E.), in southwest Illinois, near the confluence of the Mississippi and Missouri Rivers (across from what is now St. Louis). The Cahokians constructed an enormous farming settlement with monumental public buildings, spacious ceremonial plazas, and more than eighty flat-topped earthen mounds with thatch-roofed temples on top. The largest of the mounds, called Monks Mound, was ten stories tall, encompassed fourteen acres, and required 22 million cubic feet of soil. At the height of its influence, Cahokia hosted 15,000 people on some 3,200 acres, making it the largest city north of Mexico.

Cahokia, however, vanished around 1300 C.E., and its people dispersed. Its collapse remains a mystery, but the overcutting of trees to make fortress walls may have set in motion ecological changes that doomed the community when a massive earthquake struck. The loss of trees led to widespread flooding and the erosion of topsoil, which finally forced people to seek better lands. As Cahokia disappeared, its former residents took its advanced ways of life to other areas across the Midwest and into what is now the American South.

EASTERN WOODLANDS PEOPLES

After the collapse of Cahokia, the **Eastern Woodlands peoples** spread along the Atlantic Seaboard from Maine to Florida and along the Gulf coast to Louisiana. They included three regional groups distinguished by their different languages: the Algonquian, the Iroquoian, and the Muskogean. These were the indigenous societies that Europeans would first encounter when they arrived in North America.

THE ALGONQUIANS The Algonquian-speaking peoples stretched westward from the New England Seaboard to lands along the Great Lakes and into the Upper Midwest and south to New Jersey, Virginia, and the Carolinas.

Algonquian in war paint From the notebook of English settler John White, this sketch depicts a Native American chieftain.

They lived in small, round *wigwams* or in multifamily longhouses surrounded by a tall *palisade*, a timber fence to defend against attackers. Their villages typically ranged in size from 500 to 2,000 people.

The Algonquians along the Atlantic coast were skilled at fishing and gathering shellfish; the inland Algonquians excelled at hunting. They often traveled the region's waterways using canoes made of hollowed-out tree trunks (dugouts) or birch bark.

All Algonquians foraged for wild food (nuts, berries, and fruits) and practiced agriculture to some extent, regularly burning dense forests to improve soil fertility and provide grazing room for deer. To prepare their vegetable gardens, women broke up the ground with hoes tipped with sharp clamshells or the shoulder blades from deer. In the spring, they cultivated corn, beans, and squash.

THE IROQUOIANS West and south of the Algonquians were the powerful Iroquoian-speaking peoples (including the Seneca, Onondaga, Mohawk, Oneida, and Cayuga nations, as well as the Cherokee and Tuscarora), whose lands spread from upstate New York southward through Pennsylvania and into the upland regions of the Carolinas and Georgia. The Iroquois were farmer/hunters who lived in extended family groups (clans), sharing bark-covered longhouses in towns of 3,000 or more people. The oldest woman in each longhouse served as the "clan mother."

Unlike the Algonquian culture, in which men were dominant, women held the key leadership roles in the Iroquoian culture. As an Iroquois elder explained, "In our society, women are the center of all things. Nature, we believe, has given women the ability to create; therefore it is only natural that women be in positions of power to protect this function." A French priest who lived among the Iroquois for five years marveled that "nothing is more real than women's superiority. . . . It is they who really maintain the tribe."

Iroquois men and women operated in separate social domains. No woman could be a chief; no man could head a clan. Women selected the chiefs, controlled the distribution of property, supervised the slaves, and planted and harvested the crops. They also arranged marriages. After a wedding ceremony, the man moved in with the wife's family. In part, the Iroquoian matriarchy reflected the frequent absence of Iroquois men, who as skilled hunters and traders traveled extensively for long periods, requiring women to take charge of domestic life.

EASTERN WOODLANDS INDIANS The third major Native American group in the Eastern Woodlands included the peoples along the coast of the Gulf of Mexico who farmed and hunted and spoke the Muskogean language: the Creek, Choctaw, Chickasaw, Seminole, Natchez, Apalachee, and Timucua. Like the Iroquois, they were often matrilineal societies, meaning that ancestry flowed through the mother's line, but they had a more rigid class structure. The Muskogeans lived in towns arranged around a central plaza. Along the Gulf coast, many of their thatch-roofed houses had no walls because of the mild winters and hot, humid summers.

Over thousands of years, the native North Americans had displayed remarkable resilience, adapting to the uncertainties of frequent warfare, changing climate, and varying environments. They would display similar resilience against the challenges created by the arrival of Europeans.

EUROPEAN VISIONS OF AMERICA

The European exploration of the Western Hemisphere resulted from several key developments during the fifteenth century. Dramatic intellectual changes and scientific discoveries, along with sustained population growth, transformed religion, warfare, family life, and national economies. In addition, the resurgence of old vices—greed, conquest, exploitation, oppression, racism, and slavery—helped fuel European expansion abroad.

By the end of the fifteenth century, medieval feudalism's agrarian social system, in which peasant serfs worked for local nobles in exchange for living on and farming the land, began to disintegrate. People were no longer forced to remain in the same area and keep the same social status in which they were born. A new "middle class" of profit-hungry bankers, merchants, and investors emerged. They were committed to a more dynamic commercial economy fueled by innovations in banking, currency, accounting, and insurance.

The growing trade-based economy in Europe freed kings from their dependence on feudal nobles, enabling the monarchs to unify the scattered cities ruled by princes (principalities) into large kingdoms with stronger, more-centralized governments. The rise of towns, cities, and a merchant class provided new tax revenues. Over time, the new class of monarchs, merchants, and bankers displaced the landed nobility.

This process of centralizing political power was justified in part by claims that European kings ruled by divine right rather than by popular mandate: since God appointed them, only God, not the people, could hold them responsible for their actions.

THE RENAISSANCE At the same time, the rediscovery of ancient Greek and Roman writings about representative government (republics) spurred the *Renaissance* (rebirth), an intellectual revolution that transformed the arts as well as traditional attitudes toward religion and science. The Renaissance began in Italy and spread across western Europe, bringing with it a more *secular* outlook that took greater interest in humanity than in religion. Rather than emphasizing God's omnipotence, Renaissance *humanism* highlighted the power of inventive people to exert their command over nature.

The Renaissance was an essential force in the transition from medievalism to early modernism. From the fifteenth century on, educated people throughout Europe began to challenge prevailing beliefs as well as the absolute authority of rulers and churchmen. They discussed controversial new ideas, engaged in scientific research, and unleashed their artistic creativity. In the process, they fastened on a new phrase—"to discover"—which first appeared in 1553. Voyages of exploration became voyages of discovery.

The Renaissance also sparked the Age of Exploration. New knowledge and new technologies made possible the construction of larger sailing ships capable of oceanic voyages. The development of more accurate magnetic compasses, maps, and navigational instruments such as *astrolabes* and *quadrants* helped sailors determine their ship's location. The fifteenth and sixteenth centuries also brought the invention of gunpowder, cannons, and firearms—and the printing press.

THE RISE OF GLOBAL TRADE By 1500, trade between western European nations and the Middle East, Africa, and Asia was booming. The Portuguese took the lead, bolstered by crews of expert sailors and fast, three-masted ships called *caravels*. Portuguese ships roamed along the west coast of

Africa collecting grains, gold, ivory, spices, and slaves. Eventually, these mariners continued around Africa to the Indian Ocean in search of the fabled *Indies* (India and Southeast Asia). They ventured on to China and Japan, where they found spices (cinnamon, cloves, ginger, nutmeg, black pepper) to enliven bland European food, sugar made from cane to sweeten food and drink, silk cloth, herbal medicines, and other exotic goods.

Global trade was enabled by the emergence of four powerful nations in western Europe: England, France, Portugal, and, especially, Spain. The arranged marriage of King Ferdinand II of Aragon and Queen Isabella I of Castile in 1469 unified their two kingdoms into one formidable new nation, Spain. However, for years thereafter, it remained a loose confederation of separate kingdoms and jurisdictions, each with different cultural and linguistic traditions.

The new king and queen were eager to spread the Catholic faith. On January 1, 1492, after nearly eight centuries of warfare between Spanish Christians and Moorish Muslims on the Iberian Peninsula, Ferdinand and Isabella declared victory for Catholicism at Granada, the last Muslim stronghold in southern Spain. The monarchs then set about instituting a fifteenth-century version of ethnic cleansing. They gave practicing Muslims and Jews living in Spain and Portugal one choice: convert to Catholicism or leave.

The forced exile of Muslims and Jews was one of many factors that enabled Europe's global explorations at the end of the fifteenth century. Other factors—urbanization, world trade, the rise of centralized nations, advances in knowledge, technology, and firepower—all combined with natural human curiosity, greed, and religious zeal to spur efforts to find alternative routes to the Indies. More immediately, the decision of Chinese rulers to shut off the land routes to Asia in 1453 forced merchants to focus on seaborne options. For these reasons, Europeans set in motion the events that, as one historian has observed, would bind together "four continents, three races, and a great diversity of regional parts."

The Voyages of Columbus

Born in the Italian seaport of Genoa in 1451, the son of a woolen weaver, Christopher Columbus took to the sea at an early age, teaching himself geography, navigation, and Latin. By the 1480s, he was eager to spread Christianity across the globe and win glory and riches for himself.

The tall, red-haired Columbus spent a decade trying to convince European rulers to finance a western voyage across the Atlantic. England, France, Portugal, and Spain turned him down. Yet he persevered and eventually persuaded Ferdinand and Isabella to fund his voyage. The monarchs agreed to award him a one-tenth share of any riches he gathered; they would keep the rest.

COLUMBUS'S VOYAGES

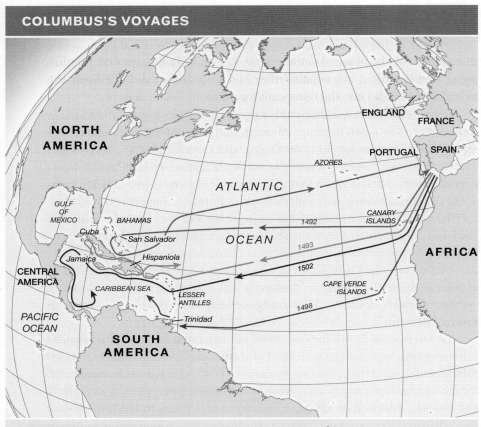

- How many voyages did Columbus make to the Americas?
- What is the origin of the name for the Caribbean Sea?
- What happened to the colony that Columbus left on Hispaniola in 1493?

CROSSING THE ATLANTIC On August 3, 1492, Columbus and a crew of ninety men and boys, mostly from Spain but from seven other nations as well, set sail on three tiny ships, the *Santa María*, the *Pinta*, and the *Niña*. They traveled first to Lisbon, Portugal, and then headed west to the Canary Islands, where they spent a month loading supplies and making repairs. On September 6, they headed west across the open sea, hoping desperately to sight the shore of east Asia. By early October, worried sailors rebelled at the "madness" of sailing blindly and forced Columbus to promise that they would turn back if land were not sighted within three days.

Then, on October 12, a sailor on watch atop the masthead yelled, "Tierra! Tierra!" ("Land! Land!"). He had spotted a small island in the Bahamas east of Florida that Columbus named San Salvador (Blessed Savior). Columbus mistakenly assumed that they must be near the Indies, so he called the native people "Indios" and named the surrounding islands the West Indies. At every encounter with the peaceful native people, known as Tainos, his first question, using sign language, was whether they had gold. If they did, the Spaniards seized it; if they did not, the Europeans forced them to search for it.

The Tainos, unable to understand or repel the strange visitors, offered gifts of food, water, spears, and parrots. Columbus described them as "well-built, with good bodies, and handsome features"—brown-skinned, with straight black hair. He marveled that they could "easily be made Christians" and "would make fine servants," boasting that "with fifty men we could subjugate them all and make them do whatever we want." He promised to bring six "natives" back to Spain for "his highnesses." Thus began the typical European bias toward the Indians: the belief that they were inferior peoples worthy of being exploited and enslaved.

EXPLORING THE CARIBBEAN   After leaving San Salvador, Columbus, excited by native stories of "rivers of gold" to the west, landed on the north shore of Cuba. He exclaimed that it was the "most beautiful land human eyes have ever beheld."

After a few weeks, Columbus sailed to the island he named Hispaniola ("the Spanish island"), present-day Haiti and the Dominican Republic. He described the island's indigenous people as the "best people in the world," full "of love and without greed." They had no weapons, wore no clothes, and led a simple life, cultivating cassava plants to make bread but spending most of their time relaxing, "seemingly without a care in the world."

Columbus decided that the Indians were "fitted to be ruled and be set to work" generating riches for Spain. He decreed that all Indians over age 14 must bring him at least a thimbleful of gold dust every three months. As it turned out, the quota was often unattainable—there was not as much gold in the Caribbean as Columbus imagined. Nevertheless, those who failed to supply enough gold had their hands cut off, causing many of them to bleed to death. If they fled, they were hunted down by dogs. Huge numbers died from overwork or disease. Others committed suicide. During fifty years of Spanish control, the Indians on Hispaniola virtually disappeared. In their place, the Spanish began importing enslaved Africans.

At the end of 1492, Columbus, still convinced he had reached an outer island of Japan, sailed back to Spain, taking a dozen Tainos as gifts for the king and queen. After receiving a hero's welcome, he promised Ferdinand and Isabella that his discoveries would provide them "as much gold as they need . . . and as many slaves as they ask."

Thanks to the newly invented printing press, news of Columbus's path-breaking voyage spread rapidly across Europe and helped spur a restless desire to explore the world. The Spanish monarchs told Columbus to prepare for a second voyage, instructing him to "treat the Indians very well and lovingly and abstain from doing them any injury." Columbus and his men would repeatedly defy this order.

Spain worked quickly to secure its legal claim to the Western Hemisphere. With the help of the Spanish-born pope, Alexander VI, Spain and Portugal signed the Treaty of Tordesillas (1494). It divided the non-Christian world, giving most of the Western Hemisphere to Spain, with Africa and what would become Brazil granted to Portugal. In practice, this meant that while Spain developed its American empire in the sixteenth century, Portugal provided it with most of its enslaved African laborers.

In 1493, Columbus returned to the New World, crossing the Atlantic with seventeen ships and 1,400 sailors, soldiers, and settlers—all men. Also on board were Catholic priests eager to convert the native peoples to Christianity. Upon his arrival back in Hispaniola, Columbus discovered that the forty men he had left behind had lost their senses, raping women, robbing villages, and, as his son later added, "committing a thousand excesses for which they were mortally hated by the Indians."

NAMING AMERICA   Columbus proved to be a much better ship captain than a colonizer and governor. His first business venture in the New World was as a slave trader. When he returned to Spain from his second voyage with hundreds of captive Indians, Queen Isabella, who detested slavery, was horrified. "Who is this Columbus who dares to give out my vassals [Indians] as slaves?"

This incident set in motion a series of investigations into Columbus's behavior. The queen sent a Spanish royal commissioner, Francis Bobadilla, to Hispaniola. The first things he saw were the corpses of six Spanish settlers hanging from a gallows; more colonists were to be hanged the next day. Bobadilla was so shocked that he canceled the executions and announced that he was supplanting Columbus as governor. When Columbus objected, Bobadilla had him jailed for two months before shipping the explorer, now nearly blind and crippled by arthritis, back to Spain in chains in 1500.

To the end of his life, in 1506, Columbus insisted that he had discovered the outlying parts of Asia. By one of history's greatest ironies, this led Europeans to name the New World not for Columbus but for another Italian sailor-explorer, Amerigo Vespucci.

In 1499, with the support of Portugal's monarchy, Vespucci sailed across the Atlantic, landing first at Brazil and then sailing along 3,000 miles of the South American coastline in search of a passage to Asia. In the end, Vespucci decided that South America was so large and so densely populated that it must be a *new* continent. In 1507, a German mapmaker paid tribute to Vespucci's navigational skills by labeling the New World using the feminine Latin variant of the explorer's first name: America.

PROFESSIONAL EXPLORERS News of the remarkable voyages of Columbus and Vespucci stimulated more expeditions. The first explorer to sight the North American continent was John Cabot, an Italian sponsored by King Henry VII of England. Cabot's landfall in 1497 at what the king called "the new founde lande," in present-day Canada, gave England the basis for a later claim to *all* of North America. On a return voyage, however, Cabot and his four ships disappeared.

The English were actually unaware that Norsemen ("Vikings") from Scandinavia (Denmark, Norway, Sweden) had been the first Europeans to "discover" and colonize areas of North America. As early as the tenth century, Norsemen had landed on the rocky, fogbound shore of Greenland, a large island off the northeast coast of North America, and established farming settlements that had lasted hundreds of years before disappearing after prolonged cold weather forced them back to Scandinavia.

RELIGIOUS CONFLICT IN EUROPE

While explorers were crossing the Atlantic, powerful religious conflicts were tearing Europe apart in ways that would shape developments in the Western Hemisphere. When Columbus sailed west in 1492, all of Europe acknowledged the thousand-year-old supremacy of the Roman Catholic Church and its pope in Rome. The pope led a huge religious empire, and the Catholics were eager to spread their faith around the world.

The often brutal efforts of the Spanish to convert native peoples in the Western Hemisphere to **Roman Catholicism** illustrated the murderous intensity with which European Christians embraced religious life in the sixteenth century. Spiritual concerns inspired, comforted, and united them. People fervently believed in heaven and hell, demons and angels, magic and miracles. And they were willing to kill and die for their religious beliefs.

Martin Luther A theologian and critic of the Catholic Church, Luther is best remembered for his ninety-five "theses," an incendiary document that served as a catalyst for the Protestant revolution.

MARTIN LUTHER

The enforced unity of Catholic Europe began to crack on October 31, 1517, when an obscure, thirty-three-year-old German monk who taught at the University of Wittenberg in the German state of Saxony, sent his ninety-five "theses" on the "corrupt" Catholic Church to church officials. Little did Martin Luther (1483–1546) know that his defiant stance and explosive charges would ignite history's fiercest spiritual drama, the **Protestant Reformation**, or that his controversial ideas would forever change the Christian world and plunge Europe into decades of religious strife.

Luther was a spiritual revolutionary who fractured Christianity by undermining the authority of the Catholic Church. He called the pope "the greatest thief and robber that has appeared or can appear on earth" who had subjected the Christian family to levels of "satanic" abuse. Luther especially criticized the widespread sale of *indulgences,* whereby priests would forgive sins in exchange for money. The Catholic Church had made a profitable business out of forgiving sins, using the revenue from indulgences to raise huge armies and build lavish cathedrals. Luther condemned indulgences as a crass form of thievery. He insisted that God alone, through the grace and mercy of Christ, offered salvation; people could not purchase it from church officials. As Luther exclaimed, "By faith alone are you saved!" To him, the Bible was the sole source of Christian truth; believers had no need for the "den of murderers"—Catholic priests, bishops, and popes.

Through this simple but revolutionary doctrine of "Protestantism," Luther sought to revitalize Christianity's original faith and spirituality. The common people, he declared, represented a "priesthood of all believers." Individuals could seek their own salvation. "All Christians are priests," he said; they "have the power to test and judge what is correct or incorrect in matters of faith" by themselves. Luther went on to produce the first Bible in a German translation so that everyone—male or female, rich or poor—could read it.

Luther's rebellion spread quickly across Europe thanks to the circulation of thousands of inexpensive pamphlets, which served as the social media of the time. Without the new printing presses, there may not have been a Protestant Reformation.

Lutheranism began as an intense religious movement, but it soon developed profound social and political implications. By proclaiming that "all" are equal before God, Protestants disrupted traditional notions of wealth, class, and monarchical supremacy. Their desire to practice a faith independent of papal or government interference contributed to the ideal of limited government. By the end of the sixteenth century, King James VI of Scotland grew nervous that his Protestant subjects were plotting to install a "democratic form of government."

THE CATHOLIC REACTION What came to be called Lutheranism quickly found enthusiastic followers, especially in the German-speaking states. In Rome, however, Pope Leo X lashed out at Luther's "dangerous doctrines," calling him "a leper with a brain of brass and a nose of iron."

Luther, aware that his life was at stake, fought back, declaring that he was "born to war" and refusing to abide by any papal decrees: "I will recant nothing!" The "die is cast, and I will have no reconciliation with the Pope for all eternity." When the pope expelled Luther from the Catholic Church in 1521 and the Holy Roman emperor sentenced him to death, civil war erupted throughout the German principalities. A powerful prince protected Luther from the church's wrath by hiding him in his castle.

Luther's conflict with the pope plunged Europe into decades of religious warfare during which both sides sought to eliminate dissent by torturing and burning at the stake those called "heretics." A settlement between Lutherans and Catholics did not come until 1555, when the Treaty of Augsburg allowed each German prince to determine the religion of his subjects. For a while, they got away with such dictatorial policies, for most people still deferred to ruling princes. Most of the northern German states, along with Scandinavia, became Lutheran.

JOHN CALVIN

If Martin Luther was the lightning that sparked the Reformation, John Calvin provided the thunder. Soon after Luther began his revolt against Catholicism, Swiss Protestants also challenged papal authority. In Geneva, a city of 16,000 people, the movement looked to John Calvin (1509–1564), a brilliant French theologian and preacher who had fled from Catholic France to Geneva at age twenty-seven and quickly brought it under the sway of his powerful beliefs.

Calvin deepened and broadened the Reformation that Luther initiated by developing a strict way of life for Protestants to follow. His chief contribution was his emphasis upon humanity's inherent sinfulness and utter helplessness before an awesome and all-powerful God who had predetermined who would be saved and who would be left to eternal damnation, regardless of their behavior.

Calvin and Luther were the twin pillars of early Protestantism, but whereas Luther was a volatile personality who loved controversy and debate, Calvin was a cool, calculating, analytical theorist who sought to create a Protestant absolutism rigidly devoid of all remnants of Catholicism. Under his leadership, Geneva became a theocracy in which believers sought to convince themselves and others that God had chosen them for salvation.

Calvin came to rule Geneva with uncompromising conviction. He summoned the citizenry to swear allegiance to a twenty-one-article confession of religious faith. No citizen could be outside the authority of the church, and Calvin viewed himself as God's appointed judge and jury. No aspect of life in Geneva escaped his strict control. Dancing, card-playing, and theatergoing were outlawed. Censorship was enforced, and informers were recruited to report wrongdoing. Visitors staying at inns had to say a prayer before dining. Everyone was required to attend church and to be in bed by nine o'clock. Even joking was outlawed.

Calvin urged that some thirty "witches" in Geneva be burned, drowned, or hanged for supposedly causing an epidemic. Overall, he had fifty-eight people put to death. Calvin also banished scores of people who fell short of his demanding standards, including members of his extended family. He exiled his sister-in-law for adultery and ordered his stepdaughter jailed for fornication. "I have found it to be true," observed a witty Genevan, "that men who know what is best for society are unable to cope with their families."

CALVINISM For all of its harshness, Calvinism as embodied in Geneva spread like wildfire across France, Scotland, and the Netherlands. It even penetrated Lutheran Germany. Calvinism formed the basis for the German Reformed Church, the Dutch Reformed Church, the Presbyterians in Scotland, and the Huguenots in France, and it prepared the way for many forms of American Protestantism. Like Luther, Calvin argued that Christians did not need popes or kings, archbishops, and bishops to dictate their search for salvation; each congregation should elect its own elders and ministers to guide their worship and nurture their faith.

Over time, Calvin exerted a greater effect upon religious belief and practice in the English colonies than did any other leader of the Reformation. His emphasis on humankind's essential depravity, his concept of predestination, his support for the primacy and autonomy of each congregation, and his belief in the necessity of theocratic government formed the ideological foundation for Puritan New England.

THE COUNTER-REFORMATION The Catholic Church furiously resisted the emergence of new "protestant" faiths by launching a "Counter-Reformation" that reaffirmed basic Catholic beliefs while addressing some of the concerns about priestly abuses raised by Luther, Calvin, and others. In Spain, the monarchy established an "Inquisition" to root out Protestants and heretics. In 1534, a Spanish soldier, Ignatius de Loyola, organized the Society of Jesus, a militant monastic order created to revitalize Catholicism. Its members, the black-robed Jesuits, fanned out across Europe and the Americas as missionaries and teachers.

Throughout the sixteenth and seventeenth centuries, Catholics and Protestants persecuted, imprisoned, tortured, and killed each other. Every major international conflict in early modern Europe became, to some extent, a religious holy war between Catholic and Protestant nations.

THE REFORMATION IN ENGLAND In England, the Reformation followed a unique course. The Church of England (the Anglican Church) emerged through a gradual process of integrating Calvinism with English Catholicism. In early modern England, the Catholic church and the national government were united and mutually supportive. The monarchy required people to attend religious services and to pay taxes to support the church. The English rulers also supervised the church officials: two archbishops, twenty-six bishops, and thousands of parish clergy, who were often instructed to preach sermons in support of government policies. As one English king explained, "People are governed by the pulpit more than the sword in time of peace."

KING HENRY VIII The English Reformation originated because of purely political reasons. King Henry VIII, who ruled between 1509 and 1547, had won from the pope the title Defender of the Faith for initially refuting Martin Luther's rebellious ideas. But Henry turned against the Catholic Church over the issue of divorce. His marriage to Catherine of Aragon, his elder brother's widow and the youngest daughter of the Spanish monarchs Ferdinand and Isabella, had produced a girl, Mary, but no boy. Henry's obsession for a male heir convinced him that he needed a new wife, and he had grown smitten with another woman, sharp-witted Anne Boleyn. But first he had to convince the pope to annul, or cancel, his twenty-four-year marriage to Catherine, who rebelled against her husband's plan. She had a powerful ally in her nephew, Charles V, king of Spain and ruler of the Holy Roman Empire, whose armies were in control of the church in Rome.

The pope refused to grant an annulment—in part because Charles V had placed him under arrest to encourage him to make the right decision. In 1533, Henry VIII responded by severing England's nearly 900-year connection with the Catholic Church. The archbishop of Canterbury then granted the annulment, thus freeing Henry to marry his mistress, the pregnant Anne Boleyn. The pope then excommunicated Henry from the Catholic Church, whereupon Parliament passed an Act of Supremacy declaring that the king, not the pope, was head of the Church of England. Henry quickly banned all Catholic "idols," required Bibles to be published in English rather than Latin, and confiscated the vast land holdings of the Catholic Church across England.

In one of history's greatest ironies, Anne Boleyn gave birth not to a male heir but to a daughter named Elizabeth. The disappointed king refused to attend the baby's christening. Instead, he accused Anne of adultery and had her beheaded, and he declared the infant Elizabeth a bastard. (He would marry four more times.) Elizabeth, however, would grow up to be a nimble, cunning, and courageous queen.

THE REIGN OF ELIZABETH In 1547, Henry VIII died and was succeeded by nine-year-old Edward VI, his son by his third wife, Jane Seymour. Edward approved efforts to further "reform" the Church of England. Priests were allowed to marry, church services were conducted in English rather than Latin, and new articles of faith were drafted and published.

When Edward grew gravely ill in 1553, he declared that his cousin, Lady Jane Grey, should succeed him, but nine days after his death, his Catholic half-sister, Mary, led an army that deposed Lady Jane and later ordered her beheaded. The following year, Queen Mary shocked many by marrying Philip, the Holy Roman emperor and king of Spain. With his blessing, she restored Catholic supremacy in England, ordering hundreds of Protestants burned at the stake and others exiled.

"Bloody Mary" died in 1558, and her Protestant half-sister, Henry VIII's daughter Elizabeth, ascended the throne at the age of twenty-five. Over the next forty-five years, despite political turmoil, religious strife, economic crises, and foreign wars, Elizabeth proved to be one of the greatest rulers in history. During her long reign, the Church of England again became Protestant, while retaining much of the tone and texture of Catholicism.

THE SPANISH EMPIRE

Throughout the sixteenth century, Spain struggled to manage its colonial empire while trying to repress the Protestant Reformation. Between 1500 and 1650, some 450,000 Spaniards, 75 percent of them poor, single, unskilled men, made their way to the Western Hemisphere. During that time, Spain's colonies in the Western Hemisphere shipped some 200 tons of gold and 16,000 tons of silver to Spain. By plundering, conquering, and colonizing the Americas and converting and enslaving its inhabitants, the Spanish planted Christianity in the Western Hemisphere and gained the financial resources to rule the world.

SPAIN IN THE CARIBBEAN The Caribbean Sea served as the gateway through which Spain entered the Americas. After establishing a trading post on Hispaniola, the Spanish proceeded to colonize Puerto Rico (1508), Jamaica (1509), and Cuba (1511–1514). Their motives, as one soldier explained, were simple: "To serve God and the king, and also to get rich." As their New World colonies grew more numerous, the monarchy created an administrative structure to govern them and a name to encompass them: New Spain.

A CLASH OF CULTURES

The often-violent encounters between Spaniards and Native Americans involved more than a clash of cultures. They involved contrasting forms of technological development. The Indians of Mexico used wooden canoes for water transportation, while the Europeans traveled in much larger, heavily armed sailing vessels. The Spanish ships also carried warhorses and fighting dogs, long steel swords, crossbows, firearms, gunpowder, and armor. "The most essential thing in new lands is horses," reported one Spanish soldier. "They instill the greatest fear in the enemy and make the Indians respect the leaders of the army."

CORTÉS'S CONQUEST The most dramatic European conquest of a major Indian civilization occurred in Mexico. On February 18, 1519, Hernán Cortés, a Spanish soldier of fortune who went to the New World "to get rich, not to till the soil like a peasant," sold his Cuban lands to buy ships and supplies, then set sail for Mexico.

Cortés's fleet of eleven ships carried nearly 600 soldiers and sailors. Also on board were 200 indigenous Cuban laborers, sixteen warhorses, greyhound fighting dogs, and cannons. The Spanish first stopped on the Yucatan Peninsula, where they defeated a group of Mayans. The vanquished chieftain gave Cortés twenty young women. Cortés distributed them to his captains but kept one of the girls ("La Malinche") for himself and gave her the name of Doña

Cortés in Mexico Page from the *Lienzo de Tlaxcala*, a historical narrative from the sixteenth century. The scene, in which Cortés is shown seated on a throne, depicts the arrival of the Spanish in Mexico.

Marina. Malinche spoke Mayan as well as Nahuatl, the language of the Aztecs, with whom she had previously lived. She became Cortés's interpreter—and his mistress; she would later bear the married Cortés a son.

After leaving Yucatan, Cortés and his ships sailed west and landed at a place he named Veracruz ("True Cross"), where they convinced the local Totomacs to join his assault against their hated rivals, the Mexica (Aztecs). To prevent his soldiers, called *conquistadores* (conquerors), from deserting, Cortés had the ships scuttled, sparing only one vessel to carry the expected gold back to Spain.

With his small army and Indian allies, Cortés brashly set out to conquer the extensive Mexica Empire, which extended from central Mexico to what is today Guatemala. The army's nearly 200-mile march through the mountains to the Mexica capital of Tenochtitlán (modern Mexico City) took almost three months.

SPANISH INVADERS As Cortés and his army marched across Mexico, they heard fabulous stories about Tenochtitlán. With some 200,000 inhabitants scattered among twenty neighborhoods, it was one of the largest cities in the world. Laid out in a grid pattern on an island in a shallow lake, divided by long cobblestone avenues, crisscrossed by canals, connected to the mainland by wide causeways, and graced by formidable stone pyramids, the city and its massive buildings seemed impregnable.

Through a combination of threats and deceptions, the Spanish entered Tenochtitlán peacefully. The emperor, Montezuma II, a renowned warrior who had ruled since 1502, mistook Cortés for the exiled god of the wind and sky, Quetzalcoatl, come to reclaim his lands. Montezuma gave the Spaniards a lavish welcome, housing them close to the palace and exchanging gifts of gold and women.

Within a week, however, Cortés executed a palace coup, taking Montezuma hostage while outwardly permitting him to continue to rule. Cortés ordered many religious statues destroyed and coerced Montezuma to end the ritual sacrifices of slaves.

In the spring of 1520, disgruntled Mexica priests orchestrated a rebellion after deciding that Montezuma was a traitor. According to Spanish accounts, the Mexica stoned the emperor to death; more recently, scholars argue that the Spanish did the deed. One account says that they poured molten gold down Montezuma's throat. Whatever the cause of the emperor's death, the Spaniards were forced to retreat from the capital city.

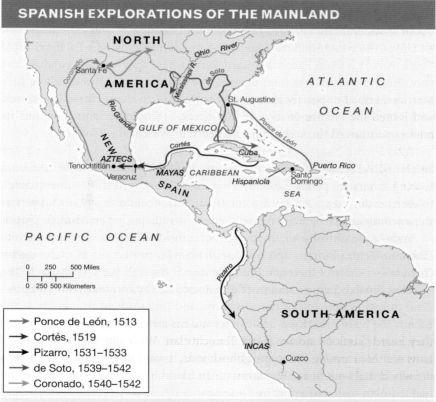

SPANISH EXPLORATIONS OF THE MAINLAND

- What were the Spanish conquistadores' goals for exploring the Americas?
- How did Cortés conquer the Mexica?
- Why did the Spanish first explore North America, and why did they establish St. Augustine, the first European settlement in what would become the United States?

Cortés, however, was undaunted. His many Indian allies remained loyal, and the Spaniards gained reinforcements from Cuba. They then laid siege to Tenochtitlán for eighty-five days, cutting off its access to water and food, and allowing a smallpox epidemic to devastate the inhabitants.

After three months, the siege came to a bloody end in August 1521. The ravages of smallpox and the support of thousands of anti-Mexica Indians help explain how such a small force of Spaniards vanquished a proud nation with millions of people. A conquistador remembered that as he entered the capital city after its surrender, the streets "were so filled with sick and dead people that our men walked over nothing but bodies.

Cortés became the first Governor General of "New Spain" and quickly began replacing the Mexica leaders with Spanish bureaucrats and church officials. He ordered that a grand Catholic cathedral be built from the stones of Montezuma's destroyed palace.

In 1531, Francisco Pizarro mimicked the conquest of Mexico when he led a band of 168 conquistadores and sixty-seven horses down the Pacific coast of South America from Panama toward Peru, where they brutally subdued the Inca Empire and its 5 million people. The Spanish killed thousands of Inca warriors, seized imperial palaces, took royal women as mistresses and wives, and looted the empire of its gold and silver. From Peru, Spain extended its control southward through Chile and north to present-day Colombia.

NEW SPAIN As the sixteenth century unfolded, the Spanish shifted from looting the native peoples to enslaving them. To reward the conquistadores, Spain transferred to America a medieval socioeconomic system known as the *encomienda*, whereby favored soldiers or officials received huge parcels of land—and control over the people who lived there. The Spanish were to Christianize the Indians and provide them with protection in exchange for "tribute"—a share of their goods and labor.

New Spain became a society of extremes: wealthy *encomenderos* and powerful priests at one end of the spectrum, and Indians held in poverty at the other. The Spaniards used brute force to ensure that the Indians accepted their role as serfs. Nuño de Guzman, a governor of a Mexican province, loved to watch his massive fighting dog tear apart rebellious Indians. But he was equally brutal with Spanish colonists. After a Spaniard talked back to him, he had the man nailed to a post by his tongue.

A CATHOLIC EMPIRE The Spanish launched a massive effort to convert the Indians into Catholic servants. During the sixteenth century, hundreds of priests fanned out across New Spain.

Most of the missionaries decided that the Indians could be converted only by force. "Though they seem to be a simple people," a priest declared in 1562, "they are up to all sorts of mischief, and without compulsion, they will never speak the [religious] truth." By the end of the sixteenth century, there were more than 300 monasteries or missions in New Spain, and Catholicism had become a major instrument of Spanish imperialism.

Some officials criticized the forced conversion of Indians and the *encomienda* system. A Catholic priest, Bartolomé de Las Casas, observed with horror the treatment of Indians by Spanish settlers in Hispaniola and Cuba. To ensure obedience, they tortured, burned, and cut off the hands and noses of the native peoples. Las Casas resolved in 1514 to spend the rest of his life aiding the Indians, and he began urging the Spanish to change their approach.

Las Casas spent the next fifty years advocating better treatment for indigenous people, earning the title "Protector of the Indians." He urged that the Indians be converted to Catholicism only through "peaceful and reasonable" means, and he eventually convinced the monarchy and the Catholic Church to issue new rules calling for better treatment of the Indians. Still, the use of "fire and the sword" continued, and angry colonists on Hispaniola banished Las Casas from the island. In 1564, two years before his death, he bleakly predicted that "God will wreak his fury and anger against Spain some day for the unjust wars waged against the Indians."

THE COLUMBIAN EXCHANGE

The first European contacts with the Western Hemisphere began the **Columbian Exchange**, a worldwide transfer of plants, animals, and diseases, which ultimately worked in favor of the Europeans at the expense of the indigenous peoples.

The plants and animals of the two worlds differed more than the peoples and their ways of life. Europeans had never encountered iguanas, buffaloes, cougars, armadillos, opossums, sloths, tapirs, anacondas, rattlesnakes, catfish, condors, or hummingbirds. Nor had the Native Americans seen the horses, cattle, pigs, sheep, goats, chickens, and rats that soon flooded the Americas.

THE EXCHANGE OF PLANTS AND FOODS The exchange of plant life between the Western Hemisphere and Europe/Africa transformed the diets of both regions. Before Columbus's voyage, Europeans had no knowledge of maize (corn), potatoes (sweet and white), or many kinds of beans (snap, kidney, lima). Other Western Hemisphere food plants included peanuts, squash, peppers, tomatoes, pumpkins, pineapples, avocados, cacao (the source of chocolate), and chicle (for chewing gum). Europeans in turn introduced rice, wheat, barley, oats, grapevines, and sugarcane to the Americas. The new crops changed diets and spurred a dramatic increase in the European population, which in turn helped provide the restless, adventurous young people who would colonize the New World.

AN EXCHANGE OF DISEASES The most significant aspect of the Columbian Exchange was, by far, the transmission of **infectious diseases**. During the three centuries after Columbus's first voyage, Europeans and enslaved Africans brought deadly diseases that Native Americans had never encountered: smallpox, typhus, malaria, mumps, chickenpox, and measles. The results were catastrophic. By 1568, just seventy-five years after Columbus's first voyage, infectious diseases had killed 80 to 90 percent of the Indian population—the greatest loss of human life in history.

Smallpox was an especially ghastly killer. In central Mexico alone, some 8 million people, perhaps a third of the entire Indian population, died of smallpox within a decade of the arrival of the Spanish. Unable to explain or cure the diseases, Native American chieftains and religious leaders often lost their stature—and their lives—as they were usually the first to meet the Spanish and thus were the first infected. As a consequence of losing their leaders, the indigenous peoples were less capable of resisting the European invaders. Many Europeans, however, interpreted such epidemics as diseases sent by God to punish those who resisted conversion to Christianity.

THE SPANISH IN NORTH AMERICA

Throughout the sixteenth century, no European power other than Spain held more than a brief foothold in the Americas. Spanish explorers had not only arrived first but had stumbled onto those regions that would produce the quickest profits. While France and England were preoccupied with political disputes and religious conflict at home, Catholic Spain had forged an authoritarian national and religious unity that enabled it to dominate Europe as well as the New World.

HISPANIC AMERICA For most of the colonial period, much of what is now the United States was governed by Spain. Spanish culture etched a lasting imprint upon America's future ways of life. Hispanic place-names—San Francisco, Santa Barbara, Los Angeles, San Diego, Santa Fe, San Antonio,

Pensacola, St. Augustine—survive to this day, as do Hispanic influences in art, architecture, literature, music, law, and food.

ST. AUGUSTINE

In 1513, Juan Ponce de León, then governor of Puerto Rico, made the earliest known European exploration of Florida. Meanwhile, Spanish explorers sailed along the Gulf coast from Florida to Mexico, scouted the Atlantic coast all the way to Canada, and established a short-lived colony on the Carolina coast.

In 1539, Hernando de Soto and 600 conquistadores landed on the western shore of La Florida (Land of Flowers) and soon set out on horseback to search for riches. Instead of gold, they found "great fields of corn, beans and squash . . . as far as the eye could see." De Soto, who a companion said was "fond of the sport of killing Indians," led the expedition north as far as western North Carolina, and then moved westward across Tennessee, Georgia, and Alabama before happening upon the Mississippi River near what today is Memphis. After crossing the Mississippi, the conquistadores went up the Arkansas River, looting and destroying Indian villages along the way. In the spring of 1542, de Soto died near Natchez, Mississippi; the next year, the survivors among his party floated down the Mississippi River, and 311 of the original adventurers made their way to Spanish Mexico.

In 1565, in response to French efforts to colonize north Florida, the Spanish king dispatched Pedro Menendez de Aviles with a ragtag group of 1,500 soldiers and colonists to found an outpost on the Florida coast. St. Augustine became the first permanent European settlement in the present-day United States. The Spanish settled St. Augustine in response to French efforts to colonize north Florida. In the 1560s, French Protestant refugees (called Huguenots) established France's first American colonies, one on the coast of what became South Carolina and the other in Florida. The settlements did not last long.

At dawn on September 20, 1565, some 500 Spanish soldiers from St. Augustine assaulted Fort Caroline, the French Huguenot colony in northeastern Florida, and hanged all the men over age fifteen. Only women, girls, and young boys were spared. The Spanish commander notified his Catholic king that he had killed all the French he "had found [in Fort Caroline] because . . . they were scattering the odious Lutheran doctrine in these Provinces." Later, when survivors from a shipwrecked French fleet washed ashore on Florida beaches after a hurricane, the Spanish commander told them they must abandon Protestantism and swear their allegiance to Catholicism. When they refused, his soldiers killed 245 of them.

THE SPANISH SOUTHWEST The Spanish eventually established other permanent settlements in what are now New Mexico, Texas, and California. From the outset, however, the settlements were sparsely populated, inadequately supplied, dreadfully poor, and consistently neglected by Spanish colonial officials.

In New Spain, civil liberties and notions of equal treatment were nonexistent; people were expected to follow orders. There was no freedom of speech, religion, or movement; no local elections; no real self-government. The military officers, bureaucrats, wealthy landowners, and priests appointed by the king regulated every detail of colonial life. Settlers could not travel within the colonies without official permission.

New Mexico The land that would later be called **New Mexico** was the first center of Catholic missionary activity in the American Southwest. In 1595, Juan de Oñate, the rich son of a Spanish family in Mexico, received a land grant for *El Norte*, the mostly desert territory north of Mexico above the Rio Grande—Texas, New Mexico, Arizona, California, and parts of Colorado. Over the next three years, he recruited colonists willing to move north with him: soldier-settlers and Mexican Indians and *mestizos* (the offspring of Spanish and indigenous parents).

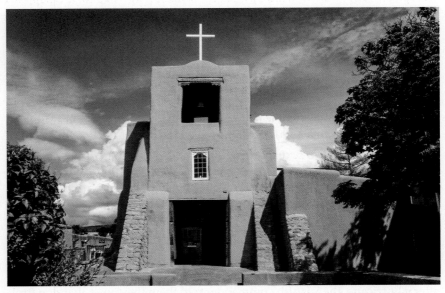

Missionaries in the New World A Spanish mission in New Mexico, established to spread the Catholic faith among the indigenous peoples.

In 1598, the caravan of 250 colonists, including women, children, horses, goats, sheep, and 7,000 cattle, began moving north from the mountains above Mexico City across the harsh desert landscape. "O God! What a lonely land!" one traveler wrote to relatives in Mexico City.

After walking more than 800 miles in seven months, they established the colony of New Mexico, the farthest outpost of New Spain. It took wagon trains eighteen months to travel to Mexico City and back. The Spanish labeled the local Indians "Pueblos" (a Spanish word meaning village) for the city-like aspect of their terraced, multistoried buildings, sometimes chiseled into the steep walls of cliffs.

Hopis, Zunis, and other Pueblo peoples sought peace rather than war, yet they were often raided by Apaches (from a Pueblo word meaning "enemy"). "Their government," Oñate noted, "is one of complete freedom, for although they have chieftains, they obey them badly and in few matters."

The goals of Spanish colonialism were to find gold, silver, and other valuable commodities while forcing the Native Americans to adopt the Spanish religion and way of life. Oñate, New Mexico's first governor, told the Pueblos that if they embraced Catholicism and followed his orders, they would receive "an eternal life of great bliss" instead of "cruel and everlasting torment."

There was, however, little gold or silver in New Mexico. Nor was there enough corn and beans to feed the Spanish invaders, who had to be resupplied by caravans traveling for months from Mexico City. Eventually Oñate forced the Indians to pay tributes (taxes) to the Spanish authorities in the form of a yard of cloth and a bushel of corn each year.

CATHOLIC MISSIONS Once it became evident that New Mexico had little gold, the Spanish focused on religious conversion. Priests forced Indians to build and support Catholic missions and to work in the fields they had once owned. They also performed personal tasks for the priests and soldiers—cooking, cleaning, even sexual favors. Whips were used to herd the Indians to church services and to punish them for not working hard enough. A French visitor reported that it "reminded us of a . . . West Indian [slave] colony."

Some Indians welcomed the Spanish as "powerful witches" capable of easing their burdens. Others tried to use the European invaders as allies against rival Indian groups. Still others rebelled. Before the end of New Mexico's first year of Spanish rule, in December 1598, the Acoma Pueblo revolted, killing eleven soldiers and two servants.

Oñate's response was even more brutal. Over three days, Spanish soldiers destroyed the entire pueblo, demolishing buildings and killing 500 Pueblo men and 300 women and children. Survivors were enslaved, and children were separated from their parents and moved into a Catholic mission, where, Oñate remarked, "they may attain the knowledge of God and the salvation of their souls."

THE MESTIZO FACTOR Few Spanish women journeyed to New Spain in the sixteenth century. Those who did had to be married and accompanied by a husband. As a result, there were so few Spanish women in North America that the government encouraged soldiers and settlers to marry Native Americans and did not discriminate against the children (*mestizos*) of the mixed marriages. By the eighteenth century, mestizos were a majority in Mexico and New Mexico. Such widespread interbreeding and intermarriage led the Spanish to adopt a more inclusive social outlook toward the Indians than the English later did in their colonies along the Atlantic coast. Since most colonial officials were mestizo themselves, they were less likely to belittle or abuse the Indians. At the same time, many Native Americans falsely claimed to be mestizo as a means of improving their legal status and avoiding having to pay annual tribute.

Smallpox Mexica victims of the 1538 smallpox epidemic are covered in shrouds (center) as two others lie dying (at right).

THE PUEBLO REVOLT In 1608, the Spanish government decided to turn New Mexico into a royal province and moved its capital to Santa Fe ("Holy Faith" in Spanish). It became the first permanent seat of government in the present-day United States. By 1630, there were fifty Catholic churches and monasteries in New Mexico as well as some 3,000 Spaniards. Roman Catholic missionaries in New Mexico claimed that 86,000 Pueblos had embraced Christianity during the seventeenth century.

In fact, however, resentment among the Indians increased as the Spanish stripped them of their ancestral ways of life. "The heathen," reported a Spanish soldier, "have conceived a mortal hatred for our holy faith and enmity [hatred] for the Spanish nation."

In 1680, a charismatic Indian spiritual leader named Popé (meaning "Ripe Plantings") organized a massive rebellion of warriors from nineteen villages. The Indians burned Catholic churches; tortured, mutilated, and executed 21 priests and 400 Spanish settlers; destroyed all relics of Christianity; and forced the 2,400 survivors to flee. The entire province of New Mexico was again in Indian hands, and the Spanish governor reported that the Pueblos "are very happy without religion or Spaniards."

The Pueblo Revolt was the greatest defeat Indians ever inflicted on European efforts to conquer the New World. It took twelve years and four military assaults for the Spanish to reestablish control over New Mexico.

Horses and the Great Plains

Another major consequence of the Pueblo Revolt was the opportunity it gave Indian rebels to acquire Spanish horses. (Spanish authorities had made it illegal for Indians to ride or own horses.) The Pueblos established a thriving horse trade with other tribes. By 1690, horses were in Texas, and soon they spread across the Great Plains.

Before the arrival of horses, Indians had hunted on foot and used dogs as their beasts of burden. Dogs are carnivores, however, and it was difficult to find enough meat to feed them. The vast grasslands of the Great Plains were the perfect environment for horses, since the prairies offered plenty of forage.

With horses, the Indians in the Great Plains gained a new source of mobility and power. Horses could haul up to seven times as much weight as dogs; their speed and endurance made the Indians much more effective hunters and warriors. Horses grew so valuable that they became a form of Indian currency and a sign of wealth and prestige. On the Great Plains, a warrior's status reflected the number of trained horses he owned. The more horses, the more wives he could support and the more buffalo robes he could exchange for more horses.

Plains Indians The horse-stealing raid depicted in this hide painting demonstrates the essential role horses played in plains life.

Horses gave the Indians on the Great Plains a new source of mobility and power. Horses could haul up to seven times as much weight as dogs; their speed and endurance made the Indians much more effective hunters and warriors. Horses grew so valuable that they became a form of Indian currency and a sign of wealth and prestige. On the Great Plains, a warrior's status reflected the number of horses he owned. The more horses, the more wives he could support and the more buffalo robes he could exchange for more horses.

By the late seventeenth century, the Indians were fighting the Spaniards on more equal terms. This helps explain why the Indians of the Southwest and Texas, unlike the Indians in Mexico, were able to sustain their cultures for the next 300 years. On horseback, they were among the most fearsome fighters in the world.

BUFFALO HUNTING The Arapaho, Cheyenne, Comanche, Kiowa, and Sioux reinvented themselves as horse-centered cultures. They left their traditional woodland villages and became nomadic buffalo hunters.

A bull buffalo could weigh more than a ton and stand five feet tall at the shoulder. Indians used virtually every part of the buffalo: meat for food; hides for clothing, shoes, bedding, and shelter; muscles and tendons for thread and bowstrings; intestines for containers; bones for tools; horns for eating utensils; hair for headdresses; and dung for fuel. They used tongues for hair brushes and tails for fly swatters. One scholar has referred to the buffalo as the "tribal department store."

Women and girls butchered and dried the buffalo meat and tanned the hides. As the value of the hides grew, Indian hunters began practicing polygamy, because more wives could process more buffalo carcasses. The rising value of wives eventually led Plains Indians to raid other tribes in search of brides.

The introduction of horses on the Great Plains was a mixed blessing; they brought prosperity and mobility but also triggered more conflicts among the Plains Indians. Over time, the Indians on horseback eventually killed more buffaloes than the herds could replace. Further, horses competed with the buffaloes for food, often depleting the prairie grass. As horse-centered culture enabled Indians to travel greater distances and encounter more people, infectious diseases spread more widely. Yet horses overall brought a better quality of life. By 1800, a white trader in Texas would observe that "this is a delightful country, and were it not for perpetual wars, the natives might be the happiest people on earth."

THE SPANISH EMPIRE IN DECLINE

During the one and a half centuries after 1492, the Spanish developed the most extensive empire the world had ever known. It spanned southern Europe and the Netherlands, much of the Western Hemisphere, and parts of Asia.

Yet the Spanish rulers overreached. The religious wars of the sixteenth and seventeenth centuries killed millions, created intense anti-Spanish feelings among the English and Dutch, and eventually helped bankrupt the Spanish government. At the same time, the Spanish Empire grew so vast that its size and complexity overtaxed the government's resources.

Spain's colonial system was mostly disastrous for the peoples of Africa and the Americas. Spanish explorers, conquistadores, and priests imposed Catholicism on the native peoples, as well as a cruel system of economic exploitation and dependence. As Bartolomé de Las Casas concluded, "The Spaniards have shown not the slightest consideration for these people, treating them (and I speak from first-hand experience, having been there from the outset) . . . as piles of dung in the middle of the road. They have had as little concern for their souls as for their bodies." In the end, the lust for empire ("God, Glory, and Gold") brought decadence and decline to Spain and much of Europe.

CHALLENGES TO THE SPANISH EMPIRE

Catholic Spain's conquests in the Western Hemisphere spurred Portugal, France, England, and the Netherlands (Holland) to begin their own explorations and exploitations of the New World.

The French were the first to pose a serious threat. Spanish treasure ships sailing home from Mexico, Peru, and the Caribbean offered tempting targets for French pirates. At the same time, the French began explorations in North America. In 1524, the French king sent Italian Giovanni da Verrazano across the Atlantic. Upon sighting land (probably at Cape Fear, North Carolina), Verrazano ranged along the coast as far north as Maine. On a second voyage, in 1528, he was killed by Caribbean Indians.

NEW FRANCE Unlike the Verrazano voyages, those of Jacques Cartier, beginning in the next decade, led to the first French effort at colonization in North America. During three voyages, Cartier ventured up the St. Lawrence River, which today is the boundary between Canada and New York. Twice he got as far as present-day Montreal, and twice he wintered at Quebec, near which a short-lived French colony appeared in 1541–1542.

France after midcentury, however, plunged into religious civil wars, and the colonization of Canada had to await the arrival of Samuel de Champlain, "the Father of New France," after 1600. Over thirty-seven years, Champlain would lead twenty-seven expeditions from France to Canada—and never lose a ship.

THE DUTCH REVOLT From the mid-1500s, greater threats to Spanish power in the New World arose from the Dutch and the English. In 1566, the Netherlands included seventeen provinces. The fragmented nation had passed by inheritance to the Spanish king in 1555, but the Dutch soon began a series of rebellions against Spanish Catholic rule.

A long, bloody struggle ensued in which Queen Elizabeth aided the Dutch, sending some 8,000 English soldiers to support their efforts. The Dutch revolt, as much a civil war as a war for national independence, was a series of different uprisings in different provinces at different times. Each province had its own institutions, laws, and rights. Although seven provinces joined together to form the Dutch Republic, the Spanish did not officially recognize the independence of the entire Netherlands until 1648.

THE DEFEAT OF THE ARMADA Almost from the beginning of the Protestant revolt in the Netherlands, the Dutch captured Spanish treasure ships in the Atlantic and carried on illegal trade with Spain's colonies. While

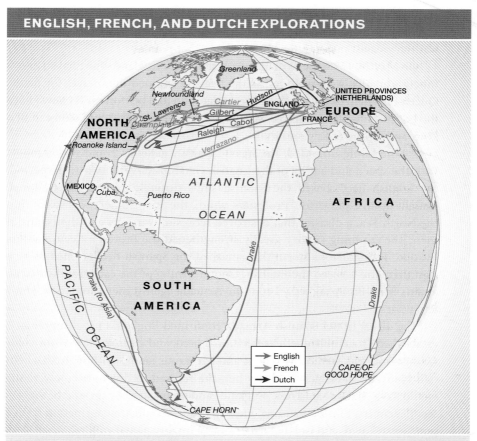

ENGLISH, FRENCH, AND DUTCH EXPLORATIONS

- Who were the first European explorers to rival Spanish dominance in the New World, and why did they cross the Atlantic?
- Why was the defeat of the Spanish Armada important to the history of English exploration?
- What was the significance of the voyages of Gilbert and Raleigh?

England's Queen Elizabeth steered a tortuous course to avoid open war with Spain, she desperately sought additional resources to defend her island nation. She encouraged English privateers such as Sir Francis Drake to attack Spanish ships and their coastal colonies in America, leading the Spanish to call her the "pirate queen."

English raids on Spanish ships and settlements continued for some twenty years before open war erupted between the two nations. Philip II, the king of Spain who was Elizabeth's brother-in-law and fiercest opponent, finally had enough and began plotting an invasion of England. To do so, he assembled the massive **Spanish Armada**: 132 warships, 8,000 sailors, and 18,000 soldiers. It was the greatest invasion fleet in history to that point.

On May 28, 1588, the Armada began sailing for England. The English navy's ninety warships were waiting. As the fleets positioned themselves for battle, Queen Elizabeth donned a silver breastplate and told her forces, "I know I have the body of a weak and feeble woman, but I have the heart and stomach of a king, and a King of England too."

As the battle unfolded, the heavy Spanish galleons could not compete with the speed and agility of the English warships. Over a two-week period, the English fleet chased the Spanish ships through the English Channel. Caught up in a powerful "Protestant wind," the Spanish fleet was swept into the North Sea, a disaster that destroyed scores of warships and thousands of men. The stunning victory greatly strengthened the Protestant cause across Europe. The ferocious storm that smashed the Spanish fleet seemed to be a sign that God favored the English. Upon learning of the catastrophic defeat, Spain's King Philip sighed, "I sent the Armada against men, not God's winds and waves."

The defeat of the Spanish Armada confirmed England's naval supremacy, established Queen Elizabeth as a national hero, and cleared the way for colonizing America's "remote heathens and barbarous lands." Although Elizabeth had many suitors eager to marry her, she refused to divide her power. She would have "but one mistress [England] and no master." By the end of the sixteenth century, Elizabethan England had begun an epic transformation from a poor, humiliated, and isolated nation into a mighty global empire.

ENGLISH EXPLORATION OF AMERICA

English efforts to colonize America began a few years before the battle with the Spanish Armada. In 1584, Queen Elizabeth asked Sir Walter Raleigh to organize a colonizing mission on the North American coast. His expedition discovered the Outer Banks of North Carolina and landed at Roanoke Island. Raleigh named the area Virginia, in honor of Elizabeth, the "Virgin Queen."

After several false starts, Raleigh in 1587 sponsored another expedition of about 100 colonists, including 26 women and children, led by Governor John White. White spent a month helping launch the settlement on Roanoke Island and then returned to England for supplies, leaving behind his daughter Elinor and his granddaughter Virginia Dare, the first English child born in the Americas.

The English in Virginia The arrival of English explorers on the Outer Banks, with Roanoke Island at left.

White's journey back to Virginia was delayed because of the naval war with Spain. When he finally returned, in 1590, the Roanoke colony had been abandoned and pillaged. On a post at the entrance to the village, someone had carved the word "CROATOAN," leading White to conclude that the settlers had set out for the island of that name some fifty miles south, where friendly Indians lived.

The English never found the "lost colonists." They may have been killed by Indians or Spaniards. The most recent evidence indicates that the "Lost Colony" suffered from a horrible drought that prevented the settlers from growing enough food to survive. While some may have gone south, most went north, to the southern shores of Chesapeake Bay, where they lived for years until Indians killed them.

Whatever the fate of the lost colonists, there were no English settlements in North America when Queen Elizabeth died in 1603. The Spanish controlled the only colonial outposts on the continent. This was about to change, however. Inspired by the success of the Spanish in exploiting the New World, the English—as well as the French and Dutch—would soon develop colonial empires of their own.

CHAPTER REVIEW

Summary

- **Native American Societies** Hunter-gatherers came across the Bering Strait by foot and settled the length and breadth of the Americas, forming groups with diverse cultures, languages, and lifestyles. Global warming enabled an agricultural revolution that allowed the hunter-gatherers to settle and build empires, such as that of the *Mexica*, whose *Aztec Empire* included subjugated peoples and a vast system of trade and tribute. Some North American peoples developed an elaborate continental trading network and impressive cities like *Cahokia*; their *burial mounds* reveal a complex and stratified social organization. The *Eastern Woodlands peoples* that the Europeans would first encounter included both patriarchal and matriarchal societies as well as extensive language-based alliances. Warfare was an important cultural component, leading to shifting rivalries and alliances among tribes and with European settlers.

- **Age of Exploration** By the 1490s, Europeans were experiencing a renewed curiosity about the larger world. Warfare, plagues, and famine undermined the agricultural feudal system in Europe, and in its place arose a middle class that monarchs could tax. Powerful new nations replaced the estates and cities ruled by princes. Scientific and technological advances led to the creation of better maps and navigation techniques, as well as new weapons and ships. Navies became the critical component of global trade and world power. Two motives drove the Spanish efforts to colonize the New World: the conversion of Indians to *Roman Catholicism* and a lust for gold and silver. The rivalries of the *Protestant Reformation* in Europe shaped the course of conquest in the Americas.

- **Conquering and Colonizing the Americas** Spanish *conquistadores,* such as Hernán Cortés, exploited their advantages in military technology, including steel, gunpowder, and domesticated animals, such as the horse, to conquer the powerful Aztec and Inca Empires. European diseases, first introduced to the New World by Columbus, did even more to ensure Spanish victories. The Spanish *encomienda* system demanded goods and labor from their new subjects. As the Indian population declined, the Portuguese and Spanish began to import enslaved Africans into the Americas.

- **Columbian Exchange** Contact between the Old World and the New resulted in the *Columbian Exchange*, sometimes called the great biological exchange. Crops native to the New World such as *maize*, beans, and potatoes became staples in Europe, and native peoples incorporated into their culture such Eurasian animals as the horse and pig. But the invaders also carried *infectious diseases* that set off pandemics of smallpox, plague, and other illnesses to which Indians had no immunity. The Americas were depopulated and cultures destroyed.

- **Spanish Legacy** Spain left a lasting legacy from California to Florida. Spanish horses eventually transformed Indian life on the plains, and Catholic missionaries contributed to the destruction of the old ways of life by exterminating "heathen" beliefs in the Southwest, a practice that led to open rebellion in *New Mexico* in 1598 and 1680. Spain's rival European nation-states began competing for gold and glory in the New World. England's defeat of the *Spanish Armada* cleared the path for English dominance in North America.

CHRONOLOGY

by 22,000 B.C.E.	Humans have migrated to the Americas
5000 B.C.E.	The agricultural revolution begins in Mexico
600–1300 C.E.	The city of Cahokia flourishes in North America
1325	The Mexica (Aztec) Empire is founded in Central Mexico
1492	Columbus makes his first voyage of discovery to the Americas
1503	Spaniards bring the first African slaves to the Americas
1517	Martin Luther launches the Protestant Reformation
1519	Cortés begins the Spanish conquest of Mexico
1531	Pizarro subdues the Inca Empire in South America for Spain
1565	Spaniards build settlement at St. Augustine, the first permanent European outpost in the present-day United States
1584–1587	Raleigh's Roanoke Island venture
1588	The English navy defeats the Spanish Armada
1680	Pueblo Revolt

KEY TERMS

maize p. 7

Mexica p. 8

Aztec Empire p. 8

burial mounds p. 12

Cahokia p. 13

Eastern Woodlands peoples p. 13

Roman Catholicism p. 21

Protestant Reformation p. 22

conquistadores p. 28

encomienda p. 30

Columbian Exchange p. 31

infectious diseases p. 32

New Mexico p. 34

Spanish Armada p. 42

 INQUIZITIVE

Go to InQuizitive to see what you've learned—and learn what you've missed—with personalized feedback along the way.

2 England's Colonies

"Ould Virginia" As one of the earliest explorers and settlers of the Jamestown colony, John Smith put his intimate knowledge of the region to use by creating this seventeenth-century map of Virginia. In the upper right-hand corner is a Susquehannock warrior, whom Smith called a "G[i]ant-like people."

For thousands of seekers and adventurers, America in the seventeenth century was a vast unknown land of new beginnings and new opportunities. The English settlers who poured into coastal America and the Caribbean islands found not a "virgin land" of uninhabited wilderness but a developed region populated by Native Americans. As was true in New Spain and New France, European diseases such as smallpox overwhelmed the Indians and wiped out whole societies. William Bradford of the Plymouth colony in Massachusetts reported that the Indians "fell sick of the smallpox, and died most miserably . . . like rotten sheep."

Native Americans dealt with Europeans in different ways. Many resisted, others retreated, and still others developed thriving trade relationships with the newcomers. In some areas, land-hungry colonists quickly displaced or decimated the Indians. In others, Indians found ways to live in cooperation with English settlers—if they were willing to adopt the English way of life.

After creating the Virginia, Maryland, and New England colonies, the English would go on to conquer Dutch-controlled New Netherland, settle Carolina, and eventually establish the rest of the thirteen original American mainland colonies. The diverse English colonies had one thing in common: To one extent or another, they all took part in the enslavement of other peoples, either Native Americans or Africans or both. Slavery, common throughout the world in the seventeenth and eighteenth centuries, enriched a few, corrupted many, and compromised the American dream of equal opportunity for all.

focus questions

1. What motivated English monarchs and investors to establish American colonies?

2. What were the characteristics of the English colonies in the Chesapeake region, the Carolinas, the middle colonies—Pennsylvania, New York, New Jersey, and Delaware—and New England prior to 1700?

3. In what ways did the English colonists and Native Americans adapt to each other's presence?

4. What role did indentured servants and the development of slavery play in colonial America?

5. How did the English colonies become the most populous and powerful region in North America by 1700?

THE ENGLISH BACKGROUND

Over the centuries, the island nation of England had developed political practices and governing principles similar to those on the continent of Europe—but
with key differences. European societies were tightly controlled hierarchies.
From birth, people learned their place in the social order. Commoners bowed
to priests, priests bowed to bishops, peasants pledged their loyalty to landowners, and nobles knelt before the monarchs, who claimed God had given them
absolute power to rule over their domain.

Since the thirteenth century, however, English monarchs had *shared* power
with the nobility and with a lesser aristocracy, the *gentry*. England's tradition
of parliamentary monarchy began with the Magna Carta (Great Charter) of
1215, a statement of fundamental rights and liberties that nobles forced the
king to approve. The Magna Carta established that England would be a nation
ruled by laws. Everyone was equal before the law, and no one was above it.

The people's representatives formed the national legislature known as
Parliament, which comprised the hereditary and appointed members of the
House of Lords and the elected members of the House of Commons. The most
important power allocated to Parliament was the authority to impose taxes. By
controlling tax revenue, the legislature exercised leverage over the monarchy.

RELIGIOUS CONFLICT AND WAR

When Queen Elizabeth, who never married, died in 1603, her cousin, James
VI of Scotland, became King James I of England. He called his joint kingdom
Great Britain. While Elizabeth had ruled through constitutional authority, James
claimed to govern by "divine right," which meant he answered only to God.

James I confronted a divided Church of England, with the reform-minded
Puritans in one camp and the Anglican establishment, headed by the archbishop and bishops, in the other. In seventeenth-century England, those who
criticized the Anglican Church were called *Dissenters*.

The Puritans believed that the Church of England needed further "purify-
ing." All "papist" (Roman Catholic) rituals must be eliminated. No use of holy
water, candles, or incense. No "Devil's bagpipes" (pipe organs). No priestly
robes (then called vestments). No lavish cathedrals, stained glass windows, or
statues of Jesus. They even sought to ban the use of the term *priest*.

The Puritans wanted to simplify religion to its most basic elements: people
worshipping God in plain, self-governing congregations without the formal
trappings of Catholic and Anglican ceremonies. They had hoped the new

king would support their efforts, but James I, who had been baptized in the Catholic faith, embraced the Anglican Church to avoid a civil war and sought to banish the Puritans from England.

Some Puritans decided that the Church of England was so corrupt and corrupting that it could not be reformed, so they created their own separate congregations, thus earning the name *Separatists*, derived in part from Paul's biblical command to "come out from among them, and be ye separate." Such rebelliousness infuriated the leaders of the Church of England, who required people by law to attend Anglican church services.

During the late sixteenth century, the Separatists (also called *Nonconformists*) were "hunted and persecuted on every side." Many left England, and some, who would eventually be known as Pilgrims, decided to sail for America. James's son, Charles I, succeeded

The Execution of Charles I Flemish artist John Weesop witnessed the king's execution and painted this gruesome scene from memory. He was so disgusted by "a country where they cut off their king's head" that he refused to visit England again.

his father in 1625 and proved to be an even more stubborn defender of absolute royal power. He raised taxes without consulting Parliament, harassed the Puritans, and actually disbanded Parliament from 1629 to 1640.

The monarchy went too far, however, when it forced Anglican forms of worship on Presbyterian Scots. In 1638, Scotland rose in revolt, and in 1640, Charles, desperate to save his skin, revived Parliament, ordering its members to raise taxes for the defense of his kingdom. Parliament, led by militant Puritans, refused.

In 1642, when the king tried to arrest five members of Parliament, a civil war erupted in England between Royalists and Parliamentarians, leading many New England Puritans to return home to fight against the Royalist army. In 1646, parliamentary forces led by Puritan Oliver Cromwell captured Charles and, in a public trial, convicted him of high treason and contempt of Parliament, labeling him a "tyrant, traitor, murderer, and public enemy." He was beheaded in 1649. As it turned out, however, the Puritans had killed a king but not slain the monarchy.

Cromwell ruled like a military dictator, calling himself Lord Protector. He outlawed Roman Catholics and Anglicans. Many Anglican Royalists, called *Cavaliers*, escaped by sailing to Virginia. After Cromwell's death in 1658, the army allowed new elections for Parliament and in 1660 supported the Restoration of the monarchy under Charles II, eldest son of the executed king.

Unlike his father, King Charles II agreed to rule jointly with Parliament. His younger brother, the Duke of York (who became King James II in 1685), was more rigid. James openly embraced Catholicism, murdered or imprisoned political opponents, and defied Parliament.

The English tolerated James II's rule so long as they expected one of his Protestant daughters, Mary or Anne, to succeed him. In 1688, however, the birth of a royal son who would be raised Roman Catholic stirred a revolt. Political, religious, and military leaders urged the king's daughter Mary and her Protestant husband, William III of Orange (the ruling Dutch prince), to oust her father and assume the English throne as joint monarchs. A month after William landed in England with a huge army, King James II fled to France.

Amid this dramatic transfer of power, which became known as the Glorious Revolution, Parliament reasserted its right to counterbalance the authority of the monarchy. Kings and queens could no longer suspend Parliament, create armies, or impose taxes without Parliament's consent. The monarchy would henceforth derive its power not from God ("divine right") but from the people through their representatives in Parliament.

AMERICAN COLONIES

PEOPLE AND PROFITS During these eventful years of the seventeenth century, all but one of England's North American colonies—Georgia— were founded. From the outset, English colonization differed in important ways from the Spanish pattern, in which the government regulated all aspects of colonial life.

The monarchy treated its original American colonies much like it dealt with neighboring Ireland. The English had brutally conquered the Irish during the reign of Queen Elizabeth and thereafter extended their control over Catholic Ireland through the "planting" of Protestant settlements in Ireland called *plantations*. By confiscating Irish lands and repopulating them with 120,000 Protestants, the government sought to reduce the influence of Roman Catholicism and smother any rebellious Irish nationalism.

English soldiers and colonizers inflicted a variety of cruelties on the Irish, whom they regarded as every bit as "savage" and "barbarous" as the Indians of North America. In time, the English would impose their rule and religion upon the Native Americans.

England envied the riches taken from the New World by Spain, especially the enormous amounts of gold and silver. Much of the wealth and lands the Spanish accumulated in the Americas, however, became the property of the monarchs who funded the conquistadores. In contrast, English colonization in the Americas was led by churches and companies: those seeking freedom from religious persecution, both Protestants and Catholics, and those seeking land and wealth.

Planting colonies in America was an expensive undertaking. Investors banded together to buy shares in what were called **joint-stock companies**. That way, large amounts of money could be raised and, if a colony failed, no single investor would suffer the entire loss. If a colony succeeded, the investors would share the profits based on the amount of stock (shares) they owned. The joint-stock companies represented the most important organizational innovation of the Age of Exploration and provided the first instruments of English colonization in America.

SELF-SUSTAINING COLONIES The English settlements in America were much more compact than those in New Spain, and the native peoples along the Atlantic coast were less numerous and less wealthy than the Mexica and the Incas.

England's colonies were also much more populous than the Spanish, French, and Dutch colonies. In 1660, for example, there were 58,000 colonists in New England, Virginia, and Maryland, compared with 3,000 in New France and 5,000 in Dutch New Netherland. By 1750, English colonists (male and female) still outnumbered the French (mostly male) nearly twenty to one, while in the northernmost areas of New Spain—the lands that became Texas, New Mexico, Arizona, Florida, and California—there were only 20,000 Spaniards.

The English government and individual investors had two primary goals for their colonies: (1) to provide valuable raw materials, such as timber for shipbuilding, tobacco for smoking, and fur pelts for hats and coats; and (2) to develop a thriving market for English manufactured goods. To populate the colonies, the English encouraged social rebels, religious dissenters, and the homeless and landless to migrate to America, thereby reducing social and economic tensions at home.

In some cases, immigrants had no choice. Some 50,000 British convicts were shipped to America as servants for hire, as were several thousand Royalist prisoners, mostly Scots. Many of them did very well. In 1665, a Scottish minister in Virginia reported that several exiled Royalist soldiers were "living better than ever their forefathers" after being "sold as slaves here."

The most powerful enticement to colonists was to offer them land and the promise of a better way of life—what came to be called the American dream. Land, plentiful and cheap, was English America's treasure—once it was taken from the Native Americans.

What virtually all immigrants shared was an impulse to escape the constraints and corruptions of the old and the courage to risk everything for a life of freedom and adventure in the new. In the process of discovering a New World of opportunities and dangers, they also re-created themselves as Americans.

THE LANDLESS ENGLISH During the late sixteenth century, England experienced a population explosion that created a surplus of landless workers. Many of the jobless laborers found their way to America. An additional social strain for the English poor was the *enclosure* of farmlands on which peasants had lived and worked for generations. As trade in woolen products grew, landlords decided to "enclose" farmlands and evict the farmworkers in favor of grazing sheep.

The enclosure movement, coupled with the rising population, generated the great number of beggars and vagrants who wandered across England during the late sixteenth century. The problems created by this uprooted peasant population provided a compelling reason to send many of them to colonies in America and the Caribbean. As the Reverend Richard Hakluyt explained, "Valiant youths rusting [from] lack of employment" would flourish in America and generate trade that would enrich England.

VIRGINIA In 1606, King James I chartered a joint-stock enterprise named the Virginia Company. It was owned by investors, called "adventurers," who sought to profit from the gold and silver they hoped to find in America. King James also gave the Virginia Company a spiritual mission by ordering the settlers to take the "Christian religion" to the Indians, who "live in darkness and miserable ignorance of the true knowledge and worship of God."

In December 1606, the Virginia Company sent to America three ships carrying 104 colonists, all men and boys. In May 1607, after five storm-tossed months at sea, they reached the broad expanse of Chesapeake Bay, which extends 200 miles along the coast of Virginia and Maryland. To avoid Spanish raiders, the colonists chose to settle about forty miles inland along a large river. They called it the James, in honor of the king, and named their settlement Jamestown.

The ill-prepared settlers had expected to find gold, friendly Indians, and easy living. Instead they found disease, drought, starvation, violence, and death. Virtually every colonist fell ill within a year. "Our men were destroyed with cruel diseases," a survivor wrote, "but for the most part they died of mere famine."

In the colony's desperate early weeks and months, the settlers struggled to find enough to eat, for many of them were either poor townsmen unfamiliar with farming or "gentlemen" who despised manual labor. All most of them did, according to one colonist, was "complain, curse, and despair." For fifteen years, the Jamestown settlers blundered their way from one mishap to another. Unwilling to invest the time and labor in growing their own food, they stole or traded for Indian corn.

The 14,000 Indians living along the Virginia coast were dominated by the **Powhatan Confederacy,** which had conquered or intimidated the other Indian peoples in the region. Powhatan, as the English called the imperial

Chief Powhatan In this 1624 line engraving from John Smith's "Generall Historie of Virginia," Cheif Powhatan holds court from a dominant, seated position.

chieftain, lorded over several hundred villages (of about 100 people each) organized into thirty chiefdoms in eastern Virginia. When the colonists arrived, Powhatan was preoccupied with destroying the Chesapeakes, who lived along the Virginia coast.

At the time, the Powhatan Confederacy may have been the most powerful group of native peoples along the Atlantic coast. Focused on raising corn and conquering their neighbors, they lived in oval-shaped houses framed with bent saplings and covered with bark or mats. Their walled villages included forts, buildings for storing corn, and temples.

Chief Powhatan lived in an imposing lodge on the York River not far from Jamestown, where he was protected by forty bodyguards and supported by 100 wives. Colonist John Smith reported that Powhatan "sat covered with a great robe, made of raccoon skins, and all the tails hanging by," flanked by "two rows of men, and behind them as many women, with all their heads and shoulders painted red."

The Powhatans, Smith observed, were "generally tall and straight," "very ingenious," and handsome. Some attached feathers and chains to their pierced ears, and many painted their bodies. During the winter, they wore fur skins; in the summer, they were mostly naked.

The Powhatans lived in family clusters. Some villages had 20 huts; others had 200. The Powhatan men, Smith stressed, avoided "woman's work." When they were not hunting, fishing, or fighting, they sat watching the "women and children do the rest of the work": gardening, making baskets and pottery, cooking, and "all the rest."

Powhatan was as much an imperialist as the English or Spanish. He forced the peoples he had conquered to give him corn. Upon learning of the English settlement at Jamestown, he planned to impose his will on the "Strangers." When Powhatans discovered seventeen Englishmen stealing their corn, they killed them, stuffing their mouths with ears of corn. Only too late did Powhatan realize that the English had not come to Virginia to trade but "to invade my people, and possess my country."

The colonists found a match for Powhatan in twenty-seven-year-old John Smith, a canny, iron-willed international mercenary (soldier for hire). At five feet three inches, he was a stocky runt of a man full of tenacity, courage, and overflowing confidence.

The Virginia Company, impressed by Smith's exploits, had appointed him to help manage the new colony. Smith imagined "abounding America" as a land of freedom and opportunity. "Here every man may be master of his own labor and land," he wrote, "so long as settlers were willing to work patiently at humble tasks such as farming and fishing."

Smith confronted a colony on the verge of collapse. Of the original 105 settlers, only 38 survived the first nine months. At one point, said Smith, all their food was gone, "all help abandoned, each hour expecting the fury of the savages." He imposed strict military discipline and forced everyone to work long days in the fields. He also bargained effectively with the Indians. Through his efforts, Jamestown survived—but only barely.

The influx of new settlers nearly overwhelmed the struggling colony. During the winter of 1609–1610, the food supply again ran out, and most of the colonists died. Desperate settlers consumed their horses, cats, and dogs, then rats, mice, and snakes. A few even ate their leather shoes and boots and the starch in their shirt collars. Some summoned the effort to "dig up dead corpses out of graves and to eat them." One hungry man killed, salted, and ate his pregnant wife. Horrified by such cannibalism, his fellow colonists tried, convicted, tortured and executed him. Still, the cannibalism continued as the starvation worsened. "So great was our famine," Smith wrote, "that a savage we slew and buried, the poorer sort [of colonists] took him up again and ate him."

In late May 1610, Sir Thomas Gates brought some 150 new colonists to Jamestown. They found the settlement in shambles. The fort's walls had been torn down, the church was in ruins, and cabins had been "rent up and burnt." Only sixty or so skeletal colonists remained, and most were bedridden from disease and malnourishment. They greeted the newcomers by shouting, "We are starved! We are starved!"

Gates loaded the surviving colonists on his ships and they made their way downriver, headed for the Chesapeake Bay and the Atlantic. But no sooner had they started than they spied three relief ships headed upriver. The ships carried a new governor, Thomas West, known as Lord De La Warr (Delaware would be named for him), several hundred men, and plentiful supplies. De La Warr ordered Gates to turn around; Jamestown would not be abandoned.

That chance encounter was a turning point for the struggling colony. After De La Warr returned to England in 1611, Gates rebuilt the settlements and imposed a strict system of laws. The penalties for running away included shooting, hanging, and burning. Gates also ordered the colonists to attend church services on Thursdays and Sundays. Religious uniformity became an essential instrument of public policy and civil duty in colonial Virginia.

Over the next several years, the Jamestown colony limped along until at last the settlers found a profitable crop: **tobacco**. The plant had been grown on Caribbean islands for years, and smoking had become a popular habit in Europe. In 1612, settlers in Virginia began growing tobacco for export to England. By 1620, the colony was shipping 50,000 pounds of tobacco each year; by 1670, Virginia and Maryland were exporting 15 million pounds annually.

Large-scale tobacco farming required additional cleared lands for planting and more laborers to work the fields. A Jamestown planter said he needed lots of "lusty laboring men . . . capable of hard labor, and that can bear and undergo heat and cold."

INDENTURED SERVANTS To support their investment in tobacco lands, planters employed **indentured servants**. The colonists who signed a contract ("indenture") exchanged several years of labor for the cost of passage to America and, they hoped, an eventual grant of land. Indentured servitude increased the flow of immigrant workers and became the primary source of laborers in English America during the colonial period. Of the 500,000 English immigrants to America from 1610 to 1775, some 350,000 came as indentured servants, most of them penniless young men and boys. In the 1630s, the gender ratio in Virginia was 6 men to every woman; by the 1650s, it had dropped to three men to every one woman.

Not all indentured servants came voluntarily. Many homeless children in London were "kid-napped" and sold into servitude in America. In addition, Parliament in 1717 declared that convicts could avoid prison or the hangman by relocating to the colonies, and some 50,000 were banished to the New World.

Once in America, servants were provided food and a bed, but life was harsh and their rights were limited. They could be sold, loaned, or rented to others, and masters could whip them or chain them in iron collars and extend their length of service as penalty for bad behavior. Marriages required the master's permission.

Being indentured was almost like being a slave, but servants, unlike slaves, could file a complaint with the local court. Elizabeth Sprigs, a servant in Maryland, told of "toiling day and night, and then [being] tied up and whipped to that degree you would not beat an animal, scarce [fed] anything but Indian corn and salt."

The most important difference between servanthood and slavery was that it did not last a lifetime. When the indenture ended, usually after four to seven years, the servant could claim the "freedom dues" set by custom and law: tools, clothing, food, and, on occasion, small tracts of land.

Some former servants did well. By 1629, seven members of the Virginia legislature had arrived as indentured servants, and by 1637, fifteen were serving in the Maryland Assembly. Such opportunities were much less common in England or Europe, giving people even more reason to travel to America.

POCAHONTAS One of the most remarkable Powhatans was Pocahontas, the favorite daughter of Chief Powhatan. In 1607, then only eleven years old, she figured in perhaps the best-known story of the settlement, her plea for the life of John Smith. After Indians attacked Smith and a group of Englishmen trespassing on their land, killing two of them and capturing the rest, Chief Powhatan asked Smith why they were on his territory. Smith lied, claiming they had been chased there by wicked Spaniards. Powhatan saw through the ruse and ordered his warriors to kill Smith. They told him to kneel and place his head on a stone altar. As they prepared to smash his skull with war clubs, according to the unreliable Smith, young Pocahontas made a dramatic appeal for his life, convincing her father to release him in exchange for muskets, hatchets, beads, and trinkets.

Schoolchildren still learn the story of Pocahontas and John Smith, but through the years the story's facts have become distorted or even falsified. Pocahontas and John Smith were friends, not Disney World lovers. Moreover, the Indian princess saved Smith on more than one occasion, before she herself was kidnapped by English settlers in an effort to blackmail Powhatan.

Pocahontas, however, surprised her English captors by choosing to join them. She embraced Christianity, was baptized and renamed Rebecca, and fell in love with John Rolfe, a twenty-eight-year-old widower who introduced tobacco to Jamestown. After their marriage, they moved in 1616 with their infant son, Thomas, to London. There the young princess drew excited attention from the royal family and curious Londoners. Just months after arriving, however, Rebecca, only twenty years old, contracted a lung disease and died.

THE VIRGINIA COMPANY PROSPERS Jamestown remained fragile until 1618, when Sir Edwin Sandys, a prominent member of Parliament, became head of the Virginia Company. He created a **headright** (land grant) program to attract more colonists. Any Englishman who bought a share in the company and could pay for passage to Virginia could have fifty acres upon arrival, and fifty more for each servant he brought along.

The Virginia Company also promised the settlers all the "rights of Englishmen," including an elected legislature, arguing that "every man will more willingly obey laws to which he has yielded his consent." Such a commitment to representative democracy was a crucial development, for the English had long enjoyed the broadest civil liberties and the least-intrusive government in Europe. Now the colonists in Virginia were to have the same rights.

They were also to have the benefits of marriage. In 1619, a ship carrying ninety young women arrived at Jamestown. Men rushed to claim them as wives by providing 125 pounds of tobacco to cover the cost of their transatlantic passage. Also in 1619, a Dutch ship, the *White Lion,* stopped near Jamestown and unloaded "20 Negars," the first enslaved Africans known to have reached English America. These captives from the Portuguese colony of Angola in West Africa were sold into slavery, the first of some 450,000 people who would be shipped from Africa to America as slaves. Thus began an inhumane system that would spur dramatic economic growth, sow moral corruption, and generate horrific suffering for African Americans.

By 1624, some 8,000 English men, women, and children had migrated to Jamestown, although only 1,132 had survived or stayed, and many of them were in "a sickly and desperate state." In 1622 alone, 1,000 colonists had died of disease or were victims of an Indian massacre. In 1624, the Virginia Company declared bankruptcy, and Virginia became a royal colony.

The settlers were now free to own property and start businesses. The king, however, would thereafter appoint their governors. Sir William Berkeley, who arrived in 1642, presided over the colony's rapid growth for most of the next thirty-five years. Tobacco prices surged, and wealthy planters began to dominate social and political life.

The Jamestown experience did not invent America, but the colony's gritty will to survive, its mixture of greed and piety, and its exploitation of both Indians and Africans formed the model for many of the struggles, achievements, and ironies that would come to define the American spirit.

BACON'S REBELLION The relentless stream of new settlers into Virginia exerted constant pressure on Indian lands and created growing tensions among whites. The largest planters sought to live like the wealthy "English gentlemen" who owned huge estates in the countryside. In Virginia, these men acquired the most fertile land along the coast and rivers, compelling freed servants to become farmworkers or forcing them inland to gain their own farms. In either case, the poorest Virginians found themselves at a disadvantage. By 1676, one-fourth of the free white men were landless. They roamed the countryside, squatting on private property, working odd jobs, poaching game, and struggling to survive.

The simmering tensions among the landless colonists contributed to what came to be called **Bacon's Rebellion**. The discontent erupted when a squabble between a white planter and Native Americans on the Potomac River led to the murder of the planter's herdsman and, in turn, to retaliation by frontier vigilantes, who killed some two dozen Indians. When five native chieftains were later murdered, enraged Indians took revenge on frontier settlements.

When Governor Berkeley refused to take action against the Indians, Nathaniel Bacon, a young planter, led more than 1,000 men determined to terrorize the "protected and darling Indians." Bacon said he would kill all the Indians in Virginia and promised to free any servants and slaves who joined him.

STRANGE NEWS

FROM

VIRGINIA;

Being a full and true

ACCOUNT

OF THE

LIFE and DEATH

OF

Nathanael Bacon Esquire,

Who was the only Cause and Original of all the late Troubles in that COUNTRY.

With a full Relation of all the Accidents which have happened in the late War there between the Christians and Indians.

LONDON,
Printed for *William Harris*, next door to the Turn-Stile without *Moor-gate.* 1677.

News of the rebellion A pamphlet printed in London provided details about Bacon's Rebellion.

Bacon's Rebellion quickly became a battle of landless servants, small farmers, and even some slaves against Virginia's wealthiest planters and political leaders. Bacon's ruthless assaults against Indians and his lust for power and land (rather than any commitment to democratic principles) sparked his conflict with the governing authorities and the planter elite.

For his part, Berkeley opposed Bacon's efforts because he didn't want to disrupt the profitable deerskin trade the colonists enjoyed with the Native Americans. Bacon issued a "Declaration of the People of Virginia" accusing Berkeley of corruption and attempted to take the governor into custody. Berkeley's forces resisted—feebly—and Bacon's men burned Jamestown in frustration.

Bacon, however, fell ill and died a month later, after which the rebellion disintegrated. Berkeley had twenty-three of the rebels hanged. For such severity, the king denounced Berkeley as a "fool" and recalled him to England, where he died within a year.

MARYLAND   In 1634, ten years after Virginia became a royal colony, a neighboring settlement appeared on the northern shore of Chesapeake Bay. Named Maryland in honor of English queen Henrietta Maria, its 12 million acres were granted to Sir George Calvert, Lord Baltimore, by King Charles I. It became the first *proprietary* colony—that is, an individual owned it, not a joint-stock company.

Calvert had long been one of the king's favorites. In 1619, he became one of two royal secretaries of state for the nation. Forced to resign after a squabble with the king's powerful advisers, Calvert announced that he had converted from Anglicanism to Catholicism. Thereafter, he asked the new king, James II, to grant him a charter for an American colony north of Virginia. However, Calvert died before the king could act, so the charter went to his devoted son Cecilius, the second Lord Baltimore, who actually founded the colony and spent the rest of his life making it sustainable.

Cecilius Calvert wanted Maryland to be a refuge for English Catholics. Yet he also wanted the colony to be profitable and to avoid antagonizing Protestants. To that aim, he instructed his brother, Leonard, the colony's first proprietary governor, to ensure that Catholic colonists worshipped in private and remained "silent upon all occasions of discourse concerning matters of religion."

In 1634, the Calverts planted the first settlement in coastal Maryland at St. Marys, near the mouth of the Potomac River, about eighty miles up the Chesapeake Bay from Jamestown. Cecilius sought to avoid the mistakes made

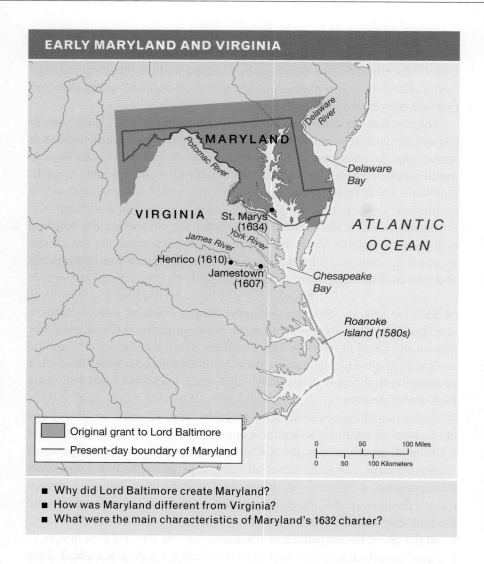

EARLY MARYLAND AND VIRGINIA

Original grant to Lord Baltimore
Present-day boundary of Maryland

- Why did Lord Baltimore create Maryland?
- How was Maryland different from Virginia?
- What were the main characteristics of Maryland's 1632 charter?

at Jamestown, so he recruited a more committed group of colonists—made up of families intending to stay rather than just single men seeking quick profits.

In addition, the Calverts did not want a colony of scattered farms and settlements vulnerable to Indian attack, like Virginia, or to be dependent solely on tobacco. They sought to create a more diversified agriculture and to build fortified towns designed to promote social interaction. The Calverts also wanted to avoid the extremes of economic wealth and poverty that had developed in Virginia. In that vein, they provided 100 acres to each adult and 50 more for each child. Maryland also had an explicit religious objective: the "conversion and civilizing of those barbarous heathens that live like beasts without the light of faith." Jesuit priests served as missionaries to the Indians. To avoid the chronic Indian wars suffered in Virginia, the Calverts resolved to purchase land from the Native Americans rather than take it by force.

Still, the early years in Maryland were as difficult as in Virginia. Nearly 30 percent of infants born in the colony died in their first year, and nearly half of the colonists died before reaching age twenty-one. Some 34,000 colonists would arrive between 1634 and 1680, but in 1680 the colony's white population was only 20,000.

The charter from the king gave the Calverts the power to make laws with the consent of the *freemen* (all property holders). Yet they could not attract enough Roman Catholics to develop a self-sustaining economy. The majority of the servants who came to the colony were Protestants, both Anglicans and Puritans. To recruit servants and settlers, the Calverts offered "a quiet life sweetened with ease and plenty" on small farms. In the end, Maryland succeeded more quickly than Virginia because of its focus on growing tobacco from the start. Its long coastline along the Chesapeake Bay gave planters easy access to shipping.

Despite the Calverts' caution "concerning matters of religion," sectarian squabbles impeded the colony's early development. Catholics and Protestants feuded as violently as they had in England. When Oliver Cromwell and the Puritans took control in England and executed King Charles I in 1649, Cecilius Calvert feared he might lose his colony.

To avoid such a catastrophe, Calvert appointed Protestants to the colony's ruling council and wrote the Toleration Act (1649), a revolutionary document that acknowledged the Puritan victory and welcomed all Christians, regardless of their denomination or beliefs. (It also promised to execute anyone who denied the divinity of Jesus.)

Still, Calvert's efforts were not enough to prevent the new government in England from installing Puritans in positions of control in Maryland. They rescinded the Toleration Act in 1654, stripped Catholic colonists of voting rights, and denied them the right to worship.

The once-persecuted Puritans had become persecutors themselves, at one point driving Calvert out of his own colony. Were it not for its success in growing tobacco, Maryland may well have disintegrated. In 1692, following the Glorious Revolution in England, Catholicism was effectively banned in Maryland. Only after the American Revolution would Marylanders again be guaranteed religious freedom.

SETTLING NEW ENGLAND

Very different English settlements were emerging north of the Chesapeake Bay colonies. Unlike Maryland and Virginia, the New England colonies were intended to be self-governing religious utopias based on the teachings of John Calvin. The New England settlers were not indentured servants as in the Chesapeake colonies; they were mostly middle-class families that could pay their own way across the Atlantic. Most male settlers were small farmers, merchants, seamen, or fishermen. New England also attracted more women than did the southern colonies.

Although its soil was not as fertile as that of the Chesapeake region and its growing season was much shorter, New England was a healthier place to live. Because of its colder climate, settlers avoided the infectious diseases like malaria that ravaged the southern colonies. Still, only 21,000 colonists arrived in New England, compared to the 120,000 who went to the Chesapeake Bay colonies. By 1700, however, New England's thriving white population exceeded that of Maryland and Virginia.

The land-hungry Pilgrims and Puritans who arrived in Massachusetts were willing to sacrifice everything to create a model Christian society. These self-described "visible saints" intended to purify their churches of *all* Catholic and Anglican rituals and enact a code of laws and a government structure based upon biblical principles. Unlike the Anglican Church, which allowed anyone, including sinners, to join, the Puritans limited membership in their churches only to saints—those who had been chosen by God for salvation. They also sought to stamp out gambling, swearing, and Sabbath breaking. Their blameless lives and holy communities, they hoped, would provide a beacon of righteousness for a wicked England to emulate.

PLYMOUTH The first permanent English settlement in New England was established by the Plymouth Company, a group of seventy British investors. Eager to make money by exporting the colony's abundant natural resources, the joint-stock company agreed to finance settlements in exchange for the furs, timber, and fish they would ship back to England for sale.

Among the first to accept the company's offer were Puritan Separatists, or Pilgrims, who were forced to leave England because of their refusal to worship in Anglican churches. The Separatist "saints" demanded that each congregation govern itself rather than be ruled by a bureaucracy of bishops and archbishops.

The Separatists, mostly simple farm folk, sought to live in "peace, love, and holiness." Tired of being "clapped up in prison," they made the heartbreaking

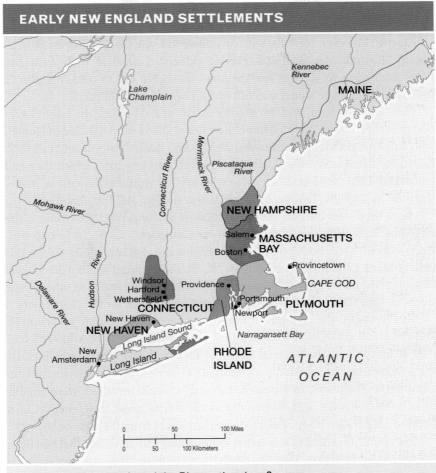

EARLY NEW ENGLAND SETTLEMENTS

- Why did Pilgrims found the Plymouth colony?
- How were the settlers of the Massachusetts Bay Colony different from those of Plymouth?
- What was the origin of the Rhode Island colony?

choice to leave England for Holland, where, over time, they worried that their children were becoming Dutch. Such concerns led them to leave Europe and create a holy community in America.

In September 1620, about 100 women, men, and children, some of whom were called "strangers" rather than saints because they were *not* part of the religious group, crammed aboard the tiny *Mayflower*, a leaky, three-masted vessel only 100 feet long, and headed across the Atlantic bound for the Virginia colony, where they had obtained permission to settle. Each colonist received one share in the enterprise in exchange for working seven years in America.

Storms, however, blew the ship off course to Cape Cod, southeast of what became Boston, Massachusetts. Having exhausted most of their food and water after sixty-six days at sea, they had no choice but to settle there in "a hideous and desolate wilderness full of wild beasts and wild men."

Now safely on land, William Bradford, who would become the colony's second governor, wrote, "they fell upon their knees and blessed the God of Heaven who had brought them over the vast and furious ocean." They would call their hillside settlement Plymouth, after the English port city from which they had embarked. Like the Jamestown colonists, they too would experience a "starving time" of drought, famine, bitter cold, desperation, and frequent deaths.

Since they were outside the jurisdiction of any organized government, the forty-one Separatists signed the **Mayflower Compact**, a covenant (group contract) to form "a civil body politic" based on "just and civil laws" designed for "our better ordering and protection." But the Mayflower Compact was not democracy in action. The saints granted themselves the rights to vote and hold office. Their inferiors—the strangers and servants—would have to wait for their civil rights.

At Plymouth, the civil government grew out of the church government, and the members of each were identical. The signers of the Mayflower Compact at first met as the General Court of Plymouth Plantation, which chose the governor and his assistants (or council). Other property owners were later admitted as members, or freemen, but only church members were eligible to join the General Court. Eventually, as the colony grew, the General Court became a legislative body of elected representatives from the various towns.

The colonists settled in a deserted Wampanoag Indian village that had been devastated by smallpox. Like the Jamestown colonists, they, too, experienced a difficult "starving time." During the first winter, half of them died, including thirteen of the eighteen married women. Only the discovery of stored Indian corn buried underground enabled the survivors to persist.

Eventually, a local Indian named Squanto taught the colonists how to grow corn, catch fish, gather nuts and berries, and negotiate with the Wampanoags. Still, when a shipload of colonists arrived in 1623, they "fell a-weeping" as they found the original colonists in such a "low and poor condition." By the 1630s, Governor Bradford was lamenting the failure of Plymouth to become the thriving holy community he and others had envisioned.

MASSACHUSETTS BAY The Plymouth colony's population never rose above 7,000, and after ten years it was overshadowed by its much larger neighbor, the Massachusetts Bay Colony. Like Plymouth, the new colony was also intended to be a holy commonwealth for Puritans, but the Massachusetts Bay Puritans were different from the Pilgrims. They remained Anglicans—they wanted to purify the Church of England from within. They were called nonseparating *Congregationalists* because their churches were governed by their congregations rather than by an Anglican bishop in England. Like the Pilgrims, the Puritans limited church membership to "visible saints"—those who could demonstrate that they had received the gift of God's grace.

In 1629, King Charles I gave a royal charter to the Massachusetts Bay Company, a group of Calvinist Puritans led by John Winthrop, a lawyer with intense religious convictions and mounting debts. Winthrop wanted the colony to be a haven for Puritans and a model Christian community where Jesus Christ would be exalted and faith would flourish. They would create "a City upon a Hill," as he declared, borrowing the phrase from Jesus's Sermon on the Mount. "The eyes of all people are on us," Winthrop said, so they must live up to their sacred destiny.

Winthrop shrewdly took advantage of an oversight in the company charter: It did not require that the joint-stock company maintain its home office in England. The Puritans took the royal charter with them, thereby transferring government authority from London to Massachusetts, where they hoped to govern themselves.

In 1630, Winthrop, his wife, three of his sons, and eight servants joined some 700 Puritan settlers on eleven ships loaded with cows, horses, supplies, and tons of beer, which remained safely drinkable much longer than did water. Unlike the first colonists in Virginia, most of the Puritans in Massachusetts arrived as family groups.

On June 12, Winthrop's ships landed at Salem. The Puritans then moved to the mouth of the Charles River, where they built a village and called it Boston, after the English town of that name. Winthrop was delighted to discover that the local Indians had been "swept away by the smallpox . . . so God hath hereby cleared

John Winthrop The first governor of the Massachusetts Bay Colony, he envisioned the colony as "a City upon a Hill."

our title to this place." Yet disease knew no boundaries. Within eight months, some 200 Puritans had died, and many others had returned to England.

Planting colonies was not for the faint-hearted. Anne Bradstreet, who became one of the first colonial poets, spoke for many when she lamented the difficult living conditions: "After I was convinced it was the way of God, I submitted to it." Such submissiveness to divine will sustained the Puritans through many trials. What allowed the Massachusetts Bay Colony eventually to thrive was a flood of additional colonists who brought money, skills, and needed supplies.

Winthrop was a commanding figure determined to enforce religious devotion and ensure social stability. He and other Puritan leaders prized law and order and hated the idea of democracy—the people ruling themselves. As the Reverend John Cotton explained, "If the people be governors, who shall be governed?" Cotton, Winthrop, and others spent much of their time trying to convince or force the growing population to conform to their beliefs.

New England villages were fractious places; people loved to argue and judge their neighbors' conduct. John Winthrop never embraced religious toleration, political freedom, social equality, or cultural diversity. The only freedom he tolerated was the freedom to do what was "good, just, and honest." He and the Puritans worked to suppress other religious views in New England. Catholics, Anglicans, Quakers, and Baptists were punished, imprisoned, banished, and sometimes executed.

Anne Hutchinson Puritans who spoke out against religious or political policies were quickly condemned. For example, Anne Hutchinson, the strong-willed wife of a prominent merchant, raised thirteen children, served as a midwife helping deliver neighbors' babies, and hosted meetings in her home to discuss sermons.

Soon, however, the discussions turned into large twice-weekly gatherings at which Hutchinson shared her passionate convictions about religious matters. According to one participant, she "preaches better Gospel than any of your black coats [male ministers]." Blessed with vast biblical knowledge and a quick wit, Hutchinson criticized mandatory church attendance and the absolute power of ministers and magistrates. Most controversial of all, she claimed to know which of her neighbors had been saved and which were damned, including ministers. Puritan leaders saw her as a "dangerous" woman who threatened their authority.

A pregnant Hutchinson was hauled before the all-male General Court in 1637. For two days she sparred with the Puritan leaders, at one point reminding them of the biblical injunction that "elder women should instruct the younger." She steadfastly refused to acknowledge any wrongdoing. Her ability to cite chapter-and-verse biblical defenses of her actions led an exasperated Governor Winthrop to explode: "We are your judges, and not you ours. . . . We do not mean to discourse [debate] with those of your sex." As the trial continued, Hutchinson was eventually lured into convicting herself by claiming direct revelations from God—blasphemy in the eyes of mainstream Puritans. In 1638, Winthrop and the General Court banished Hutchinson as a "leper" not fit for "our society."

Hutchinson initially resettled with her family and about sixty followers on an island south of Providence, Rhode Island. The hard journey took its toll, however. Hutchinson grew sick, and her baby was stillborn, leading her critics to claim that the "monstrous birth" was God's way of punishing her.

The trial of Anne Hutchinson In this nineteenth-century wood engraving, Anne Hutchinson stands her ground against charges of heresy from the all-male leaders of Puritan Boston.

Her spirits never recovered. After her husband's death in 1642, she and her followers resettled along a river in the Bronx, near New Amsterdam (New York City), which was then under Dutch control. The following year, Indians massacred Hutchinson, six of her children, and nine others. Her murder, wrote John Winthrop, was "a special manifestation of divine justice." Recent research suggests that Winthrop may have encouraged the Indian raid.

REPRESENTATIVE GOVERNMENT The transfer of the Massachusetts Bay Colony's royal charter, whereby an English trading company evolved into a provincial government, was a unique venture in colonization. Unlike "Old" England, New England had no lords or bishops, kings or queens. The Massachusetts General Court, wherein power rested under the royal charter, consisted of all shareholders, or property owners, called freemen. At first, the freemen had no power except to choose "assistants," who in turn elected the governor and deputy governor. In 1634, however, the freemen turned themselves into the General Court, with two or three deputies to represent each town.

The Puritans, having fled religious persecution, ensured that their liberties in America were spelled out and protected. Over time, membership in a Puritan church replaced the purchase of stock as the means of becoming a freeman (and thus a voter) in Massachusetts Bay. In sum, the vital godliness and zeal of the New England Puritans shaped their society and governed their lives.

RHODE ISLAND   More by accident than design, the Massachusetts Bay Colony became the staging area for other New England colonies created by people dissatisfied with Puritan ways. Roger Williams (1603–1683), who had arrived from England in 1631, was among the first to cause problems, precisely because he was the purest of Puritans—a Separatist who criticized "impure" Puritans for not abandoning the "whorish" Church of England.

Where John Winthrop cherished strict governmental and clerical authority, Williams championed individual liberty. The Puritan leaders were mistaken, he claimed, in requiring everyone, including nonmembers, to attend church. To Williams, true *puritanism* required complete separation of church and state and freedom from all coercion in matters of faith. "Forced worship," he declared, "stinks in God's nostrils."

Williams held a brief pastorate in Salem, north of Boston, and then moved south to Separatist Plymouth, where he took the time to learn Indian languages and continued to question the right of English settlers to confiscate Native American lands. He then returned to Salem, where he came to love and support the Indians.

Williams posed a radical question: If one's salvation depends solely upon God's grace, as John Calvin had argued, why bother to have churches at all? Why not give individuals the right to worship God directly, in their own way? His belief that a true church must include only those who had received God's gift of grace eventually convinced him that no true church was possible, unless perhaps it consisted of his wife and himself.

Such "dangerous opinions" threatened the foundations of New England Puritanism and led Governor Winthrop and the General Court to banish Williams to England. Before authorities could ship him back, however, he and his wife slipped away and found shelter among the Narragansett Indians. He studied their language, defended their rights as human beings, and in 1636 he bought land from them to establish a town he named Providence, at the head of Narragansett Bay. It was the first permanent settlement in Rhode Island and the first in America to allow complete freedom of religion and to give voting rights to all "free inhabitants," meaning those property owners who were not enslaved or indentured servants.

From the beginning, Rhode Island was the most democratic of the colonies, governed by the heads of households rather than by church members. The colony welcomed all who fled religious persecution. For their part, Puritans in Boston came to view Rhode Island as "Rogue Island," a refuge for rebels and radicals. A Dutch visitor reported that the colony was "the sewer of New England." Yet by the 1670s, an English official would describe Rhode Island as the "most profitable part of New England."

CONNECTICUT, NEW HAMPSHIRE, AND MAINE Other New England colonies had more conventional beginnings. In 1636, the Reverend Thomas Hooker led three church congregations from the Boston area to Connecticut, where they organized a self-governing colony and founded the town of Hartford. Hooker resented John Winthrop's iron grip on politics in the Bay Colony and believed that all men, not just church members, should be able to vote.

In 1639, the Connecticut General Court adopted the Fundamental Orders, a series of laws that provided for a "Christian Commonwealth" like that of Massachusetts, except that all freemen could vote. The Connecticut constitution specified that the Congregational Church would be the colony's official religion, and it commanded each governor to rule according to "the word of God."

In 1622, territory north of Hartford was granted to Sir Ferdinando Gorges and Captain John Mason. In 1629, Mason took the southern part, which he named the Province of New Hampshire, and Gorges took the northern part, which became the Province of Maine.

During the early 1640s, Massachusetts took over New Hampshire, and in the 1650s it extended its authority to the scattered settlements in Maine. This led to lawsuits, and in 1678 English judges decided against Massachusetts in both cases. In 1679, New Hampshire became a royal colony, but Massachusetts continued to control Maine. A new Massachusetts charter in 1691 finally incorporated Maine into Massachusetts.

THE ENGLISH CIVIL WAR IN AMERICA

By 1640, English settlers in New England and around Chesapeake Bay had established two great beachheads on the Atlantic coast, with the Dutch colony of New Netherland in between. After 1640, however, the struggle between king and Parliament in England diverted attention from colonization, and migration to America dwindled. During the English Civil War (1642–1651) and Oliver Cromwell's Puritan dictatorship (1653–1658), the mother country pretty much left its American colonies alone.

THE RESTORATION IN THE COLONIES

The restoration of Charles II to the English throne in 1660 revived interest in colonial expansion. Within twelve years, the English would conquer New Netherland and settle Carolina. In the middle region, formerly claimed by the Dutch, four new colonies would emerge: New York, New Jersey, Pennsylvania, and Delaware. The king awarded them to men (proprietors) who had remained loyal to the monarchy during the civil war. In 1663, Charles II granted a vast parcel of land south of Virginia to eight prominent supporters who became lords proprietor (owners) of the region they called Carolina, from the Latin spelling of Charles.

THE CAROLINAS From the start, the southernmost mainland colony in the seventeenth century consisted of two widely separated areas that eventually became the colonies of North Carolina and South Carolina. The northernmost, initially called Albemarle, had been settled in the 1650s by colonists from Virginia. For half a century, Albemarle was an isolated cluster of farms along the shores of Albemarle Sound. Not until 1712 would Carolina be separated into northern and southern colonies.

The eight lords proprietor focused on more-promising sites in southern Carolina. To speed their efforts to generate profits from sugarcane, they recruited English planters from the Caribbean island of Barbados, the oldest, richest, and most heavily populated colony in English America.

BARBADOS The mostly male English in Barbados had developed a hugely profitable sugar plantation system based on the hard labor of enslaved Africans. The "king sugar" colony, the easternmost island in the Caribbean, was dominated by a few extraordinarily wealthy planters who exercised powerful political influence in the mother country. In a reference to Barbados and the other "sugar colonies," an Englishman pointed out in 1666 that "these Settlements have been made and upheld by Negroes and without constant supplies of them cannot subsist."

By 1670, Barbados hosted some 25,000 whites and more than 35,000 enslaved Africans. All available land on Barbados had been claimed, and the sons and grandsons of the planter elite were forced to look elsewhere to find estates of their own. Many seized the chance to settle Carolina and bring the Barbadian plantation system to the new American colony.

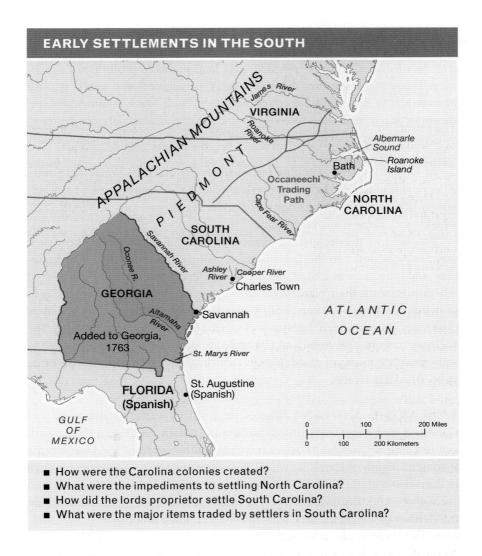

EARLY SETTLEMENTS IN THE SOUTH

- How were the Carolina colonies created?
- What were the impediments to settling North Carolina?
- How did the lords proprietor settle South Carolina?
- What were the major items traded by settlers in South Carolina?

CAROLINA The first English colonists in South Carolina arrived in 1669 at Charles Town (later Charleston). Over the next twenty years, half the colonists came from Barbados and other island colonies in the Caribbean, such as Nevis, St. Kitts, and Jamaica.

From the start, South Carolina was a slave-based colony. Planters from the Caribbean brought enormous numbers of enslaved Africans to Carolina to clear land, plant crops, and herd cattle. Carolina, a Swiss immigrant said, "looks more like a negro country than like a country settled by white people."

The government of Carolina grew out of a unique document, the Fundamental Constitutions of Carolina, drafted by one of the eight proprietors, Lord Anthony Ashley Cooper. It awarded large land grants to prominent Englishmen. From the beginning, however, every immigrant who could pay for passage across the Atlantic received headright land. The Fundamental Constitutions granted religious toleration, which gave Carolina a greater degree of religious freedom (extending to Jews and "heathens") than in England or any other colony except Rhode Island.

In 1712, the Carolina colony was formally divided into North and South. After rebelling against the lords proprietor, South Carolina became a royal colony in 1719. North Carolina remained under the proprietors' rule until 1729, when it, too, became a royal colony.

Rice became the dominant commercial crop in South Carolina because it was perfectly suited to the hot, humid growing conditions. Rice, like sugarcane and tobacco, was a labor-intensive crop, and planters preferred enslaved Africans to work their plantations, in part because West Africans had been growing rice for generations. Both Carolinas also had huge forests of yellow pine trees that provided lumber and other materials for shipbuilding. The sticky resin from pine trees could be boiled to make tar, which was needed to waterproof the seams of wooden ships (which is why North Carolinians came to be called Tar Heels).

ENSLAVING INDIANS One of the quickest ways to make money in Carolina's early years was through trade with Indians. In the late seventeenth century, English merchants began traveling southward from Virginia into the Piedmont region of Carolina, where they developed a prosperous commerce in deerskins with the Catawbas. Between 1699 and 1715, Carolina exported an average of 54,000 deerskins per year to England, where they were transformed into leather gloves, belts, hats, work aprons, and book bindings.

English traders also quickly became interested in buying enslaved Indians. To do so, the traders at times fomented war between Indian tribes; they knew that the best Indian slave catchers were other Indians. That Native Americans had for centuries captured and enslaved other indigenous peoples helped the Europeans justify and expand the sordid practice.

In Carolina, as many as 50,000 Indians were sold as slaves in Charles Town between 1670 and 1715, with many being shipped to faraway lands—Barbados, Antigua, New York. More enslaved Indians were exported during that period than Africans were imported, and thousands of others were sold to "slavers" who took them to islands in the Caribbean.

The growing commerce in people, however, triggered bitter struggles between rival Indian nations and helped ignite unprecedented violence. In 1712, the Tuscaroras of North Carolina attacked German and English colonists who had encroached upon their land. North Carolina authorities appealed to South Carolina for aid, and the colony, eager for more slaves, dispatched two expeditions made up mostly of Indian allies of the English—Yamasees, Cherokees, Creeks, and Catawbas. They destroyed a Tuscarora town, executed 162 male warriors, and took 392 women and children captive for sale in Charles Town. The surviving Tuscaroras fled north, where they joined the Iroquois.

The Tuscarora War sparked more conflict in South Carolina. The Yamasees felt betrayed when white traders paid them less for their Tuscarora captives than they wanted. In April 1715, Yamasees attacked coastal plantations and killed more than 100 whites.

The governor mobilized all white and black men to defend the colony; other colonies supplied weapons. But it wasn't until the governor bribed the Cherokees to join them that the Yamasee War ended—in 1717. The defeated Yamasees fled to Spanish-controlled Florida. By then, hundreds of whites had been killed and dozens of plantations destroyed and abandoned. To prevent another conflict, the colonial government outlawed all private trading with Indians.

THE MIDDLE COLONIES AND GEORGIA

The area between New England and the Chesapeake—Maryland and Virginia—included the "middle colonies" of New York, New Jersey, Delaware, and Pennsylvania, which were initially controlled by the Netherlands, a newly independent republic of 2 million people. By 1670, the mostly Protestant Dutch had the largest merchant fleet in the world and controlled northern European commerce. They had become one of the most diverse and tolerant societies in Europe—and England's fiercest competitor in international commerce.

NEW NETHERLAND BECOMES NEW YORK In London, King Charles II decided to pluck out that old Dutch thorn in the side of the English colonies in America: New Netherland, which was older than New England. The Dutch East India Company (organized in 1602) had hired English sea captain Henry Hudson to explore America in hopes of finding a northwest passage to the Indies. Sailing along the coast of North America in 1609, Hudson crossed Delaware Bay and then sailed ninety miles up the "wide and deep" river that eventually would be named for him in New York State.

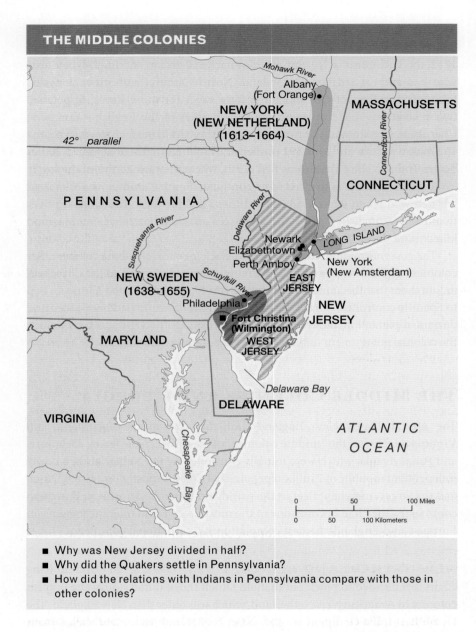

THE MIDDLE COLONIES

Mohawk River

Albany
(Fort Orange)

NEW YORK
(NEW NETHERLAND)
(1613–1664)

MASSACHUSETTS

Connecticut River

42° parallel

CONNECTICUT

P E N N S Y L V A N I A

Delaware River

Susquehanna River

Newark
Elizabethtown
Perth Amboy

LONG ISLAND

New York
(New Amsterdam)

NEW SWEDEN
(1638–1655)

Schuylkill River

EAST
JERSEY

Philadelphia

NEW
JERSEY

Fort Christina
(Wilmington)

WEST
JERSEY

MARYLAND

Delaware Bay

DELAWARE

VIRGINIA

Chesapeake Bay

ATLANTIC
OCEAN

0   50   100 Miles

0   50   100 Kilometers

- Why was New Jersey divided in half?
- Why did the Quakers settle in Pennsylvania?
- How did the relations with Indians in Pennsylvania compare with those in other colonies?

The Hudson River would become one of the most strategically important waterways in America; it was wide and deep enough for oceangoing vessels to travel far north into the interior, where the Dutch traded various goods for the fur pelts harvested by Indian trappers. In 1625, Dutch traders acquired 5,295 beaver pelts and 463 otter skins, which they shipped to the Netherlands.

Like Virginia and Massachusetts, New Netherland was created as a profit-making enterprise. "Everyone here is a trader," explained one resident. And like the French, the Dutch were interested mainly in the fur trade, as the European demand for beaver hats created huge profits. In 1610, the Dutch established fur-trading posts on Manhattan Island and upriver at Fort Orange (later called Albany).

In 1626, the Dutch governor purchased Manhattan (an Indian word meaning "island of many hills") from the Indians for 60 guilders, or about $1,000 in current values. The Dutch then built a fort and a fur-trading post at the lower end of the island. The village of New Amsterdam (eventually New York City), which grew up around the fort, became the capital of New Netherland.

New Netherland was a corporate colony governed by the newly organized Dutch West India Company. It controlled political life, appointing the colony's governor and advisory council and forbid any form of elected legislature. All commerce with the Netherlands had to be carried in the company's ships, and the company controlled the beaver trade with the Indians.

In 1629, the Dutch West India Company decided that it needed more settlers outside Manhattan to help protect the colony from Indian attacks. To encourage settlers to move into the surrounding countryside, it awarded wealthy individuals a large estate called a *patroonship* in exchange for peopling it with fifty adult settlers within four years. Like a feudal lord, the *patroon* (from the Latin word for father) provided cattle, tools, and buildings. His tenants paid him rent, used his gristmill for grinding flour, gave him first option to purchase surplus crops, and submitted to a court he established.

These arrangements, which amounted to transplanting the feudal manor to America, met with little success. Most settlers took advantage of the company's provision that they could have as farms (*bouweries*) all the lands they could improve.

Unlike most of the other European colonies in the Americas, the Dutch embraced ethnic and religious diversity, since their passion for profits outweighed their social prejudices. In 1579, the treaty creating the Dutch Republic declared that "everyone shall remain free in religion and . . . no one may be persecuted or investigated because of religion."

Both the Dutch Republic and New Netherland welcomed exiles from Europe: Spanish and German Jews, French Protestants (Huguenots), English Puritans, and Catholics. There were even Muslims in New Amsterdam, where in the 1640s the 500 residents communicated in eighteen different languages. So from its inception, New York City was America's first multiethnic community, and immigrant minorities dominated its population.

But the Dutch did not show the same tolerance for Native Americans. Soldiers regularly massacred Indians in the region around New Amsterdam. At Pound Ridge, Anglo-Dutch soldiers surrounded an Indian village, set it ablaze, and killed all who tried to escape. Such horrific acts led the Indians to respond in kind.

Dutch tolerance had other limitations. In September 1654, a French ship arrived in New Amsterdam harbor carrying twenty-three *Sephardim*, Jews of Spanish-Portuguese descent. They had come seeking refuge from Portuguese-controlled Brazil and were the first Jewish settlers to arrive in North America.

The colonial governor, Peter Stuyvesant, refused to accept them, however. A short-tempered leader who had lost a leg to a Spanish cannonball, Stuyvesant dismissed Jews as a "deceitful race" and "hateful enemies." Dutch officials in Amsterdam overruled him, however, pointing out that it would be "unreasonable and unfair" to refuse to provide the Jews a safe haven. They wanted to "allow everyone to have his own belief, as long as he behaves quietly and legally, gives no offense to his neighbor, and does not oppose the government."

It would not be until the late seventeenth century that Jews could worship in public, however. Such restrictions help explain why the American Jewish community grew so slowly. In 1773, more than 100 years after the first Jewish refugees arrived, Jews represented only one tenth of 1 percent of the entire colonial population. Not until the nineteenth century would the American Jewish community experience dramatic growth.

In 1626, the Dutch West India Company began importing enslaved Africans to meet its labor shortage. By the 1650s, New Amsterdam had one of the largest slave markets in America.

The extraordinary success of the Dutch economy also proved to be its downfall, however. Like imperial Spain, the Dutch Empire expanded too rapidly. They dominated the European trade with China, India, Africa, Brazil, and the Caribbean, but they could not control their far-flung possessions. It did not take long for European rivals to exploit the sprawling empire's weak points.

The New Netherland governors were mostly corrupt or inept autocrats who were especially clumsy at Indian relations. They depended upon a small army for defense, and the residents of Manhattan, many of whom were not Dutch, were often contemptuous of the government. In 1664, the colonists showed almost total indifference when Governor Stuyvesant called on them to defend the colony against an English flotilla carrying 2,000 soldiers. Stuyvesant finally surrendered without firing a shot.

The English conquest of New Netherland had been led by James Stuart, Duke of York, who would later become King James II. Upon the capture of

New Amsterdam, his brother, King Charles II, granted the entire region to him. The Dutch, however, negotiated an unusual surrender agreement that allowed New Netherlanders to retain their property, churches, language, and local officials. The English renamed the harbor city of New Amsterdam as New York, in honor of the duke.

NEW JERSEY Shortly after the conquest of New Netherland, the Duke of York granted the lands between the Hudson and Delaware Rivers to Sir George Carteret and Lord John Berkeley and named the territory for Carteret's native Jersey, an island in the English Channel. In 1676, by mutual agreement, the new royal colony was divided into East and West Jersey, with Carteret taking the east and Berkeley the west. Finally, in 1682, Carteret sold out to a group of investors.

New settlements gradually arose in East Jersey. Disaffected Puritans from New Haven founded Newark, Carteret's brother brought a group to found Elizabethtown, and a group of Scots founded Perth Amboy. In the west, a scattering of Swedes, Finns, and Dutch remained, but they were soon over-whelmed by swarms of English and Welsh Quakers, as well as German and Scots-Irish settlers (mostly Presbyterian Scots who had been encouraged by the English government to migrate to Ireland and thereby dilute the appeal of Catholicism). In 1702, East and West Jersey were united as the single royal colony of New Jersey.

PENNSYLVANIA The Quakers, as the Society of Friends was called (because they believed that no one could know Christ without "quaking and trembling"), became the most uncompromising and controversial of the rad-ical religious groups that emerged from the English Civil War. Founded in England in 1647 by George Fox, the Friends rebelled against *all* forms of polit-ical and religious authority, including salaried ministers, military service, and paying taxes. They insisted that everyone could experience a personal revela-tion from God, what they called the "Inner Light" of the Holy Spirit.

Quakers believed that people were essentially good rather than depraved and could achieve salvation through a personal communion with God. They demanded complete religious freedom for everyone, promoted equality of the sexes, and discarded all formal religious creeds and rituals, including an ordained priesthood. When gathered for worship, they kept silent, knowing that the "Inner Light" would move them to say what was fitting at the right moment.

The Quakers were also pacifists who stressed the need to lead lives of ser-vice to society. Some early Quakers went barefoot; others wore rags, and a

Quaker meeting The presence of women speaking at this Friends meeting is evidence of progressive Quaker views on gender equality.

few went naked and smeared themselves with excrement to demonstrate their "primitive" commitment to Christ.

The Quakers suffered often violent abuse for their odd behavior because their beliefs were so threatening to the social and religious order. Authorities accused them of disrupting "peace and order" and undermining "religion, Church order, and the state." Quakers were especially hated because they refused to acknowledge the supremacy of Puritanism. New England Puritans first banned Quakers, then lopped off their ears, pierced their tongues with a red-hot rod, and finally executed them. Still, the Quakers kept coming. In fact, they often sought out abuse and martyrdom as proof of their intense Christian commitment. As the French philosopher Voltaire (François-Marie Arouet) said, "Getting persecuted is a great way of making converts" to one's religious views.

The settling of English Quakers in West Jersey encouraged other Friends to migrate, especially to the Delaware River side of the colony, where William Penn's Quaker commonwealth, the colony of Pennsylvania, soon arose. Penn, the son of wealthy Admiral Sir William Penn, had attended Oxford University, from which he was expelled for criticizing the university's requirement that students attend daily chapel services. His furious father banished his son from their home.

The younger Penn lived in France for two years, then studied law before moving to Ireland to manage the family's estates. There he was arrested in 1666 for attending a Quaker meeting. Much to the chagrin of his parents, he became a Quaker and was arrested several more times for his religious convictions.

Upon his father's death, Penn inherited a fortune, including a huge tract of land in America, which the king urged him to settle as a means of ridding England of Quakers. The land was named, at the king's insistence, for Penn's father—Pennsylvania (literally, "Penn's Woods")—and it was larger than England itself. Penn encouraged people of different religions from different countries to settle in the new colony, which he considered a "holy experiment" for people of all faiths and nations to live together in harmony. By the end of 1681, thousands of immigrants had responded, and a bustling town emerged at the junction of the Schuylkill and Delaware Rivers. Penn called it Philadelphia (meaning "City of Brotherly Love").

The relations between the Native Americans and the Pennsylvania Quakers were unusually good because of the Quakers' friendliness and Penn's policy of purchasing land titles from the Native Americans. For some fifty years, the settlers and Native Americans lived in peace.

The colony's government, which rested on three Frames of Government drafted by Penn, resembled that of other proprietary colonies except that the freemen (owners of at least fifty acres) who professed their belief in Jesus Christ elected the council members as well as the assembly. The governor had no veto, although Penn, as proprietor, did. Penn hoped to show that a colonial government could operate in accordance with Quaker principles, that it could maintain peace and order, and that religion could flourish without government support and with absolute freedom of conscience.

Over time, however, the Quakers struggled to forge a harmonious colony. In Pennsylvania's first ten years, it went through six governors. A disappointed Penn wrote from London: "Pray stop those scurvy quarrels that break out to the disgrace of the province."

DELAWARE In 1682, the Duke of York granted Penn the area of Delaware, another part of the former Dutch territory. At first, Delaware—named for the Delaware River—became part of Pennsylvania, but after 1704 it was granted the right to choose its own assembly. From then until the American Revolution, Delaware had a separate assembly but shared Pennsylvania's governor.

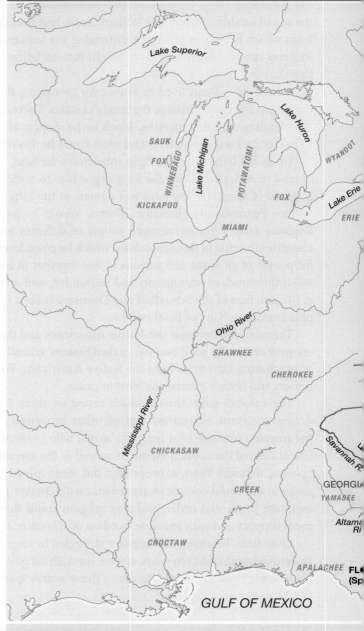

EUROPEAN SETTLEMENTS AND INDIAN

Lake Superior

Lake Huron

Lake Michigan

SAUK

FOX

WINNEBAGO

POTAWATOMI

WYANDOT

KICKAPOO

FOX

Lake Erie

ERIE

MIAMI

Ohio River

SHAWNEE

CHEROKEE

Mississippi River

Savannah R.

CHICKASAW

GEORGIA

CREEK

YAMASEE

Altama
Ri

CHOCTAW

APALACHEE FL
(Sp

GULF OF MEXICO

■ Why did European settlement lead to the expansion of
hostilities among the Indians?

■ What were the consequences of trade and commerce
between the English settlers and the southern indigenous
peoples?

■ How were the relationships between the settlers and the
members of the Iroquois League different from those between
settlers and tribes in other regions?

SOCIETIES IN EARLY NORTH AMERICA

Quebec
NEW FRANCE
Montreal
MAINE
ABENAKI
MAHICAN
Hudson R.
HURON
MOHAWK
MASSACHUSETT
Lake Ontario
ONEIDA
ONONDAGA
CAYUGA
SENECA
IROQUOIS
Albany
MA
Boston
WAMPANOAG
NAUSET
Providence
Hartford
RI
PEQUOT
NARRAGANSETT
CONNECTICUT
Delaware R.
New York
PA
NJ
Philadelphia
DELAWARE
MD
DE
Potomac R.
NANTICOKE
POWHATAN
St. Marys
VIRGINIA
James R.
Jamestown
Occaneechi Trading Path
ATLANTIC OCEAN
TUSCARORA
NORTH CAROLINA
LINE
CATAWBA
SOUTH
AROLINA
Charleston
Savannah
TIMUCUA
DA
sh)
0
100
200 Miles
0
100
200 Kilometers

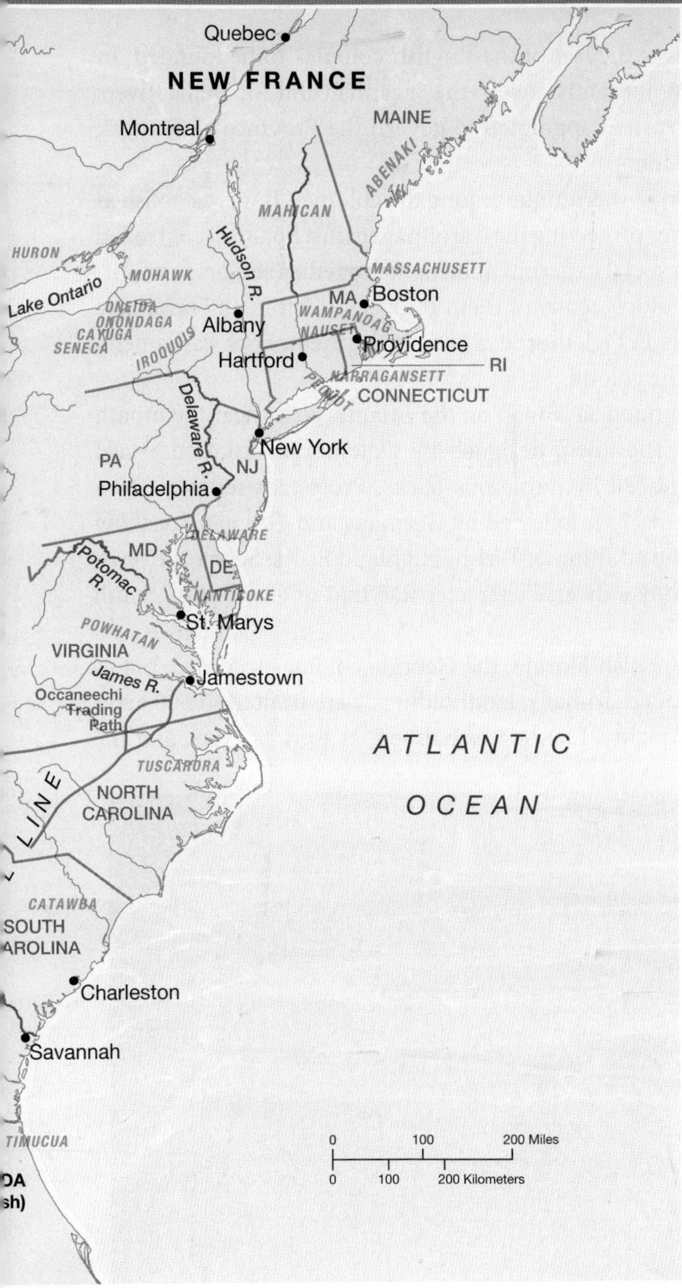

GEORGIA Georgia was the last of the English colonies to be founded. In 1732, King George II gave the land between the Savannah and Altamaha Rivers to twenty-one English trustees appointed to govern the Province of Georgia, named in honor of the king.

In two respects, Georgia was unique among the colonies. It was established to provide a military buffer protecting the Carolinas against Spanish-controlled Florida and to serve as a social experiment bringing together settlers from different countries and religions, many of them refugees, debtors, or "miserable wretches." General James E. Oglethorpe, a prominent member of Parliament, was appointed to head the colony.

In 1733, colonists founded Savannah on the Atlantic coast near the mouth of the Savannah River. The town, designed by Oglethorpe, featured a grid of crisscrossing roads graced by numerous parks. Protestant refugees from Austria began to arrive in 1734, followed by Germans and German-speaking Moravians and Swiss. The addition of Welsh, Highland Scots, Sephardic Jews, and others gave the colony a diverse character like that of Charleston, South Carolina.

As a buffer against Spanish Florida, the Georgia colony succeeded, but as a social experiment, it failed. Initially, landholdings were limited to 500 acres to promote economic equality. Liquor was banned, as were lawyers, and the

Savannah, Georgia The earliest known view of Savannah, Georgia (1734). The town's layout was carefully planned.

importation of saves was forbidden. The idealistic rules soon collapsed, however, as the olony struggled to become self-sufficient. The regulations against rum and savery were widely disregarded and finally abandoned.

In 1754, Georgia became a royal colony, and it began to grow rapidly after 1763. Georgians exported rice, lumber, beef, and pork, and they carried on a profitable trade with Caribbean islands. Almost unintentionally, the colony became an economic success and a slave-centered society.

NATIVE PEOPLES AND ENGLISH SETTLERS

Most English colonists adopted a strategy for dealing with the Indians quite different from that of the French and the Dutch, who focused on exploiting the fur trade. The thriving commerce in animal skins helped spur exploration of the vast American continent. It also enriched and devastated the lives of Indians.

To protect a steady supply of fur pelts, the French and Dutch built outposts in upper New York and along the Great Lakes, where they established friendly relations with the Hurons and Algonquians who sought French support in their wars with the Iroquois nations. In contrast to the French experience in Canada, the English colonists were more interested in pursuing their "God-given" right to hunt and farm on Indian lands and to fish in Indian waters.

NATIVE AMERICANS AND CHRISTIANITY The New England Puritans aggressively tried to convert Native Americans to Christianity and "civilized" living. They insisted that Indian converts abandon their religion, language, clothes, names, and villages, and forced them to move to what were called "praying towns" to separate them from their "heathen" brethren.

THE PEQUOT WAR Indians in the English colonies who fought to keep their lands were forced out or killed. In 1636, settlers in Massachusetts accused a Pequot of murdering two white traders. The English took revenge by burning a Pequot village. As the Indians fled, the Puritans killed them. The militia commander declared that God had guided his actions "to smite our Enemies . . . and give us their land for an Inheritance."

Sassacus, the Pequot chief, organized the survivors and counterattacked. During the ensuing Pequot War of 1637, the colonists and their Mohegan and Narragansett allies set fire to a Pequot village and killed hundreds, including women and children. William Bradford, the governor of Plymouth, admitted that it was "a fearful sight" to see the Indians "frying in the fire and the streams

King Philip's War A 1772 engraving by Paul Revere depicts Metacom (King Philip), leader of the Wampanoags.

of blood quenching the flames, but "the victory seemed a sweet sacrifice" delivered by God.

The scattered remnants of the Pequot Nation were then hunted down. Under the terms of the Treaty of Hartford (1638), the Pequot Nation was dissolved. Captured warriors and boys were sold as slaves to plantations on Barbados and Jamaica in exchange for African slaves. Pequot women were enslaved in New England as house servants.

KING PHILIP'S WAR For almost forty years after the Pequot War, relations between colonists and Indians improved somewhat, but the continuing influx of English settlers and the decline of the beaver population eventually reduced the Native Americans to poverty. In the process, the Indians and English settlers came to fear each other deeply.

The era of peaceful coexistence ended in 1675. Native American leaders, especially the chief of the Wampanoags, Metacom (known to the colonists as King Philip), resented the efforts of Europeans to take their lands and convert Indians to Christianity. In the fall of 1674, John Sassamon, a Christian Indian who had graduated from Harvard College, warned the Plymouth governor that the Wampanoags were preparing for war.

A few months later, Sassamon was found dead in a frozen pond. With little evidence to go on, colonial authorities nevertheless convicted three Wampanoags of murder and hanged them. Enraged Wampanoag warriors then burned Puritan farms on June 20, 1675. Three days later, an Englishman shot a Wampanoag; the Wampanoags retaliated by ambushing a group of Puritans, "beheading, dismembering, and mangling" the bodies in a "most inhumane" manner.

The shocking violence soon spun out of control in what came to be called **King Philip's War**, or Metacom's War. Over fourteen months, the fighting resulted in more deaths and destruction in New England in proportion to the population than any conflict since. Rival Indian nations fought on opposite sides. The colonists launched a surprise attack that killed 300 Narragansett warriors and 400 women and children. The Narragansetts retaliated by destroying Providence, Rhode Island, and threatening Boston itself, prompting a minister to call it "the saddest time with New England that was ever known." A Boston merchant lamented that unless the tide was reversed, "these colonies will soon be ruined." The situation grew so desperate that the colonies passed America's first conscription laws, drafting into the militia all males between the ages of sixteen and sixty.

In the end, 600 colonists, 5 percent of the white male population, died during the war. Some 1,200 homes were burned and 8,000 cattle killed. The Wampanoags and their allies suffered even higher casualties, perhaps as many as 4,000 dead. The colonists destroyed numerous villages and shipped off hundreds of Indians as slaves to the Caribbean islands.

The war and its aftermath slashed New England's Indian population in half, to fewer than 9,000. Those who remained were forced into villages supervised by English officials. Metacom initially escaped, only to be hunted down and killed. The victorious New Englanders marched Metacom's severed head to Plymouth, where it stayed atop a pole for twenty years, a grisly reminder of the English determination to ensure their dominance over Native Americans.

THE IROQUOIS LEAGUE The same combination of forces that wiped out the Indian populations of New England and the Carolinas affected the native peoples around New York City and the lower Hudson Valley. The inability of Indian groups to unite effectively, as well as their vulnerability to infectious diseases, doomed them to conquest and exploitation. Yet indigenous peoples throughout the colonies, drawing upon their spiritual traditions in the face of barbarous suffering, came together to reconstruct their devastated communities.

In the interior of New York, for example, the Iroquois nations—Seneca, Cayuga, Onondaga, Oneida, and Mohawk—were convinced by Hiawatha, a Mohawk, to forge an alliance. The **Iroquois League**, known to its members as the *Haudenosaunee*, or Great Peace, became so strong that the Dutch and, later, English traders were forced to work with them. By the early seventeenth century, a council of some fifty sachems (chieftains) oversaw the 12,000 members of the Iroquois League.

The League benefited from a remarkable constitution, called the Great Law of Peace, which had three main principles: peace, equity, and justice. Each person was to be a shareholder in the wealth of the nation. The constitution established a Great Council of fifty male *royaneh* (religious and political leaders), each representing one of the female-led clans of the Iroquois nations. The Great Law of Peace insisted that every time the royaneh dealt with "an especially important matter or a great emergency," they had to "submit the matter to the decision of their people," both men and women, for their consent.

The search for furs and captives led Iroquois war parties to range widely across what is today eastern North America. They gained control over a huge area from the St. Lawrence River to Tennessee and from Maine to Michigan. For more than twenty years, warfare raged across the Great Lakes region between the Iroquois (supported by Dutch and English fur traders) and the Algonquians and Hurons (and their French allies).

In the 1690s, the French and their Indian allies destroyed Iroquois crops and villages, infected them with smallpox, and reduced the male Iroquois population by more than a third. Facing extermination, the Iroquois made peace in 1701. During the first half of the eighteenth century, they stayed out of the almost constant wars between the English and French, which enabled them to play the two European powers off against each other while creating a thriving fur trade for themselves.

Algonquian ceremony celebrating harvest As with most Native Americans, the Algonquians' dependence on nature for survival shaped their religious beliefs.

SLAVERY IN THE COLONIES

SLAVERY IN NORTH AMERICA By 1700, enslaved Africans made up 11 percent of the total American population. (Slaves would comprise more than 20 percent by 1770.) But slavery differed greatly from region to region. Africans were a tiny minority in New England (about 2 percent). Because there were no large plantations there and fewer slaves were owned, "family slavery" prevailed, with masters and slaves usually living under the same roof.

Slavery was much more common in the Chesapeake colonies and the Carolinas. By 1730, the black slave population in Virginia and Maryland had achieved a self-sustaining rate of growth, enabling the population to replenish itself naturally, thereby removing the need for slaves imported from Africa.

SLAVERY'S AFRICAN ROOTS The transport of African captives to the Americas was the largest forced migration in world history. More than 10 million people eventually made the journey to the Western Hemisphere, the vast majority of them going to Portuguese Brazil or Caribbean sugar islands such as Barbados and Jamaica.

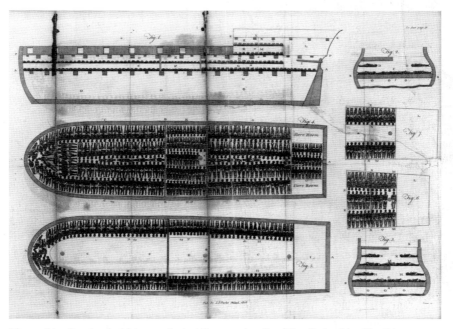

Slave ship One in six Africans died while crossing the Atlantic in ships like this one, from an American diagram ca. 1808.

THE AFRICAN SLAVE TRADE, 1500–1800

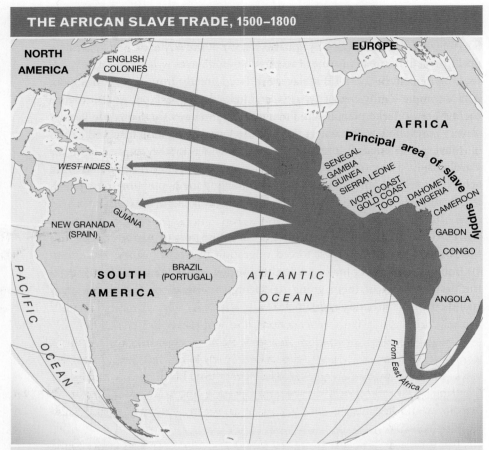

- How were Africans captured and enslaved?
- Describe how captive Africans were treated during the Middle Passage.
- How did enslaved African Americans create a new culture in the colonies?

Enslaved Africans spoke as many as fifty different languages and worshipped many different gods. In their homelands, Africans had preyed upon other Africans. Warfare was almost constant, as rival tribes conquered, kidnapped, enslaved, and sold one another.

Slavery in Africa, however, was less brutal than in the Americas. In Africa, slaves lived with their captors, and their children were not automatically enslaved. The involvement of Europeans in transatlantic slavery, whereby captives were sold and shipped to other nations, was much worse.

During the seventeenth and eighteenth centuries, African slave traders brought captives to dozens of "slave forts" along the West African coast. After languishing for weeks or months, the captured Africans would be led to waiting ships owned by Europeans. As one of them remembered, "it was a most horrible scene; there was nothing to be heard but rattling of chains, smacking of whips, and groans and cries of our fellow men."

Once purchased, the captives were branded on the back or buttocks with a company mark, put in chains, and loaded onto slave ships. They were packed below deck and subjected to a transatlantic voyage that could last up to six months. It was known as the **Middle Passage** because it served as the middle leg of the so-called *triangular trade* in which British ships traveled on the first leg to West Africa, where they exchanged rum, clothing, and guns for slaves. The slaves then were taken on the second leg to American ports, where they were sold. The ships were then loaded with commodities and timber before returning to Britain and Europe on the final leg of the triangular trade. By the mid–eighteenth century, Britain was the largest slaving nation in the world.

The rapid growth of slavery was driven by high profits and justified by a widespread racism that viewed Africans as beasts of burden rather than human beings. Once in America, Africans were treated as property (chattel), herded in chains to public slave auctions, and sold to the highest bidder.

On large southern plantations that grew tobacco, sugarcane, or rice, slaves were organized into work gangs supervised by black "drivers" and white overseers. The slaves were often quartered in barracks, fed like livestock, and issued ill-fitting clothes and shoes. They were whipped, branded, shackled, castrated, or sold away, often to the Caribbean islands, where few survived the harsh working conditions.

The enslaved Africans, however, found ingenious ways to cope. Some rebelled by resisting work orders, sabotaging crops and stealing tools, faking illness or injury, or running away. If caught, runaways faced terrible punishment. If successful, however, they faced uncertain freedom. Where would they run *to* in a society ruled by whites and governed by racism?

SLAVE CULTURE While being forced into lives of bondage, Africans forged a new identity as African Americans. At the same time, they wove into American culture many strands of their heritage, including new words such as *tabby, tote, goober, yam,* and *banana.* More significant were African influences upon American music, folklore, and religious practices. Slaves often used songs, stories, and religious preachings to circulate coded messages expressing their distaste for masters or overseers. The fundamental theme of slave religion, adapted from the Christianity that was forced upon them, was deliverance: God would free them and open the gates to heaven's promised land.

African cultural heritage in the South The survival of African culture among enslaved Americans is evident in this late eighteenth-century painting of a South Carolina plantation. The musical instruments and pottery are of African origin (probably Yoruban).

THRIVING COLONIES

By the early eighteenth century, the English colonies in the New World had outstripped those of both the French and the Spanish. English America had become the most populous, prosperous, and powerful of the European empires. Yet many settlers found hard labor, desperation, and an early death in the New World. Others flourished only because they were able to exploit Indians, indentured servants, or Africans.

The English colonists did enjoy crucial advantages over their European rivals. While the tightly controlled colonial empires of Spain and France stifled innovation, the English colonies were organized as profit-making enterprises with a minimum of royal control. Where New Spain was dominated by wealthy men who often intended to return to Spain, many English colonists ventured to America because, for them, life in England had grown intolerable. The leaders of the Dutch and non-Puritan English colonies, unlike the Spanish and French, welcomed people from a variety of nationalities and religions. Perhaps most important, the English colonies enjoyed a greater degree of self-government, which made them more dynamic and creative than their French and Spanish counterparts.

Throughout the seventeenth century, geography reinforced England's emphasis on the concentrated settlements of its American colonies. The farthest western expansion of English settlement stopped at the eastern slopes of the Appalachian Mountains. To the east lay the wide expanse of ocean, which served as a highway from Europe to America. But the ocean also served as a barrier that separated old ideas from new, allowing the English colonies to evolve from a fragile stability to a flourishing prosperity in a "new world"—while developing new ideas about economic freedom and political liberties that would emerge in the eighteenth century.

CHAPTER REVIEW

SUMMARY

- **English Background**   England's colonization of North America differed from
  that of its European rivals. While chartered by the Crown, English colonization
  was funded by *joint-stock companies*, groups of investors eager for profits. Colonial
  governments reflected the English model of a two-house Parliament and civil liberties. The colonization of the Eastern Seaboard occurred at a time of religious and
  political turmoil in England, strongly affecting colonial culture and development.

- **English Settlers and Colonization**   The early years of Jamestown and Plymouth were grim. In time, *tobacco* flourished, and its success paved the way for a
  slave-based economy in the South. To entice colonists, the Virginia and Plymouth
  companies granted *headrights*, or land grants. Sugar and rice plantations developed
  in the proprietary Carolina colonies, which operated with minimal royal intrusion.
  Family farms and a mixed economy characterized the middle and New England
  colonies. Religion was the primary motivation for the founding of several colonies.
  Puritans drafted the *Mayflower Compact* and founded Massachusetts Bay Colony
  as a Christian commonwealth. Rhode Island was established by Roger Williams,
  a religious dissenter from Massachusetts. Maryland was founded as a refuge for
  English Catholics. William Penn, a Quaker, founded Pennsylvania and invited
  Europe's persecuted sects to his colony. The Dutch allowed members of all faiths to
  settle in New Netherland.

- **Indian Relations**   Trade with the *Powhatan Confederacy* in Virginia helped
  Jamestown survive its early years, but brutal armed conflicts such as *Bacon's Rebellion* occurred as settlers invaded Indian lands. Puritans retaliated in the Pequot
  War of 1637 and in *King Philip's War* from 1675 to 1676. Among the principal
  colonial leaders, only Roger Williams and William Penn treated Indians as equals.
  The powerful *Iroquois League* played the European powers against one another to
  control territories.

- **Indentured Servants and Slaves**   The colonies increasingly relied on *indentured
  servants*, immigrants who signed contracts (indentures) that required them to
  work for several years upon arriving in America. By the end of the seventeenth
  century, enslaved Africans had become the primary form of labor in the Chesapeake. The demand for slaves in the sugar plantations of the West Indies drove
  European slave traders to organize the transport of Africans via the dreaded
  Middle Passage across the Atlantic. African cultures fused with others in the
  Americas to create a native-born African American culture.

- **Thriving English Colonies**   By 1700, England had become a great trading
  empire, and English America was the most populous and prosperous region of
  North America. Minimal royal interference in the proprietary for-profit colonies

and widespread landownership encouraged settlers to put down roots. Religious diversity attracted a variety of investors and settlers.

CHRONOLOGY

1603	James I takes the throne of England
1607	The Virginia Company establishes Jamestown
1619	First Africans arrive in English America
1620	The Plymouth colony founded by Pilgrims; Mayflower Compact
1626	The Dutch purchase Manhattan from Indians
1630	Massachusetts Bay Colony is founded by Puritans
1634	Settlement of Maryland begins
1637	The Pequot War in New England
1642–1651	The English Civil War (Puritans versus Royalists)
1649	The Toleration Act in Maryland
1660	Restoration of English Monarchy
1664	English take control of New Amsterdam (New York City)
1669	Charles Town is founded in the Carolina colony
1675–1676	King Philip's War in New England
1676	Bacon's Rebellion in Virginia
1681	Pennsylvania is established
1733	Georgia is founded

KEY TERMS

Puritans p. 48

joint-stock companies p. 51

Powhatan Confederacy p. 53

tobacco p. 55

indentured servants p. 55

headright p. 57

Bacon's Rebellion (1676) p. 58

Mayflower Compact (1620) p. 64

King Philip's War (1675–1676) p. 84

Iroquois League p. 85

Middle Passage p. 89

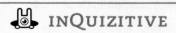 INQUIZITIVE

Go to InQuizitive to see what you've learned—and learn what you've missed—with personalized feedback along the way.

3 Colonial Ways of Life

The artisans of Boston (1766) While fishing, shipbuilding, and maritime trade dominated New England economies, many young men entered apprenticeships, learning a trade from a master craftsman in the hopes of becoming blacksmiths, carpenters, gunsmiths, printers, candlemakers, leather tanners, and more.

The daring people who colonized America during the seventeenth and eighteenth centuries were part of a massive social migration occurring throughout Europe and Africa. Everywhere, it seemed, people were in motion—moving from farms to villages, from villages to cities, and from homelands to colonies. Rapid population growth and the rise of commercial agriculture squeezed poor farmworkers off the land and into cities, where they struggled to survive. That most Europeans in the seventeenth and eighteenth centuries were desperately poor helps explain why so many were willing to migrate to the American colonies. Others sought political security or religious freedom. A tragic exception was the Africans, who were captured and transported to new lands against their will.

Whatever their origins or social status, by the late eighteenth century a French immigrant living in New York named J. Hector St. John de Crevecoeur could announce that the diverse peoples in America were being "melted into a new race of men, whose labors and posterity [children and grandchildren] will one day cause great changes in the world."

Those who initially settled in colonial America were mostly young (more than half were under twenty-five), male, single, and poor, and almost half were indentured servants or slaves. A young servant girl in Maryland wrote her father that she was "toiling almost day and night," had "scarce anything but Indian corn and salt to eat," and had "no shoes nor stockings to wear."

Once in America, many of the newcomers kept moving within and across colonies in search of better lands or business opportunities. This extraordinary

focus questions

1. What were the major factors that contributed to the demographic changes in the English colonies during the eighteenth century?

2. What roles did women play in the English colonies?

3. What were the differences and similarities between the societies and economies of the southern, New England, and middle colonies?

4. How did race-based slavery develop during the seventeenth century, and in what ways did it impact the social and economic development of colonial America?

5. In what ways did the Enlightenment and Great Awakening shape American thought?

mosaic of adventurous, resilient, and often ingenious people created America's enduring institutions and values, as well as its distinctive spirit and restless energy.

THE SHAPE OF EARLY AMERICA

Life in early America was hard and often short. Many of the first colonists died of disease or starvation; others were killed by Native Americans. The average **death rate** in the early years of settlement was 50 percent. Once colonial life became more settled, however, the colonies grew rapidly. On average, the population doubled every twenty-five years during the colonial period. By 1750, the number of colonists had passed 1 million; by 1775, it approached 2.5 million. By comparison, the combined population of England, Scotland, and Ireland in 1750 was 6.5 million. An English visitor reported in 1766 that America would surely become "the most prosperous empire the world had ever seen." But that meant trouble for Britain: "How are we to rule them?"

POPULATION GROWTH   Benjamin Franklin, a keen observer of life in British America, said that the extraordinary growth in the colonial population came about because land was plentiful and cheap, and laborers were scarce and expensive. In contrast, Europe suffered from overpopulation and expensive farmland. From this reversal of conditions flowed many of the changes that European culture underwent during the colonization of America— not the least being that more land and good fortune lured enterprising immigrants and led the colonists to have large families, in part because farm children could help in the fields.

Colonial farm This plan of a newly cleared farm shows how trees were cut and the stumps left to rot.

Colonists, men and women, tended to marry and start families at an earlier age than was common in Europe. In England, the average age at marriage for women was twenty-five or twenty-six; in America, it was twenty. The

birth rate rose accordingly, since women who married earlier had time for about two additional pregnancies during their childbearing years. On average, a married woman had a child every two to three years before menopause. Some women had as many as twenty pregnancies over their lifetimes.

Birthing children, however, was also dangerous, since most babies were delivered at home in unsanitary conditions. Miscarriages were common. Between 25 and 50 percent of women died during birthing or soon thereafter, and almost a quarter of all babies did not survive infancy, especially during the early stages of a colonial settlement. More deaths occurred among young children than any other age group.

Disease and epidemics were rampant in colonial America. Half of the children born in Virginia and Maryland died before reaching age twenty. In 1713, Boston minister Cotton Mather lost three of his children and his wife to a measles epidemic. (Mather lost eight of fifteen children in their first year of life.) Martha Custis, the Virginia widow who married George Washington, had four children during her first marriage. They all died young, at ages two, three, sixteen, and seventeen. Overall, however, mortality rates in the colonies were lower than in Europe. Between 1670 and 1700, the white population of the English colonies doubled, while the black population increased fivefold.

During the eighteenth century, the average age in the colonies was about sixteen; because the colonial population was younger, Americans were less susceptible to disease than were those living in Europe. The majority of colonists lived in sparsely populated settlements and were less likely to be exposed to infectious diseases. That began to change, however, as colonial cities grew larger and more congested, and trade and travel increased. By the mid–eighteenth century, the colonies were beginning to see levels of contagion much like those in the cities of Europe.

ANTI-IMMIGRANT PREJUDICES Nativism began to emerge in the colonies during the eighteenth century. Although Pennsylvania was founded as a haven for people from all countries and religions, by the mid-eighteenth century, concerns arose about the influx of Germans. Benjamin Franklin described the German arrivals as "the most ignorant" group in Pennsylvania. Many of them refused to learn English, and they "herded together" in their own communities. He feared that they would "soon outnumber us" and be a source of constant tension. Why, Franklin asked, "should Pennsylvania, founded by the English, become a Colony of Aliens?" He was "not against the admission of Germans in general, for they have their Virtues," but he urged that they bespread across the colonies so as not to allow them to become a majority anywhere.

WOMEN IN THE COLONIES

In contrast to New Spain and New France, English America had far more women, which largely explains the difference in population growth rates among the European empires in the Americas. More women did not mean more equality, however. As a New England minister stressed, "The woman is a weak creature not endowed with [the] strength and constancy of mind [of men]."

Women, as had been true for centuries, were expected to focus on what was called "housewifery," or the "domestic sphere." They were to obey and serve their husbands, nurture their children, and maintain their households. Governor John Winthrop insisted that a "true wife" would find contentment only "in subjection to her husband's authority." The wife's role, said another Puritan, was "to guide the house etc. and not guide the husband."

Not surprisingly, the lopsided power relationship in colonial households at times generated tensions. One long-suffering wife used the occasion of her husband's death to commission the following inscription on his tombstone: "Stranger, call this not a place of fear and gloom \ To me it is a pleasant spot— It is my husband's tomb." Another woman focused on her own tombstone. It read: "She lived with her husband fifty years / And died in confident hope of a better life."

Women in most colonies could not vote, hold office, attend schools or colleges, bring lawsuits, sign contracts, or become ministers. Divorces were allowed only for desertion or "cruel and barbarous treatment," and no matter who was named the "guilty party," the father received custody of the children. A Pennsylvania court did see fit to send a man to prison for throwing a loaf of hard bread at his wife, "which occasioned her Death in a short Time."

"WOMEN'S WORK" Virtually every member of a household worked, and no one was expected to work harder than women. As John Cotton, a Boston minister, admitted in 1699, "Women are creatures without which there is no Comfortable living for a man." Women who failed to perform the work expected of them were punished as if they were servants or slaves.

In 1643, Margaret Page of Salem, Massachusetts, was jailed "for being a lazy, idle, loitering person." In Virginia, two seamstresses were whipped for fashioning shirts that were too short, and a female indentured servant was forced to

The First, Second, and Last Scene of Mortality Prudence Punderson's needlework (ca. 1776) shows the domestic path, from cradle to coffin, followed by most affluent colonial women.

work in the tobacco fields even though she was sick. She died in a furrow, with a hoe still in her hands. Such harsh conditions prompted a song popular with women and aimed at those back in England: "The Axe and Hoe have wrought my overthrow. If you do come here, you will be weary, weary, weary."

During the eighteenth century, **women's work** typically involved activities in the house, garden, and fields. Many unmarried women moved into other households to help with children or to make clothes. Others took in children or spun thread into yarn to exchange for cloth. Still others hired themselves out as apprentices to learn a skilled trade or craft, or operated laundries or bakeries. Technically, any money earned by a married woman was the property of her husband.

Farm women usually rose and prepared breakfast by sunrise and went to bed soon after dark. They were responsible for building the fire and hauling water. They fed and watered the livestock, cared for the children throughout the day, tended the garden, prepared lunch (the main meal) and dinner, milked the cows, and cleaned the kitchen before retiring. Women also combed, spun, spooled, wove, and bleached wool for clothing; knitted linen and cotton, hemmed sheets, and pieced quilts; made candles and soap;

chopped wood, mopped floors, and washed clothes. Female indentured servants in the southern colonies commonly worked as field hands.

One of the most lucrative trades among colonial women was the oldest: prostitution. Many servants took up prostitution after their indenture was fulfilled, and port cities had thriving brothels. They catered to sailors and soldiers, but men from all walks of life frequented what were called "bawdy houses," or, in Puritan Boston, "disorderly houses." Local authorities frowned on such activities. In Massachusetts, convicted prostitutes were stripped to the waist, tied to the back of a cart, and whipped as it moved through the town. In South Carolina, several elected public officials were dismissed because they were caught "lying with wenches." Some enslaved women whose owners expected sexual favors turned the tables by demanding compensation.

Elizabeth Lucas Pinckney's dress This rare sack-back gown made of eighteenth-century silk has been restored and displayed at the Charleston Museum in South Carolina.

ELIZABETH LUCAS PINCKNEY On occasion, circumstances forced women to exercise leadership outside the domestic sphere. Such was the case with South Carolinian Elizabeth Lucas Pinckney (1722–1793). Born in the West Indies, raised on the island of Antigua, and educated in England, "Eliza" moved to Charleston, South Carolina, at age fifteen, when her father, George Lucas, inherited three plantations. The following year, however, Lucas, a British army officer and colonial administrator, was called back to Antigua, leaving Eliza to care for her ailing mother and younger sister—and to manage three plantations worked by slaves. She wrote a friend, "I have the business of three plantations to transact, which requires much writing and more business and fatigue . . . [but] by rising early I find I can go through much business."

Eliza loved the "vegetable world" and experimented with several crops before focusing on *indigo*, a West Indian plant that produced a coveted blue dye for coloring fabric, especially military uniforms. Indigo made Eliza's family a fortune, as it did for many other plantation owners. In 1744, she married Charles Pinckney, a wealthy widower twice her age, who was speaker of the South Carolina Assembly. She made him promise that she could continue to manage her plantations.

In 1758, Pinckney died of malaria. Now a thirty-six-year-old widow, Eliza responded by adding her husband's plantations to her already substantial managerial responsibilities. Self-confident and fearless, Eliza signaled the possibility of women breaking out of the confining tradition of housewifery and assuming roles of social prominence and economic leadership.

WOMEN AND RELIGION During the colonial era, no denomination allowed women to be ordained as ministers. Only the Quakers let women hold church offices and preach (exhort) in public. Puritans cited biblical passages claiming that God required "virtuous" women to submit to male authority and remain "silent" in congregational matters.

Women who challenged ministerial authority were usually prosecuted and punished. Yet by the eighteenth century, as is true today, women made up the overwhelming majority of church members. Their disproportionate attendance at services and revivals worried many ministers, since a feminized church was presumed to be a church in decline.

In 1692, the influential Boston minister Cotton Mather observed that there "are far more Godly Women in the world than there are Godly Men." In explaining this phenomenon, Mather argued that the pain associated with childbirth, which had long been interpreted as the penalty women paid for Eve's sinfulness, was in part what drove women "more frequently, & the more fervently" to commit their lives to Christ.

In colonial America, the religious roles of black women were different from those of their white counterparts. In most West African tribes, women frequently served as priests and cult leaders. Although some enslaved Africans had been exposed to Christianity or Islam, most tried to sustain their traditional African religion once they arrived in the colonies.

The acute shortage of women in the early settlement years made them more highly valued in the colonies than they were in Europe; thus over time, women's status improved slightly. The Puritan emphasis on a well-ordered family life led to laws protecting wives from physical abuse and allowing for divorce. In addition, colonial laws gave wives greater control over the property that they had brought into a marriage or that was left after a husband's death. But the age-old notion of female subordination and domesticity remained firmly entrenched in colonial America.

SOCIETY AND ECONOMY IN THE SOUTHERN COLONIES

As the southern colonies matured, inequalities of wealth became more visible, and social life grew more divided. The use of enslaved Indians and Africans to grow and process crops generated enormous wealth for a few landowners and their families. Socially, the planters and merchants increasingly became a class apart from the "common folk." They dominated the legislatures, bought luxury goods from London and Paris, and built brick mansions with formal gardens—all the while looking down upon their "inferiors," both white and black.

Warm weather and plentiful rainfall helped the southern colonies grow the profitable **staple crops** (also called cash crops) valued by the mother country: tobacco, rice, sugarcane, and indigo. Tobacco production soared during the seventeenth century. "In Virginia and Maryland," wrote a royal official in 1629, "tobacco . . . is our All, and indeed leaves no room for anything else."

The same was true for rice in South Carolina and Georgia. Using only hand tools, slaves transformed the coastal landscapes, removing trees from swamps and wetlands infested with snakes, alligators, and mosquitos. They then created a system of floodgates to allow workers to drain or flood the fields as needed. Over time, rice planters became the wealthiest group in the British colonies. As plantations grew, the demand for enslaved laborers rose dramatically.

The first English immigrants to Virginia and Maryland built primitive one-room huts that provided limited protection and rotted quickly. Eventually, colonists built cabins on stone or brick foundations, roofed with thatched straw. The spaces between the log timbers were "chinked" with "wattle and daub"—a mix of mud, sand, straw, and wooden stakes that when dried formed a sturdy wall or seam. Most colonial homes had few furnishings;

Indigo plant A sketch of an indigo plant reveals the bright appearance of this important cash crop on Southern colonial plantations.

residents slept on the floor. Rarely did they have glass to fill windows. Instead, they used wooden shutters to cover the openings.

SOCIETY AND ECONOMY IN NEW ENGLAND

Environmental, social, and economic factors contributed to the remarkable diversity among the early American colonies. New England was quite different from the southern and middle Atlantic regions: it was more governed by religious concerns, less focused on commercial agriculture, more engaged in trade, more centered on village and town life, and much less involved with slavery.

TOWNSHIPS Whenever New England towns were founded, the first public structure built was usually a church. By law, every town had to collect taxes to support a church, and every resident—church member or not—was required to attend midweek and Sunday religious services. The average New Englander heard more than 7,000 sermons in a lifetime.

The Puritans believed that God had created a *covenant*, or contract, in which people formed a congregation for common worship. This led to the idea of people joining to form governments, but the principles of democracy and equality were not part of Puritan political thought. Puritan leaders sought to do the will of God, and the ultimate source of authority was not majority rule but the Bible as interpreted by the ministers and magistrates (political leaders).

Unlike the settlers in the southern colonies or in Dutch New York, few New Englanders received huge tracts of land. *Township grants* were usually awarded to organized groups of settlers, often already gathered into a church congregation. They would request a "town" (what elsewhere was commonly called a township), then would divide the land according to a rough principle of equity. Those who invested more or had larger families or greater status might receive more land. The town retained some pasture and woodland in common and held other tracts for future arrivals.

DWELLINGS AND DAILY LIFE The first colonists in New England initially lived in caves, tents, or cabins, but they eventually built simple wood-frame houses with steeply pitched roofs to reduce the buildup of snow. By the end of the seventeenth century, most New England homes were plain but sturdy dwellings. Interior walls were often plastered and whitewashed, but it was not until the eighteenth century that the exteriors of most houses were painted, usually a deep "Indian" red, as the colonists called it. The interiors were dark, illuminated by candles or oil lamps, both of which were expensive; most people usually went to sleep soon after sunset.

There were no bathrooms ("privies"). Most families relieved themselves outside, often beside the walls of the house, indifferent to the stench. Family life revolved around the main room on the ground floor, called the hall, where meals were cooked in a fireplace and where the family lived most of the time. Hence, they came to be called *living* rooms.

Food was served at a table of rough-hewn planks, called the board, and the only eating utensils were spoons and fingers. The father was sometimes referred to as the "chair man" because he sat in the only chair (the origin of the term *chairman of the board*). The rest of the family usually stood or sat on stools or benches. A typical meal consisted of corn, boiled meat, and vegetables washed down with beer, cider, rum, or milk. Cornbread was a daily favorite, as was cornmeal mush, known as hasty pudding.

THE NEW ENGLAND ECONOMY   As John Winthrop and the Puritans prepared to embark for New England in 1630, he stressed that God had made some people powerful and rich and others helpless and poor—so that the elite would show mercy and the masses would offer obedience. He reminded the Puritans that all were given a noble "calling" by God to work hard and ensure that material pursuits never diminished the importance of spiritual devotion.

Once in New England, the Puritans implanted their Protestant work ethic, and the primacy of religion as bedrock American values. They also celebrated the idea that newness was the prime creator of culture, and they lived in the expectation of something new and dramatic: Christ's second coming and his reign on earth, the Millennium. Newness was to Americans what antiquity was to Europeans—a sign of integrity, the mark of a special relationship to history and to God. It affirmed the idea of American exceptionalism. Puritanism, in this sense, underwrote the American Revolution with its promise of political renewal.

Early New England farmers and their families led hard lives. Clearing rocks might require sixty days of hard labor per acre. The growing season was short, and no staple crops grew in the harsh climate. The crops and livestock were those familiar to the English countryside: wheat, barley, oats, some cattle, pigs, and sheep.

Many New Englanders turned to the sea for their livelihood. Codfish had been a regular element of the European diet for centuries, and the waters off the New England coast had the heaviest concentrations of cod in the world. Whales supplied ambergris, a waxy substance used in the manufacture of perfumes, as well as oil for lighting and lubrication.

New Englanders exported dried fish to Europe, with lesser grades going to the West Indies as food for slaves. The thriving fishing industry encouraged the development of shipbuilding and spurred transatlantic commerce. Rising incomes and a booming trade with Britain and Europe soon brought a taste for luxury goods in New England that clashed with the Puritan ideal of plain living and high thinking.

SHIPBUILDING The forests of New England represented a source of enormous wealth. Old-growth trees were prized for use as ships' masts and spars (on which sails were attached). Early on, the British government claimed the tallest and straightest trees, mostly white pines and oaks, for use by the Royal Navy. At the same time, British officials encouraged the colonists to develop their own shipbuilding industry, and American-built ships quickly became known for their quality and price. It was much less expensive to purchase ships built in America than to transport timber to Britain for ship construction, especially since a large ship might require as many as 2,000 trees. Nearly a third of all British ships were made in the colonies during the eighteenth century.

TRADE By the end of the seventeenth century, the New England colonies had become part of a complex North Atlantic commercial network, trading not only with the British Isles and the British West Indies but also—often illegally—with Spain, France, Portugal, the Netherlands, and their colonies.

Trade in New England and the middle colonies differed from that in the South in two respects. The lack of staple crops to exchange for English goods was a relative disadvantage, but the success of shipping and commercial enterprises worked in their favor. After 1660, to protect its agriculture and fisheries, the English government placed prohibitive duties (taxes) on fish, flour, wheat, and meat, while leaving the door open to high-demand products such as timber, furs, and whale oil. Between 1698 and 1717, New England and New York bought more from England than they exported to it, creating an unfavorable trade balance.

These circumstances gave rise to the **triangular trade**. New England merchants shipped rum to the west coast of Africa, where it was exchanged for slaves. Ships then took the enslaved Africans to Caribbean islands to sell. The

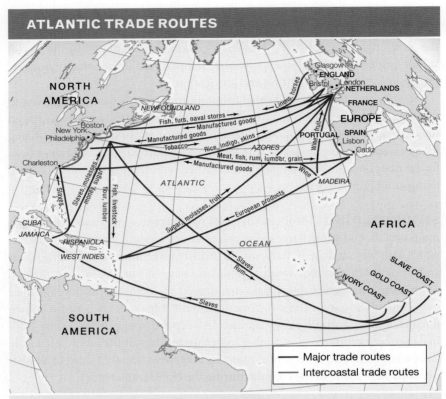

ATLANTIC TRADE ROUTES

- How was overseas trade in the South different from that in New England and the middle colonies?
- What was the "triangular trade"?
- What were North America's most important exports?

ships returned home with various commodities, including molasses, from which New Englanders manufactured rum. In another version, they shipped provisions to the Caribbean, carried sugar and molasses to England, and returned with goods manufactured in Europe.

PURITANICAL PURITANS? The Puritans were religious fundamentalists who looked to the Bible for authority and inspiration. For most, the Christian faith was a living source of daily inspiration and obligation.

Although the Puritans sailed to America to create pious, prosperous communities, the traditional caricature of the dour, black-clothed Puritan, hostile to anything that gave pleasure, is false. Yes, they banned card playing, dancing in taverns, swearing, and bowling. They even fined people for celebrating

Christmas, for in their view only pagans marked the birth date of their rulers with merrymaking. Puritans also frowned on hurling insults, disobeying parents, and disrespecting civil and religious officials. In 1631, a servant named Phillip Ratcliffe had both of his ears cut off for making scandalous comments about the governor and the church in Salem.

Yet Puritans also wore colorful clothing, enjoyed secular music, and imbibed prodigious quantities of beer and rum. "Drink is in itself a good creature of God," said the Reverend Increase Mather, "but the abuse of drink is from Satan." Drunks were arrested, and repeat offenders were forced to wear the letter *D* in public.

Moderation in all things except piety was the Puritan guideline, and it applied to sexual life as well. Although sexual activity outside of marriage was strictly forbidden, New England courts overflowed with cases of adultery and illicit sex. A man found guilty of coitus with an unwed woman could be jailed, whipped, fined, and forced to marry the woman. Female offenders were also jailed and whipped, and in some cases adulterers were forced to wear the letter *A* in public.

WITCHES IN SALEM At times, the religious zeal of Puritan communities boiled over. The strains of Massachusetts's transition from Puritan utopia to royal colony reached a tragic climax in 1692–1693 amid the witchcraft hysteria at Salem Village (now called Danvers), a community on the northern edge of Salem Town, a flourishing port some fifteen miles north of Boston.

Belief in witchcraft was widespread in the seventeenth century. Prior to the dramatic episode in Salem Village, almost 300 New Englanders (mostly middle-aged women) had been accused of practicing witchcraft, and more than 30 had been hanged.

The Salem episode was unique in its scope and intensity, however. During

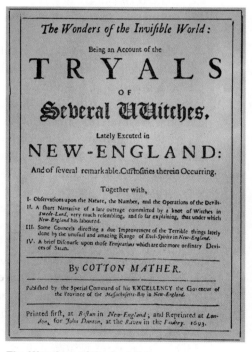

The Wonders of the Invisible World Title page of the 1693 London edition of Cotton Mather's account of the Salem witchcraft trials. Mather, a prominent Boston minister, warned his congregation that the devil's legions were assaulting New England.

the brutally cold winter of 1692, several preteen girls became fascinated with a fortune teller named Tituba, an Indian slave from Barbados. Two of the girls, nine-year-old Betty Parris and eleven-year-old Abigail Williams, the daughter and niece of the village minister, Samuel Parris, began to behave oddly. They writhed, shouted, barked, sobbed hysterically, and flapped their arms as if to fly. When asked who was tormenting them, they replied that three women— Tituba, Sarah Good, and Sarah Osborne—were Satan's servants.

Parris beat Tituba, his slave, until she confessed to doing Satan's bidding. (Under the rules of the era, those who confessed were jailed; those who denied the charges were hanged.) Tituba described one of the devil's companions as "a thing all over hairy, all the face hairy and a long nose."

Authorities arrested Tituba and the other accused women. Two of them were hanged, but not before they named other supposed witches and more young girls experienced convulsive fits. The mass hysteria extended to surrounding towns, and within a few months, the Salem Village jail was filled with more than 150 men, women, and children—and two dogs—all accused of practicing witchcraft.

When a prominent farmer, Giles Corey, was accused of supernatural crimes, his neighbors stripped off his clothes, lowered him into an open grave, placed a board over his body, and began loading it with heavy boulders to force a confession. After three days of such abuse, the defiant old man finally died, having muttered only two words: "More weight!"

As the allegations and executions multiplied and spread beyond Salem, leaders of the Massachusetts Bay Colony began to worry that the witch hunts were spinning out of control. The governor finally intervened when his wife was accused of serving the devil. He disbanded the special court in Salem and ordered the remaining suspects released.

By then, nineteen people (fourteen women and five men, including a for-mer minister) had been hanged—all justified by the biblical verse that tells believers not to "suffer a witch to live." A little over a year after it had begun, the witchcraft frenzy was finally over.

What explains Salem's mass hysteria? It may have represented nothing more than theatrical adolescents trying to enliven the dreary routine of every-day life. Others suggest community tensions may have led people to accuse neighbors, masters, relatives, or rivals as an act of spite or vengeance. Some historians have stressed that most of the accused witches were women, many of whom had in some way defied the traditional roles assigned to females.

Still another interpretation suggests that the accusations may have reflected the psychological strains caused by frequent Indian attacks just north of Salem, along New England's northern frontier. Some of the convulsing girls had seen their families killed or mutilated by Indians and suffered from what today is called post-traumatic stress disorder.

Society and Economy
in the Middle Colonies

Both geographically and culturally, the middle colonies (New York, New Jersey, Pennsylvania, Delaware, and Maryland) stood between New England and the South. They reflected the diversity of colonial life and foreshadowed the pluralism of the future nation.

AN ECONOMIC MIX The middle colonies produced surpluses of foodstuffs for export to the slave-based plantations of the South and the West Indies: wheat, barley, oats and other grains, flour, and livestock. Three great rivers—the Hudson, Delaware, and Susquehanna—and their tributaries provided access to the backcountry of Pennsylvania and New York, and to a rich fur trade with Native Americans. The region's bustling commerce thus rivaled that of New England.

Land policies followed the *headright* system prevalent in the Chesapeake colonies. In New York, the early royal governors continued the Dutch practice of the patroonship, granting vast estates to influential men (called patroons). The patroons controlled large domains farmed by tenants (renters) who paid fees to use the landlords' mills, warehouses, smokehouses, and docks. With free land available elsewhere, however, New York's population languished, and new waves of immigrants sought the promised land of Pennsylvania.

AN ETHNIC MIX In the makeup of their population, the middle colonies differed from New England's Puritan settlements and the biracial plantation colonies to the south. In New York and New Jersey, Dutch culture and language lingered. Along the Delaware River near Philadelphia, the first settlers—Swedes and Finns—were overwhelmed by an influx of Europeans. By the mid–eighteenth century, the middle colonies were the fastest-growing region in North America.

The Germans came to America (primarily Pennsylvania) mainly from the Rhineland region of Europe, where brutal religious wars had pitted Protestants against Catholics. William Penn's recruiting brochures circulated throughout central Europe, and his promise of religious freedom appealed to many persecuted sects, especially the Mennonites, German Baptists whose beliefs resembled those of the Quakers.

In 1683, a group of Mennonites founded Germantown, near Philadelphia. They represented the first wave of German migrants, most of whom were indentured servants. The large numbers of German immigrants during the eighteenth century alarmed many English colonists.

Throughout the eighteenth century, the Scots-Irish moved still farther out into the Pennsylvania backcountry. ("Scotch-Irish" is the more common but

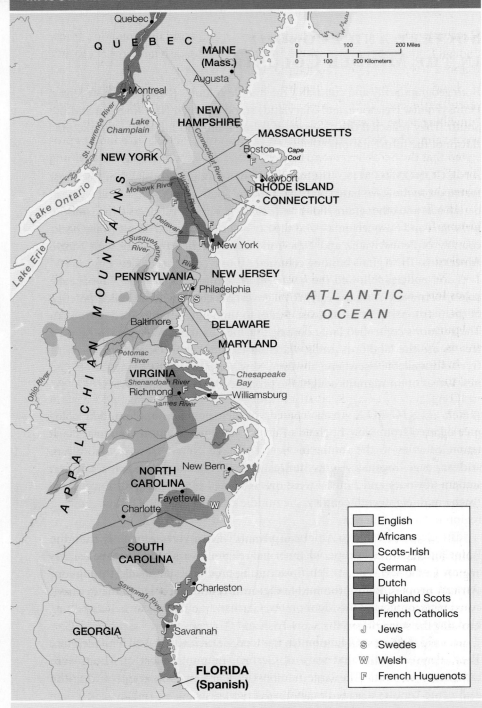

MAJOR IMMIGRANT GROUPS IN COLONIAL AMERICA

Quebec

QUEBEC

MAINE
(Mass.)

Augusta

Montreal

NEW
HAMPSHIRE

Lake
Champlain

St. Lawrence River

MASSACHUSETTS

NEW YORK

Boston   Cape
           Cod
F

Mohawk River

Newport
RHODE ISLAND
J
CONNECTICUT

Hudson River

Connecticut River

Delaware River

F

Susquehanna
River

F

New York

Lake Ontario

Lake Erie

PENNSYLVANIA

W
S S
Philadelphia

NEW JERSEY

ATLANTIC
OCEAN

Baltimore

DELAWARE

MARYLAND

Potomac
River

Ohio River

VIRGINIA
Shenandoah River
Richmond   F

Chesapeake
Bay

Williamsburg

James River

APPALACHIAN MOUNTAINS

NORTH
CAROLINA

New Bern
F

Fayetteville
W
Charlotte

SOUTH
CAROLINA

Savannah River

F F
J
Charleston

GEORGIA

J
Savannah

F

FLORIDA
(Spanish)

0   100   200 Miles
0   100   200 Kilometers

	English
	Africans
	Scots-Irish
	German
	Dutch
	Highland Scots
	French Catholics
J	Jews
S	Swedes
W	Welsh
F	French Huguenots

- What attracted German immigrants to the middle colonies?
- Why did the Scots-Irish spread across the Appalachian backcountry?
- Where did the first Jews settle in America? How were they received?

inaccurate name for the Scots-Irish, a mostly Presbyterian population trans- planted from Scotland to northern Ireland by the English government to give Catholic Ireland a more Protestant tone.)

Land was the great magnet for the poor Scots-Irish. They were, said a recruiting agent, "full of expectation to have land for nothing" and were "unwilling to be disappointed." In most cases, the lands they "squatted on" were claimed by Native Americans. In 1741, a group of Delaware Indians pro- tested that the Scots-Irish were taking "our land" without giving "us anything for it." If the colonial government did not stop the flow of whites, the Dela- wares threatened, they would "drive them off."

The Scots-Irish and Germans became the largest non-English ethnic groups in the colonies. Other ethnic minorities also enriched the popu- lation: Huguenots (French Protestants whose religious freedom had been revoked in 1685, forcing many to leave France), Irish, Welsh, Swiss, and Jews. New York had inherited from the Dutch a tradition of ethnic and reli- gious tolerance, which had given the colony a diverse population before the English conquest: French-speaking Walloons (a Celtic people of southern Belgium), French, Germans, Danes, Portuguese, Spaniards, Italians, Bohe- mians, Poles, and others, including some New England Puritans.

In the eighteenth century, the population in British North America soared, and the colonies grew more diverse. In 1790, the white population was 61 per- cent English; 14 percent Scottish and Scots-Irish; 9 percent German; 5 percent Dutch, French, and Swedish; 4 percent Irish; and 7 percent "unidentifiable," a category that included people of mixed origins as well as "free blacks." If one adds to the 3,172,444 whites in the 1790 census the 756,770 nonwhites, without even considering the almost 100,000 Native Americans who went uncounted, only about half the nation's inhabitants, and perhaps fewer, could trace their origins to England.

THE BACKCOUNTRY Pennsylvania became the great distribution point for the ethnic groups of European origin, just as the Chesapeake Bay region and Charleston, South Carolina, became the distribution points for African peoples. Before the mid–eighteenth century, settlers in the Pennsyl- vania backcountry had reached the Appalachian mountain range. Rather than crossing the steep ridges, the Scots-Irish and Germans filtered southward. Ger- mans were the first white settlers in the Upper Shenandoah Valley in southern Pennsylvania, western Maryland, and northern Virginia, and the Scots-Irish filled the lower valley in western Virginia and North Carolina. The German and Scots-Irish settlers built cabins and tended farms on Indian lands, built churches, and established isolated communities along the frontier.

RACE-BASED SLAVERY

During the late seventeenth century, slavery was legalized in all colonies but was most prevalent in the South. In 1642, Leonard Calvert paid a ship captain 24,000 pounds of tobacco for fourteen "negro men-slaves, of between 16 & 26 years old, able & sound of body and limbs." His son acknowledged that "we are naturally inclin'd to love negros [as workers] if our purses would endure it."

White colonists viewed **race-based slavery** as a normal aspect of everyday life; few considered it a moral issue. They believed that God determined one's "station in life." Slavery was therefore not a social evil but a "personal misfortune." Not until the late eighteenth century did meaningful numbers of white Europeans and Americans begin to raise ethical questions about slavery.

The first Africans in America were treated much like indentured servants, with a limited term of service, after which they gained their freedom (but not equality). Until the mid–seventeenth century, no laws in the colonies specified the meaning and scope of the word *slavery*. Gradually, however, *lifelong* slavery for blacks became the custom—and the law—of the land. By the 1660s, colonial legislatures formalized the institution of race-based slavery, with detailed **slave codes** regulating most aspects of slaves' lives. The South Carolina code, for example, defined all "Negroes, Mulattoes, and Indians" sold into bondage as slaves *for life*, as were the children born of enslaved mothers.

In 1667, the Virginia legislature declared that slaves could not serve on juries, travel without permission, or gather in groups of more than two or three. Some colonies even prohibited owners from freeing their slaves (manumission). The codes allowed owners to punish slaves by whipping them, slitting their noses, cutting their ankle cords, castrating men, or killing them. A 1669 Virginia law declared that accidentally killing a slave who was being whipped or beaten was not a serious crime. William Byrd II, a wealthy Virginia planter, confessed that the "unhappy effect of owning many Negroes is the necessity of being severe." In 1713, a South Carolina planter punished a slave by closing him up in a tiny coffin to die, only to have the trapped man's son slip in a knife so that he could kill himself rather than suffocate.

COLOR PREJUDICE More than a century before the English arrived in America, the Portuguese and Spanish had established a global trade in enslaved Africans. While English settlers often enslaved Indian captives, as had the Spanish and Portuguese before them, the Europeans did not enslave other Europeans who were captured in warfare. Color was the crucial difference, or at least the rationalization used to justify slavery and its hellish brutalities.

The English associated the color black with darkness and evil. To them, the different appearance, behavior, and customs of Africans and Native Americans represented savagery and heathenism. Colonial Virginians convinced themselves that blacks (and Indians) were naturally lazy, treacherous, and stupid.

SLAVES REPLACE SERVANTS During the seventeenth and eighteenth centuries, the profitable sugar-based economies of the French and British West Indies and Portuguese Brazil sparked greater demand for enslaved Africans, as sugar became valued almost as much as gold or silver. By 1675, the island colonies in the Caribbean had more than 100,000 slaves, while the American colonies had about 5,000.

As tobacco, rice, and indigo crops became more established in Maryland, Virginia, and the Carolinas, however, the number of African slaves in those colonies grew substantially, while the flow of white indentured servants from Britain and Europe to America slowed. Until the eighteenth century, English immigrants made up 90 percent of American colonists. After 1700, the largest number of new arrivals were enslaved Africans, who totaled more than all European immigrants combined.

Slavery was rooted in the ancient Mediterranean societies, both Christian and Muslim. By the sixteenth century, European slave traders, with the encouragement of their monarchs, had established a network of relationships with various African rulers, who provided slaves in exchange for European goods—cloth, metal objects, muskets, and rum. Over some 400 years, more than 11 million Africans were transported to the Americas.

During the late seventeenth century, the profitability of African slavery led to the emergence of dozens of new slave-trading companies both in Europe and America, thus expanding the availability of enslaved Africans and lowering the price. American colonists preferred slaves because they were officially viewed as property with no civil rights, and they (and their offspring) were servants for life. The colonists preferred Africans over enslaved Indians because they could not escape easily in a land where they stood out because of their dark skin. In short, African slaves offered a better investment.

THE MARKET IN SLAVES Once a slave ship arrived at an American port, Africans in chains would be auctioned to the highest bidder and taken away to begin lifelong work for a complete stranger. They were usually forbidden to use their native languages, practice African religions, or sustain their native cultures. With only rare exceptions, slaves were prohibited from owning anything unrelated to their work.

The vast majority of enslaved Africans worked on farms or plantations from dawn to dusk, in oppressive heat and humidity. As Jedidiah Morse, a prominent Charleston minister, admitted in the late eighteenth century, "No white man, to speak generally, ever thinks of settling a farm, and improving it for himself, without negroes."

During the eighteenth century, the demand for slaves soared in the southern colonies. By 1750, there were almost 250,000 slaves in British America. The vast majority, about 150,000, resided in Virginia and Maryland, with 60,000 in South Carolina and Georgia.

As the number of slaves grew, so, too, did their talents and expertise. Over time, slaves became skilled blacksmiths, carpenters, and bricklayers. Many enslaved women worked as household servants and midwives.

SLAVE RESISTANCE Despite the overwhelming power and authority of slave owners, slaves found ways to resist and rebel—and escape.

In a newspaper, a Georgia slave owner asked readers to be on the lookout for "a negro fellow named Mingo, about 40 years old, and his wife Quante, a sensible wench about 20 with her child, a boy about 3 years old, all this country born."

In a few cases, slaves organized rebellions in which they stole weapons, burned and looted plantations, and killed their captors. On Sunday morning, September 9, 1739, while white families were attending church, some twenty African-born slaves attacked a store in Stono, South Carolina, twenty miles southwest of Charleston. Led by a slave named Jemmy, they killed and decapitated two shopkeepers, seized weapons, and headed south toward freedom in Spanish Florida, gathering more recruits along the way. Within a few days, the slaves had burned six plantations and killed about two dozen whites, sparing one white innkeeper because he was "kind to his slaves."

The growing army of rebel slaves marched in military formation, waving a banner proclaiming "Liberty" and freeing more slaves as they moved southward. Then the well-armed and mounted militiamen caught up with them. Most of the rebels were killed, and sixty were eventually captured and decapitated by enraged planters. In the end, forty-four blacks were killed in the largest slave uprising of the colonial period.

The **Stono Rebellion** so frightened white planters that they convinced the colonial assembly to ban the importation of African slaves for ten years and pass the so-called Negro Act of 1740, which called for more oversight of slave activities and harsher punishments for rebellious behavior. Slaves could no longer grow their own food, gather in groups, learn to read or write, or earn money on the side. The new law also reduced the penalty for a white killing a slave to a minor offense and banned slaves from testifying in courts.

Slavery in New Amsterdam (1642) The significance of African slaves to the colonial economy is the focus of this engraving of the Dutch colony New Amsterdam, later known as New York City.

SLAVERY IN NEW YORK CITY In contrast to their experience in the southern colonies, most slaves in the northern colonies lived in towns or cities, which gave them more opportunities to move about. New York City had more slaves than any American city, and by 1740 was second only to Charleston in the percentage of slaves in its population.

As the number of slaves increased in the city, fears and tensions mounted— and occasionally exploded. In 1712, several dozen slaves revolted; they started fires and used swords, axes, and guns to kill whites who attempted to fight the fires. Called out to restore order, the militia captured twenty-seven slaves, six of whom committed suicide. The rest were executed; some were burned alive. (Authorities postponed the execution of two pregnant African women at the request of their owners so that they could enslave the babies and thereby recover their investment.) New York officials thereafter passed a citywide *black code* that strictly regulated slave behavior.

The harsh regulations did not prevent another major racial incident. In the bitterly cold March of 1741, city dwellers worried that slaves were setting a series of suspicious fires, including one at the governor's house. "The Negroes are rising!" shouted terrified whites.

The frantic city council launched an investigation. Mary Burton, a sixteen-year-old white indentured servant, told authorities that slaves and poor whites were plotting to "burn the whole town" and kill the white men. The plotters were supposedly led by John Hughson, a white trafficker in stolen goods. His wife, two slaves, and a prostitute were charged as coconspirators. Despite their denials, all were convicted and hanged. Within weeks, more than half of the adult male slaves in the city were in jail. What came to be called the Conspiracy of 1741 finally ended after seventeen slaves and four whites were hanged. Thirteen more blacks were burned at the stake, while many others were deported.

At its most basic level, slavery is a system in which the powerless are brutalized by the powerful. Many slaves who ran away in colonial America faced ghastly punishments when caught. Antonio, a West African man shipped as a slave to New Amsterdam and then to Maryland, worked in the tobacco fields. He tried to escape several times. After his last attempt, in 1656, his owner, a young Dutch planter named Syman Overzee, tortured and killed him. Authorities charged Overzee with murder—and an all-white jury acquitted him.

Slavery in the Western Hemisphere was a rapidly growing phenomenon by the time of the American Revolution. White Europeans believed they were justified in dehumanizing an entire class of human beings because of the supposed "backwardness" of Africans and Indians. Not even the American Revolution's ideals of freedom and equality (for whites) would change that attitude.

First Stirrings of a Common Colonial Culture

By the middle of the eighteenth century, the thirteen colonies were growing and maturing. Schools and colleges were springing up, and the standard of living was rising. More and more colonists were able to read about the latest ideas circulating in London and Paris while purchasing the latest consumer goods from Europe.

The rage for luxury goods, especially jewelry, fine clothing, and beaver hats, heightened the recognition of social inequality, particularly in the cities. Many ministers complained that wealthy Americans were ignoring their commitment to Christian ideals. In 1714, a Bostonian regretted the "great extravagance that people are fallen into, far beyond their circumstances, in their purchases, buildings, families, expenses, apparel—generally in their whole way of living."

English merchants required Americans to buy their goods only with *specie* (gold or silver coins). This left little "hard money" in the colonies. American merchants tried various ways to get around the shortage of specie. Some engaged in *barter*, using commodities such as tobacco or rice as currency in exchange for manufactured goods and luxury items. The issue of money—what kind and how much—would become one of the major areas of dispute between the colonies and Britain.

COLONIAL CITIES

Throughout the seventeenth and eighteenth centuries, the colonies were mostly populated by farmers or farmworkers. But a handful of cities blossomed into dynamic centers of political and social life. Economic opportunity drove most city dwellers.

Colonial cities hugged the coastline or, like Philadelphia, sprang up on rivers large enough to handle oceangoing vessels. Never comprising more than 10 percent of the colonial population, the large coastal cities had a disproportionate influence on commerce, politics, society, and culture. By the end of the colonial period, Philadelphia, with some 30,000 people, was the largest city in the colonies, and New York City, with about 25,000, ranked second. Boston numbered 16,000; Charleston, South Carolina, 12,000; and Newport, Rhode Island, 11,000.

THE SOCIAL AND POLITICAL ORDER The urban social elite was dominated by wealthy merchants and property owners served by a middle class of shop owners, innkeepers, and skilled craftsmen. Almost two thirds of urban male workers were artisans—carpenters and coopers (barrel makers), shoemakers and tailors, silversmiths and blacksmiths, sailmakers, stonemasons, weavers, and potters. At the bottom of the social order were sailors, manual laborers, servants, and slaves.

Colonial cities were busy, crowded, and dangerous. Epidemics such as cholera, malaria, and yellow fever were common. The use of open fireplaces caused frequent fires, which in turn led to the development of fire companies. Rising crime and violence required increased policing by sheriffs and local militias.

Colonists also were concerned about the poor and homeless. The number of Boston's poor receiving aid rose from 500 in 1700 to 4,000 in 1736; in

New York City, it rose from 250 in 1698 to 5,000 in the 1770s. Those designated "helpless" were often provided money, food, clothing, and fuel. In some towns, "poorhouses" were built to house the homeless and provide them with jobs.

THE URBAN WEB The first American roads were Indian trails that were widened with frequent travel. Overland travel was initially by horse or by foot. Inns and taverns (also called public houses, or pubs) were essential social institutions, since travel at night was treacherous—and Americans loved to drink. (It was said that when the Spanish settled an area, they would first build a church; the Dutch would first erect a fort; and the English would first construct a tavern.)

Taverns and inns were places to eat, relax, read a newspaper, play cards, gossip and conduct business, and enjoy alcoholic beverages: beer, hard cider, and rum. But ministers and magistrates began to worry that the pubs were promoting drunkenness and social rebelliousness. Not only were poor whites drinking heavily but also Indians, which, one governor told the assembly, would have "fatal consequences to the Government."

Early in the eighteenth century, ministers succeeded in passing an anti-tavern law in Massachusetts Bay Colony. The Act Against Intemperance, Immorality, and Profaneness targeted taverns that had become "nurseries of intemperance." It tightened the process of issuing licenses for the sale of liquor,

Taverns A tobacconist's business card from 1770 captures men talking in a Philadelphia tavern while they drink ale and smoke pipes.

eliminated fiddle-playing in pubs, called for public posting of the names of "common drunkards," and banned the sale of rum and brandy, the most potent beverages.

After a few years, however, the law was rarely enforced, but the concerns remained. In 1726, a Bostonian declared that "the abuse of strong Drink is becoming Epidemical among us, and it is very justly Supposed . . . that the Multiplication of Taverns has contributed not a little to this Excess of Riot and Debauchery." The failed law was the last legislative effort to restrict alcohol consumption before the Revolution.

By the end of the seventeenth century, there were more taverns in America than any other business. They were the most important social institutions in the colonies—and the most democratic. They were places where rich and poor intermingled, and by the mid–eighteenth century, they would become gathering spots for protests against British rule.

Long-distance communication was a more complicated matter. Postal service was almost nonexistent—people gave letters to travelers or sea captains in hopes that they would be delivered. Under a parliamentary law of 1710, the postmaster of London named a deputy in charge of the colonies. A postal system eventually emerged along the Atlantic Seaboard, providing the colonies with an effective means of communication that would prove crucial in the growing controversy with Great Britain. More reliable mail delivery also spurred the growing popularity of newspapers.

CITIZENSHIP IN THE EMPIRE Prior to the eighteenth century, the individual colonies, except New Hampshire, competed for immigrants from around the world. They needed settlers to generate economic growth and to conquer Native Americans. One way to entice colonists was to give them the opportunity to acquire the same civil rights as those born in the colonies ("birthright citizenship"). To that end, the colonies developed "naturalization" policies outlining the path to citizenship. Each colony had slightly different rules, but the rights of naturalization typically included acquiring property, voting and holding office, and receiving royal grants of land.

From the start, therefore, British America was an immigrant-welcoming society. The preamble to Virginia's naturalization acts of 1680 and 1705 urged "persons of different nations to transport themselves hither with their families and stocks, to settle, plant or reside, by investing them with all the rights and privileges of his majesty's natural free born subjects within the said colony."

But why were the colonies so welcoming? Because, as South Carolina's law explained, immigrants, "by their industry, diligence and trade, have very much enriched and advanced this colony and settlement thereof."

By contrast, England sought to restrict immigration to the home country, fearing that Protestant sects such as Presbyterians, Baptists, and Methodists would undermine the authority of the Church of England. Others feared that naturalized immigrants, if given the right to vote and hold office, "might endanger our ancient polity and government, and by frequent intermarriages go a great way to blot out and extinguish the English race."

To sustain high levels of immigration to British America, Parliament in 1740 passed the Naturalization Act. It announced that immigrants ("aliens") living in America for seven years would become subjects in the British Empire after swearing a loyalty oath and providing proof that they were Protestants. While excluding "papists" (Roman Catholics), the new law did make exceptions for Jews.

THE ENLIGHTENMENT IN AMERICA

The most significant of the new European ideas circulating in eighteenth-century America grew out of a burst of intellectual activity known as the **Enlightenment**. The Enlightenment celebrated rational inquiry, scientific research, and individual freedom. Enlightened people sought the truth, wherever it might lead, rather than remain content with believing ideas and dogmas passed down through the ages or taken from the Bible.

Immanuel Kant, the eighteenth-century German philosopher, summed up the Enlightenment point of view: "Dare to know! Have the courage to use your own understanding." He and others used the power of reason to analyze the workings of nature, and they employed new tools like microscopes and telescopes to engage in close observation, scientific experimentation, and precise mathematical calculation.

THE AGE OF REASON The Enlightenment, often called the Age of Reason, was triggered by a scientific revolution in the sixteenth century that transformed the way educated people observed and understood the world. Just as early explorers alerted Europeans to the excitement of new geographical discoveries, early modern scientists began to realize that social "progress" could occur through a series of intellectual and technological discoveries enabled by the adaptation of mathematical techniques for observing the natural world. The engines of curiosity and inventiveness drove a scientific revolution whose findings over the course of 150 years would prove astonishing.

The ancient Christian view that the God-created earth was at the center of the universe, with the sun revolving around it, was overthrown by the controversial solar system described by Nicolaus Copernicus, a Polish astronomer and Catholic priest. In 1533, Copernicus asserted that the earth and other planets orbit the sun. Catholic officials scorned his theory until it was later confirmed by other scientists using telescopes.

In 1687, Englishman Isaac Newton announced his transformational theory of the earth's gravitational pull. Using both astronomy and mathematical physics, especially calculus, Newton challenged biblical notions of the world's workings by depicting a changing, dynamic universe moving in accordance with natural laws that could be grasped by human reason and explained by mathematics. He implied that natural laws (rather than God) govern all things, from the orbits of the planets to the effects of gravity to the science of human relations: politics, economics, and society.

Some enlightened people, called **Deists**, carried Newton's scientific outlook to its logical conclusion, claiming that God created the world and designed its "natural laws," which governed the operation of the universe. In other words, Deism maintained that God planned the universe and set it in motion, but no longer interacted directly with the earth and its people. Their rational God was nothing like the intervening God of the Christian tradition, to whom believers prayed for daily guidance and direct support.

Evil, according to the Deists, resulted not from humanity's inherent *sinfulness* as outlined in the Bible but from human *ignorance* of the rational laws of nature. Therefore, the best way to improve society and human nature, according to Deists such as Thomas Jefferson and Benjamin Franklin, was by cultivating Reason, which was the highest Virtue. (Followers of the Enlightenment thinkers often capitalized both words.)

By using education, reason, and scientific analysis, societies were bound to improve their knowledge as well as their quality of life. In this sense, the word *enlightenment* meant that people were learning to think for themselves rather than blindly accept what tradition, the Bible, and political and religious elites directed them to believe. In sum, the perspectives of the Enlightenment helped people to stop fearing nature and to begin controlling and manipulating it to improve the quality of life—for all.

Enlightened "freethinkers" refused to allow church and state to limit what they could study and investigate. In this sense, the Enlightenment was a disruptive and even dangerous force in European thought. It spawned not just revolutionary ideas but revolutionary movements.

Faith in the possibility of human progress was one of the most important beliefs of the Enlightenment. Equally important was the notion of political freedom. Both Thomas Jefferson and Benjamin Franklin, among many other eighteenth-century British Americans, were intrigued by English political philosopher John Locke, who maintained that "natural law" called for a

Benjamin Franklin A champion of rational thinking and common sense behavior, Franklin was an inventor, philosopher, entrepreneur, and statesman.

government that rested on the consent of the governed and respected the "natural rights" of all. Those "rights" included the basic civic principles of the Enlightenment—human rights, political liberty, religious toleration—that would later influence colonial leaders' efforts to justify a revolution.

THE AMERICAN ENLIGHTENMENT Benjamin Franklin epitomized the American version of the Enlightenment. Born in Boston in 1706, he left home at the age of seventeen, bound for Philadelphia. Six years later, he bought a print shop and began editing and publishing the *Pennsylvania Gazette* newspaper. When he was twenty-six, he published *Poor Richard's Almanack*, a collection of seasonal weather forecasts, puzzles, household tips, and witty sayings.

Franklin was a pragmatist who focused on getting things done and relished helping people learn to work together and embrace the necessity of compromise. Most of all, he celebrated the virtue and benefit of public service. Before he retired from business at the age of forty-two, Franklin had founded a public library, started a fire company, helped create what became the University of Pennsylvania, and organized a debating club that grew into the American Philosophical Society.

Franklin became a highly regarded diplomat, politician, and educator. Above all, he was an inventive genius devoted to scientific investigation. His wide-ranging experiments extended to the fields of medicine, meteorology, geology, astronomy, and physics. He developed the Franklin stove, the lightning rod, bifocal spectacles, and a glass harmonica.

Although raised as a Presbyterian, Franklin was no churchgoer. A Deist who prized science, reason, and a robust social life, he did not believe in the sacredness of the Bible or the divinity of Jesus. Like the European Deists, Franklin came to believe that God had created a universe directed by natural laws, but thereafter the Creator was not a daily force in human life.

For Franklin and others, to be *enlightened* meant exercising an all-encompassing curiosity about life that in turn nurtured the confidence and capacity to think critically. For them, it was intolerable to accept what tradition dictated as truth without first testing its legitimacy.

EDUCATION IN THE COLO-NIES White colonial Americans were among the most literate people in the world. Almost 90 percent of men (more than in England) could read. The colonists were concerned about educating their young, and education in the traditional ideas and manners of society—even literacy itself—was primarily the responsibility of family and church. (The modern concept of free public education would not be fully embraced until the nineteenth century.)

The Puritan emphasis on reading Scripture, which all Protestants shared to some degree, led to the strong focus on literacy. In 1647, the Massachusetts Bay Colony required every town to support a grammar school (a "Latin school" that could prepare a student for college).

Colonial education A page from the rhymed alphabet of *The New England Primer*, a popular American textbook first published in the 1680s.

The Dutch in New Netherland were as interested in education as the New England Puritans. In Pennsylvania, the Quakers established private schools. In the southern colonies, however, schools were rare. The wealthiest southern planters and merchants hired tutors or sent their children to England for schooling.

THE GREAT AWAKENING

The growing popularity of Enlightenment rationalism posed a direct threat to traditional religious life in Europe and America. But Christianity has always shown remarkable resilience. This was certainly true in the early eighteenth century, when the American colonies experienced a revival of spiritual zeal designed to restore the primacy of emotion in the religious realm.

Between 1700 and 1750, when the controversial ideas of the Enlightenment were circulating among the best-educated colonists, hundreds of new Christian congregations were founded. Most Americans (85 percent) lived in colonies with an "established" church, meaning that the colonial government endorsed—and collected taxes to support—a single official denomination.

The Church of England, also known as Anglicanism, was the established church in Virginia, Maryland, Delaware, and the Carolinas. Puritan Congregationalism was the official faith in most of New England. In New York, Anglicanism vied with the Dutch Reformed Church for control. Pennsylvania had no state-supported church, but Quakers dominated the legislative assembly. New Jersey and Rhode Island had no official denomination and hosted numerous Christian splinter groups.

Most colonies organized religious life around local parishes, which defined their theological boundaries and defended them against people who did not hold to the same faith. In colonies with official tax-supported religions, people of other faiths could not preach without the permission of the parish. In the 1730s and 1740s, the parish system was thrown into turmoil by the arrival of traveling evangelists, called *itinerants*, who claimed that most of the local parish ministers were incompetent. In their emotionally charged sermons, the itinerants, several of whom were white women and African Americans, insisted that Christians must be "reborn" in their convictions and behavior.

REVIVALISM During the early 1730s, worries about the erosion of religious fervor helped spark a series of emotional revivals known as the **Great Awakening**. The revivals spread up and down the Atlantic coast, divided congregations, towns, and families, and fueled popular new denominations, especially the Baptists and Methodists, who accounted for most of the growth. A skeptical Benjamin Franklin admitted that the Awakening was having a profound effect on social life: "Never did the people show so great a willingness to attend sermons. Religion is become the subject of most conversation."

JONATHAN EDWARDS In 1734–1735, a remarkable spiritual transformation occurred in the congregation of Jonathan Edwards, a prominent Congregationalist minister in the Massachusetts town of Northampton. One of America's most brilliant philosophers and theologians, Edwards had entered Yale College in 1716, at age thirteen, and graduated at the top of his class four years later.

When Edwards arrived in Northampton in 1727, he was shocked by the town's lack of religious conviction. He claimed that the young people were preoccupied with sinful pleasures and indulged in "lewd practices" that "corrupted others." He warned that Christians had become obsessed with making and spending money, and that the ideas associated with the Enlightenment were eroding the importance of religious life.

Edwards rushed to restore the emotional side of religion. "Our people," he said, "do not so much need to have their heads stored [with new scientific knowledge] as to have their hearts touched [with spiritual intensity]."

Edwards was fiery and charismatic, and his vivid descriptions of the torments of hell and the delights of heaven helped rekindle spiritual intensity among his congregants. By 1735, he reported that "the town seemed to be full of the presence of God; it never was so full of love, nor of joy."

In 1741, Edwards delivered his most famous sermon, "Sinners in the Hands of an Angry God," in which he

Jonathan Edwards One of the foremost preachers of the Great Awakening, Edwards dramatically described the torments that awaited sinners in the afterlife.

reminded the congregation that hell is real and that God "holds you over the pit of hell, much as one holds a spider, or some loathsome insect, over the fire, abhors you, and is dreadfully provoked. . . . He looks upon you as worthy of nothing else, but to be cast into the fire." When he finished, he had to wait several minutes for the congregants to quiet down before he could lead them in a closing hymn.

GEORGE WHITEFIELD The most celebrated promoter of the Great Awakening was a young English minister, George Whitefield, whose reputation as a spellbinding evangelist preceded him to the colonies.

Whitefield set out to restore the fires of religious intensity in America. In the autumn of 1739, the twenty-five-year-old evangelist began a fourteen-month tour, preaching to huge crowds in every colony. His critics were as fervent as his admirers. A disgusted Bostonian described a revival meeting's theatrics: "The meeting was carried on with . . . some screaming out in Distress and Anguish . . . some again jumping up and down . . . some lying along on

George Whitefield The English minister's dramatic eloquence roused Americans, inspiring many to experience a religious rebirth.

the floor. . . . The whole with a very great Noise, to be heard at a Mile's Distance, and continued almost the whole night."

Whitefield enthralled audiences with his golden voice, flamboyant style, and unparalleled eloquence. Even Benjamin Franklin, a confirmed rationalist who saw Whitefield preach in Philadelphia, was so excited by the sermon that he emptied his pockets into the collection plate.

Whitefield urged his listeners to experience a "new birth"—a sudden, emotional moment of conversion and salvation. By the end of his sermon, one listener reported, the entire congregation was "in utmost Confusion, some crying out, some laughing, and Bliss still roaring to them to come to Christ, as they answered, I will, I will, I'm coming, I'm coming."

RADICAL EVANGELISTS Edwards and Whitefield inspired many imitators, the most radical of whom carried emotional evangelism to extremes, stirring up women as well as those at the bottom of society— laborers, seamen, servants, slaves, and landless farm folk—and ordaining their own ministers.

William Tennent, an Irish-born Presbyterian, charged that local ministers were "cold and sapless," afraid to "thrust the nail of terror into sleeping souls." Tennent's oldest son, Gilbert, also an evangelist, defended his tactics by explaining that he and other traveling preachers invaded parishes only when the local minister showed no interest in the "Getting of Grace and Growing in it."

The Tennents urged people to renounce their ministers and pursue salvation on their own. They also attacked the excesses of the wealthy and powerful. Worried members of the colonial elite charged that the radical revivalists were spreading "anarchy, levelling, and dissolution."

Equally unsettling to the elite was the Reverend James Davenport, who urged Christians to renounce "rationalist" ministers influenced by the Enlightenment and become the agents of their own salvation through a purely emotional conversion experience. A Connecticut minister warned that Davenport and other extremists were "frightening people out of their senses."

WOMEN AND REVIVALS

The Great Awakening's most controversial element was the emergence of women who defied convention by speaking in religious services. Among them was Sarah Haggar Osborne, a Rhode Island schoolteacher who organized prayer meetings that eventually included men and women, black and white. When concerned ministers told her to stop, she refused to "shut my mouth and doors and creep into obscurity."

Similarly, in western Massachusetts, Bathsheba Kingsley spread the gospel among her neighbors because she had received "immediate revelations from heaven." When her husband tried to intervene, she pummeled him with "hard words and blows," praying loudly that he "go quick to hell."

For all the turbulence created by the revivals, however, churches remained male bastions of political authority.

A CHANGING RELIGIOUS LANDSCAPE The Great Awakening made religion intensely personal by creating both a deep sense of spiritual guilt and an intense yearning for redemption. Yet it also undermined many of the established churches by emphasizing that all individuals, regardless of wealth or social status, could receive God's grace without the guidance of ministers. Denominations became bitterly divided as "Old Light" conservatives criticized democratic revivalism and sparred with "New Light" evangelicals who delighted in provoking emotional outbursts and celebrating individual freedom in matters of faith.

New England religious life would never be the same, as the Great Awakening shattered the Puritan ideal of religious uniformity. Isaac Stiles, a crusty Connecticut minister, denounced the "intrusion of choice into spiritual matters" and charged that the "multitudes were seriously, soberly, and solemnly out of their wits" in their embrace of ultra-emotional religion. John Henry Goetschius, a Dutch Reformed evangelist, shot back that Stiles and other Old Lights were determined to "impose on many people, against their will, their old, rotten, and stinking routine religion."

In the more sedate churches of Boston, a focus on rational or enlightened religion gained the upper hand; ministers found Puritan theology too cold and forbidding, and they considered irrational the Calvinist concept that people could be forever damned by predestination. They embraced Enlightenment rationalism, arguing that God created laws of nature that people could discover and exploit.

RELIGIOUS COLLEGES In reaction to taunts that "born-again" revivalist ministers lacked learning, the Awakening gave rise to denominational colleges that became a distinctive characteristic of American higher education. The three colleges already in existence had religious origins: Harvard College in Massachusetts, founded in 1636 because the Puritans dreaded "to leave an illiterate ministry to the church when our present ministers shall lie in the dust"; the College of William and Mary in Virginia, created in 1693 to strengthen the Anglican ministry; and Yale College, set up in 1701 to educate the Puritans of Connecticut, who believed that Harvard was drifting from the strictest orthodoxy. The College of New Jersey, later Princeton University, was founded by Presbyterians in 1746.

In close succession came King's College (1754) in New York, later renamed Columbia University, an Anglican institution; the College of Rhode Island (1764), later called Brown University, which was Baptist; New Jersey's Queens College (1766), later known as Rutgers, which was Dutch Reformed; and Dartmouth College (1769) in New Hampshire, which was Congregationalist.

THE HEART VERSUS THE HEAD Like a ferocious fire that burned intensely before dying out, the Great Awakening subsided by 1750. Like the Enlightenment, however, it influenced the forces leading to the revolution against Great Britain and set in motion powerful currents that still flow in American life.

The Awakening implanted in American culture the evangelical impulse and the emotional appeal of revivalism, weakened the status of the old-fashioned clergy and state-supported churches, and encouraged believers to exercise their own individual judgment. By encouraging the proliferation of denominations, it heightened the need for toleration of dissent.

In some respects, however, the Awakening and the Enlightenment, one stressing the urgings of the spirit and the other celebrating the cold logic of reason, led by different roads to similar ends. Both movements spread across the mainland colonies and thereby helped bind the regions together. Both emphasized the power and right of individual decision-making, and both aroused hopes that America would become the promised land in which people might attain the perfection of piety or reason, if not both.

By urging believers to exercise their own spiritual judgment, revivals weakened the authority of the established churches and their ministers, just as resentment of British economic regulations would later weaken colonial loyalty to the king. As such, the Great Awakening and the Enlightenment helped nurture a growing commitment to individual freedom and resistance to authority that would play a key role in the rebellion against British "tyranny" in 1776.

CHAPTER REVIEW

SUMMARY

- **Colonial Demographics**   Cheap land lured poor immigrants to America. The initial shortage of women eventually gave way to a more equal gender ratio and a tendency to earlier marriage than in Europe, leading to higher *birth rates* and larger families. *Death rates* were lower in the colonies than in Europe, which led to rapid population growth.

- **Women in the Colonies**   English colonists brought their beliefs and prejudices with them to America, including convictions about the inferiority of women. Colonial women remained largely confined to *women's work* in the house, yard, and field. Over time, though, necessity created opportunities for women outside their traditional roles.

- **Colonial Differences**   A thriving colonial trading economy sent raw materials such as fish, timber, and furs to England in return for manufactured goods. The expanding economy created new wealth and a rise in the consumption of European goods, and it fostered the expansion of slavery. Tobacco was the *staple crop* in Virginia, rice in the Carolinas. Plantation agriculture based on slavery became entrenched in the South. New England's shipping industry created a profitable *triangular trade* among Africa, America, and England. By 1790, German, Scots-Irish, Welsh, and Irish immigrants, as well as other European ethnic groups, had settled in the middle colonies, along with Quakers, Jews, Huguenots, and Mennonites.

- **Race-Based Slavery**   Deep-rooted prejudice led to *race-based slavery*. Africans were considered "heathens" whose supposed inferiority entitled white Americans to use them as slaves. Africans brought diverse skills to help build America's economy. The use of African slaves was concentrated in the South, where landowners used them to produce lucrative staple crops, such as tobacco, rice, and indigo. But slaves lived in cities, too, especially New York. As the slave population increased, race relations grew tense, and *slave codes* were created to regulate the movement of enslaved people. Sporadic slave uprisings, such as the *Stono Rebellion*, occurred in both the North and South.

- **The Enlightenment and the Great Awakening**   Printing presses, education, and city life created a flow of new ideas that circulated via long-distance travel, tavern life, the postal service, and newspapers. The attitudes of the *Enlightenment* were transported along international trade routes. Sir Isaac Newton's scientific discoveries culminated in the belief that reason could improve society. Benjamin Franklin, who believed that people could shape their own destinies, became the face of the Enlightenment in America. *Deism* expressed the religious views of the Age of Reason. By the 1730s, a revival of faith, the *Great Awakening*, swept through the colonies. New congregations formed as evangelists insisted that Christians be "reborn." Individualism, not orthodoxy, was stressed in this first popular religious movement in America's history.

CHRONOLOGY

1619	First Africans arrive at Jamestown
1636	Harvard College is established
1667	Virginia enacts slave code declaring that enslaved children who were baptized as Christians remained slaves
1692–1693	Salem witchcraft trials
1730s–1740s	Great Awakening
1739	Stono Rebellion
	George Whitefield preaches his first sermon in America, in Philadelphia
1741	Jonathan Edwards preaches "Sinners in the Hands of an Angry God"

KEY TERMS

death rate p. 96

birth rate p. 97

women's work p. 99

staple crops p. 102

triangular trade p. 105

race-based slavery p. 112

slave codes p. 112

Stono Rebellion (1739) p. 114

Enlightenment p. 120

Deists p. 121

Great Awakening p. 124

 INQUIZITIVE

Go to InQuizitive to see what you've learned—and learn what you've missed—with personalized feedback along the way.

4

From Colonies to States

Boston Tea Party Disguised as Native Americans, a swarm of Patriots boarded three British ships and dumped more than 300 chests of East India Company tea into Boston Harbor.

Four great European naval powers—Spain, France, England, and the Netherlands (Holland)—created colonies in North America during the sixteenth and seventeenth centuries as part of their larger fight for global supremacy. Throughout the eighteenth century, wars raged across Europe, mostly pitting the Catholic nations of France and Spain against Protestant Great Britain and the Netherlands. The conflicts spread to the Americas, and by the middle of the eighteenth century, North America had become a primary battleground, involving both colonists and Native Americans allied with different European powers.

Spain's sparsely populated settlements in the borderlands north of Mexico were small and weak compared to those in the British colonies. Spain had failed to create substantial colonies with robust economies. Instead, it emphasized the conversion of native peoples to Catholicism, prohibited manufacturing within its colonies, strictly limited trade with Native Americans, and searched—in vain—for gold.

The French and British colonies developed a thriving trade with Native Americans at the same time that the fierce rivalry between Great Britain and France gradually shifted the balance of power in Europe. By the end of the eighteenth century, Spain and the Netherlands were in decline, leaving France and Great Britain to fight for dominance. Their nearly constant warfare led Great Britain to tighten its control over the American colonies to raise the funds needed to combat Catholic France and Spain. Tensions over these British efforts to preserve their empire at the expense of American freedoms would lead to rebellion and eventually to revolution.

focus questions

1. What were the similarities and differences in the way that the British and French Empires administered their colonies before 1763?

2. Analyze how the French and Indian War changed relations among the European powers in North America.

3. Describe how after the French and Indian War the British tightened their control over the colonies, and then summarize the colonial responses.

4. What were the underlying factors in the events of the 1770s that led the colonies to declare their independence from Britain?

COMPETING NEIGHBORS

The bitter rivalry between Great Britain and France fed France's desire to challenge the English presence in the Americas by establishing Catholic settlements in the Caribbean, Canada, and the region west of the Appalachian Mountains. Yet the French never invested enough people or resources in North America. During the 1660s, the population of New France was less than that of the tiny English colony of Rhode Island. By the mid–eighteenth century, the residents of New France numbered less than 5 percent of British Americans.

NEW FRANCE

The actual settlement of New France began in 1605, when soldier-explorer Samuel de Champlain founded Port-Royal in Acadia, along the Atlantic coast of Canada. Three years later, Champlain established Quebec, to the west, along the St. Lawrence River. Until his death in 1635, Champlain governed New France on behalf of trading companies looking to create a prosperous commercial colony tied to fur trade with the Indians and fishing opportunities off the Atlantic coast.

In 1627, however, the French government ordered that only Catholics could live in New France. This restriction stunted the settlement's growth—as did the harsh winter climate. As a consequence, the number of French who colonized Canada was *much* smaller than the number of British, Dutch, and Spanish colonists in other North American colonies, and they were almost all men. From the start, France spent far more to maintain its North American colony than it gained from the furs and fish exported to France for sale.

Champlain knew that the French could survive only by befriending the native peoples. To that end, he dispatched trappers and traders to live with the indigenous nations, learn their languages and customs, and marry their women. Many of these hardy woodsmen pushed into the forested regions around the Great Lakes and developed a flourishing fur trade.

In 1663, French King Louis XIV converted New France into a royal colony led by a governor-general who modeled his rule after that of the absolute monarchy. New France was fully subject to the French king; colonists had no political rights or elected legislature.

To solidify New France, Louis XIV dispatched soldiers and settlers, including shiploads of young women to be wives for the mostly male colonists. He also awarded large grants of land, called *seigneuries*, to lure aristocratic settlers. The poorest farmers usually rented land from the *seigneur*.

Champlain in New France Samuel de Champlain firing at a group of Iroquois, killing two chieftains (1609).

Still, only about 40,000 French immigrants came to the Western Hemisphere during the seventeenth and eighteenth centuries. By 1750, when the British colonists in North America numbered about 1.5 million, the total French population was only 70,000.

From their Canadian outposts along the Great Lakes, French explorers in the early 1670s moved down the Mississippi River to the Gulf of Mexico. Louis Jolliet, a fur trader born in Quebec, teamed with Father Jacques Marquette, a Jesuit priest fluent in Indian languages, to explore the Wisconsin River south to the Mississippi. Traveling in canoes, they paddled to within 400 miles of the Gulf of Mexico, where they turned back for fear of encountering Spanish soldiers.

Other French explorers followed. In 1682, René-Robert Cavelier, sieur de La Salle, organized an expedition that started in Montreal, crossed the Great Lakes, and went down the Mississippi to the Gulf of Mexico, the first European to do so. Near what is today Venice, Mississippi, La Salle erected a cross, claiming for France the vast Ohio and Mississippi Valleys—all the way to the Rocky Mountains. He named the region Louisiana, after Louis XIV. New France had one important advantage over the British: access to the great inland rivers that led to the heartland of the continent and thus to the pelts of such fur-bearing animals as beaver, otter, and mink.

Settlement of the Louisiana Territory finally began in 1699, when the French established a colony near Biloxi, Mississippi. The main settlement then moved to Mobile Bay and, in 1710, to the present site of Mobile, Alabama.

For nearly fifty years, the driving force in Louisiana was Jean-Baptiste Le Moyne, sieur de Bienville. In 1718, he founded New Orleans, which soon became the capital of the sprawling Louisiana colony encompassing much of the interior of the North American continent.

That same year, the Spanish, concerned about the French presence in Louisiana, founded San Antonio in the Texas province of New Spain. They built a Catholic mission (later called the "Alamo") and a fort (*presidio*) to convert the indigenous people and to fend off efforts by the French to expand into Texas.

THE BRITISH COLONIAL SYSTEM

The diverse British colonies in North America were different from those of New France. Colonial governments were typically headed by a royal governor or proprietor who could appoint and remove officials, command the militia, and grant pardons to people convicted of crimes.

Yet the British colonists enjoyed rights and powers absent in Britain—as well as in New France. In particular, they had *elected* legislatures. Representatives in the "lower" houses were chosen by popular vote, but only adult males owning a specified amount of property could vote. Because property holding was so widespread in America, however, a greater proportion of the male population could vote in the colonies than could anywhere else in the world.

The most important political trend in eighteenth-century America was the growing power of the colonial legislatures. Like Parliament, the colonial assemblies controlled the budget and could pass laws and regulations. Most assemblies exercised influence over the royal governors by paying their salaries. Throughout the eighteenth century, the assemblies expanded their power and influence. Self-government in British America became first a habit, then a cherished "right."

MERCANTILISM The English Civil War during the 1640s sharply reduced the flow of money and people to America and forced English Americans to take sides in the conflict between Royalists and Puritans.

Oliver Cromwell's victory over the monarchy in 1651 had direct effects in the colonies. As England's new ruler, Cromwell embraced a more rigidly enforced **mercantilism**, a political and economic policy adopted by most European monarchs during the seventeenth century in which the government controlled all economic activities. Key industries were regulated, taxed, or "subsidized" (supported by payments from the government), and people with specialized skills or knowledge of new technologies, such as textile machinery, were not allowed to leave the country.

Mercantilism also supported the creation of global empires. Colonies, it was assumed, enriched the mother country in several ways: (1) by providing silver and gold as well as crucial raw materials [furs, fish, grains, timber, sugar, tobacco, indigo, tar, etc.]; (2) by creating a captive market of colonial consumers who were forced to buy goods created in the home country; (3) by relieving social tensions and political unrest in the home country, because colonies could become a haven for the poor, unemployed, and imprisoned; and (4) by not producing goods that would compete with those produced in the home country.

NAVIGATION ACTS Such mercantilist assumptions prompted Oliver Cromwell to adopt the first in a series of **Navigation Acts** intended to increase control over the colonial economies. The Navigation Act of 1651 required that all goods going to and from the colonies be carried *only* in English-owned ships. The law was intended to hurt the Dutch, who had developed a flourishing shipping business between America and Europe. Dutch shippers charged much less to transport goods than did the English, and they actively encouraged smuggling in the American colonies as a means of defying the Navigation Acts. By 1652, England and the Netherlands were at war—the first of three naval conflicts between 1652 and 1674 involving the two Protestant rivals.

After the monarchy was restored to power in England in 1660, the Royalist Parliament passed the Navigation Act of 1660, which specified that certain colonial products (such as tobacco) were to be shipped *only* to England or other colonies. The Navigation Act of 1663, called the Staples Act, required that *all* shipments from Europe to America first stop in Britain to be offloaded and taxed before being sent to the colonies.

In 1664, English warships conquered New Netherland, removing the Dutch from North America. By 1700, the English had surpassed the Dutch as the world's leading maritime power, and most products sent to and from America via Europe and Africa were carried in English ships. What the English government did not expect was that the mercantile system would arouse intense resentment in the colonies.

COLONIAL RESENTMENT Colonial merchants and shippers complained about the Navigation Acts, but the English government refused to

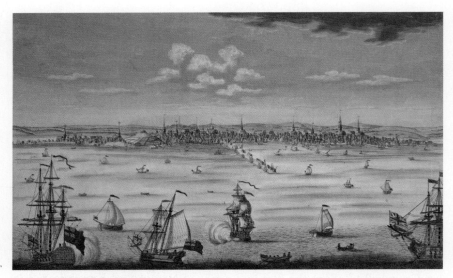

Boston from the southeast This view of eighteenth-century Boston shows the importance of shipping and its regulation in the colonies.

lift the restrictions. New England was particularly hard hit. In 1678, a defiant Massachusetts legislature declared that the Navigation Acts had no legal standing. In 1684, King Charles II tried to teach the rebellious colonists a lesson by revoking the royal charter for Massachusetts.

The following year, Charles died and his brother, King James II, succeeded him, becoming the first Catholic monarch in more than 100 years. To demonstrate his power, the new king reorganized the New England colonies into a single supercolony called the Dominion of New England.

In 1686, a new royal governor, the authoritarian Sir Edmund Andros, arrived in Boston. Andros stripped New Englanders of their civil rights, imposed new taxes, ignored town governments, strictly enforced the Navigation Acts, and punished smugglers.

THE GLORIOUS REVOLUTION

In 1688, the Dominion of New England added the former Dutch provinces of New York, East Jersey, and West Jersey to its control, just a few months before the **Glorious Revolution** erupted in England. People called the revolution "glorious" because it took place with little bloodshed. Catholic James II, fearing imprisonment in the Tower of London, fled to France and was replaced by the king's daughter Mary and her husband William III, the ruling Dutch Prince. Both were Protestants.

William III and Mary II would govern England as constitutional monarchs, their powers limited by Parliament. They soon issued a religious Toleration Act and a Bill of Rights to ensure that there never again would be an absolute monarchy in England.

In 1689, Americans in Boston staged their own revolution. A group of merchants, ministers, and militiamen (citizen-soldiers) arrested Governor Andros and his aides and removed Massachusetts Bay Colony from the new Dominion of New England. Within a few weeks, the other colonies that had been absorbed into the Dominion also restored their independence.

William and Mary, however, were determined to crack down on smuggling and rebelliousness. They appointed new royal governors in Massachusetts, New York, and Maryland. In Massachusetts, the governor was given authority to veto acts of the colonial assembly, and he removed the requirement that only church members could vote in elections.

JOHN LOCKE ON REVOLUTION The removal of King James II in the Glorious Revolution showed that a monarch could be deposed according to constitutional principles. In addition, the long-standing geographical designation "Great Britain" for the united kingdoms of England, Scotland, and Wales would soon be revived as the nation's official name.

A powerful justification for revolution appeared in 1690 when English philosopher John Locke published *Two Treatises on Government*, which had an enormous impact on political thought in the colonies. Locke rejected the traditional "divine" right of monarchs to govern with absolute power and insisted that people are endowed with **natural rights** to life, liberty, and property. He noted that it was the need to protect those natural rights that led people to establish governments in the first place. When rulers failed to protect the property and lives of their subjects, Locke argued, the people had the right—in extreme cases—to overthrow the monarch and change the government.

AN EMERGING COLONIAL SYSTEM

In early 1689, New Yorkers sent a message to King William thanking him for delivering England from "tyranny, popery, and slavery." Many colonists were disappointed, however, when the king cracked down on American smugglers. The Act to Prevent Frauds and Abuses of 1696 required royal governors to enforce the Navigation Acts, allowed customs officials in America to use "writs of assistance" (general search warrants that did not have to specify the place to be searched), and ordered that accused smugglers be tried in royal *admiralty* courts (because juries in colonial courts rarely convicted their peers).

Soon, however, British efforts to enforce the Navigation Acts waned. King George I and George II, German princes who were descendants of James I, showed much less interest in enforcing colonial trade laws. Robert Walpole, the long-serving prime minister (1721–1742) and lord of the treasury, decided that the American colonies should be left alone to export needed raw materials (timber, tobacco, rice, indigo) and to buy manufactured goods from the mother country.

Under Walpole's leadership, Britain followed a policy of "salutary neglect" of the Navigation Acts, allowing the colonies greater freedom to pursue their economic interests, in part because the British did not want to pay the huge expense of enforcing the imperial regulations. What Walpole did not realize was that **salutary neglect** would create among many colonists an independent attitude that would eventually blossom into revolution.

THE HABIT OF SELF-GOVERNMENT Government within the American colonies evolved during the eighteenth century as the colonial assemblies acquired powers, particularly with respect to government appointments, which Parliament had yet to exercise itself.

The English colonies in America benefited from elected legislative assemblies. Whether called the House of Burgesses (Virginia), Delegates (Maryland), Representatives (Massachusetts), or simply the assembly, the "lower" houses were chosen by popular vote. Only male property owners could vote. Because property holding was much more widespread in America than in Europe, a greater proportion of the male population could vote and hold office. Members of the colonial assemblies tended to be wealthy, but there were exceptions. One unsympathetic colonist observed in 1744 that the New Jersey Assembly "was chiefly composed of mechanicks and ignorant wretches; obstinate to the last degree."

The most profound political trend during the eighteenth century was the growing power and influence of the colonial assemblies. They controlled the budget through their vote on taxes and expenditures, and they held the power to initiate legislation. Most of the assemblies also exerted leverage on the royal governors by controlling their salaries. By midcentury, the colonies had become largely self-governing.

WARFARE IN THE COLONIES

The Glorious Revolution of 1688 transformed relations among the great powers of Europe. Protestants William and Mary, for example, were passionate foes of Catholic France's Louis XIV. They organized an alliance of European nations against the French in a transatlantic war known in the American colonies as King William's War (1689–1697).

It would be the first of four major wars fought in Europe and the colonies over the next seventy-four years pitting Britain and its European allies against France or Spain and their allies. By the end of the eighteenth century, the struggle between the British and French would shift the balance of power in Europe.

The prolonged warfare had a devastating effect on New England, especially Massachusetts, which was closest to the battlefields of French Canada. It also reshaped the relationship between America and Great Britain, which emerged from the wars as the most powerful nation in the world. Thereafter, international commerce became increasingly essential to the expanding British Empire, thus making the American colonies even more strategically significant.

THE FRENCH AND INDIAN WAR The most important conflict between Britain and France (and its Catholic ally Spain) in North America was the **French and Indian War** (1756–1763), globally known as the **Seven Years' War**. Unlike the three earlier wars, the French and Indian War started in America and ended with a decisive victory. It was sparked by French and British competition for the ancestral Indian lands in the vast Ohio Valley; whichever nation or colony (both Pennsylvania and Virginia claimed jurisdiction over it) controlled the "Ohio Country" would control the entire continent because of the strategic importance of the Ohio and Mississippi Rivers.

To defend their interests, the French pushed south from Canada and built forts in the Ohio Country. When Virginia's governor learned of the forts, he sent a twenty-two-year-old militia officer, Major George Washington, to warn the French to leave. But Washington was rudely rebuffed by the French.

A few months later, in the spring of 1754, Washington, now a lieutenant colonel, went back to the Ohio Country with 150 volunteer soldiers and Indian allies. They planned to build a fort where the Allegheny, Monongahela, and Ohio Rivers converged (where the city of Pittsburgh later developed). The so-called Forks of the Ohio was the key strategic gateway to the vast territory west of the Appalachian Mountains, and both sides were determined to control it.

After two months of travel through densely forested, hilly terrain, Washington learned that French soldiers had beaten him to the site and built Fort Duquesne in western Pennsylvania. Washington decided to camp about forty miles away. The next day, the Virginians ambushed a French scouting party, killing ten soldiers, including the commander—the first fatalities in what would become the French and Indian War.

Washington and his troops, reinforced by more Virginians and British soldiers dispatched from South Carolina, hastily constructed a tiny circular stockade. They called it Fort Necessity. Washington remarked that the valley provided "a charming field for an encounter," but there was nothing charming about the battle that erupted when a large French force surrounded and attacked on July 3, 1756.

After the day-long, lopsided Battle of Great Meadows, Washington surrendered, having seen a third of his 300 men killed or wounded. The French and their Indian allies lost only three men. The French commander then forced Washington to surrender his French prisoners and admit that he had "assassinated" the group of French soldiers at the earlier encounter. On July 4, 1754, Washington and the defeated Virginians began trudging home.

France was now in undisputed control of the Ohio Country. Yet Washington's bungled expedition wound up triggering what would become a massive world war. As a British politician exclaimed, "the volley fired by a young Virginian in the backwoods of America set the world on fire."

THE ALBANY PLAN British officials in America, worried about war with the French and their Indian allies, urgently called a meeting of the northern colonies. Twenty-one representatives from seven colonies gathered in Albany, New York. It was the first time that a large group of colonial delegates had met to take joint action.

At the urging of Pennsylvania's Benjamin Franklin, the Albany Congress (June 19–July 11, 1754) approved the **Albany Plan of Union**. It called for eleven colonies to band together, headed by a president appointed by the king. Each colonial assembly would send two to seven delegates to a "grand council," which would have legislative powers. The Union would have jurisdiction over Indian affairs.

The Albany Plan of Union was too radical for the time, however. British officials and the colonial legislatures, eager to maintain their powers, wanted simply a military alliance against Indian attacks, so they rejected the Albany Plan. Franklin later maintained that the Plan of Union, had it been approved, might have postponed or eliminated the eventual need for a full-scale colonial revolution. His proposal, however, would become the model for the form of governance (Articles of Confederation) created by the new American nation in 1777.

WAR IN NORTH AMERICA With the failure of the Albany Plan, the British decided to force a showdown with the "presumptuous" French. In June 1755, a British fleet captured the French forts protecting Acadia, along the Atlantic coast of Canada. The British then expelled 11,500 Acadians, the Catholic French residents. Hundreds of them eventually found their way to French Louisiana, where they became known as Cajuns.

In 1755, the British government sent 1,000 soldiers to dislodge the French from the Ohio Country. The arrival of unprecedented numbers of "redcoat" soldiers on American soil would change the dynamics of British North America. Although the colonists endorsed the use of force against the

French, they later would oppose the use of British soldiers to enforce colonial regulations.

BRADDOCK'S DEFEAT The British commander in chief in America, General Edward Braddock, was a stubborn, overconfident officer who refused to recruit large numbers of Indian allies. Braddock viewed Indians with contempt, telling those willing to fight with him that he would not reward them with land: "No savage should inherit the land." His dismissal of the Indians and his ignorance of unconventional warfare would prove fatal.

With the addition of some American militiamen, including George Washington as a volunteer officer, Braddock's force left northern Virginia to confront the French, hacking a 125-mile-long road west through the Allegheny Mountains toward Fort Duquesne.

On July 9, 1755, as the British neared the fort, they were ambushed by French soldiers, Canadian militiamen, and Indians; they suffered shocking losses. Braddock was shot; he died three days later. Washington, his coat riddled by four bullets, helped lead a hasty retreat.

What came to be called the Battle of Monongahela was one of the worst British defeats in history. The French and Indians captured the British cannons and supplies and killed 63 of 86 British officers and 914 of 1,373 soldiers. The

The first American political cartoon Benjamin Franklin's plea to the colonies to unite against the French in 1754 would become popular again twenty years later, when the colonies faced a different threat.

Indians burned alive twelve wounded British soldiers left behind on the battlefield. A devastated Washington wrote his brother that the vaunted British redcoats had "been scandalously beaten by a trifling body of men" and had "broke & run as sheep pursued by hounds." The Virginians, he noted, "behaved like Men and died like Soldiers."

A WORLD WAR While Braddock's defeat sent shock waves through the colonies, Indians allied with the French began attacking American farms throughout western Pennsylvania, Maryland, and Virginia, killing, scalping, or capturing hundreds of men, women, and children. Desperate to respond, the Pennsylvania provincial government offered 130 Spanish dollars for each male Indian scalp and 50 dollars for female scalps.

Indians and colonists killed each other mercilessly throughout 1755 and 1756. It was not until May 1756, however, that Protestant Britain and Catholic France formally declared war in Europe. The first true "world war," the Seven Years' War in Europe (the French and Indian War in North America) would eventually be fought on four continents and three oceans. In the end, it would redraw the political map of North America.

France, governed by the inept Louis XV, entered the war without excitement, fought with little distinction, and emerged battered, humiliated, and bankrupt. When the war began, the British had the smaller army but three times as many warships. By the end, the French had lost nearly 100 ships, and the British had captured more than 64,000 French sailors.

The onset of war brought into office a new British government,

From La Roque's Encyclopedie des Voyages An Iroquois warrior in an eighteenth-century French engraving.

with William Pitt as prime minister. Pitt determined that defeating the French required a different military policy. Realizing that the colonial legislatures had largely resisted British efforts to coerce American colonists into embracing the war as their own, he decided to treat the colonies as allies rather than inferiors. Instead of forcing them to help finance the war, he provided funds that convinced the legislatures to become full partners in the quest to oust the French from Canada.

Pitt's shrewd approach enabled British commanders to assemble a force of 45,000 British troops and American militiamen, and in August 1759, they captured French forts near the Canadian border at Ticonderoga, Crown Point, and Niagara.

THE BATTLE OF QUEBEC In 1759, the French and Indian War reached its climax with a series of British triumphs. The most decisive victory was at Quebec, the hilltop fortress city and the capital of French Canada. During the dark of night, some 4,500 British troops scaled the cliffs above the St. Lawrence River and at dawn surprised the French defenders in a battle that lasted only ten minutes. The French surrendered four days later.

The Battle of Quebec marked the turning point in the war. Thereafter, the conflict in North America ebbed, although the fighting dragged on until 1763. In the South, fighting flared between the Carolina settlers and the Cherokee Nation. A force of British regulars and colonial militia broke Cherokee resistance in 1761.

A NEW BRITISH KING On October 25, 1760, the ailing British King George II arose at 6 A.M., drank his chocolate milk, and adjourned to his toilet closet. A few minutes later, a servant heard a strange noise, opened the door, and found the king dead, the result of a ruptured artery. His death shocked the nation and brought an untested new king—George II's twenty-two-year-old grandson—to the throne.

Although initially shy and insecure, King George III would surprise his

George III The young king of a victorious empire.

family by becoming a strong-willed leader who oversaw the military defeat of France and Spain in the Seven Years' War.

THE TREATY OF PARIS (1763) The **Treaty of Paris**, signed in February 1763, gave Britain control of important French colonies around the world, including many in India, several highly profitable "sugar island" colonies in the Caribbean, and all of France's North American possessions east

NORTH AMERICA, 1713

HUDSON BAY

HUDSON'S BAY COMPANY

UNEXPLORED

NEWFOUNDLAND

NEW FRANCE

NOVA SCOTIA

NEW ENGLAND

Mississippi River

LOUISIANA

ENGLISH COLONIES

VIRGINIA

PACIFIC OCEAN

CAROLINAS

ATLANTIC OCEAN

NEW SPAIN

FLORIDA

GULF OF MEXICO

CUBA

HISPANIOLA

CARIBBEAN SEA

England
France
Spain

0   500   1000 Miles
0   500   1000 Kilometers

NEW GRANADA

- What events led to the first clashes between the French and the British in the late seventeenth century?
- Why did New England suffer more than other regions of North America during the wars of the eighteenth century?
- What were the long-term financial, military, and political consequences of the wars between France and Britain?

of the Mississippi River. This encompassed all of Canada and what was then called Spanish Florida, including much of present-day Alabama and Mississippi. As compensation, the treaty gave Spain control over the vast Louisiana Territory, including New Orleans and all French land west of the Mississippi. France was left with no territory on the North American continent.

British Americans were delighted with the outcome of the war. As a New England minister declared, Great Britain had reached the "summit of earthly grandeur and glory." The French menace had been removed, and British

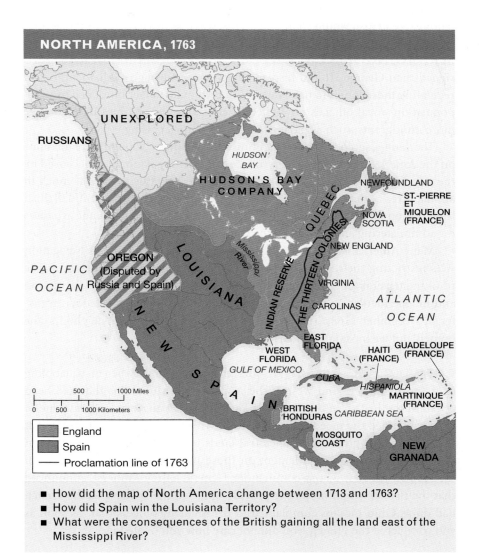

NORTH AMERICA, 1763

UNEXPLORED

RUSSIANS

HUDSON BAY

HUDSON'S BAY COMPANY

NEWFOUNDLAND

ST.-PIERRE ET MIQUELON (FRANCE)

QUEBEC

NOVA SCOTIA

NEW ENGLAND

Mississippi River

OREGON (Disputed by Russia and Spain)

PACIFIC OCEAN

LOUISIANA

INDIAN RESERVE

THE THIRTEEN COLONIES

VIRGINIA

CAROLINAS

ATLANTIC OCEAN

NEW SPAIN

EAST FLORIDA

WEST FLORIDA

GULF OF MEXICO

CUBA

HAITI (FRANCE)

GUADELOUPE (FRANCE)

HISPANIOLA

MARTINIQUE (FRANCE)

BRITISH HONDURAS

CARIBBEAN SEA

MOSQUITO COAST

NEW GRANADA

0   500   1000 Miles
0   500   1000 Kilometers

- England
- Spain
— Proclamation line of 1763

- How did the map of North America change between 1713 and 1763?
- How did Spain win the Louisiana Territory?
- What were the consequences of the British gaining all the land east of the Mississippi River?

Americans could now enjoy the highest quality of life of any people in the Western Hemisphere.

Yet Britain's spectacular military success on land and sea created massive challenges. The national debt had doubled during the war, and the new cost of maintaining the sprawling North American empire, including the permanent stationing of thousands of British soldiers in the colonies, was staggering. Moreover, British leaders developed what one historian has called an "arrogant triumphalism," which led them to tighten—and ultimately lose—their control over the Indians and colonists in North America. In managing a vastly larger empire, the British would soon find themselves at war with their own colonies.

MANAGING A NEW EMPIRE No sooner was the Treaty of Paris signed than George III and his cabinet, working through Parliament, began regulating the colonies in new ways. With Britain no longer burdened by overpopulation, royal officials now rejected efforts by the colonies to encourage more immigrants, such as paying for their Atlantic crossing.

The king also encouraged his ministers to enforce economic regulations on the American colonies to help reduce the crushing national debt caused by the war. In 1763, the average British citizen paid twenty-six times as much in annual taxes as did the average American colonist. With that in mind, British leaders thought it only fair that the Americans should pay more of the expenses for administering and defending the colonies.

Many Americans disagreed, however, arguing that the various Navigation Acts restricting their economic activity were already a form of taxation. The resulting tension set in motion a chain of events that would lead to revolution and independence. "It is truly a miserable thing," said a Connecticut minister in December 1763, "that we no sooner leave fighting our neighbors, the French, but we must fall to quarreling among ourselves."

PONTIAC'S REBELLION After the war, colonists began squabbling over Indian-owned land west of the Appalachian Mountains that had been ceded to the British in the Treaty of Paris. Native American leaders, none of whom attended the meetings leading to the treaty, were shocked to learn that the French had "given" their ancestral lands to the British, who were intent upon imposing a harsh settlement on those Indians who had been allies of the French. The new British commander, General Jeffrey Amherst, announced that the British would no longer provide "gifts" to the Indians, as the French had done. Ohio Indians complained to British army officers that "as soon as you conquered the French, you did not care how you treated us."

The frustrated Indians fought back in the spring of 1763, capturing most of the British forts around the Great Lakes and in the Ohio Valley. "Never was panic more general," reported the *Pennsylvania Gazette*, "than that of the Back[woods] Inhabitants, whose terrors at this time exceed that followed on the defeat of General Braddock."

Native Americans also raided colonial settlements in Pennsylvania, Maryland, and Virginia, destroying farms and killing thousands. "Every day, for some time past," reported a Marylander, "has offered the melancholy scene of poor distressed families . . . who have deserted their plantations, for fear of falling into the cruel hands of our savage enemies."

The widespread Indian attacks came to be called **Pontiac's Rebellion** because of the prominent role played by the Ottawa chieftain in trying to unify several tribes in the effort to stop British expansion. Pontiac told a British official that the "French never conquered us, neither did they purchase a foot of our Country, nor have they a right to give it to you."

In December 1763, frontier ruffians in Pennsylvania took the law into their own hands. Outraged at the unwillingness of pacifist Quakers in the Pennsylvania assembly to protect white settlers on the frontier from marauding Indians, a group called the Paxton Boys, Scots-Irish farmers from Paxton, near Harrisburg, took revenge by massacring and scalping peaceful Conestogas— men, women, and children. Then they threatened to kill the so-called Moravian Indians, a group of Christian converts living near Bethlehem. When the Indians took refuge in Philadelphia, some 1,500 Paxton Boys marched on the capital, where Benjamin Franklin helped persuade them to return home.

THE PROCLAMATION LINE To help keep peace with the Indians and to abide by the terms of an earlier agreement with the Delawares and Shawnees, King George III issued the **Royal Proclamation of 1763**, which drew an imaginary line along the crest of the Appalachian Mountains from Canada to Georgia. Americans ("our loving subjects") were forbidden to go west of the line to ensure that the Indians would not be "molested or disturbed" on their ancestral lands.

For the first time, royal officials were curtailing territorial expansion, and Americans did not like it. Virginia planter George Washington was among those who objected. Like thousands of other British Americans, he wanted "to secure some of the most valuable lands in the King's part" even if it meant defying "the Proclamation that restrains it at present." He interpreted the Proclamation Line as a short-term way to appease Indian concerns about colonial expansion into their ancestral lands.

In practice, the Proclamation Line ended the activities of speculators buying huge tracts of Indian lands but did not keep land-hungry settlers from pushing across the Appalachian ridges into the Indian lands in the Ohio Valley. By 1767, an Indian chief was complaining that whites were "making more encroachments on their Country than ever they had before."

IMMIGRATION SOARS One unexpected result of the war's end was a surge in European immigration to the American colonies. With the French no longer a threat, colonists were more comfortable in testing the American wilderness. Between 1763 and 1775, more than 30,000 English, 55,000 Protestant Irish, and 40,000 Scots left the British Isles for the colonies. In addition, 12,000 German and Swiss settlers came in search of a better life. At the same time, some 85,000 enslaved Africans were brought to America's southern colonies, especially the Carolinas and Virginia. It was the greatest mass migration in history to that point, and it provided the foundation for much of America's development thereafter.

Most of the new arrivals were young males who had served as apprentices to learn a craft or trade. Many others were poor farm families who emigrated as a group. Half of them could not afford to pay the cost of crossing the Atlantic and therefore arrived as indentured servants.

The settlers were entering an exotic new civilization that had no rigid aristocracy. America was a fluid environment in which people could make their way on their abilities alone. A young English farmer wrote to say that he missed his friends but valued more his chance to become "independent" in ways unavailable at home.

REGULATING THE COLONIES

As Britain tightened its hold over the colonies—and the Indians—after 1763, Americans reminded Parliament that their original charters guaranteed that they should be treated as if they were English citizens, with all the rights and liberties protected by the nation's constitutional traditions. Why should they be governed by a distant legislature in which they had no elected representatives? Such arguments, however, fell on deaf ears in Parliament. As one member explained, the British were determined "to make North America pay [for] its own army."

GRENVILLE'S COLONIAL POLICY Just as the Proclamation of 1763 was being drafted, a new British government, led by prime minister George Grenville, began to grapple with the huge debts the government had accumulated during the Seven Years' War, along with the added expenses of maintaining troops in America. Grenville insisted that the Americans must pay for the soldiers defending them. He also resented the large number of American merchants who engaged in smuggling to avoid paying British taxes on imported goods. Grenville ordered colonial officials to tighten enforcement of the Navigation Acts and sent warships to capture smugglers.

THE SUGAR ACT Grenville's effort to enforce the Navigation Acts posed a serious threat to New England's prosperity. Distilling rum out of molasses, a sweet syrup made from sugarcane, had become quite profitable, especially if the molasses could be smuggled in from Caribbean islands still controlled by the French.

To generate more money from the colonies, Grenville put through the American Revenue Act of 1764, commonly known as the Sugar Act, which cut the tax on molasses in half. Doing so, he believed, would reduce the temptation to smuggle French molasses or to bribe royal customs officers. The Sugar Act, however, also added new *duties* (taxes) on other goods (sugar, wines, coffee, spices) imported into America. The new revenues, Grenville believed, would help pay for "the necessary expenses of defending, protecting, and securing, the said colonies."

With the Sugar Act, Parliament, for the first time, adopted a policy designed to raise *revenues* from the colonies and not merely to *regulate* trade with other nations. Colonists claimed that the Sugar Act taxed them without their consent, since they had no elected representatives in Parliament. British officials argued, however, that Parliament's power over the colonies was absolute and indivisible. If the Americans accepted parliamentary authority in *any* area, they had to accept it in *every* area. In the end, however, the cost of enforcing the new sugar tax proved to be four times greater than the revenue it generated.

THE CURRENCY ACT The colonies had long faced a chronic shortage of "hard" money (gold and silver coins, called *specie*), which kept flowing overseas to pay debts in England. To address the lack of specie, many colonies issued their own paper money, which could not be used in other colonies. British creditors feared payment in a currency of such fluctuating value, so Grenville implemented the Currency Act of 1764, a set of regulatory measures that prohibited the colonies from coining or printing money, while requiring that all payments for imported British goods be in gold or silver coins or in a commodity like tobacco. By banning paper money, the value of existing paper money plummeted. As a Philadelphia newspaper complained, "The Times are Dreadful, Dismal, Doleful, Dolorous, and dollar-less."

THE STAMP ACT Grenville excelled at repeatedly doing the wrong thing. In 1765, for example, he persuaded Parliament to pass the Quartering Act, which required Americans to feed and house British troops. Most Americans saw no need for so many British soldiers. If the British were there to defend against Indians, why were they positioned in cities far from the frontier?

Some colonists decided that the Quartering Act was actually an effort to bully them. William Knox, a British colonial official, admitted as much in 1763 when he said that the "main purpose" of keeping an army in America was "to secure the dependence of the colonies on Great Britain."

In February 1765, Grenville aggravated colonial concerns by pushing through an even more controversial measure. The **Stamp Act** required colonists to purchase paper with an official government stamp for virtually every possible use: newspapers, pamphlets, bonds, leases, deeds, licenses, insurance policies, college diplomas, even playing cards. The requirement was to go into effect November 1.

The Stamp Act was the first effort by Parliament to place a tax directly on American goods and services rather than levying an "external" tax on imports and exports, and it offended just about everyone. Benjamin Franklin's daughter Sarah ("Sally") wrote to her father in London, where he was representing the colonies. She reported that the only subject of conversation in America was the Stamp Act, "and nothing else is talked of. . . . everybody has something to say" about the hated tax, in part because, when combined with the Sugar and Currency Acts, it promised to bring economic activity to a halt.

THE WHIG POINT OF VIEW Grenville's colonial policies especially outraged Americans living in the large port cities: Boston, New York, Philadelphia, and Charleston. Unwittingly, the prime minister had stirred up protests and set in motion a violent debate about the proper relationship between Great Britain and her colonies. In the late eighteenth century, the Americans who opposed British policies began to call themselves Patriots, or *Whigs*, a name earlier applied to British critics of royal power. In turn, Whigs labeled the king and his "corrupt" government ministers and Parliamentary supporters as *Tories*, a term of abuse meaning friends of the king.

In 1764 and 1765, American Whigs felt that Grenville was violating their rights in several ways. A professional army was usually a weapon used by tyrants, and with the French defeated and Canada solidly under British control, thousands of British soldiers remained in America. Were the troops there to protect the colonists or scare them into obedience?

The Whigs also argued that although British citizens had the right to be taxed only by their elected representatives in Parliament, Americans had no such representatives. British leaders countered that the colonists enjoyed **virtual representation**, but William Pitt, a staunch supporter of American rights in Parliament, dismissed virtual representation as "the most contemptible idea that ever entered into the head of a man." Many others, in both Britain and America, agreed. Sir Francis Bernard, the royal governor of Massachusetts, correctly predicted that the new stamp tax "would cause a great Alarm & meet much Opposition" in the colonies.

PROTESTS IN THE COLONIES   The Stamp Act did arouse fierce resentment and resistance. In a flood of pamphlets, speeches, resolutions, and street protests, critics repeated a slogan familiar to Americans: "No taxation without representation [in Parliament]."

Protesters, calling themselves **Sons of Liberty**, emerged in every colony, often meeting beneath "liberty trees"—in Boston a great elm, in Charleston a live oak. In Virginia, Patrick Henry convinced the assembly to pass the "Stamp Act Resolutions," which asserted that the colonists could not be taxed without being first consulted by the British government or represented in Parliament by their own elected members.

THE NONIMPORTATION MOVEMENT   Since the mid–seventeenth century, colonial consumers could not get enough imported British manufactured goods—textiles, ceramics, glassware, and printed products. Now, however, militants saw such consumerism as a bold new weapon of political protest. To put economic pressure on the British government and show that they had not become "dependent" on Britain's "empire of goods," patriots by the thousands signed nonimportation agreements pledging not to buy or consume British goods.

The nonimportation movement of the 1760s and 1770s united Whigs from different communities and different colonies. It also enabled women to play a role in the resistance. Calling themselves **Daughters of Liberty**, many colonial women stopped buying imported British clothes and quit drinking British tea to "save this abused Country from Ruin and Slavery." Using herbs and flowers, they made "Liberty Tea" instead.

The Daughters of Liberty also participated in public "spinning bees," whereby they would gather in the town square to spin yarn and wool into fabric, known as "homespun." In 1769, the *Boston Evening Post* reported that the "industry and frugality of American ladies" were enabling "the political salvation of a whole continent."

COLONIAL UNITY The boycotts worked; imports of British goods fell by 40 percent. At the same time, the Virginia House of Burgesses struck the first official blow against the Stamp Act with the Virginia Resolves, a series of resolutions inspired by the fiery Patrick Henry. Virginians, Henry declared, were entitled to all the rights of Englishmen, and Englishmen could be taxed only by their elected representatives. Because Virginians had no elected representatives in Parliament, they could only be taxed by the Virginia legislature, for example. Newspapers spread the Virginia Resolves throughout the colonies, and other assemblies hastened to follow Virginia's example.

In 1765, the Massachusetts House of Representatives invited the other colonial assemblies to send delegates to New York City to discuss opposition to the Stamp Act. Nine responded, and from October 7 to October 25, the Stamp Act Congress formulated a Declaration of the Rights and Grievances of the Colonies. The delegates insisted that they would accept no taxes being "imposed on them" without "their own consent, given personally, or by their representatives."

REPEAL OF THE STAMP ACT The storm over the Stamp Act had scarcely erupted before Grenville, having lost the confidence of King George III, was replaced by Lord Rockingham in July 1765. The growing violence in America and the success of the nonimportation movement convinced Rockingham that the Stamp Act was a mistake, and a humiliated Parliament repealed it in February 1766. To save face, Parliament passed the Declaratory Act, in which it asserted its power to govern the colonies "in all cases whatsoever." The repeal of the Stamp Act set off excited demonstrations throughout the colonies.

A British newspaper reported that the debate over the Stamp Tax had led some Americans to express a desire for "independence." The editor predicted that eventually the colonies would "shake off all subjection. If we yield to them . . . by repealing the Stamp Act, it is all over."

THE TOWNSHEND ACTS In July 1766, George III replaced Lord Rockingham with William Pitt, the former prime minister who had exercised heroic leadership during the Seven Years' War. For a time, the guiding force in the Pitt ministry was Charles Townshend, the treasury chief whose "abilities were superior to those of all men," said a colleague, "and his judgment [common sense] below that of any man."

In 1767, Townshend pushed through Parliament an ill-fated plan to generate more colonial revenue. A few months later, he died at age forty-two, leaving behind a bitter legacy: the **Townshend Acts**. The Revenue Act of 1767, which

The Repeal, or The Funeral Procession of Miss Americ-Stamp This 1766 cartoon shows Grenville carrying the dead Stamp Act in its coffin. In the background, trade with America starts up again.

taxed colonial imports of glass, lead, paint, paper, and tea, was the most hated. It posed an even more severe threat than Grenville's taxes had, for Townshend planned to use the new tax revenues to pay the salaries of the royal governors in the colonies. Until that point, the colonial assemblies paid the salaries, thus giving them leverage over the governors. John Adams observed that Townshend's plan would make the royal governor "independent of the people" and disrupt "that balance of power which is essential to all free governments." Writing in the *Boston Gazette*, Adams insisted that such "an INDEPENDENT ruler, [is] a MONSTER in a free state."

DISCONTENT ON THE FRONTIER

While the disputes over British regulatory policy raged along the seaboard, parts of the backcountry stirred with quarrels that had nothing to do with the Stamp and Townshend Acts. Rival claims to lands east of Lake Champlain pitted New York against New Hampshire. Eventually, the residents of the disputed area would form their own state of Vermont, which would be recognized as a member of the Union in 1791.

In South Carolina, frontiersmen issued a chorus of complaints about the lack of military protection from horse thieves, cattle rustlers, and Indians. They organized societies, called Regulators, to administer vigilante justice in the region, and refused to pay taxes until they gained effective government. The assembly finally set up six circuit courts in the region but did not respond to demands for representation.

In North Carolina, the protests were less over the lack of government than over abuses and extortion by appointees from the eastern part of the colony. Western farmers felt especially oppressed by the government's refusal to issue paper money or accept produce in payment of taxes, and in 1766 they organized to resist. The efforts of these Regulators to stop seizures of property and other court proceedings led to more disorders and the enactment of a bill that made the rioters guilty of treason. That the Regulators tended to be Baptists, Methodists, and Presbyterians who preached plain living, while the coastal elite tended to be wealthy Anglicans, injected a religious and social element into the squabbles.

In the spring of 1771, William Tryon, the royal governor of North Carolina, led 1,200 militiamen to victory over some 2,000 ill-organized Regulators in the Battle of Alamance. Tryon's men then ranged through the backcountry, forcing some 6,500 Piedmont settlers to sign an oath of allegiance to the king.

These disputes and revolts illustrated the diversity of opinion and outlook among Americans on the eve of the Revolution. Colonists were of many minds about many things, including British rule, but they also differed with one another about how best to protest against their particular grievances.

THE CRISIS GROWS

The Townshend Acts surprised and angered many colonists. As American rage bubbled over, Samuel ("Sam") Adams of Boston, a failed beer brewer who had become one of the most radical rebels, decided that a small group of determined Whigs could generate a mass movement. "It does not take a majority to prevail," Adams insisted, "but rather an irate, tireless minority, keen on setting brushfires of freedom in the minds of men."

Early in 1768, Adams and Boston attorney James Otis Jr. convinced the Massachusetts Assembly to circulate a letter that restated the illegality of taxation without representation and invited the support of the other colonies. British officials ordered the Massachusetts Assembly to withdraw the letter. They refused, and the king ordered the assembly dissolved.

In October 1768, in response to an appeal by the royal governor concerned about keeping order, 4,000 British troops arrived in Boston, the hotbed of colonial resistance. **Loyalists**, as the Americans who supported the king and Parliament were often called, welcomed the soldiers; **Patriots**, those rebelling against British authority, viewed the troops as an occupation force. Meanwhile, in London, the king appointed still another new chief minister, Frederick, Lord North.

THE FIRST BLOODSHED In 1765, Benjamin Franklin had predicted that although British soldiers sent to America would "not find a rebellion; they may indeed make one." The growing tensions triggered several violent incidents. The first, called the Battle at Golden Hill, occurred in New York City, where "Liberty Boys" kept erecting "liberty poles," only to see British soldiers knock them down. The soldiers, cursed as "lobsterbacks" or "redcoats," also began posting signs declaring that the Sons of Liberty were "the real enemies of society."

On January, 18, 1770, a group of Patriots captured two British soldiers. Soon an angry crowd formed around the twenty British soldiers sent to rescue their comrades, and the outnumbered soldiers retreated. When they reached Golden Hill, more soldiers arrived. At that point, the redcoats turned on the crowd. They attacked, and in the confusion, several on both sides were seriously hurt. The first blood had been shed over American liberties, and it was soon followed by more violence.

THE BOSTON MASSACRE (1770) In Boston, the presence of thousands of British soldiers had become a constant source of irritation. Crowds frequently heckled the soldiers, many of whom had earned the abuse by harassing Americans.

On the evening of March 5, 1770, two dozen "saucy" Boston rowdies—teens, Irishmen, blacks, and sailors—began throwing icicles and oyster shells at Hugh White, a British soldier guarding the Customs House. Someone rang the town fire bell, drawing a larger crowd to the scene, as the taunting continued: "Kill him, kill him, knock him down. Fire, damn you, fire, you dare not fire!"

A squad of soldiers arrived to help White, but the surly crowd surrounded them. When someone knocked a soldier down, he arose and fired his musket. Others joined in. After the smoke had cleared, five people lay dead or dying on the cobblestone street, and eight more were wounded. The first one killed, or so the story goes, was Crispus Attucks, a former slave who worked at the docks. The *Boston Gazette* called it a "horrid massacre."

The Bloody Massacre   Paul Revere's engraving of the Boston Massacre (1770).

The next day, nine British soldiers were arrested and jailed. Never before in Massachusetts had a trial generated such passion and excitement. Samuel Adams and other firebrands demanded quick justice. Months passed, however, before the trial convened. Finally, in late October, two of the British soldiers, convicted of manslaughter, were branded on the thumb.

The so-called **Boston Massacre** sent shock waves throughout the colonies and all the way to London. Virtually the entire city of Boston attended the funerals for the deceased. Only the decision to postpone the trial for six months allowed tensions to subside. At the same time, the impact of the colonial boycott of British products persuaded prime minister Lord North to modify the Townshend Acts.

Late in April 1770, Parliament repealed all the Townshend duties except for the tea tax, which the king wanted to keep as a symbol of Parliament's authority. Colonial discontent subsided for two years. The redcoats left Boston but remained in Canada, and the British navy still patrolled the New England coast looking for smugglers.

THE GASPÉE INCIDENT In June 1772, a naval incident further eroded the colonies' fragile relationship with the mother country. Near Warwick, Rhode Island, the HMS *Gaspée*, a British warship, ran aground while chasing smugglers. Its hungry crew seized local sheep, hogs, and chickens. An enraged crowd, some poorly disguised as Mohawk Indians, then boarded the *Gaspée*, shot the captain, removed the crew, and looted and burned the ship.

The *Gaspée* incident symbolized the intensity of growing anti-British feelings among Americans. When the British tried to take the suspects to London for trial, Patriots organized in protest. Thomas Jefferson said it was the threat of transporting Americans for trials in Britain that reignited anti-British activities in Virginia.

In response to the *Gaspée* incident, Samuel Adams organized the **Committee of Correspondence**, which issued a statement of American rights and grievances and invited other towns to do the same. Similar committees sprang up across the colonies, forming a unified network of resistance. "The flame is kindled and like lightning it catches from soul to soul," reported Abigail Adams, the high-spirited wife of future president John Adams. By 1772, Thomas Hutchinson, the royal governor of Massachusetts, could tell the colonial assembly that the choice facing Americans was stark: They must choose between obeying "the supreme authority of Parliament" and "total independence."

THE BOSTON TEA PARTY The British prime minister, Lord North, soon provided the spark to transform resentment into rebellion. In 1773, he tried to bail out the struggling East India Company, which had in its warehouses some 17 million pounds of tea that it desperately needed to sell before it rotted. Parliament passed the Tea Act of 1773 to allow the company to send its tea directly to America without paying any taxes. British tea merchants could thereby undercut the prices charged by their American competitors, most of whom were smugglers who bought tea from the Dutch. At the same time, King George III told Lord North to "compel obedience" in the colonies.

In Massachusetts, the Committees of Correspondence alerted colonists that the British government was trying to purchase colonial submission with cheap tea. ("Tea stands for Tyranny!") The reduction in the price of tea was a clever trick to make colonists accept taxation without consent. In Boston, furious citizens decided that their passion for liberty outweighed their love for tea. On December 16, 1773, scores of Patriots dressed as Indians boarded three

British ships in Boston Harbor and dumped overboard 342 chests filled with forty-six tons of East India Company tea.

The **Boston Tea Party** pushed British officials in London to the breaking point. The destruction of so much valuable tea convinced the king and his advisers that a forceful response was required. "The colonists must either submit or triumph," George III wrote to Lord North, who decided to make Boston an example to the rest of the colonies.

THE COERCIVE ACTS In 1774, Lord North convinced Parliament to punish Boston and the province of Massachusetts by passing a cluster of harsh laws, called the **Coercive Acts**. (Americans renamed them the "Intolerable" Acts.) The Port Act closed Boston harbor until the city paid for the lost tea. (It never did.) Many people lost their jobs, and the cost of consumer goods skyrocketed as trade ceased. A new Quartering Act ordered colonists to provide lodging for British soldiers. The Impartial Administration of Justice Act said that any royal official accused of a major crime would be tried in London rather than in the colony.

Finally, the Massachusetts Government Act stripped Americans of their representative governments, effectively disenfranchising them. It gave the royal governor the authority to appoint the colony's legislative council, which until then had been elected by the people, as well as local judges and sheriffs. It also banned town meetings. In May, Lieutenant General Thomas Gage, commander in chief of British forces in North America, became governor of Massachusetts and assumed command of the British soldiers who had returned to Boston.

The Intolerable Acts shocked colonists. No one had expected such a severe reaction to the Boston Tea Party. Many towns held meetings in violation of the new laws, and voters elected their own unauthorized provincial legislative assemblies—which ordered town governments to quit paying taxes to the royal governor. By August 1774, Patriots across Massachusetts had essentially taken control of local governments. They also began stockpiling weapons and gunpowder in anticipation of an eventual clash with British troops.

Elsewhere, colonists across America rallied to help Boston by raising money, sending supplies, and boycotting, burning, or dumping British tea. In Virginia, George Washington found himself in a debate with Bryan Fairfax, an old friend and self-described Royalist. Fairfax blamed the Boston rebels for the tensions with London. Washington disagreed, defending the "quiet and steady conduct of the people of the Massachusetts Bay." It was time, he added, for Americans to stand up for their rights or "submit" to being treated like "abject slaves."

In Williamsburg, when the Virginia assembly (House of Burgesses) met in May, a member of the Committee of Correspondence, Thomas Jefferson, suggested that June 1, the effective date of the Boston Port Act, become an official day of fasting and prayer.

The royal governor responded by dissolving the assembly, whose members then retired to the Raleigh Tavern and decided to form a Continental Congress to represent all the colonies. As Samuel Savage, a Connecticut colonist, wrote in May 1774, the conflict had come down to a single question: "Whether we shall or shall not be governed by a British Parliament." Each step the colonists might take next was fraught with risk, but the opposition to "tyranny" was growing.

THE FIRST CONTINENTAL CONGRESS On September 5, 1774, the fifty-five delegates from twelve colonies (Georgia was absent) making up the First Continental Congress assembled in Philadelphia, the largest American city. Never before had representatives from all the colonies met to coordinate resistance to British policies. Now the Continental Congress was serving as a provisional national government. Over seven weeks, the Congress endorsed the Suffolk Resolves, which urged Massachusetts to resist British tyranny with force. The Congress then adopted a Declaration of American Rights, which proclaimed once again the rights of Americans as British citizens and denied Parliament's authority to regulate internal colonial affairs. "We demand no new rights," said the Congress. "We ask only for peace, liberty, and security."

Finally, the Congress adopted the Continental Association of 1774, which recommended that every colony organize committees to enforce a complete boycott of all imported British goods, a dramatic step that would be followed by a refusal to export American goods to Britain. The Association was designed to show that Americans could deny themselves the "baubles of Britain" and demonstrate their commitment to colonial liberties and constitutional rights.

The county and city committees forming the Continental Association became the organizational network for the resistance movement. Seven thousand men across the colonies served on the local committees, and many more women helped put the boycotts into practice. The committees required colonists to sign an oath refusing to purchase British goods. In East Haddam, Connecticut, Patriots tarred, feathered, and rubbed pig dung on a Loyalist, who refused to join the boycott. Such violent incidents led Loyalists to claim that it was better to be a slave to the king than to be enslaved by a Patriot mob.

Thousands of men and women participated in the boycott of British goods, and their sacrifices provided the momentum leading to revolution. It was common people who enforced the boycott, volunteered in Patriot militia units, attended town meetings, and ousted royal officials. As Pittsfield, Massachusetts, affirmed in a petition, "We have always believed that the people are the fountain of power."

Royal officials marveled at the colonists' ability to thwart British authority. "The ingenuity of these people," declared an army officer, "is singular in their modes of mischief." Loyalist Thomas Hutchinson, however, assured the king that the Americans could not remain united. "A union of the Colonies was utterly impracticable," he wrote, because "the people were greatly divided among themselves in every colony." Hutchinson had no doubt "that all America would *submit*, and that they *must*, and moreover would, *soon*."

Hutchinson could not have been more wrong. The rebellion now extended well beyond simple grievances over taxation. Patriots decided that there was a *conspiracy* against their liberties among Parliament, the king, and his ministers. By the end of 1774, more and more colonists came to reject the authority of Parliament. Across the colonies, Patriots ousted royal governors, forcing them to take refuge on British ships, and replaced them with provisional "committees of safety" committed to independence. Many committees began secretly purchasing weapons and gunpowder from European nations.

The colonies were mobilizing, and growing numbers of people came to expect an explosion. "Government has now devolved upon the people," wrote an irritated Tory in 1774, "and they seem to be for using it." In Boston, an increasingly nervous General Thomas Gage requested more British troops to suppress the growing "flames of sedition." He reported that "civil government is near its end, the Courts of Justice expiring one after another."

LAST-MINUTE COMPROMISE In London, King George fumed. He wrote Lord North that "blows must decide" whether the Americans "are to be subject to this country or independent." In early 1775, Parliament declared that Massachusetts was officially "in rebellion" and prohibited the New England colonies from trading with any nation outside the British Empire. A few Whigs stood in Parliament to defend the Americans. Edmund Burke, a prominent Irish statesman, stressed that the "fierce spirit of liberty is stronger in the English Colonies probably than in any other people on earth."

London officials hired Samuel Johnson, a distinguished poet, essayist, and ardent Tory, to write a pamphlet called *Taxation No Tyranny* (1775), expressing the government's perspective on the colonists and their slogan, "No taxation without representation." The people who settled America, Johnson wrote, had left Britain, where they had the vote but little property, for a colonial life where they had no vote but lots of property. However much Americans might complain about taxes, they remained British subjects who should obey government actions. If the Americans wanted to participate in Parliament, Johnson suggested, they could move to England and purchase an estate. Whatever the case, Johnson expressed confidence that the dispute between England and America would be resolved through "English superiority and American obedience."

BOLD TALK OF WAR   While most Patriots believed that Britain would back down, Patrick Henry of Virginia dramatically declared that war was unavoidable. The twenty-nine-year-old Henry, a full-throated farmer and storekeeper turned lawyer, claimed that the colonies had "done everything that could be done to avert the storm which is now coming on," but had been met only by "violence and insult." Freedom, Henry shouted, could be bought only with blood: "We must fight!" If forced to choose, he supposedly shouted, "Give me liberty"—he then paused dramatically, clenched his fist as if it held a dagger, and plunged it into his chest—"Or give me death."

As Henry predicted, events quickly moved toward armed conflict. By mid-1775, the king and Parliament had effectively lost control; they could neither persuade nor force the Patriots to accept new regulations and revenue measures. In Boston, General Gage warned that armed conflict would unleash the "horrors of civil war." But Lord Sandwich, head of the British navy, dismissed the rebels as "raw, undisciplined, cowardly men" without an army or navy. Major John Pitcairn, a British army officer, agreed, writing from Boston that "one active campaign, a smart action, and burning two or three of their towns, will set everything to rights."

LEXINGTON AND CONCORD   Major Pitcairn soon had his chance to quash the resistance. On April 14, 1775, the British army received secret orders to stop the "open rebellion" in Massachusetts. General Gage had decided to arrest rebel leaders such as Samuel Adams and seize the militia's gunpowder stored at Concord, sixteen miles northwest of Boston.

After dark on April 18, some 800 British soldiers secretly boarded boats and crossed the Charles River to Cambridge, then set out on foot to Lexington, about eleven miles away. When Patriots got wind of the plan, Paul Revere and William Dawes mounted their horses for their famous "midnight ride" to warn rebel leaders that the British were coming.

In the gray dawn of April 19, an advance unit of 238 redcoats found American Captain John Parker and about 70 "Minutemen" (Patriot militia who could

The Battle of Lexington Amos Doolittle's impression of the Battle of Lexington as shooting begins between the Royal Marines and the Minutemen.

assemble at a "minute's" notice) lined up on the Lexington town square, while dozens of villagers watched. "Stand your ground," shouted Parker. "Don't fire unless fired upon; but if they mean to have a war, let it begin here!"

Parker and his men intended only a silent protest, but Major Pitcairn rode onto the Lexington Green, swinging his sword and yelling, "Disperse, you damned rebels! You dogs, run!" The outnumbered militiamen were backing away when someone fired. (Both sides blamed the other for shooting first.) The British then shot at the Minutemen and charged them with bayonets amid a "continual roar of musketry," leaving eight dead and ten wounded.

The British officers brought their men under control and led them west to Concord, where they destroyed hidden military supplies. While marching out of the town, they encountered American riflemen. Shots were fired, and a dozen or so British soldiers were killed or wounded. More important, the short skirmish and ringing church bells alerted nearby rebel farmers, ministers, craftsmen, and merchants to grab their muskets. They were, as one of them said, determined to "be free or die."

By noon, the exhausted redcoats began a ragged retreat back to Lexington. It soon turned into a disaster. Less than a mile out of Concord, they suffered the first of many ambushes. The narrow road turned into a gauntlet of death as rebel marksmen fired from behind stone walls, trees, barns, and houses. "It was a day full of horror," one of the soldiers recalled.

By nightfall, the redcoat survivors were safely back in Boston, having marched some forty miles and suffered three times as many dead and wounded as the Americans. A British general reported that the colonists had earned his respect: "Whoever looks upon them as an irregular mob will find himself much mistaken." The Salem newspaper reported that now "we are involved in the horrors of a civil war." Others found the news exhilarating. When Samuel Adams heard the firing at Lexington, he shouted: "O what a glorious morning is this!"

Warfare may be glorious when heard from long distance, but its deadly results bring home its tragic reality. Hannah Davis, a mother of four living in Acton, was awakened on April 19 by the alarm bells calling the militiamen to assemble. She dutifully helped her thirty-year-old husband Isaac get his musket and powder horn. "He said but little that morning. He seemed serious and thoughtful; but never seemed to hesitate." His only words were: "Take care of the children." That afternoon, she recalled, "he was brought home a corpse."

Until the Battles of Lexington and Concord, both sides had mistakenly assumed that the other would back down. Instead, the clash turned a resistance movement into a war of rebellion. Masses of ordinary people were determined to fight for their freedoms against a British Parliament and king bent on denying them their civil and legal rights. In Virginia, Thomas Jefferson reported that the news from Concord and Lexington had unleashed "a frenzy of revenge" among "all ranks of people." In Georgia, the royal governor noted that "a general rebellion throughout America is coming on suddenly and swiftly."

Joseph Warren, a Bostonian, warned: "Our all is at stake. Death and devastation are the instant consequences of delay. Every moment is infinitely precious. An hour lost may deluge our country in blood, and entail perpetual slavery."

THE SPREADING CONFLICT

On June 15, 1775, the Second Continental Congress unanimously selected forty-three-year-old George Washington to lead the new Continental Army. His service in the French and Indian War had made him one of the few experienced American officers. He was also admired for his success as a planter, surveyor, and land speculator, as well as for his service in the Virginia legislature and the Continental Congress. Perhaps more important, he *looked* like a leader. Standing more than six feet tall and weighing 200 pounds, Washington was a fearless fighter accustomed to command. His courage in battle, perseverance after defeat, and integrity in judgment would earn him the respect of his troops and the nation.

Attack on Bunker Hill The Battle of Bunker Hill and the burning of Charlestown Peninsula.

Washington humbly accepted the responsibility of leading the American war effort and refused to be paid. Poet Mercy Otis Warren wrote a friend in London that Washington was "a man whose military abilities & public & private virtue place him in the first class of the Good & the Brave." Washington's first act was to draft a will and write his wife, Martha, explaining that he had done his best to avoid being considered for the position, but that in the end it seemed his "destiny" to lead the revolution.

THE BATTLE OF BUNKER HILL On Saturday, June 17, the day that George Washington was named commander in chief, Patriot militiamen engaged British forces in their first major clash, the Battle of Bunker Hill (Breed's Hill was the battle's actual location).

In an effort to strengthen their control over the area around Boston, some 2,400 British troops based in the city boarded boats and crossed over the Charles River to the Charlestown Peninsula, where they formed lines and advanced up Breed's Hill in tight formation through waist-high grass and across pasture fences, as the American defenders watched from behind their earthworks.

"Don't fire until you see the whites of their eyes," yelled Israel Putnam as he rode along the American lines. "Fire low because you are shooting downhill—and focus your fire on the officers." The militiamen, mostly farmers, waited until the redcoats had come within thirty paces, then loosed a volley that sent the attackers retreating in disarray. An American said the British fell like "grass when mowed."

The British re-formed their lines and attacked again, but the Patriot riflemen forced them back a second time. General William Howe could not believe his eyes. All his aides had been killed or wounded, and his professional soldiers were being stymied by a "rabble" of untrained farmers. It was, he said, "a moment that I never felt before."

During the third British assault, the colonists ran out of gunpowder and retreated in panic and confusion, but the British were too tired to follow. They had suffered 1,054 casualties, more than twice the American losses. "A dearly bought victory," said British general Henry Clinton. A British officer reported to London that "we have lost a thousand of our best men and officers" because of "an absurd and destructive confidence, carelessness, or ignorance."

There followed a nine-month stalemate around Boston, with each side hoping for a negotiated settlement of the dispute. Abigail Adams wrote that the Patriots still living in Boston, where the British army governed by martial law, were being treated "like abject slaves under the most cruel and despotic of tyrants."

Thirty-eight days later, word of the Battle of Bunker Hill reached London. The king and Lord North agreed that this meant all-out war. George III issued a Proclamation of Rebellion that said all his subjects ("unhappy people") were "bound by law . . . to disclose all traitorous conspiracies . . . against us, our Crown and Dignity." If the American colonies were lost, the king believed, Britain's other colonies in the West Indies and around the world would fall like dominoes.

"OPEN AND AVOWED ENEMIES" Three weeks after the Battle of Bunker Hill, in July 1775, the Continental Congress sent King George the Olive Branch Petition, urging him to negotiate. When the petition reached London, however, he arrogantly dismissed it and denounced the Americans as "open and avowed enemies."

OUTRIGHT REBELLION Resistance had grown into outright rebellion, but few Patriots were ready to call for independence. They still considered themselves British subjects. When the Second Continental Congress convened at Philadelphia on May 10, 1775, most delegates still wanted Parliament to restore their rights so that they could resume being loyal British colonists.

Meanwhile, the British army in Boston was under siege by American militia units and small groups of musket-toting men who had arrived from across

New England to surround the city. They were still farmers and shopkeepers, not trained soldiers, and the uprising still had no organized command structure or effective support system. The Patriots also lacked training, discipline, ammunition, and blankets. What they did have was a growing sense of confidence and resolve. As a Massachusetts Patriot said, "Our all is at stake. Death and devastation are the instant consequences of delay. Every moment is infinitely precious."

With each passing day, war fever infected more and more colonists. "Oh that I were a soldier!" John Adams wrote home to his wife, Abigail, from Philadelphia. "I will be. I am reading military books. Everybody must, and will, and shall be a soldier."

The fever of war excited men of faith as well as militiamen. In early 1776, the Reverend Peter Muhlenberg told his congregation in Woodstock, Virginia: "The Bible tells us 'there is a time for all things.' And there is a time to preach and a time to pray. But the time for me to preach has passed away; and there is a time to fight, and that time has now come." He then stepped down from the pulpit and took off his robe to reveal a Continental army uniform. Drums then sounded outside the church as husbands kissed their wives goodbye and walked down the aisle to enlist. Within an hour, 162 men had followed their minister's call to arms.

Independence

The Revolutionary War was well under way in January 1776 when Thomas Paine, a thirty-nine-year-old English immigrant who had found work as a radical journalist in Philadelphia, published a stirring pamphlet titled **Common Sense**. Until it appeared, most Patriots had directed their grievances at Parliament. Paine, however, directly attacked the king.

The "common sense" of the matter, Paine stressed, was that King George III, "the royal brute unfit to be the ruler of a free people," had caused the rebellion and had ordered the denial of American rights. "Even brutes do not devour their young," he wrote, "nor savages make war upon their families." Paine urged Americans to abandon the monarchy: "The blood of the slain, the weeping voice of nature cries, 'TIS TIME TO PART.'" It was time for those who "oppose not only the tyranny but the tyrant [King George] to stand forth! . . . Time hath found us!" The "cause of America," he proclaimed, "is the cause of all mankind." It was America that had long "been the asylum for the persecuted lovers of civil and religious liberty from every part of Europe," and

The coming revolution The Continental Congress votes for independence, July 2, 1776.

Paine urged Revolutionaries to ensure that America would always be a haven for the oppressed peoples of the world.

Paine's fiery pamphlet changed the course of history by convincing American rebels that independence was inevitable. Only by declaring independence, he predicted, could the colonists gain the crucial support of France and Spain: "The cause of America is in great measure the cause of all mankind." The rest of the world, he said, would welcome and embrace an independent America; it would be the "glory of the earth." Paine concluded that the "sun had never shined on a cause of greater worth."

Within three months, more than 150,000 copies of *Common Sense* were circulating throughout the colonies and around the world, an enormous number for the time. "*Common Sense* is working a powerful change in the minds of men," George Washington reported.

BREAKING THE BONDS OF EMPIRE *Common Sense* inspired the colonial population from Massachusetts to Georgia and helped convince British subjects still loyal to the king to embrace the radical notion of independence. "Without the pen of Paine," remembered John Adams, "the sword of Washington would have been wielded in vain." During the spring and summer of 1776, some ninety local governments, towns, and colonial legislatures issued declarations of independence.

Momentum for independence was building in the Continental Congress, too, but John Dickinson of Pennsylvania urged delay. On June 1, he warned that independence was a dangerous step since America had no national government or European allies. But his was a lone voice of caution.

The Declaration of Independence The Declaration in its most frequently reproduced form, an 1823 engraving by William J. Stone.

In June 1776, one by one, the colonies authorized their delegates in the Continental Congress to take the final step. On June 7, Richard Henry Lee of Virginia moved "that these United Colonies are, and of right ought to be, free and independent states." At first, six colonies were not ready, but Lee's resolution finally passed on July 2, a date that John Adams predicted would "be the most memorable" in the history of America.

The more memorable date, however, became July 4, 1776, when the Congress formally adopted the **Declaration of Independence** creating the "United States of America." A few delegates refused to sign the document; others, said Adams, "signed with regret . . . and with many doubts." Most, however, signed wholeheartedly, knowing full well that by doing so they were likely to be hanged if captured by British troops. Benjamin Franklin acknowledged how high the stakes were: "Well, Gentlemen," he told the Congress, "we must now hang together, or we shall most assuredly hang separately." Portly Benjamin Harrison injected needed wit at that point, noting that when it was his turn to try on a British noose, his plentiful weight would bring him a mercifully swift death.

JEFFERSON'S DECLARATION In Philadelphia, thirty-three-year-old Thomas Jefferson, a brilliant Virginia planter and attorney serving in the Continental Congress, had drafted a statement of independence that John Adams and Benjamin Franklin then edited.

The Declaration of Independence was crucially important not simply because it marked the creation of a new nation but because of the ideals it expressed and the grievances it listed. Over the previous ten years, colonists had deplored acts of Parliament that impinged on their freedoms. Now, Jefferson directed colonial resentment at King George III himself, arguing that the monarch should have reined in Parliament's efforts to "tyrannize" the colonies.

In addition to highlighting the efforts to tax the colonists and restrict their liberties, Jefferson also noted the king's 1773 decree that sought to restrict population growth in the colonies by "obstructing the laws for the naturalization of foreigners." British authorities had grown worried that the mass migration to America threatened to "de-populate" the home country. So, beginning in 1767, the government began banning "bounties" offered to immigrants by many colonies and ended the practice of providing large land grants in America to encourage settlement.

After listing the objections to British actions, Jefferson asserted that certain truths were self-evident: that "all men are created equal and independent" and have the right to create governments of their own choosing. Governments, he explained, derive "their just powers from the consent of the people," who are entitled to "alter or abolish" those governments when denied their "unalienable rights" to "life, liberty, and the pursuit of happiness." Because King George III was trying to impose "an absolute tyranny over these states," the "Representatives of the United States of America" declared the thirteen "United Colonies" of British America to be "Free and Independent States."

THE CONTRADICTIONS OF FREEDOM Once the Continental Congress chose independence, its members revised Jefferson's draft declaration before sending it to London. Southern representatives insisted on deleting Jefferson's section criticizing George III for perpetuating the African slave trade. In doing so, they revealed the major contradiction at work in the movement for independence. The rhetoric of freedom that animated the Revolution did not apply to the widespread system of slavery that fueled the southern economy. Slavery was the absence of liberty, yet few Americans confronted the inconsistency of their protests in defense of freedom—for whites.

In 1764, a group of slaves in Charleston watching a demonstration against British tyranny by white Sons of Liberty got caught up in the moment and began chanting, "Freedom, freedom, freedom." But that was not what southern planters wanted for African Americans. In 1774, when a group of slaves killed four whites in a desperate attempt to gain their freedom, Georgia planters captured the rebels and burned them alive.

James Otis, a Harvard-educated lawyer, was one of the few Whigs who demanded freedom for blacks and women. In 1764, he had argued that "the colonists, black and white, born here, are free British subjects, and entitled to all the essential civil rights of such." He went so far as to suggest that slavery itself should be ended, since "all men . . . white or black" were "by the law of nature freeborn."

Otis also asked, "Are not women born as free as men? Would it not be infamous to assert that the ladies are all slaves by nature?" His sister, Mercy Otis Warren, became a tireless advocate of

Phillis Wheatley An autographed portrait of America's first African American poet.

American resistance to British "tyranny" through her poems, pamphlets, and plays. In a letter to a friend, she noted that British officials needed to realize that America's "daughters are politicians and patriots and will aid the good work [of resistance] with their female efforts."

Slaves insisted on independence too. In 1773, a group of enslaved African Americans in Boston appealed to the royal governor of Massachusetts to free them just as white Americans were defending their freedoms against British tyranny. In many respects, the slaves argued, they had a more compelling case for liberty: "We have no property, We have no wives! No children! No city! No country!"

A few months later, a group of four Boston slaves addressed a public letter to the town government in which they referred to the hypocrisy of slave-holders who protested against British regulations and taxes. "We expect great things from men who have made such a noble stand against the designs of their fellow-men to enslave them," they noted. But freedom in 1776 was a celebration to which slaves were not invited.

George Washington himself acknowledged the contradictory aspects of the Revolutionary movement when he warned that the alternative to declaring independence was to become "tame and abject slaves, as the blacks we rule over with such arbitrary sway [absolute power]." Washington and other slaveholders at the head of the Revolutionary movement, such as Thomas Jefferson, were in part so resistant to "British tyranny" because they witnessed every day what actual slavery was like—for the blacks under their control.

Jefferson admitted the hypocrisy of slave-owning Revolutionaries. "Southerners," he wrote to a French friend, are "jealous of their own liberties but trampling on those of others." Phillis Wheatley, the first African American writer to publish her poetry in America, highlighted the "absurdity" of white colonists claiming their freedom while continuing to exercise "oppressive power" over enslaved Africans.

"WE ALWAYS HAD GOVERNED OURSELVES" Historians still debate the causes of the American Revolution. Americans in 1775–1776 were not desperately poor; overall, they probably enjoyed a higher standard of living than most other societies and lived under the freest institutions in the world. Their diet was better than that of Europeans, as was their average life span. In addition, the percentage of free property owners in the thirteen colonies was higher than in Britain or Europe. At the same time, the new taxes forced on Americans after 1763 were not as great as those imposed on the British people. And many American colonists, perhaps as many as half, were indifferent, hesitant, or actively opposed to rebellion.

So why did the Americans revolt? Historians have highlighted many factors: the clumsy British efforts to tighten their regulation of colonial trade, the restrictions on colonists eager to acquire western lands, the growing tax burden, the mounting debts to British merchants, the lack of American representation in Parliament, and the role of radicals such as Samuel Adams and Patrick Henry in stirring up anti-British feelings.

Yet other reasons were not so selfless or noble. Many wealthy New Englanders and New Yorkers most critical of tighter British regulations, such as Boston merchant John Hancock, were smugglers; paying more British taxes would have cost them a fortune. Likewise, South Carolina's Henry Laurens and Virginia's Landon Carter, both prosperous planters, worried that the British might abolish slavery.

Overall, however, what Americans most resented were the British efforts to constrict colonists' civil liberties, thereby denying their rights as British citizens. As Hugh Williamson, a Pennsylvania physician, explained, the Revolution resulted not from "trifling or imaginary" injustices but from "gross and palpable" violations of American rights that had thrown "the miserable colonists" into the "pit of despotism."

Yet how did the diverse colonies develop such a unified resistance? Although most Patriots were of English heritage, many other peoples were represented: Scots, Irish, Scots-Irish, Welsh, Germans, Dutch, Swedes, Finns, Swiss, French, and Jews, as well as growing numbers of Africans and diminishing numbers of Native Americans.

What most Americans—regardless of their backgrounds—had come to share by 1775 was a defiant attachment to the civil rights and legal processes guaranteed by the English constitutional tradition. This outlook, rooted in the defense of sacred constitutional principles, made the Revolution conceivable. Armed resistance made it possible, and independence, ultimately, made it achievable.

The Revolution reflected the shared political notion that all citizens were equal and independent, and that all governmental authority had to be based on longstanding constitutional principles and the consent of the governed. This "republican ideal" was the crucial force that transformed a prolonged effort to preserve rights and liberties enjoyed by British citizens into a movement to create an independent nation. With their declaration of independence, the Revolutionaries—men and women, farmers, artisans, mechanics, sailors, merchants, tavern owners, and shopkeepers—had become determined to develop their own society. Americans wanted to trade freely with the world and to expand what Jefferson called their "empire of liberty" westward, across the Appalachian Mountains.

The Revolutionaries knew the significance of what they were attempting. They were committing themselves, stressed John Adams, to "a Revolution, the most complete, unexpected, and remarkable of any in the history of nations."

Perhaps the last word should belong to Levi Preston, a Minuteman from Danvers, Massachusetts. Asked late in life about the British efforts to impose new taxes and regulations on the colonists, Preston responded, "What were they? Oppressions? I didn't feel them." He was then asked, "What, were you not oppressed by the Stamp Act?" Preston replied that he "never saw one of those stamps . . . I am certain I never paid a penny for one of them." What about the tax on tea? "Tea-tax! I never drank a drop of the stuff; the boys threw it all overboard." His interviewer finally asked why he decided to fight for independence. "Young man," Preston explained, "what we meant in going for those redcoats was this: we always had governed ourselves, and we always meant to. They didn't mean we should."

CHAPTER REVIEW

SUMMARY

- **British and French Colonies** New France followed the Spanish model of absolute power in governing its far-flung trading outposts. On the other hand, Great Britain's policy of *salutary neglect* allowed the colonies a large degree of self-government, until its decision to enforce more rigidly its policy of *mercantilism*, as seen in such measures as the *Navigation Acts*, became a means to enrich its global empire. The *Glorious Revolution* in Great Britain inspired new political philosophies that challenged the divine right of kings with the *natural rights* of free men.

- **The French and Indian War** Four European wars between the British and French and their allies affected America between 1689 and 1763. The *Seven Years' War*, known as the *French and Indian War* (1756–1763) in the colonies, eventually was won by the British. Early in the war, the colonies created the *Albany Plan of Union*, which formed an early blueprint for an independent American government. In the *Treaty of Paris* (1763), France lost all its North American possessions, Britain gained Canada and Florida, and Spain acquired the vast Louisiana Territory. The Indians fought to regain control of their ancestral lands in *Pontiac's Rebellion*, and Great Britain, weary of war, negotiated the *Royal Proclamation of 1763* to keep colonists out of Indian lands.

- **British Colonial Policy** After the French and Indian War, the British government was saddled with enormous debt. To reduce that burden, prime minister George Grenville implemented various taxes to compel colonists to pay for their own defense. The colonists resisted, claiming that they could not be taxed because they were not represented in Parliament. British officials countered that the colonists had *virtual representation* in Parliament, since each member was supposed to represent his district as well as the empire as a whole. Colonial reaction to the *Stamp Act* of 1765 was the first intimation of real trouble for British authorities. Conflicts between Whigs and Tories intensified when the *Townshend Acts* imposed additional taxes. The *Sons of Liberty* and the *Daughters of Liberty* mobilized resistance, particularly through boycotts of British goods.

- **Road to the American Revolution** But the crisis worsened. Spontaneous resistance led to the *Boston Massacre*; organized protesters later staged the *Boston Tea Party*. The British response, called the *Coercive Acts*, sparked further violence between *Patriots* and *Loyalists*. The First Continental Congress formed *Committees of Correspondence* to organize and spread resistance. Thomas Paine's pamphlet *Common Sense* helped kindle revolutionary fervor and plant the seed of independence, and the Continental Congress delivered its *Declaration of Independence*.

Chronology

Key Terms

 INQUIZITIVE

Go to InQuizitive to see what you've learned—and learn what you've missed—with personalized feedback along the way.

part two

BUILDING A NATION

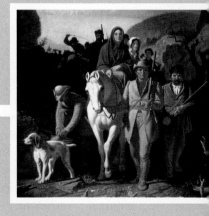

In August 1776, Benjamin Rush, a Philadelphia physician and dedicated Revolutionary,
recognized that the thirteen diverse colonies
somehow had to behave like a united nation.
"We are now a new Nation . . . dependent on each other—not totally
independent states."

Yet it was one thing for Patriot leaders to declare independence
and quite another to win it on the battlefield. The odds greatly favored
the British; fewer than half of the 2.5 million colonists were Patriots who *actively* supported the Revolution, and many others—the

Loyalists—fought against it. Still others sought just to stay alive, often by changing sides "with the circumstances of every day," as Thomas Paine groaned. Many Americans were initially worried and confused by the course of events, suspicious of both sides, and hesitant to embrace an uncertain cause.

The thirteen independent states had new, untested governments; the Continental Congress struggled to serve as a national government with few powers; and General George Washington found himself in charge of an inexperienced and poorly equipped army of amateurs facing the world's greatest military power.

Yet the Revolutionaries would persevere and prevail. As a military leader, Washington proved to be more dogged than brilliant. He did have extensive knowledge of the nation's geography and used it to his advantage. He chose excellent advisers and generals, inspired loyalty among his troops, and quickly perceived that politics was as crucial to victory as gunpowder.

Equally important to the Revolutionary cause was the decision by the French (and later the Spanish and Dutch) to join the fight against Britain. The Franco-American alliance, negotiated in 1778, was the turning point in the war. In 1783, after eight years of sporadic fighting and heavy human and financial losses, the British gave up their American colonies.

While fighting the British, the Patriots also had to create new governments for themselves. The deeply ingrained resentment of British imperial rule led Americans to give more power to the individual states than to the weak new national government, called the Confederation. As Thomas Jefferson declared, "Virginia is my country."

Such powerful local ties help explain why the Articles of Confederation, the original constitution organizing the thirteen states, provided only minimal national authority when it was finally ratified in 1781. After the Revolutionary War, the flimsy political bonds authorized by the Articles of Confederation could not meet the needs of the new nation. This realization led to the calling of the Constitutional Convention in 1787. The process of drafting and approving the new constitution generated heated debate about the respective powers granted to the states and the national government, a debate that became the central theme of American political thought.

The Revolution also helped reshape American society. What would be the role of women, African Americans, and Native Americans? How would the diverse regions of the new United States develop different economies? Who would control access to the vast Native American ancestral lands to the west? How would the United States relate to the world?

These questions gave birth to the first national political parties. During the 1790s, the Federalist party, led by George Washington, John Adams, and Alexander Hamilton, and the Democratic-Republican party, led by Thomas Jefferson and James Madison, furiously debated the political and economic future of the new nation.

With Jefferson's election as president in 1800, the Democratic-Republicans gained the upper hand in national politics and would remain dominant for the next quarter century. In the process, they presided over a maturing republic that expanded westward at the expense of Native Americans, embraced industrial development, engaged in a second war with Great Britain, and witnessed growing tensions between North and South over slavery.

5 The American Revolution
1776–1783

The Death of General Mercer at the Battle of Princeton (ca. 1789–1831) After the
American victory at Trenton, New Jersey, George Washington (center, on horseback)
launched a surprise attack on the British at the Battle of Princeton. The Americans
won the battle, but one of the casualties was Washington's close friend, General Hugh
Mercer (bottom), whose death created a rallying symbol for the Revolution.

Few Europeans thought the untested Americans could win a war against the world's most powerful empire. Although the British did win most of the major battles in the Revolutionary War, the Patriots outlasted them and eventually forced them to grant independence to the upstart United States of America.

This stunning result reflected the tenacity of the Patriots as well as the difficulties the British faced in fighting a prolonged war 3,000 miles from home and in adjusting to the often unorthodox American ways of warfare.

What began as a war for independence became both a *civil war* between Americans (Patriots/Whigs versus Loyalists/Tories), joined by their Indian allies, and a *world war* involving numerous "allied" European nations. The crucial development in the war was the ability of the United States to forge military alliances with France, Spain, and the Netherlands, all of which were eager to humble Great Britain. As Britain's adversaries, they provided the Revolutionaries with money, supplies, weapons, soldiers, and warships. The French and Spanish also sent warships to the English Channel, which forced much of the Royal Navy to remain at home and thus weakened the British effort to blockade American ports.

The war for independence unleashed unexpected social and political changes, as it required "common people" to take a more active role in governments at all levels—local, state, and national. Ordinary folk readily took advantage of their new opportunities. In Virginia, voters in 1776 elected a new state legislature that, an observer noted, "was composed of men not quite so well dressed, nor so politely educated, nor so highly born" as had been the case in the past.

focus questions

1. What challenges did the British and American military leaders face in the Revolutionary War?

2. What were some of the key turning points in the Revolutionary War? How did they change its direction?

3. In what ways did the American Revolution function as a civil war?

4. How was the Revolutionary War an "engine" for political and social change?

5. How did the Revolutionary War impact African Americans, women, and Native Americans?

MOBILIZING FOR WAR

The British Empire sent some 35,000 soldiers and half its huge navy across the Atlantic to put down the American rebellion. The British also hired foreign soldiers (mercenaries), as some 30,000 professional German soldiers served in the British armies. Most were from the German state of Hesse-Cassel. Americans called them **Hessians**.

The British also recruited Loyalists, Native Americans, and African Americans to fight on their behalf, but there were never as many enlisting as they had hoped. Further, the British initially assumed that there would be enough food for their troops and forage for their horses in America. As the war ground on, however, most of their supplies had to come from Britain. The war's increasing costs—in human lives and war debt—demoralized the British.

The British government under Lord North also never had a consistent war strategy. At first, the British tried to use their naval superiority to blockade New England's seaports and strangle American commerce. When that failed, they sought to destroy George Washington's troops in New York. Despite early success, the British commanders failed to pursue and eliminate the retreating Continental army. They next tried to drive a wedge between New England and New York, splitting the colonies in two. That too would fail, leading to the final British strategy: moving the main army into the southern colonies in hopes of rallying Loyalists in the region.

THE CONTINENTAL ARMY   While the Patriots had the advantage of fighting on their home ground, they also had to create an army and navy from scratch, and with little money. Before the war, **citizen-soldiers** (militiamen) were primarily civilians summoned from their farms and shops. Once the immediate danger passed, they quickly dispersed and returned to their homes. Many militiamen were unreliable and ungovernable. They were, reported General Washington, "nasty, dirty, and disobedient." They "come in, you cannot tell how, go, you cannot tell when, and act, you cannot tell where, consume your provisions, exhaust your stores [supplies], and leave you at last at a critical moment."

Washington knew that militiamen alone could not win against the veteran British and German soldiers. He therefore convinced the Continental Congress to create a professional *Continental army* with full-time, well-trained soldiers. About half of the 200,000 Americans who served in the war were militiamen ("Minutemen") and half were in the Continental army. They were relatively poor farmers, laborers, indentured servants, or recently arrived immigrants, and most were young and single. Some 5,000 African Americans also served.

What the Continental army needed most at the start of the war were capable officers, intensive training, modern weapons, reliable supplies, and multiyear enlistment contracts. Its soldiers also needed strict discipline, for they had no room for error against the British. As Washington and his officers began whipping the army into shape, those who violated the rules were jailed, flogged, sent packing, or even hanged as an example to others.

Many Patriots found army life unbearable and combat horrifying. As General Nathanael Greene, a Rhode Island Quaker who abandoned pacifism for the war effort and became Washington's ablest commander, pointed out, few Patriots had engaged in mortal combat, and they were hard-pressed to "stand the shocking scenes of war, to march over dead men, to hear without concern the groans of the wounded."

Desertions grew as the war dragged on. The Continental army became an ever-shifting group, "part turnstile and part accordion." At times, Washington could put only a few thousand men in the field. Eventually, Congress provided more generous enticements, such as land grants and cash bonuses, to encourage recruits to serve in the army for the duration of the war.

PROBLEMS OF FINANCE AND SUPPLY Financing the Revolution was much harder for the Americans than it was for Great Britain. Lacking the power to impose taxes, the Confederation Congress could only *ask* the states to provide funds for the national government. Yet the states rarely provided their expected share of the war's expenses, and the Congress reluctantly had to allow Patriot armies to take supplies directly from farmers in return for written promises of future payment.

In a predominantly agricultural society like America, turning farmers into soldiers hurt the national economy. William Hooper, a North Carolinian who signed the Declaration of Independence, grumbled that "a soldier made is a farmer lost." Many states found a ready source of revenue in the sale of abandoned Loyalist homes, farms, and plantations. Nevertheless, Congress and the states still fell short of funding the war's cost and were forced to print more and more paper money, which eroded its value.

NATIVE AMERICANS AND THE REVOLUTION Both the British and Americans recruited Indians to fight with them, but the British were far more successful at it, largely because they had longstanding relationships with chieftains and promised to protect Indian lands. The tribes making up the Iroquois League split their allegiances, with most Mohawks, Onondagas,

Cayugas, and Senecas joining the British, and most Oneidas and Tuscaroras supporting the Patriots. In the Carolinas, the Cherokees joined the British in hopes of driving out American settlers who had taken their lands. Most Indians in New England tried to remain neutral or sided with the Patriots.

DISASTER IN CANADA In July 1775, the Continental Congress authorized a military expedition in Canada against Quebec in the vain hope of convincing the French Canadians to become allies.

The Americans, having spent six weeks struggling through dense forests, crossing roaring rapids, and wading through frost-covered marshes, arrived outside Quebec in September, tired, exhausted, freezing, and hungry. A silent killer then ambushed them: smallpox. As the virus raced through the American camp, General Richard Montgomery faced a brutal dilemma. Most of his soldiers had signed up for short tours of duty, and many were scheduled for discharge at the end of the year. Because of the impending departure of his men, Montgomery could not afford to wait until spring for the smallpox to subside. Seeing little choice but to fight, he ordered an attack on the British forces defending Quebec on December 31, 1775.

The assault was a disaster. More than 400 Americans were taken prisoner; the rest of the Patriot force retreated to their camp outside the walled city and appealed to the Continental Congress for reinforcements. The British, sensing weakness, attacked and sent the Patriots on a frantic retreat up the St. Lawrence River to the American-held city of Montreal, and eventually back to New York and New England.

By the summer of 1776, the Patriots had come to realize that their quest for independence would be neither short nor easy. George Washington confessed to his brother that his efforts to form an effective army out of "the great mixture of troops" were filled with "difficulties and distresses."

WASHINGTON'S NARROW ESCAPE During the summer of 1776, the British decided to invade New York City, hoping to capture the new nation's leading commercial seaport. By the end of summer, two-thirds of the British army, veterans of many campaigns around the world, were camped on Staten Island, just a mile off the coast of Manhattan.

The British commanders, General William Howe and his brother, Admiral Richard Howe, sympathized with American grievances but felt strongly that the rebellion must be crushed. They met with Patriot leaders in an attempt to negotiate a settlement. After the negotiations failed, a British fleet of 427 ships carrying 32,000 troops, including 8,000 hired German soldiers, began landing on Long Island near New York City. It was the largest seaborne military expedition in history to that point.

After ousting the British from Boston earlier in the year, George Washington had moved his forces to defensive positions around New York City in February 1776. Although it was too small an army to protect New York, the Continental Congress insisted that the city be defended at all costs. As John Adams explained, New York was the "key to the whole continent."

Washington had never commanded a large force. He confessed to the Continental Congress that he had no "experience to move [armies] on a large scale" and had only "limited . . . knowledge . . . in military matters." He was still learning the art of generalship. The British invasion of New York taught him some painful lessons.

In late August 1776, the Americans entrenched on Long Island waited for the British to attack. Washington walked back and forth behind his outnumbered men with two loaded pistols, warning them that he would shoot anyone who turned tail and ran. He assured them that he would "fight as long as I have a leg or an arm."

Many Americans lost arms and legs as the Battle of Long Island and White Plains unfolded. A Marylander reported that a British cannonball careened through the American lines. It "first took the head off . . . a stout heavy man; then took off Chilson's arm, which was amputated . . . It then struck Sergeant Garret . . . on the hip. . . . What a sight that was to see . . . men with legs and arms and packs all in a heap."

The inexperienced American army suffered a humiliating defeat. In the face of steadily advancing ranks of British soldiers with bayonet-tipped muskets, many American defenders and their officers had panicked. Washington had urged his soldiers to fight "like men, like soldiers," but the more numerous redcoats overwhelmed the Patriots.

The smoke and chaos of battle, the "confusion and horror," disoriented the untested Americans. The disorganized, undisciplined, and indecisive Americans steadily gave ground, leading British commanders to assume that the Revolution was about to end. On August 28, while fighting continued in Brooklyn Heights, Admiral Lord Richard Howe hosted two captured American generals aboard his flagship. Over dinner, he shared his ideas for ending the war and restoring British authority over the wayward colonies.

At the same time Admiral Howe was discussing the end of the war, General Washington had decided there would be no surrender as the redcoats continued to maul his Patriots. On August 29, Washington realized the only hope for his battered army was to organize a hasty retreat that night. Thanks to a timely rainstorm and the heroic efforts of experienced New England boatmen, the 9,500 Americans and their horses and equipment were rowed across the East River to Manhattan through the night. An early morning fog cloaked the final stages of the risky retreat. The British did not realize what was happening until it was too late. Admiral Howe's hopes for a quick end to the Revolution were dashed.

Had General William Howe's army moved more quickly in pursuit of the retreating Patriots, it could have trapped Washington's entire force. Rather than sustaining their momentum, however, the British rested as the main American army made a miraculous escape over the next several weeks, crossing the Hudson River and retreating into New Jersey, and then over the Delaware River into Pennsylvania.

Washington was "wearied almost to death" as the ragged remnants of his army outraced their British pursuers over 170 miles in two months. "In one thing only" did the British fail, reported an observer; "they could not run as fast as their Foe."

New York City became the headquarters of both the Royal Navy and the British army. Local Loyalists, or "Tories" as the Patriots mockingly called them, excitedly welcomed the British occupation. "Hundreds in this colony are against us," a New York City Patriot wrote to John Adams. "Tories openly express their sentiments in favor of the enemy."

By December 1776, the American Revolution was near collapse. A British officer reported that many "rebels" were "without shoes or stockings, and several were observed to have only linen drawers . . . without any proper shirt. They must suffer extremely" in the winter weather. Indeed, the Continental army was shrinking before Washington's eyes. He had only 3,000 men left. Unless a new army could be raised quickly, he warned, "I think the game is pretty near up."

Thomas Paine Thomas Paine originally published his inspiring pamphlet *Common Sense* anonymously because the British viewed it as treasonous.

Then, almost miraculously, help emerged from an unexpected source: the English-born war correspondent, Thomas Paine. Having opened the eventful year of 1776 with his inspiring pamphlet *Common Sense*, Paine now composed *The American Crisis*, in which he wrote these stirring lines:

> These are the times that try men's souls: The summer soldier and the sunshine patriot will, in this crisis, shrink from the service of his country; but he that stands it NOW deserves the love and thanks of man and woman. Tyranny, like Hell, is not easily conquered. Yet we have this consolation with us, that the harder the conflict, the more glorious the triumph.

Paine's rousing pamphlet boosted the Patriots' flagging spirits. Washington had *The American Crisis* read aloud to his dwindling army. Members of the Continental Congress were also emboldened, and on December 27, 1776, Congress gave Washington "large powers" to strengthen the war effort, including the ability to offer recruits cash, land, clothing, and blankets.

Washington had learned some hard lessons. The feisty frontier militiamen he had relied upon to bolster the Continental army came and went as they pleased, in part because they resisted traditional forms of military discipline. Washington acknowledged that "a people unused to restraint must be led; they will not be driven."

His genius was to learn from his mistakes and to use resilience and flexibility as weapons. With soldiers deserting every day, Washington modified his conventional top-down approach in favor of allowing soldiers to tell him their concerns and offer suggestions. What he heard led him to change his strategy. The British would not be defeated in large battles. He needed to use his limited forces in surprise attacks, hit-and-run campaigns that would confuse the British and preserve his struggling army. Unknowingly, the British fell into his trap.

In December 1776, General William Howe, commander of the British forces in North America, decided to wait out the winter in New York City. (Eighteenth-century armies rarely fought during the winter months.) By not pursuing the Americans into Pennsylvania, Howe had lost a great opportunity to end the Revolution. He instead settled down with his "flashing blonde" Loyalist mistress (twenty-five-year-old Elizabeth Loring, the wife of a New England Tory). One American general quipped that Howe "shut his eyes, fought his battles, drank his bottle and had his little whore."

A DESPERATE GAMBLE   George Washington, however, was not ready to hibernate. He decided that the Revolutionary cause desperately needed "some stroke" of good news. So he hatched a plan to surprise the British forces before more of his soldiers decided to return home.

On a fearfully cold Christmas night in 1776, Washington secretly led some 2,400 men, packed into forty-foot-long boats, across the ice-clogged Delaware

George Washington at Princeton
Commissioned for Independence Hall in Philadelphia, this 1779 painting by Charles Willson Peale portrays Washington as the hero of the Battle of Princeton.

River into New Jersey. It was a risky endeavor, made even riskier by the weather and the rough river currents. Twice the Americans had to turn back, but on the third try they made it across the river. It had taken nine hours, and the howling winds, sleet, and blinding snow continued to slow their progress as they marched inland.

Near sunrise at Trenton, the Americans surprised 1,500 sleeping Hessians. The **Battle of Trenton** was a total rout. Just two of Washington's men were killed, and only four wounded. After the battle, Washington hurried his men and their German captives back across the river, urging his troops to treat the prisoners "with humanity, and let them have no reason to complain of our copying the brutal example of the British army."

Four days later, the Americans again crossed the Delaware River, won another battle at Trenton, and then headed north to attack British forces around Princeton before taking shelter in winter quarters at Morristown, New Jersey. A British officer grumbled that the Americans had "become a formidable enemy."

The American victories at Princeton and Trenton saved the cause of independence and shifted the war's momentum. A fresh wave of Patriots signed up to serve in the army, and Washington regained the confidence of his men.

A British officer recognized that the victories at Trenton and Princeton would "revive the dropping spirits of the rebels and increase their force." British war correspondents claimed that Washington was more talented than any of their commanders. Yet although the "dark days" of late 1776 were over, unexpected challenges quickly chilled the Patriots' excitement.

WINTER IN MORRISTOWN During the record-cold winter in early 1777, George Washington's ragged army was again much diminished, as six-month enlistment contracts expired and deserters fled the hardships caused by the brutal weather, inadequate food, and widespread disease. One soldier

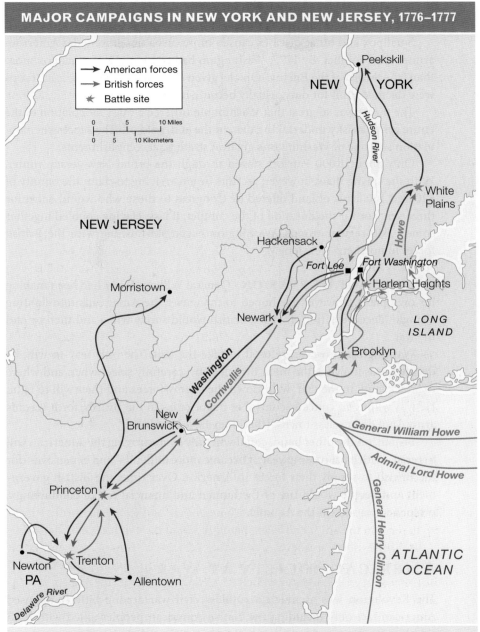

MAJOR CAMPAIGNS IN NEW YORK AND NEW JERSEY, 1776–1777

→ American forces
→ British forces
✳ Battle site

0   5   10 Miles
0   5   10 Kilometers

NEW YORK

Peekskill

Hudson River

White Plains

NEW JERSEY

Hackensack

Fort Lee   Fort Washington

Howe

Harlem Heights

Morristown

Newark

LONG ISLAND

Washington   Cornwallis

Brooklyn

New Brunswick

General William Howe

Admiral Lord Howe

Princeton

General Henry Clinton

ATLANTIC OCEAN

Newton

Trenton

PA

Allentown

Delaware River

- Why did General Washington lead his army from Brooklyn to Manhattan and from there to New Jersey?
- How could the British army commander, General William Howe, have ended the rebellion in New York?
- What was the significance of the Battle of Trenton?

recalled that "we were absolutely, literally starved. . . . I saw several of the men roast their old shoes and eat them."

Smallpox and other diseases caused more casualties among the American armies than combat. By 1777, Washington had come to dread smallpox more than "the Sword of the Enemy." On any given day, a fourth of American troops were deemed unfit for duty, usually because of smallpox.

The threat was so great that Washington ordered a mass inoculation of the entire army, a risky undertaking that, in the end, paid off. The successful inoculation was one of Washington's greatest strategic accomplishments.

Only about 1,000 Patriots stayed through the brutal New Jersey winter. With the spring thaw, however, recruits began arriving to claim the bounty of $20 and 100 acres of land offered by Congress to those who would enlist for three years or for the duration of the conflict, if less. Having cobbled together some 9,000 regular troops, Washington began skirmishing with the British forces in northern New Jersey.

A STRATEGY OF EVASION   General William Howe had been making his own plans, however. He hoped to maneuver the Americans into fighting a single "decisive action" that the British would surely win—and thereby end the war.

Washington, however, refused to take the bait. The only way to win, he decided, was to evade the main British army, carefully select when and where to attack, and, in the end, wear down the enemy forces and their will to fight. He was willing to concede control of major cities to the British, for it was his army, "not defenseless towns, [that] they have to subdue."

Britain, on the other hand, could win only by destroying the American will to resist. With each passing year, it became more difficult—and expensive—for the British to supply their forces in America. Over time, the British government and people would tire of the human and financial toll of conducting a prolonged war across the Atlantic.

AMERICAN SOCIETY AT WAR

The Revolution was as much a ruthless civil war among bitterly opposed American factions (including the Native American peoples allied with both sides) as it was a prolonged struggle against Great Britain. The necessity of choosing sides divided families and friends, towns and cities.

Benjamin Franklin's illegitimate son, William, for example, was the royal governor of New Jersey. An ardent Loyalist, he sided with Great Britain. His

Patriot father later removed him from his will. Similarly, eighteen-year-old Bostonian Lucy Flucker defied her Loyalist father's wishes and married bookseller Henry Knox in 1774. (Knox would become an American general.) Lucy's estranged family fled with the British army when it left Boston in 1776, and she never saw them again. "I have lost my father, mother, brother, and sister, entirely lost them," she wrote.

Overall, the colonists were generally divided into three groups: (1) Patriots, who formed the Continental army and fought in state militias; (2) Loyalists, or Tories, siding with Britain and the king; and, (3) a less committed middle group that sought to remain neutral but were eventually swayed by the better organized and more energetic Patriots. Loyalists may have represented 20 percent of the American population, but Patriots were the largest of the three groups.

Some Americans (like Benedict Arnold) switched sides during the war, some as many as four or five times. Both the Patriots and the British, once they took control of a city or community, would often require the residents to swear an oath of loyalty to their cause. In Pennsylvania, Patriots tied a rope around the neck of John Stevens, a Loyalist, and dragged him behind a canoe in the Susquehanna River because he refused to sign a loyalty oath to the American cause.

The Loyalists, whom George Washington called "abominable pests of society," viewed the Revolution as an act of treason. The British Empire, they felt, was much more likely than an independent America to protect them from foreign foes and enable them to prosper. As the Reverend Mather Byles explained, "They call me a brainless Tory, but tell me . . . which is better—to be ruled by one tyrant 3,000 miles away or by 3,000 tyrants [Patriots] one mile away?"

Loyalists were most numerous in the seaport cities, especially New York and Philadelphia, as well as the Carolinas, and they came from all walks of life. Governors, judges, and other royal officials were almost all Loyalists; most Anglican ministers also preferred the mother country. Many small farmers who had largely been unaffected by the controversies over British efforts to tighten colonial regulations rallied to the British side. More New York men joined Loyalist regiments than enlisted in the Continental army. In few places, however, were there enough Loyalists to assume control without the support of British troops.

The Loyalists did not want to "dissolve the political bands" with Britain, as the Declaration of Independence demanded. Instead, as some 700 of them in New York City said in a petition to British officials, they "steadily and uniformly opposed" this "most unnatural, unprovoked Rebellion."

***Four Soldiers* (ca. 1781)** This illustration drawn by a French lieutenant captures the varied uniforms worn by Patriot forces in the war (left to right): a black soldier (freed for joining the 1st Rhode Island Regiment), a New England militiaman, a frontiersman, and a French soldier.

The British, however, were repeatedly frustrated by both the failure of Loyalists to materialize in strength and the collapse of Loyalist militia units once British troops departed. Because Patriot militias quickly returned whenever the British left an area, Loyalists faced a difficult choice: either accompany the British and leave behind their property, or stay and face the wrath of the Patriots. Even more disheartening was what one British officer called "the licentiousness of the [Loyalist] troops, who committed every species of rapine and plunder" and thereby converted potential friends to enemies.

The Patriots, both moderates and radicals, supported the war because they realized that the only way to protect their liberty was to separate themselves from British control. They also wanted to establish an American republic that would convert them from being *subjects* of a king to being *citizens* with the power to elect their own government and pursue their own economic interests.

SETBACKS FOR THE BRITISH (1777)

In 1777, the British launched a three-pronged assault on the state of New York. The complicated plan called for an army, based in Canada and led by General John Burgoyne, to advance southward from Quebec via Lake Champlain to the Hudson River. At the same time, another British force would move eastward from Oswego, in western New York. General William Howe would lead a third army up the Hudson River from New York City. All three armies would eventually converge in central New York and wipe out any remaining Patriot resistance.

The British armies, however, failed in their execution—and in their communications with one another. At the last minute, Howe changed his mind and decided to move south from New York City to attack the Patriot capital, Philadelphia. General Washington withdrew most of his men from New Jersey to meet the threat in Pennsylvania, while other American units banded together in upstate New York to deal with the British there.

On September 11, 1777, at Brandywine Creek, southwest of Philadelphia, the British overpowered Washington's army and occupied Philadelphia, then the largest and wealthiest American city. Caught up in the fighting, the members of the Continental Congress fled. Battered but still intact, Washington and his army withdrew to winter quarters twenty miles away at Valley Forge, while Howe and his men remained in Philadelphia.

THE CAMPAIGN OF 1777 Meanwhile, an overconfident General Burgoyne (nicknamed "General Swagger") led his army southward from Canada, eventually reaching Lake Champlain in June 1777. The British then pushed south toward the Hudson River. Eventually, they ran short of food and provisions, leaving them no choice but to make a desperate attempt to reach Albany. Growing numbers of Patriot soldiers slowed their advance, however.

The American army commander in New York was General Horatio Gates. Thirty-two years earlier, in 1745, he and Burgoyne had served as officers in the same British regiment. Now they were commanding opposing armies.

As Patriot militiamen converged from across central New York, Burgoyne pulled his forces back to the village of Saratoga (now called Schuylerville), where the reinforced American army surrounded the British. In the ensuing three-week-long **Battles of Saratoga**, the British, desperate for food and ammunition, twice tried—and failed—to break through the encircling Americans. On October 17, 1777, Burgoyne surrendered his outnumbered army. "The fortunes of war," he told Gates, "have made me your prisoner." Burgoyne also turned over 5,800 troops, 7,000 muskets, and 42 cannons to the Americans.

The news from New York unhinged King George. He fell "into agonies on hearing the account." The Saratoga campaign was the greatest loss that the British had ever suffered, and they would never recover. William Pitt, the former British

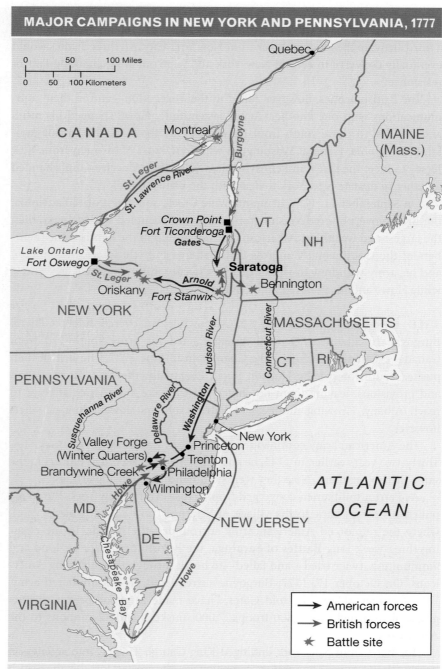

MAJOR CAMPAIGNS IN NEW YORK AND PENNSYLVANIA, 1777

0   50   100 Miles
0   50   100 Kilometers

Quebec

CANADA   Montreal

Burgoyne

MAINE (Mass.)

St. Lawrence River

St. Leger

Lake Ontario
Fort Oswego

Crown Point
Fort Ticonderoga
Gates

VT

NH

St. Leger

Saratoga

Arnold

Oriskany   Fort Stanwix

Bennington

NEW YORK

Hudson River

Connecticut River

MASSACHUSETTS

CT   RI

PENNSYLVANIA

Susquehanna River

Delaware River

Washington

Valley Forge
(Winter Quarters)

Brandywine Creek

New York

Princeton
Trenton
Philadelphia

Wilmington

Howe

ATLANTIC
OCEAN

MD

DE

NEW JERSEY

Chesapeake Bay

Howe

VIRGINIA

→ American forces
→ British forces
✳ Battle site

- What were the consequences of Burgoyne's strategy of dividing the colonies by invading upstate New York from Canada?
- How did life in the American winter camp at Valley Forge transform the army?
- Why were the Battles of Saratoga a turning point in the American Revolution?

prime minister, made a shocking prediction to Parliament after the defeat:
"You cannot conquer America."

ALLIANCE WITH FRANCE The
surprising victory at Saratoga was a strategic turning point for the new nation
because it brought about an **alliance
with France**, which had lost four wars to
the British in the previous eighty years.

Under the Treaty of Alliance, on
February 6, 1778, the parties agreed,
first, that if France entered the war,
both countries would fight until American independence was won; second,
that neither would conclude a "truce
or peace" with Great Britain without
"the formal consent of the other"; and,
third, that each would guarantee the
other's possessions in America "from
the present time and forever against all
other powers." France further agreed

General John Burgoyne Burgoyne was
commander of Britain's northern forces.
He and most of his troops surrendered
to the Americans at Saratoga on
October 17, 1777.

not to seek Canada or other British possessions on the mainland of North
America.

In the end, the French intervention determined the outcome of the war. The
Americans would also form important alliances with the Spanish (1779) and
the Dutch (1781), but neither provided as much direct support as the French.

After the British defeat at Saratoga and the news of the French alliance
with the United States, Parliament tried to end the war by granting all the
demands the Americans had made before they had declared independence.
The Continental Congress, however, would not negotiate until Britain officially recognized American independence and withdrew its forces. King
George refused.

1778: BOTH SIDES REGROUP

VALLEY FORGE AND STALEMATE For George Washington's
army at **Valley Forge**, near Philadelphia, the winter of 1777–1778 was a time
of intense suffering. The 12,000 Patriots, including some twelve-year-old

soldiers accompanied by their mothers, lacked shoes and blankets. All were miserably hungry, and their makeshift log-and-mud huts offered little protection from the harsh weather. Bare feet froze, turned black, and were amputated. "Why are we sent here to starve and freeze?" wrote a Connecticut Patriot. "Poor food . . . hard logging . . . cold weather . . . it snows . . . I'm sick . . . I can't endure it. . . . Lord, Lord, Lord."

By February 1778, some 7,000 troops were too ill for duty. More than 2,500 soldiers died at Valley Forge; another 1,000 deserted, and several hundred officers resigned or left before winter's end. Washington sent urgent messages to Congress, warning that if fresh food and supplies were not provided, the army would be forced "to starve, dissolve, or disperse."

Fortunately for the Revolutionaries, the plodding General Howe again remained content to ride out the winter in the company of his charming companion, Mrs. Loring, this time amid the comforts of Philadelphia. Their cozy relationship prompted a Patriot to pen a bawdy song:

> Sir William, he, snug as a flea
> Lay all this while a snoring;
> Nor dream'd of harm as he lay warm
> In bed with Mrs. Loring.

Yet there was little singing among the Americans. Desperate to find relief for his long-suffering soldiers, Washington sent troops across New Jersey, Delaware, and the Eastern Shore of Maryland to confiscate horses, cattle, and hogs in exchange for "receipts" promising future payment.

In the early spring of 1778, Washington sought to boost morale and distract the soldiers from their challenges by organizing a rigorous training program. To do so, he turned to an energetic, heavy-set Prussian soldier of fortune, Friedrich Wilhelm, Baron von Steuben, who volunteered without rank or pay.

Soon after his arrival at Valley Forge on February 23, 1778, Steuben reported being shocked by the "horrible conditions" he found. Knowing no more English than "Goddamn," Steuben used an interpreter as he issued instructions to the haggard Americans, teaching them how to march, shoot, and attack in formation. Once, when Steuben had grown frustrated at the soldiers' lack of attentiveness, he screamed for his translator: "These fellows won't do what I tell them. Come swear for me!" In Europe, he complained, soldiers blindly followed orders; in America, they demanded to know *why* they should listen to officers.

Steuben was one of several foreign volunteers who joined the American army at Valley Forge. Another was a nineteen-year-old, red-haired French orphan

named Gilbert du Motier, Marquis de Lafayette.
A wealthy idealist excited by the American cause,
Lafayette offered to serve in the Continental
army for no pay in exchange for being named
a major general. He then gave $200,000 to
the war effort, outfitted a ship, recruited
other French volunteers, and left behind
his pregnant wife and year-old daughter to
join the "grand adventure."

Washington was initially skeptical of
the young French aristocrat, but Lafayette
soon became the commander in chief's
most trusted aide. Washington noted that
Lafayette possessed "a large share of bravery
and military ardor." The young French general
also proved to be an able diplomat in forging the military alliance with France.

Lafayette Marquis de Lafayette,
portrayed in this colored mezzotint
by Charles Willson Peale, was a key
figure in the Revolutionary War. The
French statesman and soldier lived
from 1757 to 1834.

Patriot morale had risen when the
Continental Congress promised extra pay
and bonuses after the war, and again with
the news of the military alliance with
France. In the spring of 1778, British
forces withdrew from Pennsylvania to New York City, with the American army
in hot pursuit. From that time on, the combat in the north settled into a long
stalemate.

WAR IN THE WEST   The Revolution had created two wars. In addition
to the main conflict in the east, a frontier guerrilla war of terror and vengeance
pitted Indians and Loyalists against isolated Patriot settlers living along the
northern and western frontiers. In the Ohio Valley, as well as western New York
and Pennsylvania, the British urged frontier Loyalists and their Indian allies to
raid settlements and offered to pay bounties for American scalps.

To end the English-led attacks, early in 1778 George Rogers Clark took
175 Patriot frontiersmen on flatboats down the Ohio River. On the evening of
July 4, the Americans captured English-controlled Kaskaskia, in present-day
Illinois. Then, without bloodshed, Clark took Cahokia (in Illinois across the
Mississippi River from St. Louis) and Vincennes (in present-day Indiana).

After the British retook Vincennes, Clark led his men across icy rivers and
flooded prairies to attack the British garrison. Clark's rugged frontiersmen,
called Rangers, captured five Indians carrying American scalps. He ordered

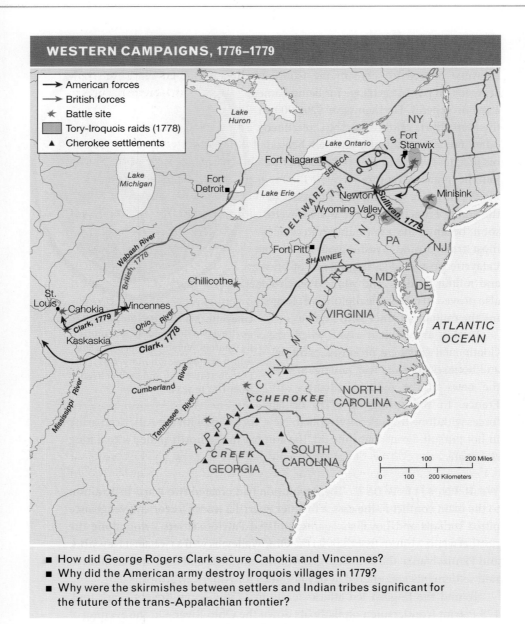

WESTERN CAMPAIGNS, 1776–1779

- How did George Rogers Clark secure Cahokia and Vincennes?
- Why did the American army destroy Iroquois villages in 1779?
- Why were the skirmishes between settlers and Indian tribes significant for the future of the trans-Appalachian frontier?

them to kill the Indians in sight of the fort. After watching the executions, the British surrendered.

While Clark's Rangers were in Indiana, a much larger U.S. force moved against Iroquois strongholds in western New York, where Loyalists (Tories) and their Indian allies had been terrorizing frontier settlements. The Iroquois attacks had killed hundreds of Patriot militiamen.

In response, George Washington sent 4,000 men under General John Sullivan to crush "the hostile tribes" and "the most mischievous of the Tories." At Newtown, New York, on August 29, 1779, Sullivan's soldiers did as ordered: they destroyed about forty Seneca and Cayuga villages, which broke the power of the Iroquois Confederacy.

The Patriots also desecrated Indian graves, raped native women, and mutilated warriors they had killed. An Indian chieftain reported that the Americans "put to death all the women and children, excepting some of the young women, whom they carried away for the use of the soldiers and were afterwards put to death in a more shameful manner."

In the Kentucky Territory, legendary frontiersman Daniel Boone and his small band of settlers repeatedly clashed with the Shawnees and their British and Loyalist allies. In 1778, Boone and some thirty men, aided by their wives and children, held off an assault by more than 400 Indians at Boonesborough. In early 1776, a delegation of northern Indians—Shawnees, Delawares, and Mohawks—had talked the Cherokees into attacking frontier settlements in Virginia and the Carolinas. Swift retaliation had followed as Carolina militiamen, led by Andrew Pickens, burned dozens of Cherokee villages. By weakening the major Indian tribes along the frontier, the American Revolution cleared the way for white settlers to seize Indian lands after the war.

THE WAR MOVES SOUTH

In late 1778, the British launched their southern strategy, built on the assumption that large numbers of Loyalists in the Carolinas, Virginia, and Georgia would join their cause. Once the British gained control of the southern colonies, they would have the shrinking United States pinched between Canada and the South.

In December 1778, General Sir Henry Clinton, the new commander in chief of British forces, sent 3,000 redcoats, Hessians, and Loyalists to take the port city of Savannah, on the southeast Georgia coast, and roll northeast from there. He enlisted support from local Loyalists and the Cherokees, led by Chief Dragging Canoe, who promised to leave the ground "dark and bloody."

BRITISH MOMENTUM Initially, Clinton's southern strategy worked beautifully. Within twenty months, the British and their allies had defeated three American armies; seized the strategic cities of Savannah and Charleston; occupied Georgia and much of South Carolina; and killed, wounded, or captured some 7,000 American soldiers. This success led Lord George Germain, the British official in London overseeing the war, to predict a "speedy and happy termination of the American war."

Germain's optimistic prediction, however, fell victim to three developments: first, the Loyalist strength in the South was weaker than estimated; second, the British effort to unleash Indian attacks convinced many undecided backcountry settlers to join the Patriot side; and, third, some British and Loyalist soldiers behaved so harshly that they drove Loyalists to switch sides.

WAR IN THE CAROLINAS   The Carolina campaign took a major turn when British forces, led by generals Clinton and Charles Cornwallis, bottled up an entire American army on the Charleston Peninsula for six weeks. Benjamin Lincoln, the inexperienced U.S. commander, begged local planters to arm their slaves and let them join the defense of the city, but the slaveholders refused. Prominent South Carolina leaders then used their control of local militia units to prevent Lincoln and his army from escaping.

On May 12, 1780, Lincoln surrendered Charleston and its 5,500 defenders. It was the greatest Patriot loss of the war. Soon thereafter, General Cornwallis, in charge of the British troops in the South, defeated a much larger American force led by General Horatio Gates at Camden, South Carolina. The British leader sought to intimidate other Revolutionaries by hanging captured Patriots.

Cornwallis had Georgia and most of South Carolina under British control by 1780. Then he made a tactical blunder by sending lieutenants into the countryside to organize Loyalist fighters to assault Patriots. In doing so, they mercilessly burned homes and murdered surrendering rebels. Their behavior alienated many poor rural folk who had been neutral. Francis Kinlock, a Loyalist, warned a British official that "the lower sort of people, who were in many parts . . . originally attached to the British government, have suffered so severely and been so frequently deceived, that Great Britain now has a hundred enemies where it had one before."

In mid-1780, small bands of Patriots based in the swamps and forests of South Carolina launched a successful series of hit-and-run raids. Led by colorful fighters such as Francis Marion, "the Swamp Fox," and Thomas Sumter, "the Carolina Gamecock," the Patriot guerrillas gradually wore down British confidence and morale. By August 1780, the British commanders were forced to admit that South Carolina was "in an absolute state of rebellion."

Warfare in the Carolinas was especially brutal. Neighbors fought neighbors, and families were split. Fathers fought sons, and brothers killed brothers. Both sides looted farms and plantations and tortured, scalped, and executed prisoners. Edward Lacey, a young South Carolina Patriot who commanded a militia unit, had to tie his Tory father to a bedstead to prevent him from informing the British of his whereabouts. In Virginia, planter Charles Lynch set up vigilante courts to punish Loyalists by "lynching" them—which in this case meant whipping them. Others were covered with bubbling-hot tar and feathers.

In the "backcountry" of the Carolinas and Georgia, British commanders encouraged their poorly disciplined Loyalist allies to wage a scorched-earth war of terror, arson, and intimidation. British general Charles Cornwallis urged his commanders to use the "most *vigorous* measures to *extinguish the rebellion*."

Tory militiamen took civilian hostages, assaulted women and children, plundered and burned houses and churches, stole property, bayoneted wounded Patriots, and tortured and executed unarmed prisoners. Vengeful Patriots responded in kind.

THE BATTLE OF KINGS MOUNTAIN Cornwallis's most cold-blooded cavalry officers, Sir Banastre Tarleton and Major Patrick Ferguson, were in charge of training Loyalist militiamen. The British officers often let their men burn Patriot farms, liberate slaves, and destroy livestock.

Yet they eventually overreached. Ferguson sealed his doom when he threatened to march over the Blue Ridge Mountains, hang the mostly Scots-Irish Presbyterian Patriot leaders ("backwater barbarians"), and destroy their farms "with fire and sword." Instead, the feisty "over the mountain men" from southwestern Virginia and western North and South Carolina, all experienced hunters and riflemen who had often fought Cherokees, went hunting for Ferguson and his army of Loyalists in late September 1780.

On October 7, the two sides clashed near Kings Mountain, a heavily wooded ridge along the border between North and South Carolina. In a ferocious hour-long battle, Patriot sharpshooters devastated the Loyalist troops.

Major Ferguson, resplendent in a black and red checkered coat, had boasted beforehand that "all the rebels in hell could not push him off" Kings Mountain. By the end of the battle, his lifeless body was pocked with seven bullets, and both his arms were broken. Seven hundred Loyalists were captured, and nine of them were later hanged. "The division among the people is much greater than I imagined," an American officer wrote to one of General Washington's aides. The Patriots and Loyalists, he said, "persecute each other with . . . savage fury."

As with so many confrontations in the South, the Battle of Kings Mountain resembled an extended family feud. Seventy-four sets of brothers fought on opposite sides, and twenty-nine sets of fathers and sons.

Five brothers in the Goforth family from Rutherford County, North Carolina, fought at Kings Mountain; three were Loyalists, and two were Patriots.

Only one of them survived. Two of the brothers, Preston and John Preston, fighting on opposite sides, recognized each other during the battle, took deadly aim as if in a duel, and fired simultaneously, killing each other.

The American victory at Kings Mountain undermined the British strategy in the South. Afterward, Cornwallis's forces retreated to South Carolina—and found it virtually impossible to recruit more Loyalists.

SOUTHERN RETREAT   In late 1780, the Continental Congress chose a new commander for the American army in the South: General Nathanael Greene, "the fighting Quaker" of Rhode Island. A former blacksmith blessed with unflagging persistence, he was bold and daring, and well-suited to a drawn-out war.

Greene arrived in Charlotte, North Carolina, to find himself in charge of a "shadow army." The 2,200 troops lacked everything "necessary either for the Comfort or Convenience of Soldiers." Greene wrote General Washington that the situation was "dismal, and truly distressing." Yet he also knew that if his army were not victorious, the South would be "re-annexed" to Britain.

Like Washington, Greene adopted a hit-and-run strategy. From Charlotte, he moved his army eastward while sending General Daniel Morgan and about 700 riflemen on a sweep to the west of Cornwallis's headquarters at Winnsboro, South Carolina.

On January 17, 1781, Morgan's force took up positions near Cowpens in northern South Carolina, about twenty-five miles from Kings Mountain. There he lured Sir Banastre Tarleton's army into an elaborate trap. Tarleton rushed his men forward, only to be ambushed by Morgan's cavalry. Tarleton escaped, but 110 British soldiers died and more than 700 were taken prisoner. Cowpens was the most complete victory for the Americans in the Revolution and was one of the few times that the Patriots won a battle in which the two sides were evenly matched.

Morgan's army then moved into North Carolina and linked up with Greene's troops. Greene lured the starving British army north, then attacked the redcoats at Guilford Courthouse (near what became Greensboro, North Carolina) on March 15, 1781.

The Americans lost the Battle of Guilford Courthouse but inflicted such heavy losses that Cornwallis left behind his wounded and marched his weary men toward Wilmington, on the North Carolina coast, to lick their wounds and take on supplies from British ships. The British commander reported that the Americans had "fought like demons."

Greene then resolved to go back into South Carolina, hoping to draw Cornwallis after him or force the British to give up the state. Greene connected with local guerrilla bands led by Francis Marion, Andrew Pickens, and

MAJOR CAMPAIGNS IN THE SOUTH, 1778–1781

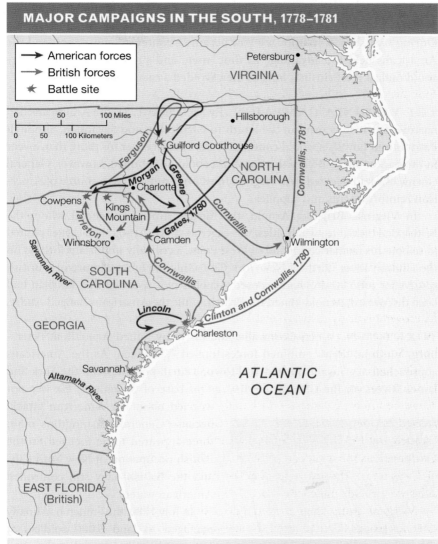

- Why did the British suddenly shift their military campaign to the South?
- Why were the battles at Savannah and Charleston major victories for the British?
- How did General Greene undermine British control of the Lower South?

Thomas Sumter. By targeting outlying British units and picking them off one by one, the guerrillas eventually forced the British back into Charleston and Savannah. George Washington praised Greene for having done "great things with little means."

A War of Endurance

During 1780, the Revolutionary War became a contest of endurance, and the Americans held the advantage in time, men, and supplies. They knew they could outlast the British as long as they avoided a catastrophic defeat.

THE VIRGINIA CAMPAIGN By September 1781, the Americans had narrowed British control in the South to Charleston and Savannah, although Patriots and Loyalists would continue to battle each other for more than a year in the backcountry. Before the Carolinas could be subdued, however, General Cornwallis had decided that Virginia must be eliminated as a source of American reinforcements and supplies.

In Virginia, Benedict Arnold, the former American general whom the British had bribed to switch sides, was eager to strike. Arnold had earlier plotted to sell out his former command of West Point, a critically important fortress on the Hudson River north of New York City. Only the lucky capture of a British spy, Major John André, had exposed Arnold's plot. Warned that his plan had been discovered, Arnold joined the British, while the Americans hanged André.

YORKTOWN When Cornwallis and his army joined Arnold's at Petersburg, Virginia, their combined forces totaled 7,200 men. As the Americans approached, Cornwallis picked Yorktown, a small port between the York and James Rivers on the Chesapeake Bay, as his base of operations. He was not worried about an American attack, because General Washington's main force appeared to be focused on the British occupation of New York City, and the British navy still controlled American waters.

In July 1780, the French had finally managed to land 6,000 soldiers at Newport, Rhode Island, but they had been bottled up there for a year, blockaded by the British fleet. As long as the British navy maintained supremacy along the coast, the Americans could not hope to win the war.

In May 1781, however, the elements for a combined French-American action suddenly fell into

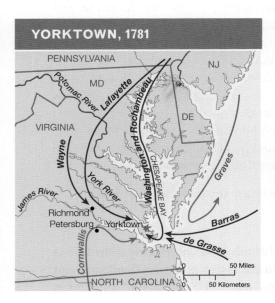

YORKTOWN, 1781

place. As Cornwallis's army moved into Virginia, Washington persuaded the commander of the French army in Rhode Island to join an attack on the British in New York City. Before they could strike, however, word came from the Caribbean that Admiral François-Joseph-Paul de Grasse was headed for the Chesapeake Bay with his fleet of French warships and some 3,000 soldiers.

This unexpected news led Washington to change his plans. He immediately begin moving his army south toward Yorktown. At the same time, French ships slipped out of the British blockade at Newport and also headed south. Somehow, in an age when communications were difficult, the French and Americans coordinated a secret plan to combine naval and army forces and destroy the main British army. Success depended on the French fleet getting to the Chesapeake Bay before the British navy did.

On August 30, Admiral de Grasse's twenty-four warships won the race to Yorktown, and French troops joined the Americans. The allies were about to spring their trap. Once Cornwallis realized what was happening, it was too late. The British commander sent an urgent plea for reinforcements: "If you cannot relieve me very soon, you must be prepared to hear the worst."

On September 6, the day after a British fleet appeared, de Grasse attacked and forced the British navy to abandon Cornwallis's surrounded army, leaving him with no access to fresh food and supplies. De Grasse then sent ships up the Chesapeake to ferry down the soldiers who had marched south from New York, bringing the combined American and French armies to 19,000 men—more than double the size of Cornwallis's army.

The **Battle of Yorktown** began on September 28. The American and French troops soon closed off Cornwallis's last escape route and began bombarding the British with cannons, sending some 3,600 shells raining down on the French lines. The British held out for three grim weeks, but on October 17, 1781—the anniversary of the American victory at Saratoga—Cornwallis surrendered. Two days later, the 7,000 British soldiers laid down their weapons as the band played "The World Turned Upside Down."

Claiming to be ill but sick only with humiliation, Cornwallis sent a painfully brief report to the British commander in chief in New York: "I have the mortification to inform your Excellency that I have been forced to surrender the troops under my command."

THE TREATY OF PARIS (1783)

Although Cornwallis had surrendered, the war was not yet over. The British still had more than 20,000 troops in America. They controlled New York City, Charleston, and Savannah, and their warships still blockaded other American ports. Yet any lingering British hopes of a military victory vanished at York-town. In London, prime minister Lord North exclaimed, "Oh God, it is all over."

In December 1781, King George decided against sending more troops to America. Early in 1782, the British contacted Benjamin Franklin in Paris to ask if the Americans would be willing to sign a peace treaty without involving the French. Franklin replied that the United States had no intention of desert-ing its "noble" French ally to sign a treaty with "an unjust and cruel Enemy."

On February 27, 1782, Parliament voted to begin negotiations to end the war, and on March 20, Lord North resigned. In part, the British leaders chose peace in America so that they could concentrate on their continuing global war with France and Spain. At the same time, France let Franklin know that it was willing to let the United States negotiate its own treaty with Great Britain.

A NEGOTIATED PEACE   Upon learning of the British decision to negotiate, the Continental Congress named a group of prominent Americans to go to Paris to discuss terms. They included John Adams, who was then representing the United States in the Netherlands; John Jay, minister (ambas-sador) to Spain; and Benjamin Franklin, already in France. The cranky Adams was an odd choice since, as Thomas Jefferson said, "He hates [Benjamin] Franklin, he hates John Jay, he hates the French, he hates the English." In the end, Franklin and, especially, Jay did most of the work.

The negotiations dragged on for months until, on September 3, 1783, the war-ring nations signed the Treaty of Paris. Its provisions were surprisingly favorable to the United States. Great Britain recognized the independence of the thirteen former colonies and agreed that the Mississippi River was America's western boundary, thereby more than doubling the territory of the new nation. Native Americans had no role in the negotiations, and they were by far the biggest losers.

The treaty's unclear references to America's northern and southern borders would be a source of dispute for years. Florida, as it turned out, passed back to Spain. As for the prewar debts owed by Americans to British merchants, the U.S. negotiators promised that British merchants should "meet with no legal impediment" in seeking to collect money owed them.

However imperfect the peace treaty was, the upstart Americans had hum-bled the British Empire. "A great revolution has happened," acknowledged Edmund Burke, a prominent British politician. "A revolution made, not by chopping and changing of power in any one of the existing states, but by the appearance of a new state, of a new species, in a new part of the globe."

In winning the war, the Americans had acquired a robust sense of their own power and an awareness of the limitations of British power. Most important, the Americans had earned their legitimate right to decide their own future.

Whatever the failings and hypocrisies of the Revolution, it severed America's connection with monarchical rule and provided the catalyst for the creation of a representative democracy.

In late November 1783, the remaining British troops left New York City for home. On December 23, George Washington appeared before the Continental Congress in Annapolis, Maryland. With trembling hands and a rasping voice, he asked the members to accept his retirement. "Having now finished the work assigned to me, I retire from the great theater of Action . . . and take my leave of all employments of public life."

WAR AS AN ENGINE OF CHANGE

Like all major wars, the American war for independence had unexpected effects on political, economic, and social life. It upset traditional social relationships and affected the lives of people who had long been discriminated against—African Americans, women, and Indians. In important ways, then, the Revolution was an engine for political experimentation and social change, and it ignited a prolonged debate about what new forms of government would best serve the new American republic.

REPUBLICAN IDEOLOGY American Revolutionaries embraced a **republican ideology** instead of the aristocratic or monarchical outlook that had long dominated Europe. The new republic was not a democracy in the purest sense of the word. In ancient Greece, the Athenians had practiced *direct democracy*, which meant that citizens voted on all major decisions affecting them. The new United States, however, was technically a *representative democracy*, in which property-holding white men governed themselves through the concept of republicanism—they elected representatives, or legislators, to make decisions on their behalf. As Thomas Paine observed, representative democracy had many advantages over monarchies, one of which was greater transparency: "Whatever are its excellencies and defects, they are visible to all."

To preserve the delicate balance between liberty and power, Revolutionary leaders believed that they must protect the rights of individuals and states from being violated by the national government. The war for independence thus sparked a wave of new **state constitutions**. Not only was a nation coming into being as a result of the Revolutionary War, but new state-level governments were being created, all of which were designed to reflect the principles of the republican ideology limiting the powers of government so as to protect the rights of the people.

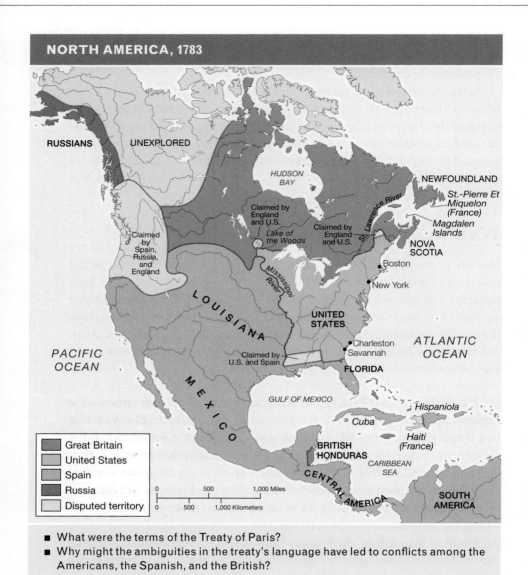

NORTH AMERICA, 1783

RUSSIANS   UNEXPLORED

HUDSON
BAY

NEWFOUNDLAND

St.-Pierre Et
Miquelon
(France)

Claimed by
England
and U.S.

Claimed by
England
and U.S.

Magdalen
Islands

Lake of
the Woods

St. Lawrence River

NOVA
SCOTIA

Claimed
by
Spain,
Russia,
and
England

Mississippi
River

Boston

New York

L O U I S I A N A

UNITED
STATES

ATLANTIC
OCEAN

PACIFIC
OCEAN

Charleston
Savannah

Claimed by
U.S. and Spain

FLORIDA

M E X I C O

GULF OF MEXICO

Hispaniola

Cuba

Haiti
(France)

	Great Britain
	United States
	Spain
	Russia
	Disputed territory

BRITISH
HONDURAS

CARIBBEAN
SEA

0   500   1,000 Miles

0   500   1,000 Kilometers

CENTRAL AMERICA

SOUTH
AMERICA

- What were the terms of the Treaty of Paris?
- Why might the ambiguities in the treaty's language have led to conflicts among the Americans, the Spanish, and the British?

STATE GOVERNMENTS Most of the political experimentation between 1776 and 1787 occurred at the state level in the form of written constitutions in which the people granted limited authority to their governments. The first state constitutions created governments during the War of Independence much like the colonial governments, but with *elected* governors and senates instead of royally *appointed* governors and councils. Most of the constitutions also included a bill of rights that protected freedom of speech, trial by jury, and freedom from self-incrimination, while limiting the powers of governors and strengthening the powers of the legislatures.

THE ARTICLES OF CONFEDERATION   Once the colonies had declared their independence in 1776, the Patriots needed to form a *national* government. Before March 1781, the Continental Congress had exercised emergency powers without any legal or official authority.

Plans for a permanent form of government emerged quickly. As early as July 1776, a committee appointed by the Continental Congress had produced a draft constitution called the *Articles of Confederation and Perpetual Union*. When the **Articles of Confederation** were finally ratified in March 1781, they essentially legalized the way things had been operating since independence had been declared, although the Continental Congress became the Confederation Congress.

The Confederation reflected the long-standing fears of monarchy by not allowing for a president or chief executive. In the Confederation government, Congress had full power over foreign affairs and disputes between the states. Yet the Confederation had no national courts and no power to enforce its resolutions and ordinances. It could not levy taxes, and its budgetary needs depended on requisitions from the states, which state legislatures often ignored.

The states were in no mood to create a strong central government. The Confederation Congress, in fact, was granted less power than the colonists had once accepted in the British Parliament, since it could not regulate interstate and foreign commerce. For certain important acts, moreover, a "special majority" in the Confederation Congress was required. Nine states had to approve measures dealing with war, treaties, coinage, finances, and the military. Unanimous approval from the states was needed to impose tariffs (often called "duties," or taxes) on imports and to amend the Articles.

For all its weaknesses, however, the Confederation government represented the most practical structure for the new nation. After all, the Revolution had yet to be won, and an America besieged by British armies and warships could not risk divisive debates over the distribution of power.

EXPANSION OF POLITICAL PARTICIPATION   The new political opportunities afforded by the creation of state governments led more citizens to participate than ever before. Property qualifications for voting, which already allowed an overwhelming majority of white men to vote, were lowered after 1776. As a group of farmers explained, "No man can be free and independent" unless he possesses "a voice . . . in the most important offices in the legislature." In Pennsylvania, Delaware, North Carolina, and Georgia, any male taxpayer could vote, regardless of how much, if any, property he owned. Farmers, tradesmen, and shopkeepers were soon elected to state legislatures. In general, a higher percentage of American males could vote in the late eighteenth and early nineteenth century than could their counterparts in Great Britain.

THE SOCIAL REVOLUTION

The American Revolution was fought in the name of liberty, a virtuous ideal that proved elusive—even in victory. What did the Revolution mean to the workers, servants, farmers, and freed slaves who participated? Many hoped that it would remove the elite's traditional political and social advantages. Wealthy Patriots, on the other hand, would have been content to replace royal officials with the rich, the wellborn, and the able—and let it go at that.

In the end, the new republic's social fabric and political culture were visibly different after the war. The energy created by the concepts of liberty, equality, and democracy changed the dynamics of social and political life in ways that people could not have imagined in 1776.

THE EXODUS OF LOYALISTS The Loyalists suffered for their stubborn support of King George III and their refusal to pledge allegiance to the new United States. During and after the Revolution, their property was confiscated or destroyed, and many were assaulted, brutalized, and executed by Patriots (and vice versa).

After the American victory at Yorktown, tens of thousands of panicked Loyalists made their way to seaports to board British ships and flee the United States. Thousands of African Americans, mostly runaway slaves, also flocked to New York City, Charleston, and Savannah, with many of their owners in hot pursuit. Boston King, a runaway, said he saw white slave owners grabbing their escaped slaves "in the streets of New York, or even dragging them out of their beds."

General Guy Carleton, commander in chief of British forces in North America, organized the mass evacuation. He intentionally violated the provisions of the Treaty of Paris by refusing to return slaves to their owners, defiantly telling a furious George Washington that his slaves from Mount Vernon had already escaped and boarded British ships bound for Canada.

Some 80,000 desperate refugees—white Loyalists, free blacks, freed slaves, and Native Americans who had allied with the British—dispersed throughout the British Empire. Among those who resettled in Canada were 3,500 former slaves who had been freed in exchange for joining the British army. Some 2,000 freed blacks chose to go to Sierra Leone, where British abolitionists helped them create an experimental colony called Freetown.

About 12,000 Georgia and South Carolina Loyalists, including thousands of their slaves (the British granted freedom only to the slaves of Patriots), went to British-controlled East Florida, only to see their new home handed over to Spain in 1783. Spanish authorities gave them a hard choice: swear allegiance to the Spanish king and convert to Catholicism, or leave. Most of them left.

Some of the doubly displaced Loyalists sneaked back into the United States, but most went to British islands in the Caribbean. "We are all cast off," complained one Loyalist. "I shall ever tho' remember with satisfaction that it was not I deserted my King [George III], but my King that deserted me." The largest number of exiles landed in Canada.

The departure of so many Loyalists from America was one of the most important social consequences of the Revolution. Their confiscated homes, lands, and vacated jobs created new social, economic, and political opportunities for Patriots.

Religious development The Congregational Church developed a national presence in the early nineteenth century. Lemuel Haynes, depicted here, was its first African American minister.

FREEDOM OF RELIGION The Revolution also tested traditional religious loyalties and set in motion important changes in the relationship between church and government. Before the Revolution, Americans *tolerated* religious dissent; after the Revolution, they insisted on complete *freedom* of religion as embodied in the principle of separation of church and state.

The Anglican Church, established as the official religion in five colonies and parts of two others, was especially vulnerable to changes prompted by the war. Anglicans tended to be pro-British, and non-Anglicans, notably Baptists and Methodists, outnumbered Anglicans in all states except Virginia. All but Virginia eliminated tax support for the church before the fighting was over, and Virginia did so soon afterward. Although Anglicanism survived in the form of the new Episcopal Church, it never regained its pre-Revolutionary stature.

In 1776, the Virginia Declaration of Rights had guaranteed the free exercise of religion. Ten years later, the **Virginia Statute of Religious Freedom** (written by Thomas Jefferson) declared that "no man shall be compelled to frequent or support any religious worship, place or ministry whatsoever" and "that all men shall be free to profess, and by argument to maintain, their opinions in matters of religion." These statutes, and the Revolutionary ideology that justified them, helped shape the course that religious life would take in the United States: diverse and voluntary rather than monolithic and enforced by the government.

SLAVES AND THE REVOLUTION

The sharpest irony of the American Revolution was that Great Britain offered enslaved blacks more opportunities for freedom than did the United States. In November 1775, the British royal governor of Virginia, John Murray (Lord Dunmore), himself a slave owner, announced that all slaves and indentured servants would gain their freedom if they joined the Loyalist cause. Within a month, the British had attracted more than 300 former servants and slaves to what came to be called the "Ethiopian Regiment." The number soon grew to almost 1,000 males and twice as many women and children.

The British recruitment of slaves outraged George Washington, Thomas Jefferson, and other white plantation owners in Virginia, where 40 percent of the population was black. Washington predicted that if Dunmore's efforts were "not crushed" soon, the number of slaves joining the British army would "increase as a Snow ball by Rolling."

Jefferson expressed the same concerns after twenty-three slaves escaped from his plantation outside Charlottesville. He eventually reclaimed six of them, only to sell them for their "disloyalty."

In 1775, authorities in Charleston, South Carolina executed Thomas Jeremiah, a free man of color who was the wealthiest black man in North America. A harbor pilot, Jeremiah owned slaves himself. His crime? He supposedly incited a rebellion by telling slaves that British troops were coming "to help the poor Negroes."

At Jeremiah's "trial" in a "slave court," which had no judge, jury, or attorneys, Henry Laurens, a planter and former slave trader who would be elected president of the Continental Congress, charged that Jeremiah "was a forward fellow, puffed up by prosperity, ruined by Luxury & debauchery" and prone to "vanity & ambition." Lau-

The Death of Major Peirson, 1783
In this detail of the John Singleton Copley painting, a free Black soldier is depicted fighting on the side of the British in the Revolutionary War.

rens demanded that "nothing less than Death Should be the Sentence." On August 18, 1775, authorities hanged Jeremiah and burned his body to ashes.

Such brutalities led a British abolitionist to remark that America during its Revolution was "the land of the brave and the land of the slave." Many southern revolutionaries were fighting less for independence from "British tyranny" than to retain their slave-labor system.

SOUTHERN BACKLASH   In the end, the British policy of recruiting slaves backfired. The "terrifying" prospect of British troops arming slaves persuaded many fence-straddling southerners to join the Patriot cause. Edward Rutledge of South Carolina said that the British decision to arm slaves did more to create "an eternal separation between Great Britain and the colonies than any other expedient."

For Rutledge and many other southern whites, the Revolution became primarily a war to defend slavery. Racial prejudice thus helped fuel revolutionary rebellion. What South Carolinians wanted from the Revolutionary War, explained Pierce Butler, "is that their slaves not be taken from them."

In response to the British recruitment of enslaved African Americans, at the end of 1775 a desperate General Washington authorized the enlistment of free blacks—but not slaves—into the American army. In February 1776, however, southern representatives convinced the Continental Congress to instruct Washington to enlist no more African Americans, free or enslaved. Two states, South Carolina and Georgia, refused to allow any blacks to serve. As the American war effort struggled, however, Massachusetts organized two all-black army units, and Rhode Island organized one, which also included Native Americans. About 5,000 African Americans fought on the Patriot side, most of them free blacks from northern states.

While thousands of free blacks and runaway slaves fought in the war, the vast majority of African Americans did not choose sides so much as they chose freedom. Several hundred thousand enslaved blacks, mostly in the southern states, took advantage of the disruptions caused by the war to seize their freedom. Others used the impetus of the Revolution to promote freedom for all.

As early as the summer of 1776, Lemuel Haynes, a free black who served in the Massachusetts militia, borrowed the language of the Declaration of Independence for an abolitionist sermon. He highlighted the "self-evident truth" that all men had the "unalienable right" to liberty, which was "as precious to a black man, as it is to a white one, and bondage as equally as intolerable to the one as it is to the other."

In the North, which had far fewer slaves than the South, the ideals of liberty and freedom led most states to end slavery, either during the war or shortly afterward. But those same ideals had little to no impact in the southern states. These contrasting attitudes toward slavery would continue to shape the political disputes of the young nation.

THE STATUS OF WOMEN The ideal of liberty spawned by the Revolution applied to the status of women as much as to that of African Americans. The legal status of women was governed by British common law, which essentially treated them like children, limiting their roles to child rearing and maintaining the household. Women could not vote or hold office. Few had access to formal education. Boys were taught to read and write; girls were taught to read and sew. Until married, women were subject to the dictates of their fathers.

Once a woman married, she essentially became the possession of her husband, and all property she brought to the marriage became his. A married woman had no right to buy, sell, or manage property. Technically, any wages a wife earned belonged to the husband. Women could not sign contracts, file lawsuits, or testify in court. A husband could beat and even rape his wife without fearing legal action. Divorces were extremely difficult to obtain.

Yet the Revolution offered women opportunities to broaden their social roles and to support the armies in various ways. They handled supplies, served as messengers or spies, and worked as "camp followers," cooking, washing, sewing, and nursing in exchange for daily rations. Some officers paid women to be their personal servants.

Often women had no choice but to follow their husbands into war because they had no place to live or food to eat. Some camp followers tended cattle, sheep, or hogs, and guarded supplies. Others sold various items. A few of the single women were prostitutes. In 1777, George Washington ordered that commanders take measures to "prevent an inundation of bad women [prostitutes] from Philadelphia." He also urged that soldiers fraternize only with "clean" women to prevent the spread of venereal diseases.

Wives who were camp followers sometimes brought along their children, again because they had no choice. Washington would have preferred to ban women and children, but he was forced to accept them because he was afraid to lose "a number of men, who very probably would have followed their wives" home.

Women risked their lives in battle, tending the wounded or bringing water to the soldiers. On occasion, wives took the place of their soldier-husbands. In 1777, some 400 armed women mobilized to defend Pittsfield, Vermont. The men of the town had gone off to fight when a band of Loyalists and Indians approached the village. The women held off the attackers until help arrived.

Several women disguised themselves and fought as ordinary soldiers. Deborah Sampson joined a Massachusetts regiment as "Robert Shurtleff" and served from 1781 to 1783 thanks to the "artful concealment" of her gender. Ann Bailey did the same. In 1777, eager to get the enlistment bonus payment, she cut her hair, dressed like a man, and used a husky voice to join the Patriot army in New York as "Samuel Gay." Bailey performed so well that she was promoted to corporal, only to be discovered as a woman, dismissed, jailed, and fined.

WOMEN AND LIBERTY   America's war against Great Britain led some women to demand their own independence. Early in the struggle, Abigail Adams, one of the most learned and spirited women of the time, wrote to her husband John: "In the new Code of Laws which I suppose it will be necessary for you to make, I desire you would remember the Ladies. . . . Do not put such unlimited power into the hands of the Husbands." Since men were "Naturally

Tyrannical," she wrote, "why then, not put it out of the power of the vicious and the Lawless to use us with cruelty and indignity with impunity." Otherwise, "if particular care and attention is not paid to the Ladies we are determined to foment a Rebellion, and will not hold ourselves bound by any Laws in which we have no voice, or Representation."

John Adams could not help but "laugh" at his wife's radical proposals. He insisted on retaining the traditional privileges enjoyed by males: "Depend upon it, we know better than to repeal our Masculine systems." If women were to be granted equality, he warned, then "children and apprentices" and "Indians and Negroes" would also demand equal rights and freedoms.

Thomas Jefferson shared Adams's outlook. In his view, women should not "wrinkle their foreheads with politics" but instead "soothe and calm the minds of their husbands." Improvements in the status of women would have to wait.

NATIVE AMERICANS AND THE REVOLUTION   Most Native Americans sought to remain neutral in the war, but both British and American agents urged the chiefs to fight on their side. The result was chaos. Indians on both sides attacked villages, burned crops, and killed civilians.

During and after the war, the new government assured its Indian allies that it would respect their lands and their rights. But many white Americans used the disruptions of war to destroy and displace Native Americans. Once the war ended and independence was secured, there was no peace for the Indians. By the end of the eighteenth century, land-hungry Americans were again pushing into Indian territories on the western frontier.

THE EMERGENCE OF AN AMERICAN NATIONALISM

On July 2, 1776, when the Second Continental Congress had resolved "that these United Colonies are, and of right ought to be, free and independent states," John Adams had written Abigail that future generations would remember that date as their "day of deliverance." Adams got everything right but the date. As luck would have it, July 4, the date the Declaration of Independence was approved, became Independence Day rather than July 2, when independence was formally declared.

The celebration of Independence Day quickly became the most important public ritual in the United States. People suspended their normal routines to devote a day to parades, patriotic speeches, and fireworks displays. In the process, the infant republic began to create its own myth of national identity.

The new nation was not rooted in antiquity. Its people, except for the Native Americans, had not inhabited it over many centuries, nor was there any notion of a common ethnic descent. "The American national consciousness," one observer wrote, "is not a voice crying out of the depth of the dark past, but is proudly a product of the enlightened present, setting its face resolutely toward the future."

Many people, at least since the time of the Pilgrims, had thought of the New World as singled out by God for a special mission. John Adams proclaimed the opening of America "a grand scheme and design in Providence for the illumination and the emancipation of the slavish part of mankind all over the earth."

This sense of providential mission provided much of the energy for America's development as a new republic. From the democratic rhetoric of Thomas Jefferson to the pragmatism of George Washington to heady toasts bellowed in South Carolina taverns, patriots everywhere claimed a special role for American leadership. People believed that God was guiding the United States to lead the world toward greater liberty and equality. Benjamin Rush, a Philadelphia doctor and scientist, issued a prophetic statement in 1787: "The American war is over: but this is far from being the case with the American Revolution. On the contrary, but the first act of the great drama is closed."

George Washington acknowledged that important work remained. While retiring from military service, he penned a letter to the thirteen colonies in which he told the American people it would be "their choice . . . and conduct" that would determine whether the United States would become "respectable and prosperous, or contemptible and miserable as a Nation." Yet he remained hopeful, for Americans had already done the impossible: winning their independence on the battlefield. So he urged the citizenry to rejoice and be grateful as they set about demonstrating to a skeptical world that a large and unruly republic could survive and flourish.

CHAPTER REVIEW

SUMMARY

- **Military Challenges**   In 1776, the British had the mightiest army and navy in the world, and they supplemented their might by hiring professional German soldiers called *Hessians* to help put down the American Revolution. The Americans had to create an army—the Continental army—from scratch. George Washington realized that the Americans had to turn unreliable *citizen-soldiers* into a disciplined fighting force and try to wage a long, costly war that would force the British army, fighting thousands of miles from its home base, to cut its losses and eventually give up.

- **Turning Points**   After forcing the British to evacuate Boston, the American army suffered a string of defeats before George Washington surprised the Hessians at the *Battle of Trenton* at the end of 1776. The victory bolstered American morale and prompted more enlistments in the Continental army. The French were likely allies for the colonies from the beginning because they resented their losses to Britain in the Seven Years' War. After the British defeat at the *Battles of Saratoga (1777)*, the colonies brokered an *alliance with France*. Washington's ability to hold his ragged forces together, despite daily desertions and especially difficult winters in Morristown and *Valley Forge (1777–1778)*, provided another turning point. The British lost support on the frontier and in the southern colonies when terrorist tactics backfired. The Battle of Kings Mountain drove the British into retreat, and French supplies and the French fleet helped tip the balance and ensure the American victory at the *Battle of Yorktown (1781)*.

- **Civil War**   The American Revolution was also a civil war, dividing families and communities. There were at least 100,000 Loyalists in the colonies. They included royal officials, Anglican ministers, wealthy southern planters, and the elite in large seaport cities; they also included many humble people, especially recent immigrants. After the hostilities ended, many Loyalists, including slaves who had fled plantations to support the British cause, left for Canada, the West Indies, or England.

- **A Political and Social Revolution**   The American Revolution disrupted and transformed traditional class and social relationships. Revolutionaries embraced a *republican ideology*, and more white men gained the right to vote as property requirements were removed. But fears of a monarchy being reestablished led colonists to vest power in the states rather than in a national government under the *Articles of Confederation*. New *state constitutions* instituted more elected positions, and most included bills of rights that protected individual liberties. The *Virginia Statute of Religious Freedom (1786)* led the way in guaranteeing the separation of church and state, and religious toleration was transformed into religious freedom.

- **African Americans, Women, and Native Americans**   Northern states began to free slaves, but southern states were reluctant. Although many women had undertaken nontraditional roles during the war, afterward they remained largely confined to the domestic sphere, with no changes to their legal or political status. The Revolution had catastrophic effects on Native Americans, regardless of which side they had allied with during the war. American settlers seized Native American land, often in violation of existing treaties.

CHRONOLOGY

1776	British forces seize New York City
	General Washington's troops defeat British forces at the Battle of Trenton
	States begin writing new constitutions
1777	American forces defeat British in a series of battles at Saratoga
1778	Americans and French form a military alliance
	George Rogers Clark's militia defeats British troops in Mississippi Valley
1779	American forces defeat the Iroquois Confederacy at Newtown, New York
1780	Patriots defeat Loyalists at the Battle of Kings Mountain
1781	British invasion of southern colonies turned back at the Battles of Cowpens and Guilford Courthouse
	American and French forces defeat British at Yorktown, Virginia
	Articles of Confederation are ratified
	Continental Congress becomes Confederation Congress
1783	Treaty of Paris is signed, formally ending the Revolutionary War
1786	Virginia adopts the Statute of Religious Freedom

KEY TERMS

Hessians p. 184

citizen-soldiers p. 184

Battle of Trenton (1776) p. 190

Battles of Saratoga (1777) p. 195

alliance with France p. 197

Valley Forge (1777–1778) p. 197

Battle of Yorktown (1781) p. 207

republican ideology p. 209

state constitutions p. 209

Articles of Confederation p. 211

Virginia Statute of Religious Freedom (1786) p. 214

 INQUIZITIVE

Go to InQuizitive to see what you've learned—and learn what you've missed—with personalized feedback along the way.

6 Strengthening the New Nation

***Washington as a Statesman at the Constitutional Convention* (1856)** This painting by Junius Brutus Stearns is one of the earliest depictions of the drafting of the Constitution, capturing the moment after the convention members, including George Washington (right), completed the final draft.

During the 1780s, the United States of America was rapidly emerging as the lone large republic in an unstable world dominated by monarchies. The new nation was distinctive in that it was born out of a conflict over ideas, principles, and ideals rather than from centuries-old racial or ancestral bonds, as in Europe and elsewhere.

America was a democratic republic "brought forth" by certain self-evident political ideals—that people should govern themselves through their elected representatives, that everyone should have an equal opportunity to prosper ("the pursuit of happiness"), and that governments exist to protect liberty and promote the public good. Those ideals were captured in lasting phrases: All men are created equal. Liberty and justice for all. *E pluribus unum* ("Out of many, one"—the phrase on the official seal of the United States). How Americans understood, applied, and violated these ideals shaped the nation's development after 1783.

POWER TO THE PEOPLE

The American Revolution created not only an independent republic but also a different conception of politics than prevailed in Europe. What Americans most feared was governmental abuse of power. Memories of the "tyranny" of Parliament, King George III, his prime ministers, and royal colonial governors were still raw. Freedom from such arbitrary power had been the ideal guiding

focus questions

1. What were the strengths and weaknesses of the Articles of Confederation? How did they prompt the creation of a new U.S. constitution in 1787?

2. What political innovations did the 1787 Constitutional Convention develop for the new nation?

3. What were the debates surrounding the ratification of the Constitution? Explain how they were resolved.

4. In what ways did the Federalists' vision for the United States differ from that of their Republican opponents during the 1790s?

5. Assess how the attitudes toward Great Britain and France shaped American politics in the late eighteenth century.

the American Revolution, while the freedom to "pursue happiness" became the ideal driving the new nation.

To ensure their new freedoms, the Revolutionaries wrestled with a fundamental question: What is the proper role and scope of government? In answering that question, they eventually developed new ways to divide power among the various branches of government so as to manage the tensions between ensuring liberty and maintaining order.

But America after the war was a nation in name only. The Confederation was less a national government of "united states" than a league of thirteen independent, squabbling states. After all, the Articles of Confederation had promised that "Each state retains its sovereignty, freedom, and independence." The quest for true nationhood after the Revolution was the most significant political transformation in modern history, for Americans would insist that sovereignty (ultimate power) resided not with a king or aristocracy but with "the people," the mass of ordinary citizens.

FORGING A NEW NATION Americans had little time to celebrate victory in the Revolutionary War. As Alexander Hamilton, a brilliant army officer turned congressman, noted in 1783, "We have now happily concluded the great work of independence, but much remains to be done to reach the fruits of it."

The transition from war to peace was neither simple nor easy. America was independent but not yet a self-sustaining nation. In fact, the Declaration of Independence never mentioned the word *nation*. Its official title was "the unanimous Declaration of the thirteen united States of America."

Forging a new *nation* out of a *confederation* of thirteen rebellious colonies-turned-"free-and-independent"-states posed huge challenges, not the least of which was managing what George Washington called a "deranged" economy suffocating in war-related debts. The accumulated debt was $160 million, a huge amount at the time.

The period from the drafting of the Declaration of Independence in 1776, through the creation of the new federal constitution in 1787, and ending with the election of Thomas Jefferson as president in 1800, was fraught with instability and tension. From the start, the new nation experienced political divisions, economic distress, and foreign troubles.

Three fundamental questions shaped political debate during the last quarter of the eighteenth century. Where would sovereignty reside in the new nation? What was the proper relationship of the states to each other and to the national government? And what was required for the new republic to flourish as an independent nation? The efforts to answer those questions created powerful tensions that continue to complicate American life.

THE CONFEDERATION GOVERNMENT

John Quincy Adams, a future president, called the years between 1783 and 1787 the "Critical Period" when American leaders developed sharp differences about economic policies, international relations, and the proper relationship of the states to the national government. Debates over those issues unexpectedly gave birth to the nation's first political parties and, to this day, continue to influence the American experiment in **federalism** (the sharing of power among national, state, and local governments).

After the war, many Patriots who had feared government power and criticized British officials for abusing it now directed their attacks at the new state and national governments. At the same time, state legislatures desperate for funds to pay off their war debts sparked unrest and riots by raising taxes.

The clashes between the working poor and state governments were a great disappointment to Washington, John Adams, and other Revolutionary leaders. For them and others disillusioned by the surge of "democratic" rebelliousness, the Critical Period was a time of hopes frustrated, a story shaded by regret at the absence of national loyalty and international respect. The weaknesses of the Articles of Confederation in dealing with the postwar turmoil led political leaders to design an entirely new national constitution and federal government.

A LOOSE ALLIANCE OF STATES The **Articles of Confederation**, formally approved in 1781, had created a loose alliance (confederation) of thirteen independent states that were united only in theory. In practice, each state government acted on its own. The first major provision of the Articles insisted that "each state retains its sovereignty, freedom, and independence."

The weak national government under the Articles had only one component, a one-house legislature. There was no president, no executive branch, no national judiciary (court system). State legislatures, not voters, appointed the members of the Confederation Congress, in which each state, regardless of size or population, had one vote. This meant that Rhode Island, with 68,000 people, had the same power in the Congress as Virginia, with more than 747,000 inhabitants.

George Washington called the Confederation "a half-starved, limping government." It could neither regulate trade nor create taxes to pay off the country's war debts. It could approve treaties but had no power to enforce their terms. It could call for raising an army but could not force men to serve.

The Congress, in short, could not enforce its own laws, and its budget relied on "voluntary" contributions from the states. In 1782, for example, the Confederation asked the states to provide $8 million for the national government; they sent $420,000. The lack of state support forced the Congress to print paper money, called Continentals, whose value plummeted to 2 cents on the dollar as more and more were printed, leading to the joking phrase, "Not worth a Continental." Virtually no gold and silver coins remained in circulation; they had all gone abroad to purchase items for the war.

It was hard to find people to serve in such a weak Congress, and people openly doubted the stability of the new republic. As John Adams wrote to Thomas Jefferson, "The Union is still to me an Object of as much Anxiety as ever independence was."

ROBERT MORRIS The closest thing to an executive leader of the Confederation was Robert Morris, who as superintendent of finance in the final years of the war became the most influential figure in the government. Morris wanted to make both himself and the Confederation government more powerful. He envisioned a program of taxation and debt management to make the national government financially stable. "A public debt supported by public revenue will prove the strongest cement to keep our confederacy together," he confided to a friend.

The powerful financiers who had lent the new government funds to buy supplies and pay its bills, Morris believed, would give stronger support to a government committed to paying its debts. He therefore welcomed the chance to enlarge the national debt by issuing new government bonds that would help pay off wartime debts. With a sounder federal Treasury—one with the power to raise taxes—the bonds could be expected to rise in value, creating new capital with which to finance banks and economic development.

To anchor his plan, Morris in 1781 secured a congressional charter for the Bank of North America, which would hold government cash, lend money to the government, and issue currency. Though a national bank, it was in part privately owned and was expected to turn a profit for Morris and other shareholders, in addition to performing a crucial public service. Morris's program, however, depended upon the government having a secure income, and it foundered on the requirement of unanimous state approval for amendments to the Articles of Confederation.

LAND POLICY In ending the Revolutionary War, the Treaty of Paris doubled the size of the United States, extending the nation's western boundary to the Mississippi River. Under the Articles of Confederation, land outside the boundaries of the thirteen original states became *public domain*, owned and administered by the national government.

Between 1784 and 1787, the Confederation Congress created three major ordinances (policies) detailing how the lands in the West would be surveyed, sold, and developed. These ordinances rank among the Confederation's greatest achievements, for they provided the framework for western settlement that would shape much of the nation's development during the nineteenth century.

Thomas Jefferson drafted the Land Ordinance Act of 1784, which urged states to drop their competing claims to Indian-held territory west of the Appalachian Mountains so that the vast, unmapped area could be divided into as many as fourteen self-governing *territories* of equal size. In the new territories, all adult white males would be eligible to vote, hold office, and write constitutions for their territorial governments. When a territory's population equaled that of the smallest existing state (Rhode Island), it would be eligible for statehood. In other words, the western territories would not be treated as American colonies but as future states governed by republican principles.

Jefferson assumed that individual pioneers should be allowed to settle the western territories. George Washington and others, however, predicted chaos if migration were unregulated. Clashes with Indians would generate constant warfare, and disputes over land and boundaries would foster incessant bickering.

So before Jefferson's plan could take effect, the Confederation Congress created the Land Ordinance of 1785. It called for organizing the Northwest Territory on America's immediate western border (what would become the states of Ohio, Michigan, Indiana, Illinois, and Wisconsin) into townships of thirty-six square miles that would be surveyed, sold for less than a dollar an acre, and settled. Then the surveyors would keep moving westward, laying out more townships for settlement.

Wherever Indian lands were purchased—or taken—they were surveyed and divided into six-mile-square townships laid out along a grid running east–west and north–south. Each township was in turn divided into thirty-six sections one mile square (640 acres), with each section divided into four farms. The 640-acre sections of "public lands" were to be sold at auctions, the proceeds of which would go to the national Treasury.

THE NORTHWEST ORDINANCE Two years after passage of the Land Ordinance of 1785, the Confederation Congress passed the **Northwest Ordinance** of 1787. It set forth two key principles to better manage western expansion: the new western territories would eventually become coequal states, as Jefferson had originally proposed, and slavery would be banned from the region north of the Ohio River. (Slaves already living there would remain slaves.) The Northwest Ordinance also included a promise, which would be repeatedly broken, that Indian lands "shall never be taken from them without their consent."

For a new territory to become a state, the Northwest Ordinance specified a three-stage process. First, Congress would appoint a territorial governor and other officials to create a legal code and administer justice. Second, when the population of adult males reached 5,000, they could elect a territorial legislature. Third, when a territory's population reached 60,000 "free inhabitants," the adult males could draft a constitution and apply to Congress for statehood.

DIPLOMACY After the Revolutionary War, relations with Great Britain and Spain remained tense because both nations retained trading posts, forts, and soldiers on American soil, and both encouraged Indians to resist American efforts to settle on tribal lands. The British refused to remove their troops stationed south of the Canadian border in protest of the failure of Americans to pay their prewar debts. Another major irritant was the American seizure of Loyalist property during the war.

With Spain, the chief issues pertained to disputes about the location of the southern boundary of the United States and the right for Americans to send boats or barges down the Mississippi River, which Spain then controlled. After the Seven Years' War in 1763, Spain had acquired the Louisiana Territory, which included the port of New Orleans, the Mississippi River, and all the area west to the Rocky Mountains. After the Revolution, Spain closed the Mississippi to American use, infuriating settlers in Kentucky and Tennessee. Spain had also regained ownership of Florida, which then included southern Alabama. Thereafter, the Spanish governor in Florida provided firearms to Creek Indians, who resisted American encroachment on their lands in south Georgia.

TRADE AND THE ECONOMY More troublesome than the behavior of the British and the Spanish was the fragile state of the American economy. Seven years of warfare had nearly bankrupted the new nation. At the same time, many who had served in the army had never been paid. Nor had civilians who had loaned money, supplies, crops, and livestock to the war effort been reimbursed.

THE OLD NORTHWEST, 1785

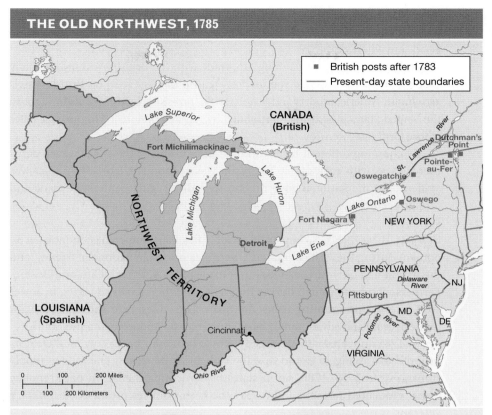

- How did the Northwest Ordinance of 1787 revise Jefferson's earlier plan for territorial government?
- How were settlement patterns in the Northwest territories different from those on the frontier near the South?
- How did the United States treat Native American claims to their ancestral lands in the West?

After the war, the British treated the United States as an enemy nation, insisting that all Americans who had been born in England were still bound by allegiance to King George III. British warships began stopping and boarding American ships in the Atlantic, kidnapping English-born American sailors, and "impressing" them into service in the Royal Navy.

The British also closed their profitable Caribbean island colonies to American commerce. New England shipowners and southern planters were especially hard-hit, as exports of tobacco, rice, rum, and other commodities remained far below what they had been before the war. After 1783, merchant ships were allowed to deliver American products to England and return to the United States with English goods. But U.S. vessels could not carry British goods anywhere else.

To punish Britain for banning U.S. trade with the British West Indies, many state governments imposed special taxes (called tonnage fees) on British vessels arriving in American ports and levied tariffs (taxes) on British goods brought to the United States. The British responded by sending their ships to ports in states whose tariff rates were lower.

By charging different tariffs on the same products, the states waged commercial war with each other. The result was economic chaos. By 1787, it was evident that the national government needed to regulate interstate trade and foreign relations.

SCARCE MONEY   Complex financial issues also hampered economic development during the Critical Period. There was no stable national currency, and the nation had only three banks—in Philadelphia, New York City, and Boston. Farmers who had profited during the war found themselves squeezed by lower crop prices and mounting debts and taxes. The widespread shortage of "hard money" (gold and silver coins) caused people to postpone paying their bills.

By 1785, indebted citizens urged states to print new paper currency. Debtors believed that doing so would ease their plight by increasing the money supply (inflation). In 1785–1786, seven states began issuing their own paper money to help indebted farmers and to pay the cash bonuses promised to military veterans.

The "Gathering Crisis"

The economic difficulties weakening the Confederation were compounded by growing fears among wealthy "gentlemen" leaders ("natural aristocrats") that the democratic energies unleashed by the Revolution were undermining the authority of the social and economic elite. Class distinctions were disappearing as many among the working poor and "middling classes" stopped deferring to their "betters."

The so-called better sort of people were appalled at the "leveling" behavior of the "antifederal peasants," "little folks," and "demagogues." A Virginia aristocrat grumbled that the "spirit of independency" that inspired the Revolution was being "converted into equality."

The political culture was also changing. More men could vote and hold office as property-owning qualifications were reduced or eliminated in several states. The nation, said wealthy New Yorker John Jay, was headed toward "Evils and Calamities" because the masses were gaining power and often taking the law into their own hands. At the same time, Jay declared the federal government "incompetent." Achieving nationhood had become more challenging than gaining independence. The Confederation was less a government than an association of independent states.

No sooner was the war over than Americans with large debts again began to protest taxes. To pay their war debts, most state legislatures had sharply increased taxes. In fact, during the 1780s, most Americans paid three times as much in taxes as they had under British "tyranny." Earlier, they had objected to taxation *without* representation; now, they objected to taxation *with* representation.

In New Hampshire, in what was called the Exeter Riot, hard-pressed farmers surrounded the legislative building, demanding that the representatives print paper money to ease their plight. Similar appeals occurred in other states. The economic and political elites were horrified that the "new men" were endangering the real value of property by encouraging the printing of more money, for doing so would inflate the money supply and thereby reduce the purchasing power of currency.

SHAYS'S REBELLION Fears of a taxpayer "revolt from below" became all too real in western Massachusetts, when struggling farmers, many of them former Revolutionary soldiers, demanded that the state issue more paper money and give them additional time to pay "unjust" taxes. Farmers also resented the new state constitution because it *raised* the property qualifications for voting and holding elected office, thus stripping poorer men of political power.

When the merchant-dominated Massachusetts legislature refused to provide tax relief, three rural counties erupted in a disorganized revolt in 1786. Armed groups of angry farmers, called Regulators, banded together to force judges and sheriffs to stop seizing the cattle and farms of those who could not pay their taxes. "Close down the courts," they shouted.

Shays's Rebellion Shays and his followers demanded that states issue paper currency to help ease the payment of debts and the right to postpone paying taxes until the postwar agricultural depression lifted.

The situation worsened when a ragtag "army" of unruly farmers that included thirty-nine-year-old Daniel Shays, a distinguished war veteran, marched on the federal arsenal at Springfield in the winter of 1787. The state government responded by sending 4,400 militiamen, who scattered the debtor army with a single cannon blast that left four farmers dead and many wounded. Shays fled to Vermont. Several rebels were arrested, and two were hanged. The rebels nevertheless earned a victory of sorts, as the legislature agreed to eliminate some of the taxes and fees.

News of **Shays's Rebellion** sent shock waves across the nation. In Massachusetts, Abigail Adams, the wife of future president John Adams, dismissed Shays and his followers as "ignorant, restless desperadoes, without conscience or principles." George Washington was equally concerned. America, he said, needed a "government by which our lives, liberty, and properties will be secured." Unless an alternative could be found to the weak Confederation government, "anarchy and confusion will inevitably ensue."

CREATING THE CONSTITUTION

In the wake of Shays's Rebellion, a collective shiver passed through what John Jay called "the better kind of people." Many among the "rich and well-born" agreed with George Washington that the nation was "tottering." The time had come to empower the national government to bring social order and economic stability.

THE "CRISIS IS ARRIVED" During the 1780s, newspapers warned that the nation's situation had grown "critical and dangerous." The states were behaving like thirteen ungovernable nations, pursuing their own trade regulations and foreign policies. "Our present federal government," said Henry Knox, a Boston bookseller and much-celebrated Revolutionary War general, "is a name, a shadow, without power, or effect."

Such concerns led political leaders to revise their assessment of the republic. It was time, said James Madison, to create a new federal constitution that would repair the "vices of the political system" and "decide forever the fate of republican government." Alexander Hamilton urged that a national gathering of delegates be given "full powers" to revise the Articles of Confederation.

THE CONSTITUTIONAL CONVENTION In 1787, the Confederation Congress responded by calling for a special "federal" convention to gather in the East Room of Philadelphia's State House (now known as Independence

Hall) for the "purpose of revising the Articles of Confederation." Only Rhode Island refused to participate. That the delegates would be meeting in the same room where the Declaration of Independence had been debated and signed gave the convention added significance.

The delegates began work on May 25, 1787, meeting five hours a day, six days a week. Although the states appointed fifty-five delegates, there were never that many in attendance. Some quit in disgust; others were distracted by other priorities. Yet after fifteen weeks of deliberations, thirty-nine delegates signed the new federal constitution on September 17. Only three refused to sign.

The durability of the Constitution reflects the thoughtful and talented men who created it. They were all white; their average age was forty-two, with the youngest being twenty-six. Most were members of the political and economic elite. Twenty-

James Madison This 1783 miniature shows Madison at thirty-two years old, just four years before he would assume a major role in drafting the Constitution.

six were college graduates, two were college presidents, and thirty-four were lawyers. Others were planters, merchants, bankers, and clergymen.

About twenty-five delegates owned slaves, including George Washington and James Madison. In fact, Washington arrived in Philadelphia with three of his slaves, one of whom, Billy Lee, stood behind his chair at every session, tending to his owner's personal needs.

Yet the "Founding Fathers" were also practical men of experience. Of the twenty-two who had fought in the Revolutionary War, five had been captured and imprisoned. Seven had been state governors, and eight had helped write their state constitutions. Most had been members of the Continental or Confederation Congresses, and eight had signed the Declaration of Independence.

DRAFTING THE CONSTITUTION George Washington was unanimously elected as the presiding officer at the Federal Convention (later renamed the Constitutional Convention). He participated little in the debates, however, for fear that people would take his opinions too seriously. The governor of Pennsylvania, eighty-one-year-old Benjamin Franklin, the oldest delegate, was in such poor health that he had to be carried to the meetings in a special chair, borne aloft by four husky inmates from the Walnut Street jail. Like Washington, Franklin said little from the floor but provided a wealth of experience, patience, wit, and wisdom behind the scenes.

Most active at the Convention was James Madison of Virginia, the ablest political theorist in the group. A thirty-six-year-old attorney who owned a huge tobacco plantation called Montpelier, not far from Thomas Jefferson's Monticello, Madison had arrived in Philadelphia with trunks of books about government—and a head full of ideas.

Barely five feet tall and weighing only 130 pounds (a colleague said he was "no bigger than half a piece of soap"), Madison was too frail and sickly to serve in the Revolutionary army. Madison "speaks low, his person [body] is little and ordinary," and he was "too timid in his politics," remarked Fisher Ames of Massachusetts.

Although shy and soft-spoken, Madison had an agile mind, a huge appetite for learning, and a commitment to public service. He had served in the Continental Congress, where he had become a full-blooded nationalist. Now he resolved to ensure the "supremacy of national authority." The logic of his arguments—and his willingness to compromise—proved decisive in shaping the new constitution. "Every person seems to acknowledge his greatness," said a Georgia delegate.

Most delegates agreed with Madison that the republic needed a stronger national government, weaker state legislatures, and the power to restrain the "excessive" democratic impulses unleashed by the Revolution. "The evils we experience," said Elbridge Gerry of Massachusetts, "flow from the excess of democracy."

Two interrelated assumptions guided the Constitutional Convention: that the national government must have direct authority over the citizenry rather than governing through the state governments, and that the national government must derive its legitimacy from the "genius of the people" rather than from the state legislatures. Thus, the final draft of the Constitution begins: "We the people of the United States, in Order to form a more perfect Union, . . . do ordain and establish this Constitution for the United States of America."

The insistence that the voters were "the legitimate source of all authority," as James Wilson of Pennsylvania stressed, was the most important political innovation since the Declaration of Independence. No other nation endowed "the people" with such authority. By declaring the Constitution to be the voice of the people, the founders authorized the federal government to limit the powers of the states.

The delegates realized, too, that an effective national government needed authority to collect taxes, borrow and issue money, regulate commerce, fund an army and navy, and make laws. This meant that the states must be stripped of the power to print paper money, make treaties, wage war, and levy taxes and tariffs on imported goods. This concept of dividing authority between the national government and the states came to be called federalism.

THE VIRGINIA AND NEW JERSEY PLANS James Madison drafted the framework for the initial discussions at the Constitutional Convention. His proposals, called the Virginia Plan, started with a radical suggestion: that the delegates scrap their original instructions to *revise* the Articles of Confederation and instead create a *new* constitution.

Madison's Virginia Plan called for a "*national* government [with] a *supreme* legislative, executive, and judiciary." It proposed a Congress divided into two houses (bicameral): a lower House of Representatives chosen by the "people of the several states" and an upper house of senators elected by the state legislatures. The more populous states would have more representatives in Congress than the smaller states. Madison also wanted to give Congress the power to veto state laws.

The Virginia Plan sparked furious disagreements. When asked why the small states were so suspicious of the plan, Gunning Bedford of Delaware replied: "I do not, gentlemen, trust you."

On June 15, Bedford and other delegates submitted an alternative called the New Jersey Plan, developed by William Paterson of New Jersey. It sought to keep the existing equal representation of the states in a unicameral (one-house) national legislature. It also gave Congress the power to collect taxes and regulate commerce and the authority to name a chief executive as well as a supreme court, but not the right to veto state laws.

THE THREE BRANCHES OF GOVERNMENT

The intense debate over congressional representation was resolved in mid-July by the so-called Great Compromise, which used elements of both plans. Roger Sherman of Connecticut suggested that one chamber of the proposed Congress have its seats allotted according to population, with the other preserving the principle of one vote for each state. And that is what happened. The more populous states won apportionment (the allocation of delegates to each state) by population in the proposed House of Representatives, while the delegates who sought to protect state power won equality of representation in the Senate, where each state would have two members elected by the legislatures.

THE LEGISLATURE The Great Compromise embedded the innovative concept of **separation of powers** in the new Congress. While Madison believed that in "a republican government, the legislative authority necessarily predominates," he and others also sought to keep the Congress from becoming too powerful. To do so, they divided it into two separate houses, with the House of Representatives representing voters at large and the Senate representing state legislatures.

The House of Representatives would be, in George Mason's words, "the grand repository of the democratic principle of the Government." Its members would be elected by voters every *two* years. (Under the Articles of Confederation, members of Congress had been chosen by state legislatures.) Madison argued that allowing individual citizens to elect the people's House was "essential to every plan of free government." Indeed, such representative democracy centered on majority rule was the essence of a republican form of government.

Several delegates did not share such faith in representative democracy. The problems arising since the end of the war, according to Elbridge Gerry, "flow from an excess of democracy." Yet, as Benjamin Franklin countered, if the "common people" and "lower classes" were noble enough to fight for independence, then they were capable of exercising good citizenship. Madison agreed. The citizens of the American republic should be the "People of the United States"—"not the rich, more than the poor; not the learned more than the ignorant; not the haughty heirs of distinguished names, more than the humble sons of obscure fortune."

The Framers viewed the upper house, or Senate, as a check on the excesses of democracy. It would be a more elite group of substantial property holders, its members elected by state legislatures for *six*-year terms. The Senate could use its power to overrule the House or the president. Madison explained that the Senate would help "protect the minority of the opulent against the majority."

THE PRESIDENCY The Constitutional Convention struggled over issues related to the executive branch. Some delegates wanted a powerful president who could veto acts of Congress. Others felt that the president should simply "execute" the laws as passed by Congress. Still others, like Benjamin Franklin, wanted a "plural executive" rather than a single man governing the nation.

The eventual decision to have a single chief executive, a "natural born Citizen" at least thirty-five years old of any or no religion, caused many delegates "considerable pause," according to Madison. George Mason of Virginia feared that a single president might start behaving like a king.

In the end, several compromises ensured that the president would be powerful enough to counterbalance the Congress. The president, to be elected for four-year terms, could veto acts of Congress, which would then be subject to being overridden by a two-thirds vote in each house. The president became the nation's chief diplomat and commander in chief of the armed forces, and was responsible for implementing the laws made by Congress.

Yet the president's powers were also limited in key areas. The chief executive could neither declare war nor make peace; only Congress could. Moreover, the president could be removed from office. The House of Representatives could impeach (bring to trial) the chief executive—and other civil officers—on charges of treason, bribery, or "other high crimes and misdemeanors." An impeached president must leave office if two-thirds of the Senate voted for conviction.

To preserve the separation of the three branches of government, the president would be elected every four years by a group of highly qualified "electors" chosen by "the people" in local elections. Each state's number of electors would depend upon the combined number of its congressional representatives and senators. This "electoral college" was a compromise between those wanting the president elected by Congress and those preferring a direct vote of qualified citizens.

THE JUDICIARY The third proposed branch of government, the judiciary, sparked little debate. The Constitution called for a supreme national court headed by a chief justice. The court's role was not to make laws (a power reserved to Congress) or to execute and enforce the laws (reserved to the presidency), but to *interpret* the laws and to ensure that every citizen received *equal justice* under the law.

The U.S. Supreme Court had final authority in interpreting the Constitution and in settling constitutional disputes between states. Furthermore, Article VI of the Constitution declared that the federal Constitution, federal laws, and treaties were "the supreme Law of the Land."

THE LIMITS OF THE CONSTITUTION

The men who drafted the new constitution claimed to be representing all Americans. In fact, however, as Senator Stephen Douglas of Illinois would note seventy years later, the Constitution was "made by white men, for the benefit of white men and their posterity [descendants] forever."

Important groups were left out of the Constitution's protections. Native Americans, for example, could not be citizens unless they paid taxes, which

Signing the Constitution, September 17, 1787 Thomas Pritchard Rossiter's painting shows George Washington presiding over what Thomas Jefferson called "an assembly of demi-gods" in Philadelphia.

few did. The Constitution declared that Native American "tribes" were not part of the United States but instead were separate "nations."

SLAVERY Of all the issues that emerged during the Constitutional Convention of 1787, none was more explosive than slavery. As James Madison stressed, "the great division of interest" among the delegates "did not lie between the large & small states: it lay between the Northern & Southern," primarily from "their having or not having slaves."

When the Patriots declared independence in 1776, slavery existed in every state. By 1787, however, Massachusetts, Pennsylvania, Connecticut, and Rhode Island had abolished the dreadful system.

Many of the framers viewed slavery as an embarrassing contradiction to the principles of liberty and equality embodied in the Declaration of Independence and the new Constitution. A New Jersey delegate declared that owning human beings was "utterly inconsistent with the principles of Christianity and humanity."

By contrast, most southern delegates stoutly defended slavery. "Religion and humanity [have] nothing to do with this [slavery] question," argued John Rutledge of South Carolina. "Interest alone is the governing principle of nations." His fellow South Carolinian, Charles Pinckney, stressed the practical reality in the southern states: "South Carolina and Georgia cannot do without slaves."

Most southern delegates would have walked out of the convention had there been an attempt to abolish slavery. So in drafting the new constitution, the framers decided not to include any plan for limiting or ending slavery, nor did they view the enslaved as human beings with civil rights.

If the slaves were not to be freed or their rights to be acknowledged, however, how were they to be counted? Since the size of state delegations in the proposed House of Representatives would be based on population, southern delegates argued that slaves should be counted to help determine how many representatives their state would have. Northerners countered that it made no sense to count slaves for purposes of congressional representation when they were treated as property.

The delegates finally agreed to a compromise in which three-fifths of "all other persons" (the enslaved) would be included in population counts as a basis for apportioning a state's congressional representatives. In a constitution intended to "secure the blessings of liberty to ourselves and our posterity," the three-fifths clause was a glaring example of compromise being divorced from principle.

The corrupt bargain over slavery would bedevil the nation for the next seventy-five years, for the more slaves southern states imported from Africa, the more seats in Congress they would gain. Gouverneur Morris of New York, who would draft the final version of the Constitution, asked the delegates to imagine a Georgian or Carolinian going to Africa, where, "in defiance of the most sacred laws of humanity, [he] tears away his fellow creatures from their dearest connections & damns them to the most cruel bondages." By doing so, the southern slaveholder "shall have more votes in a Govt. instituted for the protection of the rights of mankind than the citizen of Pennsylvania or New Jersey who views with a laudable horror so nefarious a practice."

Charles Calvert and His Slave
(1761) In military regalia, the five-year-old descendant of Lord Baltimore, founder of Maryland, towers over his slave, who is dressed as a drummer boy.

In another concession to southerners, the original Constitution never mentions the word *slavery*. As slaveholder James Madison explained, it would be "wrong to admit in the Constitution the idea that there could be property in men." Instead, the document speaks of "free persons" and "all other persons" and of persons "held to service of labor." The word *slavery* would not appear in the Constitution until the Thirteenth Amendment (1865) abolished it.

Delaware's John Dickinson protested that "omitting of the WORD will be regarded [by the world] as an Endeavor to conceal a principle of which we are ashamed." As it was. The Constitution openly violated Thomas Jefferson's idealistic assertion in the Declaration of Independence that "all men are created equal."

THE ABSENCE OF WOMEN   The delegates at the Constitutional Convention dismissed any discussion of political rights for women. Yet not all women were willing to maintain their subordinate role. Just as the Revolutionary War enabled many African Americans to seize their freedom, it also inspired some brave women to demand political equality.

Eliza Yonge Wilkinson, born in 1757 to a wealthy plantation family near Charleston, South Carolina, lost her husband early in the war. In June 1780, after Wilkinson was assaulted and robbed by "inhuman" British soldiers, she became a fiery Patriot who "hated Tyranny in every shape." She assured a friend, "We may be *led*, but we never will be *driven*!"

Likewise, Wilkinson expected greater freedom for women after the war. "The men say we have no business [with politics]," she wrote to a friend. "I won't have it thought that because we are the weaker sex as to bodily strength, my dear, we are capable of nothing more than minding the dairy, visiting the poultry-house, and all such domestic concerns." Wilkinson demanded more. "They won't even allow us the liberty of thought, and that is all I want."

Judith Sargent Murray, a Massachusetts writer, argued that the rights and liberties fought for by Patriots belonged not just to men but to women, too. In her essay "On the Equality of the Sexes," published in 1790, she challenged the prevailing view that men had greater intellectual capacities than women. She insisted that any differences resulted from prejudice and discrimination that prevented women from having access to formal education and worldly experience.

The arguments for gender equality, however, fell mostly on deaf ears. The Constitution does not even include the word *women*. Writing from Paris,

Thomas Jefferson expressed the hope that American "ladies" would be "contented to soothe and calm the minds of their husbands returning ruffled from political debate."

IMMIGRATION   Although America was a nation of immigrants, leaders of the new nation had differing views about whether the United States should remain a nation open to foreigners of all sorts. Thomas Jefferson, for example, worried that many immigrants would not understand or embrace the new republic's democratic premises. Would not the new nation, he asked, be "more homogeneous, more peaceful, more durable" without large-scale immigration?

The Constitution said little about immigration and naturalization (the process of gaining citizenship), and most of what it said was negative. In Article II, Section 1, it prohibits any future immigrant from becoming president, limiting the office to a "born Citizen." On defining citizenship, the Constitution gives Congress the authority "to establish a uniform Rule of Naturalization" but offers no further guidance. As a result, naturalization policy has changed repeatedly over the years in response to fluctuating social attitudes, economic needs, and political moods.

THE FIGHT FOR RATIFICATION

On September 17, 1787, the Federal Convention reported that it had completed the new constitution. George Washington was the first to sign. "Gentlemen," announced Benjamin Franklin, "you have a republic, if you can keep it."

Then, for the first time in world history, the people were invited to discuss, debate, and vote on the national constitution. The Confederation Congress sent the final draft of the Constitution to thirteen special state conventions for approval (ratification). Over the next ten months, people from all walks of life debated the new constitution's merits. As Alexander Hamilton noted, the debate would reveal whether the people could establish good government "by reflection and choice" or by "accident and force."

CHOOSING SIDES   Advocates for the Constitution assumed the name *Federalists*; opponents became **anti-Federalists**. The two sides formed the seeds for America's first two-party political system.

The Federalists, led by James Madison and Alexander Hamilton, had several advantages. First, they had a concrete proposal, the draft constitution itself; their opponents had nothing to offer but criticism. Second, their leaders were, on average, ten to twelve years younger and more energetic than the anti-Federalists; many of them had been members of the Constitutional Convention and were familiar with the disputed issues in the document. Third, the Federalists were more unified and better organized.

The anti-Federalist leaders—Virginians Patrick Henry, George Mason, Richard Henry Lee, and future president James Monroe; George Clinton of New York; Samuel Adams, Elbridge Gerry, and Mercy Otis Warren of Massachusetts; Luther Martin and Samuel Chase of Maryland—were a diverse group. Some wanted to retain the Confederation. Others wanted to start over. Still others wanted to revise the proposed constitution. Patrick Henry wanted the preamble to read "We the states" rather than "We the people," and he worried about a new constitution that "squints toward monarchy" by creating a powerful presidency.

Most anti-Federalists feared that the new government would eventually grow corrupt and tyrannical. A Philadelphia writer denounced those who drafted the Constitution as representing "the Aristocratic Party" intent upon creating a "monarchical" national government.

The anti-Federalists especially criticized the absence of a "bill of rights" to protect individuals and states from the growing power of the national government. Other than the bill of rights, however, the anti-Federalists had no comprehensive alternative to the Constitution.

THE FEDERALIST Among the supreme legacies of the debate over the Constitution is what came to be called **The Federalist Papers**, a collection of eighty-five essays published in New York newspapers between 1787 and 1788. Written by James Madison, Alexander Hamilton, and John Jay, the essays defended the concept of a strong national government and outlined the major principles and assumptions embodied in the Constitution. Thomas Jefferson called *The Federalist Papers* the "best commentary on the principles of government which ever was written."

In the most famous of the *Federalist* essays, No. 10, Madison warned that democracies "have in general been as short in their lives as they have been violent in their deaths." Their inherent flaw was the tendency of majorities to tyrannize minorities. As Benjamin Franklin explained, a "democracy is two wolves and a lamb voting on what to have for lunch."

Madison stressed that the greatest threat to rule by the people was the rise of "factions," special interest groups whose goals conflict with the interests and welfare of the greater community. Yet any effort to eliminate factions would require tyrannical controls. The goal instead should be to minimize the negative effects of factions.

To that end, Madison turned the conventional wisdom about republics on its head. From ancient times, it had been assumed that self-governing republics survived only if they were small and homogeneous. Madison, however, argued that small republics usually fell victim to warring factions. In the United States, he explained, the size and diversity of the expanding nation would make it impossible for any single faction to form a majority that could corrupt the federal government—or society at large. The contending factions would, in essence, cancel each other out. In addition, he argued that it was the responsibility of the Congress to regulate "these various and interfering interests." Madison and the other framers created a legal and political system designed to protect minorities from a tyranny of the majority.

Given a federal government in which power was shared among the three federal branches, a large republic could work better than a small one to balance "clashing interests" and keep them in check. "Extend the [geographic] sphere," Madison wrote, "and you take in a greater variety of parties and interests; you make it less probable that a majority of the whole will have a common motive to invade the rights of other citizens."

If men were angels, Madison noted in *Federalist* No. 51, all forms of government would be unnecessary. In framing a national government "which is to be administered by men over men," however, "the great difficulty lies in this: you must first enable the government to control the governed; and in the next place oblige it to control itself."

THE STATES DECIDE Delaware, New Jersey, and Georgia were among the first states to ratify the Constitution. Massachusetts, still sharply divided in the aftermath of Shays's Rebellion, was the first state in which the outcome was close, approving the Constitution by 187 to 168 on February 6, 1788.

On June 21, 1788, New Hampshire became the ninth state to ratify the Constitution, thereby reaching the minimum number of states needed for approval. The Constitution, however, could hardly succeed without the approval of Virginia, the largest, wealthiest, and most populous state, or New York, which had the third-highest population and occupied a key position geographically. Both states included strong opposition groups who were eventually won over by an agreement to add a bill of rights.

Upon notification of New Hampshire's decision to ratify the Constitution, the Confederation Congress chose New York City as the national

New beginnings An engraving from the title page of *The Universal Asylum and Columbian Magazine* (published in Philadelphia in 1790). America is represented as a woman laying down her shield to engage in education, art, commerce, and agriculture.

capital and called for the new government to assume power in 1789. The Constitution was adopted, but the resistance to it convinced the new Congress to propose the first ten constitutional amendments, now known as the Bill of Rights.

"Our Constitution is in actual operation," Benjamin Franklin wrote a friend in 1789. "Everything appears to promise that it will last; but in this world nothing is certain but death and taxes." George Washington was even more uncertain, predicting that the Constitution would not "last for more than twenty years."

The Constitution has lasted much longer, of course, and its complexity and adaptability have provided a model of resilient republican government in which, as Jefferson noted, power was "created and constrained at the same time." The Constitution was by no means perfect (after all, it has been amended twenty-seven times); it was a bundle of messy compromises and concessions that left many issues, notably slavery, undecided or ignored. But most of its supporters believed that it was the best frame of government obtainable and that it would continue to evolve and improve. It laid the groundwork and

RATIFICATION OF THE CONSTITUTION

ORDER OF RATIFICATION	STATE	DATE OF RATIFICATION
1	Delaware	December 7, 1787
2	Pennsylvania	December 12, 1787
3	New Jersey	December 18, 1787
4	Georgia	January 2, 1788
5	Connecticut	January 9, 1788
6	Massachusetts	February 6, 1788
7	Maryland	April 28, 1788
8	South Carolina	May 23, 1788
9	New Hampshire	June 21, 1788
10	Virginia	June 25, 1788
11	New York	July 26, 1788
12	North Carolina	November 21, 1789
13	Rhode Island	May 29, 1790

provided the ideals for later generations to build upon, and it remains the oldest national constitution in the world.

The Constitution confirmed that the United States would be the first *democratic republic* in history. The founders believed that they were creating a unique political system based on a "new science of politics" combining the best aspects of democracies and republics. In a democracy, the people rule; in a republic, officials elected by the people rule. At the Constitutional Convention, the delegates combined elements of both approaches so that they balanced and regulated each other, and ensured that personal freedoms and the public welfare were protected.

THE FEDERALIST ERA

The Constitution was ratified because it promised to create a more powerful national government better capable of managing a rapidly growing republic. Yet it was one thing to ratify a new constitution and quite another to make the new government run smoothly.

With each passing year, the United States debated how to interpret and apply the provisions of the new constitution. During the 1790s, the federal government would confront rebellions, states threatening to secede, international tensions, and foreign wars, as well as the formation of competing political parties—Federalists and Democratic Republicans, more commonly known as **Jeffersonian Republicans**, or simply as Republicans.

The two parties came to represent different visions for America. The Democratic Republicans were mostly southerners, like Virginians Thomas Jefferson and James Madison, who wanted the country to remain a rural nation of small farmers dedicated to republican values. They distrusted the national government, defended states' rights, preferred a "strict" interpretation of the Constitution, and placed their trust in the masses. "The will of the majority, the natural law of every society," Jefferson insisted, "is the only sure guardian of the rights of men."

The Federalists, led by Alexander Hamilton and John Adams, were clustered in New York and New England. They embraced urban culture, industrial development, and commercial growth. Federalists feared the "passions" of the common people and advocated a strong national government and a flexible interpretation of the Constitution. As Hamilton stressed, "the people are turbulent and changing; they seldom judge or determine right."

THE FIRST PRESIDENT On March 4, 1789, the new Congress convened in New York City. A few weeks later, the presiding officer of the Senate certified that George Washington, with 69 electoral college votes, was the nation's first president. John Adams of Massachusetts, with 34 votes, the second-highest number, became vice president. (At this time, no candidates ran specifically for the vice presidency; the presidential candidate who came in second, regardless of party affiliation, became vice president.)

Washington greeted the news of his unanimous election with a "heart filled with distress," likening himself to "a culprit who is going to the place of his execution." He would have preferred to stay in "retirement" at Mount Vernon, his "peaceful" Virginia plantation, but agreed to serve because he had been "summoned by [his] country."

Some complained that Washington's personality was too cold and aloof, and that he lacked sophistication. Adams groused that Washington was "too illiterate, unlearned, [and] unread" to be president. As a French diplomat observed, however, Washington had "the soul, look, and figure of a hero in action."

Born in Virginia in 1732, Washington was a largely self-educated former surveyor, land speculator, and soldier whose father had died when he was eleven. In 1759 he married Martha Dandridge Custis, a young widow with two small children and one of the largest fortunes in Virginia. In the years that followed, he became a prosperous tobacco planter and land speculator. Although reserved and dignified in public, Washington loved riding horses, hunting foxes, playing cards or billiards, fishing, hosting oyster roasts, and drinking wine.

The fifty-seven-year-old Washington brought to the presidency both a detached reserve and a remarkable capacity for leadership. Although capable of angry outbursts, he was honest, honorable, and disciplined; he had extraordinary stamina and patience, integrity and resolve, courage and resilience. And he exercised sound judgment and remarkable self-control. Most of all, he was fearless. Few doubted that he was the best person to lead the new nation. People already were calling him the "father of his country."

In his inaugural address, Washington appealed for unity, pleading with the Congress to abandon "local prejudices" and "party animosities" to create the "national" outlook necessary for the fledgling republic to thrive. Within a few months, he would see his hopes dashed. Personal rivalries, sectional tensions, and political infighting would dominate life in the 1790s.

WASHINGTON'S CABINET President Washington faced massive challenges, and he knew full well that every decision he made would be invested with special significance. "The eyes of America—perhaps of the world—are turned to this Government," he said. He was entering "untrodden ground" and therefore must ensure that his actions were based on "true principles."

During the summer of 1789, Congress created executive departments corresponding to those formed under the Confederation. To head the Department of State, Washington named Thomas Jefferson. To lead the Department of the Treasury, he appointed Alexander Hamilton, who was widely read in matters of government finance. Henry Knox was secretary of war and John Jay became the first chief justice of the Supreme Court.

Washington routinely called his chief staff members together to discuss matters of policy. This was the origin of the president's *cabinet*, an advisory body for which the Constitution made no formal provision. The office of vice president also took on what would become its typical character. "The Vice-Presidency," John Adams wrote his wife Abigail, is the most "insignificant office . . . ever . . . contrived."

THE BILL OF RIGHTS To address concerns raised by opponents of the new federal government, James Madison, now a congressman from Virginia, presented to Congress in May 1789 a set of constitutional amendments intended to protect individual rights. As Thomas Jefferson explained, such a "bill of rights is what the people are entitled to against every government on earth, general or particular, and what no just government should refuse." After considerable debate, Congress approved twelve amendments in September 1789. By the end of 1791, the necessary three-fourths of the states had approved *ten* of the twelve proposed amendments, now known as the **Bill of Rights**.

The Bill of Rights provided safeguards for individual rights of speech, assembly, religion, and the press; the right to own firearms; the right to refuse to house soldiers; protection against unreasonable searches and seizures; the right to refuse to testify against oneself; the right to a speedy public trial, with an attorney present, before an impartial jury; and protection against "cruel and unusual" punishments. The Tenth Amendment addressed the widespread demand that powers not delegated to the national government "are reserved to the States respectively, or to the people."

The amendments were written in broad language that seemed to exclude no one. In fact, however, they technically applied only to property-owning white males. Native Americans were entirely outside the constitutional system, an "alien people" in their own land. And, like the Constitution itself, the Bill of Rights gave no protections to enslaved Americans. Similar restrictions applied to women, who could not vote in most state and national elections. Equally important, the Bill of Rights had a built-in flaw: it did not protect citizens from states violating their civil rights.

Still, the United States was the first nation to put such safeguards into its government charter. While the Constitution had designed a vigorous federal government binding together the thirteen states, the Bill of Rights provided something just as necessary: codifying the individual rights and freedoms without which the government or a tyrannical majority might abuse "the people."

RELIGIOUS FREEDOM The debates over the Constitution and the Bill of Rights generated a religious revolution as well as a political revolution. Unlike the New England Puritans, whose colonial governments enforced their particular religious beliefs, the Christian men who drafted and amended the Constitution made no direct mention of God. They were determined to protect religious life from government interference and coercion.

In contrast to the monarchies of Europe, the United States would keep the institutions of church and government separate and allow people to choose their own religions ("freedom of conscience"). To that end, the First Amendment declared that "Congress shall make no law respecting an establishment of religion or prohibiting the free exercise thereof." This statement has since become one of the most important—and controversial—principles of American government.

The First Amendment created a framework within which people of all religious persuasions could flourish and prohibited the federal government from endorsing or supporting any denomination or interfering with the religious choices that people make. As Thomas Jefferson later explained, the First Amendment erected a "wall of separation between church and State."

IMMIGRATION AND NATURALIZATION In the list of grievances against King George in the Declaration of Independence, Thomas Jefferson had charged that the monarch had "endeavored to prevent the population of these States" by "obstructing the laws for naturalization of foreigners, [and] refusing to pass others to encourage their migration hither."

To ensure that America continued to share its "blessings of liberty" with immigrants, the Constitution called upon Congress to create policies to accommodate the continuing stream of immigrants from around the world. George Washington had strong feelings on the matter. He viewed America's open embrace of refugees and immigrants as one of the nation's most important values.

In 1783, amid the excitement of the end of the Revolutionary War, General Washington had assured a group of recent Irish immigrants that "the bosom of America is open to receive not only the opulent & respectable Stranger, but the oppressed & persecuted of all Nations & Religions." Five years later, he reiterated his desire for America to continue to be "a safe and agreeable asylum to the virtuous and persecuted part of mankind, to whatever nation they might belong." He and many other founders viewed a growing population as a national blessing.

President Washington, in his first address to Congress in 1790, urged the legislators to craft a "liberal" naturalization law to attract immigrants. Congress responded with the Naturalization Act of 1790, which specified that any "free white person" could gain citizenship ("naturalization") after living at least two years

A BILL to eſtabliſh an uniform Rule of Naturalization, and to enable Aliens to hold Lands under certain Reſtrictions.

Naturalization in 1790 A detail of the bill that established "an uniform Rule of Naturalization" that made it possible for immigrants to hold lands.

in the United States. (In 1795, Congress increased the residency requirement to five years.) This law established an important principle: immigrants were free to renounce their original citizenship to become American citizens.

During the 1790s, some 100,000 European immigrants arrived in the United States, beginning a process that would grow with time. Because of its liberal naturalization policy, the United States has admitted more people from more places than any other nation in the world.

HAMILTON'S VISION OF A PROSPEROUS AMERICA

In 1776, the same year that Americans were declaring their independence, Adam Smith, a Scottish philosopher, published a revolutionary book titled *An Inquiry into the Nature and Causes of the Wealth of Nations*. It provided the first full description of what would come to be called a modern *capitalist* economy and its social benefits. (The term *capitalism* would not appear until 1850.)

Alexander Hamilton The powerful Secretary of the Treasury from 1789 to 1795.

The Wealth of Nations was a declaration of independence from Great Britain's mercantilist system. Under *mercantilism*, national governments had exercised tight control over economic life. Smith argued that instead of controlling economic activity, governments should allow individuals and businesses to compete freely for profits in the marketplace. By liberating individual self-interest and entrepreneurial innovation from the constraints of government authority, he theorized, the welfare of society would be enhanced. The poverty that had entrapped the masses of Europe for centuries would end to the extent that governments allowed for "free enterprise," by which individuals, through their hard work and ingenuity, could at last gain earthly happiness and prosperity.

Smith also explained that the strongest national economies would be those in which *all* the major sectors were flourishing—agriculture, trade, banking, finance, and manufacturing. By allowing investors to funnel cash into productive enterprises, jobs would increase, profits would soar, and economic growth would ensue.

Alexander Hamilton greatly admired *The Wealth of Nations*, and as secretary of the Treasury he took charge of managing the nation's complicated financial affairs. He grasped the complex issues of government finance and envisioned what America would become: the world's most prosperous capitalist nation. He believed that the federal government should encourage the creative spirit that distinguished Americans from other peoples.

Hamilton was a self-made and self-educated aristocrat—and he was also an immigrant. Born out of wedlock in the West Indies in 1755, he was deserted at age ten by his Scottish father and left an orphan at thirteen by the death of his mother. With the help of friends and relatives, he found his way to New Jersey in late 1772 before moving a year later to New York City. There he entered King's College (now Columbia University).

When the war with Britain erupted, Hamilton joined the Continental army as a captain at the age of nineteen. He distinguished himself in the battles of Trenton and Princeton and became one of General Washington's favorite aides. After the war, he established a thriving legal practice in New York City, married into a prominent family, and served as a member of the Confederation Congress.

Hamilton became the foremost advocate for an "energetic government" promoting vibrant economic development. In contrast to Jefferson, the southern planter, Hamilton, the urban financier, believed that the United States was too dependent on agriculture. He championed trade, banking, finance, investment, and manufacturing, as well as bustling commercial cities, as the most essential elements of America's future.

HAMILTON'S ECONOMIC REFORMS The United States was born in debt. To fight the war for independence, it had borrowed heavily from the Dutch and the French. After the war, it had to find a way to pay off the debts. Yet there was no national bank, no national currency, and few mills and factories. In essence, the American republic was bankrupt. It fell to Alexander Hamilton to determine how the debts should be repaid and how the new national government could balance its budget.

Governments have four basic ways to pay their bills: (1) impose taxes or fees on individuals and businesses; (2) levy tariffs (taxes on imported goods); (3) borrow money by selling interest-paying government bonds to investors; and, (4) print money.

Under Hamilton's leadership, the United States did all these things—and more. To raise funds, Congress, with Hamilton's support, enacted tariffs of 5 to 10 percent on a variety of imported items. Tariffs were hotly debated because they were the source of most of the federal government's annual revenue, and they "protected" American manufacturers by taxing their foreign competitors, especially those in Britain.

By discriminating against imported goods, tariffs enabled American manufacturers to charge higher prices for their products sold in the United States. This penalized consumers, particularly those in the southern states that were most dependent upon imported goods. In essence, tariffs benefited the nation's young manufacturing sector, most of which was in New England, at the expense of the agricultural sector, since farm produce was rarely imported. Tariff policy soon became an explosive political issue.

DEALING WITH DEBTS The levying of tariffs marked but one element in Alexander Hamilton's plan to put the new republic on sound financial footing. In a series of "Reports on Public Credit" submitted to Congress between January 1790 and December 1791, Hamilton outlined his visionary program for the economic development of the United States.

The first report dealt with how the federal government should refinance the massive debt the states and the Confederation government had accumulated. Hamilton insisted that the debts be repaid. After all, he explained, a robust economy depended upon its integrity and reliability: debts being paid, contracts being enforced, and private property being protected.

Selling government bonds to pay the interest due on the war-related debts, Hamilton argued, would provide investors ("the monied interest") a direct stake in the success of the new government. He also insisted that the federal government pay ("assume") the state debts from the Revolutionary War because they were a *national* responsibility; all Americans had benefited from the war for independence. "The debt of the United States," he stressed, "was the price of liberty." A well-managed federal debt that absorbed the state debts, he claimed, would be a "national blessing," provide a "mechanism for national unity," and promote long-term prosperity.

SECTIONAL DIFFERENCES Hamilton's far-sighted proposals created a storm of controversy, in part because many people, then and since, did not understand their complexities. James Madison, Hamilton's close ally in the fight for the new constitution, broke with him over the federal government "assuming" the states' debts.

Madison was troubled that northern states owed far more than southern states. Four states (Virginia, North Carolina, Georgia, and Maryland) had already paid off most of their war debts. The other states had not been as conscientious. Why should the southern states, Madison asked, subsidize the debts of the northern states?

Madison's fierce opposition to Hamilton's debt-assumption plan ignited a vigorous debate in Congress. In April 1790, the House of Representatives voted down the "assumption" plan, 32–29. Hamilton did not give up, however. After failing to get members of Congress to switch their votes, he asked Jefferson, the new secretary of state, to help break the impasse. In June 1790, Jefferson invited Hamilton and Madison to join him for dinner at his lodgings in New York City.

By the end of the evening, they had reached a famous compromise. First, they agreed that the national capital should move from New York City to Philadelphia for the next ten years, and then move to a new city to be built in a ten-mile-square "federal district" astride the Potomac River, sandwiched between the slave states of Maryland and Virginia. Hamilton agreed to find the votes in Congress to approve the move in exchange for Madison pledging to find the two votes needed to pass the debt-assumption plan.

The Compromise of 1790 went as planned. Congress voted as hoped, and the federal government moved in late 1790 to Philadelphia. Ten years later, the nation's capital moved again, this time to the new city of Washington, in the federal District of Columbia.

Hamilton's debt-funding scheme proved a success. The bonds issued by the federal government in 1790 were quickly snatched up by investors, providing money to begin paying off the war debts. In addition, Hamilton obtained new loans from European governments.

To raise additional revenue, Hamilton convinced Congress to create *excise* taxes on particular products, such as carriages, sugar, and salt. By 1794, the nation had a higher financial credit rating than all the nations of Europe. By making the new nation financially solvent, Hamilton set in motion the greatest economic success story in world history.

A NATIONAL BANK   Part of the opposition to Hamilton's debt-financing scheme grew out of opposition to Hamilton himself. The young Treasury secretary, arrogant and headstrong, viewed himself as President Washington's prime minister. That his Department of Treasury had *forty* staff members while Thomas Jefferson's State Department had *five* demonstrated the priority that Washington gave to the nation's financial situation.

Hamilton was on a mission to develop an urban-centered economy anchored in finance and manufacturing. After securing congressional approval of his debt-funding scheme, he called for a national bank modeled after the Bank of England. Such a bank, Hamilton believed, would enable much greater "commerce among individuals" and provide a safe place for the federal government's cash.

By their nature, Hamilton explained, banks were essential. They would increase the nation's money supply by issuing currency in amounts greater than the actual "reserve"—gold and silver coins and government bonds—in their vaults. By issuing loans and thereby increasing the amount of money in circulation, banks served as the engines of prosperity: "industry is increased, commodities are multiplied, agriculture and manufactures flourish, and herein consist the true wealth and prosperity" of a "genuine nation."

Once again, Madison and Jefferson led the opposition, arguing that, since the Constitution said nothing about creating a national bank, the government could not start one. Jefferson also believed that Hamilton's proposed bank would not help most Americans. Instead, a small inner circle of self-serving financiers and investors would, over time, exercise corrupt control over Congress.

Hamilton, however, had the better of the argument. Representatives from the northern states voted 33–1 in favor of the national bank; southern congressmen opposed it 19–6. The lopsided vote illustrated the growing political division between the North and South.

Before signing the bill, President Washington sought the advice of his cabinet, where he found an equal division of opinion. The result was the first great debate on constitutional interpretation. Were the powers of Congress only those *explicitly* stated in the Constitution, or were other powers *implied*? The argument turned chiefly on Article I, Section 8, which authorized Congress to "make all Laws which shall be necessary and proper for carrying into Execution the foregoing Powers."

Such language left lots of room for disagreement and led to a savage confrontation between Jefferson and Hamilton. The Treasury secretary had come to view Jefferson as a man of "profound ambition & violent passions," a "contemptible hypocrite" who was guided by an "unsound & dangerous" agrarian economic philosophy.

Thomas Jefferson A 1791 portrait by Charles Willson Peale.

Jefferson hated commerce, speculators, factories, banks, and bankers— almost as much as he hated the "monarchist" Hamilton. To thwart the proposed national bank, Jefferson pointed to the Tenth Amendment of the Constitution, which reserves to the states and the people powers not explicitly delegated to Congress. Jefferson argued that a bank might be a convenient aid to Congress in collecting taxes and regulating the currency, but it was not *necessary*, as Article I, Section 8 specified.

In a 16,000-word report to the president, Hamilton countered that the power to charter corporations was an "implied" power of any government. As he pointed out, the three banks already in existence had been chartered by states, none of whose constitutions specifically mentioned the authority to incorporate banks.

Hamilton convinced Washington to sign the bank bill. In doing so, the president had, in Jefferson's words, opened up "a boundless field of power," which in coming years would lead to a further broadening of the president's implied powers, with the approval of the Supreme Court.

The new **Bank of the United States** (B.U.S.), based in Philadelphia, had three primary responsibilities: (1) to hold the government's funds and pay its bills; (2) to provide loans to the federal government and to other banks to promote economic development; and (3) to manage the nation's money supply by regulating the power of state-chartered banks to issue paper currency or banknotes. The B.U.S. could issue national banknotes as needed to address the chronic shortage of gold and silver coins. By 1800, the B.U.S. had branches in four cities, and four more were soon added.

ENCOURAGING MANUFACTURING Hamilton's bold economic vision was not yet complete. In the last of his recommendations to Congress, the "Report on Manufactures," distributed in December 1791, he set in place the capstone of his design for a modern capitalist economy: the active governmental promotion of new manufacturing and industrial enterprises (mills, mines, and factories). Industrialization, Hamilton believed, would bring diversification to an American economy dominated by agriculture and dangerously dependent on imported British goods; improve productivity through greater use of machinery; provide work for those not ordinarily employed outside the home, such as women and children; and encourage immigration of skilled industrial workers from other nations.

To foster industrial development, Hamilton recommended that the federal government increase tariffs on imports, three quarters of which came from Britain, while providing financial incentives (called bounties) to key industries making especially needed products such as wool, cotton cloth, and window glass. Such government support, he claimed, would enable new industries to compete "on equal terms" with long-standing European enterprises. Finally, Hamilton asked Congress to fund major transportation improvements, including the development of roads, canals, and harbors.

Few of Hamilton's pro-industry ideas were enacted because of strong opposition from Jefferson, Madison, and other southerners. Hamilton's proposals, however, provided arguments for future advocates of manufacturing and federally funded transportation projects (called "internal improvements").

HAMILTON'S VISIONARY ACHIEVEMENTS Hamilton's leadership was monumental. During the 1790s, as the Treasury department began to pay off the Revolutionary War debts, foreign capitalists and banks invested heavily in the American economy, and European nations as well as China began a growing trade with the United States. Economic growth, so elusive in the 1780s, blossomed as the number of new businesses soared. A Bostonian reported that the nation had never "had a brighter sunshine of prosperity. . . . Our agricultural interest smiles, our commerce is blessed, our manufactures flourish."

All was not well, however. By championing the values and institutions of a bustling capitalist system and the big cities and industries that went with it, Hamilton upset many people, especially in the agricultural South and along the western frontier. Thomas Jefferson and James Madison had grown increasingly concerned that Hamilton's urban-industrial economic program and his political deal making threatened American liberties. Hamilton recognized that his successes had led Jefferson and Madison to form a party "hostile to me," one intent on making Jefferson the next president.

The political competition between Jefferson and Hamilton boiled over into a feud of pathological intensity. Both were visionaries, but where Hamilton envisioned a developing American economy and society modeled on that of Britain, Jefferson preferred to follow the example of France. The two men also had markedly different hopes for the nation's economic development and contrasting views of how the Constitution should be interpreted.

Jefferson told President Washington that Hamilton's efforts to create a capitalist economy would "undermine and demolish the republic" and lead to "the most corrupt government on earth." Hamilton, he added, was "really a colossus [giant] to the anti-republican party." In turn, Hamilton called Jefferson an "intriguing incendiary" who had circulated "unkind whispers" about him. He accused Jefferson of being an agrarian romantic who failed to see that manufacturing, industry, and banking would drive the nation's economic future.

Jefferson's intensifying opposition to Hamilton's politics and policies fractured Washington's cabinet. Jefferson wrote that he and Hamilton "daily pitted in the cabinet like two cocks [roosters]." Washington urged them to rise above their toxic "dissensions," but it was too late. They had become mortal enemies, as well as the leaders of the first loosely organized political parties, the Federalists and the Democratic Republicans.

FEDERALISTS AND DEMOCRATIC REPUBLICANS

The Federalists were centered in New York and New England, and were also powerful among the planter elite in South Carolina. Generally, they feared the excesses of democracy, distrusted the "common people," and wanted a strong central government led by the wisest leaders who would be committed to economic growth, social stability, and national defense. What most worried the Federalists, as Alexander Hamilton said, was the "poison" of "DEMOCRACY." The people, he stressed, were "turbulent and changing; they seldom judge or determine right [wisely]."

By contrast, the Democratic Republicans, led by Thomas Jefferson and James Madison, were most concerned about threats to individual freedoms and states' rights posed by a strong national government. They trusted the people. As Madison said, "Public Opinion sets bounds to every government and is the real sovereign in every free one." The Democratic Republicans were strongest in the southern states—Virginia, North Carolina, and Georgia. Most Democratic Republicans promoted an agricultural economy.

Unexpected events in Europe influenced the two parties. In July 1789, violence erupted in France when masses of the working poor, enraged over soaring prices for bread and in part inspired by the American Revolution, revolted against the absolute monarchy of Louis XVI.

The **French Revolution** captured the imagination of many Americans, especially Jefferson and the Democratic Republicans, as royal tyranny was displaced by a democratic republic that gave voting rights to all adult men regardless of how much property they owned. Americans formed forty-two Democratic-Republican clubs that hosted rallies on behalf of the French Revolution and in support of local Republican candidates.

FOREIGN AND DOMESTIC CRISES

During the nation's fragile infancy, George Washington was the only man able to rise above party differences. In 1792, he was unanimously reelected to a second term—and quickly found himself embroiled in the cascading consequences of the French Revolution.

In 1791, the monarchies of Prussia and Austria had invaded France to stop the revolutionary movement from infecting their absolutist societies. The invaders, however, only inspired the French revolutionaries to greater efforts to spread their ideal of democracy.

By early 1793, the most radical of the French revolutionaries, called *Jacobins*, had executed the king and queen, as well as hundreds of aristocrats and priests. The Jacobins not only promoted democracy, religious toleration, and human rights, but social, racial, and sexual equality. Then, on February 1, 1793, the French revolutionary government declared war on Great Britain, Spain, and the Netherlands, thus beginning a European-wide conflict that would last twenty-two years.

As the French republic plunged into warfare, the Revolution entered its worst phase, the so-called Reign of Terror. In 1793–1794, Jacobins executed thousands of "counterrevolutionary" political prisoners and Catholic priests, along with many revolutionary leaders. Barbarism ruled the streets.

Secretary of State Thomas Jefferson, who loved French culture and democratic ideals, wholeheartedly endorsed the Revolution. He even justified the Reign of Terror by asserting that the "tree of liberty must be refreshed from time to time with the blood of patriots and tyrants." By contrast, Alexander Hamilton and John Adams saw the French Revolution as vicious and godless, and they sided with Great Britain and its allies. Such conflicting attitudes transformed the first decade of American politics into one of the most fractious periods in the nation's history—an "age of passion."

The European war tested the ability of the United States to remain neutral in world affairs. Both France and Britain purchased goods from America, and each sought to stop the other from trading with the United States, even if it meant attacking U.S. merchant ships.

As President Washington began his second term in 1793, he faced an awkward decision. By the 1778 Treaty of Alliance, the United States was a *perpetual* ally of France. Americans, however, wanted no part of the war.

Hamilton and Jefferson agreed that entering the conflict would be foolish. Where they differed was in how best to stay out. Hamilton wanted to declare the military alliance formed with the French during the American Revolution invalid because it had been made with a monarchy that no longer existed. Jefferson preferred to use the alliance with France as a bargaining point with the British.

In the end, Washington took a wise middle course. On April 22, 1793, he issued a neutrality proclamation that declared the United States "friendly and impartial toward the belligerent powers" and warned U.S. citizens that they might be prosecuted for "aiding or abetting hostilities" or taking part in other unneutral acts. Instead of settling matters in his cabinet, however, the neutrality proclamation brought to a boil the ugly feud between Jefferson and Hamilton.

CITIZEN GENÊT At the same time that President Washington issued the neutrality proclamation, he accepted Thomas Jefferson's argument that the United States should officially recognize the French revolutionary government and welcome its ambassador to the United States, the cocky, twenty-nine-year-old Edmond-Charles Genêt.

In April 1793, Citizen Genêt, as he became known, landed at Charleston, South Carolina, to a hero's welcome. He then openly violated U.S. neutrality by recruiting four American privateers (privately owned warships) to capture English and Spanish merchant vessels.

After five weeks in South Carolina, Genêt traveled to the American capital, Philadelphia, where his efforts to draw America into the war on France's side embarrassed his friends in the Republican party. When Genêt threatened to go around President Washington and appeal directly to the American people, even Thomas Jefferson disavowed "the French monkey." In August 1793, Washington, at Hamilton's urging, demanded that the French government replace Genêt.

The growing excesses of the radicals in France were quickly cooling U.S. support for the Revolution. Jefferson, however, was so disgusted by his feud with Hamilton and by Washington's refusal to support the French that he resigned as secretary of state at the end of 1793 and returned to his Virginia home, eager to be rid of the "hated occupation of politics."

Vice President Adams greeted Jefferson's departure by saying "good riddance." President Washington felt the same way. He never forgave Jefferson and Madison for organizing Democratic-Republican clubs to oppose his policies. After accepting Jefferson's resignation, Washington never spoke to him again.

JAY'S TREATY During 1794, tensions between the United States and Great Britain threatened to renew warfare between the old enemies. The Treaty of Paris (1783) that ended the Revolutionary War had left the western and southern boundaries of the United States in dispute. In addition, in late 1793, British warships violated international law by seizing U.S. merchant ships that carried French goods or were sailing for a French port. By early 1794, several hundred American ships had been confiscated, and their crews were given the terrible choice of joining the British navy, a process called "impressment," or being imprisoned. At the same time, British troops in the Ohio Valley gave weapons to Indians, who in turn attacked American settlers.

On April 16, 1794, President Washington sent Chief Justice John Jay to London to settle the major issues between the two nations. Jay agreed to the British demand that America not sell products to France for the construction of warships. The British refused, however, to stop intercepting American merchant ships and "impressing" their sailors. Finally, Jay conceded that the British need not compensate U.S. citizens for the enslaved African Americans who had escaped to the safety of British forces during the Revolutionary War.

In return, Jay won three important promises from the British: They would (1) evacuate their six forts in northwest America by 1796; (2) reimburse Americans for the seizures of ships and cargo in 1793–1794; and, (3) grant U.S. merchants the right to trade again with the island economies of the British West Indies.

When the terms of **Jay's Treaty** were disclosed, many Americans, especially Republicans, were outraged. The wildly unpopular treaty deepened the division between Federalists and Republicans. Jefferson dismissed the treaty as an "infamous act" intended to "undermine the Constitution." The uproar created the most serious crisis of Washington's presidency. Some called for his impeachment. Yet the president decided that the proposed agreement was the only way to avoid a war with Britain that the United States was bound to lose.

In 1795, with Washington's support, Jay's Treaty barely won the necessary two-thirds majority in the Senate. Some 80 percent of the votes *for* the treaty came from New England or the middle Atlantic states; 74 percent of those opposed were southerners, most of them Jeffersonian Republicans.

Washington sighed that he had ridden out "the Storm," but he could never forget the "pernicious" figures "disseminating the acidic poison" against him. Weary of partisan squabbles, he longed to return home to Virginia. But Washington had given the young nation a precious gift—peace. No other leader could have pushed the controversial treaty through Congress.

FRONTIER TENSIONS Meanwhile, new conflicts erupted in the Ohio Valley between American settlers and Native Americans. In the fall of 1793, General "Mad" Anthony Wayne led a military expedition into the Northwest Territory's "Indian Country." His troops marched north from Cincinnati, built Fort Greenville in western Ohio, and soon went on the offensive in what became known as the Northwest Indian War, a conflict that arose after the British transferred the Ohio Country to the United States. The Native Americans living in the region insisted that the British had no right to give away their ancestral lands. As pioneers moved into the Northwest Territory, the various Indian nations formed the Western Confederacy to resist American settlement.

In August 1794, the Western Confederacy of some 2,000 Shawnee, Ottawa, Chippewa, Delaware, and Potawatomi warriors, supported by the British and reinforced by Canadian militiamen, attacked General Wayne's troops and Indian allies in the Battle of Fallen Timbers, along the Michigan-Ohio border. The Americans decisively defeated the Indians, destroyed their crops and villages, and built a line of forts in northern Ohio and Indiana. The Indians finally agreed to the Treaty of Greenville, signed in August 1795, by which the United States bought most of the territory that would form the state of Ohio and the cities of Detroit and Chicago. The treaty also established clear boundaries between Indian and American territories.

THE WHISKEY REBELLION Soon after the Battle of Fallen Timbers, the Washington administration displayed another show of strength in the backcountry, this time against the so-called **Whiskey Rebellion**.

Alexander Hamilton's 1791 tax on "distilled spirits" had ignited resistance among cash-poor farmers throughout the western frontier. Liquor made from grain or fruit was the region's most valuable product; it even was used as a form of currency. When efforts to repeal the tax failed, many turned to violence and intimidation. Beginning in September 1791, angry groups of farmers, militiamen, and laborers attacked federal tax collectors and marshals.

In the summer of 1794, the discontent exploded into rebellion in western Pennsylvania, home to a fourth of the nation's whiskey stills. A mob of angry farmers threatened to assault nearby Pittsburgh, loot the homes of the rich, and set the town ablaze. After negotiations failed, a U.S. Supreme Court justice declared on August 4, 1794, that western Pennsylvania was in a "state of rebellion." It was the first great domestic challenge to the federal government, and George Washington responded decisively.

At Hamilton's urging, Washington ordered the whiskey rebels ("enemies of order") to disperse by September 1 or he would send in the militia. When the rebels failed to respond, some 12,500 militiamen from several states began marching to western Pennsylvania. Washington donned his military uniform and rode on horseback to greet the soldiers. It was the first and last time that a sitting president would lead troops in the field.

The huge army, commanded by Virginia's governor, Henry "Lighthorse Harry" Lee, panicked the whiskey rebels, who vanished into the hills. Two dozen were charged with high treason; two were sentenced to hang, only to be pardoned by Washington.

Whiskey Rebellion George Washington as commander in chief reviews the troops mobilized to quell the Whiskey Rebellion in Pennsylvania in 1794.

The government had made its point, and the show of force led the rebels and their sympathizers to change their tactics. Rather than openly defying federal laws, they voted for Republicans, who won heavily in the next Pennsylvania elections.

PINCKNEY'S TREATY While events were unfolding in Pennsylvania, the Spanish began negotiations over control of the Mississippi River and the disputed northern boundary of their Florida colony, which they had acquired at the end of the Revolutionary War. U.S. negotiator Thomas Pinckney pulled off a diplomatic triumph in 1795 when he convinced the Spanish to accept a southern American boundary at the 31st parallel in west Florida, along the northern coast of the Gulf of Mexico (the current boundary between Florida and Georgia). The Spanish also agreed to allow Americans to ship goods, grains, and livestock down the Mississippi River to Spanish-controlled New Orleans. Senate ratification of Pinckney's Treaty (also called the Treaty of San

Lorenzo) came quickly, for westerners were eager to transport their crops and livestock to New Orleans.

WESTERN SETTLEMENT

The treaties signed by John Jay and Thomas Pinckney spurred a new wave of settlers into the western territories. Their lust for land aroused a raging debate in Congress over what the federal government should do with the vast areas it had acquired or taken from the British, the Spanish, and the Native Americans.

LAND POLICY Federalists wanted the government to charge high prices for western lands to keep the East from losing both political influence and a labor force important to the growth of manufacture. They also preferred that government-owned lands be sold in large parcels to speculators, rather than in small plots to settlers. Thomas Jefferson and James Madison were reluctantly prepared to go along with these policies for the sake of reducing the national debt, but Jefferson preferred that government-owned land be sold to farmers rather than speculators.

For the time being, the Federalists prevailed. With the Land Act of 1796, Congress doubled the price of federal land (public domain) to $2 per acre. Half the townships would be sold in 640-acre sections, making the minimum cost $1,280, a price well beyond the means of ordinary settlers. By 1800, federal land offices had sold fewer than 50,000 acres. Criticism of the policies led to the Land Act of 1800, which reduced the minimum parcel to 320 acres and spread payments over four years. Thus, with a down payment of $160, one could buy a farm.

THE WILDERNESS ROAD The lure of western lands led thousands of settlers to follow pathfinder Daniel Boone into the territory known as Kentucky, or Kaintuck, from the Cherokee KEN-TA-KE (Great Meadow). In the late eighteenth century, the Indian-held lands in Kentucky were a farmer's dream and a hunter's paradise, with their fertile soil, bluegrass meadows, abundant forests, and countless buffalo, deer, and wild turkeys.

Born on a small farm in 1734 in central Pennsylvania, Boone became one of America's first folk heroes, a larger-than-life figure known as the "Columbus of the Woods." He was a deadeye marksman, experienced farmer, and accomplished woodsman.

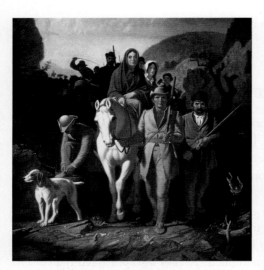

**Daniel Boone Escorting Settlers
through the Cumberland Gap**
Painting by George Caleb Bingham.

After hearing numerous reports about the lands over the Appalachian Mountains, he set out in 1769 to find a trail into Kentucky. He discovered what was called the Warriors' Path, a narrow foot trail that buffalo, deer, and Native Americans had worn along the steep ridges over the centuries.

In 1773, Boone led a group of white settlers into Kentucky. Two years later, he and thirty woodsmen used axes to widen the 208-mile-long Warriors' Path into what became known as the Wilderness Road, a passageway that more than 300,000 settlers would use over the next twenty-five years.

At a point where a branch of the Wilderness Road intersected with the Kentucky River, near what is now Lexington, Boone built the settlement of Boonesborough.

TRANSFER OF POWER

In 1796, President Washington decided that serving two terms in office was enough. Weary of the criticism directed at him, he was eager to retire to Mount Vernon. He would leave behind a formidable record of achievement, including the organization of a new national government, a prosperous economy, the recovery of territory from Britain and Spain, a stable northwestern frontier, and the admission of three new states: Vermont (1791), Kentucky (1792), and Tennessee (1796). Of the nine presidents who were slave owners, he alone would grant his slaves their freedom upon his death.

WASHINGTON'S FAREWELL On September 17, 1796, Washington delivered a farewell address in which he criticized the rising spirit of political partisanship and the emergence of political parties. They endangered the republic, he felt, because they pursued the narrow interests of minorities rather than the good of the nation. In foreign relations, Washington advised, the United States should stay away from Europe's quarrels by avoiding "permanent alliances with any portion of the foreign world." His warning would serve as a fundamental principle in U.S. foreign policy until the early twentieth century.

THE ELECTION OF 1796 With Washington out of the race, the United States had its first contested election for president. The Federalist "caucus," a group of leading congressmen, chose high-spirited Vice President John Adams as their candidate. As expected, the Republicans chose Thomas Jefferson. Aaron Burr, a young New York attorney and senator, also ran as a Republican.

The campaign was nasty. The Federalists were attacked for unpopular taxes, excessive spending, and abuses of power. Republicans called the pudgy John Adams "His Rotundity" and labeled him a monarchist because he loved symbols of power and despised "the people." Federalists countered that Jefferson was a French-loving atheist eager for another war with Great Britain and charged that he was not decisive enough to be president.

Adams won the election with 71 electoral votes, but in an odd twist, Jefferson, who received 68 electoral votes, became vice president. The Federalists won control of both houses of Congress.

THE ADAMS ADMINISTRATION

Vain and prickly, opinionated and stubborn, John Adams had long lusted for the presidency, but he was a much better political theorist than he was a political leader. An independent thinker with a combative spirit and volcanic temper, he fought as often with his fellow Federalists, especially Alexander Hamilton, as with his Republican opponents. Benjamin Franklin said Adams was "always an honest man, often a wise one, but sometimes . . . absolutely out of his senses."

Widely recognized as the hardest-working member of the Continental Congress, Adams had authored the Massachusetts state constitution. During the Revolution, he had served as an exceptional diplomat in France, Holland, and Great Britain, and he had been George Washington's vice president.

In contrast to the tall, lanky Jefferson, the short, stocky Adams feared democracy and despised equality. He once referred to ordinary Americans as the "common herd of mankind." He also felt that he was never properly appreciated—and he may have been right. Yet on the essential issue of his presidency, war and peace, he kept his head when others about him were losing theirs—probably at the cost of his reelection.

John Adams Political philosopher and politician, Adams was the first president to take up residence in the Executive Mansion, in the new national capital of Washington, D.C., in 1801.

THE WAR WITH FRANCE As America's second president, John Adams inherited a "Quasi War" with France, a by-product of the angry French reaction to Jay's Treaty between the United States and Great Britain. The navies of both nations were capturing U.S. ships headed for the other's ports. By the time of Adams's inauguration, in 1797, the French had plundered some 300 American vessels and broken diplomatic relations with the United States.

Adams sought to ease tensions by sending three Americans to Paris to negotiate an end to the attacks on U.S. ships. When the Americans arrived, however, they were accosted by three French officials (labeled X, Y, and Z by Adams in his report to Congress) who announced that negotiations could begin only if the United States paid a bribe of $250,000 and loaned France $12 million.

Such bribes were common in the eighteenth century, but the answer from the American side was "no, no, not a sixpence." When the so-called XYZ Affair became public, American hostility toward France soared. Many Republicans—with the exception of Vice President Jefferson—joined with Federalists in calling for war.

Federalists in Congress voted to construct warships and triple the size of the army. Adams asked George Washington to command the army again. Washington reluctantly agreed on the condition that his favorite lieutenant, Alexander Hamilton, be appointed a major general. By the end of 1798, French and American ships were engaged in an undeclared naval war in the Caribbean Sea.

THE WAR AT HOME The conflict with France sparked an intense debate between Federalists eager for a formal declaration of war and Republicans sympathetic to France. Amid the superheated emotions, Vice President Jefferson observed that a "wall of separation" divided the nation's leaders.

For his part, Adams had tried to take the high ground. Soon after his election, he had invited Jefferson to join him in creating a bipartisan administration.

Conflict with France A cartoon indicating the anti-French sentiment generated by the XYZ Affair. The three American negotiators (at left) reject the Paris Monster's demand for bribery money before discussions could begin.

Jefferson refused, saying that he would not be a part of the cabinet and would only preside over the Senate as vice president, as the Constitution specified. Within a year, he and Adams were at each other's throats. Adams regretted losing Jefferson as a friend but "felt obliged to look upon him as a man whose mind is warped by prejudice." Jefferson, he claimed, had become "a child and the dupe" of the Republicans in Congress.

Jefferson and other Republicans were convinced that the real purpose of the French crisis was to give Federalists an excuse to quiet their American critics. Perhaps no issue was more divisive in the 1790s than that posed by the immigrants coming from the war-torn European nations. Federalists worried that in the shadow of the French Revolution, the newcomers would bring social and political radicalism with them.

The **Alien and Sedition Acts of 1798** confirmed Republican suspicions that the Federalists were willing to go to any lengths to suppress freedom of speech. These partisan laws, passed amid a wave of patriotic war fervor, gave the president extraordinary powers to violate civil liberties protected by the Bill of Rights, all in a clumsy effort to stamp out criticism of the administration. They limited freedom of speech and of the press, as well as the liberty of "aliens" (immigrants who had not yet gained citizenship).

Adams's support of the Alien and Sedition Acts ("war measures") would prove to be the greatest mistake of his presidency. Timothy Pickering, his secretary of state, claimed that Adams agreed to the acts without consulting "any member of the government and for a reason truly remarkable—because he knew we should all be opposed to the measure."

Three of the four Alien and Sedition Acts reflected hostility toward French and Irish immigrants, many of whom had supported the French Revolution or the Irish Rebellion against British authority and had become militant Democratic Republicans in America. The Naturalization Act lengthened from five to fourteen years the residency requirement for immigrants ("aliens") to gain U.S. citizenship. It also required all immigrants to register with the federal government. The Alien Friends Act empowered the president to jail and deport "dangerous" aliens, and the Alien Enemies Act authorized the president in wartime to expel or imprison aliens from enemy nations. Finally, the Sedition Act outlawed writing, publishing, or speaking anything of "a false, scandalous and malicious" nature against the government or any of its officers.

Of the ten people convicted under the Sedition Act, all were Republicans. The case of Matthew Lyon, a Democratic-Republican congressman from Vermont, reveals how the prosecutions not only failed to silence those critical of the Adams administration, but created martyrs of the dissidents.

Lyon, who had come to America from Ireland in 1764, had accused Adams of "an unbounded thirst for ridiculous pomp, foolish adulation, and selfish avarice." Charged with defaming the president, Lyon was so bold as to ask the Federalist trial judge if he had "dined with the President and observed his ridiculous pomp and parade." The judge replied that he never saw the president engage in "pomp and display" but instead found Adams remarkable in his "plainness and simplicity."

The jury convicted Lyon, and the judge sentenced him to four months in prison. The defiant Lyon, who was up for reelection, centered his campaign on his prosecution, claiming that the Sedition Act was unconstitutional. His strategy worked, as he became the first congressman to win reelection while in prison. Democratic-Republican supporters paid his fines, for he had become a hero in the cause of free speech and civil liberties.

To counter what Jefferson called the "reign of witches" unleashed by the Alien and Sedition Acts, he and James Madison drafted the Kentucky and Virginia Resolutions, which were passed by the legislatures of those two states in late 1798. The resolutions were as troubling as the acts they denounced. While Jefferson appropriately described the Alien and Sedition Acts as "alarming infractions" of constitutional rights, he threatened disunion in claiming that state legislatures should "nullify" (reject and ignore) acts of Congress that violated the constitutional guarantee of free speech.

Meanwhile, Adams was seeking peace with France. In 1799, he dispatched another team of diplomats to negotiate with a new French government under First Consul Napoléon Bonaparte, whose army had overthrown the republic. In a treaty called the Convention of 1800, the Americans won the best terms they could. They dropped their demands to be repaid for the ships taken by the French, and the French agreed to end the military alliance with the United States dating to the Revolutionary War. The Senate quickly ratified the agreement, which became effective on December 21, 1801.

REPUBLICAN·VICTORY IN 1800 The furor over the Alien and Sedition Acts influenced the pivotal presidential election of 1800. The Federalists nominated Adams, although Alexander Hamilton publicly questioned Adams's fitness to be president, citing his "disgusting egotism." Adams reciprocated by telling a friend that Hamilton was "devoid of every moral principle."

Thomas Jefferson and Aaron Burr, the Republican candidates, once again represented the alliance of the two most powerful states, Virginia and New York. The Federalists claimed that Jefferson's election would bring civil war and anarchy. A Federalist newspaper predicted that if the "godless" Jefferson were elected, "murder, robbery, rape, adultery, and incest will be openly taught and practiced."

Not to be outdone, a Republican newspaper dismissed Adams as a "hideous hermaphroditical character with neither the force nor firmness of a man nor the gentleness and sensibility of a woman," adding that he was a "blind, bald, crippled, toothless man who wants to start a war with France."

In the raucous **election of 1800**, Jefferson and Burr, the two Republicans, emerged with 73 electoral votes each. Adams received 65. When Burr shockingly refused to withdraw in favor of Jefferson, the tie vote in the electoral college sent the election into the House of Representatives (a constitutional defect corrected in 1804 by the Twelfth Amendment).

The tie vote created an explosive political crisis. Federalist Fisher Ames predicted that Burr "might impart vigor to the country," while Jefferson "was absurd enough to believe his own nonsense."

The three months between the House vote for president in December 1800 and Jefferson's inauguration in March 1801 were so tense that people talked openly of civil war. There were even wild rumors of plots to assassinate Jefferson. In the end, it took thirty-six ballots for the House to choose Jefferson over Burr.

THE ELECTION OF 1800

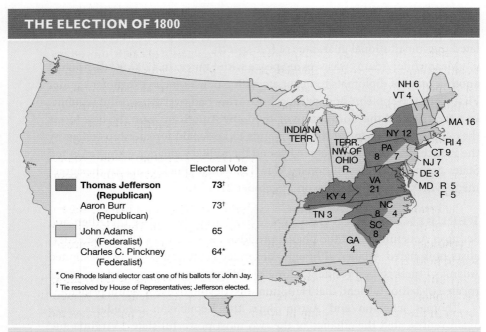

	Electoral Vote
Thomas Jefferson **(Republican)**	**73†**
Aaron Burr (Republican)	73†
John Adams (Federalist)	65
Charles C. Pinckney (Federalist)	64*

* One Rhode Island elector cast one of his ballots for John Jay.
† Tie resolved by House of Representatives; Jefferson elected.

- Why was the election of 1800 a key event in American history?
- What voting patterns emerged in the election of 1800?
- How did Congress break the tie between Thomas Jefferson and Aaron Burr?

Before the Federalists turned over power on March 4, 1801, President Adams and Congress passed the Judiciary Act of 1801. Adams intended it to ensure Federalist control of the judicial system by creating sixteen federal circuit courts, with a new judge for each. It also reduced the number of Supreme Court justices from six to five in an effort to deprive the next president of appointing a new member. Before he left office, Adams appointed Federalists to all the new positions. The Federalists, quipped Jefferson, had "retired into the judiciary as a stronghold." They never again would exercise significant political power.

A NEW ERA The election of 1800 did not resolve the fundamental political tensions that had emerged between ardent nationalists like Adams and Hamilton and those like Jefferson and Madison who clung to ideals of states' rights and an agriculture-based economy. In fact, the election further divided the young republic into warring political factions and marked a major turning point in the nation's history. It was the first time one party had relinquished presidential power to the opposition party, and it was the only election that pitted a sitting president (Adams) against his own vice president (Jefferson).

Jefferson's hard-fought victory signaled the emergence of a new, more democratic political culture dominated by bitterly divided parties and wider public participation. Before and immediately after independence, socially prominent families—the "rich, the able, and the wellborn"—still dominated political life. However, the political battles of the late 1790s, culminating with Jefferson's election, established the right of "common" men to play a more active role in governing the young republic. With the gradual elimination of the requirement that citizens must own property to vote, the electorate expanded enormously in the early nineteenth century.

Jefferson called his election the "Revolution of 1800," for it marked the triumph of the Republican party and the slaveholding South. Three Republican slaveholders from Virginia—Jefferson, James Madison, and James Monroe—would hold the presidency for the next twenty-four years.

A bitter John Adams was so upset by his defeat (as well as by the death of his alcoholic son Charles) that he refused to participate in Jefferson's inauguration in the new federal capital in Washington, D.C. He and Jefferson would not communicate for the next twelve years.

As Adams returned to work on his Massachusetts farm with his wife, Abigail, he told his eldest son, John Quincy, who would become the nation's sixth president, that anyone governing the United States "has a hard, laborious, and unhappy life." Jefferson would soon feel the same way.

CHAPTER REVIEW

SUMMARY

- **Confederation Government** Despite its many weaknesses, the national government created by the *Articles of Confederation* managed to construct important alliances during the Revolutionary War, help win the War of Independence, and negotiate the Treaty of Paris (1783). It created executive departments and established, through the *Northwest Ordinance (1787),* the process by which new western territories would be organized and governments formed before they applied for statehood. Yet the Articles of Confederation did not allow the national government to raise taxes to fund its debts. *Shays's Rebellion (1786–1787)* made many Americans fear that such uprisings would eventually destroy the new republic unless the United States formed a stronger national government.

- **Constitutional Convention** Delegates gathered at the convention in Philadelphia in 1787 to revise the existing government, but almost immediately they decided to scrap the Articles of Confederation and start over. An entirely new document emerged, creating a system called *federalism* in which a strong national government with *separation of powers* among executive, legislative, and judicial branches functioned alongside state governments with clearly designated responsibilities. Arguments about how best to ensure that the rights of individual states were protected and that "the people" were represented in the new Congress were resolved by establishing a Senate, with equal representation for each state, and a House of Representatives, the number of whose delegates was determined by population counts.

- **Ratification of the Constitution** Ratification of the Constitution was hotly contested. *Anti-Federalists,* such as Virginia's Patrick Henry, opposed the new structure of government because the absence of a bill of rights would lead to a loss of individual and states' rights. To sway New York State toward ratification, Alexander Hamilton, James Madison, and John Jay wrote *The Federalist Papers.* Ratification became possible only when the Federalists promised to add a *Bill of Rights (1791).*

- **Federalists versus Republicans** Alexander Hamilton and the Federalists wanted to create a diverse economy in which agriculture was balanced by trade, finance, and manufacturing. As secretary of the Treasury, Hamilton crafted a federal budget that funded the national debt through tariff and tax revenues, and he created a national bank, the first *Bank of the United States (1791).* Thomas Jefferson and others, known as *Jeffersonian Republicans,* worried that Hamilton's plans violated the Constitution and made the federal government too powerful. They envisioned a nation dominated by farmers and planters where the rights of states would be protected against federal power.

- **Trouble Abroad** During the *French Revolution*, George Washington's policy of neutrality violated the terms of the 1778 treaty with France. At the same time, Americans sharply criticized *Jay's Treaty (1794)* with the British for giving too much away. French warships began seizing British and American ships, and an undeclared war was under way. Federalists supported Washington's approach, while Republicans were more supportive of France.

CHRONOLOGY

1781	Articles of Confederation take effect
1783	Treaty of Paris ends the War of Independence
1786–1787	Shays's Rebellion
1787	Northwest Ordinance
	The Constitutional Convention is held in Philadelphia
1787–1788	*The Federalist Papers* are published
1789	President George Washington is inaugurated
1791	Bill of Rights is ratified
	Bank of the United States is created
1793	Washington issues a proclamation of neutrality
1794	Jay's Treaty is negotiated with England
	Whiskey Rebellion in Pennsylvania
	U.S. Army defeats Western Confederacy of Indian nations in the Battle of Fallen Timbers
1796	John Adams is elected president
1798	Alien and Sedition Acts are passed
1800	Thomas Jefferson is elected president

KEY TERMS

federalism p. 225

Articles of Confederation p. 225

Northwest Ordinance (1787) p. 228

Shays's Rebellion (1786–1787) p. 232

separation of powers p. 236

anti-Federalists p. 241

The Federalist Papers p. 242

Jeffersonian Republicans p. 246

Bill of Rights (1791) p. 248

Bank of the United States (1791) p. 255

French Revolution p. 257

Jay's Treaty (1794) p. 260

Whiskey Rebellion (1794) p. 261

Alien and Sedition Acts of 1798 p. 267

election of 1800 p. 269

 INQUIZITIVE

Go to InQuizitive to see what you've learned—and learn what you've missed—with personalized feedback along the way.

7 The Early Republic
1800–1815

We Owe Allegiance to No Crown **(ca. 1814)** The War of 1812 generated a renewed spirit of nationalism, inspiring Philadelphia sign painter John Archibald Woodside to create this patriotic painting.

W hen President Thomas Jefferson took office in 1801, the United States and its western territories reached from the Atlantic Ocean to the Mississippi River. Nine of ten Americans lived on farms, but entrepreneurs were rapidly developing a worldwide commercial economy. Everywhere people were on the make and on the move, leading one newspaper to claim that what made America different from other nations was "the almost universal ambition to get forward." The desire for profits was, according to Congressman Henry Clay, "a passion as unconquerable as any with which nature has endowed us. You may attempt to regulate [it]—[but] you cannot destroy it."

Intoxicated by their freedom, Americans were a people of possibilities in a land of dreams. They excelled at westward expansion, economic development, rapid population growth, and intense political activity because they believed in a brighter future. Former president John Adams observed that "there is no people on earth so ambitious as the people of America . . . because the lowest can aspire as freely as the highest."

Thomas Jefferson described the United States in the early nineteenth century as an "empire of liberty" spreading westward. In 1800, people eager to own their own farms bought 67,000 acres of government-owned land; the next year, they bought 498,000 acres. Native Americans resisted the invasion of their ancestral lands but ultimately succumbed to a federal government (and army) determined to relocate them.

Most whites, however, were more concerned with seizing their own economic opportunities than the plight of Native Americans. Isaac Weld, a British visitor, remarked that Americans were "always on the lookout for something

focus questions

1. What were the major domestic political developments during Thomas Jefferson's administration?

2. Describe how foreign events affected the United States during the Jefferson and Madison administrations.

3. What were the primary causes of the American decision to declare war on Great Britain in 1812?

4. What were the significant outcomes of the War of 1812 on the United States?

better or more profitable." Restless mobility and impatient striving soon came to define the American way of life.

JEFFERSONIAN REPUBLICANISM

The 1800 presidential campaign between Federalists and Jeffersonian Republicans had been so fiercely contested that some predicted civil war as the House of Representatives decided the outcome of the election. On March 4, 1801, however, fifty-seven-year-old Thomas Jefferson was inaugurated without incident. It was the first democratic election in modern history that resulted in the orderly transfer of power from one political party to another.

Jefferson's installation marked the emerging dominance of the nation's political life by Republicans—and Virginians. The nation's most populous state, Virginia supplied a quarter of the Republican congressmen in the House of Representatives that convened in early 1801.

Politics in the young republic was becoming increasingly sectional. Another Federalist, former secretary of state Timothy Pickering of Massachusetts, acknowledged that the northeastern states, where Federalism was centered, could no longer "reconcile their habits, views, and interests with those of the South and West," two fast-growing regions that were beginning to rule the nation with "a rod of iron."

Jefferson was the first president inaugurated in the new national capital of Washington, District of Columbia. The unfinished city of barely 3,000 people was crisscrossed with muddy avenues connecting a few buildings clustered around two unfinished centers, Capitol Hill and the "Executive Mansion." (It would not be called the White House until 1901.) Cows grazed along the Mall while pigs prowled the unpaved streets. Workers, many of them enslaved, had barely completed building the Capitol and the Executive Mansion before Jefferson was sworn in.

THE "PEOPLE'S PRESIDENT"   During his inauguration, Jefferson emphasized his connection to the "plain and simple" ways of the "common" people. Instead of wearing a ceremonial sword and riding in a horse-drawn carriage, as George Washington and John Adams had done, Jefferson left his boardinghouse on New Jersey Avenue and walked to the Capitol building, escorted by members of Congress and Virginia militiamen. He read his inaugural address in a "femininely soft," high-pitched voice, then took the presidential oath administered by Chief Justice John Marshall, his cousin, with whom he shared a cordial hatred.

Jefferson's deliberate display of **republican simplicity** set the tone for his administration. He wanted Americans to notice the difference between the monarchical style of the Federalists and the simplicity and frugality of the Republicans.

In his eloquent inaugural address, Jefferson imagined America as "a rising nation, spread over a wide and fruitful land, traversing all the seas with the productions of their industry, engaged in commerce" across the globe. Although determined to overturn many Federalist policies and programs, he urged Americans to work together. "We are all Republicans—we are all Federalists," Jefferson stressed, noting that "every difference of opinion is not a difference of principle."

It was a splendid message, but Jefferson's appeal for unity proved illusory, in part because of his fierce partisanship and bitter anti-Federalist prejudices. In a letter to a British friend, Jefferson said he feared that Federalists, a "herd of traitors," wanted to destroy "the liberties of the people" and convert the republic into a monarchy.

A MORE DEMOCRATIC AMERICA Jefferson's inauguration ushered in a more democratic political culture in which common people played a much larger role. During and after the Revolutionary War, an increasing proportion of white males, especially small farmers, wage laborers, artisans, mechanics, and apprentices, gained the right to vote or hold office as states reduced or eliminated requirements that voters and candidates own a specified amount of property.

Many among the founding generation of leaders in both political parties worried that men of humble origins, some of whom were uneducated and illiterate, were replacing the social and political elite ("natural aristocracy") in the state legislatures. "Since the war," a Massachusetts Federalist complained, "blustering ignorant men . . . have been attempting to push themselves into office." A Virginian noted the rising evidence of the "turbulence and follies of democracy."

As the nineteenth century unfolded, voters were not content to be governed solely by "their betters"; they wanted to do the governing themselves. And indeed, more than half of the members of the Republican-controlled Congress elected in 1800 were first-time legislators. Federalist John Adams so detested the democratic forces transforming politics and social life that he despaired for the nation's future: "Oh my Country," he moaned, "how I mourn over . . . thy contempt of Wisdom and Virtue and overweening admiration of fools and knaves! the never failing effects of *democracy*!"

A CONTRADICTORY GENIUS Thomas Jefferson, who owned hundreds of slaves, was a unique bundle of contradictions. He was progressive and enlightened in some areas, self-serving and hypocritical in others. He loathed political skullduggery, yet was a master at it. He championed government frugality, yet nearly went bankrupt buying expensive wines, paintings, silverware, and furniture. Jefferson, who had written in the Declaration of Independence that "all men are created equal," also bought, bred, flogged, and sold slaves while calling slavery "an abominable crime" and a "hideous blot" on civilization.

Jefferson wrote about the evils of racial mixing because of the "inferior" attributes of African Americans, yet after his wife Martha died, he used her half-sister, a beautiful mulatto slave named Sarah "Sally" Hemings, as his concubine; she gave birth to six of his children. For Jefferson, Hemings became what a friend called his "substitute for a wife" in a plantation world where complicated power relationships were hidden behind a veil of silence. Political foes used Jefferson's relationship with Sally against him, but he never responded.

Like George Washington, Jefferson was a wealthy planter with expensive tastes. He was also an inventive genius of staggering learning and exceptional abilities. As a self-trained architect, he designed the state capitol in Richmond, Virginia, as well as his thirty-three-room mountaintop mansion near Charlottesville called *Monticello* (Little Mountain). He was an expert in constitutional law, civil liberties, and political philosophy; religion and ethics; classical history; progressive education; natural science, paleontology, and mathematics; music and linguistics; and farming, gardening, cooking, and wine.

Yet while Jefferson lived the luxurious life, he championed the "honest heart" of the common people. His faith in expanding the number of eligible voters and his determination to reduce the power of the national government opened a more democratic era in American life.

JEFFERSON IN OFFICE For all his natural shyness and admitted weakness as a public speaker, Thomas Jefferson was the first president to pursue the role of party leader, and he openly cultivated congressional support at frequent social gatherings.

In his cabinet, the leading figures were Secretary of State James Madison, his best friend and political ally, and Secretary of the Treasury Albert Gallatin, a Pennsylvania Republican whose financial skills had won him the respect of Federalists and Republicans alike.

In filling lesser offices, however, Jefferson often succumbed to pressure from Republicans to remove Federalists, only to discover that there were few qualified candidates to replace some of them. When Gallatin asked if he might appoint women to some posts, Jefferson revealed the limits of his

The Capitol building This 1806 watercolor was painted by the building's architect, Benjamin Henry Latrobe, and inscribed to Thomas Jefferson. A prominent dome would be added later, after the building was damaged in the War of 1812.

liberalism: "The appointment of a woman to office is an innovation for which the public is not prepared, nor am I."

MARBURY V. MADISON In one area—the federal judiciary—the new president decided to remove most of the offices altogether, in part because the court system was the only branch of the government still controlled by Federalists. In 1802, at Jefferson's urging, the Republican-controlled Congress repealed the Judiciary Act of 1801, which the Federalists had passed just before the transfer of power to the Jeffersonian Republicans. The Judiciary Act had ensured Federalist control of the judicial system by creating sixteen federal circuit courts and appointing—for life—a Federalist judge for each. The controversial effort to repeal the judgeships sparked the landmark case of *Marbury v. Madison* (1803).

The case went to the Supreme Court, presided over by Chief Justice John Marshall, a Virginia Federalist who had served in the army during the Revolutionary War, attended law school at the College of William and Mary, and become a respected Richmond attorney. In 1788, Marshall helped Madison convince Virginians to ratify the U.S. Constitution. He later served in Congress and became secretary of state under President Adams, who appointed him chief justice early in 1801.

Blessed with a keen intellect and an analytical mind, Marshall was a fierce critic and lifelong enemy of Jefferson, whom he considered a war-shirking aristocrat who prized the states over the national government.

In 1801, John Jay, the first chief justice, admitted that the Supreme Court did not have "the energy, weight, and dignity" necessary to serve its role in balancing the powers of Congress and the presidency. Jefferson and the Republicans liked it that way. Marshall, however, set out to strengthen the judiciary. By the time he completed thirty-five years of service on the Supreme Court (1801–1835), he had made it the most powerful court in the world, distinctive for its emphasis on protecting individual rights while insisting upon the supremacy of the national government over the states, a principle that put him at odds with Jefferson.

The Marbury case involved the appointment of Maryland Federalist William Marbury as justice of the peace in the District of Columbia. Marbury's letter of appointment (called a commission), signed by President Adams two days before he left office, was still undelivered when James Madison took office as secretary of state, and Jefferson directed Madison to withhold it. Marbury then sued for a court order directing Madison to deliver his commission.

In the unanimous *Marbury v. Madison* ruling, Marshall and the Court held that Marbury deserved his judgeship. Marshall, however, denied that the Court had jurisdiction in the case. The Federal Judiciary Act of 1789, which gave the Court authority in such proceedings, was unconstitutional, Marshall ruled, because the Constitution specified that the Court should have original jurisdiction only in cases involving foreign ambassadors or nations. The Court, therefore, could issue no order in the case.

With one bold stroke, Marshall had elevated the stature of the Court by reprimanding Jefferson while avoiding an awkward confrontation with an administration that might have defied his order. More important, the ruling subtly struck down a federal law, the Judiciary Act of 1789, because it violated provisions of the Constitution, the "fundamental and paramount law of the nation." Marshall stressed that the Supreme Court was "emphatically" empowered "to say what the law is," even if it meant overruling both Congress and the president.

The *Marbury* decision granted the Supreme Court a power not mentioned in the Constitution: the right of what came to be called *judicial review*, whereby the Court determines whether acts of Congress (and the presidency) are constitutional. Marshall established that the Supreme Court was the final authority in all constitutional interpretations.

Jefferson fumed over the "irregular" ruling. Giving judges "the right to decide which laws are constitutional, and what not," he wrote Abigail Adams, "would make the judiciary a despotic branch."

Jefferson, however, would lose that argument. Although the Court did not declare another federal law unconstitutional for fifty-four years, it has since struck down more than 150 acts of Congress and more than 1,100 "unconstitutional" acts of state legislatures, all in an effort to protect individual liberties and civil rights. Marshall essentially created American constitutional law, making the unelected, life-tenured justices of the Supreme Court more-effective allies of a strong national government than even the framers had imagined.

JEFFERSON'S ECONOMIC POLICIES President Jefferson's first term did include some triumphs. Surprisingly, he did not dismantle Alexander Hamilton's Federalist economic program. Instead, following the advice of Treasury Secretary Albert Gallatin, Jefferson, who like many other southern planters never understood the function of banks, learned to accept the national bank as essential to economic growth.

Jefferson, however, rejected Hamilton's argument that a federal debt was a national "blessing" because it gave bankers and investors who bought government bonds a financial stake in the success of the new republic. If the debt were not eliminated, Jefferson told Gallatin, "we shall be committed to the English career of debt, corruption, and rottenness, closing with revolution."

To pay down the debt, Jefferson slashed the federal budget. He fired all federal tax collectors and cut the military budget in half, saying that state militias and small navy gunboats provided adequate protection against foreign enemies. Jefferson's was the first national government in history to *reduce* its own scope and power.

Jefferson also repealed the whiskey tax that Hamilton and George Washington had implemented in 1791. In doing so, he admitted that he had a peculiar affection for the "men from the Western side of the mountains"—grain farmers and backwoods distillers for whom whiskey was often the primary source of income.

The nation's prosperous economy helped the federal budget absorb the loss of the whiskey taxes. In addition, revenues from federal tariffs on imports rose with the growing European trade, and the sale of government-owned western lands soared as Americans streamed westward.

THE BARBARY PIRATES Upon assuming the presidency, Jefferson promised "peace, commerce, and honest friendship with all nations," but some nations preferred war. On the Barbary Coast of North Africa, the Islamic rulers of Morocco, Algiers, Tunis, and Tripoli had for centuries preyed upon unarmed European and American merchant ships. The U.S. government made numerous blackmail payments to the **Barbary pirates** in exchange for captured American merchant ships and crews.

***Burning of the Frigate* Philadelphia** Lieutenant Stephen Decatur set fire to the captured *Philadelphia* during the United States' standoff with Tripoli over the enslavement of American sailors in North Africa.

In 1801, however, the ruler of Tripoli upped his blackmail demands and declared war on the United States. Jefferson sent warships to blockade Tripoli, and a sporadic naval war dragged on until 1805, punctuated in 1804 by the notable exploits of Lieutenant Stephen Decatur, who slipped into Tripoli Harbor by night and set fire to the frigate *Philadelphia,* which had been captured after it ran aground. A force of U.S. Marines marched 500 miles across the desert to assault Derna, Tripoli's second largest town, a feat highlighted in the Marine Corps hymn ("to the shores of Tripoli"). The Tripoli ruler finally agreed to a $60,000 ransom and released the *Philadelphia*'s crew. It was still blackmail (called "tribute" in the nineteenth century), but less than the $300,000 the pirates had demanded and much less than the cost of an outright war.

WESTERN EXPANSION

Where Alexander Hamilton always faced east, looking to Great Britain for his model of national greatness, Thomas Jefferson looked to the west for his inspiration, across the mountains and even across the Mississippi River. Only by expanding westward, he believed, could America avoid the social turmoil and misery common in the cities of Europe—and remain a nation primarily of self-sufficient farmers.

To ensure continuing westward settlement, Jefferson and the Republicans strove to reduce the cost of federal lands. Ohio's admission to the Union in 1803 increased the number of states to seventeen. Government land sales west of the Appalachian Mountains skyrocketed as settlers shoved Indians aside and established homesteads. Jefferson, however, wanted more western land, and in 1803 a stroke of good fortune allowed him to double the new nation's size.

THE LOUISIANA PURCHASE In 1801, American diplomats in Europe heard rumors that Spain had been forced to transfer its huge Louisiana province back to France, now led by Napoléon Bonaparte. The French First Consul had a massive ego, remarkable self-confidence, and a single-minded hunger for victory and power. Short of stature but a giant on the battlefield, Napoléon had gone from penniless immigrant to army general by the age of twenty-six. He was a military genius, the most feared ruler in the world, conqueror of Egypt and Italy. After taking control of the French government in 1799, Napoléon set out to restore his country's North American empire (Canada and Louisiana) that had been lost to Great Britain in 1763.

President Jefferson referred to Napoléon as both a "scoundrel" and "a gigantic force" threatening the future of the United States. A weak Spain controlling the territory west of the Mississippi River could have been tolerated, Jefferson explained, but Napoleonic France in control of the Mississippi Valley would lead to "eternal friction" and eventually war.

To prevent France from seizing the Mississippi River, Jefferson sent New Yorker Robert R. Livingston to Paris in 1801 as ambassador to France. Livingston's primary objective was to acquire the strategic port city of New Orleans, situated at the mouth of the Mississippi River. Jefferson told Livingston that purchasing New Orleans and West Florida (the territory along the Gulf coast from Pensacola, Florida, to New Orleans) was of absolute importance, for "the day that France takes possession of New Orleans, . . . we must marry ourselves to the British fleet and nation" for protection.

Over the years, New Orleans had become a dynamic crossroads where some 50,000 people of different nationalities readily intermingled, garnering huge profits from the vast amount of goods floating down the Mississippi. For years, Americans living in Tennessee and Kentucky had threatened to secede if the federal government did not ensure that they could send their crops and goods downriver to New Orleans.

In early 1803, Jefferson grew so concerned about the stalled negotiations in Paris that he sent James Monroe, his trusted friend and Virginia neighbor, to assist the sixty-six-year-old Livingston. "All eyes, all hopes, are now fixed on you," Jefferson told Monroe.

No sooner had Monroe arrived than Napoléon surprisingly offered to sell not just New Orleans but *all* of the immense, unmapped Louisiana Territory, from the Mississippi River west to the Rocky Mountains and from the Canadian border south to the Gulf of Mexico.

The unpredictable Napoléon had reversed himself because his large army on the Caribbean island of Saint-Domingue (Haiti) had been decimated by epidemics of malaria and yellow fever and by a massive slave revolt led by Touissaint L'Ouverture, who had proclaimed the Republic of Haiti. It was the first successful slave rebellion in history, and it panicked slaveholders in the southern states who feared that news of the revolt would spread to America.

Napoléon had tried to regain control of Saint-Domingue because it was a profitable source of coffee and sugar. He also had hoped to connect New Orleans and Haiti as a first step in expanding France's North American trading empire. But after losing more than 24,000 soldiers to disease and warfare, Napoléon decided to cut his losses by selling the Louisiana Territory to the United States and using the proceeds to finance his "inevitable" next war with Great Britain.

By the Treaty of Cession, dated May 2, 1803, the United States agreed to pay the modest sum of $15 million (3¢ an acre) for the entire Louisiana Territory. When Livingston and Monroe asked Charles-Maurice de Talleyrand, Napoléon's negotiator, about the precise extent of the territory they were buying, the Frenchman replied: "I can give you no direction. You have made a noble bargain for yourselves. I suppose you will make the most of it." A delighted Livingston said that "from this day the United States take their place among the powers of the first rank." He called the land transfer the "noblest work of our whole lives."

The arrival of the signed treaty in Washington, D.C., presented Jefferson, who for years had criticized the Federalists for stretching the meaning of the Constitution, with a political dilemma. Nowhere did the Constitution mention the purchase of territory. Was such an action legal?

In the end, Jefferson's desire to double the size of the republic trumped his concerns about an unconstitutional exercise of executive power. Acquiring the Louisiana Territory, the president explained, would serve "the immediate interests of our Western citizens" and promote "the peace and security of the nation in general" by removing the French threat and creating a protective buffer separating the United States from the rest of the world. Jefferson also imagined that the region might be a place to relocate Indian nations or freed slaves, since he feared a multiracial society.

New England Federalists strongly opposed the purchase. Fisher Ames of Massachusetts argued that the Louisiana Territory was a waste of money, a "wilderness unpeopled with any beings except wolves and wandering Indians." Ames and others feared that adding the vast territory would weaken New England and the Federalist party, since the new western states were likely to be settled by wage laborers from New England seeking cheap land and by southern slaveholders, all of whom were Jeffersonian Republicans. As a newspaper editorialized, "Will [Jefferson and the] Republicans, who glory in their sacred regard to the rights of human nature, purchase an *immense wilderness* for the purpose of cultivating it with the labor of slaves?"

In a reversal of traditional stances, Federalists found themselves arguing for strict construction of the Constitution in opposing the Louisiana Purchase. "We are to give money of which we have too little for land of which we already have too much," argued a Bostonian in the *Columbian Centinel*. Eager to close the deal, Jefferson called a special session of Congress on October 17, 1803, at which the Senate ratified the treaty by a vote of 26–6. On December 20, 1803, U.S. officials took formal possession of the Louisiana Territory. The purchase included 875,000 square miles of land (529,402,880 acres). Six states in their entirety, and most or part of nine more, would be carved out of the Louisiana Purchase, from Louisiana north to Minnesota and west to Montana.

The **Louisiana Purchase** was the most significant event of Jefferson's presidency and one of the most important developments in American history. It spurred western exploration and expansion, and it enticed cotton growers to settle in the Old Southwest—Alabama, Mississippi, and Louisiana.

THE LEWIS AND CLARK EXPEDITION (1804–1806) To learn more about the Louisiana Territory's geography, plants, and animals, as well as its prospects for trade and agriculture, Jefferson asked Congress to fund an expedition to find the most "practicable water communication across this continent." The president then appointed two friends, army captains Meriwether Lewis and William Clark, to lead what came to be known as the **Lewis and Clark expedition**. The twenty-nine-year-old Lewis was Jefferson's private secretary. Jefferson admired his "boldness, enterprise, and discretion." Thirty-three-year-old Clark, from Louisville, Kentucky, was an accomplished frontiersman and "as brave as Caesar."

On a rainy May morning in 1804, Lewis and Clark's "Corps of Discovery," numbering about thirty "stout" men, set out from Wood River, a village near the former French town of St. Louis. They traveled in two large dugout canoes (called *pirogues*) and one large, flat-bottomed, single-masted keelboat filled with food, weapons, medicine, and gifts for the Indians. They traveled up the

EXPLORATIONS OF THE LOUISIANA PURCHASE, 1804–1807

■ How did the United States acquire the Louisiana Purchase?
■ What was the mission of Lewis and Clark's expedition?
■ What were the consequences of Lewis and Clark's widely circulated reports about the western territory?

Mississippi to the mouth of the treacherous Missouri River, where they added a dozen more men before proceeding through some of the most rugged territory in North America. Unsure of where they were going and what or whom they might encounter, they were eager to discover if the Missouri made its way to the Pacific Ocean.

Six months later, near the Mandan Sioux villages in what would become Bismarck, North Dakota, the Corps of Discovery built Fort Mandan and wintered in relative comfort, sending downriver a barge loaded with maps, soil samples, the skins and skeletons of weasels, wolves, and antelope, and live specimens of prairie dogs and magpies, previously unknown in America.

In the spring of 1805, the Corps of Discovery added two guides: a French fur trader and his remarkable wife, a Shoshone woman named Sacagawea ("Bird Woman"). In appreciation for Lewis and Clark's help in delivering her baby boy, Baptiste, Sacagawea provided crucial assistance as a guide, translator, and negotiator as they explored the Upper Missouri and encountered various Native Americans, most of whom were "hospitable, honest, and sincere people."

From Fort Mandan, the adventurers headed out, crossing the Rocky Mountains and descending the Snake and Columbia Rivers to the Pacific Ocean, where they arrived in November. "Ocean in view! O! the joy!" Clark wrote in his journal. Near the future site of Astoria, Oregon, at the mouth of the Columbia River, they built Fort Clatsop, where they spent a cold, rainy winter.

Sacagawea Of the many memorials devoted to Sacagawea, this statue by artist Alice Cooper was unveiled at the 1905 Lewis and Clark Centennial Exposition.

In the spring of 1806 they headed back to St. Louis, having been forced to eat their dogs and horses. Tough characters all, they had weathered blizzards, broiling sun, fierce rapids, pelting hail, grizzly bears, injuries, illnesses, and swarms of mosquitoes. "I have been wet and as cold in every part as I ever was in my life," Clark noted. "Indeed I was at one time fearful my feet would freeze in the thin moccasins which I wore." Only one member of the group died, and that was because of a ruptured appendix.

The expedition, which lasted twenty-eight months and covered some 8,000 miles, returned with remarkably extensive journals that described their experiences and observations while detailing some 180 plants and 125 animals. Their splendid maps attracted traders and trappers to the region and led the United States to claim the Oregon Country (the entire Pacific Northwest) by right of discovery and exploration.

POLITICAL SCHEMES The Lewis and Clark expedition and the Louisiana Purchase strengthened Thomas Jefferson's already solid support in the South and West. In New England, however, Federalists panicked because they assumed that new states carved out of the Louisiana Territory would be dominated by Jeffersonian Republicans. To protect their interests, Federalists hatched a scheme to link New York politically to New England by trying to elect Vice President Aaron Burr, Jefferson's ambitious Republican rival, as governor of New York. Burr chose to drop his Republican affiliation and run as an independent candidate.

Several leading Federalists opposed the scheme, however. Alexander Hamilton urged Federalists not to vote for Burr, calling him "a dangerous man, and one who ought not to be trusted with the reins of government." Burr ended up losing the election to the Republican candidate, who had been endorsed by Jefferson.

A furious Burr blamed Hamilton's "base slanders" for his defeat and challenged him to a duel "on the field of honor." At dawn on July 11, 1804, the two men met near Weehawken, New Jersey, on the Hudson River above New York City. Hamilton, whose son had been killed in a duel at the same location, fired first but intentionally missed as a demonstration of his religious and moral principles, knowing full well that it might cost him his life. Burr showed no such scruples. He shot Hamilton in the hip; the bullet ripped through his liver and lodged in his spine. He died the next day. Burr, who was still the nation's vice president, was charged with murder. He fled to South Carolina, where his daughter lived.

JEFFERSON REELECTED In the meantime, the presidential campaign of 1804 began. A congressional caucus of Republicans renominated Jefferson and chose George Clinton of New York as the vice presidential candidate. To avoid the problems associated with parties running multiple candidates for the presidency, in 1803, Congress had ratified the Twelfth Amendment to the Constitution, stipulating that the members of the electoral college must use separate ballots to vote for the president and vice president.

Given Jefferson's first-term achievements, the Federalist candidates, South Carolinian Charles C. Pinckney and New Yorker Rufus King, never had a chance. Jefferson had accomplished much: the Louisiana Purchase, a prosperous economy, and a reduced federal government budget and national debt.

A Massachusetts Republican claimed that the United States was "never more respected abroad. The people were never more happy at home." Jefferson and Clinton won 162 of 176 electoral votes.

DIVISIONS IN THE REPUBLICAN PARTY Jefferson's landslide victory, however, created problems within his own party. Freed from strong opposition—Federalists made up only a quarter of the new Congress in 1805—the Republican majority began to divide into warring factions, one calling itself the Jeffersonian or Nationalist Republicans, and the other, the anti-Jeffersonian Old Republicans.

Fiery Virginian John Randolph was initially a loyal Jeffersonian, but over time he emerged as the most colorful of the radically conservative "Old Republicans"—a group mostly of southern agrarian political purists for whom protecting states' rights was more important than the need for a strong national government. Randolph, for example, broke with Jefferson over the Louisiana Purchase.

The imperious Randolph, another of the president's cousins, was the Senate's most flamboyant character. He often entered the chamber wearing a long white coat and white boots with spurs, trailed by a hunting hound that would sleep under his desk. He lubricated his speeches with gulps of whiskey and described himself as an old-fashioned "aristocrat. I love liberty. I hate equality."

Randolph and other Old Republicans were best known for what they opposed: any compromise with the Federalists, any expansion of federal authority at the expense of states' rights, any new taxes or tariffs, and any change in the South's agrarian way of life rooted in slavery.

The Jeffersonian Republicans, on the other hand, were more moderate, pragmatic, and nationalistic. They were willing to compromise their states' rights principles to maintain national tariffs on imports, preserve a national bank, and stretch the "implied powers" of the Constitution to accommodate the Louisiana Purchase. Such compromises, said Randolph, were catastrophic. "The old Republican party," he claimed, "is already ruined, past redemption."

THE BURR CONSPIRACY Meanwhile, Aaron Burr continued to connive and scheme. After the controversy over his duel with Alexander Hamilton subsided, he tried to carve out his own personal empire in the West. What came to be known as the Burr Conspiracy was hatched when Burr and General James Wilkinson, an old friend then serving as senior general of the U.S. Army, plotted to use a well-armed force of volunteers to separate part of the Louisiana Territory from the Union. The plan was then to declare it an independent republic, with New Orleans as its capital and Burr as its ruler. Burr claimed that "the people of the western country were ready for revolt."

In late 1806, Burr floated down the Ohio and Mississippi Rivers toward New Orleans with 100 volunteers, only to have Wilkinson turn on him and alert Jefferson to the scheme. The president ordered that Burr be arrested. Militiamen captured Burr in February 1807 and took him to Richmond, Virginia, where, in August, he was tried for treason before Chief Justice John Marshall.

Jefferson was hellbent on seeing Burr hanged, claiming that he had tried to separate "the western states from us, of adding Mexico to them, and of placing himself at their head." In the end, however, Burr was acquitted because of a lack of evidence. Marshall had instructed the jury that a verdict of treason required an "act of war" against the United States confirmed by at least two witnesses.

Jefferson was disgusted. "It now appears we have no law but the will of the judge," he wrote a friend. The president considered proposing a constitutional amendment to limit the power of the judiciary and even thought about asking Congress to impeach Marshall. In the end, however, he did nothing. With further charges pending, the slippery Burr skipped bail and took refuge first in England, then in France. He returned to America in 1812 and resumed practicing law in New York.

ENDING THE SLAVE TRADE While shrinking the federal budget and reducing the national debt, Jefferson signed a landmark bill that outlawed the importation of enslaved Africans into the United States, in part because southerners had come to believe that African-born slaves were prone to revolt. The new law took effect on January 1, 1808. At the time, South Carolina was the only state that still permitted the purchase of enslaved Africans. For years to come, however, illegal global trafficking in African slaves would continue; as many as 300,000 were smuggled into the United States between 1808 and 1861.

WAR IN EUROPE

In the spring of 1803, soon after completing the sale of Louisiana to America, Napoléon Bonaparte declared war on Great Britain. The conflict would last eleven years and eventually involve all of Europe. Most Americans wanted to remain neutral, but the British and French were determined to keep that from happening.

NAVAL HARASSMENT During 1805, the spreading war reached a stalemate: the French army controlled most of Europe, and the British navy dominated the seas. In May 1806, Britain issued a series of declarations called

Orders in Council that imposed a naval blockade of the European coast to prevent merchant ships from other nations, including the United States, from making port in France. Although British leaders recognized America's independence in principle, they were eager to humble and humiliate the upstart republic by asserting their dominance over Atlantic trade.

Soon British warships began seizing American merchant ships bound for France. An angry Congress responded by passing the Non-Importation Act, which banned the importation of British goods. In early 1807, Napoléon announced that French warships would blockade the ports of Great Britain. The British responded that they would no longer allow foreign ships to trade with the French-controlled islands in the Caribbean. Soon thereafter, British warships appeared along the American coast and began stopping and searching U.S. merchant vessels as they headed for the Caribbean or Europe.

The tense situation posed a dilemma for American shippers. If they agreed to British demands to stop trading with the French, the French would retaliate by seizing U.S. vessels headed to and from Great Britain. If they agreed to French demands that they stop trading with the British, the British would seize American ships headed to and from France. Some American merchants decided to risk becoming victims of the Anglo-French war—and many paid a high price for their pursuit of overseas profits. During 1807, British and French warships captured hundreds of American ships.

IMPRESSMENT For American sailors, the danger on the high seas was heightened by the practice of *impressment*, whereby British warships stopped U.S. vessels, boarded them, and kidnapped sailors they claimed were British citizens. American merchant ships attracted British deserters because they paid more than twice as much as did the Royal Navy. Fully half the sailors on American ships, about 9,000 men, had been born in Britain.

The British often did not bother to determine the citizenship of those they "impressed" into service. As a British

Preparation for War to Defend Commerce Shipbuilders, like those pictured here constructing the *Philadelphia*, played an important role in America's early wars.

officer explained, "It is my duty to keep my ship manned, & I will do so wherever I find men that speak the same language with me." Between 1803 and 1811, some 6,200 American sailors were "impressed" into the British navy.

THE *CHESAPEAKE* INCIDENT (1807) The crisis boiled over on June 22, 1807, when the British warship HMS *Leopard* stopped a smaller U.S. vessel, the *Chesapeake*, eight miles off the Virginia coast. After the *Chesapeake's* captain refused to allow the British to search his ship for English deserters, the *Leopard* opened fire without warning, killing three Americans and wounding eighteen. A search party then boarded the *Chesapeake* and seized four men, one of whom, an English deserter, was hanged.

The attack on the *Chesapeake* was both an act of war and a national insult. Public anger was so great that President Jefferson could have declared war on the spot. "We have never, on any occasion, witnessed . . . such a thirst for revenge," the *Washington Federalist* reported.

In early July, Jefferson met with his cabinet before issuing a proclamation banning all British warships from American waters. He also called on state governors to mobilize their militias. Like John Adams before him, however, Jefferson resisted war fever, in part because the undersized U.S. Army and Navy were not prepared to fight. Jefferson's caution outraged his critics.

THE EMBARGO President Jefferson decided on a strategy of "peaceable coercion" to force Britain and France to stop violating American rights. Late in 1807, he somehow convinced enough Republicans in Congress to cut off *all* American foreign trade. As Jefferson said, his choices were "war, embargo, or nothing."

The unprecedented **Embargo Act** (December 1807) stopped all American exports by prohibiting U.S. ships from sailing to foreign ports to "keep our ships and seamen out of harm's way." Jefferson and his secretary of state, James Madison, mistakenly assumed that the embargo would force the warring European nations to quit violating American rights. They were wrong.

With each passing month, the embargo devastated the Republicans and the economy while reviving the political appeal of the Federalists, especially in New England, where merchants howled because the embargo cut off their primary industry: oceangoing commerce. The value of U.S. exports plummeted from $48 million in 1807 to $9 million a year later, and federal revenue from tariffs plunged from $18 million to $8 million. Shipbuilding declined by two-thirds, and farmers and planters in the South and West suffered as prices for exported farm crops were cut in half. New England's once-thriving port cities became ghost towns; thousands of ships and sailors were out of work. Meanwhile, smuggling soared, especially along the border with British Canada.

Americans raged at what critics called "Jefferson's embargo." One letter writer told the president that he had paid four friends "to shoot you if you don't take off the embargo," while another addressed the president as "you red-headed son of a bitch."

The embargo turned American politics upside down. To enforce it, Jefferson, once the leading advocate for *reducing* the power of the federal government, now found himself *expanding* federal power into every aspect of the nation's economic life. In effect, the United States used its own warships to blockade its own ports. Jefferson even activated the New York state militia in an effort to stop smuggling across the Canadian border.

Congress finally voted 70–0 to end the embargo effective March 4, 1809, the day the "splendid misery" of Jefferson's second presidential term ended. The dejected Jefferson left the presidency feeling like a freed prisoner. No one, he said, could be more relieved "on shaking off the shackles of power." His stern critic, Congressman John Randolph, declared that never had a president "left the nation in a state so deplorable and calamitous."

Jefferson learned a hard lesson that many of his successors would also discover: a second presidential term is rarely as successful as the first. As he admitted, "No man will ever carry out of that office the reputation which carried him into it."

In the election of 1808, the presidency passed to another prominent Virginian, Secretary of State James Madison. The Federalists, again backing Charles C. Pinckney of South Carolina and Rufus King of New York, won only 47 electoral votes to Madison's 122.

JAMES MADISON AND THE DRIFT TO WAR   In his inaugural address, President Madison acknowledged that he inherited a situation "full of difficulties." He soon made things worse. Although Madison had been a talented legislator and the "Father of the Constitution," he proved to be a weak, indecisive chief executive. He was a persuader, not a commander.

Madison's sparkling wife, Dolley, was the only truly excellent member of the president's inner circle. Seventeen years younger than her husband, she was a superb First Lady who excelled at entertaining political leaders and foreign dignitaries. Journalists called her the "Queen of Washington City."

From the beginning, Madison's presidency was entangled in foreign affairs and crippled by his lack of executive experience. Like Jefferson, Madison and his advisers repeatedly overestimated the young republic's diplomatic leverage and military strength. The result was international humiliation.

Madison insisted on upholding the principle of freedom of the seas for the United States and other neutral nations, but he was unwilling to create a navy strong enough to enforce it. He continued the policy of "peaceable coercion" against the European nations, which was as ineffective for him as it had been for Jefferson.

In place of the disastrous embargo, Congress passed the Non-Intercourse Act (1809), which reopened trade with all countries *except* France and Great Britain and their colonies. It also authorized the president to reopen trade with France or Great Britain if either should stop violating American rights on the high seas.

In December 1810, France issued a vague promise to restore America's neutral rights, whereupon Madison gave Great Britain three months to do the same. The British refused, and the Royal Navy continued to seize American vessels, their cargoes, and crews.

A reluctant Madison asked Congress to declare war against the United Kingdom of Great Britain and Ireland on June 1, 1812. If the United States did not defend its maritime rights, he explained, then Americans were "not independent people, but colonists and vassals."

The congressional vote to declare war was the closest in America's history of warfare. On June 5, the House of Representatives voted for war 79–49. Two weeks later, the Senate followed suit, 19–13. Every Federalist in Congress opposed "Mr. Madison's War," while 80 percent of Republicans supported it. The southern and western states wanted war; the New England states opposed it.

By declaring war, Madison and the Republicans hoped to unite the nation and discredit the Federalists. They also planned to end British-led Indian attacks along the Great Lakes and in the Ohio Valley by invading British Canada. To generate popular support, Jefferson advised Madison that he needed, above all, "to stop Indian barbarities. The conquest of Canada will do this." Jefferson presumed that the French Canadians were eager to rise up against their British rulers. With their help, the Republicans predicted, American armies would conquer Britain's vast northern colony. It did not work out that way.

The War of 1812

The War of 1812 marked the first time that Congress declared war. Great Britain was preoccupied with defeating Napoléon in Europe, and in fact, on June 16, 1812, it had promised to quit interfering with American shipping. President Madison and the Republicans, however, believed that only war would end the practice of impressment and stop British-inspired Indian attacks along the western frontier.

SHIPPING RIGHTS AND NATIONAL HONOR Why the United States chose to start the war is still debated by historians. Its main cause—the repeated British violations of American maritime rights and the practice of "impressing" sailors—dominated President Madison's war message. Most of the votes in Congress for war came from legislators representing rural regions, from Pennsylvania southward and westward, where the economic interests of farmers and planters were being hurt by the raids on American merchant ships. However, the representatives from the New England states, which bore the brunt of British attacks on U.S. shipping, voted 20–12 *against* the declaration of war.

One explanation for this seeming inconsistency is that many Americans in the South and West, especially Tennessee, Kentucky, and South Carolina, voted for war because they believed America's national *honor* was at stake. Andrew Jackson, a proud anti-British Tennessean who was the state's first congressman, announced that he was eager to fight "for the re-establishment of our national character."

NATIVE AMERICAN CONFLICTS Another factor leading to war was the growing number of Indian attacks, supported by the British, in the Ohio Valley. The story took a new turn with the rise of two Shawnee leaders, Tecumseh and his half brother, Tenskwatawa, who lived in a large village called Prophetstown on the Tippecanoe River in northern Indiana.

Tecumseh ("Shooting Star") knew that the fate of the Indians depended on their being unified. He hoped to create a single nation powerful enough, with British assistance, to fend off further American expansion. Tenskwatawa (the

Tecumseh The Shawnee leader, who tried to unite Native American peoples across the United States in defense of their lands, was killed in 1813 at the Battle of the Thames.

"Open Door"), who was known as "the Prophet," gained a large following among Native Americans for his predictions that white Americans ("children of the devil") were on the verge of collapse. He demanded that the indigenous peoples abandon all things European: clothing, customs, Christianity, and especially liquor. If they did so, the Great Spirit would reward them by turning the whites' gunpowder to sand.

A "TRAIL OF BLOOD"   Inspired by his brother's spiritual message, Tecumseh attempted to form alliances with other Native American nations in 1811. In Alabama, he told a gathering of 5,000 Indians that they should "let the white race perish" because "they seize your land; they corrupt your women; they trample on the ashes of your dead!" The whites "have driven us from the sea to the lakes," he noted. "We can go no further."

William Henry Harrison, governor of the Indiana Territory, met with Tecumseh twice and described him as "one of those uncommon geniuses who spring up occasionally to produce revolutions and overturn the established order of things."

Yet in the fall of 1811, Harrison gathered 1,000 troops and advanced on Prophetstown. What became the Battle of Tippecanoe was a disastrous defeat for the Native Americans, as Harrison's troops burned the village and destroyed its supplies. **Tecumseh's Indian Confederacy** went up in smoke, and he fled to Canada.

THE LUST FOR CANADA AND FLORIDA   Some Americans wanted war with Great Britain because they sought to seize control of Canada. That there were nearly 8 million Americans and only 300,000 Canadians led many to believe that doing so would be quick and easy. Thomas Jefferson, for instance, wrote President Madison that the "acquisition of Canada" was simply a "matter of marching" north with a military force.

The British were also vulnerable far to the south. East Florida, which had returned to Spain's control in 1783, posed a threat because Spain was too weak, or too unwilling, to prevent Indian attacks across the border with Georgia. In the absence of a strong Spanish presence, British agents and traders remained in East Florida, smuggling goods and conspiring with Indians against Americans.

Spanish Florida had also long been a haven for runaway slaves from Georgia and South Carolina. Many Americans living along the Florida-Georgia border hoped that the war would enable them to oust the British and the Spanish from Florida.

WAR HAWKS In the Congress that assembled in late 1811, new anti-British representatives from southern and western districts shouted for war to defend "national honor" and rid the Northwest of the "Indian problem" by invading Canada. Among the most vocal "war hawks" were Henry Clay of Kentucky and John C. Calhoun of South Carolina.

Clay, the brash young Speaker of the House, was "for resistance by the *sword*." He boasted that the Kentucky militia alone could conquer Canada. His bravado inspired others. "I don't like Henry Clay," Calhoun said. "He is a bad man, an imposter, a creator of wicked schemes. I wouldn't speak to him, but, by God, I love him" for wanting war against Britain. When Calhoun learned that President Madison had finally decided on war, he threw his arms around Clay's neck and led his colleagues in a mock Indian war dance.

In New England and much of New York, however, there was little enthusiasm for war. Great Britain remained those states' largest trading partner; the sentiment was that military conflict could cripple the shipping industry. Both Massachusetts and Connecticut refused to send soldiers to fight, and merchants openly sold supplies to British troops in Canada.

WAR PREPARATIONS One thing was certain: the United States was woefully unprepared for war, both financially and militarily, and James Madison lacked the leadership ability and physical stature to inspire public confidence and military resolve.

The national economy was weak, too. In 1811, Republicans had let the charter of the Bank of the United States expire. Many Republican congressmen owned shares in state banks and wanted the B.U.S. dissolved because it both competed with and regulated the local banks. Once the B.U.S. shut down, however, the number of unregulated state banks mushroomed, all with their own forms of currency, creating commercial chaos.

Once war began, it did not go well. The mighty British navy blockaded American ports, which caused federal tariff revenues to tumble. In March 1813, Treasury Secretary Gallatin warned Madison that the United States had "hardly enough money to last till the end of the month." Furthermore, Republicans in Congress were so afraid of public criticism that they delayed approving tax increases needed to finance the war.

The military situation was almost as bad. In 1812, the British had 250,000 professional soldiers and the most powerful navy in the world. By contrast, the U.S. Army numbered only 3,287 ill-trained and poorly equipped men, led by mostly incompetent officers with little combat experience. In January 1812, Congress authorized an army of 35,000 men, but a year later, just

18,500 had been recruited—many of them Irish American immigrants who hated the English and were enticed to enlist by congressional promises of cash and land.

President Madison, who refused to allow free blacks or slaves to serve in the army, had to plead with state governors to provide militiamen, only to have the Federalist governors in anti-war New England decline. The British, on the other hand, had thousands of soldiers stationed in Canada and the West Indies. And, as was true during the Revolutionary War, the British recruited more Native American allies than did the Americans.

The U.S. Navy was in better shape than the army, with able officers and well-trained seamen, but it had only 16 warships compared to Britain's 600. The lopsided military strength of the British led Madison to mutter that the United States was in "an embarrassing situation."

A CONTINENTAL WAR   For these reasons and more, the War of 1812 was one of the strangest wars in history. In fact, it was three wars fought on three fronts. One theater of conflict was the Chesapeake Bay along the coast of Maryland and Virginia, including Washington, D.C. The second was in the South—Alabama, Mississippi, and West and East Florida—where American forces led by Andrew Jackson invaded lands owned by the Creeks and the Spanish. The third front might be more accurately called the Canadian-American War. It began in what is now northern Indiana and Ohio, southeastern Michigan, and the contested border regions around the Great Lakes. The fighting raged back and forth across the border as the United States repeatedly invaded British Canada, only to be repulsed.

THE WAR IN THE NORTH   Like the American Revolution, the War of 1812, often called America's second war for independence, was very much a civil war. The Canadians, thousands of whom were former American Loyalists who had fled north after the Revolutionary War, remained loyal to the British Empire, while the Americans and a few French Canadians and Irish Canadians sought to push Britain out of North America and annex Canada.

In some cases, Americans fought former Americans, including families that were divided in their allegiances. Siblings even shot each other. Once, after killing an American militiaman, a Canadian soldier began taking the clothes off the corpse, only to realize that it was his brother. He grumbled that it served him right to have died for a bad cause.

Indians armed by the British dominated the wooded borderlands around the Great Lakes. Michigan's governor recognized that "The British cannot hold Upper Canada [Ontario] without the assistance of the Indians," but the "Indians

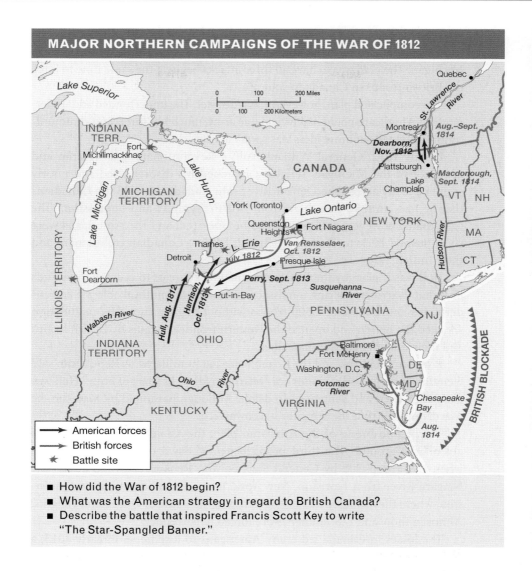

MAJOR NORTHERN CAMPAIGNS OF THE WAR OF 1812

Legend:
- → American forces
- → British forces
- ✶ Battle site

- How did the War of 1812 begin?
- What was the American strategy in regard to British Canada?
- Describe the battle that inspired Francis Scott Key to write "The Star-Spangled Banner."

cannot conduct a war without the assistance of a civilized nation [Great Britain]." So the American assault on Canada involved attacking Indians, Canadians, and British soldiers.

INVADING CANADA President Madison approved a three-pronged plan for the invasion of British Canada. It called for one army to move north through upstate New York, along Lake Champlain, to take Montreal, while another was to advance into Upper Canada by crossing the Niagara River between Lakes Ontario and Erie. The third attack would come from the west, with an American force moving east into Upper Canada from Detroit, Michigan. The plan was to have all three attacks begin at the same time to force the British troops in Canada to split up.

The complicated plan, however, was a disaster. The underfunded and under-manned Americans could barely field one army, much less three, and communication among the commanders was spotty at best.

In July 1812, General William Hull, a Revolutionary War veteran and governor of the Michigan Territory, marched his disorganized and poorly supplied army across the Detroit River into Canada. He told the Canadians that he had come to free them from British "tyranny and oppression." The Canadians, however, did not want to be liberated, and the Americans were soon pushed back to Detroit by British troops, Canadian militiamen, and their Indian allies.

Hull was tricked by the British commander's threats to unleash thousands of Indian warriors. Fearing a massacre, Hull did the unthinkable: he surrendered his entire force of 2,500 troops without firing a shot. His capitulation shocked the nation and opened the western frontier to raids by British troops and their Canadian and Indian allies.

President Madison and the Republicans felt humiliated. A Republican said General Hull must be a "traitor" or "nearly an idiot" or "part of both." Hull was eventually tried and sentenced to death. Although pardoned by Madison, he was dismissed from the army for his cowardice.

The second prong of the American plan, the assault on Montreal, never got off the ground. The third prong began at dawn on October 13, 1812, when U.S. troops led by General Stephen Van Rensselaer rowed across the Niagara River from Lewiston, New York, to the Canadian village of Queenston, where they suffered a crushing defeat in the Battle of Queenston Heights. Almost a thousand U.S. soldiers were forced to surrender.

The losses in Canada led many Americans to lose hope. In early 1813, a Kentuckian warned that any more military disasters would result in "disunion" and that the "cause of Republicanism will be lost."

Then there was a glimmer of good news. In April 1813, Americans led by General Zebulon Pike attacked York (later renamed Toronto), the provincial capital of Upper Canada. The British and Canadian militiamen surrendered, and over the next several days, in part because Pike had been killed, the U.S. soldiers rampaged out of control, plundering the city and burning government buildings.

After the burning of York, the Americans sought to gain naval control of the Great Lakes and other inland waterways along the Canadian border. If they could break the British naval supply line and secure Lake Erie, they could divide the British from their Indian allies.

In 1813, at Presque Isle, Pennsylvania, near Erie, twenty-eight-year-old Oliver Hazard Perry supervised the construction of warships from timber cut in nearby forests. By the end of the summer, Commodore Perry's new warships set out in search of the British, finally finding them at Lake Erie's Put-in-Bay on September 10.

Two British warships pounded the *Lawrence*, Perry's flagship. After four hours, none of the *Lawrence*'s guns was working, and most crew members were dead or wounded. Perry refused to quit, however. He switched to another vessel, kept fighting, and, miraculously, ended up accepting the surrender of the entire British squadron. Hatless and bloodied, Perry famously reported, "We have met the enemy and they are ours."

American control of Lake Erie forced the British to evacuate Upper Canada. They gave up Detroit and were defeated at the Battle of the Thames in southern Canada on October 5, 1813. During the battle, the British fled, leaving the great chief Tecumseh and 500 warriors to face the wrath of the Americans. When Tecumseh was killed, the remaining Indians retreated.

Perry's victory and the defeat of Tecumseh enabled the Americans to recover control of most of Michigan and seize the Western District of Upper Canada. Thereafter, the war in the north lapsed into a military stalemate, with neither side able to dislodge the other.

THE CREEK WAR War also flared in the South in 1813. The Creek Indians in western Georgia and Alabama had split into two factions: the Upper Creeks (called Red Sticks because of their bright-red war clubs), who opposed American expansion and sided with the British, and the Lower Creeks, who wanted to remain on good terms with the Americans. On August 30, Red Sticks attacked Fort Mims on the Alabama River and massacred hundreds of white and African American men, women, and children.

Americans were incensed. Thirsting for revenge, Andrew Jackson, commanding general of the Army of West Tennessee, recruited about 2,500 volunteer militiamen and headed south. With him were David Crockett, a famous sharpshooter, and Sam Houston, a nineteen-year-old Virginia frontiersman who would later lead the Texas War for Independence against Mexico.

Jackson was a natural warrior and gifted commander. His soldiers nicknamed him "Old Hickory" in recognition of his toughness. From a young age, he had embraced violence, gloried in it, and prospered by it. He told all "brave Tennesseans" that their "frontier [was] threatened with invasion by the savage

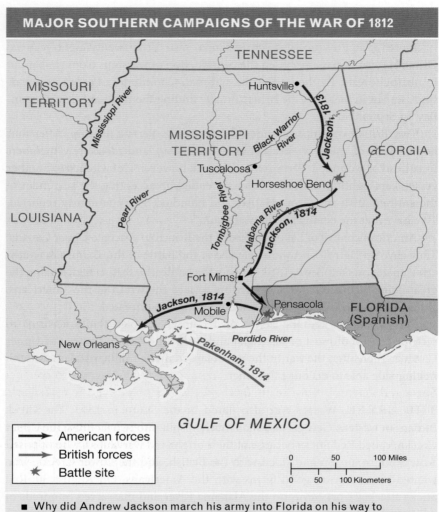

MAJOR SOUTHERN CAMPAIGNS OF THE WAR OF 1812

TENNESSEE

MISSOURI
TERRITORY

Huntsville

Mississippi River

MISSISSIPPI
TERRITORY

Black Warrior River

Jackson, 1813

GEORGIA

Tuscaloosa

Horseshoe Bend

Pearl River

Tombigbee River

Alabama River

LOUISIANA

Jackson, 1814

Fort Mims

Jackson, 1814

Mobile

Pensacola

FLORIDA
(Spanish)

New Orleans

Perdido River

Pakenham, 1814

GULF OF MEXICO

→ American forces
→ British forces
✳ Battle site

0	50	100 Miles
0	50	100 Kilometers

- Why did Andrew Jackson march his army into Florida on his way to New Orleans?
- What advantages did the American defenders have in the Battle of New Orleans?
- Why was the Battle of New Orleans important to the Treaty of Ghent?

foe" and that the Indians were advancing "with scalping knives unsheathed, to butcher your wives, your children, and your helpless babes. Time is not to be lost."

Jackson's expedition across Alabama was not easy. It was difficult to keep his men fed and supplied. Some of the men went home once their enlistment period ended. A few deserted or rebelled. When a seventeen-year-old soldier threatened an officer, he was tried and sentenced to death. Jackson had the young man shot in front of the rest of the army to demonstrate his steely determination to win the war.

Jackson's grizzled volunteers crushed the Red Sticks in a series of bloodbaths in Alabama. The decisive battle occurred on March 27, 1814, on a peninsula formed by the Horseshoe Bend on the Tallapoosa River. Jackson's soldiers, with crucial help from Cherokee and Creek allies, surrounded a Red Stick fort, set fire to it, and shot the Indians as they tried to escape. Nine hundred were killed, including 300 who drowned in a desperate effort to cross the river. Jackson reported that the "*carnage was dreadful*." Fewer than fifty of his soldiers were killed.

The Battle of Horseshoe Bend was the worst defeat ever inflicted upon Native Americans, and it effectively ended the Creeks' ability to wage war. With the Treaty of Fort Jackson, signed in August 1814, the Red Stick Creeks gave up two-thirds of their land—some 23 million acres—including southwest Georgia and much of Alabama. Red Eagle, chief of the Red Sticks, told Jackson: "I am in your power. . . . My people are all gone. I can do no more but weep over the misfortunes of my nation." President Madison rewarded Jackson by naming him a major general in the regular U.S. Army.

Events in Europe soon took a dramatic turn when the British, Spanish, and Portuguese armies repelled French emperor Napoléon's attempt to conquer Spain and Portugal. Now free to focus on the American war, the British sent 16,000 soldiers to try yet again to invade America from Canada. The British navy also received reinforcement, enabling it to extend its blockade to New England ports and to bombard coastal towns from Delaware to Florida. The final piece of the British plan was to seize New Orleans and sever American access to the Mississippi River.

FIGHTING ALONG THE CHESAPEAKE BAY In February 1813, the British had more warships in the Chesapeake Bay than were in the entire American navy, and they frequently captured and burned American merchant vessels. The British also launched numerous raids along the Virginia and Maryland shore, in effect mocking the Madison administration's ability to defend the nation.

The presence of British ships on the coast and inland rivers led many slaves to escape or revolt. As had happened during the Revolutionary War, British naval commanders promised freedom to slaves who aided or fought with them. More than 3,000 slaves in Maryland and Virginia escaped to the safety of British ships.

In September 1813, the British organized some 400 former slaves into an all-black military unit called the Colonial Marines. The recruits were provided uniforms, meals, and $6 a month in wages. News of the Colonial Marines panicked whites along the Chesapeake Bay; they feared that the former slaves would "have no mercy on them." Virginia's John Randolph spoke for many when he insisted that the "question of slavery, as it is called, is to us a question of life and death."

THE BURNING OF WASHINGTON During the late summer of 1814, U.S. forces suffered their most humiliating experience of the war when British troops captured and burned Washington, D.C.

In August, 4,000 British soldiers landed at Benedict, Maryland, routed the American militia at Bladensburg, and headed for the nation's capital a few miles away. Thousands fled the city. President Madison frantically called out the poorly led and untrained militia, then left Washington, D.C. to help rally the troops. His efforts failed, however, as the American defense disintegrated.

On August 24, British redcoats marched unopposed into the American capital. Madison and his wife, Dolley, fled just in time after first saving a portrait of George Washington and a copy of the Declaration of Independence. The vengeful British, aware that American troops had burned York, the Canadian capital, torched the Executive Mansion, the Capitol, the Library of Congress, and other government buildings before heading north to assault Baltimore. A tornado the next day compounded the damage.

The destruction of Washington, D.C., shocked, embarrassed, and infuriated Americans. Even worse, people had lost confidence in the government and the military. David Campbell, a Virginia congressman, told his brother that America was "ruled by fools and the administration opposed by knaves."

John Armstrong, the secretary of war, resigned. Madison replaced him with James Monroe, who was also secretary of state. A desperate Monroe soon proposed enlisting free blacks into the army. But many worried that such changes were too few and too late. A Virginia official noted that without a miracle, "*This union is inevitably dissolved.*"

President Madison called an emergency session of Congress and appealed to Americans to "expel the invaders." A Baltimore newspaper reported that the "spirit of the nation is roused." That determination showed itself when fifty British warships sailed into Baltimore Harbor on September 13, while 4,200 British soldiers, including the all-black Colonial Marines, assaulted

***Washington Burning*, 1814**   In this illustration by Joseph Boggs Beale, Washington residents evacuate the city as the White House and the Capitol blaze with flames in the background.

the city by land. About 1,000 Americans held Fort McHenry on an island in the harbor.

Throughout the night of September 13, the British bombarded Fort McHenry. "The portals of hell appeared to have been thrown open," an observer reported. Yet the Americans refused to surrender. At daybreak, the soldiers in the battered fort stood defiant, guns at the ready. The frustrated British sailed away.

Francis Scott Key, a slaveholding lawyer from an old Maryland plantation family who later would become district attorney for Washington, D.C., watched the assault from a British warship, having been sent to negotiate the release of a captured American. The sight of the massive U.S. flag still flying over Fort McHenry at dawn inspired Key to scribble the verses of what came to be called "The Star-Spangled Banner," which began, "Oh, say can you see, by the dawn's early light?"

Later revised and set to the tune of an English drinking song, it became America's national anthem in 1931. Less well known is that Key was a rabid white supremacist who declared that Africans in America were "a distinct and inferior race of people, which all experience proves to be the greatest evil that afflicts a community."

The lesser-known third stanza of the "Star-Spangled Banner" refers to the slaughtering of those slaves who had joined the British army in exchange for their freedom:

No refuge could save the hireling and the slave
From the terror of night or the gloom of the grave
And the star-spangled banner in triumph doth wave
O'er the land of the free and the home of the brave.

Just weeks before, Key had served as a volunteer aide to a U.S. Army general during the Battle of Bladensburg near Washington, D.C. The Colonial Marines, composed of runaway slaves, had played a crucial role in the rout of American troops that day.

THE BATTLE OF LAKE CHAMPLAIN The failure to conquer Baltimore nixed British hopes of a quick victory while giving the Americans a desperately needed morale boost. More good news soon arrived from upstate New York, where the outnumbered Americans at Plattsburgh, along Lake Champlain, were saved by the ability of Commodore Thomas Macdonough, commander of the U.S. naval squadron.

On September 11, 1814, just days after the burning of Washington, D.C., British soldiers attacked at Plattsburgh while their navy engaged Macdonough's warships in a battle that ended with the entire British fleet either destroyed or captured. The Battle of Lake Champlain (also called the Battle of Plattsburgh) forced the British to abandon the northern campaign—their main military push in the war—and retreat into Canada.

In November, an army led by Andrew Jackson in Florida seized Spanish-controlled Pensacola, on the Gulf coast, preventing another British army from landing and pushing northward into the southern states. The American victories in New York and Florida convinced Congress not to abandon Washington, D.C. Instead, the members voted to rebuild the Capitol and the Executive Mansion.

THE AFTERMATH OF THE WAR

While the fighting raged, U.S. diplomats, including Henry Clay and John Quincy Adams, son of the former president, had begun meeting with British officials in Ghent, near Brussels in present-day Belgium, to discuss ending the war. Negotiations dragged on for weeks, but on Christmas Eve 1814, the diplomats finally reached an agreement.

THE TREATY OF GHENT The weary British decided to end the war in part because of military setbacks but also because London merchants were eager to renew trade with America.

By the **Treaty of Ghent (1814)**, the two countries agreed to return each side's prisoners and restore the previous boundaries. This was a godsend for the Americans, since British forces at the time still controlled eastern Maine, northern Michigan, a portion of western New York, and several islands off the coast of Georgia. The British also pledged to stop supporting Indian attacks along the Great Lakes.

What had begun as an American effort to protect its honor, end British impressment, and conquer Canada had turned into a second war of independence. At the end of the negotiations, John Quincy Adams wrote to his wife that he had had the honor of "redeeming our union." Although the Americans lost the war for Canada and saw their national capital destroyed, they won the southern war, defeating the Indians and taking their lands. More important, the Treaty of Ghent saved the splintered republic from possible civil war and financial ruin.

THE BATTLE OF NEW ORLEANS Because it took six weeks for news of the Treaty of Ghent to reach the United States, fighting continued at the end of 1814. On December 1, Andrew Jackson arrived in New Orleans to prepare for a British invasion of the strategic city. He announced that he "would drive the British into the sea, or perish in the effort." Jackson declared martial law and transformed New Orleans into an armed camp.

On December 12, a British fleet with sixty ships and thousands of soldiers took up positions on the coast of Louisiana, hoping to capture New Orleans and gain control of the Mississippi River. But British general Sir Edward Pakenham's painfully careful preparation for an assault gave Jackson time to organize hundreds of slaves "loaned" by planters. They dug trenches, built ramparts bristling with cannons, stacked cotton bales and barrels of sugar, and dug a ten-foot-wide moat for protection.

The 4,500 Americans—including militiamen, Choctaws, African Americans, Tennessee and Kentucky sharpshooters, and Creole pirates—built an almost-invulnerable position at Chalmette Plantation seven miles south of New Orleans. Sporadic fighting occurred for more than three weeks before Pakenham rashly ordered a frontal assault at dawn on Sunday, January 8, 1815. His 5,300 soldiers marched in two columns, each eighty men abreast, into a murderous hail of artillery shells and rifle fire. When the smoke cleared, a Kentucky militiaman said that the battlefield looked first like "a sea of blood. It was not blood itself, but the red coats in which the British soldiers were dressed. The field was entirely covered in prostrate bodies."

In just 25 minutes, the British had lost some 2,100 men, including Pakenham. The Americans suffered only seventy-one killed or wounded. A British naval officer wrote that there "never was a more complete failure."

Although the **Battle of New Orleans** occurred after the Treaty of Ghent had been signed, it was vitally important psychologically. Had the British won, they might have tried to revise the treaty in their favor. Jackson's victory ensured that both governments would act quickly to approve the treaty. The unexpected American triumph also generated a wave of patriotism. As a Washington, D.C., newspaper crowed, "ALMOST INCREDIBLE VICTORY!"

Such pride in the Battle of New Orleans would later help transform Jackson into a dynamic presidential candidate eager to move the nation into an even more democratic era in which the "common man" would be celebrated and empowered. Jackson, wrote a southerner in April 1815, "is everywhere hailed as the savior of the country. . . . He has been feasted, caressed, & I may say idolized."

THE HARTFORD CONVENTION   A few weeks before the Battle of New Orleans, many New England Federalists, frustrated by the rising expense of "Mr. Madison's War," which they had opposed, tried to take matters into their own hands at the **Hartford Convention** in Hartford, Connecticut.

On December 15, 1814, the convention assembled with delegates from Massachusetts, Rhode Island, Connecticut, Vermont, and New Hampshire. Over the next three weeks, they proposed seven constitutional amendments designed to limit Republican (and southern) influence. The amendments included abolishing the counting of slaves in determining a state's representation in Congress, requiring a two-thirds supermajority rather than a simple majority vote to declare war or admit new states, prohibiting trade embargoes lasting more than sixty days, excluding immigrants from holding federal office, limiting the president to one term, and barring successive presidents from the same state (a provision clearly directed at Virginia).

The delegates also discussed the possibility that some New England states might "secede" from the United States if their demands were dismissed. Yet the threat quickly evaporated. In February 1815, when messengers from the convention reached Washington, D.C., they found the capital celebrating the good news from New Orleans. Ignored by Congress and the president, the delegates turned tail for home. The sorry episode proved fatal to the Federalist party, which never recovered from the shame of disloyalty stamped on it by the Hartford Convention.

The victory at New Orleans and the arrival of the peace treaty from Europe transformed the national mood. Almost overnight, President Madison went from being denounced and possibly impeached to being hailed a national hero.

THE WAR'S LEGACIES   There was no clear military victor in the War of 1812, nor much clarification about the issues that had ignited the war.

For all the clumsiness with which the war was managed, however, it generated an intense patriotism across much of the nation and reaffirmed American independence. The young republic was at last secure from British or European threats. As James Monroe said, "we have acquired a character and a rank among the other nations, which we did not enjoy before."

Americans soon decided that the war was a glorious triumph. The people, observed Treasury Secretary Albert Gallatin, "are more American; they feel and act more as a nation; and I hope that the permanency of the Union is thereby better secured." Yet the war also revealed the limitations of relying on militiamen and the need for a larger professional army.

Soon after the official copy of the Treaty of Ghent arrived in Washington, D.C., in February 1815, Virginian William H. Cabell wrote his brother that the "glorious peace for America . . . has come exactly when we least expected but when we most wanted it." Another Virginian, Colonel John Taylor, recognized the happy outcome as largely resulting from "a succession of lucky accidents" that "enabled the administration to get the nation out of the war."

The war also propelled the United States toward economic independence, as the interruption of trade with Europe forced America to expand its own manufacturing sector and become more self-sufficient. The British blockade of the coast created a shortage of cotton cloth in the United States, leading to the creation of the nation's first cotton-manufacturing industry, in Waltham, Massachusetts.

By the end of the war, there were more than 100 cotton mills in New England and 64 more in Pennsylvania. Even Thomas Jefferson admitted in 1815 that his beloved agricultural republic had been transformed: "We must now place the manufacturer by the agriculturalist." The new American republic was emerging as an agricultural, commercial, and industrial world power.

Perhaps the strangest result of the War of 1812 was the reversal of attitudes among Republicans and Federalists. For James Madison, the British invasion of Washington, D.C., convinced him of the necessity of a strong army and navy. In addition, the lack of a national bank had hurt the federal government's efforts to finance the war; state banks were so unstable that it was difficult to raise the funds needed to pay military expenses. In 1816, Madison created the Second Bank of the United States. The rise of new industries prompted manufacturers to call for increased tariffs on imports to protect American companies from unfair foreign competition. Madison went along, despite his criticism of tariffs in the 1790s.

While Madison reversed himself by embracing nationalism and a broader interpretation of the Constitution, the Federalists similarly reversed themselves and took up Madison's and Jefferson's original emphasis on states' rights and strict construction of the Constitution to defend the special interests of their regional stronghold, New England. It was the first great reversal of partisan political roles in constitutional interpretation. It would not be the last.

The War of 1812 proved devastating to the eastern Indian nations, most of which had fought with the British. The war accelerated westward settlement, and Native American resistance was greatly diminished after the death of Tecumseh and his Indian Confederacy. The British essentially abandoned their Indian allies, and none of their former lands were returned to them.

Lakota chief Little Crow expressed the betrayal felt by Native Americans when he rejected the consolation gifts from the local British commander: "After we have fought for you, endured many hardships, lost some of our people, and awakened the vengeance of our powerful neighbors, you make peace for yourselves. . . . You no longer need our service; you offer us these goods to pay us for [your] having deserted us. But no, we will not take them; we hold them and yourselves in equal contempt."

As the Indians were pushed out, tens of thousands of Americans moved into the Great Lakes region and into Georgia, Alabama, and Mississippi, occupying more territory in a single generation than had been settled in the 150 years of colonial history. The federal government hastened western migration by providing war veterans with 160 acres of land between the Illinois and Mississippi Rivers.

The trans-Appalachian population soared from 300,000 to 2 million between 1800 and 1820. By 1840, more than 40 percent of Americans lived west of the Appalachians in eight new states. At the same time, the growing dispute over slavery and its expansion into new western territories set in motion an explosive debate that would once again test the grand experiment in republican government.

CHAPTER REVIEW

SUMMARY

- **Jefferson's Administration** The Jeffersonian Republicans did not dismantle much of Hamilton's economic program, but they did repeal the whiskey tax, cut government expenditures, and usher in a *republican simplicity* that championed the virtues of smaller government and plain living. While Republicans idealized the agricultural world that had existed prior to 1800, the first decades of the nineteenth century were a period of transformational economic and population growth in the United States. Commercial agriculture and exports to Europe flourished; Americans moved to the West in huge numbers. The *Louisiana Purchase (1803)* dramatically expanded the boundaries of the United States. Thomas Jefferson's *Lewis and Clark expedition (1804–1805)* explored the new region and spurred interest in the Far West. In *Marbury v. Madison (1803)*, the Federalist chief justice of the Supreme Court, John Marshall, declared a federal act unconstitutional for the first time. With that decision, the Court assumed the right of judicial review over acts of Congress and established the constitutional supremacy of the federal government over state governments.

- **War in Europe** Jefferson sent warships to subdue the *Barbary pirates* in North Africa and negotiated with the Spanish and French to ensure that the Mississippi River remained open to American commerce. Renewal of war between Britain and France in 1803 complicated matters for American commerce. Neither country wanted its enemy to purchase U.S. goods, so both blockaded each other's ports. In retaliation, Jefferson convinced Congress to pass the *Embargo Act (1897)*, which prohibited all foreign trade.

- **War of 1812** President James Madison ultimately declared war against Great Britain over the issue of neutral shipping rights and the fear that the British were inciting Native Americans to attack frontier settlements. Indian nations took sides in the war. Earlier, at the Battle of Tippecanoe (1811), U.S. troops had defeated elements of *Tecumseh's Indian Confederacy*, an alliance of Indian nations determined to protect their ancestral lands. At the Battle of the Thames (1813), Tecumseh was killed. The Confederacy disintegrated soon thereafter.

- **Aftermath of the War of 1812** The *Treaty of Ghent (1814)* ended the war by essentially declaring it a draw. A smashing American victory in January 1815 at the *Battle of New Orleans* helped to ensure that the treaty would be ratified and enforced. The conflict established the economic independence of the United States, as many goods previously purchased from Britain were now manufactured at home. During and after the war, Federalists and Republicans seemed to exchange roles. Delegates from the waning Federalist party met at the *Hartford Convention (1814)* to defend states' rights and threaten secession, while Republicans promoted nationalism and a broad interpretation of the Constitution.

CHRONOLOGY

1800	U.S. population surpasses 5 million
1801	Thomas Jefferson inaugurated as president in Washington, D.C.
	Barbary pirates harass U.S. shipping
	The pasha of Tripoli declares war on the United States
1803	Supreme Court issues *Marbury v. Madison* decision
	Louisiana Purchase
1804–1806	Lewis and Clark expedition
1804	Jefferson overwhelmingly reelected
1807	British interference with U.S. shipping increases
1808	International slave trade ended in the United States
1811	Defeat of Tecumseh Indian Confederacy at the Battle of Tippecanoe
1812	Congress declares war on Britain
	U.S. invasion of Canada
1813–1814	"Creek War"
1814	British capture and burn Washington, D.C.
	Hartford Convention assembles
1815	Battle of New Orleans
	News of the Treaty of Ghent reaches the United States

KEY TERMS

republican simplicity p. 277

Marbury v. Madison (1803) p. 279

Barbary pirates p. 281

Louisiana Purchase (1803) p. 285

Lewis and Clark expedition (1804–1806) p. 285

Embargo Act (1807) p. 292

War of 1812 (1812–1815) p. 294

Tecumseh's Indian Confederacy p. 296

Treaty of Ghent (1814) p. 307

Battle of New Orleans (1815) p. 308

Hartford Convention (1814) p. 308

🐰 INQUIZITIVE

Go to InQuizitive to see what you've learned—and learn what you've missed—with personalized feedback along the way.

part three

AN EXPANDING NATION

During the nineteenth century, the United States experienced wrenching changes. With each passing decade, its predominantly agrarian society gave way to a more diverse economy and urban society, with factories and cities emerging alongside farms and towns. The pace of life quickened with industrialization. Between 1790 and 1820, the nation's boundaries expanded, and its population—both white and black—soared, while the number of Native Americans continued to decline. Immigrants from Ireland, Germany, Scandinavia, and China poured

into the United States seeking land, jobs, and freedom. By the early 1820s, the number of enslaved Americans was more than two and a half times greater than in 1790, and the number of free blacks had doubled. The white population grew just as rapidly.

Accompanying the emergence of an industrial economy in the Northeast was relentless westward expansion. Until the nineteenth century, most of the American population was clustered near the seacoast and along rivers flowing into the Atlantic Ocean or the Gulf of Mexico. After 1800, the great theme of American development was the migration of millions across the Allegheny and Appalachian Mountains into the Ohio Valley and the Middle West. Waves of adventurous Americans then crossed the Mississippi River and spread out across the Great Plains. By the 1840s, American settlers had reached the Pacific Ocean.

These developments—the emergence of a market-based economy, the impact of industrial development, and dramatic territorial expansion—made the second quarter of the nineteenth century a time of optimism and rapid change. As a German visitor noted, "Ten years in America are like a century elsewhere."

Americans were nothing if not brash and self-assured. In 1845, an editorial in the *United States Journal* claimed that "we, the American people, are the most independent, intelligent, moral, and happy people on the face of the earth." Many observers commented on the "rise of the common man" in politics and culture as the republic governed by "natural aristocrats" such as Thomas Jefferson, James Madison, James Monroe, and John Quincy Adams gave way to the frontier democracy promoted by Andrew Jackson and Henry Clay.

During the first half of the nineteenth century, two very different societies—North and South—grew more competitive with one another. The North, the more dynamic and faster-growing region, embraced industrial growth, large cities, foreign immigrants, and the ideal of "free labor" as opposed to the system of slavery in the southern states. The South remained rural, agricultural, and increasingly committed to enslaved labor as the backbone of its cotton-centered economy. Two underlying fears worried southerners: the threat of mass slave uprisings and the possibility that a northern-controlled Congress might abolish slavery. The planter elite's determination to preserve and expand slavery stifled change and reform in the South and ignited a prolonged political controversy that would eventually lead to civil war.

8

The Emergence of a Market Economy

1815–1850

***Lackawanna Valley* (1855)** Often hailed as the father of American landscape painting, George Inness was commissioned by a railroad company to capture its trains coursing through the lush Lackawanna Valley in northeastern Pennsylvania. New inventions and industrial development would continue to invade and transform the rural landscape.

No sooner had the celebrations marking the end of the war of 1812 subsided than Americans busily set about transforming their young nation. Prosperity returned as British and European markets again welcomed American ships and commerce. During the war, the loss of trade with Britain and Europe had forced the United States to develop more factories and mills of its own, spurring the growth of the diverse economy that Alexander Hamilton had envisioned in the 1790s.

Between 1815 and 1850, the United States also became a transcontinental power, expanding all the way to the Pacific coast. Hundreds of thousands of land-hungry people streamed westward. Between 1815 and 1821, six new states joined the Union: Alabama, Illinois, Indiana, Mississippi, Missouri, and Maine.

Nineteenth-century Americans were a restless, ambitious people, and the country's energy and mobility were dizzying. A Boston newspaper commented that the entire American "population is in motion." Everywhere, it seemed, people were moving to the next town, the next farm, the next opportunity. In many cities, half the population moved every ten years. In 1826, the newspaper editor in Rochester, New York, reported that 120 people left the city every day while 130 moved in. Frances Trollope, an English traveler, said that Americans were "a busy, bustling, industrious population, hacking and hewing their way" westward.

The lure of cheap land and plentiful jobs, as well as the promise of political and religious freedom, attracted millions of hardworking immigrants. This great wave of humanity was not always welcomed, however. Ethnic prejudices, anti-Catholicism, and language barriers made it difficult for many immigrants,

focus questions

1. How did changes in transportation and communication alter the economic landscape during the first half of the nineteenth century?

2. How did industrial development impact the way people worked and lived?

3. In what ways did immigration alter the nation's population and shape its politics?

4. How did the expanding "market-based economy" impact the lives of workers, professionals, and women?

especially the Irish, Germans, and Chinese, to assimilate themselves into American society and culture.

In the Midwest, large-scale commercial agriculture emerged as big farms raised corn, wheat, pigs, and cattle to be sold in distant markets and across the Atlantic. In the South, cotton became so profitable that it increasingly dominated the region's economy, luring farmers and planters (wealthy farmers with hundreds or even thousands of acres worked by large numbers of slaves) into the new states of Alabama, Mississippi, Louisiana, and Arkansas.

Cotton from the American South provided most of the clothing for people around the world. As the cotton economy expanded, it required more enslaved workers, many of whom were sold by professional slave traders and relocated from Virginia and the Carolinas to the Old Southwest—western Georgia and the Florida Panhandle, Alabama, Mississippi, Louisiana, and Arkansas.

Meanwhile, the Northeast experienced a surge of industrial development. Labor-saving machines and water- and steam-powered industries reshaped the region's economic and social life. Mills and factories began to transform the way people labored, dressed, ate, and lived. With the rise of the factory system, more and more economic activity occurred outside the home and off the farm. "The transition from mother-daughter power [in the home] to water and steam power" in the mills and factories, said a farmer, was producing a "complete revolution in social life and domestic manners." An urban middle class began to emerge as Americans, including young women, moved to towns and cities, lured by jobs in new mills, factories, stores, and banks.

By 1850, the United States boasted the world's fastest-growing economy. The industrial economy changed politics, the legal system, family dynamics, and social values. These developments in turn helped expand prosperity and freedom for whites and free blacks.

They also sparked vigorous debates over economic policies, transportation improvements, and the extension of slavery into the new territories. In the process, the nation began to divide into three regions—North, South, and West—whose shifting alliances and disputes would shape political life until the Civil War.

THE MARKET REVOLUTION

A market revolution that had begun before the war for independence accelerated the transformation of the American economy into a global powerhouse. In the eighteenth century, most Americans were isolated farmers who produced just enough food, livestock, and clothing for their own family's needs and perhaps a little more to barter (exchange) with their neighbors. Their lives revolved around a regular farmstead routine.

As the nineteenth century unfolded, however, more and more farm families began engaging in *commercial* rather than *subsistence* agriculture, producing surplus crops and livestock to sell for cash in regional and even international markets. In 1851, the president of the New York Agricultural Society noted that until the nineteenth century, "'production for consumption' was the leading purpose" of the farm economy. Now, however, "no farmer could find it profitable to do everything for himself. He now sells for money." With the cash they earned, farm families were able to buy more land, better equipment, and the latest manufactured household goods.

Such farming for sale rather than for consumption, the first stage of a "**market-based economy**," produced boom-and-bust cycles and was often built upon the backs of slave laborers, immigrant workers, and displaced Mexicans. Overall, however, the standard of living rose, and Americans enjoyed unprecedented opportunities for economic gain and geographic mobility. What the market economy most needed were "internal improvements"—deeper harbors, lighthouses, and a national network of canals, bridges, roads, and railroads—to improve the flow of goods. In 1817, for example, South Carolina congressman John C. Calhoun expressed his desire to "bind the Republic together with a perfect system of roads and canals." As the world's largest republic, the United States desperately needed a national transportation system.

Calhoun's idea sparked a fierce debate over how to fund such infrastructure improvements: Should it be the responsibility of the federal government, the individual states, or private corporations? Since the Constitution said nothing about the federal government's role in funding transportation improvements, many argued that such projects must be initiated by state and local governments. Others insisted that the Constitution gave the federal government broad powers to promote the "general welfare," which included enhancing transportation and communication. The debate over internal improvements would continue throughout the nineteenth century.

BETTER ROADS Until the nineteenth century, travel had been slow, tedious, uncomfortable, and expensive. It took a horse-drawn coach, for example, four days to go from New York City to Boston. Because of long travel times, many farm products could be sold only locally before they spoiled. That soon changed, as an array of innovations—larger horse-drawn wagons (called *Conestogas*), new roads, canals, steamboats, and railroads—knit together the expanding national market for goods and services and greatly accelerated the pace of life.

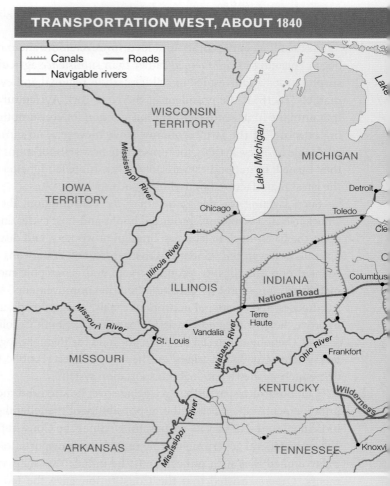

TRANSPORTATION WEST, ABOUT 1840

Canals   Roads
Navigable rivers

WISCONSIN TERRITORY

Mississippi River

Lake Michigan

MICHIGAN

IOWA TERRITORY

Detroit

Chicago

Toledo

Cle

Illinois River

ILLINOIS

INDIANA

National Road

Columbus

C

Missouri River

St. Louis

Vandalia

Terre Haute

Wabash River

Ohio River

Frankfort

MISSOURI

KENTUCKY

Wilderness

Arkansas

Mississippi River

TENNESSEE

Knoxvi

- Why were river towns important commercial centers?
- What was the economic impact of the steamboat and the flatboat in the West?
- How did the Erie Canal transform the economy of New York and the Great Lakes region?

Better roads led to faster travel. In 1803, when Ohio became a state, Congress ordered that 5 percent of the money from land sales in the state should go toward building a National Road from the Atlantic coast across Ohio and westward. Construction finally began in 1811. Originally called the Cumberland Road, it was the first interstate roadway financed by the federal government. By 1818, the road was open from Cumberland, Maryland, to

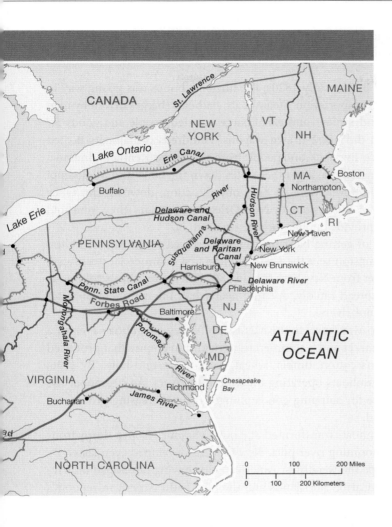

Wheeling, Virginia (now West Virginia), where it crossed the Ohio River. By 1838, the National Road extended 600 miles farther westward to Vandalia, Illinois.

The National Road quickened the settlement of the West and the emergence of a truly national market economy by reducing transportation costs, opening up new markets, and stimulating the growth of towns. Farmers increasingly took their produce and livestock to sell in distant markets.

To the northeast, a movement for paved roads gathered momentum after the Philadelphia-Lancaster Turnpike opened in 1794. (The term *turnpike* derived from a pole, or pike, at the tollgate, which was turned to admit the traffic in exchange for a small fee, or toll.) By 1821, some 4,000 miles of turnpikes had been built, and stagecoach and freight companies emerged to move more people and cargo at lower rates.

WATERWAYS By the early 1820s, the turnpike boom was giving way to advances in water transportation. Steamboats, flatboats (barges driven by men using long poles and mules), and canal barges carried people and goods far more cheaply than did horse-drawn wagons. Hundreds of flatboats floated goods, farm produce, livestock, and people from Tennessee, Kentucky, Indiana, Ohio, western Pennsylvania, and other states down the Ohio and Mississippi Rivers. Flatboats, however, went in only one direction: downstream. Once unloaded in Natchez, Mississippi, or New Orleans, Louisiana, they were sold and dismantled to provide lumber for construction.

The difficulties of getting back upriver were solved when Robert Fulton and Robert R. Livingston sent the *Clermont*, the first commercial steamboat, up the Hudson River from New York City in 1807. Thereafter, the use of wood-fired **steamboats** spread rapidly, opening nearly half the continent to water traffic along the major rivers.

By bringing two-way travel to the Mississippi Valley, steamboats created a transcontinental market and a commercial agricultural empire that produced much of the nation's cotton, timber, wheat, corn, cattle, and hogs. By 1836, there were 750 steamboats operating on American rivers. As steamboat use increased, the price for shipping goods plunged, thus increasing profits and stimulating demand.

The use of steamboats transformed St. Louis, Missouri, from a sleepy frontier village into a booming river port. New Orleans developed even faster. By 1840, it was perhaps the wealthiest American city, having developed a thriving trade with the Caribbean islands and the new Latin American republics that had overthrown Spanish rule. A thousand steamboats a year visited New Orleans. The annual amount of trade shipped through the river city doubled that of New York City by 1843, in large part because of the explosion in cotton production.

Wood-burning steamboats were a risky form of transportation. Accidents, explosions, and fires were common, and sanitation was poor. Passengers crowded on board along with pigs and cattle. There were no toilets on steamboats until the 1850s; passengers shared the same two washbasins and towels. Despite the inconveniences, however, steamboats were the fastest and most convenient form of transportation in the first half of the nineteenth century.

Canals also sped the market revolution. The historic **Erie Canal** in central New York connected the Great Lakes and the Midwest to the Hudson River and New York City. New York Governor DeWitt Clinton took the lead in promoting the risky project, which Thomas Jefferson dismissed as "little short of madness." Clinton, however, boasted that New York had the opportunity to "create a new era in history, and to erect a work more stupendous, more magnificent, and more beneficial, than has hitherto been achieved by the human race."

It was not an idle boast. After the Erie Canal opened in 1825, having taken eight years to build, it drew eastward much of the midwestern trade (furs, lumber, textiles) that earlier had been forced to go to Canada or make the long journey down the Ohio and Mississippi Rivers to New Orleans and the Gulf of Mexico. Thanks to the Erie Canal, the backwoods village of Chicago developed into a bustling city because of its commercial connection via the Great Lakes to New York City, and eventually to Europe.

The Erie Canal was a triumph of engineering audacity. Forty feet wide and four feet deep, it was the longest canal in the world, extending 363 miles across New York from Albany in the east to Buffalo and Lake Erie in the west, and rising some 675 feet in elevation.

The canal was built by thousands of laborers, mostly German and Irish immigrants who were paid less than a dollar a day to drain swamps, clear forests, build stone bridges and aqueducts, and blast through solid rock. It brought a "river of gold" to New York City in the form of an unending stream

The Erie Canal *Junction of the Erie and Northern Canals* (1830–1832), by John Hill.

of lumber, grain, flour, and other goods, and it unlocked the floodgates of western settlement. The canal also reduced the cost of moving a ton of freight from $100 to $5. It was so profitable that it paid off its construction costs in just seven years.

The Erie Canal also had enormous economic and political consequences, as it tied together the regional economies of the Midwest and the East while further isolating the Deep South. The Genesee Valley in western New York became one of the most productive grain-growing regions in the world; Rochester became a boom town, processing wheat and corn into flour and meal. Syracuse, Albany, and Buffalo experienced similarly dramatic growth.

The business of moving goods and people along the canal involved some 4,000 boats and more than 25,000 workers. Canal boats, usually eleven feet wide and seventy feet long, were pulled by teams of horses or mules walking along a towpath adjacent to the canal. The success of the Erie Canal and the entire New York canal system inspired other states to build some 3,000 miles of waterways by 1837. Canals spurred the economy by enabling speedier and less expensive transport of goods and people. They also boosted real estate prices for the lands bordering them and transformed sleepy villages into booming cities.

RAILROADS   The canal era was short-lived, however. During the second quarter of the nineteenth century, a much less expensive but much more efficient and versatile form of transportation emerged: the railroad.

In 1825, the year the Erie Canal was completed, the world's first steam-powered railway began operating in England. Soon thereafter, a railroad-building "epidemic" infected the United States. In 1830, the nation had only twenty-three miles of railroad track. Over the next twenty years, railroad coverage grew to 30,626 miles.

The railroad quickly surpassed other forms of transportation because trains could move people and freight faster, farther, and cheaper than could wagons or boats. The early **railroads** averaged ten miles per hour, more than twice the speed of stagecoaches and four times that of boats and barges. That locomotives were able to operate year-round gave rail travel a huge advantage over canals that froze in winter and dirt roads that became rivers of mud during rainstorms.

Railroads also provided indirect benefits by encouraging western settlement and the expansion of commercial agriculture. A westerner reported that the opening of a new rail line resulted in the emergence of three new villages along the line. The depot or rail station became the central building in every town, a public place where people from all walks of life converged.

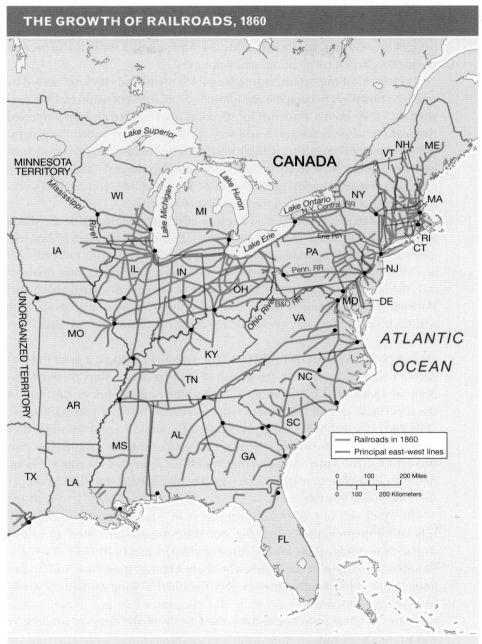

THE GROWTH OF RAILROADS, 1860

Railroads in 1860	
Principal east-west lines	

0   100   200 Miles
0   100   200 Kilometers

- Why did the number of railroads expand rapidly from 1850 to 1860?
- What were the principal east–west lines?

Building railroads stimulated the national economy not only by improving transportation but by creating a huge demand for iron, wooden crossties, bridges, locomotives, freight cars, and other equipment. Railroads also became the nation's largest corporations and employers.

Perhaps most important, railroads enabled towns and cities not served by canals or turnpikes to compete economically. Rail transportation transformed what had once been a cluster of mostly local markets into an interconnected national marketplace for goods and services. Railroads expanded the geography of American capitalism, making possible larger industrial and commercial enterprises from coast to coast. Railroads were also the first "big" businesses, huge corporations employing thousands of people while exercising extraordinary influence over the life of the regions they served.

Railroad mania, however, had negative effects as well. Its quick and shady profits frequently led to political corruption. Railroad titans often bribed legislators. By facilitating access to the trans-Appalachian West, the railroads also accelerated the decline of Native American culture. In addition, they dramatically increased the tempo, mobility, and noise of everyday life. Writer Nathaniel Hawthorne spoke for many when he said that the locomotive, with its startling whistle, brought "the noisy world into the midst of our slumberous space."

OCEAN TRANSPORTATION The year 1845 brought a great innovation in ocean transport with the launch of the first clipper ship, the *Rainbow*. Built for speed, the **clipper ships** were the nineteenth-century equivalent of the supersonic jetliner. They were twice as fast as the older merchant ships. Long and lean, with taller masts and larger sails than conventional ships, they cut dashing figures during their brief but colorful career, which lasted less than two decades. The American thirst for Chinese tea prompted the clipper boom. Asian tea leaves had to reach markets quickly after harvest, and the fast clipper ships made this possible.

The discovery of gold in California in 1848 lured thousands of prospectors and entrepreneurs. When the would-be miners generated an urgent demand for goods on the West Coast, the clippers met it. In 1854, the *Flying Cloud* took eighty-nine days and eight hours to travel from New York to San Francisco, around South America, less than half as long as the trip would have taken in a conventional ship. But clippers, while fast, lacked ample space for cargo or passengers. After the Civil War, the clippers would give way to the steamship.

COMMUNICATIONS Innovations in transportation also helped spark improvements in communications, which knit the nation even closer together.

Building a clipper ship This 1833 oil painting captures the Messrs. Smith & Co.
Ship Yard in Manhattan, where shipbuilders are busy shaping timbers to construct a
clipper ship.

At the beginning of the nineteenth century, traveling was slow and difficult. It
often took days or weeks for news to travel along the Atlantic Seaboard. For
example, after George Washington died in 1798 in Virginia, word of his death
did not appear in New York City newspapers until a week later. By 1829, however, it was possible to deliver Andrew Jackson's inaugural address from Washington, D.C., to New York City by relay horse riders in less than twenty hours.

Mail deliveries also improved. The number of post offices soared from 75
in 1790 to 28,498 in 1860. In addition, new steam-powered printing presses
enabled the mass production of newspapers, reducing their cost from 6¢ to a
penny each.

But the most important advance in communications was the national elec-
tromagnetic **telegraph system**, invented by Samuel F. B. Morse. In May 1844,
Morse sent the first intercity telegraph message from Washington, D.C., to
Baltimore, Maryland. It read: "What Hath God Wrought?"

By the end of the decade, most major cities benefited from telegraph lines.
By allowing people to communicate faster and more easily across long distances, the telegraph system triggered many changes, not the least of which
was helping railroad operators schedule trains more precisely and thus avoid
collisions. A New Orleans newspaper claimed that, with the invention of the
telegraph, "scarcely anything now will appear to be impossible."

THE ROLE OF GOVERNMENT Steamboats, canals, and railroads connected the western areas of the country with the East, boosted trade, helped open the Far West for settlement, and spurred dramatic growth in cities. Between 1800 and 1860, an undeveloped nation of scattered farms, primitive roads, and modest local markets became an engine of capitalist expansion, urban energy, and global reach.

The national government bought stock in turnpike and canal companies and, after the success of the Erie Canal, awarded land grants to several western states to support canal and railroad projects. In 1850, Stephen A. Douglas, a powerful Democratic senator from Illinois, convinced Congress to provide a major land grant to support a north–south rail line connecting Chicago and Mobile, Alabama. The 1850 congressional land grant set a precedent for other bounties that totaled about 20 million acres by 1860. However, this would prove to be a small amount when compared to the land grants that Congress would award transcontinental railroads during the 1860s and after.

INDUSTRIAL DEVELOPMENT

The concentration of huge numbers of people in commercial and factory cities, coupled with the transportation and communication revolutions, greatly increased the number of potential customers for given products. Such expanding market demand in turn gave rise to a system of *mass production*, whereby companies used new technologies (labor-saving machines) to produce greater quantities of products that could be sold at lower prices to more people, thus generating higher profits.

The introduction of steam engines, as well as the application of new technologies to make manufacturing more efficient, sparked a wave of unrelenting **industrialization** in Europe and America from the mid–eighteenth century to the late nineteenth century. "It is an extraordinary era in which we live," reported Daniel Webster in 1847. "It is altogether new. The world has seen nothing like it before."

New machines and improvements in agricultural and industrial efficiency led to a remarkable increase in productivity. By 1860, one farmer, miner, or mill worker could produce twice as much wheat, twice as much iron, and more than four times as much cotton cloth as in 1800.

AMERICAN TECHNOLOGY Improvements in productivity were enabled by the inventiveness of Americans. Between 1790 and 1811, the U.S. Patent Office approved an annual average of 77 patents certifying new inventions;

by the 1850s, the Patent Office was approving more than 28,000 new inventions each year.

Many inventions generated dramatic changes. In 1844, for example, Charles Goodyear patented a process for "vulcanizing" rubber, making it stronger, more elastic, waterproof, and winter-proof. Vulcanized rubber was soon being used for everything from shoes and boots to seals, gaskets, hoses and, eventually, tires.

In 1846, Elias Howe patented his design of the sewing machine. It was soon improved upon by Isaac Merritt Singer, who founded the Singer Sewing Machine Company, which initially produced only industrial sewing machines for use in textile mills but eventually offered machines for home use. The availability of sewing machines helped revolutionize "women's work" by dramatically reducing the time needed to make clothes at home, thus freeing up more leisure time for many women.

Technological advances improved living conditions; houses could be larger, better heated, and better illuminated. The first sewer systems helped rid city streets of human and animal waste. Mechanization of factories meant that more goods could be produced faster and with less labor, and machines helped industries produce "standardized parts" that could be assembled by unskilled wage workers. Machine-made clothes using standardized forms fit better and were less expensive than those sewn by hand; machine-made newspapers and magazines were more abundant and affordable, as were clocks, watches, guns, and plows.

THE IMPACT OF THE COTTON GIN In 1792, New Englander Eli Whitney visited Mulberry Grove plantation on the Georgia coast, where he "heard much said of the difficulty of ginning cotton"—that is, separating the fibers from the seeds. Cotton had been used for clothing and bedding from ancient times, but until the nineteenth century, cotton cloth was rare and expensive because it took so long to separate the lint (fibers) from the sticky seeds. One person working all day could separate barely one pound by hand.

At Mulberry Grove, Whitney learned that the person who could invent a "machine" to gin cotton would become wealthy overnight. Within a few days, he had devised what he called "an absurdly simple contrivance" using nails attached to a roller, to remove the seeds from cotton bolls. Over time, Whitney continued to refine his gin until it was patented in 1794. The **cotton gin** (short for *engine*) proved to be fifty times more productive than a hand laborer. Almost overnight, it made cotton America's most profitable crop. In the process, it transformed southern agriculture, northern industry, race-based slavery, national politics, and international trade.

KING COTTON Southern-grown **cotton** became the dominant force driving both the national economy and the controversial efforts to expand slavery into the western territories. Cotton, or "white gold," brought enormous wealth to southern planters and merchants, New England mill owners, and New York shipowners.

Because of the widespread use of cotton gins, by 1812 the cost of producing cotton yarn had plunged by 90 percent, and the spread of textile mills overseas had created a growing global market for southern cotton. By the mid–nineteenth century, people worldwide were wearing more-comfortable and easier-to-clean cotton clothing. When British textile manufacturers chose the less brittle American cotton over the varieties grown in the Caribbean, Brazil, and India, the demand for southern cotton skyrocketed, as did its price.

Cotton became America's largest export product and the primary driver of the nation's extraordinary economic growth. By 1860, British textile mills were processing a billion pounds a year, 92 percent of which came from the American South.

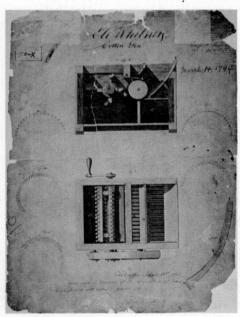

Whitney's cotton gin Eli Whitney's drawing, which accompanied his 1794 federal patent application, shows the side and top of the machine as well as the sawteeth that separated the seeds from the fiber.

Cotton growing first emerged in the Piedmont region of the Carolinas and Georgia. After the War of 1812, it migrated into the contested Indian lands to the west—Tennessee, Alabama, Florida, Mississippi, Louisiana, Arkansas, and Texas. New Orleans became a bustling port—and active slave market—because of the cotton grown throughout the region and shipped down the Mississippi River. From the mid-1830s to 1860, cotton accounted for more than half of American exports. Planter capitalists in the South harvested raw cotton, and northern buyers and shipowners carried it to New England, Great Britain, and France, where textile mills spun the fiber into thread and fabric. Bankers in New York City and London financed the growth of global cotton capitalism.

THE EXPANSION OF SLAVERY Because cotton was a labor-intensive crop, growers were convinced that only slaves could make their farms and plantations profitable. As a result, the price of slaves soared. When farmland in Maryland and Virginia lost its fertility after years of relentless tobacco planting, many whites shifted to growing corn and wheat, since the climate was too cold for cotton, and they sold their surplus slaves to work in the new cotton-growing areas in Georgia, Alabama, Mississippi, and Louisiana. In 1790, planters in Virginia and Maryland had owned 56 percent of all the slaves in the United States; by 1860, they owned only 15 percent.

Cotton created boom times. A cotton farmer in Mississippi urged a friend in Kentucky to sell his farm and join him: "If you could reconcile it to yourself to bring your negroes to the Mississippi Territory, they would certainly make you a handsome fortune in ten years by the cultivation of Cotton." Slaves became so valuable that stealing them became a common problem in the southern states.

FARMING THE MIDWEST By 1860, more than half the nation's population lived west of the Appalachian Mountains. The flat, fertile farmlands in the Midwest—Ohio, Michigan, Indiana, Illinois, and Iowa—drew farmers from the rocky hillsides of New England and the exhausted soils of Virginia. By 1860, an estimated 30 to 40 percent of Americans born in New England had moved west, looking to start fresh on their *own* land made available by the government.

After land was cleared, corn was typically the first crop grown. Women and children often planted the seeds in small mounds about three feet apart. Once the corn sprouted, pumpkin, squash, or bean seeds would be planted around the seedlings. Corn kernels could be boiled to make porridge or ground up to make flour and cornmeal that was baked into a bread called johnnycake, and corn stalks were stored to provide winter feed for the cattle and hogs.

Over time, technological advances led to greater agricultural productivity. The development of durable iron plows (replacing wooden ones) eased the backbreaking job of tilling the soil. In 1819, Jethro Wood of New York introduced an iron plow with separate parts that were easily replaced when needed. Further improvements would follow, including Vermonter John Deere's steel plow (1837), whose sharp edges could cut through the tough prairie grass in the Midwest and Great Plains.

Other technological improvements quickened the growth of commercial agriculture. By the 1840s, new mechanical seeders had replaced the process of sowing seed by hand. Even more important, in 1831 twenty-two-year-old Virginian Cyrus Hall McCormick invented a mechanical reaper to harvest wheat, a development as significant to the agricultural economy of the Midwest, Old Northwest, and Great Plains as the cotton gin was to the South.

In 1847, **McCormick reapers** began selling so fast that McCormick moved to Chicago and built a manufacturing plant. Within a few years, he had sold thousands of his machines, in the process transforming the scale of commercial agriculture. Using a handheld sickle, a farmer could harvest a half acre of wheat a day; with a McCormick reaper, two people could work twelve acres a day.

EARLY TEXTILE MANUFACTURERS While technological breakthroughs quickened agricultural development and created a national and international marketplace, other advances altered the economic landscape even more profoundly. Industrial capitalists who financed and built the first factories were the revolutionaries of the nineteenth century.

Mills and factories were initially powered by water wheels, then coal-fired steam engines. The shift from water to coal as a source of energy initiated a worldwide industrial era destined to end Britain's long domination of the global economy.

The foundations of Britain's advantage were the invention of the steam engine in 1705, its improvement by James Watt in 1765, and a series of additional inventions that mechanized the production of textiles (including thread, fabric, bedding, and clothing). Britain carefully guarded its industrial secrets, forbidding the export of machines or the publication of descriptions of them, and even restricting the emigration of skilled mechanics.

In 1800, the output of America's mills and factories amounted to only one sixth of Great Britain's production, and the growth rate remained slow until Thomas Jefferson's embargo in 1807 stimulated the domestic production of cloth. By 1815, hundreds of textile mills in New England, New York, and Pennsylvania were producing thread, cloth, and clothing.

After the War of 1812, however, British textile companies blunted America's industrial growth by flooding the United States with cheap cotton cloth in an effort to regain their customers who had been shut off by the war. Such postwar "dumping" nearly killed the American textile industry. A delegation of New England mill owners traveled to Washington, D.C., to demand a federal tariff (tax) on imported British cloth to make American textile mills more competitive. Their efforts created a culture of industrial lobbying for congressional tariff protection against imported products that continues to this day.

What the mill owners neglected to admit was that import tariffs hurt consumers by forcing them to pay higher prices. Over time, as Scotsman Adam Smith explained in *The Wealth of Nations* (1776), consumers not only pay higher prices for foreign goods as a result of tariffs, but higher prices for domestic goods, since businesses invariably seize opportunities to raise the prices charged for their products.

Tariffs helped protect American industries from foreign competition, but competition is the engine of innovation and efficiency in a capitalist economy. New England shipping companies opposed higher tariffs because they would reduce the amount of goods carried in their vessels across the Atlantic from Britain and Europe. Many southern planters opposed tariffs because of fears that Britain and France would retaliate by imposing tariffs on American cotton and tobacco shipped to their ports.

In the end, Congress passed the Tariff Bill of 1816, which placed a tax of 25¢ on every yard of imported cloth. By impeding foreign competition, the tariffs enabled American manufacturers to dominate the national marketplace.

THE LOWELL SYSTEM The factory system, centered on wage-earning workers, emerged at Waltham, Massachusetts, in 1813, when a group known as the Boston Associates constructed the first textile mill in which the mechanized processes of spinning yarn and weaving cloth were brought together under one roof.

In 1822, the Boston Associates, led by Francis Cabot Lowell, developed another cotton mill at a village along the Merrimack River twenty-eight miles north of Boston. Renamed Lowell, it soon became the model for textile mill towns throughout New England.

The founders of the **Lowell system** sought not just to improve efficiency but to develop model industrial communities. They located their four- and five-story brick-built mills along rivers in the countryside.

The mill owners hired mostly young women ages fifteen to thirty from farm families. The owners preferred women laborers because of their skill in operating textile machines. Also valued was their general ability to endure the mind-numbing boredom of operating

Mill girls Massachusetts mill workers of the mid–nineteenth century, photographed holding shuttles used in spinning thread and yarn.

spinning machines and looms for a wage of $2.50 per week—a wage lower than that paid to men for the same work. At the time, these jobs offered the highest wages, for women, of any in the world.

Moreover, by the 1820s, New England had a surplus of women because so many men had migrated westward. In the early 1820s, a steady stream of single women began flocking to Lowell. To reassure worried parents, mill owners promised to provide the "Lowell girls" with tolerable work, prepared meals, comfortable boardinghouses (four girls to a room), moral discipline, and educational and cultural opportunities.

Initially the "Lowell idea" worked. The Lowell girls lived in dormitories staffed by housemothers who enforced church attendance and evening curfews. Despite thirteen-hour work days and five-and-a-half day work weeks (longer hours than those imposed upon prison inmates), some of the women found time to form study groups, publish a literary magazine, and attend lectures. By 1840, there were thirty-two mills and factories in Lowell.

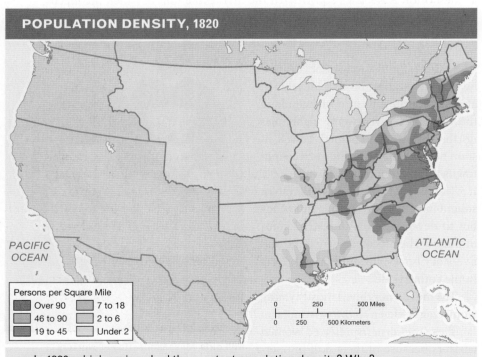

POPULATION DENSITY, 1820

PACIFIC OCEAN

ATLANTIC OCEAN

Persons per Square Mile

- Over 90
- 46 to 90
- 19 to 45
- 7 to 18
- 2 to 6
- Under 2

0 — 250 — 500 Miles
0 — 250 — 500 Kilometers

- In 1820, which regions had the greatest population density? Why?
- How did the changes in the 1820 land law encourage western expansion?
- What events caused the price of land to decrease between 1800 and 1841?

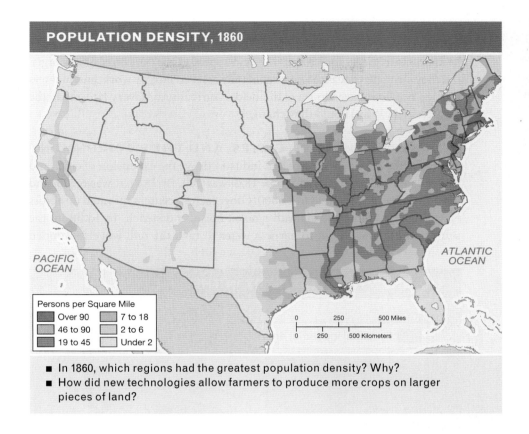

POPULATION DENSITY, 1860

PACIFIC OCEAN

ATLANTIC OCEAN

Persons per Square Mile

- Over 90
- 46 to 90
- 19 to 45
- 7 to 18
- 2 to 6
- Under 2

0   250   500 Miles

0   250   500 Kilometers

- In 1860, which regions had the greatest population density? Why?
- How did new technologies allow farmers to produce more crops on larger pieces of land?

As Lowell grew, however, the once rural village became a grimy industrial city. Mill owners produced too much cloth, which depressed prices. To maintain their profits, they cut wages and quickened the pace of work. As a worker said, "We go in at five o'clock [in the morning]; at seven we come out to breakfast; at half-past seven we return to our work, and stay until half past twelve. At one . . . we return to our work, and stay until seven at night."

In 1834, about a sixth of the native-born Lowell women mill workers went on strike to protest their working and living conditions. The mill owners labeled the 1,500 striking women "ungrateful" and "unfeminine"—and tried to get rid of the strike's leaders.

Two years later, the Lowell workers again walked out, this time in protest of the owners raising rents in the company-owned boarding houses. Although the owners backed down, they soon began hiring Irish immigrants who were so desperate for jobs that they rarely complained about the working conditions. By 1850, some 40 percent of the mill workers were Irish.

The economic success of the New England textile mills raises an obvious question: Why didn't the South build its own mills close to the cotton fields to keep profits in the region? A few mills did appear in the Carolinas and Georgia, but they struggled because whites generally resisted factory work, and planters refused to allow slaves to leave the fields. Agricultural slavery had made the planters rich. Why should they change?

INDUSTRIALIZATION, CITIES, AND THE ENVIRONMENT
The rapid growth of commerce and industry drove the expansion of cities and mill villages. Lowell's population in 1820 was 200. By 1830, it was 6,500, and ten years later it had soared to 21,000. Other factory centers sprouted up across New England, filling the air with smoke, noise, and stench. In addition, the profusion of dams—built to harness water to turn the mill wheels—flooded

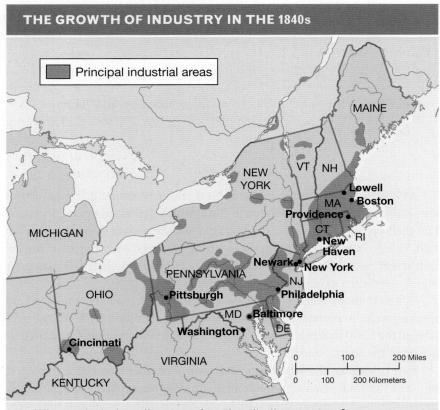

THE GROWTH OF INDUSTRY IN THE 1840s

Principal industrial areas

MAINE

NEW YORK

VT   NH

Lowell

MA   Boston

Providence

CT

New Haven   RI

MICHIGAN

Newark   New York

PENNSYLVANIA

NJ

OHIO   Pittsburgh   Philadelphia

MD   Baltimore

Washington   DE

Cincinnati

VIRGINIA

KENTUCKY

0   100   200 Miles

0   100   200 Kilometers

■ What made the Lowell system of textile mill villages unique?
■ What were the consequences of industrial expansion in the Northeast?

pastures, decimated fish populations, and spawned rapid urban growth that polluted rivers.

Between 1820 and 1840, the number of Americans engaged in manufacturing increased 800 percent, and the number of city dwellers more than doubled. As Thomas Jefferson and other agrarians had feared, the United States was rapidly becoming a global industrial power.

Between 1790 and 1860, the proportion of urban to rural populations grew from 3 percent to 16 percent. New Orleans became the nation's fifth-largest city because of its location and role in shipping goods floated down the Mississippi River for distribution to the East Coast and to Europe. By 1860, New York had become the first city to surpass 1 million in population, largely because of its superior harbor and its unique access to commerce along the Erie Canal and the Atlantic Ocean.

POPULAR CULTURE

During the colonial era, working-class Americans had little time for amusement. Most adults worked from dawn to dusk six days a week. In rural areas, free time was often spent in communal activities, such as barn raisings, shooting matches, and footraces, while coastal residents sailed and fished. In cities, people attended dances, went on sleigh rides and picnics, and played "parlor games" such as billiards, cards, and chess.

By the early nineteenth century, however, an increasingly urban society enjoyed more diverse forms of recreation. A distinctive urban culture emerged, and laborers and shopkeepers sought new forms of leisure and entertainment.

URBAN RECREATION Social drinking was pervasive during the first half of the nineteenth century. In 1829, the secretary of war estimated that three quarters of the nation's laborers drank at least four ounces of "hard liquor" daily. Taverns and social or sporting clubs served as centers of recreation and leisure.

So-called blood sports were also popular, especially among the working poor. Cockfighting and dogfighting attracted frenzied betting, but prizefighting (boxing) eventually displaced the animal contests and proved popular with all social classes. The early contestants tended to be Irish or English immigrants who fought with bare knuckles, and the results were brutal. A match ended only when a contestant could not continue. One bout in 1842 lasted 119 rounds and ended when a fighter died in his corner. Such deaths prompted several cities to outlaw boxing, only to see it reappear as an underground activity.

Bare Knuckles Blood sports emerged as popular urban entertainment for men of all social classes, but especially among the working poor.

THE POPULAR ARTS Theaters became the most popular form of indoor entertainment. People from all walks of life flocked to opera houses, playhouses, and music halls to watch a wide spectrum of performances: Shakespeare's tragedies, "blood and thunder" melodramas, comedies, minstrel shows, operas, and local pageants. Audiences were predominantly men. "Respectable" women rarely attended, as the prevailing "cult of domesticity" kept them at home.

The 1830s brought the first uniquely American form of mass entertainment: blackface minstrel shows, featuring white performers made up as blacks. "Minstrelsy," which drew upon African American folklore and reinforced racial stereotypes, featured banjo and fiddle music, "shuffle" dances, and lowbrow humor. Between the 1830s and the 1870s, minstrel shows were immensely popular, especially among northern working-class ethnic groups and southern whites.

The most popular minstrel songs were written by a white composer named Stephen Foster. In 1846, he composed "Oh! Susanna," which immediately became a national favorite. Its popularity catapulted Foster into the limelight, and he responded with equally well-received tunes such as "Old Folks at Home" (popularly known as "Way Down upon the Swanee River"), "Massa's in de Cold, Cold Ground," "My Old Kentucky Home," and "Old Black Joe," all of which perpetuated the sentimental myth of contented slaves.

The Crow Quadrilles This sheet-music cover, printed in 1837, shows vignettes caricaturing African Americans. Minstrel shows enjoyed nationwide popularity while reinforcing racial stereotypes.

IMMIGRATION

More than ever, the United States continued to be a nation of immigrants. Warfare in Europe at the start of the nineteenth century restricted travel to America. After 1815, however, when Napoléon was defeated and forced into exile, new U.S. territories and states in the West actively recruited immigrants from Europe, often offering special incentives such as voting rights after only six-months' residency.

Why did people risk their lives and abandon their homelands to come to the United States? America offered jobs, higher wages, lower taxes, cheap and fertile land, no entrenched aristocracy, religious freedom, and voting rights.

After 1837, a worldwide economic slump accelerated the pace of immigration. American employers recruited foreigners, in large part because they were often willing to work for lower wages than native-born Americans. The *Chicago Daily Tribune* observed that the tide of German immigrants was perfect for the "cheap and ingenious labor of the country." A German laborer was willing "to live as cheaply and work infinitely more intelligently than the negro."

The years from 1845 to 1854 marked the greatest proportional influx of immigrants in U.S. history, 2.4 million, or about 14.5 percent of the total population in 1845. By far the largest number of immigrants between 1840 and 1860 came from Ireland and Germany.

THE IRISH No nation proportionately sent more of its people to America than Ireland. A prolonged agricultural crisis caused many Irish to flee their homeland in the mid–nineteenth century. Irish farmers primarily grew potatoes; a third of them were dependent on the potato harvest for survival.

In 1845, a fungus destroyed the potato crop and triggered what came to be called the Irish Potato Famine. More than a million people died, and almost 2 million more left Ireland, whose total population was only 8 million. Most traveled to Canada and the United States. By the 1850s, the Irish made up more than half the population of Boston and New York City and were almost as dominant in Philadelphia. Most of them were crowded into filthy, poorly ventilated tenement apartments, and Irish neighborhoods were plagued by crime, diseases, prostitution, and alcoholism. The archbishop of New York described the Irish as "the poorest and most wretched population that can be found in the world."

The Irish often took on the hardest and most dangerous jobs. A visiting Irish journalist wrote that there were "several sorts of power working at the fabric of the Republic: water-power, steam-power, horse-power, and Irish power. The last works hardest of them all." It was mostly Irish men who built the canals and railroads, and mostly Irish women who worked in the textile mills and cleaned the houses of upper-middle-class Americans. One Irishman groaned that he worked like "a slave for the Americans."

Irish immigrants were stereotyped as filthy, bad-tempered, and heavy drinkers. They also encountered anti-Catholic prejudice among native-born Protestants. Many employers posted signs reading "No Irish Need Apply."

Irish Americans, however, could be equally mean-spirited toward other groups, such as free African Americans, who competed with them for low-wage, mostly unskilled jobs. In 1850, the *New York Tribune* expressed concern that the Irish, having escaped from "a galling, degrading bondage" in their homeland, opposed equal rights for blacks and frequently arrived at the polls shouting, "Down with the Nagurs! Let them go back to Africa, where they belong."

Many African Americans viewed the Irish with equal contempt. In 1850, a slave noted that his "master" "treats me badly as if I were a common Irishman." Irish immigrants often worked as waiters, dockworkers, and deliverymen—jobs that had long been held by African Americans. One frustrated free black said that the Irish were "crowding themselves into every place of business and labor, and driving the poor colored American citizen out."

Some enterprising Irish immigrants did forge remarkable careers in America, however. Twenty years after arriving in New York, Alexander T. Stewart became the owner of the nation's largest department store and vast real estate holdings. Michael Cudahy, who began working at age fourteen in a Milwaukee meatpacking business, became head of the Cudahy Packing Company and developed a process for the curing of meats under refrigeration. Dublin-born Victor Herbert emerged as one of America's most revered composers, and Irish dancers and playwrights came to dominate the stage.

By the start of the Civil War, Irish immigrants had energized American trade unions, become the most important ethnic group supporting the Democratic party, and made the Roman Catholic Church the nation's largest denomination. Years of persecution had instilled a fierce loyalty to the Catholic Church as "the supreme authority over all the affairs of the world." Such passion for Catholicism generated unity among Irish Americans—and fear among Protestants.

THE GERMANS German immigrants were almost as numerous as the Irish. Unlike the Irish, however, the Germans included skilled craftsmen and well-educated professional people—doctors, lawyers, teachers, engineers—some of whom were refugees from the failed German revolution of 1848.

The Germans brought with them a variety of religious preferences. Most were Protestants (usually Lutherans), a third were Roman Catholics, and a significant number were Jews. Among the Germans who prospered in the New World were Heinrich Steinweg, a piano maker who in America changed his name to Steinway and became famous for the quality of his instruments, and Levi Strauss, a Jewish tailor who followed the gold rush to California and began making work pants, later dubbed "Levi's."

Germans settled more often in rural areas. Many were independent farmers, skilled workers, and shopkeepers who were able to establish themselves immediately. More so than the Irish, they migrated in families and groups. This clannish quality helped them better sustain elements of their language and culture. More of them also returned to Germany. About 14 percent eventually went back to their homeland, compared with 9 percent of the Irish.

THE BRITISH, SCANDINAVIANS, AND CHINESE Immigrants from Great Britain and Canada continued to arrive in large numbers during the first half of the nineteenth century. They included professionals, independent farmers, and skilled workers. Two other large groups of immigrants were from Scandinavia and China. Norwegians and Swedes, mostly farmworkers, gravitated to Illinois, Wisconsin, and the Minnesota Territory, where the cold climate and dense forests reminded them of home. By the 1850s, the rapid development of California was attracting a growing number of Chinese, who, like the Irish in the East, did the heavy work of construction, especially on railroad tracks and bridges.

NATIVISM Not all Americans welcomed the flood of immigrants. A growing number of "nativists," people born in the United States who resented the newcomers, sought to restrict or stop immigration altogether. The flood of Irish and German Catholics especially angered Protestants. A Boston minister described Catholicism as "the ally of tyranny, the opponent of material prosperity, the foe of thrift, the enemy of the railroad, the caucus, and the school."

Nativists eventually organized to stop the tide of immigrants. The Order of the Star-Spangled Banner, founded as an oath-bound secret society in New York City in 1849, soon spread to most other large cities. In the early 1850s, it had grown into a powerful political group known in some cities as the American party. In 1855, the American party became a national organization. Members pledged never to vote for foreign-born or Catholic candidates. When asked about their secretive organization, they were told to say, "I know nothing," a phrase which gave rise to the informal name for the party: the **Know-Nothings**.

For a while, the Know-Nothings appeared to be on the brink of major-party status, especially during the 1850s, when the number of immigrants was five times as large as it had been during the 1840s. In the state and local campaigns of 1854, they swept the Massachusetts legislature, winning all but two seats in the lower house, and that fall they elected more than forty congressmen.

A Know-Nothing cartoon This cartoon shows the Catholic Church supposedly attempting to control American religious and political life through Irish immigration.

The Know-Nothings demanded that immigrants and Roman Catholics be excluded from public office and that the waiting period for naturalization (earning citizenship) be extended from five to twenty-one years. The party, however, was never strong enough to enact such legislation. For a while, the Know-Nothings threatened to control New England, New York, and Maryland, but the anti-Catholic movement subsided when slavery became the focal issue of the 1850s, and after 1856 members opted either for the Republican or Democratic parties.

ORGANIZED LABOR AND NEW PROFESSIONS

While most Americans continued to work as farmers, a growing number found employment in textile mills, shoe factories, banks, railroads, publishing, retail stores, teaching, preaching, medicine, law, construction, and engineering. Technological innovations (steam power, mechanized tools, and new modes of transportation) and their social applications (mass communication, turnpikes, the postal service, banks, and corporations) fostered an array of new industries and businesses that transformed the nature of work for both men and women.

The shoe factory When Philadelphia shoemakers went on strike in 1806, a court found them guilty of a "conspiracy to raise wages." Here, shoemakers work at a Massachusetts factory.

EARLY UNIONS In 1800, only 12 percent of Americans worked for wages; by 1860, that number had grown to 40 percent. The rapid growth of wage workers often came at the expense of skilled, self-employed artisans and craftsmen who owned small shops where they made or repaired carriages, shoes, hats, saddles, silverware, jewelry, glass, ropes, furniture, boats, and a broad array of other products. Other skilled craftsmen were blacksmiths, printers, or barrel makers.

Throughout the first half of the nineteenth century, the number of self-employed craftsmen steadily declined as the number of factories and mills increased. Those who emphasized quality and craftsmanship in their custom-made products found it increasingly hard to compete with the low prices for similar products made in much larger numbers in factories and mass-production workshops.

The production of shoes, for example, was transformed by the shift to mass manufacturing. Until the nineteenth century, boots and shoes were made by hand for local customers. Working in their own home or small shop, shoemakers might also employ one or two journeymen (assistants) as well as an apprentice, a young man learning the skilled trade.

That changed during the early nineteenth century, as the number and size of shoe shops increased in New England, largely driven by the demand for inexpensive shoes, many of which were shipped south for the rapidly growing slave population. Shoe shops were displaced by factories, and the master shoemaker became a manager rather than an artisan. Instead of creating a shoe from start to finish, workers were given specific tasks, such as cutting the leather or stitching the "uppers" onto the soles.

Symbols of organized labor
A pocket watch with an International Typographical Union insignia.

Skilled workers forced to make the transition to mass production and a strict division of labor often resented the change. A Massachusetts worker complained that the factory owners were "little stuck up, self-conceited individuals" who forced workers to follow their orders or be fired. In 1850, the Board of Health in Lynn, Massachusetts, reported that the life expectancy of a shoe worker was almost twenty years shorter than a farmer.

A growing fear that they were losing status led artisans in the major cities to become involved in politics and unions. At first, these workers organized into interest groups representing their individual skills or trades. Philadelphia furniture craftsmen, for example, called for their peers to form a "union" to protect "their mutual independence."

Such "trade associations" were the first type of labor unions. They pressured politicians for tariffs to protect their industries from foreign imports, provided insurance benefits, and drafted regulations to improve working conditions. In addition, they sought to control the number of tradesmen in their profession so as to maintain wage levels.

Early labor unions faced major legal obstacles—in fact, they were prosecuted as unlawful conspiracies. In 1842, though, the Massachusetts Supreme Judicial Court issued a landmark ruling in *Commonwealth v. Hunt* declaring that forming a trade union was not in itself illegal, nor was a demand that employers hire only members of the union. The court also said that union workers could strike if an employer hired laborers who refused to join the union.

Until the 1820s, labor organizations took the form of local trade unions, each confined to one city and one craft or skill. From 1827 to 1837, however, organization on a larger scale began to take hold. In 1834, the **National Trades' Union** was formed to organize local trade unions into a stronger national association. At the same time, shoemakers, printers, carpenters, and weavers established their own national craft unions.

Women also formed trade unions. Sarah Monroe, who helped organize the New York Tailoresses' Society, said that if it was "unfashionable for men to bear [workplace] oppression in silence, why should it not also become unfashionable

Tailoresses at work in New York A line engraving of a workroom inside Douglas & Sherwood's skirt factory in New York. Many tailoresses doing work such as this would go on to join labor unions to combat the poor working conditions and paltry wages in the textile industry.

with the women?" In 1831, the women tailors went out on strike demanding a "just price for labor."

Skilled workers also formed political organizations to represent their interests. A New York newspaper reported that people were organizing Workingmen's political parties to protect "those principles of liberty and equality unfolded in the Declaration of our Independence." Workingmen's parties called for laws to regulate banks and abolish the practice of imprisoning people who could not pay their debts.

THE RISE OF THE PROFESSIONS

The dramatic changes in everyday life opened up an array of new **professions**. Bustling new towns required new services—retail stores, printing shops, post offices, newspapers, schools, banks, law firms, medical practices. In 1849, Henry Day delivered a lecture titled "The Professions" at the Western Reserve School of Medicine. He declared that the most important social functions in modern life were the professional skills and claimed that society had become utterly dependent upon "professional services."

TEACHING   Teaching was one of the fastest-growing professions in the first half of the nineteenth century. Horace Mann of Massachusetts was instrumental in promoting the idea of free public education as the best way to transform children into disciplined, judicious citizens. Many states, especially in the North, agreed, and the number of schools exploded. New schools required teachers, and Mann helped create "normal schools" to train future teachers. Public schools initially preferred men as teachers, usually hiring them at age seventeen or eighteen. The pay was so low that few stayed in the profession their entire career, but for many educated young adults, teaching offered independence and social status, as well as an alternative to the rural isolation of farming. Church groups and civic leaders started private academies, or seminaries, for girls.

LAW, MEDICINE, AND ENGINEERING   Teaching was a common stepping-stone for men who became lawyers. In the decades after the American Revolution, young men would teach for a year or two before joining an experienced attorney as an apprentice (what today would be called an *intern*). They would learn the practice of law in exchange for their labors. (There were no law schools yet.)

Like attorneys, physicians often had little formal academic training. Healers of every stripe assumed the title of *doctor* and established medical practices. Most were self-taught or had assisted a physician for several years, while occasionally taking classes at the handful of medical schools. By 1860, there were 60,000 self-styled physicians, many of whom were "quacks" or frauds. As a result, the medical profession lost the public's confidence until the emergence of formal medical schools.

The industrial expansion of the United States also spurred the profession of engineering, a field that would eventually become the nation's largest professional occupation for men. Specialized expertise was required to build canals and railroads, develop machine tools and steam engines, and construct roads, bridges, and factories.

"WOMEN'S WORK"   Most women still worked primarily in the home or on a farm. The only professions readily available to them were nursing (often midwifery, the delivery of babies) and teaching. Many middle-class women did religious and social-service work. Then as now, women were the backbone of most churches.

A few women, however, courageously pursued careers in male-dominated professions. Elizabeth Blackwell of Ohio managed to gain admission to Geneva Medical College (now Hobart and William Smith College) in western New York despite the disapproval of the faculty. When she arrived at her first class, a hush fell upon the students "as if each member had been struck with paralysis." Blackwell had the last laugh when she finished first in her class in 1849, but thereafter the medical school refused to admit more women. The first American woman to earn a medical degree, Blackwell went on to start the New York Infirmary for Women and Children and later had a long career as a professor of gynecology at the London School of Medicine for Women.

EQUAL OPPORTUNITIES

The market-based economy that emerged during the first half of the nineteenth century helped spread the idea that individuals should have equal opportunities to better themselves through their abilities and hard work. Equality of opportunity, however, did not assume equal outcomes. Americans wanted an equal chance to earn unequal amounts of wealth.

The same ideals that prompted so many white immigrants to come to the United States were equally appealing to African Americans and women. By the 1830s, they, too, began to demand their right to "life, liberty, and the pursuit of happiness." Such desires for equality of opportunity would quickly spill over into the political arena. Still, progress in those arenas was achingly slow. The prevailing theme of American political life in the first half of the nineteenth century would be the continuing democratization of opportunities for white men, regardless of income or background, to vote and hold office.

CHAPTER REVIEW

Summary

- **Transportation and Communication Revolutions**   Canals and other improvements in transportation, such as the *steamboat*, allowed goods to reach markets more quickly and cheaply and transformed the more isolated "household economy" of the eighteenth century into a *market-based economy* in which people bought and sold goods for profit. *Clipper ships* shortened the amount of time it took to transport goods across the oceans. The *railroads* (which expanded rapidly during the 1850s) and the *telegraph system* diminished the isolation of the West and united the country economically and socially. The *Erie Canal (1825)* contributed to New York City's emerging status as the nation's economic center even as it boosted the growth of Chicago and other midwestern cities. Improvements in transportation and communication linked rural communities to a worldwide marketplace.

- **Industrialization**   New machine tools and technology as well as innovations in business organization spurred a wave of *industrialization* during the nineteenth century. The *cotton gin* dramatically increased cotton production, and a rapidly spreading *cotton* culture boomed in the South, with a resultant increase in slavery. Other inventions, such as John Deere's steel plow and the mechanized *McCormick reaper*, helped Americans, especially westerners, farm more efficiently and more profitably. In the North, mills and factories, powered first by water and eventually by coal-fired steam engines, spread rapidly. Mills produced textiles for clothing and bedding from southern cotton, as well as iron, shoes, and other products. The federal government's tariff policy encouraged the growth of domestic manufacturing, especially cotton textiles, by reducing imports of British cloth. Between 1820 and 1840, the number of Americans engaged in manufacturing increased 800 percent. Many mill workers, such as the women in the *Lowell system* of New England textile factory communities, worked long hours for low wages in unhealthy conditions. Industrialization, along with increased commerce, helped spur the growth of cities. By 1860, urban areas held 16 percent of the country's population.

- **Immigration**   The promise of cheap land and good wages drew millions of immigrants to America. By 1844, about 14.5 percent of the population was foreign born. The devastating potato famine led to an influx of destitute Irish Catholic families. By the 1850s, they represented a significant portion of the urban population in the United States, constituting a majority in New York and Boston. German migrants, many of them Catholics and Jews, migrated during this same time. Not all native-born Americans welcomed the immigrants. *Nativists* became a powerful political force in the 1850s, with the *Know-Nothings* nearly achieving major-party status with their message of excluding immigrants and Catholics from the nation's political community.

- **Workers, Professionals, and Women**   Skilled workers (artisans) formed trade associations to protect their members and lobby for their interests. As industrialization spread, some workers expanded these organizations nationally, forming the *National Trades' Union*. The growth of the market economy also expanded opportunities for those with formal education to serve in new or emerging *professions*. The number of physicians, teachers, engineers, and lawyers grew rapidly. By the mid–nineteenth century, women, African Americans, and immigrants began to agitate for equal social, economic, and political opportunities.

CHRONOLOGY

1794	Eli Whitney patents the cotton gin
	Philadelphia-Lancaster Turnpike is completed
1807	Robert Fulton and Robert Livingston launch steamship transportation on the Hudson River near New York City
1825	Erie Canal opens in upstate New York
1831	Cyrus McCormick invents a mechanical reaper
1834	National Trades' Union is organized
1837	John Deere invents the steel plow
1842	Massachusetts Supreme Judicial Court issues *Commonwealth v. Hunt* decision
1845	The *Rainbow*, the first clipper ship, is launched
	Irish Potato Famine
1846	Elias Howe invents the sewing machine
1855	Know-Nothing party (American party) formed

KEY TERMS

market-based economy p. 321

steamboats p. 324

Erie Canal (1825) p. 324

railroads p. 326

clipper ships p. 328

telegraph system p. 329

industrialization p. 330

cotton gin p. 331

cotton p. 332

McCormick reapers p. 334

Lowell system p. 335

nativists p. 344

Know-Nothings p. 344

National Trades' Union p. 347

professions p. 348

 INQUIZITIVE

Go to InQuizitive to see what you've learned—and learn what you've missed—with personalized feedback along the way.

9 Nationalism and Sectionalism

1815–1828

***Parade of the Victuallers* (1821)** On a beautiful day in March 1821, Philadelphia butcher William White organized a parade celebrating America's high-quality meats. This watercolor by John Lewis Krimmel captures the new, vibrant nationalism that emerged in America after the War of 1812.

A fter the War of 1812, the British stopped interfering with American shipping. The United States could now develop new industries and exploit new markets around the globe. Yet it was not simply Alexander Hamilton's financial initiatives and the capitalistic energies of wealthy investors and entrepreneurs that sparked America's dramatic economic growth. Prosperity also resulted from the willingness of ordinary men and women to take risks, uproot families, use unstable paper money issued by unregulated local banks, and tinker with new machines, tools, and inventions.

By 1828, the young agrarian republic was poised to become a sprawling commercial nation connected by networks of roads and canals as well as regional economic relationships—all enlivened by a restless spirit of enterprise, experimentation, and expansion.

For all the energy and optimism exhibited by Americans after the war, however, the fundamental tension between *nationalism* and *sectionalism* remained: how to balance the economic and social needs of the nation's three growing regions—Northeast, South, and West?

Nationalists promoted the interests of the country as a whole, an outlook that required each region to recognize that no single section could get all it wanted without threatening the survival of the nation. Many sectionalists, however, were single-mindedly focused on their region's priorities: shipping, manufacturing, and commerce in the Northeast; slave-based agriculture in the South; low land prices and transportation improvements in the West. Of all the issues dividing the young republic, the passions aroused by the expansion of slavery proved to be the most difficult to resolve.

focus questions

1. How did the new spirit of nationalism that emerged after the War of 1812 affect economic and judicial policies?

2. What issues and ideas promoted sectional conflict?

3. How did the "Era of Good Feelings" emerge? What factors led to its demise?

4. What were the federal government's diplomatic accomplishments during this era? What was their impact?

5. What developments enabled Andrew Jackson to become president? How did he influence national politics in the 1820s?

A New Nationalism

After the War of 1812, Americans experienced a wave of patriotic excitement. They had won their independence from Britain for a second time, and a postwar surge of prosperity fed a widespread sense of optimism.

POSTWAR NATIONALISM In a message to Congress in late 1815, President James Madison revealed how much the challenges of the war, especially the weaknesses of the armed forces and federal financing, had changed his attitudes about the role of the federal government.

Now, Madison and other leading southern Republicans acted like nationalists rather than states' rights sectionalists. They abandoned many of Thomas Jefferson's presidential initiatives (for example, his efforts to reduce the armed forces and his opposition to the national bank) in favor of the *economic nationalism* advanced by Federalists Alexander Hamilton and George Washington. Madison now supported a larger army and navy, a new national bank, and tariffs to protect American manufacturers from foreign competition. "The Republicans have out-Federalized Federalism," one New Englander commented after Madison's speech.

THE BANK OF THE UNITED STATES After President Madison and congressional Republicans allowed the charter for the First Bank of the United States to expire in 1811, the nation's finances fell into a muddle. States began chartering local banks with little or no regulation, and their banknotes (paper money) flooded the economy with different currencies of uncertain value.

In response to the growing financial turmoil, Madison in 1816 urged Congress to establish the **Second Bank of the United States** (B.U.S.), and with the help of powerful congressmen Henry Clay of Kentucky and John C. Calhoun of South Carolina, Congress followed through. The B.U.S. was intended primarily to support a stable national currency that would promote economic growth. In return for issuing paper money and opening branches in every state, it was to handle all federal government funds without charge, lend the government up to $5 million upon demand, and pay the government $1.5 million.

The bitter debate over the B.U.S., then and later, helped set the pattern of regional alignment for most other economic issues. Generally speaking, westerners opposed the national bank because it catered to eastern customers.

The controversy over the B.U.S. was also noteworthy because of the leading roles played by the era's greatest statesmen: Calhoun, Clay, and Daniel Webster of New Hampshire (and later Massachusetts). Calhoun introduced the banking bill and pushed it through, justifying its constitutionality by citing the congressional power to regulate the currency.

Clay, who had long opposed a national bank, now argued that new economic circumstances had made it indispensable. Webster led the opposition among New England Federalists, who feared the growing financial power of Philadelphia. Later, Webster would return to Congress as the champion of a much stronger national government—at the same time that unexpected events would steer Calhoun away from economic nationalism and toward a defiant embrace of states' rights, slavery, and even secession.

A PROTECTIVE TARIFF The long controversy with Great Britain over shipping rights convinced most Americans of the need to develop their own manufacturing sector to end their dependence on imported British goods. Efforts to develop iron and textile industries, begun in New York and New England during the embargo of 1807, had accelerated during the War of 1812 when America lost access to European goods.

After the war ended, however, British companies flooded U.S. markets with less-expensive products, which undercut their American competitors. In response, northern manufacturers lobbied Congress for federal tariffs to protect their infant industries from what they called "unfair" British competition.

Congress responded by passing the **Tariff of 1816**, which placed a 20 to 25 percent tax on a long list of imported goods. Tariffs benefited some regions (the Northeast) more than others (the South), thus aggravating sectional grievances. Debates over tariffs would dominate national politics throughout the nineteenth century, in part because tariffs provided much of the annual federal revenue and in part because they benefited manufacturers rather than consumers.

The few southerners who voted for the tariff, led by John C. Calhoun, did so because they hoped that the South might also become a manufacturing center. Within a few years, however, New England's manufacturing sector would roar ahead of the South, leading Calhoun to do an about-face and begin opposing tariffs.

INTERNAL IMPROVEMENTS The third major element of economic nationalism involved federal financing of "**internal improvements**," what is today called *infrastructure*—the construction of roads, bridges, canals, and harbors. Most American rivers flowed from north to south, so the nation needed a network of roads running east to west, including what became known as the National Road connecting the Midwest with the East Coast.

In 1817, John C. Calhoun urged the House to fund internal improvements. He believed that a federally financed network of roads and canals in the West would help the South by opening up trade between the two regions. Support for Calhoun's proposal came largely from the West, which badly needed transportation infrastructure. Opposition centered in New England, which expected to gain the least from such projects.

POSTWAR NATIONALISM AND THE SUPREME COURT The postwar emphasis on economic nationalism also surfaced in the Supreme Court, where Chief Justice John Marshall strengthened the constitutional powers of the federal government at the expense of states' rights. In the path-breaking case of *Marbury v. Madison* (1803), the Court had, for the first time, declared a federal law unconstitutional. In *Martin v. Hunter's Lessee* (1816) and *Cohens v. Virginia* (1821), the Court ruled that the Constitution could remain the supreme law of the land only if the Court could review and at times over-turn the decisions of state courts.

PROTECTING CONTRACT RIGHTS The Supreme Court made two major decisions in 1819 that strengthened the power of the federal govern-ment. One, **Dartmouth College v. Woodward**, involved the New Hampshire legislature's effort to change the Dartmouth College charter to stop the col-lege's trustees from electing their own successors. In 1816, the state's legislature created a new board of trustees. The original trustees sued to block the move. They lost in the state courts but won on appeal to the Supreme Court.

The college's original charter, wrote John Marshall in drafting the Court's opinion, was a valid contract that the state legislature had impaired, an act forbidden by the Constitution. This decision implied an enlarged definition of *contract* that seemed to put corporations beyond the reach of the states that chartered them. Thereafter, states commonly wrote into the charters incorpo-rating businesses and other organizations provisions making charters subject to modification. Such provisions were then part of the "contract."

PROTECTING A NATIONAL CURRENCY The second major Supreme Court case of 1819 was Chief Justice Marshall's most signifi-cant interpretation of the constitutional system: **McCulloch v. Maryland**. James McCulloch, a B.U.S. clerk in Baltimore, had refused to pay state taxes on B.U.S. currency as required by a Maryland law. The state indicted McCulloch. He appealed to the Supreme Court, which ruled unanimously that Congress had the authority to charter the B.U.S. and that states had no right to tax the national bank.

Speaking for the Court, Marshall ruled that given the "implied powers" granted it, Congress had the right to take any action not forbidden by the Constitution as long as the purpose was within the "scope of the Constitution." One great principle that "entirely pervades the Constitution," Marshall wrote, is "that the Constitution and the laws made in pursuance thereof are supreme: . . . They control the Constitution and laws of the respective states, and cannot be controlled by them." The effort by a state to tax a federal bank therefore was unconstitutional, for the "power to tax involves the power to destroy."

REGULATING INTERSTATE COMMERCE John Marshall's last major decision, ***Gibbons v. Ogden*** (1824), affirmed the federal government's supremacy in regulating *interstate* commerce.

In 1808, the New York legislature granted Robert Fulton and Robert R. Livingston the sole right to operate steamboats on the state's rivers and lakes. Fulton and Livingston then gave Aaron Ogden the exclusive right to ferry people and goods up the Hudson River between New York and New Jersey. Thomas Gibbons, however, operated ships under a federal license that

Steamboat Travel on the Hudson River (1811) This watercolor of an early steamboat was painted by a Russian diplomat, Pavel Petrovich Svinin, who was fascinated by early technological innovations and the unique culture of America.

competed with Ogden. On behalf of a unanimous Court, Marshall ruled that the monopoly granted by the state to Ogden conflicted with the federal license issued to Gibbons.

Thomas Jefferson detested John Marshall's judicial nationalism. The Court's ruling in the *Gibbons* case, said the eighty-two-year-old former president, revealed how "the Federal branch of our Government is advancing towards the usurpation of all the rights reserved to the States, and the consolidation in it lf of all powers, foreign and domestic."

DEBATES OVER THE AMERICAN SYSTEM

The major economic initiatives debated by Congress after the War of 1812— the national bank, federal tariffs, and federally financed roads, bridges, ports, and canals—were interrelated pieces of a comprehensive economic plan called the **American System**.

The term was coined by Henry Clay, the powerful young Kentucky congressman who would serve three terms as Speaker of the House before becoming a U.S. senator. Clay wanted to free America's economy from its dependence on Great Britain while tying together the diverse regions of the nation politically. He said, "I know of no South, no North, no East, no West to which I owe my allegiance. The Union is my country."

In promoting his American System, Clay sought to give each section of the country its top economic priority. He argued that high tariffs on imports were needed to block the sale of British products in the United States and protect new industries in New England and New York from unfair foreign competition.

To convince the western states to support the tariffs, Clay first called for the federal government to use tariff revenues to build much-needed infrastructure—roads, bridges, canals, and other internal improvements—in the frontier West to enable speedier travel and faster shipment of goods to markets.

Second, his American System would raise prices for federal lands sold to the public and distribute the revenue from the land sales to the states to help finance more roads, bridges, and canals. Third, Clay endorsed a strong national bank to create a national currency and to regulate the often unstable state and local banks.

Clay's program depended on each section's willingness to compromise. For a while, it worked. Critics, however, argued that higher prices for federal lands would discourage western migration and that tariffs benefited the northern manufacturing sector at the expense of southern and western farmers and the "common" people, who had to pay more for the goods produced by tariff-protected industries. Many westerners and southerners also feared that the Second Bank of the United States would become so powerful and corrupt that it could dictate the nation's economic future at the expense of states' rights and the needs of particular regions. Missouri senator Thomas Hart Benton predicted that cash-strapped western towns would be at the mercy of the national bank in Philadelphia. Westerners, Benton worried, "are in the jaws of the monster! A lump of butter in the mouth of a dog! One gulp, one swallow, and all is gone!"

"AN ERA OF GOOD FEELINGS"

Near the end of his presidency, James Madison turned to James Monroe, a fellow Virginian, to be his successor. In the 1816 election, Monroe overwhelmed his Federalist opponent, Rufus King of New York, by a 183–34 margin in the electoral college. The "Virginia dynasty" of presidents continued.

Soon after his inauguration, Monroe embarked on a goodwill tour of New England, the stronghold of the Federalist party. In Boston, a Federalist newspaper complimented the Republican president for striving to "harmonize feelings, annihilate dissentions, and make us one people." Those words of praise were printed under the heading "Era of Good Feelings," which became a popular label for Monroe's administration.

JAMES MONROE Like George Washington, Thomas Jefferson, and James Madison, James Monroe was a slaveholding planter from Virginia. At the outbreak of the Revolutionary War, he dropped out of the College of William and Mary to join the army. He served under Washington, who called him a "brave, active, and sensible army officer."

James Monroe Portrayed as he began his presidency in 1817.

After studying law under Jefferson, Monroe served as a representative in the Virginia Assembly, as governor, as a representative in the Confederation Congress, as a U.S. senator, and as U.S. minister (ambassador) to Paris, London, and Madrid. Under President Madison, he was secretary of state and doubled as secretary of war during the War of 1812. John C. Calhoun said that Monroe was "among the wisest and most cautious men I have ever known." Jefferson described him as "a man whose soul might be turned wrong side outwards without discovering a blemish to the world."

Although Monroe's presidency began peacefully enough, two major events signaled the end of the Era of Good Feelings and warned of stormy times ahead: the financial Panic of 1819 and the political conflict over statehood for Missouri.

THE PANIC OF 1819 The young republic experienced its first economic depression when the **Panic of 1819** led to a prolonged financial slowdown. Like so many other economic collapses, it resulted from greed: too many people trying to get rich too quickly.

After the War of 1812, European demand for American products, especially cotton, tobacco, and flour, soared, leading farmers and planters to increase production. To fuel the roaring postwar economy, unsound local and state banks made it easy—too easy—for people and businesses to get loans. The B.U.S. aggravated the problem by issuing risky loans, too.

At the same time, the federal government sold vast tracts of public land, which spurred reckless real estate speculation by people buying large parcels with the intention of reselling them. On top of all that, good weather in Europe led to a spike in crop production there, thus reducing the need to buy American commodities. Prices for American farm products plunged.

The Panic of 1819 was ignited by the sudden collapse of cotton prices after British textile mills quit buying high-priced American cotton—the nation's leading export—in favor of cheaper cotton from other parts of the world. As the price of cotton fell and the flow of commerce slowed, banks began to fail, and unemployment soared. The collapse of cotton prices was especially devastating for southern planters, but it also reduced the world demand for other American goods. Owners of new factories and mills, most of them in New England, New York, and Pennsylvania, struggled to find markets for their goods and to fend off more-experienced foreign competitors.

As the financial panic deepened, a widespread distrust of banks and bankers emerged. Tennessee congressman David Crockett dismissed the "whole Banking system" as nothing more than "swindling on a large scale." Thomas Jefferson told John Adams that "the paper [money] bubble is then burst. This is what you and I, and every reasoning man . . . have long foreseen."

Other factors caused the financial panic to become a depression. Business owners, farmers, and land speculators had recklessly borrowed money to expand their ventures or to purchase more land. With the collapse of crop prices and the decline of land values, both speculators and settlers saw their income plummet.

The equally reckless lending practices of the numerous new state banks compounded the problems. To generate more loans, the banks issued more paper money. Even the Second Bank of the United States, which was supposed to provide financial stability, got caught up in the easy-credit mania.

In 1819, newspapers uncovered extensive fraud and embezzlement in the Baltimore branch of the B.U.S. The scandal prompted the appointment of Langdon Cheves, a former South Carolina congressman, as the bank's new president. Cheves restored confidence in the national bank by forcing state banks to keep more gold coins in their vaults to back up the loans they were making. State banks in turn put pressure on their debtors, who found it harder to renew old loans or to get new ones.

The depression lasted about three years, and many blamed the B.U.S. After the panic subsided, many Americans, especially in the South and the West, remained critical of the national bank.

THE MISSOURI COMPROMISE In the midst of the financial panic, another dark cloud appeared on the horizon: the onset of a fierce sectional controversy over expanding slavery into the western territories. The possibility of western territories becoming "slave states" created the greatest political debate of the nineteenth century. By 1819, the country had an equal number of slave and free states—eleven of each. The Northwest Ordinance (1787) had banned slavery north of the Ohio River, and the Southwest Ordinance (1790) had authorized slavery south of the Ohio.

West of the Mississippi River, however, slavery had existed since France and Spain first colonized the area. St. Louis became the crossroads through which southerners brought slaves into the Missouri Territory.

In 1819, Missouri Territory residents asked the House of Representatives to let them draft a constitution and apply for statehood, as the region's population had passed the minimum of 60,000 white settlers. (There were also some 10,000 slaves.) It would be the first state west of the Mississippi River.

At that point, Representative James Tallmadge Jr., a New York Republican, proposed a resolution to ban the transport of any more slaves into Missouri. Tallmadge's resolution enraged southern slaveholders, many of whom had developed a profitable business selling slaves to traders, who resold them in the western territories. Any effort to restrict slavery in the western territories, they believed, could lead to "disunion" and civil war.

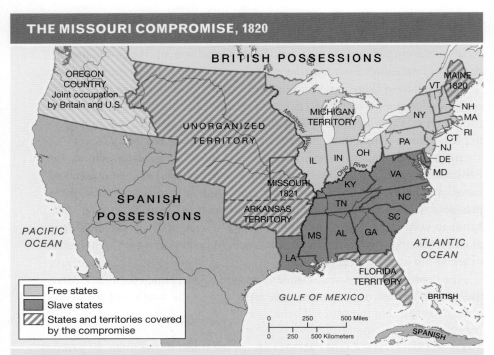

THE MISSOURI COMPROMISE, 1820

BRITISH POSSESSIONS

OREGON COUNTRY
Joint occupation by Britain and U.S.

UNORGANIZED TERRITORY

SPANISH POSSESSIONS

MICHIGAN TERRITORY

MISSOURI 1821

ARKANSAS TERRITORY

Mississippi River

IL IN OH
Ohio River

MISSOURI 1821 KY
TN

MS AL GA

LA

FLORIDA TERRITORY

PACIFIC OCEAN

MAINE 1820
VT
NH
NY MA
RI
PA CT
NJ
DE
VA MD
NC
SC

ATLANTIC OCEAN

GULF OF MEXICO

BRITISH

SPANISH

Free states
Slave states
States and territories covered by the compromise

0   250   500 Miles
0   250   500 Kilometers

- What caused the sectional controversy over slavery in 1819?
- What were the terms of the Missouri Compromise?
- What was Henry Clay's solution to the Missouri constitution's ban on free blacks in that state?

Southerners also worried that the addition of Missouri as a free state would tip the balance of power in the Senate against the slave states. Their fears were heightened when Congressman Timothy Fuller, an anti-slavery Republican from Massachusetts, declared that it was both "the right and duty of Congress" to stop the spread "of the intolerable evil and the crying enormity of slavery." After fiery debates, the House, with its northern majority, passed the Tallmadge Amendment on an almost strictly sectional vote. The Senate, however, rejected it—also along sectional lines.

At about the same time, Maine, which had been part of Massachusetts, applied for statehood. The Senate decided to link Maine's request for statehood with Missouri's, voting in 1820 to admit a year later Maine as a free state and Missouri as a slave state, thus maintaining the political balance between free and slave states.

Illinois senator Jesse Thomas revised the so-called **Missouri Compromise** (1820) by introducing an amendment to exclude slavery in the rest of the Louisiana Purchase north of latitude 36°30', Missouri's southern border. Slavery thus would continue in the Arkansas Territory and in Missouri but would be excluded from the remainder of the area west of the Mississippi River. By a narrow margin, the Thomas Amendment passed.

Then another issue arose. The pro-slavery faction in Missouri's constitutional convention inserted in the proposed state constitution a provision excluding free blacks and mulattoes (mixed-race people) from residing in the state. This threatened to unravel the deal to admit Maine and Missouri as states until Henry Clay fashioned a "second" Missouri Compromise in which Missouri would be admitted only if its legislature pledged never to deny free blacks their constitutional rights. On August 10, 1821, Missouri became the twenty-fourth state, and the twelfth where slavery was allowed.

Nationalists praised the Missouri Compromise, but it actually settled little. Instead, it hardened positions on both sides and revealed a widening divide in the country among the Northeast, dominated by shipping, commerce, and manufacturing; the Midwest, centered on small farms; and the South, more and more dependent on cotton and slavery.

NATIONALIST DIPLOMACY

Henry Clay's support of economic nationalism and John Marshall's decisions affirming *judicial* nationalism were reinforced by efforts to practice *diplomatic* nationalism. President Monroe's secretary of state, John Quincy Adams, son of former president John Adams, worked to clarify and expand the nation's boundaries. He also wanted Europeans to recognize America's dominance in the Western Hemisphere.

RELATIONS WITH BRITAIN The Treaty of Ghent (1814) had ended the War of 1812, but it left unsettled several disputes between the United States and Great Britain. Adams oversaw the negotiations of two important treaties, the Rush-Bagot Treaty of 1817 (named after the diplomats who arranged it) and the Convention of 1818.

In the Rush-Bagot Treaty, the two nations limited the number of warships on the Great Lakes. The Convention of 1818 was even more important. It settled the disputed northern boundary of the Louisiana Purchase by extending it along the 49th parallel westward, from what would become Minnesota to the Rocky Mountains. West of the Rockies, the Oregon Country would be jointly occupied by the British and the Americans.

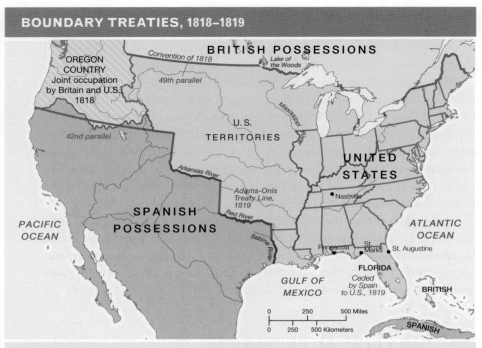

BOUNDARY TREATIES, 1818–1819

BRITISH POSSESSIONS

OREGON COUNTRY
Joint occupation by Britain and U.S. 1818

Convention of 1818

Lake of the Woods

49th parallel

Mississippi River

42nd parallel

U.S. TERRITORIES

UNITED STATES

Arkansas River

Adams-Onis Treaty Line, 1819

• Nashville

SPANISH POSSESSIONS

Red River

PACIFIC OCEAN

Sabine River

ATLANTIC OCEAN

Pensacola   St. Marks   • St. Augustine

FLORIDA

GULF OF MEXICO

Ceded by Spain to U.S., 1819

BRITISH

0   250   500 Miles
0   250   500 Kilometers

SPANISH

- How did the Convention of 1818 settle boundary disputes between Spain and the United States?
- How did Andrew Jackson's aggressive military actions in Florida help John Quincy Adams claim territory from Spain?

FLORIDA Still another disputed boundary involved western Florida. Spanish control over Florida during the early nineteenth century was more a technicality than an actuality. Spain was now a declining power, unable to enforce its obligations under Pinckney's Treaty of 1795 to keep Indians in the region from making raids into south Georgia.

In 1816, U.S. soldiers clashed with runaway slaves in West Florida, in the present-day Florida Panhandle. At the same time, Seminole warriors fought white settlers in the area. In 1817, Americans burned a Seminole village on the border, killing five Indians.

At that point, Secretary of War John C. Calhoun ordered General Andrew Jackson to lead an army from Tennessee into Florida, igniting what became known as the First Seminole War. Calhoun told Jackson to pursue marauding Indians into Spanish Florida but not to attack Spanish forts. Jackson, frustrated by the restrictions, wrote President Monroe that if the United States wanted Spanish Florida, he could conquer it in sixty days.

Massacre of the Whites by Indians and Blacks in Florida **(1836)** Published in a southerner's account of the Seminole War, this is one of the earliest known depictions of African Americans and Native Americans fighting as allies.

In early 1818, Jackson's force of 2,000 federal soldiers, volunteer Tennessee militiamen, and Indian allies moved into Spanish Florida. In April, they assaulted a Spanish fort at St. Marks and destroyed several Seminole villages along the Suwannee River.

Jackson's soldiers also captured and court-martialed two British traders accused of provoking Indian attacks. When told that a military trial of the British citizens was illegal, Jackson replied that the laws of war did not "apply to conflicts with savages."

Jackson ordered the immediate execution of the British troublemakers, which outraged the British government and alarmed Monroe's cabinet. But the impulsive Jackson kept moving. In May, he captured Pensacola, the Spanish capital of West Florida, where he established a provisional American government.

While Jackson's conquests excited expansionists, Spain demanded the return of its territory and that Jackson be punished for violating international law. Monroe's cabinet was at first prepared to disavow Jackson's illegal acts. Privately, Calhoun criticized Jackson for disobeying orders—a stand that would later cause bad blood between them.

Jackson, however, remained a hero to most Americans. He also had an important friend in the cabinet—Secretary of State John Quincy Adams, who realized that Jackson's unauthorized conquest of Florida had strengthened his own hand in negotiating with the Spanish to purchase the territory.

In 1819, Adams convinced the Spanish to sign the **Transcontinental Treaty** (also called the Adams-Onís Treaty), in which the United States acquired all of Florida for $5 million in exchange for abandoning any claims to Texas. In 1821, Florida became a U.S. territory; in 1845, it would become a state.

John Quincy Adams A brilliant man but an ineffective leader, he appears here in his study in 1843. He was the first U.S. president to be photographed.

The treaty also clarified the contested western boundary separating the Louisiana Territory from New Spain. The boundary would run from the Gulf of Mexico north to the 42nd parallel and then west to the Pacific coast. The United States finally spanned the continent.

Adams also reaffirmed George Washington's belief that the United States should avoid "entangling" itself in European affairs. It would sympathize with democratic movements abroad, but it would not become embroiled in wars supporting such causes. In 1821, Adams declared that America "goes not abroad in search of monsters to destroy. She is the well-wisher to the freedom and independence of all. She is the champion and vindicator only of her own."

THE MONROE DOCTRINE The most important diplomatic policy crafted by President Monroe and Secretary of State Adams involved a determined effort to prevent any future European colonialism in the Western Hemisphere. The Spanish, British, French, Portuguese, Dutch, and Russians still controlled one or more colonies in the Americas.

One consequence of the Napoleonic Wars in Europe was the French occupation of Spain and Portugal. The turmoil in those two nations helped trigger independence movements among their colonies in the Americas. Within little more than a decade after the flag of rebellion was raised in 1809 in Ecuador, Spain had lost almost its entire empire in the Americas: La Plata (later Argentina), Bolivia, Chile, Ecuador, Peru, Colombia, Mexico, Paraguay, Uruguay, and Venezuela had all proclaimed their independence, as had Portuguese Brazil. The only areas still under Spanish control were the islands of Cuba and Puerto Rico and the colony of Santo Domingo on the island of Hispaniola.

In 1823, rumors reached America that the monarchs of Europe were planning to help Spain recover its Latin American colonies. The British foreign minister, George Canning, told the United States that the two countries should jointly oppose any new incursions by European nations in the Western Hemisphere. Monroe initially agreed—if the London government would recognize the independence of the new nations of Latin America. The British refused.

Adams, however, advised Monroe to go it alone in prohibiting further European involvement in the hemisphere, stressing that "it would be more candid as well as more dignified" for America to ban further European intervention than to tag along with a British statement.

Monroe agreed. In his annual message to Congress in December 1823, he outlined the four major points of what became known as the **Monroe Doctrine**: (1) That "the American continents . . . are henceforth not to be considered as subjects for future colonization by any European powers"; (2) that the United States would consider any attempt by a European nation to intervene "in this hemisphere as dangerous to our peace and safety"; (3) that the United States would not interfere with existing European-controlled colonies in the Americas; and (4) that the United States would keep out of the internal affairs of European nations.

Reaction to the Monroe Doctrine was mixed. In France, Marquis de Lafayette, the freedom-loving volunteer in the American Revolution, hailed the policy "as the best little bit of paper that God had ever permitted any man to give to the world." Others were not as impressed. No European nation recognized the validity of the Monroe Doctrine.

To this day, the Monroe Doctrine has no official standing in international law. Symbolically, however, it has been an important statement of American intentions to prevent European involvement in the Western Hemisphere and an example of the young nation's determination to take its place among the world's powers. Since it was announced, not a single Latin American nation has lost its independence to an outside invader.

THE RISE OF ANDREW JACKSON

After the War of 1812, the United States had become a one-party political system. The refusal of the Federalists to support the war had virtually killed the party. In 1820, President Monroe was reelected without opposition.

While the Democratic Republican party was dominant for the moment, however, it was about to follow the Federalists into oblivion. If Monroe's first term was the Era of Good Feelings, his second became an Era of Bad Feelings, as sectional controversies erupted into violent disputes that gave birth to a new political party, the Democrats, led by Andrew Jackson.

ANDREW JACKSON Born in 1767 along the border between the Carolinas, Jackson grew up in a struggling single-parent household. His father was killed in a farm accident three weeks before Andrew was born, forcing his widowed mother, Elizabeth, to scratch out a living as a housekeeper while raising three sons.

During the Revolution, the Jackson boys fought against the British. One of them, sixteen-year-old Hugh, died of heat exhaustion during a battle; another, Robert, died while trudging home from a prisoner-of-war camp.

In 1781, fourteen-year-old Andrew was captured. When a British officer demanded that the boy shine his boots, Jackson refused, explaining that he was a prisoner of war and expected "to be treated as such." The angry officer slashed him with his sword, leaving ugly scars on Andrew's head and hand. Soon after he was released, Elizabeth Jackson, who had helped nurse injured American soldiers, died of cholera. Her orphaned son thereafter despised the British.

After the Revolution, Jackson went to Charleston, South Carolina, where he learned to love racehorses, gambling, and fine clothes. He returned home and tried saddle-making and teaching before moving to Salisbury, North Carolina, where he earned a license to practice law. He also enjoyed life. A friend recalled that Jackson was "the most roaring, rollicking, game-cocking, card-playing, mischievous fellow that ever lived in Salisbury."

In 1788, at age twenty-one, Jackson moved to Nashville and became a frontier attorney.

In 1796, when Tennessee became a state, voters elected Jackson to the U.S. House and later to the Senate, where he served only a year before returning to Tennessee and becoming a judge. Jackson also made a lot of money, first as an attorney, then as a buyer and seller of horses, land, and slaves. He eventually owned 100 slaves on his cotton plantation, called the Hermitage. He had no moral reservations about slavery and could be a cruel master.

Many American political leaders cringed at the thought of the combative, short-tempered Jackson, who had run roughshod over international law in his war against the British and Seminoles in Florida, presiding over the nation. "His passions are terrible," said Thomas Jefferson. John Quincy Adams scorned Jackson "as a barbarian and savage who could scarcely spell his name." Jackson dismissed such criticism as an example of the "Eastern elite" trying to maintain control of American politics. He responded to Adams's criticism by commenting that he never trusted a man who could think of only one way to spell a word.

PRESIDENTIAL POLITICS No sooner had James Monroe started his second presidential term, in 1821, than leading Republicans began positioning themselves to be the next president, including three members of the cabinet: secretary of war, John C. Calhoun; secretary of the Treasury, William H. Crawford; and secretary of state, John Quincy Adams. The Speaker of the House, Henry Clay, also hungered for the presidency. And there was Andrew Jackson, who was elected to the Senate in 1823. The emergence of so many viable candidates revealed how fractured the Republican party had become.

In 1822, the Tennessee legislature named Jackson its long-shot choice to succeed Monroe. Two years later, Pennsylvania Republicans endorsed Jackson for president and chose Calhoun for vice president. Meanwhile, the Kentucky legislature had nominated its favorite son, Clay, in 1822. The Massachusetts legislature nominated Adams in 1824. That same year, a group of Republican congressmen nominated Crawford, a cotton planter from Georgia.

Crawford's friends emphasized his devotion to states' rights. Clay continued to promote the economic nationalism of his American System. Adams, the only non-slaveholder in the race, shared Clay's belief that the national government should finance internal improvements to stimulate economic development, but he was less strongly committed to tariffs.

Jackson declared himself the champion of the common people and the foe of the entrenched social and political elite. He claimed to represent the "old republicanism" of Thomas Jefferson. But Jefferson believed Jackson lacked the education, polish, and prudence to be president. "He is," Jefferson told a friend, "one of the most unfit men I know." Jefferson supported Crawford.

As a self-made military hero, Jackson was an attractive candidate, especially to voters of Irish background. The son of poor Scots-Irish colonists, he was beloved for having defeated the hated English in the Battle of New Orleans. In addition, his commitment to those he called the "common men" resonated with many Irish immigrants who associated aristocracy with centuries of English rule over Ireland.

THE "CORRUPT BARGAIN" The initial results of the 1824 presidential election were inconclusive. Jackson won the popular vote and the electoral college, where he had 99 votes, Adams 84, Crawford 41, and Clay 37. But Jackson did not have the necessary majority of electoral votes. In such a circumstance, as in the 1800 election, the Constitution specified that the House of Representatives would make the final decision from among the top three vote-getters. By the time the House could convene, however, Crawford had suffered a stroke and was ruled out. So the election came down to Adams and Jackson.

Henry Clay's influence as Speaker of the House would be decisive. While Adams and Jackson courted Clay's support, he scorned them both, claiming they provided only a "choice of evils." But he regarded Jackson as a "military chieftain," a frontier Napoléon unfit for the presidency. Jackson's election, Clay predicted, would "be the greatest misfortune that could befall the country."

Henry Clay of Kentucky Clay entered the Senate at twenty-eight, despite the requirement that senators be at least thirty years old. Here, Clay is pictured in an oil painting by Charles Willson Peale.

Although Clay and Adams disliked each other, the nationalist Adams supported most of the policies that Clay wanted, particularly high tariffs, transportation improvements, and a strong national bank. Clay also expected Adams to name him secretary of state, the office that usually led to the White House. In the end, they made a deal on January 9, 1825. Clay convinced the House of Representatives to elect Adams.

The controversial victory proved costly for Adams, however, as it united his foes and crippled his administration before it began. A furious Jackson dismissed Clay as the "Judas of the West" who had entered into a **"corrupt bargain"** with Adams. Their "corruptions and intrigues," he charged, had "defeated the will of the People." American politics had now entered an Era of Bad Feelings.

Almost immediately, Jackson's supporters launched a campaign to undermine the Adams administration and elect their hero in 1828. Crawford's supporters soon joined the Jackson camp, as did the new vice president, John C. Calhoun, who quickly found himself at odds with President Adams.

JOHN QUINCY ADAMS Adams was one of the ablest men, hardest workers, and finest intellects ever to enter the White House. Groomed for greatness by his parents, John and Abigail Adams, he had been ambassador to four European nations, a U.S. senator, a Harvard professor, and an outstanding secretary of state. He had helped negotiate the end to the War of 1812 and had drafted the Monroe Doctrine.

Yet for all his accomplishments, Adams proved to be an ineffective president, undercut from the start by the controversy surrounding his deal with Henry Clay. Strong-willed and intelligent, but socially awkward and a stubborn moralist, Adams lacked the common touch and the politician's gift for compromise. He was easy to admire but hard to like and impossible to love.

His sour personality was shaped in part by family tragedies: He saw two brothers and two sons die from alcoholism. He also suffered from bouts of depression that reinforced his grim self-righteousness and tendency toward self-pity, qualities that did not endear him to others. Poet Ralph Waldo Emerson said Adams was so stern and irritable that he must be taking sulfuric acid with his tea. Even Adams's son Charles Francis admitted that his father "makes enemies by perpetually wearing the iron mask."

Adams detested the democratic politicking that Andrew Jackson represented. He worried, as had his father, that republicanism was rapidly turning into democracy, and that government *of* the people was degenerating into government *by* the people, many of whom, in his view, were uneducated and incompetent. He wanted politics to be a "sacred" arena for the "best men," a profession limited to the "most able and worthy" leaders motivated by a sense of civic duty rather than a selfish quest for power and stature. Poet Walt Whitman wrote that although Adams was "a virtuous man—a learned man . . . he was not a man of the People."

Adams was determined to create an activist federal government with expansive goals. His first State of the Union message, in December 1825, included a grand blueprint for national development, but it was set forth so bluntly that it became a political disaster.

The federal government, Adams stressed, should finance a national transportation network (internal improvements—new roads, canals, harbors, and bridges), create a great national university in Washington, D.C., support scientific explorations of the Far West, build an astronomical observatory ("lighthouse of the skies"), and establish a Department of the Interior to manage the extensive government-owned lands. He challenged Congress to approve his proposals and not be paralyzed "by the will of our constituents."

Reaction was overwhelmingly negative. Newspapers charged that Adams was behaving like an aristocratic tyrant, and Congress quickly revealed that it would approve none of his proposals. The disastrous start shattered Adams's confidence. He wrote in his diary that he was in a "protracted agony of character and reputation."

Adams's effort to expand the powers of the federal government was so divisive that the Democratic-Republican party split, creating a new party system. Those who agreed with the economic nationalism of Adams and Clay began calling themselves National Republicans. The opposition—made up of those who supported Andrew Jackson and states' rights—began calling themselves Democrats. They were strongest in the South and West, as well as among the working class in large eastern cities.

The Democrats were the first party in America to recruit professional state organizers, such as Martin Van Buren of New York, who developed sophisticated strategies for mobilizing voters and orchestrating grassroots campaigns featuring massive rallies, barbecues, and parades.

Perhaps most important, the Democrats convinced voters that their primary allegiance should be to their party rather than to any particular candidate. Party loyalty became the most powerful weapon the Democrats could muster against the "privileged aristocracy" running the state and federal governments.

Adams's opponents sought to use the always controversial tariff issue against him. In 1828, anti-Adams congressmen introduced a new tariff bill designed to help elect Jackson. The bill placed duties (taxes) on imported raw materials such as wool, hemp, and iron that were also produced in key states where Jackson needed support: Pennsylvania, New York, Ohio, Kentucky, and Missouri.

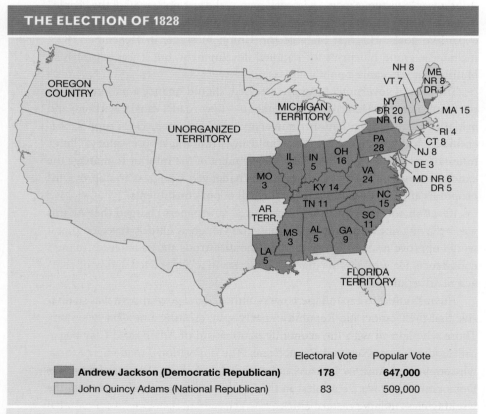

THE ELECTION OF 1828

	Electoral Vote	Popular Vote
Andrew Jackson (Democratic Republican)	178	647,000
John Quincy Adams (National Republican)	83	509,000

- How did the two presidential candidates, John Quincy Adams and Andrew Jackson, portray each other?
- Why did Jackson seem to have the advantage in the election of 1828?
- How did the broadening of voting rights affect the presidential campaign?

The measure passed, only to be condemned as the "Tariff of Abomina-tions" by the cotton states of the Lower South. John C. Calhoun wrote the *South Carolina Exposition and Protest* (1828), in which he ominously declared that a state could nullify an act of Congress that it found unconstitutional, such as the new tariff.

JACKSON'S ELECTION These maneuverings launched the savage **election campaign of 1828** between John Quincy Adams and Andrew Jackson, the National Republicans versus the Jacksonian Democrats.

Both sides launched vicious personal attacks. Adams's supporters denounced Jackson as a hot-tempered, ignorant barbarian, a gambler and slave trader who thrived on confronta-tion and violence and whose fame rested upon his reputation as a cold-blooded killer.

Their most scurrilous charge was that Jackson had lived in adultery with his wife, Rachel Donelson Robards. In fact, they had lived together as husband and wife for two years in the mistaken belief that her divorce from her first hus-band was final. As soon as the divorce was official, Andrew and Rachel had remarried to end all doubts about their status. A furi-ous Jackson blamed Henry Clay for spreading the slurs, calling the Kentuckian "the basest, meanest scoundrel that ever disgraced the image of his god."

Andrew Jackson The controversial general was painted by Anna Claypoole Peale in 1819, the year of his military exploits in Florida. She captured Jackson's confident demeanor that made him so popular.

The Jacksonians, for their part, condemned Adams as "a lordly, purse-proud" aristocrat, a career politician who had never had a real job and had been corrupted in the courts of Europe. Adams's opponents even claimed that during his time as ambassador to Russia, he had allegedly acted as a pimp, delivering young girls to serve the lust of Czar Alexander I. Adams was left to gripe about the many "forgeries now swarming in the newspapers against me."

As a fabled Indian fighter, Jackson was beloved as the "people's cham-pion" by farmers and working men, and as a planter, lawyer, and slaveholder, he had the trust of the southern political elite. He supported a small federal government, individual liberty, an expanded military, and white supremacy. Above all, he was a nationalist committed to preserving the Union.

Jackson benefited from a growing spirit of democracy in which many viewed Adams as an elitist. Jackson insisted that the election came down to one question: "Shall the government or the people rule?" As president, he promised, he would fight against the entrenched power of the wealthy and powerful.

When Adams's supporters began referring to Jackson as a "jackass," Jackson embraced the name, using the animal as a symbol for his "tough" campaign. The jackass eventually became the enduring symbol of the Democratic party.

THE "COMMON MAN" IN POLITICS Andrew Jackson's campaign explicitly appealed to the common voters, many of whom were able to vote in a presidential election for the first time. By 1824, twenty-one of the twenty-four states had dropped property-owning requirements for voting. Only Virginia and the Carolinas, still dominated by the planter elite, continued to resist the democratizing trend. This "democratization" of politics also affected many free black males in northern states, half of which allowed blacks to vote.

The extension of voting rights to common men led to the election of politicians sprung from "the people" rather than from the social elite. Jackson, a frontiersman of humble origin and limited education who had scrambled up the political ladder by sheer tenacity, symbolized this emerging democratic ideal.

LABOR POLITICS With the widespread removal of property qualifications for voting, the working class (laborers paid hourly wages) became an important political force in the form of the Working Men's parties. They were first organized in 1828 in Philadelphia, the nation's largest manufacturing center.

The Working Men's parties promoted the interests of laborers, such as shorter working hours and allowing all males to vote regardless of the amount of property they owned. But their overarching concern was the widening inequality of wealth in America.

The Working Men's parties faded quickly, however. The inexperience of labor politicians left them vulnerable to manipulation by political professionals. In addition, major national parties, especially the Jacksonian Democrats, co-opted many of their issues.

Yet the working-class parties succeeded in drawing attention to their demands. They promoted free public education for all children, called for an end to imprisoning people for indebtedness, and supported a ten-hour workday to prevent employers from abusing workers. Union members loved Andrew Jackson, and the new Democratic party proved adept at building a national coalition of working-class supporters.

PRESIDENT JACKSON When the 1828 election returns came in, Jackson had won handily, taking every state west and south of Pennsylvania. Equally important was the surge in voter turnout; more than twice as many men voted as in the 1824 election.

As Andrew Jackson prepared to enter the White House, he was determined to be the "people's president." He would launch a new "democratic" era that would silence his critics, restore government to "the people," and take power away from the "Eastern elite." In doing so, he would transform the nation's political landscape—for good and for ill, as it turned out.

CHAPTER REVIEW

SUMMARY

- **Nationalism**   After the War of 1812, the federal government pursued many policies to strengthen the *national* economy. The *Tariff of 1816* protected American manufacturing, and the *Second Bank of the United States* provided a stronger currency. Led by John Marshall, the Supreme Court strengthened the power of the federal government in *Dartmouth College v. Woodward (1819)* and *McCulloch v. Maryland (1819)*. The Marshall court interpreted the Constitution as giving Congress the right to take any action not forbidden by the Constitution as long as the purpose of such laws was within the "scope of the Constitution." In *Gibbons v. Ogden (1824)*, the Court established the federal government's supremacy over interstate commerce, thereby promoting growth of the national economy.

- **Sectionalism**   Henry Clay's *American System* supported economic nationalism by endorsing a national bank, a protective tariff, and federally funded *internal improvements* such as roads and canals. Many Americans, however, were more tied to the needs of their particular sections of the country. People in the different regions—Northeast, South, and Midwest—disagreed about which economic policies best served their interests. As settlers streamed west, the extension of slavery into the new territories became the predominant political concern, eventually requiring both sides to compromise repeatedly to avoid civil war.

- **Era of Good Feelings**   James Monroe's term in office began with peace and prosperity. Two major events, however, ended the Era of Good Feelings: the financial *Panic of 1819* and the Missouri Compromise (1820). The explosive growth of the cotton culture transformed life in the South, in part by encouraging the expansion of slavery, which moved west with migrating southern planters. In 1819, however, the sudden collapse of world cotton prices devastated the southern economy. The *Missouri Compromise (1820)*, a short-term solution to the issue of allowing slavery in the western territories, exposed the emotions and turmoil that the expansion of slavery generated.

- **National Diplomacy**   The main diplomatic achievements after the War of 1812 extended America's boundaries and enabled the resumption of trade with Great Britain. To the north, U.S. diplomatic achievements established borders with Canada. To the south, the *Transcontinental Treaty (1819)* with Spain extended the boundaries of the United States. The *Monroe Doctrine (1823)* declared that the Americas were no longer open to European colonization.

- **The Election of 1828**   The demise of the Federalists left the Republicans as the only national political party. The Republicans' seeming unity was shattered by the election of 1824, which Andrew Jackson lost as a result of what he believed was a *corrupt bargain* between John Quincy Adams and Henry Clay. Jackson won the presidency in the *election campaign of 1828* by rallying southern and western voters with his promise to serve the interests of the common people.

CHRONOLOGY

1816	Second Bank of the United States is established
	First protective tariff goes into effect
1817	Rush-Bagot Treaty between the United States and Great Britain
1818	The Convention of 1818 establishes the northern border of the Louisiana Purchase at the 49th parallel
1819	Panic of 1819
	Supreme Court issues *McCulloch v. Maryland* decision
	United States and Spain agree to the Transcontinental (Adams-Onís) Treaty
1820	Congress accepts the Missouri Compromise
1821	Maine and Missouri become states
	Florida becomes a territory
1823	President Monroe announces the Monroe Doctrine
1824	Supreme Court issues *Gibbons v. Ogden* decision
	John Quincy Adams wins the presidential election by what some claim is a "corrupt bargain" with Henry Clay
1828	Andrew Jackson wins presidency

KEY TERMS

Second Bank of the United States (B.U.S.) p. 354

Tariff of 1816 p. 355

internal improvements p. 355

Dartmouth College v. Woodward (1819) p. 356

McCulloch v. Maryland (1819) p. 356

Gibbons v. Ogden (1824) p. 357

American System p. 358

Panic of 1819 p. 360

Missouri Compromise (1820) p. 362

Transcontinental Treaty (Adams-Onís Treaty) (1819) p. 365

Monroe Doctrine (1823) p. 367

corrupt bargain p. 370

election campaign of 1828 p. 373

 INQUIZITIVE

Go to InQuizitive to see what you've learned—and learn what you've missed—with personalized feedback along the way.

10 The Jacksonian Era

1828–1840

Hard times in the Jacksonian era Although Andrew Jackson championed the "poor and humble," his economic policies contributed to the Panic of 1837, a financial crisis that hit the working poor the hardest. This cartoon illustrates New York City during the seven-year depression: A frantic mob storms a bank, while in the foreground, a widow begs on the street with her child, surrounded by a banker or landlord and a barefoot sailor. At left are a drunken member of the Bowery Toughs gang and a down-on-his-luck militiaman. The cartoonist places the blame on Jackson, whose hat, glasses, and pipe overlook the scene. The white flag at left wryly states: "July 4, 1837, 61st Anniversary of Our Independence."

Andrew Jackson was a unique personality and a transformational leader. He was the first president from a western state (Tennessee), the first to have been born in a log cabin, the first *not* from a prominent colonial family, the last to have participated in the Revolutionary War, and the first to carry two bullets lodged in his lung and arm from a duel and a barroom brawl. Most important, Jackson was the polarizing emblem of a new democratic era.

Jackson was short-tempered and thin-skinned, proud and insecure. If his prickly sense of honor were challenged or his authority questioned, he never hesitated to fight or get even. For Jackson, politics was personal and combative.

Jackson believed in simple pleasures. He smoked a corncob pipe and chewed—and spit—tobacco. (He installed twenty spittoons in the White House.) Tall and lean, Jackson weighed only 140 pounds but was an intimidating figure with his penetrating blue eyes, long nose, jutting chin, silver-gray hair, and intense, iron-willed personality. "Old Hickory," however, was not in good health when he assumed the presidency. He suffered from blinding headaches and other ailments that led rival Henry Clay to describe him as "feeble in body and mind."

Despite his physical challenges, Jackson remained sharply focused and keenly sure of himself. More than previous presidents, he loved the rough-and-tumble combat of the raucous new democratic political culture. "I was born for a storm," he once boasted. "A calm [life] does not suit me."

Jackson took the nation by storm. No political figure was so widely loved or more deeply despised. As a self-made soldier, lawyer, planter, and politician, he helped create and shape the Democratic party, and he ushered in new

focus questions

1. What were Andrew Jackson's major beliefs regarding democracy, the presidency, and the proper role of government in the nation's economy?

2. What was Jackson's legacy regarding the status of Indians in American society?

3. How did Jackson respond to the nullification crisis?

4. What brought about the economic depression of the late 1830s and the emergence of the Whig party?

5. What were the strengths and weaknesses of Jackson's transformational presidency?

elements of modern presidential campaigning into electoral politics. Jackson continued to champion the emergence of the "common man" in politics (by which he meant white men only), and he stamped his name and, more important, his ideas, personality, and values on an entire era of American history.

JACKSONIAN DEMOCRACY

Andrew Jackson's election marked the culmination of thirty years of democratic innovations in politics. During the 1820s and 1830s, as America grew in population and people continued to move westward, most white men, whether they owned property or not, were allowed to vote and hold office. "The principle of universal suffrage," announced the *U.S. Magazine and Democratic Review*, "meant that white males of age constituted the political nation." Jackson promised to protect "the poor and humble" from the "tyranny of wealth and power." His populist goal was to elevate the "laboring classes" of white men who "love liberty and desire nothing but equal rights and equal laws."

Such democratization gave previously excluded white men equal status as citizens, regardless of wealth or background. No longer was politics an exclusive arena for only the most prominent and wealthiest white Americans.

POLITICAL DEMOCRACY   Campaigning was also democratized. Politics became the most popular form of mass entertainment, as people from all walks of life were remarkably well informed about public policy issues. Politics was "the only pleasure an American knows," observed visiting Frenchman Alexis de Tocqueville. "Even the women frequently attend public meetings and listen to political harangues as a recreation from their household labors."

Jackson was the most openly partisan and politically involved president in history to that point. Unlike previous presidents, who viewed campaigning as unseemly, he actively sought votes among the people, lobbied congressmen, and formed "Hickory Clubs" to campaign for him. Jackson also benefited from a powerful Democratic party "machine" run by his trusted secretary of state (later his vice president), Martin Van Buren, a shrewd New York lawyer.

Democracy, of course, is a slippery and elastic concept, and Jacksonians rarely defined what they meant by the "rule of the people." Noah Webster, the Connecticut Federalist who produced the nation's first reliable dictionary of homegrown American English, complained that "the men who have preached these doctrines [of democracy] have never defined what they mean by the *people*, or what they mean by *democracy*, nor how the *people* are to govern themselves." Jacksonian Democrats also showed little concern for the *undemocratic* constraints on African Americans, Native Americans, and women of every race, all of whom were denied basic political and civil rights.

ANTI-DEMOCRATIC FORCES Many southern slaveholders worried that the surge of democratic activism would eventually threaten the slave system. Virginian Muscoe Garnett, a planter and attorney, declared that "democracy is indeed incompatible with slavery, and the whole system of Southern society." His fellow Virginian, George Fitzhugh, was more explicit in his disdain for democratic ideals. In every society, he asserted, "some were born with saddles on their backs, and others booted and spurred to ride them."

DEMOCRACY UNLEASHED The inauguration of President Jackson symbolized the democratization of political life. Dressed in a black mourning suit in honor of his recently deceased wife, America's seventh president stepped out of the Capitol Building at noon on March 4, 1829. Waiting for him in the cold were 15,000 people who collectively roared and waved their hats when he emerged. "I never saw anything like it before," marveled Daniel Webster, the distinguished senator from Massachusetts.

Once the wild cheering subsided, Jackson bowed with great dignity, acknowledging the crowd's excitement and urging them to settle down. He then delivered a typically brief speech in which he committed his administration to "the task of reform" in the federal government, taking jobs out of "unfaithful or incompetent hands" and balancing states' rights with the exercise of national power. He also pledged to pursue the will of the people.

After being sworn in by Chief Justice John Marshall, Jackson mounted his white horse and rode down Pennsylvania Avenue to the White House, then called the Executive Mansion, where a wild celebration ensued. The huge crowd of jubilant western Democrats turned into a drunken mob. Dishes, glasses, and furniture were smashed, and muddy-booted revelers broke windows, ripped down draperies, and trampled on rugs. A Washington lady marveled at the arrival of frontier democracy in the nation's capital: "What a scene we did witness! The majesty of the people had disappeared, and a rabble, a mob, of boys, negroes, women, children, scrambling, fighting, romping. What a pity, what a pity!"

Those already skeptical of Jackson's qualifications for office saw the boisterous inaugural party as a symbol of all that was wrong with the "democratic" movement. Supreme Court Justice Joseph Story said he had never seen such "a mixture" of rowdy people, from the "highest and most polished down to the most vulgar and gross in the nation."

To his supporters, Jackson was a military hero and gifted leader. To his opponents, he was a self-serving tyrant. One critic dismissed as "humbug" the "mischievous popularity of this illiterate, violent, vain, and iron-willed soldier."

All Creation Going to the White House In this depiction of Andrew Jackson's inauguration party, satirist Robert Cruikshank draws a visual parallel to Noah's Ark, suggesting that people from all walks of life were now welcome in the White House.

JACKSON AS PRESIDENT

Andrew Jackson sought to increase the powers of the presidency at the expense of the legislative and judicial branches. One of his opponents noted that previous presidents had assumed that Congress was the primary branch of government. Jackson, however, believed that the presidency was "superior." The ruling political and economic elite must be removed, he said, for "the people" are the government, and too many government officials had grown corrupt and self-serving at the expense of the public interest.

To dislodge the "corrupt" eastern political elite, Jackson launched a policy he called "rotation in office," whereby he replaced many federal officials with his supporters. Government jobs—district attorneys, federal marshals, customs collectors—belonged to the people, not to career bureaucrats. Democracy, he believed, was best served when "newly elected officials" appointed new government officials. Such partisan behavior came to be called "the spoils system," since, as a prominent New York Democrat declared, "to the victor belong the spoils."

Jackson also sought to cut federal spending, to help pay off the federal debt. He supported internal improvements that were national in scope, promoted a "judicious tariff," hoped to destroy the Second Bank of the United States

(B.U.S.), and called for the relocation of the "ill-fated race" of Indians still liv-ing in the East to western lands across the Mississippi River. He claimed that displacing the Indians was for their own protection, but his primary motive was to enable whites to exploit Indian ancestral lands.

THE EATON AFFAIR Yet Jackson soon found himself preoccupied with squabbles within his cabinet. From the outset, his administration was divided between supporters of Secretary of State Martin Van Buren of New York and those allied with Vice President John C. Calhoun of South Carolina, both of whom wanted to succeed Jackson as president. Jackson did not trust Calhoun, a Yale graduate of towering intellect and fiery self-interest, who in many ways was a loner distrusted by members of both parties. Although once a Republican nation-alist, Calhoun now focused on defending southern interests, especially the pres-ervation of the slave-based cotton economy that had made him a wealthy planter.

In his rivalry with Calhoun, Van Buren would eventually take full advan-tage of a juicy scandal known as the Peggy Eaton affair. Widower John Eaton, a former U.S. senator from Tennessee and one of Jackson's closest friends, had long been associated with Margaret "Peggy" O'Neale Timberlake, a dev-astatingly attractive Washington temptress married to John Timberlake, a naval officer frequently at sea. While her husband was away, the flirtatious Mrs. Timberlake enjoyed "the attentions of men, young and old." She took special delight in Senator John Eaton.

In April 1828, John Timberlake died at sea. Although the official cause of death was respiratory failure, rumors swirled that he had committed suicide after learning of his wife's affair with Eaton.

Soon after the 1828 presidential election, John Eaton had written President-elect Jackson about the spiteful gossip aimed at himself and Peggy Timberlake. Jackson responded quickly and firmly: "Marry her and you will be in a posi-tion to defend her." Eaton did so on January 1, 1829.

Eaton's enemies quickly criticized the "unseemly haste" of the marriage and continued to savage Peggy Eaton as a whore. Louis McLane, a U.S. sen-ator from Delaware who would later serve in Jackson's cabinet, sneered that John Eaton, soon to be named Jackson's secretary of war, "has just married his mistress, and the mistress of eleven dozen others." Floride Calhoun, the vice president's imperious wife, especially objected to Peggy Eaton's unsavory past. At Jackson's inaugural ball, she openly ignored her, as did the other cabinet members' wives.

The constant gossip led Jackson to explode: "I did not come here [to Washington] to make a Cabinet for the Ladies of this place, but for the Nation." Peggy Eaton's plight reminded him of the mean-spirited gossip that had plagued

King Andrew the First Opponents considered Jackson's veto of the Maysville Road Bill an abuse of power. This cartoon shows "King Andrew" trampling on the Constitution, internal improvements, and the Bank of the United States.

his own wife, Rachel. Intensely loyal to John Eaton, the president defended Peggy, insisting that she was as pure "as a virgin." His cabinet members, however, were unable to cure their wives of what Martin Van Buren dubbed "the Eaton Malaria." The rumoring and sniping became a time-consuming distraction for the president.

Jackson blamed the Eaton scandal, also known as the "Petticoat Affair," on Henry Clay and John C. Calhoun. The president assumed that Calhoun and his wife had targeted John Eaton because Eaton did not support Calhoun's desire to be president. One of Calhoun's friends wrote in April 1829 that the United States was "governed by the President—the President by the Secretary of War—and the latter by his Wife." Jackson concluded that Calhoun "would sacrifice his friend, his country, and forsake his god, for selfish personal ambition." For his part, Calhoun dismissed Jackson as a "self-infatuated man . . . blinded by ambition [and] intoxicated by flattery and vanity!"

THE MAYSVILLE ROAD VETO When President Jackson was not dealing with the Petticoat Affair, he used his executive authority to limit the role of the federal government—while delivering additional blows to John C. Calhoun and Henry Clay.

In 1830, Congress passed a bill pushed by Calhoun and Clay that authorized the use of federal monies to build a sixty-mile-long road across the state of Kentucky from the city of Maysville to Lexington, Clay's hometown. Jackson, urged on by Martin Van Buren, who wanted to preserve the Erie Canal's monopoly over western trade, vetoed the bill on the grounds that the proposed road was a "purely local matter," being solely in the state of Kentucky and thus outside the domain of Congress, which had authority only over *interstate* commerce. Federal funding for such local projects would thus require a constitutional amendment.

Clay was stunned. "We are all shocked and mortified by the rejection of the Maysville road," he wrote a friend. But he had no luck convincing Congress to override the veto.

THE EASTERN INDIANS

President Jackson's forcible removal of Indians from their ancestral lands was his highest priority and one of his lowest moments. Like most white frontiersmen, he saw Indians as barbarians who were to be treated as "subjects," not "nations." He claimed that Indians and land-hungry white settlers could never live in harmony, so the Indians had to go if they were to survive. Henry Clay felt the same way, arguing that the Indians were "destined to extinction" and not "worth preserving."

After Jackson's election in 1828, he urged that the remaining eastern Indians (east of the Mississippi River) be moved to reservations west of the Mississippi, in what became Oklahoma. Jackson believed that moving the Indians would serve their best interests as well as the national interest, for the states in the Lower South, especially the Carolinas, Georgia, and Alabama, were aggressively restricting the rights of Indian nations and taking their land. Jackson often told Indian leaders that he was their "Great Father" trying to protect them from greedy state governments. He claimed that relocating the eastern Indians was a "wise and humane policy" that would save them from "utter annihilation" if they tried to hold on to their lands in the face of state actions.

INDIAN REMOVAL In 1830, Jackson submitted to Congress the **Indian Removal Act**, which authorized him to ignore commitments made by previous presidents and to convince the Indians remaining in the East and South to move to federal lands west of the Mississippi River. The federal government, the new program promised, would pay for the Indian exodus and give them initial support in their new lands ("Indian Territory") in Oklahoma.

Indian leaders were skeptical. As a federal agent reported, "They see that our professions are insincere, that our promises are broken, that the happiness of the Indian is a cheap sacrifice to the acquisition of new lands."

Jackson's proposal also provoked heated opposition among reformers who distrusted his motives and doubted the promised support from the federal government. Critics flooded Congress with petitions that criticized the policy and warned that Jackson's plan would bring "enduring shame" on the nation.

But to no avail. In late May 1830, the Senate passed the Indian Removal Act by a single vote, and Jackson eagerly signed it. The Cherokees responded by announcing that "we see nothing but ruin before us."

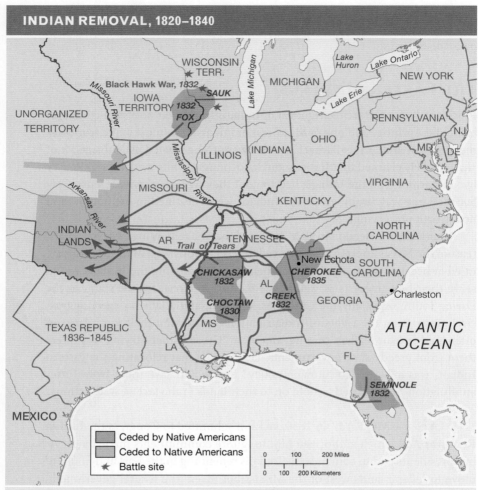

INDIAN REMOVAL, 1820–1840

- Why did Congress relocate the Choctaws, Chickasaws, Creeks, Seminoles, and Cherokees to territory west of Arkansas and Missouri?
- How far did the exiled Indians have to travel, and what were the conditions on the journey?
- Why were they not forced to move before the 1830s?

RESISTANCE Most northern Indians were relocated. In Illinois and the Wisconsin Territory, however, Sauk and Fox Indians fought to regain their ancestral lands. The Black Hawk War erupted in April 1832, when Chief Black Hawk led 1,000 Sauks—men, women, and children who had been relocated to the Iowa Territory—back across the Mississippi River to their homeland in Illinois, land shared with the Fox Nation. After several skirmishes, Indiana and Illinois militia chased the Sauk and Fox into the Wisconsin Territory and caught them on the eastern bank of the Mississippi, a few miles downstream from the mouth of the Bad Axe River.

The soldiers misinterpreted the Indians' effort to surrender, and fighting erupted. In what became known as the Bad Axe Massacre, the militiamen murdered hundreds of women and children as they tried to escape. The soldiers then scalped the dead Indians and cut long strips of flesh from several of them for use as strops to sharpen razors. Six weeks later, Black Hawk was captured and imprisoned.

In Florida, the Seminoles, led by Osceola (called by U.S. soldiers "the still unconquered red man"), ferociously resisted the federal removal policy. For eight years, the Seminoles would fight a guerrilla war in the swamps of the Everglades—the longest, most costly, and deadliest war ever fought by Native Americans. Some 1,500 were killed on both sides. At times, Seminole women killed their children rather than see them captured.

But Seminole resistance waned after 1837, when Osceola was treacherously captured under a white flag of truce, imprisoned, and left to die of malaria at Fort

Hiding in a Mangrove Swamp An armed group of Seminoles crouch under a mangrove in the Florida Everglades during the Second Seminole War, out of sight of the American sailors passing by.

Moultrie near Charleston, South Carolina. After 1842, only a few hundred Seminoles remained. It was not until 1934 that the surviving Seminoles in Florida became the last Native American tribe to end its war with the United States.

THE CHEROKEES The Cherokee Nation also tried to defy the federal removal policy. Cherokees had long occupied northwest Georgia and the mountainous areas of northern Alabama, eastern Tennessee, and western North Carolina. In 1827, relying upon their established treaty rights, they adopted a constitution as an independent nation in which they declared that they were not subject to the laws or control of any state or federal government. Georgia officials had other ideas.

In 1828, shortly after Andrew Jackson's election, the Georgia government announced that after June 1, 1830, the authority of state law would extend to the Cherokees. The "barbarous and savage tribes" must give way to the march of white civilization. Under the new state laws, they would not be allowed to vote, own property, or testify against whites in court.

The discovery of gold in north Georgia in 1829 had increased whites' lust for Cherokee land, attracted trespassing prospectors, and led to the new law. It prohibited the Cherokees from digging for gold on their own lands. The Cherokees sought relief in the Supreme Court, arguing that "we wish to remain on the land of our fathers. We have a perfect and original right to remain without interruption or molestation."

In *Cherokee Nation v. Georgia* (1831), Chief Justice John Marshall ruled that the Cherokees had "an unquestionable right" to maintain control of their ancestral lands, but the Court could not render a verdict because of a technicality: the Cherokees had filed suit as a "foreign nation," but in Marshall's view they were "domestic dependent nations." If it were true that "wrongs have been inflicted," Marshall explained, "this is not the tribunal which can redress the past or prevent the future."

The following year, the Supreme Court *did* rule in favor of the Cherokees in *Worcester v. Georgia* (1832). The case arose when Georgia officials arrested a group of white Christian missionaries who were living among the Cherokees in violation of a state law forbidding such interaction. Two of the missionaries, Samuel Worcester and Elihu Butler, were sentenced to four years at hard labor. They appealed to the Supreme Court.

In the *Worcester* case, John Marshall said the missionaries must be released. The anti-Cherokee laws passed by the Georgia legislature, he declared, had violated "the Constitution, laws, and treaties of the United States." He added that the Cherokee Nation was "a distinct political community" within which Georgia law had no force.

President Jackson, however, refused to enforce the Court's "wicked" decisions, claiming that he had no constitutional authority to intervene in Georgia. A New York newspaper editor reported that Jackson said, "John Marshall has made his decision, now let him enforce it."

Thereafter, Jackson gave the Cherokees and other Indian nations a terrible choice: either abide by discriminatory new state laws or relocate to federal lands west of the Mississippi River, which would be theirs "forever." Jackson told the Creeks that they and whites could not live "in harmony and peace" if they remained on their ancestral lands and that "a speedy removal" to the West was their only option. Soon, Georgia officials began selling Cherokee lands.

The irony of the new Georgia policy was that of all the southern tribes, the Cherokees had come closest to adopting the customs of white America. They had abandoned traditional hunting practices to develop farms, build roads, schools, and churches, and create trading posts and newspapers. Many Cherokees had married whites, adopted their clothing and food, and converted to Christianity. And the Cherokees owned some 2,000 enslaved African Americans.

THE TRAIL OF TEARS The federal officials responsible for implementing the Indian Removal Act developed a strategy of divide and conquer with the Cherokees. In 1835, for example, a minority faction of the Cherokees signed the fraudulent Treaty of New Echota, in which they agreed to move to the Indian Territory in Oklahoma. The treaty was rejected by 90 percent of the Cherokee people but readily accepted by the U.S. Senate and enforced by the U.S. Army.

In 1838, after President Jackson had left office and Martin Van Buren was president, 17,000 Cherokees were evicted and moved West under military guard on the **Trail of Tears**, an 800-mile forced journey marked by the harshness of soldiers and the neglect of irresponsible private contractors assigned to manage the process. Some 4,000 refugees died along the way. For his part, Van Buren told Congress in December 1838 that he took "sincere pleasure" in reporting that the entire Cherokee Nation had been relocated.

The Trail of Tears was, according to a white Georgian, "the cruelest work I ever knew." A few Cherokees held out in the mountains of North Carolina; they became known as the "Eastern Band" of Cherokees. The Creeks and Chickasaws followed the Trail of Tears a few years later, after Alabama and Mississippi took control of their tribal lands.

Some 100,000 eastern Indians were relocated to the West during the 1820s and 1830s, and the government sold some 100 million acres of Indian land,

Trail of Tears Thousands of Cherokees died on a nightmarish march from Georgia to Oklahoma after being forced from their native lands.

most of it in the prime cotton-growing areas of Georgia, Alabama, and Mississippi, known as the Old Southwest.

THE BANK WAR

Andrew Jackson showed the same principled stubbornness in dealing with the national bank as he did in removing the Indians. The charter for the First Bank of the United States (B.U.S.) had expired in 1811 but was renewed in 1816 as the Second Bank of the United States. It soon became the largest corporation in the nation and the only truly national business enterprise.

The second B.U.S. (the federal government owned only 20 percent of the bank's capital) was a private corporation with extensive public responsibilities—and powers. To benefit the government, the B.U.S. held all federal funds, including tax collections (mostly from land sales and tariff revenues), and disbursed federal payments for its obligations, all in exchange for an annual $1.5 million fee. The B.U.S., however, conducted other business like a commercial bank and was free to use the government deposits in its vaults as collateral for loans to businesses. Headquartered in Philadelphia and supported by twenty-nine branches around the nation, the B.U.S. competed with state-chartered banks for local business.

The B.U.S. helped accelerate business expansion by making loans to individuals, businesses, and state banks. It also helped promote a stable money supply and deter excessive lending by requiring the 464 state banks to keep enough gold and silver coins (called specie) in their vaults to back their own paper currency, which they in turn loaned to individuals and businesses. The primary benefit of the B.U.S. was its ability to monitor and regulate many of the state banks.

With federal revenues soaring from land sales during the early 1830s, the B.U.S., led by Nicholas Biddle, had accumulated massive amounts of money—and economic clout. Even though the B.U.S. benefited the national economy, state banks, especially in the South and West, feared its growing "monopolistic" power. Critics claimed that Biddle and the B.U.S. were restricting lending by state banks and impeding businesses from borrowing as much as they wanted.

Andrew Jackson, like many westerners, had always hated banks and bankers, whom he called "vipers and thieves." His prejudice grew out of his experiences in the 1790s, when he had suffered huge financial losses. Now, he claimed to speak for ordinary Americans who felt that banks favored the "rich and powerful" in the East.

Jackson distrusted banks because they printed too much paper money, causing prices to rise (inflation). He wanted only gold and silver coins to be used for economic transactions. Jackson also disliked Biddle because he was everything that Jackson was not: an Easterner born to wealth, highly educated, financially sophisticated, and a world traveler. Ironically, Biddle had voted for Jackson.

The **Bank War** between Jackson and Biddle revealed that the president never truly understood the national bank's role or policies, and he let personal animosity drive many of his policy decisions. The B.U.S. had provided a stable monetary system for the expanding economy, as well as a mechanism for controlling the pace and integrity of economic growth by regulating the ability of branch banks and state banks to issue paper currency.

THE RECHARTER EFFORT Although the Second Bank's charter ran through 1836, leaders of the newly named National Republican party, especially Senators Henry Clay and Daniel Webster (who was a paid legal counsel to the B.U.S.), told Nicholas Biddle that the charter needed to be renewed before the 1836 presidential election. They assured him that Congress would renew the charter, leading Biddle to grow overconfident about the bank's future. Jackson, he said, "thinks because he has scalped Indians . . . he is to have his way with the Bank."

Rechartering the Bank Jackson's effort to defeat the recharter of the B.U.S. is likened to fighting a hydra, a many-headed serpent from Greek mythology. Just as the hydra would sprout two heads when one was severed, for each B.U.S. supporter that Jackson subdued, even more would emerge to take his place.

Biddle and his allies, however, failed to appreciate Jackson's tenacity or the depth of his hatred for the B.U.S. And most voters were on Jackson's side. In the end, Biddle, Clay, and the National Republicans unintentionally handed Jackson a popular issue on the eve of the 1832 election. At their nominating convention in December 1831, the National Republican party, also called the Anti-Jackson party, endorsed Clay as their presidential candidate and approved the renewal of the B.U.S.

Early in the summer of 1832, both houses of Congress passed the bank recharter bill, in part because Biddle used bribes to win votes. Upon learning of such shenanigans, Jackson's chief of staff concluded that the B.U.S. was "becoming desperate: *caught in its own net.*"

Biddle, Webster, and Clay assumed that Jackson would not veto the recharter bill because doing so might cost him reelection. On July 10, 1832, however, Jackson nixed the bill, sending it back to Congress and harshly criticizing the bank for making the "rich richer and the potent more powerful" while discriminating against "the humble members of society—the farmers, mechanics, and laborers."

Webster accused Jackson of using the bank issue "to stir up the poor against the rich." To Clay, Jackson's veto represented another example of the president's desire to concentrate "all power in the hands of one man." Clay and Webster, however, could not convince the Senate to override the veto, thus setting the stage for a nationwide debate and a dramatic presidential campaign.

The overriding issue in the election was the future of the Bank of the United States. Let the people decide, Jackson argued. "I have now done my duty to the citizens of this country," he said in explaining his veto. "If sustained by my fellow-citizens [in the upcoming election], I shall be grateful and happy; if not, I shall find in the motives which impel me ample grounds for contentment and peace."

NULLIFICATION

Andrew Jackson eventually would veto twelve congressional bills, more than all previous presidents combined. Critics claimed that his behavior was "monarchical." Jackson, however, believed that the president represented *all* the people, unlike congressmen who were elected locally. His commitment to nationalism over sectionalism was nowhere more evident than in his handling of the nullification crisis in South Carolina.

CALHOUN AND THE TARIFF Vice President John C. Calhoun became President Jackson's fiercest critic—and vice versa. In part because of his feud with the president, Calhoun had become the leading states' rights advocate for the South.

Changing economic conditions in his home state frustrated Calhoun. The financial panic of 1819 had sparked a nationwide depression, and through the 1820s, South Carolina continued to suffer from falling cotton prices. The state lost almost 70,000 people during the decade as residents moved West in search of cheaper and more-fertile land for growing cotton. Twice as many would leave during the 1830s.

Most South Carolinians blamed their woes on the Tariff of 1828, which was labeled the **Tariff of Abominations**. By taxing British cloth coming into U.S. markets, the tariff hurt southern cotton growers by reducing British demand for raw cotton from America. It also hurt southerners by raising prices for imported products.

In a pamphlet called the *South Carolina Exposition and Protest* (1828), Calhoun claimed that the Tariff of 1828 favored the interests of New England textile manufacturing over southern agriculture. Under such circumstances, he argued, a state could "nullify," or veto, a federal law it deemed unconstitutional.

Webster Replying to Senator Hayne (1848) The eloquent Massachusetts senator challenges the argument for nullification in the Webster–Hayne debate.

Nullification was the ultimate weapon for those determined to protect states' rights against federal authority. As Jackson and others pointed out, however, allowing states to pick and choose which federal laws they would follow would create national chaos.

CLASH OF TITANS—WEBSTER VERSUS HAYNE The controversy over the Tariff of 1828 simmered until 1830, when the Webster–Hayne debate in Congress sharpened the lines between states' rights and national authority. In a fiery speech, Senator Robert Y. Hayne of South Carolina argued that the anti-slavery Yankees were invading the South, "making war upon her citizens, and endeavoring to overthrow her principles and institutions." In Hayne's view, the Union was created by the states, and the states therefore had the right to nullify, or ignore, federal laws they disliked. The independence of the states was to him more important than the preservation of the Union.

Massachusetts senator Daniel Webster challenged Hayne's arguments. Blessed with a thunderous voice and a theatrical flair, Webster pointed out that the U.S. Constitution was created not by the states but by the American people. If states were allowed to nullify a federal law, the Union would be nothing but a "rope of sand." South Carolina's defiance of federal authority, he charged, "is nothing more than resistance by *force*—it is disunion by *force*—it is secession by *force*—it is civil war."

Webster's powerful closing statement—"Liberty and Union, now and for-ever, one and inseparable"—was printed in virtually every newspaper in the nation. Abraham Lincoln later called it "the very best speech ever delivered." Even Hayne was awestruck. He told Webster that "a man who can make such speeches as that ought never to die." In the end, Webster had the better argument.

CALHOUN VERSUS JACKSON That Jackson, like Calhoun, was a cotton-planting slaveholder led many southerners to assume that the president would support their resistance to the federal tariff. Jackson was sympathetic—until Calhoun and others in South Carolina threatened to nullify federal laws.

On April 13, 1830, the Democratic party hosted scores of congressmen and political leaders at the first annual Jefferson Day dinner. When it was Jackson's turn to salute Thomas Jefferson's memory, he rose to his feet, raised his glass, and, glaring at Calhoun, growled: "Our Union—it must be preserved!"

People gasped, knowing that the vice president must reply to Jackson's threat to nullification. Calhoun, trembling with emotion, countered with a defiant toast to "the Union, next to our liberty the most dear!" In that dramatic exchange, Jackson and Calhoun laid bare the fundamental tension between federal authority and states' rights that has remained an animating theme of the American republic.

Soon thereafter, another incident deepened the animosity between the two men. On May 12, 1830, the president saw for the first time a letter from 1818 in which Calhoun, then secretary of war under James Monroe, had wanted to discipline Jackson for his unauthorized invasion of Spanish-held Florida. After exchanging heated letters about the incident with Calhoun, Jackson told a friend that he was finally through with the "double dealing of J.C.C."

The rift prompted Jackson to take a dramatic step suggested by Secretary of State Martin Van Buren, his closest adviser. During one of their daily horse-back rides together, Van Buren offered himself up as a sacrifice as a way to remove all Calhoun supporters from the cabinet and thereby end the ongoing Eaton affair that had fractured the administration.

As the first step in the cabinet coup, Van Buren convinced John Eaton to resign as secretary of war on April 4, 1831. Four days later, Van Buren resigned as secretary of state. "The long agony is over," crowed Samuel Ingham, the secretary of the Treasury, in a letter to Attorney General John Berrien. "Mr. V. B. and Major Eaton have resigned." What Ingham and Berrien did not realize was that a few days later, Jackson would force them—both Calhoun supporters—to resign as well. Jackson now had a clean slate on which to create another cabinet.

Critics saw through the secretary of state's scheme: "Mr. Van Buren may be called the 'Great Magician,'" wrote the *New York Courier*, "for he *raises his wand, and the whole Cabinet disappears*." Others claimed that the cabinet purge showed that Jackson did not have the political skill to lead the nation. One newspaper announced that the ship of state "is sinking and the rats are flying! The hull is too leaky to mend, and the hero of two wars and a half has not the skill to keep it afloat."

The next act in the running political drama occurred when John Eaton challenged Ingham to a duel. The ousted Treasury secretary chose instead to retreat to his home in Pennsylvania. After the Eatons left Washington, D.C., a gloating Henry Clay retrieved William Shakespeare's characterization of Egyptian queen Cleopatra to mark Peggy's departure: "Age cannot wither nor time stale her infinite virginity."

NEW CABINET By the end of August 1831, President Jackson had appointed a new cabinet. At the same time, he increasingly relied upon the advice of Martin Van Buren and others making up his so-called "kitchen cabinet," an informal group of close friends and supporters, many of them Democratic newspaper editors.

The kitchen cabinet soon convinced Jackson to drop his pledge to serve only one term. They explained that it would be hard for Van Buren, the president's chosen successor, to win the 1832 Democratic nomination because Calhoun would do everything in his power to stop him—and might win the nomination himself.

THE ANTI-MASONIC PARTY In 1832, for the first time in a presidential election, a third political party entered the field. The Anti-Masonic party grew out of popular hostility toward the Masonic fraternal order, a large, all-male social organization that had originated in Great Britain. The Freemasons often claimed to be the natural leaders of their communities, the "best men." By 1830, more than 2,000 Masonic "lodges" were scattered across the United States with about 100,000 Freemason members, including Andrew Jackson and Henry Clay.

The new Anti-Masonic party owed its origins to William Morgan, a fifty-two-year-old unemployed bricklayer in Batavia, New York. Morgan had been thrown out of the Masons because of his joblessness. Seeking revenge, he convinced a local printer to publish a widely circulated pamphlet revealing the secret rituals of the Masonic order. Masons then burned the print shop where the pamphlet had been published. They also had Morgan arrested on a trumped-up charge of indebtedness.

Soon thereafter, on September 12, 1826, someone paid for Morgan's release from jail and spirited him away. A year later, a man's decomposed body washed up in Oak Orchard Creek, near Lake Ontario. Morgan's grieving wife confirmed that it was her husband. Governor Dewitt Clinton, himself a Mason, offered a reward for anyone who would identify the kidnappers.

The Morgan mystery became a major political issue. New York launched more than twenty investigations into Morgan's disappearance (and presumed murder) and conducted a dozen trials of several Masons but never gained a conviction. Each legal effort aroused more public indignation because most of the judges, lawyers, and jurors were Masons.

People began to fear that the Masons had become a self-appointed aristocracy lacking the education and character necessary for self-denying civic leadership. John Quincy Adams said that disbanding the "Masonic institution" was the most important issue facing "us and our posterity."

Suspicion of the Masonic order gave rise to the Anti-Masonic party, whose purpose was to protect republican values from corruption by self-serving, power-hungry Masonic insiders. The Anti-Masons claimed that they were determined to "hand down to posterity unimpaired the republic we inherited from our forefathers."

The Verdict of the People George Caleb Bingham's painting depicts a socially diverse electorate, suggesting the increasingly democratic politics of the Jacksonian era.

The new party drew most of its support from New Englanders and New Yorkers alienated by both the Democratic and National Republican parties. Anti-Masonic adherents tended to be rural evangelical Protestants, many of whom also opposed slavery.

Although opposition to a fraternal organization was hardly the foundation upon which to build a lasting political coalition, the Anti-Masonic party had three important "firsts" to its credit: In addition to being the first third party with a national base of support, it was the first political party to hold a national convention to nominate a presidential candidate, and the first to announce a formal platform of specific policy goals.

THE 1832 ELECTION In preparing for the 1832 election, the Democrats and National Republicans followed the example of the Anti-Masonic party by holding nominating conventions of their own. In December 1831, the National Republicans nominated Henry Clay.

The Democratic convention first adopted the two-thirds rule for nomination (which prevailed until 1936, when the requirement became a simple majority), and then named Martin Van Buren as Andrew Jackson's running mate. The Democrats, unlike the other two parties, adopted no formal platform and relied to a substantial degree upon the popularity of the president to carry their cause.

Nicholas Biddle invested the vast resources of the Bank of the United States into the campaign against Jackson and paid for thousands of pamphlets promoting Clay. By the summer of 1832, Clay declared that "the campaign is over, and I think we have won the victory." But his blinding ego prevented him from seeing the sources of Jackson's popularity. Where he dismissed Jackson as a power-hungry military chief, most Americans saw the president as someone fighting for them.

Clay also failed to understand Jackson's effectiveness as a political candidate. The *National Intelligencer*, a newspaper that supported Clay, acknowledged that Jackson's eager participation in campaign events was "certainly a new mode of electioneering. We do not recollect before to have heard of a President of the United States descending in person into the political arena." Jackson gave stump speeches, dived into crowds to shake hands, and walked in parades or ate barbecue with supporters who cheered and mobbed him.

In the end, Jackson earned 219 electoral votes to Clay's 49 and enjoyed a solid victory in the popular vote, 688,000 to 530,000. William Wirt, the Anti-Masonic candidate, carried only Vermont, winning 7 electoral votes. Dazzled by the president's strong showing, Wirt observed that Jackson could "be President for life if he chooses."

THE NULLIFICATION CRISIS

In the fall of 1831, President Jackson tried to defuse the confrontation with South Carolina by calling on Congress to reduce tariff rates. Congress responded with the Tariff of 1832, which lowered rates on some products but kept them high on British cotton fabric and clothing.

The new tariff disappointed John C. Calhoun and others eager for the British to buy more southern cotton. South Carolinians seethed with resentment toward the federal government. Living in the only state where enslaved Africans were a majority of the population, they feared that if the northern representatives in Congress were powerful enough to create tariffs that proved so harmful to the South, they might eventually vote to end slavery itself. Calhoun declared that the "peculiar domestic institutions of the southern states" (slavery) were at stake.

SOUTH CAROLINA NULLIFIERS In November 1832, just weeks after Andrew Jackson was reelected, a special convention in South Carolina passed an Ordinance of Nullification that disavowed the "unconstitutional" federal tariffs of 1828 and 1832, declaring them "null, void, and no law." If federal authorities tried to use force to collect the tariffs on foreign goods unloaded in Charleston Harbor, South Carolina would secede from the Union, they vowed. The state legislature then selected Senator Robert Hayne as governor and named Calhoun to replace him as U.S. senator. Calhoun resigned as vice president so that he could defend his nullification theory in Congress and oppose Jackson's "tyrannical" actions.

JACKSON SAYS NO TO NULLIFICATION President Jackson's public response was measured yet forthright. He promised to use "firmness and forbearance" with South Carolina but stressed that nullification "means insurrection and war; and the other states have a right to put it down."

In private, however, Jackson was furious. He asked the secretary of war how many soldiers it would take to go to South Carolina and "crush the monster [nullification] in its cradle." He also threatened to hang Calhoun and other "nullifiers" if there were any bloodshed.

During the fall of 1832, most northern state legislatures passed resolutions condemning the nullificationists. Southern states expressed sympathy for South Carolina, but none endorsed nullification. "We detest the tariff," explained a Mississippian, "but we will hold to the Union." South Carolina was left standing alone.

On December 10, 1832, the unyielding Jackson issued his official response to the people of South Carolina. In his blistering proclamation, he dismissed nullification as "an absurdity," a "mad project of disunion" that was "*incompatible with the existence of the Union, contradicted expressly by the letter of the Constitution, unauthorized by its spirit, inconsistent with every principle on which It was founded, and destructive of the great object for which it was formed.*" He warned that nullification would lead to secession (formal withdrawal of a state from the United States), and secession meant civil war. "Be not deceived by names. Disunion by armed force is TREASON. Are you really ready to incur its guilt?"

CLAY STEPS IN   President Jackson then sent federal soldiers and a warship to Charleston to protect the federal customs house where tariffs were applied to products imported from Europe. Governor Hayne responded by mobilizing the state militia. A South Carolina Unionist reported to Jackson that many "reckless and dangerous men" were "looking for civil war and scenes of bloodshed." While taking forceful actions, Jackson still wanted "peaceably to nullify the nullifiers."

In early 1833, the president requested from Congress the authority to use the U.S. Army to "force" compliance with federal law in South Carolina. Calhoun exploded on the Senate floor, exclaiming that he and the others defending his state's constitutional rights were being threatened by what they called the **Force Bill** "to have our throats cut, and those of our wives and children." The greatest threat facing the nation, he argued, was not nullification but presidential despotism.

Calhoun and the nullifiers, however, soon backed down, and the South Carolina legislature postponed implementation of the nullification ordinances in hopes that Congress would pass a more palatable tariff bill.

Passage of a compromise bill, however, depended upon the support of Senator Henry Clay, himself a slaveholding planter, who finally yielded to those urging him to step in and save the day. A senator told Clay that these "South Carolinians are good fellows, and it would be a pity to see Jackson hang them."

Clay agreed. On February 12, 1833, he circulated a plan suggested by Jackson to gradually reduce the federal tariff on key imported items. Clay urged Congress to treat South Carolina with respect and display "that great principle of compromise and concession which lies at the bottom of our institutions." The tariff reductions were less than South Carolina preferred, but Clay's compromise helped the nullifiers out of the dilemma they had created. Calhoun supported the compromise: "He who loves the Union must desire to see this agitating question [the tariff] brought to a termination."

On March 1, 1833, Jackson signed into law the compromise tariff and the Force Bill, the latter being a symbolic statement of the primacy of the Union. Calhoun rushed home to convince the rebels to back down. The South Carolina convention then met and rescinded its nullification of the tariff acts. In a face-saving gesture, the delegates nullified the Force Bill, which Jackson no longer needed.

Both sides felt they had won. Jackson had defended the supremacy of the Union without firing a shot, and South Carolina's persistence had brought tariff reductions. Joel Poinsett, a South Carolina Unionist, was overjoyed with the resolution but added that the next crisis would force a choice between "union and disunion."

Despite the compromise, southern slaveholders felt increasingly threatened by anti-slavery sentiment in the North. "There is no liberty—no security for the South," groused South Carolina radical Robert Barnwell Rhett. Jackson concluded that the "tariff was only the pretext [for the nullification crisis], and disunion and southern confederacy the real object. The next pretext will be the negro, or slavery question." Two days after the nullification crisis was resolved, Jackson was sworn in for a second term as president.

WAR OVER THE B.U.S.

Jackson interpreted his lopsided reelection as a "decision of the people against the bank." Having vetoed the renewal of the Bank of the United States charter, Jackson ordered the Department of the Treasury to transfer federal monies from the national bank to twenty-three mostly western state banks—called "pet banks" by Jackson's critics because many were run by the president's allies. When the Treasury secretary balked, Jackson fired him.

BIDDLE'S RESPONSE B.U.S. head Nicholas Biddle responded by ordering the bank to quit making loans and demanded that state banks exchange their paper currency for gold or silver coins. Through such deflationary policies, Biddle was trying to bring the economy to a halt, create a depression, and thus reveal the importance of maintaining the national bank. An enraged Jackson said the B.U.S. under Biddle was "trying to kill me, *but I will kill it!*"

Biddle's plan worked. Northern Democrats worried that the president's "lawless and reckless" Bank War would ruin the party. But Jackson refused to flinch. When state bankers visited the White House to plead for relief, Jackson said, "We have no money here, gentlemen. Biddle has all the money."

In the Senate, Calhoun and Clay argued that Jackson's transfer of government cash from the B.U.S. to the pet banks was illegal. On March 28, 1834,

Clay convinced a majority in the Senate to *censure* Jackson for his actions. Jackson was so angry that he wanted to challenge Clay to a duel so that he could "bring the rascal to a dear account."

THE NEW WHIG PARTY The president's war on the bank led his opponents to create a new political party. They claimed that he was ruling like a monarch, dubbed him "King Andrew the First," and called his Democratic supporters *Tories*. The new anti-Jackson coalition called themselves **Whigs**, a name that had also been used by the Patriots of the American Revolution (as well as by the parliamentary opponents of the Tories in Britain).

The Whig party grew directly out of the National Republican party led by John Quincy Adams, Henry Clay, and Daniel Webster. The Whigs also found support among Anti-Masons and even some Democrats who resented Jackson's war on the national bank. Of the forty-one Democrats in Congress who had voted against Jackson on rechartering the national bank, twenty-eight had joined the Whigs by 1836.

The Whigs, like the National Republicans they replaced, were economic nationalists who wanted the federal government to promote manufacturing, support a national bank, and finance a national road network. In the South, the Whigs tended to be bankers and merchants. In the West, they were mostly farmers who valued government-funded internal improvements. Unlike the Democrats, who attracted Catholic voters from Germany and Ireland, northern Whigs tended to be native-born Protestants—Congregationalists, Presbyterians, Methodists, and Baptists—who advocated the abolition of slavery and efforts to restrict alcoholic beverages. For the next twenty years, the Whigs and the Democrats would be the two major political parties.

KILLING THE B.U.S. In the end, a relentless President Jackson won his battle with Nicholas Biddle's bank. The B.U.S. would shut down completely by 1841, and the United States would not have a central banking system until 1914. Jackson exulted in his "glorious triumph," but his controversial efforts to destroy the B.U.S. aroused so much opposition that some in Congress talked of impeaching him. He received so many death threats that he decided his political opponents were trying to kill him.

In January 1835, the threat became real. After attending a funeral for a member of Congress, Jackson was leaving the Capitol when an unemployed housepainter named Richard Lawrence emerged from the shadows and, from point-blank range, aimed a pistol at the president's heart. When Lawrence pulled the trigger, however, the gun misfired. Jackson lifted his walking stick and charged at the man, who pulled out another pistol, but it, too, miraculously misfired, enabling police to arrest him.

Jackson assumed that his political foes had planned the attack. A jury, however, decided that Lawrence, the first person to attempt to assassinate a U.S. president, was insane and ordered him confined in an asylum.

The destruction of the B.U.S. illustrated Jackson's strengths and weaknesses. He was a cunning and ferocious fighter. Yet his determination to destroy the B.U.S. ended up hurting the national economy. Without the B.U.S., there was nothing to regulate the nation's money supply or its banks. The number of state banks more than doubled between 1829 and 1837. Of even greater concern, however, was that the dollar amount of loans made by these unregulated banks quadrupled, preparing the way for a financial panic and a terrible depression.

Jackson and the Democrats grew increasingly committed to the expansion of slavery westward into the Gulf coast states, driven by an unstable banking system. "People here are run mad with [land] speculation," wrote a traveler through northern Mississippi. "They do business in a kind of frenzy." Gold was scarce but paper money was plentiful, and people rushed to buy lands freed up by the removal of Indians. With the restraining effects of Biddle's national bank removed, scores of new state banks sprouted like mushrooms in the cotton belt, each irresponsibly printing its own paper currency that was often lent recklessly to land speculators and new businesses, especially in cotton-growing states like Mississippi and Louisiana.

The result was chaos. Too many banks had inadequate capital and expertise. As Senator Thomas Hart Benton, one of Jackson's most loyal supporters, said in 1837, he had not helped the president kill the B.U.S. to create a "wilderness of local banks. I did not join in putting down the paper currency of a national bank to put up a national paper currency of a thousand local banks."

But that is what happened. After 1837, anyone who could raise a certain minimum amount of money ("capital") could open a bank. And many did. With no central bank to regulate and oversee the "wildcat" banks, many of them went bankrupt after only a few months or years, leaving their depositors empty handed.

THE MONEY QUESTION During the 1830s, the federal government acquired huge amounts of money from the sale of government-owned lands. Initially, the Treasury department used the annual surpluses from land sales to pay down the accumulated federal debt, which it eliminated completely in 1835—the first time any nation had done so. By 1836, the federal budget was generating an annual surplus, which led to intense discussions about what to do with the increasingly worthless paper money flowing into Treasury's vaults.

The surge of unstable paper money peaked in 1836, when two key initiatives endorsed by the Jackson administration devastated the nation's financial system and threw the economy into a sudden tailspin.

First, in June 1836, Congress approved the **Distribution Act**, initially proposed by Henry Clay and Daniel Webster. It required the federal government to "distribute" to the states surplus federal revenue from land sales. The surpluses would be "deposited" into eighty-one state banks in proportion to each state's representation in Congress. The state governments would then draw upon those deposits to fund roads, bridges, and other internal (infrastructure) improvements.

A month later, Jackson issued the Specie Circular, which announced that the federal government would accept only specie (gold or silver coins) in payment for land purchased by speculators. (Farmers could still pay with paper money.) The Specie Circular upset westerners because most of the government land sales were occurring in their states. They helped convince Congress to pass an act overturning Jackson's policy. The president, however, vetoed it.

Once enacted, the Deposit and Distribution Act and the Specie Circular put added strains on the nation's already tight supplies of gold and silver. Eastern banks had to transfer much of their gold and silver reserves to western banks. In doing so, they had to reduce their lending. Soon, the once-bustling economy began to slow as the money supply contracted, and it became much more difficult for individuals and businesses to get loans. Nervous depositors rushed to their local banks to withdraw their money, only to learn that there was not enough specie to redeem their deposits. In killing the B.U.S., Jackson had unwittingly thrown the economy into chaos.

CENSORING THE MAIL While concerns about the strength of the economy grew, slavery emerged again as a flashpoint issue. In 1835, northern organizations began mailing anti-slavery publications to prominent white southerners, hoping to convince them to end the "peculiar institution." They found little support. Angry pro-slavery South Carolinians in Charleston broke into the federal post office, stole bags of the abolitionist mailings, and ceremoniously burned them; southern state legislatures passed laws banning such "dangerous" publications. Jackson asked Congress to pass a federal censorship law that would prohibit "incendiary" materials intended to incite "the slaves to insurrection."

Congress took action in 1836, but instead of banning abolitionist materials, a bipartisan group of Democrats and Whigs reaffirmed the sanctity of the federal mail. Southern post offices began censoring the mail anyway, arguing that federal authority ended when the mail arrived at the post office door. Jackson decided not to enforce the congressional action, creating what would become a growing split in the Democratic party over the future of slavery.

New Method of Assorting the Mail, As Practised by Southern–Slave Holders, Or Attack on the Post Office, Charleston S.C. **(1835)** On the wall of the post office a sign reads "$20,000 Reward for Tappan," referring to the bounty placed on the head of Arthur Tappan, founder and president of the American Anti-Slavery Society.

The controversy over the mails proved to be a victory for the growing abolitionist movement. One anti-slavery publisher said that instead of stifling their efforts, Jackson and the southern radicals "put us and our principles up before the world—just where we wanted to be." Abolitionist groups started mailing their pamphlets and petitions to members of Congress. James Hammond, a pro-slavery South Carolinian, called for Congress to ban such petitions. When his proposal failed, Congress in 1836 adopted an informal solution suggested by Martin Van Buren: Whenever a petition calling for the end of slavery was introduced, someone would immediately move that it be tabled. The plan, Van Buren claimed, would preserve the "harmony of our happy Union."

The supporters of this "gag rule" soon encountered a formidable obstacle in John Quincy Adams, the former president who now was a congressman from Massachusetts. He devised an array of procedures to get around the rule. Henry Wise of Virginia called Adams "the acutest, the astutest, the archest enemy of southern slavery that ever existed." In the 1838–1839 session of Congress, thanks to Adams, some 1,500 anti-slavery petitions were filed with 163,845

Martin Van Buren Van Buren earned the nickname the "Great Magician" for his "magical" ability to exploit his political and social connections.

signatures. Andrew Jackson dismissed Adams, his old rival, as "the most reckless and depraved man living."

THE ELECTION OF 1836 In 1835, eighteen months before the presidential election, the Democrats nominated Jackson's handpicked successor, Vice President Martin Van Buren. The Whig coalition, united chiefly by its opposition to Jackson, adopted a strategy of nominating multiple candidates, hoping to throw the election into the House of Representatives.

The Whigs put up three regional candidates: New Englander Daniel Webster, Hugh Lawson White of Tennessee, and William Henry Harrison of Indiana. But the strategy failed. In the popular vote of 1836, Van Buren defeated the entire Whig field, winning 170 electoral votes while the others combined to collect only 113.

THE EIGHTH PRESIDENT Martin Van Buren was a skillful politician. Elected governor of New York in 1828, he had resigned to join Andrew Jackson's cabinet, first as secretary of state, and then as vice president in 1833. He was the first New Yorker to be elected president.

Van Buren had been Jackson's closest political adviser and most trusted ally, but many considered him too self-centered to do the work of the people. John Quincy Adams wrote that Van Buren was "by far the ablest" of the Jacksonians, but that he had wasted "most of his ability upon mere personal intrigues. His principles are all subordinate to his ambition." Van Buren's rival, John C. Calhoun, was even more cutting. "He is not of the race of the lion or the tiger." Rather, he "belongs to a lower order—the fox."

At his inauguration, Van Buren promised to follow "in the footsteps" of the enormously popular Jackson. Before he could do so, however, the nation's financial sector began collapsing. On May 10, 1837, several large state banks in New York, running out of gold and silver, suddenly refused to convert customers' paper money into coins. Other banks quickly did the same, creating a panic among depositors across the nation. More than a third of the banks went under. This financial crisis would become known as the **Panic of 1837** and would soon mushroom into the country's worst depression, lasting some seven years.

THE PANIC OF 1837 The causes of the financial crisis went back to the Jackson administration, but Van Buren got the blame. The problem actually started in Europe. During the mid-1830s, Great Britain, America's largest trading partner, experienced an acute financial crisis when the Bank of England, worried about a run on the gold and silver in its vaults, curtailed its loans. This forced most British companies to reduce their trade with America. As British demand for American cotton plummeted, so did the price paid for cotton. On top of everything else, in 1836 there had been a disastrous U.S. wheat crop.

As creditors hastened to foreclose on businesses and farms unable to make their debt payments, government spending plunged. Many canals under construction were shut down, and many state governments could not repay their debts. In April 1837, some 250 businesses failed in New York City alone. By early fall, 90 percent of the nation's factories had closed down.

Not surprisingly, the economic crisis frightened people. As a newspaper editorial complained in December 1836, the economy "has been put into confusion and dismay by a well-meant, but *extremely mistaken*" pair of decisions by Congress and President Jackson: the Specie Circular and the elimination of the B.U.S.

In April 1836, *Niles' Weekly Register*, the nation's leading business journal, reported that the economy was "approaching a momentous crisis." The federal government was lucky to sell land for $3 an acre that had been going for $10 an acre. More and more people could not pay their debts. Many fled their creditors altogether by moving to Texas, then a province of Mexico. Forty percent of the state banks shut their doors. The federal government itself, having put most of its gold and silver in state banks, was verging on bankruptcy. The *National Intelligencer* newspaper reported in May that the federal Treasury "has not a dollar of gold or silver in the world!"

The poor, as always, were particularly hard hit. By the fall of 1837, one third of the nation's workers were jobless, and those still fortunate enough to be employed had their wages cut by 30 to 50 percent within two years. At the same time, prices for food and clothing soared. As the winter of 1837 approached, a New York City journalist reported that 200,000 people were "in utter and hopeless distress with no means of surviving the winter but those provided by charity." The nation had a "poverty-struck feeling."

POLITICS AMID THE DEPRESSION The unprecedented economic calamity sent shock waves through the political system. Critics among the Whigs called the president "Martin Van Ruin" because he did not believe that he or the federal government had any responsibility to rescue farmers, bankers, or businessmen, or to provide relief for the jobless and homeless. Van Buren insisted that any efforts to help people in distress must come from the states.

How best to deal with the unprecedented depression clearly divided Democrats from Whigs. Unlike Van Buren, Whig Henry Clay insisted that suffering people were "entitled to the protecting care of a parental Government." To him, an enlarged role for the federal government was the price of a maturing, expanding republic in which elected officials had an obligation to promote the "safety, convenience, and prosperity" of the people. Van Buren and the Democrats believed that the government had no such obligations. Clay and others savaged the president for his "cold and heartless" attitude.

AN INDEPENDENT TREASURY Martin Van Buren believed that the federal government should stop risking its cash deposits in the insecure "pet" state banks that Jackson had selected. Instead, Van Buren wanted to establish an Independent Treasury system whereby the government would keep its funds in its own vaults and do business entirely in gold or silver. He wanted the federal government to regulate the nation's supply of gold and silver and let the marketplace regulate the supply of paper currency.

It took him more than three years to convince Congress to pass the **Independent Treasury Act**. Although it lasted little more than a year (the Whigs repealed it in 1841), it would be restored in 1846. But it was a political disaster. The state banks that lost control of the federal funds howled in protest. Moreover, it did nothing to end the widespread suffering caused by the deepening depression.

THE 1840 CAMPAIGN By 1840, an election year, President Van Buren and the Democrats were in deep trouble. Aside from the growing financial crisis, the hot potato of Texas was also an issue. In 1837, Van Buren had decided *not* to annex the Republic of Texas, claiming that there was no provision in the Constitution for absorbing another nation and that doing so would trigger a war with Mexico. The decision outraged his political mentor, Andrew Jackson, and aroused strong criticism among southern Democrats.

The Whigs now sensed that they could win the presidency. At their nominating convention, they passed over Henry Clay, Jackson's longtime foe, in favor of William Henry Harrison, whose credentials were impressive: victor at the Battle of Tippecanoe against Tecumseh's Shawnees in 1811, former governor of the Indiana Territory, and former congressman and senator from Ohio.

To balance the ticket geographically, the Whigs nominated John Tyler of Virginia as their vice president. Clay was bitterly disappointed, complaining that "my friends are not worth the powder and shot it would take to kill them. I am the most unfortunate man in the history of parties."

THE ELECTION OF 1840

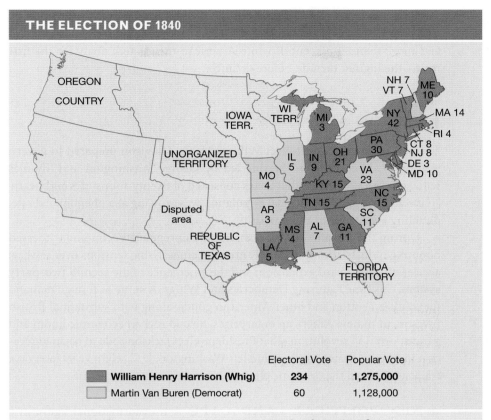

	Electoral Vote	Popular Vote
William Henry Harrison (Whig)	**234**	**1,275,000**
Martin Van Buren (Democrat)	60	1,128,000

- Why did Van Buren carry several western states but few others?
- How did the Whigs achieve a decisive electoral victory over the Democrats?
- How was the Whig strategy in 1840 different from their campaign in 1836?

The Whigs refused to take a stand on major issues. They did, however, seize upon a catchy campaign slogan: "Tippecanoe and Tyler Too." When a Democratic newspaper declared that Harrison was the kind of man who would spend his retirement "in a log cabin [sipping apple cider] on the banks of the Ohio [River]," the Whigs chose the cider and log cabin symbols to depict Harrison as a humble man sprung from the working poor, in contrast to Van Buren's aristocratic lifestyle. (Harrison was actually from one of Virginia's wealthiest families.)

Harrison defeated Van Buren easily, winning 234 electoral votes to 60. The Whigs had promised a return to prosperity without explaining how it would happen. It was simply time for a change.

What was most remarkable about the election of 1840 was the turnout. By this time almost every state had dropped property qualifications for voting, and more than 80 percent of white American men voted, many for the first time—the highest turnout before or since.

Jackson's Legacy

The nation that President-elect William Henry Harrison prepared to govern was vastly different from the one led by George Washington and Thomas Jefferson. In 1828, the United States consisted of twenty-four states and nearly 13 million people. The national population was growing at a phenomenal rate, doubling every twenty-three years.

During the so-called Jacksonian era, the unregulated economy witnessed booming industrialization; rapidly growing cities; rising tensions over slavery; accelerating westward expansion; and the emergence of the **second two-party system**, this time featuring Democrats and Whigs. A surge in foreign demand for southern cotton and other American goods, along with substantial British investment in new American enterprises, helped fuel an economic boom and a transportation revolution. That President-elect Jackson rode to his inauguration in a horse-drawn carriage and left Washington, D.C., eight years later on a train symbolized the dramatic changes occurring in American life.

A NEW POLITICAL LANDSCAPE A transformational figure in a transformational era, Andrew Jackson helped reshape the American political landscape. Even his ferocious opponent, Henry Clay, acknowledged that Jackson had "swept over the Government . . . like a tropical tornado."

In his 1837 farewell address, Jackson stressed his crusade on behalf of "the farmer, the mechanic, and the laboring classes of society—the bone and sinew of the country—men who love liberty and desire nothing but equal rights and equal laws."

Jackson championed opportunities for the "common man" to play a greater role in the political arena at the same time that working men were forming labor unions to increase their economic power and political clout. He helped establish the modern Democratic party and attracted to it the working poor and immigrants from eastern cities, as well as farmers from the South and East. Through a nimble combination of force and compromise, he saved the Union by suppressing the nullification crisis.

And, with great fanfare on January 1, 1835, Jackson announced that the government had paid off the national debt accumulated since the Revolutionary

War, which he called a "national curse." The *Washington Globe* noted that the elimination of the debt coincided with the twentieth anniversary of the Battle of New Orleans, writing that "New Orleans and the National Debt—the first of which paid off our scores to *our enemies*, whilst the latter paid off the last cent to *our friends*."

Jackson's concept of "the people," however, was limited to a "white men's democracy," as it had been for all previous presidents. The phenomenon of Andrew Jackson, the heroic symbol of the common man and the democratic ideal, continues to spark historical debate, as it did during his lifetime.

In 1828, William P. Anderson, who had been one of Jackson's horse-racing friends and political supporters but turned into an outspoken opponent, wrote an open letter to the presidential candidate that was published in several newspapers. He brutally outlined Jackson's faults: "Your besetting sins are ambition and the love of money. . . . You are naturally and constitutionally irritable, overbearing and tyrannical. . . . When you become the enemy of any man, you will put him down if you can, no matter by what means, fair or foul. . . . You are miserably deficient in principle, and have seldom or never had power without abusing it."

Although the criticism was too harsh, it contained more than a grain of truth. Jackson was so convinced of the rightness and righteousness of his ideals that he was willing to defy constitutional limits on his authority when it suited his interests and satisfied his rage. He was both the instrument of democracy and its enemy, protecting "the humble people" and the Union by expanding presidential authority in ways that the founders had never envisioned, including removing federal money from the national bank, replacing government officials with party loyalists, censoring the mails, and ending nullification in South Carolina.

Jackson often declared that the only justification for using governmental power was to ensure equal treatment for everyone. Yet his own use of government force was at times contradictory and even hypocritical. While he threatened to "kill" the B.U.S. and hang John Calhoun and other South Carolina nullifiers, he refused to intervene when Georgia officials violated the legal rights of Cherokees. His inconsistent approach to executive power both symbolized and aggravated the perennial tension in the American republic between a commitment to democratic ideals and the exercise of presidential authority.

CHAPTER REVIEW

Summary

- **Jackson's Views and Policies**   The Jacksonians sought to democratize the political process and expand economic opportunity for the "common man" (that is, "poor and humble" white men). As the representative of "the people," Andrew Jackson expanded the role of the president in economic matters, reducing federal spending and eliminating the powerful Second Bank of the United States. His *Bank War* was hugely popular, but Jackson did not understand its long-term consequences. In addition, his views on limited government were not always reflected in his policies. He left the high taxes from the *Tariff of Abominations (1828)* in place until opposition in the South created a national crisis.

- **Indian Removal Act (1830)**   The *Indian Removal Act* authorized the relocation of eastern Indians to federal lands west of the Mississippi River. The Cherokees used the federal court system to block this relocation. Despite the Supreme Court's decisions in their favor, President Jackson forced them to move; the event and the route they took came to be called the *Trail of Tears (1832–1840)*. By 1840, only a few Seminoles and Cherokees remained in remote areas of the Southeast.

- **Nullification Controversy**   The concept of *nullification*, developed by South Carolina's John C. Calhoun, enabled a state to disavow a federal law. When a South Carolina convention nullified the Tariffs of 1828 and 1832, Jackson requested that Congress pass a *Force Bill (1833)* authorizing the U.S. Army to compel compliance with the tariffs. After South Carolina, under the threat of federal military force, accepted a compromise tariff put forth by Henry Clay, the state convention nullified the Force Bill. The immediate crisis was over, with both sides claiming victory.

- **Democrats and Whigs**   Jackson's arrogant behavior, especially his use of the veto, led many to regard him as "King Andrew the First." Groups who opposed him coalesced into a new party, the *Whigs*, thus producing the country's *second two-party system*. Two acts—the *Distribution Act (1836)* and the Specie Circular— ultimately destabilized the nation's economy. Jackson's ally and vice president, Martin Van Buren, succeeded him as president, but Jacksonian bank policies led to the financial *Panic of 1837* and an economic depression. Congress and Van Buren responded by passing the *Independent Treasury Act (1840)* to safeguard the nation's economy but offered no help for individuals in distress. The economic calamity ensured a Whig victory in the election of 1840.

- **The Jackson Years**   Andrew Jackson's America was very different from the America of 1776. Most white men had gained the vote, but political equality did not mean economic equality. Jacksonian Democrats wanted every American to have an equal chance to compete in the marketplace and in the political arena, but they never promoted equality of results. Inequality between rich and poor widened during the Jacksonian era.

CHRONOLOGY

1828	Tariff of Abominations goes into effect
1830	Congress passes the Indian Removal Act
	Andrew Jackson vetoes the Maysville Road Bill
1831	Supreme Court issues *Cherokee Nation v. Georgia* decision
1832	Supreme Court issues *Worcester v. Georgia* decision
	South Carolina passes Ordinance of Nullification
	Andrew Jackson vetoes the Bank Recharter Bill
1833	Congress passes the Force Bill, authorizing military force in South Carolina
	Congress passes Henry Clay's compromise tariff with Jackson's support
1836	Democratic candidate Martin Van Buren is elected president
1837	Financial panic deflates the economy
1832–1840	Eastern Indians are forced West on the Trail of Tears
1840	Independent Treasury established
	Whig candidate William Henry Harrison is elected president

KEY TERMS

Indian Removal Act (1830) p. 385

Trail of Tears (1832–1840) p. 389

Bank War p. 391

Tariff of Abominations (1828) p. 393

nullification p. 394

Force Bill (1833) p. 400

Whigs p. 402

Distribution Act (1836) p. 404

Panic of 1837 p. 406

Independent Treasury Act (1840) p. 408

second two-party system p. 410

 INQUIZITIVE

Go to InQuizitive to see what you've learned—and learn what you've missed—with personalized feedback along the way.

11 The South, Slavery, and King Cotton
1800–1860

The Old South One of the enduring myths of the Old South is captured in this late-nineteenth-century painting of a plantation on the Mississippi River: muscular slaves tending the lush cotton fields, a steamboat easing down the wide river, and the planter's family relaxing in the cool shade of their white-columned mansion. Novels and films like *Gone with the Wind* (1939) would perpetuate the notion of the Old South as a stable, paternalistic agrarian society led by white planters who were the "natural" aristocracy of virtue and talent within their communities.

O f all the regions of the United States during the first half of the nineteenth century, the pre–Civil War Old South was the most distinctive. What had once been a narrow band of settlements along the Atlantic coast dramatically expanded westward and southward to form a subcontinental empire rooted in cotton.

The southern states remained rural and agricultural long after the rest of the nation had embraced cities, immigrants, and factories. Yet the Old South was also instrumental in the nation's capitalist development and its growing economic stature. After the War of 1812, southern-grown cotton became the key raw material driving industrial growth and feeding the textile mills of Great Britain and New England, where wage workers toiling over newly invented machines fashioned it into thread, yarn, and clothing.

The price of raw cotton doubled in the first year after the war, and the profits made by cotton producers flowed into the hands of northern and British bankers, merchants, and textile-mill owners, many of whom made loans to Southerners to buy more land and more slaves. Northerners also provided the cotton industry with insurance, financing, and shipping.

The story of how southern cotton clothed the world, spurred the expansion of global capitalism, and transformed history was woven with the threads of tragedy, however. The revolution spawned by the mass production of cotton accelerated the spread of slavery across the South and into Texas. A group of slaves in Virginia recognized the essential role they played when they asked, "Didn't we clear the land, and raise the crops of corn, of tobacco, rice, of sugar,

focus questions

1. What factors made the South distinct from the rest of the United States during the early nineteenth century?

2. What role did cotton production and slavery play in the South's economic and social development?

3. What were the major social groups within southern white society? Why did each group support the expansion of slavery?

4. What was the impact of slavery on African Americans, both free and enslaved, throughout the South?

5. How did enslaved peoples respond to the inhumanity of their situation?

of everything? And then didn't the large cities in the North grow up on the cotton and the sugars and the rice that we made?"

THE DISTINCTIVENESS OF THE OLD SOUTH

People have long debated what set the Old South apart from the rest of the nation. Most arguments focus on the region's climate and geography. Its warm, humid climate was ideal for cultivating profitable crops such as tobacco, cotton, rice, indigo, and sugarcane, which led to the plantation system of large commercial agriculture and its dependence upon enslaved labor.

Unlike the North, the South had few large cities or banks, and few railroads, factories, or schools. Most southern commerce was related to the storage, distribution, and sale of agricultural products, especially cotton. With the cotton economy booming, investors focused on buying land and slaves; there was little reason to create a robust industrial sector. "We want no manufactures; we desire no trading, no mechanical, or manufacturing classes," an Alabama politician told an English visitor.

Profitable farming thus remained the South's ideal pursuit of happiness. Education was valued by the planter elite for their sons, but there was little interest in public schooling for the masses. The illiteracy rate in the South was three times higher than in the North.

A BIRACIAL CULTURE What made the Old South most distinctive was not its climate or soil but its system of race-based slavery. The majority of southern whites did not own slaves, but they supported what John C. Calhoun called the South's "**peculiar institution**" because it was so central to their way of life. Calhoun's carefully crafted phrase allowed Southerners to avoid using the charged word *slavery*, while the adjective *peculiar* implied that slavery was *unique* to the South, as it essentially was.

The profitability and convenience of owning slaves created a sense of social unity among whites that bridged class differences. Poor whites who owned no slaves and resented the planters ("cotton snobs") could still claim racial superiority over enslaved blacks ("niggers"). Because of race-based slavery, explained Georgia attorney Thomas Reade Cobb, every white "feels that he belongs to an elevated class. It matters not that he is no slaveholder; he is not of the inferior race; he is a free-born citizen."

The Old South also differed from other sections of the country in its high proportion of native-born Americans. The region attracted few European immigrants after the Revolution in part because the main shipping routes from Britain and Europe took immigrants to northern port cities. Because most immigrants were penniless, they could not afford to travel to the South. Moreover, European immigrants, most of whom were manual laborers, could not compete with slave labor.

CONFLICTING MYTHS Southerners, a North Carolina editor wrote, are "a mythological people, created half out of dream and half out of slander, who live in a still legendary land." Myths are beliefs made up partly of truths and partly of lies. During the nineteenth century, a powerful myth emerged among white Southerners—that the South was both different from *and* better than the North. This blended notion of distinctiveness and superiority became central to Southerners' self-image. Even today, many Southerners tenaciously cultivate a separate identity from the rest of the nation.

In defending their way of life, Southerners claimed that their region was morally superior. Kind planters, according to the prevailing myth, provided happy slaves with food, clothing, shelter, and security—in contrast to a North

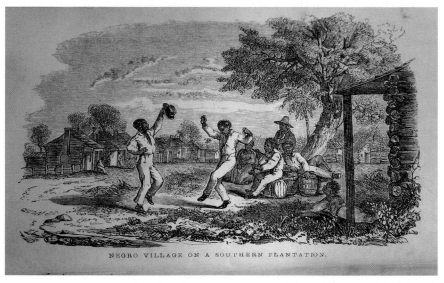

NEGRO VILLAGE ON A SOUTHERN PLANTATION.

Negro Village on a Southern Plantation This line drawing of slaves dancing after a day of work in the cotton fields is an example of the "happy slave" myth, wherein white Southerners glossed slavery as somehow cheerful and harmonious rather than oppressive. The drawing is from Mrs. Mary H. Eastman's *Aunt Phillis's Cabin; or, Southern Life as It Is*—a pro-slavery novel published in 1853 in response to Harriet Beecher Stowe's anti-slavery novel *Uncle Tom's Cabin*.

populated with greedy bankers and heartless factory owners who treated their wage laborers worse than slaves. John C. Calhoun insisted that in northern states the quality of life for free people of color had "become worse" since slavery there had been banned, whereas in the South the standard of living among enslaved African Americans had "improved greatly in every respect."

In this mythic version of the Old South, slavery benefited both slaves and owners. In *Aunt Phillis's Cabin; or, Southern Life as It Is* (1852), novelist Mary Henderson Eastman stressed "the necessity of the existence of slavery at present in our Southern States," and claimed "that, as a general thing, the slaves are comfortable and contented, and their owners humane and kind."

The agrarian ideal and the southern passion for guns, horsemanship, hunting, the military, and manly honor completed the self-gratifying image of the Old South. Its defenders viewed it as a region of honest small farmers, aristocratic gentlemen, young belles, and beautiful ladies who led leisurely lives of well-mannered graciousness, all the while sipping mint juleps in a carefree world of white-columned mansions.

The contrasting myth of the Old South was much darker. Northern abolitionists (those who wanted an immediate end to slavery) pictured the region as being trapped in an immoral economic system dependent on the exploitation of blacks and the displacement of Native Americans. In this version, the theme of violence—physical, mental, and emotional—ran deep.

Northern abolitionists such as Harriet Beecher Stowe portrayed southern planters as cunning capitalists who raped enslaved women, brutalized slaves, and lorded over their communities. They broke up their slaves' families and sold slaves "down the river" to toil in Louisiana sugar mills and on rice plantations. An English woman traveling in the South in 1830 noted that what slaves in Virginia and Maryland feared most was being "sent to *the south and sold.* . . . The sugar plantations [in Louisiana] and, more than all, the rice grounds of Georgia and the Carolinas, are the terror of the American negroes."

MANY SOUTHS The contradictory elements of these myths continue to fight for supremacy in the South, each pressing its claim to legitimacy, in part because both descriptions are built upon half-truths and fierce prejudices. The South has long been defined by two souls, two hearts, two minds competing for dominance. The paradoxes associated with southern mythmaking provided much of the region's variety, for the Old South, like the New South, was not a single culture but a diverse section with multiple interests and perspectives.

The Old South included three subsections with distinct patterns of economic development and diverging degrees of commitment to slavery. Throughout the first half of the nineteenth century, the seven states of the Lower South

(South Carolina, Georgia, Florida, Alabama, Mississippi, Louisiana, and parts of Texas) grew increasingly dependent upon commercial cotton production supported by slave labor. By 1860, slaves represented nearly half the population of the Lower South, largely because they were the most efficient producers of cotton in the world.

The states of the Upper South (Virginia, North Carolina, Tennessee, and Arkansas) had more-varied agricultural economies—a mixture of large commercial plantations and small family farms ("yeoman farms"), where crops were grown mostly for household use. Many states also had large areas without slavery, especially in the mountains of Virginia, the western Carolinas, eastern Tennessee, and northern Georgia, where the soil and climate were not suited to cotton or tobacco.

In the Border South (Delaware, Maryland, Kentucky, and Missouri), slavery was slowly disappearing because cotton could not thrive there. By 1860, approximately 90 percent of Delaware's black population and half of Maryland's were already free. Slave owners in the Lower South, however, had a much larger investment in slavery. They believed that only constant supervision, intimidation, and punishment would keep the fast-growing population of enslaved workers under control, in part because the working and living conditions were so brutal. "I'd rather be dead," said a white overseer in Louisiana, "than a nigger in one of those big [sugarcane] plantations."

THE COTTON KINGDOM

After the Revolution, as the tobacco fields in Virginia and Maryland lost their fertility, tobacco farming spread into Kentucky and as far west as Missouri. Rice continued to be grown in the coastal areas ("low country") of the Carolinas and Georgia, where fields could easily be flooded and drained by tidal rivers flowing into the ocean. Sugarcane, like rice, was also an expensive crop to produce, requiring machinery to grind the cane to release the sugar syrup. During the early nineteenth century, only southern Louisiana focused on sugar production.

In addition to such "cash crops," the South led the nation in the production of livestock: hogs, horses, mules, and cattle. Southerners, both black and white, fed themselves largely on pork. John S. Wilson, a Georgia doctor, called the region the "Republic of Porkdom." Corn was on southern plates as often as pork. During the early summer, corn was boiled on the cob; by late summer and fall, it was ground into cornmeal, a coarse flour. Cornbread and hominy, as well as a "mush" or porridge made of whole-grain corn mixed with milk, were almost daily fare.

Captaining the Cotton Kingdom This photograph offers a glimpse of the staggering scale of cotton production. These 500-pound cotton bales are densely packed and plentiful on this steamboat photographed on the Mississippi River in Louisiana.

KING COTTON During the first half of the nineteenth century, cotton surpassed rice as the most profitable cash crop in the South, and its revenues spread far beyond the region. By the 1850s, New York City, where much of the cotton was bought, sold, and shipped abroad, garnered 40 percent of the revenue. Southern cotton (called "white gold") drove much of the national economy.

Cotton shaped the lives of the enslaved who cultivated it, the planters who grew rich by it, the mill girls who sewed it, the merchants who sold it, the people who wore it, and the politicians who warred over it. "Cotton is King," exclaimed the *Southern Cultivator* in 1859, "and wields an astonishing influence over the world's commerce." In 1832, more than eighty of America's largest companies were New England textile mills.

The Cotton Kingdom resulted largely from two crucial developments. Until the late eighteenth century, cotton fabric was a rarity produced by women in India using handlooms. Then British inventors developed machinery to convert raw cotton into thread and cloth. The mechanical production of cotton made Great Britain the world's first industrial nation, and the number of British textile mills grew so fast that owners could not get enough cotton fiber to meet their needs. American Eli Whitney solved the problem by constructing the first cotton gin, which mechanized the labor-intensive process of manually removing the sticky seeds from the bolls of what was called short-staple cotton.

Taken together, these breakthroughs helped create the world's largest industry—and transformed the South in the process. By 1815, just months after Andrew Jackson's victory over the British at New Orleans, some thirty British ships were docked at the city's wharves because, as an American merchant reported, "Europe must, and will have, cotton for her manufacturers." To be sure, other nations joined the cotton-producing revolution—India, Egypt, Brazil, and China—but the American South was the driving force of cotton capitalism.

THE OLD SOUTHWEST Because of its warm climate and plentiful rainfall, the Lower South became the global leader in cotton production. The region's cheap, fertile land, and the profits to be made in growing cotton, generated a frenzied mobility in which people constantly searched for more and better opportunities. Henry Watson, a New Englander who moved to Alabama, complained in 1836 that "nobody seems to consider himself settled [here]; they remain one, two, three or four years & must move on to some other spot."

The cotton belt moved south and west during the first half of the nineteenth century. As the oldest southern states—Virginia and the Carolinas—experienced soil exhaustion from the overplanting of tobacco and cotton, restless farmers moved to the **Old Southwest**—western Georgia, Alabama, Mississippi, Louisiana, Arkansas and, eventually, Texas.

In 1820, Virginia, the Carolinas, and Georgia had produced two thirds of the nation's cotton. By 1830, the Old Southwest states were the dominant cotton producers. An acre of land in South Carolina produced about 300 pounds of cotton, while an acre in Alabama or in the Mississippi Delta, a 200-mile-wide strip of fertile soil between the Yazoo and Mississippi Rivers, could generate 800 pounds. It was the most profitable farmland in the world.

Such profits, however, required backbreaking labor, most of it performed by enslaved blacks driven by the brutal efficiency of overseers. In marshy areas near the Gulf coast, slaves were put to work removing trees and stumps from the swampy muck. "None but men as hard as a Savage," said one worker, could survive such conditions.

The formula for growing rich was simple: cheap land, cotton seed, and slaves driven to exhaustion by profit-seeking planters who viewed them as property. Between 1810 and 1840, the combined population of Georgia, Alabama, and Mississippi increased from about 300,000 (252,000 of whom were

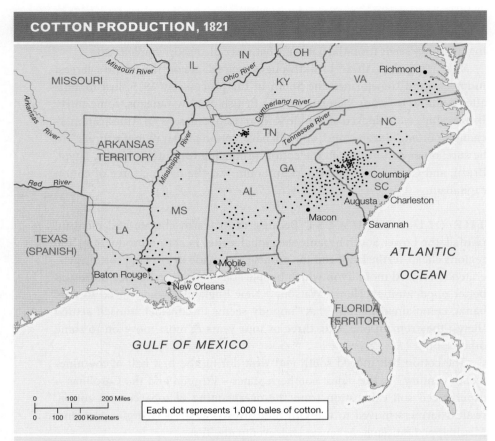

COTTON PRODUCTION, 1821

Each dot represents 1,000 bales of cotton.

- Why was cotton so profitable?
- What regions produced the most cotton in 1821?
- What innovations enabled farmers to move inland and produce cotton more efficiently?

in Georgia) to 1,657,799. Annual cotton production in the United States grew from 150,000 bales (a bundle of cotton weighing 500 pounds) in 1815 to 4 *million* bales in 1860.

THE SOUTHERN FRONTIER Farm families in the Old Southwest tended to be large. "There is not a cabin but has ten or twelve children in it," reported a traveling minister. "When the boys are eighteen and the girls are fourteen, they marry—so that in many cabins you will see . . . the mother looking as young as the daughter."

Women were a minority among migrants from Virginia and the Carolinas to the Old Southwest. Many resisted moving to what they had heard was

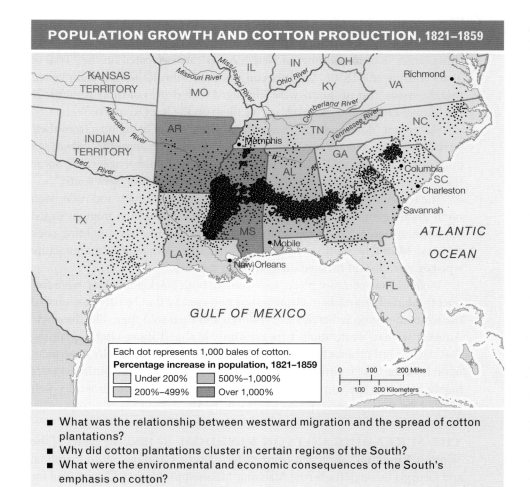

POPULATION GROWTH AND COTTON PRODUCTION, 1821–1859

Each dot represents 1,000 bales of cotton.
Percentage increase in population, 1821–1859
- Under 200%
- 200%–499%
- 500%–1,000%
- Over 1,000%

- What was the relationship between westward migration and the spread of cotton plantations?
- Why did cotton plantations cluster in certain regions of the South?
- What were the environmental and economic consequences of the South's emphasis on cotton?

a disease-ridden, male-dominated, violent, and primitive territory. Others feared that life on the southern frontier would produce a "dissipation" of morals. They had heard wild stories of lawlessness, drunkenness, gambling, and whoring. A woman newly arrived in frontier Alabama wrote home that the farmers around her "live in a miserable manner. They think only of making money, and their houses are hardly fit to live in."

Enslaved blacks had many of the same reservations. Almost a million captive African Americans in Maryland, Virginia, and the Carolinas were forced to move to the Old Southwest during the first half of the nineteenth century. Herded onto steamboats or slave ships or forced to walk hundreds of miles handcuffed in pairs and manacled in iron collars and chains ("coffles"), they lived in "perpetual dread" of the Gulf states' harsh working conditions, heat, and humidity.

The forced resettlement of enslaved men, women, children, and babies along the "Slave Trail" from the tobacco South to the cotton South was twenty times larger than the number of Native Americans relocated on the "Trail of Tears" during the 1830s. Virginia congressman John Randolph complained that the roads near his home were "thronged with droves of these wretches & the human carcass-butchers, who drive them on the hoof to market."

Slaves sent "downriver" were also despondent about being torn from their wives, children, and friends. One song expressed their anguish: "Massa sell poor negro, ho, heave, O! / Leave poor wife and children, ho, heave, O!" Some tried to run away. Others maimed themselves to avoid being "sent south."

The frontier environment in the Old Southwest was rough and rude. Men often drank, gambled, and fought. In 1834, a South Carolina migrant urged his brother to join him in the west because "you can live like a fighting cock with us." Most Old Southwest plantations had their own stills to manufacture whiskey. Alcoholism ravaged many frontier families.

Violence was commonplace, and women, both black and white, were frequently abused. An Alabama woman was outraged by the "beastly passions" of the white men who fathered slave children and then sold them like livestock. Another woman wrote about a friend whose husband abused her, explaining that she had little choice but to suffer in silence, for she was "wholly dependent upon his care." The contrasting gender experiences in the Old Southwest were highlighted in a letter in which a woman reported: "All the men is very well pleased but the women is not very well satisfied."

THE SPREADING COTTON KINGDOM By 1860, the center of the "**Cotton Kingdom**" stretched from eastern North Carolina, South Carolina, and Georgia through the fertile Alabama-Mississippi "black belt" (so called for the color of the soil), through Louisiana, on to Texas, and up the Mississippi Valley as far as southern Illinois.

Steamboats made the Mississippi River the cotton highway by transporting millions of bales to New Orleans, where sailing ships took the cotton to New York, New England, Great Britain, and France. King Cotton accounted for more than half of all U.S. exports.

By 1860, Alabama, Mississippi, and Louisiana were the top-producing cotton states, and two thirds of the richest Americans lived in the South. The rapid expansion of the cotton belt ensured that the South became more dependent on enslaved black workers.

Slavery was, as John Quincy Adams wrote in his diary, "the great and foul stain" upon the nation's commitment to liberty and equality. It persisted because it was a powerful engine of economic development—and a tangible sign of economic success. Enterprising young white men judged wealth and status by the number of slaves owned. By 1860, the dollar value of enslaved blacks outstripped the value of *all* American banks, railroads, and factories combined.

The soaring profitability of cotton also fostered a false sense of security—and bred cockiness. In 1860, a Mississippi newspaper boasted that the South, "safely entrenched behind her cotton bags . . . can defy the world—for the civilized world depends on the cotton of the South." In a speech to the U.S. Senate in 1858, South Carolina's former governor, James Henry Hammond, who owned a huge cotton plantation worked by more than 100 slaves, warned critics in the North: "You dare not make war on cotton. No power on earth dares make war upon it. Cotton is King."

What Hammond failed to acknowledge was that the southern economy had grown dangerously dependent on European demand for raw cotton. By 1860, Great Britain was importing more than 80 percent of its cotton from the American South. Southern leaders did not anticipate what they could least afford: a sudden collapse in demand for their cotton. In 1860, the expansion of the British textile industry peaked, and the price paid for southern cotton began a steady decline. By then, however, the Lower South was committed to large-scale cotton production for generations to come.

WHITES IN THE OLD SOUTH

The culture of cotton and slavery shaped the South's social structure and provided much of its political power. Unlike in the North and Midwest, southern society was dominated by an elite group of planters and merchants.

WHITE PLANTERS Although there were only a few giant plantations in each southern state, their owners exercised overwhelming influence. As a Virginian observed in the mid-1830s, "the old slaveholding families exerted a great deal of control . . . and they affected the manner and prejudices of the slaveholding part of the state."

The richest planters and merchants were determined to control southern society, in part because of self-interest and in part because they assumed they were the region's natural leaders. "The planters here are essentially what the nobility are in other countries," claimed James Henry Hammond. "They stand at the head of society and politics. . . . Slavery does indeed create an aristocracy—an aristocracy of talents, of virtue, of generosity, and courage." Planters themselves rarely engaged in manual labor. They focused on managing the overseers and handling the marketing and sale of cotton, tobacco, rice, or sugar.

What distinguished a plantation from a farm, in addition to its size, was the use of a large number of slaves supervised by drivers and overseers. If, as historians have agreed, one had to own at least twenty slaves to be called a **planter**, only 1 out of 30 whites in 1860 qualified. Eleven planters, among the wealthiest people in the nation, owned 500 slaves each, and one planter, a South Carolina rice grower, owned 1,000. The 10,000 most powerful planters, making up less than 3 percent of white men in the South, held more than half the slaves. The total number of slaveholders was only 383,637 out of a white population of 8 million.

Over time, planters and their wives grew accustomed to being waited on by slaves day and night. A Virginia planter told a British visitor that a slave girl slept in the master bedroom with him and his wife. When his guest asked why, he replied: "Good heaven! If I wanted a glass of water during the night, what would become of me?"

The planter elite indulged expensive habits and tastes that they often could neither afford nor control. Living the storied life of a planter was the focus of their energies, their honor, and often their indebtedness. As a plantation slave recalled, his master on Sundays liked to "gamble, run horses, or fight game-cocks, discuss politics, and drink whisky, and brandy and water all day long."

Most planters began their careers as land traders, investors, cotton merchants (called "factors"), and farmers. Over time, they made enough money to acquire a plantation. Success required careful monitoring of the markets for cotton, land, and slaves, as well as careful management of the workers and production.

Most southern white men embraced an unwritten social code centered on a prickly sense of personal respectability in which they defended their reputations with words, fists, knives, or guns. Duels to the death (called "affairs of honor") were the ultimate expressions of manly honor.

Dueling was much more common in the South than in the rest of the nation, a fact that gave rise to the observation that Southerners were excessively polite until they grew angry enough to kill you. Many prominent southern leaders—congressmen, senators, governors, editors, and planters—engaged in duels with pistols, although dueling was technically illegal in many states. The roster of participants included President Andrew Jackson of Tennessee and Senator Henry Clay of Kentucky. But men of all classes were ready to fight at the first sign of disrespect.

THE PLANTATION MISTRESS The South, like the North, was a male-dominated society, only more so because of the slave system. A prominent Georgian, Christopher Memminger, explained that slavery heightened the need for a hierarchical social and family structure. White wives and children needed to be as subservient and compliant as enslaved blacks. "Each planter," he declared, "is in fact a Patriarch—his position compels him to be a ruler in his household," and he requires "obedience and subordination."

The **plantation mistress** was no frail, helpless creature focused solely on planning parties and balls. Although she had slaves to attend to her needs, she supervised the household in the same way as the planter took care of the cotton business. Overseeing the supply and preparation of food and linens, she also managed the housecleaning and care of the sick, the birthing of babies, and the operations of the dairy.

A plantation slave remembered that her mistress "was with all the slave women every time a baby was born. Or, when a plague of misery hit the folks, she knew what to do and what kind of medicine to chase off the aches and pains." The son of a Tennessee slaveholder remembered that his mother and grandmother were "the busiest women I ever saw," in part because they themselves had babies every year or so.

Mary Boykin Chesnut, a plantation mistress in South Carolina, complained that "there is no slave, after all, like a wife." She admitted that she had few rights in the large household she managed, since her husband was the "master of the house."

A wife was expected to love, honor, obey, and serve her husband. Virginian George Fitzhugh, a Virginia attorney and writer, spoke for most southern men when he said that a "man loves his children because they are weak, helpless, and dependent. He loves his wife for similar reasons."

Planters had little interest in educated wives. When people tried to raise funds for a woman's college in Georgia, a planter angrily refused to contribute, explaining that "all that a woman needs to know is how to read the New Testament and to spin and weave clothing for her family. I would not have one of your graduates for a wife, and I will not give you a cent for any such project."

White southern women were expected to be examples of Christian

Mary Boykin Chesnut Her diary describing life in the Confederacy during the Civil War was republished in 1981 and won the Pulitzer Prize.

morality and sexual purity, even as their husbands, brothers, and sons often engaged in gambling, drinking, carousing, and sexually assaulting enslaved women. Such a double standard reinforced the arrogant authoritarianism of many white planters for whom the rape of slave women was common practice. In the secrecy of her famous diary, Mary Boykin Chesnut used sexual metaphors to express the limitations of most of the Carolina planters, writing that they "are nice fellows, but slow to move; impulsive but hard to keep moving. They are wonderful for a spurt, but that lets out all of their strength."

Yet for all their private complaints and daily burdens, few plantation mistresses spoke out. They largely accepted the role assigned them by men such as George Howe, a South Carolina religion professor. In 1850, he complimented southern women for understanding their subordinate place. "Born to lean upon others, rather than to stand independently by herself, and to confide in an arm stronger than hers," the southern woman had no desire for "power" outside the home, he said. The few women who were demanding equality were "unsexing" themselves and were "despised and detested" by their families and communities.

OVERSEERS AND DRIVERS On large plantations, *overseers* managed the slaves and were responsible for maintaining the buildings, fences, and grounds. They usually were white farmers or skilled workers, the sons of planters, or poor whites eager to rise in stature. Some were themselves slaveholders.

Overseers moved often in search of better wages and cheaper land. A Mississippi planter described white overseers as "a worthless set of vagabonds." Frederick Douglass, who escaped from slavery in Maryland, said his overseer was "a miserable drunkard, a profane swearer, and a savage monster" always armed with a blood-stained bullwhip and a club that he used so cruelly that he even "enraged" the plantation owner. The overseer tolerated no excuses or explanations. "To be accused was to be convicted, and to be convicted was to be punished," Douglass said.

Although there were a few black overseers, the highest managerial position a slave could usually hope for was that of *driver*, whose job was to supervise a small group ("gang") of slaves, getting them up and organized each morning by sunrise, and directing their work (and punishing them) until dark. Over the years, there were numerous examples of slaves murdering drivers for being too cruel.

"PLAIN WHITE FOLK" About half of white Southerners were small farmers (yeomen), **plain white folk** who were often illiterate and forced to scratch out lives of bare self-sufficiency. These yeomen typically lived with their families in simple two-room cabins on fifty acres or less. They raised a few pigs and chickens, grew enough corn and cotton to live on, and traded with neighbors more than they bought from stores.

Women on these farms worked in the fields during harvest time but spent most of their days doing household chores while raising lots of children. Farm children grew up fast. By age four they could carry a water bucket from the well to the house and collect eggs from the henhouse. Young boys could feed livestock, milk cows, and plant, weed, and harvest crops.

The average slaveholder was a small farmer working alongside five or six slaves. Such "middling" farmers usually lived in a log cabin rather than a columned mansion. In the backcountry and mountainous regions of the South, where slaves and plantations were scarce, small farmers dominated the social structure.

Southern farmers tended to be fiercely independent and suspicious of government authority, and they overwhelmingly identified with the Democratic party of Andrew Jackson. Although a minority of middle-class white farmers owned slaves, most of them supported the slave system. They feared that slaves, if freed, would compete with them for land and jobs, and they also enjoyed the privileged social status that race-based slavery afforded them. James Henry Hammond and other rich planters frequently reminded their white neighbors who owned no slaves that "in a slave country, every freeman is an aristocrat" because blacks were beneath them in the social order. Such racist sentiments pervaded the Lower South—and much of the nation—throughout the nineteenth century.

"POOR WHITES" Visitors to the Old South often had trouble telling small farmers apart from the "poor whites," the desperately poor people who were relegated to the least desirable land and lived on the fringes of society. The "poor whites," often derided as "crackers," "hillbillies," or "trash," were usually day laborers or squatters who owned neither land nor slaves. Some 40 percent of white Southerners worked as "tenants," renting land or, as farm laborers, toiling for others. They frequently took refuge in the pine barrens, mountain hollows, and swamps after having been pushed aside by the more enterprising and the more successful. They often made their own clothing and barely managed to keep their families warm, dry, and fed.

BLACK SOCIETY IN THE SOUTH

Southern society was literally black and white. Whites had the power and often treated enslaved blacks as property rather than people. "We believe the negro to belong to an inferior race," one planter declared. Thomas Reade Cobb proclaimed that African Americans were better off "in a state of bondage."

Effective slave management therefore required teaching slaves to understand that they were supposed to be treated like animals. As Henry Garner, an escaped slave, explained, the aim of slaveholders was "to make you as much like brutes as possible." Some justified slavery as a form of benevolent paternalism. George Fitzhugh said that the enslaved black was "but a grown-up child, and must be governed as a child."

Such self-serving paternalism had one ultimate purpose: profits. Planters, explained a Southerner, "care for nothing but to buy Negroes to raise cotton & raise cotton to buy Negroes." In 1818, James Steer in Louisiana predicted that enslaved blacks would be the best investment that Southerners could make. Eleven years later, in 1829, the North Carolina Supreme Court declared that slavery existed to increase "the profit of the Master."

Those in the business of buying and selling slaves reaped huge profits. One of them reported in the 1850s that "a nigger that wouldn't bring over $300, seven years ago, will fetch $1000, cash, quick, this year." Thomas Clemson of South Carolina, the son-in-law of John C. Calhoun, candidly explained that "my object is to get the most I can for the property [slaves]. . . . I care but little to whom and how they are sold, whether together [as families] or separated."

Owning, working, and selling slaves was the quickest way to wealth and social status in the South. The wife of a Louisiana planter complained in 1829 that white people talked constantly about how the profits generated by growing cotton enabled them to buy "plantations & negroes." In 1790, the United States had fewer than 700,000 enslaved African Americans. By 1830, it had more than 2 million, and by 1860, there were 4 million, virtually all of them in the South and border states.

THE SLAVE SYSTEM Most southern whites viewed slaves as property rather than people. Babies became slaves at birth; slaves could be moved, sold, rented out, whipped, or raped, as their master saw fit. As the enslaved population grew, slaveholders developed an increasingly complex *system* of rules, regulations, and restrictions. Formal **slave codes** in each state regulated the treatment of slaves to deter runaways or rebellions. Slaves could not leave their owner's land or household without permission or stay out after dark without an identification pass. Some codes made it a crime for slaves to learn to read and write, for fear that they might pass notes to plan a revolt. Frederick Douglass said that slaveholders assumed that allowing slaves to learn to read and write "would spoil the best nigger in the world."

Slaves in most states could not testify in court, legally marry, own firearms, or hit a white man, even in self-defense. They could also be abused, tortured, and whipped. Despite such restrictions and brutalities, however, the enslaved managed to create their own communities and cultures, forging bonds of care, solidarity, recreation, and religion.

"FREE PERSONS OF COLOR" African Americans who were not enslaved were called free persons of color. They occupied an uncertain and often vulnerable social status between bondage and freedom. Many lived in constant fear of being kidnapped into slavery.

To be sure, free blacks had more rights than slaves. They could enter into contracts, marry, own property (including slaves of their own), and pass on their property to their children. They were not viewed or treated as equal to whites, however. In most states, they were treated as if they were enslaved: they could not vote, own weapons, attend white church services, or testify against whites in court. In South Carolina, free people of color had to pay an annual tax and were not allowed to leave the state. After 1823, they were required to have a white "guardian" and an identity card.

Some slaves were able to purchase their freedom, and others were freed ("manumitted") by their owners. By 1860, approximately 250,000 free blacks lived in the slave states, most of them in coastal cities such as Baltimore, Charleston, Savannah, Mobile, and New Orleans. Many were skilled workers. Some were tailors, shoemakers, or carpenters; others were painters, bricklayers, butchers, blacksmiths, or barbers. Still others worked on the docks or on steamships. Free black women usually worked as seamstresses, laundresses, or house servants.

Among the free black population were a large number of **mulattoes**, people of mixed racial ancestry. The census of 1860 reported 412,000 mulattoes in the United States, or about 10 percent of the black population—probably a drastic undercount. In cities such as Charleston and, especially, New Orleans, "colored" society occupied a shifting status somewhere between that of blacks and that of whites.

Yarrow Mamout As an enslaved African Muslim, Mamout purchased his freedom, acquired property, and settled in present-day Washington, D.C. Charles Willson Peale painted this portrait in 1819, when Mamout was over 100 years old.

Free black persons These badges, issued in 1860 in Charleston, South Carolina, were worn by free black persons so that they would not be mistaken for someone's "property."

Although most free people of color were poor, some mulattoes built substantial fortunes and even became slaveholders themselves. William Ellison was the richest freedman in the South. Liberated by his white father in 1816, he developed a thriving business in South Carolina making cotton gins while managing his own 900-acre plantation worked by more than sixty slaves. In Louisiana, a mulatto, Cyprien Ricard, paid $250,000 for an estate that had ninety-one slaves. In Natchez, Mississippi, William Johnson, son of a white father and a mulatto mother, operated three barbershops, owned 1,500 acres of land, and held several slaves.

Black or mulatto slaveholders were few in number, however. The 1830 census reported that 3,775 free blacks, about 2 percent of the total free black population, owned 12,760 slaves. Many of the African American slaveholders were men who bought or inherited their own family members.

THE TRADE IN SLAVES The rapid rise in the slave population during the early nineteenth century mainly occurred naturally, through slave births, especially after Congress and President Thomas Jefferson outlawed the purchase of slaves from Africa in 1808. By 1820, more than 80 percent of slaves had been born in America.

Once the African slave trade was outlawed, the slave-trading network *within* the United States became much more important—and profitable. Between 1800 and 1860, the average price of slaves *quadrupled*, in large part because of the dramatic expansion of the cotton culture in the Old Southwest.

In Virginia, slave breeding became the state's most profitable industry and primary cash crop. Over a twenty-year period, a Virginia plantation owned

by John Tayloe III recorded 252 slave births and 142 slave deaths, thus providing Tayloe with 110 extra slaves to be deployed on the plantation, given to
his sons, or sold to traders. Thomas Jefferson bragged to George Washington
that the numerous births of black children were increasing Virginia's wealth
by 4 percent per year.

To manage the growing slave trade, markets and auction houses sprang
up in every southern city. New Orleans alone had twenty slave-trading businesses. Each year, thousands of slaves circulated through the city's "slave pens."
There they were converted from people into products. They were bathed and
groomed; "fattened up" with bacon, milk, and butter, like cattle; assigned cate-
gories such as Prime, No. 1, No. 2, and Second Rate; and "packaged" (dressed)
for sale in identical blue suits or dresses. On auction day, they were paraded
into the sale room. The tallest, strongest, and "blackest" young men brought
the highest prices. As a slaver stressed, "I must have if possible the *jet black*
Negroes, for they stand the climate best."

Buyers physically inspected each slave on the "auction block" as if they
were horses or cattle. They squeezed their muscles, felt their joints, and pried
open their mouths to examine their teeth and gums. They forced the slaves
to strip and carefully inspected their naked bodies, looking for signs of disease or deformities. They particularly focused on any scars from whipping. As
Solomon Northup noted, "scars on a slave's back were considered evidence of
a rebellious or unruly spirit, and hurt [his chances for] sale."

Slave markets in New Orleans also featured the "fancy trade," which meant
selling women as forced sexual partners. One reporter spied on the auction
block "one of the most beautiful women I had ever saw. She was about sixteen, dressed in a cheap striped woolen gown, and bareheaded." Her name was
Hermina, and she was "sold for $1250 [$35,000 today] to one of the most lech-
erous brutes I ever set eyes on." The same reporter noted that "a noble-looking
woman" and her "bright-eyed seven-year-old" son were offered for sale as a
pair. When no one bid on them, the auctioneer offered them separately. A man
from Mississippi bought the boy, while the mother went to a Texan. As her son
was dragged away, his mother "burst forth into the most frantic wails that ever
despair gave utterance to."

SLAVERY AS A WAY OF LIFE The lives of slaves depended in part on the
personality of their owner; in part on whether they cultivated rice, sugar, tobacco,
or cotton, and in part on whether they were on farms or in cities. Although many
slaves were artisans or craftsmen (carpenters, blacksmiths, furniture makers,
butchers, boatmen, house servants, cooks, nurses, maids, weavers, basket makers, etc.), the vast majority were **field hands** who were often organized into work

THE SLAVE POPULATION, 1820

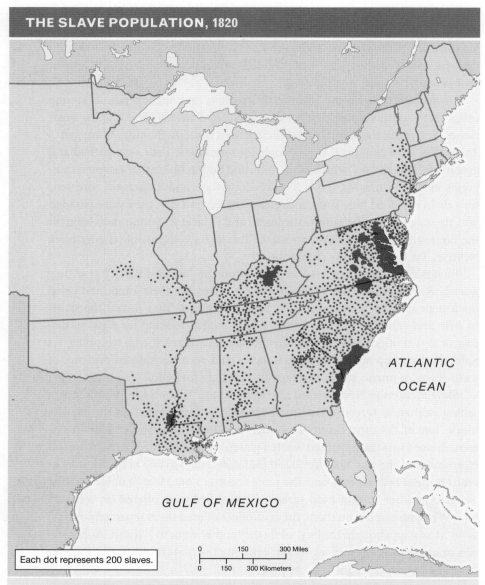

ATLANTIC

OCEAN

GULF OF MEXICO

Each dot represents 200 slaves.

0   150   300 Miles

0   150   300 Kilometers

- Consider where the largest populations of slaves were clustered in the South in 1820. Why were most slaves living in these regions and not in others?
- How was the experience of plantation slavery different for men and women?

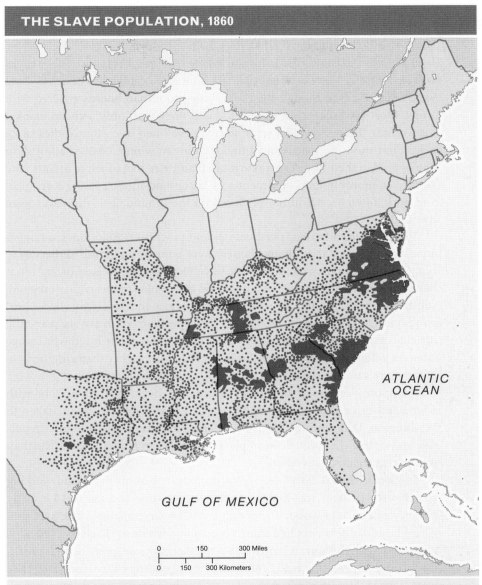

THE SLAVE POPULATION, 1860

ATLANTIC OCEAN

GULF OF MEXICO

| 0 | 150 | 300 Miles |

| 0 | 150 | 300 Kilometers |

- Compare this map with the map of cotton production on page 423. What patterns do you see?
- Why did many slaves resist migrating West?

gangs supervised by a black driver or white overseer. Some slaves were hired out to other planters or to merchants, churches, or businesses. Others worked on Sundays or holidays to earn cash of their own.

Plantation slaves were usually housed in one- or two-room wooden shacks with dirt floors. The wealthiest planters built slave cabins out of brick. Beds were a luxury, even though they were little more than boards covered with straw. Most slaves slept on the cold, damp floor with only a cheap blanket for warmth. They received a set of inexpensive linen or cotton clothes twice a year, but shoes were generally provided only in winter. About half of slave babies died in their first year, a rate more than twice that of white infants. The weekly or monthly food allotment was cheap and monotonous: corn meal and pork, often served in bowls placed on the ground, as if the slaves were livestock.

Planters varied in their personalities and practices. Philip Jones, a Louisiana slave, observed that "many planters were humane and kind." Others were not. "Massa was purty good," one ex-slave recalled. "He treated us jus' 'bout like you would a good mule." Another said his owner "fed us reg'lar on good, substantial food, jus' like you'd tend to your hoss [horse], if you had a real good one." A slave born in 1850 had a life expectancy of thirty-six years; the life expectancy of whites was forty years. Some slaveholders hired white wage laborers, often Irish immigrants, for dangerous work rather than risk the lives of the more valuable slaves.

Solomon Northup, a freeborn African American from New York with a wife and three children, was kidnapped in 1845 by slave traders, taken to Washington, D.C., and then to New Orleans, and eventually sold to a "repulsive and coarse" Louisiana cotton planter. More than a decade later, Northup was able to regain his freedom.

In *Twelve Years a Slave* (1853), Northup described his living and working conditions. His bed "was a plank twelve inches wide and ten feet long. My pillow was a stick of wood. The bedding was a coarse blanket." The log cabin where he and others slept had a dirt floor and no windows. Each day, "an hour before daylight, the horn is blown. Then the slaves arouse, prepare their breakfast . . . and hurry to the field." If found in their "quarters after daybreak," they were flogged. "It was rarely that a day passed by without one or more whippings. . . . The crack of the lash, and the shrieking of the slaves, can be heard from dark till bed time."

Field hands worked from sunrise to sunset, six days a week. At times they worked at night as well, ginning cotton, milling sugarcane, grinding corn, or doing other indoor tasks. Women, remembered a slave, "had to work all day in de fields an' den come home an' do the housework at night." Sundays were precious days off. Slaves used the Sabbath to hunt, fish, dance, tell stories, or tend their own small gardens.

Beginning in August and lasting several months, the focus was on picking cotton. The productivity per slave increased dramatically during the first half of the nineteenth century, in large part because of the implementation of the "pushing system." During harvest season, each slave was assigned a daily quota of cotton to be picked, an amount that increased over the years.

Gangs of slaves, men and women, would sweep across a field, pull the bolls from the thorny pods, and stuff them in large sacks or baskets which they dragged behind them. All the while, an overseer, bullwhip in hand, would force them to keep up the pace. Solomon Northup remembered picking cotton until it was "too dark to

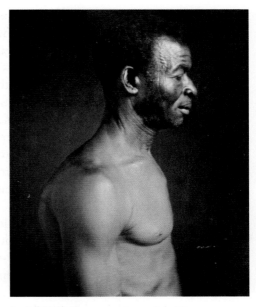

Jack **(1850)** Daguerreotype of a slave identified only as Jack, on the plantation of B. F. Taylor in Columbia, South Carolina.

see, and when the moon is full, they oftentimes labor till the middle of the night." Each evening, the baskets would be weighed and the number of pounds recorded on a slate board by each picker's name. Those who fell short of their quota were scolded and whipped.

THE VIOLENCE OF SLAVERY Although some owners and slaves developed close and even affectionate relationships, slavery on the whole was a system rooted in brutality. The difference between a good owner and a bad one, according to one slave, was the difference between one "who did not whip you too much" and one who "whipped you till he'd bloodied you and blistered you."

Allen Sidney, a slave, recalled an incident on a Mississippi plantation that illustrated the ruthlessness of cotton production. A slave who fell behind in his work resisted when a black driver started to "whip him up." Upon seeing the fracas, the white overseer, mounted on horseback, galloped over and shot the resisting slave, killing him. "None of the other slaves," Sidney noted, "said a word or turned their heads. They kept on hoeing as if nothing had happened."

At times, whites turned the punishment of slaves into grisly spectacles to strike fear into anyone considering rebellion or escape. In Louisiana, whippings often followed a horrific procedure, as a visitor reported: "Three stakes is drove into the ground in a triangular manner, about six feet apart. The culprit [slave] is told to lie down . . . flat on his belly. The arms is extended out, sideways, and each hand tied to a stake hard and fast. The feet is both tied to the third stake, all stretched tight." The overseer would then step back "seven, eight or ten feet and with a rawhide whip about 7 feet long . . . lays on with great force and address across the Buttocks," cutting strips of flesh "7 or 8 inches long at every stroke."

URBAN SLAVERY Slaves in cities such as Richmond, Memphis, Atlanta, New Orleans, or Charleston had a much different experience from those on isolated farms and plantations. "A city slave is almost a freeman," claimed a Maryland slave.

Slaves in urban households tended to be better fed and clothed and had more privileges. They interacted not only with their white owners but with the extended interracial community—shopkeepers and police, neighbors and strangers. Some were hired out to others and allowed to keep a portion of their wages.

ENSLAVED WOMEN Although enslaved men and women often per-formed similar chores, especially on farms, they did not experience slavery in the same way. Once slaveholders realized how profitable a fertile female slave could be by giving birth to babies that could later be sold, they "encour-aged" the women to have as many children as possible. Sometimes a woman would be locked in a cabin with a male slave, whose task was to impregnate her. Pregnant slaves were given less work and more food. Some plantation owners rewarded new mothers with dresses and silver dollars.

But if motherhood provided enslaved women with greater stature and ben-efits, it also was exhausting. Within days after childbirth, mothers were put back to work spinning, weaving, or sewing. A few weeks thereafter, they were sent back to the fields; breast-feeding mothers were often forced to take their babies with them, strapped to their backs. Enslaved women were expected to do "man's work": cut trees, haul logs, spread fertilizer, plow fields, dig ditches, slaughter animals, hoe corn, and pick cotton.

Once women passed their childbearing years, their workload increased. Slaveholders put middle-aged women to work full-time in the fields or per-forming other outdoor labor. On large plantations, elderly women, called *grannies*, tended the children during the day. Slave women also worked as cooks and seamstresses, midwives and nurses, healers and folk doctors.

Enslaved girls and women faced the constant threat of sexual abuse. Hun-dreds of thousands of mulattoes provided physical proof of interracial sexual assault. Mary Boykin Chesnut noted in her diary that "like the patriarchs of old, our men live all in one house with their wives & their concubines, & the Mulattoes one sees in every family exactly resemble the white children—& every lady tells you who is the father of all the Mulatto children in everybody's household, but those in her own, she seems to think drop from the clouds."

James Henry Hammond, the prominent South Carolina planter, confessed that he was a man of passion who nurtured a "system of roguery" among his female slaves. He had a long affair with young Sally Johnson, who bore several of his children. Later, to the horror of his long-suffering wife, Hammond began another affair with one of his and Sally's daughters, twelve-year-old Louisa, and fathered more children with her. (Hammond also forced himself upon four "lovely and luscious" teen-aged nieces and two daughters of his sister-in-law).

CELIA Slaves often could improve their circumstances only by making horrible choices that offered no guarantee of success. The tragic story of a slave girl named Celia reveals the moral complexity of slavery for African American women and the limited legal options available to them.

In 1850, fourteen-year-old Celia was purchased by Robert Newsom, a Missouri farmer who told his daughters that he had bought the girl to be their servant. In fact, however, the recently widowed Newsom wanted a sexual slave. After purchasing Celia, he raped her, and for the next five years, he treated her as his mistress, even building her a brick cabin fifty yards from his house. During that time, she gave birth to two children.

On June 23, 1855, the sixty-five-year-old Newsom entered Celia's cabin, ignored her frantic appeals, and kept assaulting her until she struck and killed him with a large stick and then burned his body in the fireplace. Celia was not allowed to testify at her murder trial because she was a slave. The judge and jury, all white men, pronounced her guilty, and on December 21, 1855, she was hanged.

Celia's grim story illustrates the lopsided power structure in southern society at the time. She bore a double burden, being both a slave and a woman living in a male-dominated society rife with racism and sexism.

FORGING A SLAVE COMMUNITY

Despite being victims of terrible injustice and abuse, enslaved African Americans displayed endurance, resilience, and achievement. Wherever they could, they forged their own sense of community, asserted their individuality, and devised ingenious ways to resist. Many on the largest plantations would gather at secret "night meetings" where they would drink stolen alcohol, dance, sing, and tell stories of resistance. The stories often were derived from African tales, such as that of "Brer [Brother] Rabbit," who used his wits to elude the larger animals stalking him by hiding in a patch of prickly briars. Such stories impressed upon slaves the importance of deceiving those with power over them.

Many religious **spirituals** also contained double meanings, often expressing a longing to get to a "free country," what slaves called "Sweet Canaan" or the "promised land." The spiritual "Wade in the Water," for example, contained underlying instructions to runaways about how to evade capture by avoiding dry land and running in creek beds ("wading in the water"). Songs such as "The Gospel Train" and "Swing Low, Sweet Chariot" included disguised references to the Underground Railroad, the secret organization that helped slaves escape to the North.

Frederick Douglass recalled that the spirituals also were a form of protest. They "breathed the prayer and complaint of souls overflowing with the bitterest anguish. . . . The songs of the slave represent the sorrows of his heart, rather than his joys. Like tears, they were a relief to aching hearts."

THE SLAVE FAMILY Although states did not recognize slave marriages, they did not prevent men and women from choosing life partners and forging families within the slave system. Many slaveholders considered unofficial marriages a stabilizing influence; a black man who supported a family, they assumed, would be more reliable and obedient. Sometimes slaveholders performed "weddings" in the slave quarters or had a minister conduct the service. Whatever the formalities, the norm for the slave community, as for the white, was the nuclear family, with the father as head of the household.

Enslaved African Americans often reached out to those who worked with them, with older slave women being addressed as "granny," or coworkers as "sis" or "brother." Such efforts to create a sense of extended family resembled kinship practices in Africa. One white teacher visiting a slave community observed that they "all belonged to one immense family."

Religion in the Old South

The Old South was made up of God-fearing people whose faith sustained them. Although there were pockets of Catholicism and Judaism in the large coastal cities—Baltimore, Richmond, Charleston, Savannah, and New Orleans—the vast majority of Southerners, white and black, embraced evangelical Protestant denominations such as Baptists and Methodists, both of which wanted to

Slave family in a Georgia cotton field The invention of the cotton gin sent production soaring, deepening the South's dependence on slavery in the process.

create a Kingdom of God on earth before the millennium, when Jesus would return (the "second coming").

SLAVERY AND RELIGION In the late eighteenth century, Baptists and Methodists had condemned slavery, welcomed blacks to their congregations, and given women important roles in their churches. Some slaveholders, led by George Washington and Thomas Jefferson, had agonized over the immorality of slavery.

By the 1830s, however, criticism of slavery in the southern states had virtually disappeared. Most preachers switched from attacking slavery to defending it as a divinely ordained, Bible-sanctioned social system. Alexander Glennie, a white minister, told slaves that their life of bondage was the "will of God." Most ministers who refused to promote slavery left the region.

AFRICAN AMERICAN RELIGION Among the most important elements of African American culture was its dynamic religion, a mixture of

Plantation Burial (1860) The slaves of Mississippi governor Tilghman Tucker gather in the woods to bury and mourn one of their own. The painter of this scene, Englishman John Antrobus, would serve in the Confederate army during the Civil War.

African, Caribbean, and Christian elements. Religion provided slaves both relief for the soul and release for their emotions.

Most Africans brought with them to the Americas belief in a Creator, or Supreme God, whom they could recognize in the Christian God, and whom they might identify with Christ, the Holy Ghost, and the saints. But they also believed in spirits, magic, charms, and conjuring—the casting of spells. A conjurer, it was believed, was like a witch doctor or a voodoo priest who could suddenly make someone sick or heal the afflicted.

Whites usually tried to eliminate African religion and spirituality from the slave experience. Slaves responded by gathering secretly in what were called camp meetings, or bush meetings, to worship in their own way and share their joys, pains, and hopes.

By 1860, about 20 percent of adult slaves had joined Christian denominations. Many others practiced aspects of the Christian faith but were not considered Christians. As a white minister observed, some slaves had "heard of Jesus Christ, but who he is and what he has done for a ruined world, they cannot tell." Few whites, however, fully understood the dynamics or power of slave religion.

Slaves found the Bible inspiring in its support for the poor and oppressed, and they embraced its promise of salvation through the sacrifice of Jesus. Likewise, the lyrics of religious spirituals helped slaves endure the strain of field labor and express their dreams of gaining freedom in "the promised land." One popular spiritual, "Go Down, Moses," derived from the plight of the ancient Israelites held captive in Egypt, says: "We need not always weep and moan, / Let my people go. / And wear these slavery chains forlorn, / Let my people go."

Many white planters assumed that Christianized slaves would be more passive and obedient. A south Georgia planter declared that a Christian slave "is more profitable than an unfaithful one. He will do more and better work, be less troublesome, and [even] less liable to disease."

SLAVE REBELLIONS

The greatest fear of whites in the Lower South was an organized slave revolt, as had occurred in 1791 in the French-controlled sugar colony of Saint-Domingue, which eventually became the independent Republic of Haiti. The slaves rose up and burned plantations, destroyed cane fields, and killed white planters and their families.

The unprecedented rebellion in Saint-Domingue, the world's richest colony and leading source of sugar and coffee, sent shock waves across the United States. Many terrified whites who fled Haiti arrived in Charleston, where they told of the horrors they had experienced. Despite repeated attempts by both French and British armies to reconquer Haiti, the former slaves, led by Touissaint L'Ouverture, defeated them all.

The revolt in Haiti was the southern slaveholder's greatest nightmare. As a prominent Virginian explained, a slave uprising would "deluge the southern country with blood." Any sign of resistance or rebellion among the enslaved therefore risked a brutal and even gruesome response.

In 1811, for example, two of Thomas Jefferson's nephews, Lilburn and Isham Lewis, tied a seventeen-year-old slave named George to the floor of their Kentucky cabin and killed him with an axe in front of seven other slaves, all because George had run away several times. They then handed the axe to one of the slaves and forced him to dismember the body and put the pieces in the fireplace. The Lewises, who had been drinking heavily, wanted "to set an example for any other uppity slaves."

THE PROSSER CONSPIRACY The overwhelming authority and firepower of southern whites made organized resistance risky. The nineteenth-century South witnessed only four major slave insurrections. The first occurred in 1800, when a slave named Gabriel Prosser, a blacksmith on a plantation near Richmond, Virginia, hatched a revolt involving hundreds of slaves. They planned to seize key points in the city; capture the governor, James Monroe; and overthrow the white elite.

Gabriel expected the "poor white people" to join their effort. But it did not happen. Someone alerted whites to the scheme, and a ferocious rainstorm forced "Gabriel's army" to scatter. Gabriel and twenty-six of his "soldiers" were captured and hanged, while ten others were deported to the West Indies.

REVOLT IN LOUISIANA In early 1811, the largest slave revolt in American history occurred just north of New Orleans, where sugarcane planters had acquired a large population of slaves, many of whom were ripe for revolt because of the harshness of their working conditions.

Late on January 8, a group of slaves led by Charles Deslondes, a trusted black overseer, broke into their owner's plantation house along the east bank of the Mississippi River. The planter was able to escape, but his son was hacked to death. Deslondes and his fellow rebels seized weapons, horses, and militia uniforms. Reinforced by more slaves and emboldened by liquor, they headed toward New Orleans, some fifty miles away. Along the way, they burned houses, killed whites, and gathered more recruits. Over the next two days, their ranks swelled to more than 200.

Their victories were short-lived, however. The territorial governor mobilized a group of angry whites—as well as several free blacks who were later praised for their "tireless zeal and dauntless courage"—to suppress the insurrection. U.S. Army units and militia joined in. Dozens of slaves were killed or wounded, and most of those who fled were soon captured.

Deslondes had his hands chopped off and was shot in both thighs and his chest. As he was slowly bleeding to death, a bale of hay was scattered over him and ignited. As many as 100 slaves were tortured, killed, and beheaded, and the severed heads were placed on poles along the Mississippi River. A month after the rebellion, a white resident noted that "all the negro difficulties have subsided and gentle peace prevails."

DENMARK VESEY The Denmark Vesey plot in Charleston, South Carolina, involved a similar effort to assault the white population. Vesey was a Caribbean slave who, in 1785, was taken to Charleston, where, like many urban slaves, he was allowed to work for pay in his free time, at nights, and on Sundays. In 1799, he purchased a lottery ticket and won $1,500, which he used to buy his freedom and start his own carpentry shop. He learned to read and write and organized a Bible study class for other free blacks in the African Methodist Episcopal (AME) Church. Yet he retained a simmering hatred for whites and for the slave system.

In 1822, Vesey and several other blacks developed a plan for a massive slave revolt. They would first capture the city's arsenal and distribute hundreds of rifles to both free and enslaved blacks. All whites in the city would then be killed, along with any blacks who refused to join the rebellion. Vesey then planned to burn the city, seize ships, and head for the black republic of Haiti.

The plot never got off the ground, however. A slave told his owner about the planned rebellion, and soon Vesey and 135 others were captured, arrested, tried, and convicted. Vesey and thirty-four others were executed; three dozen more were transported to Spanish-controlled Cuba and sold into slavery. The Emanuel AME church in Charleston was closed and demolished. (The congregation continued to worship in secret and rebuilt the church following the Civil War.) When told that he would be hanged, Vesey replied that "the work of insurrection will go on."

Vesey's planned rebellion led South Carolina officials to place additional restrictions on the mobility of free blacks and black religious gatherings. It also influenced John C. Calhoun to abandon the nationalism of his early political career and become the South's most outspoken advocate for states' rights and slavery.

NAT TURNER'S REBELLION Nat Turner, a trusted black overseer in Southampton County, Virginia, where blacks were the majority, was also a preacher and healer who believed God had instructed him to "proclaim liberty to the captive" slaves and lead a rebellion that would enact "the day of vengeance of our God." He interpreted a solar eclipse in February 1831 as God's signal for him to act. Turner chose August 21 as the day to launch his insurrection in part because it was the fortieth anniversary of the Haitian slave rebellion.

The revolt began when Turner, in the middle of the night, unlocked the door of his master's house and let in a small group of slaves armed with axes. They methodically murdered the owner, Joseph Travis, and his wife Sally, their twelve-year-old son, a young apprentice, and a baby. The rebels, about forty in all, then repeated the process at other farmhouses, where more slaves and some free blacks joined them. Some slaves tried to protect or hide their owners. Before the two-day revolt ended, fifty-seven whites had been killed, most of them women and children, including ten students at a school.

Federal troops, Virginia militiamen, and volunteers crushed the revolt, indiscriminately killing nearly 200 slaves in the process. A newspaper described the behavior of the white vigilantes as comparable in "barbarity to the atrocities of the insurgents." Twenty African Americans were hanged, including three free blacks; several were decapitated, and their severed heads were placed on poles along the road. Turner, called the "blood-stained monster," was arrested, tried, and found guilty. While waiting to be hanged, he was asked if the revolt was worth it. "Was not Christ crucified?" he replied. His dead body was dismembered, with body parts given to the victims' families.

More than any other slave uprising, news of **Nat Turner's Rebellion** terrified whites across the South. The Virginia legislature debated whether slavery should be abolished. That proposal was defeated; instead, the delegates restricted the ability of slaves to learn to read, write, and gather for religious meetings. A state legislator claimed that people suspected "that a Nat Turner might be in every family, that the same bloody deed could be acted over at any time."

In response to Turner's rebellion, states created more armed patrols to track down runaways. A former slave highlighted the "thousand obstacles thrown in the way of the flying slave. Every white man's hand is raised against him—the patrollers are watching for him—the hounds are ready to follow on his track, and the nature of the country is such as renders it impossible to pass through it with any safety."

THE LURE OF FREEDOM Yet thousands of escaped slaves (called "fugitives") made it to freedom in spite of the obstacles facing them. The fugitive slaves were a powerful example of the enduring lure of freedom and the extraordinary courage of those who yearned for it. On average, some 50,000 enslaved people tried to escape each year. Others ran away for short periods of time, usually to avoid being beaten.

The odds were stacked against escape, however, in part because most slaves could not read, had no maps, and could not use public transportation such as stagecoaches, steamboats, and railroads. Whether free or enslaved, blacks had to have an identity pass or official emancipation papers to go anywhere on their own. Runaways, the vast majority of whom were young males, often were forced to return when they ran out of food or lost their way. Others were tracked down by bloodhounds or bounty hunters. Even in the 1850s—the height of efforts by many Northerners to help runaways—only 1,000 to 1,500 slaves each year made it to freedom.

Slaves who did not escape found other ways to resist. They often exasperated, enraged, and manipulated their owners. Some faked illness, stole or broke tools, destroyed crops, or secretly slaughtered and ate livestock. Others slacked off when unsupervised. As a slave song confessed, "You may think I'm working / But I ain't." Yet there were constraints on such rebellious behavior, for laborers would likely eat better on a prosperous plantation than on a struggling one. And the shrewdest slaveholders knew that offering rewards was more profitable than inflicting pain.

THE SOUTH—A REGION APART

The rapid settlement of the western territories during the first half of the nineteenth century set in motion a ferocious competition between North and South for political influence in the West. Would the new western territories and states be "slave" or "free"? Congressmen from the newly admitted western states would tip the delicate political balance one way or the other.

Because of the rapidly growing profitability of slave-grown cotton, Southerners exercised immense political power, both to protect and expand the system of slavery and to embed the economy of cotton into national and world markets.

The aggressive efforts to expand slavery westward ignited a prolonged political controversy that would end in civil war. As the 1832 nullification controversy in South Carolina had revealed, Southerners despised being told what to do by outsiders, and they especially resented the growing demands to abolish slavery.

The recurring theme of southern politics and culture from the 1830s to the outbreak of civil war in 1861 was the region's determination to remain a society dominated by whites who lorded over people of color. A South Carolinian asserted that "slavery with us is no abstraction—but a great and vital fact. Without it, our every comfort would be taken from us."

Protecting their right to own, transport, and sell slaves in the new western territories became the overriding focus of southern political leaders during the 1830s and after. Race-based slavery provided the South's prosperity as well as its growing sense of separateness—and defensiveness—from the rest of the nation.

Throughout the 1830s, southern state legislatures were "one and indivisible" in their efforts to preserve and expand slavery. Virginia's General Assembly, for example, declared that only the southern states had the right to control slavery and that such control must be "maintained at all hazards." The Georgia legislature agreed, announcing that "upon this point there can be no discussion—no compromise—no doubt."

With each passing year, the leaders of the Old South equated the survival of their region with the preservation of slavery. The increasingly militant efforts of Northerners to restrict or abolish slavery helped reinforce southern unity while provoking an emotional defensiveness that would lead to secession and war—and the unexpected end of slavery and the Cotton Kingdom it enabled.

CHAPTER REVIEW

Summary

- **Southern Distinctiveness**   The South remained rural and agricultural in the first half of the nineteenth century as the rest of the nation embraced urban industrial development. The region's climate favored the growth of cash crops such as tobacco, rice, indigo, and, increasingly, cotton. These crops led to the spread of the plantation system of large commercial agriculture dependent upon enslaved labor. The southern planter elite sought to preserve and expand slavery, despite growing criticism of the *peculiar institution*.

- **A Cotton Economy**   The Old South became increasingly committed to a cotton economy based on slave labor. Despite efforts to diversify the economic base, the wealth and status associated with cotton, as well as soil exhaustion and falling prices from Virginia to Georgia, prompted the westward expansion of the plantation culture to the *Old Southwest*. Slaves worked in harsh conditions as they prepared the terrain for cotton cultivation and experienced the breakup of their families. By 1860, the *Cotton Kingdom* stretched from the Carolinas and Georgia through eastern Texas and up the Mississippi River to Illinois. More than half of all slaves worked on cotton plantations. As long as cotton prices rose, southern planters searched for new land and invested in slaves.

- **Southern White Culture**   White society was divided between the planter elite— those who owned twenty slaves or more—and the rest. *Planters* represented only around 4 percent of the white population but exercised a disproportionately powerful political and social influence. Other whites owned a few slaves, but most owned none. A majority of whites were *plain white folk*—simple farmers who raised corn, cotton, hogs, and chickens. Southern farmers were highly mobile and willing to move West. Southern white women spent most of their time on household chores. The *plantation mistress* supervised her home and household slaves. Most whites were fiercely loyal to the institution of slavery. Even those who owned no slaves feared the competition they believed they would face if slaves were freed, and they enjoyed the privileged status that race-based slavery gave them.

- **Slave Culture**   As the southern economy became more dependent on slave labor, the enslaved faced more regulations and restrictions. The vast majority of southern blacks served as *field hands*. They could be bought and sold at any time; their movements were severely limited, and they had no ability to defend themselves. Any violations could result in severe punishments. Most southern blacks were slaves, but a small percentage were free. Many of the free blacks were *mulattoes*, having mixed-race parentage. Free blacks often worked for wages in towns and cities.

- **African American Resistance and Resilience** During the colonial period, slaves were treated more as indentured servants and were eligible for freedom after a specified number of years. But *slave codes* eventually codified the practice of treating slaves as property rather than as people. Although many slaves attempted to escape, only a few openly rebelled because the consequences were so harsh. Organized revolts such as *Nat Turner's Rebellion (1831)* in Virginia were rare. Most slaves survived by relying on their own communities, family ties, and Christian faith, and by developing their own culture, such as the singing of *spirituals* to express frustration, sorrow, and hope for their eventual deliverance.

CHRONOLOGY

1790	The enslaved population of the United States is almost 700,000
1791	Slave revolt in Saint-Domingue (Haiti)
1800	Gabriel Prosser conspiracy in Richmond, Virginia
1808	U.S. participation in the international slave trade is outlawed
1811	Charles Deslondes revolt in Louisiana
1815	Annual cotton production in the United States is 150,000 bales
1822	Denmark Vesey conspiracy is discovered in Charleston, South Carolina
1830	U.S. slave population exceeds 2 million
1831	Nat Turner leads slave insurrection in Virginia
1840	Population in the Old Southwest tops 1.5 million
1860	Annual cotton production in the United States reaches 4 million bales
	Slave population in the United States reaches 4 million

KEY TERMS

peculiar institution p. 416

Old Southwest p. 421

Cotton Kingdom p. 424

planters p. 426

plantation mistress p. 427

plain white folk p. 428

slave codes p. 430

mulattoes p. 431

field hands p. 433

spirituals p. 440

Nat Turner's Rebellion (1831) p. 446

 INQUIZITIVE

Go to InQuizitive to see what you've learned—and learn what you've missed—with personalized feedback along the way.

12 Religion, Romanticism, and Reform

1800–1860

***The Voyage of Life: Childhood* (1839–1840)** In his *Voyage of Life* series, Thomas Cole drew upon both the religious revivalism and Romantic ideals of the period to depict the four stages of a man's life: childhood (shown above), youth, manhood, and old age. In this painting, an infant drifts along the River of Life with his guardian angel into the fertile landscape from the dark cave, meant to be "emblematic of our earthly origin, and the mysterious Past."

During the first half of the nineteenth century, the United States was overflowing with restless energy and expansive optimism. Confidence was the American creed. "America is the country of the Future," Massachusetts philosopher-poet Ralph Waldo Emerson observed. "It is a country of beginnings, of projects, of designs, and expectations."

However, the dynamic young republic was also experiencing growing pains as the market revolution widened economic inequality. At the same time, sectional tensions over economic policies and increasingly heated debates over the morality and future of slavery created a combative political environment whose struggles overflowed into social and cultural life.

After the Revolution, Americans also became as interested in religious salvation as they were in exercising political rights. The country experienced a theological revolution whereby many people rejected Calvinist determinism. Salvation, they argued, was open to everyone, not just the "elect." By this logic, sin was voluntary rather than innate and inevitable. People were not helplessly depraved; they were free agents who could choose salvation and improve themselves and society.

Such notions democratized Christianity by giving everyone the path to salvation. So-called free-will ministers assured people that they could *choose* to be saved simply by embracing Jesus's promise of salvation, just as more men in Jacksonian America were allowed to vote and *choose* their elected officials.

Evangelicals assumed that America had a God-mandated mission to provide a shining example of representative government, much as Puritan New England had once stood as an example of an ideal Christian community. The concept of a God-given *mission* to create an ideal society (often called "manifest destiny") still carried strong spiritual overtones.

focus questions

1. What major changes took place in the practice of religion in the early nineteenth century? What impact did they have on American society?

2. How did transcendentalism emerge in the early nineteenth century?

3. What were the origins of the major social-reform movements in the early nineteenth century? How did they influence American society and politics?

4. What were the impacts of the anti-slavery movement on society and politics?

It also contained an aspiration toward perfectionism: People could become more and more perfect by reforming themselves and society. Throughout the first half of the nineteenth century, reformers fanned out across the United States to root out injustice or suffering. The combination of religious energy and intense social activism brought major advances in human rights. It also triggered cynicism and disillusionment.

A MORE DEMOCRATIC RELIGION

The energies of the rational Enlightenment and the spiritual Great Awakening flowed from the colonial period into the nineteenth century. In different ways, these two powerful modes of thought, one scientific and rational and the other religious and optimistic, eroded the Calvinist view that people were innately sinful and that God had chosen only a select few (the elect) for salvation ("predestination").

During the nineteenth century, many Christians embraced the more democratic religious outlook that offered salvation to everyone. Just as Enlightenment rationalism stressed humanity's natural goodness and encouraged belief in progress through democratic reforms and individual improvement, Protestant churches stressed that all people were capable of perfection through the guiding light of Christ and their own activism.

RATIONAL RELIGION Enlightenment ideas, including the religious concept of *Deism*, inspired prominent leaders such as Thomas Jefferson and Benjamin Franklin. Deists believed in a rational God—the creator of the rational universe—and that all people were created as equals in the eyes of God. Deists prized science and reason over traditional religion and unquestioning faith.

Interest in Deism increased after the American Revolution. Through the use of reason and scientific research, Deists believed, people might grasp the natural laws governing the universe. Deists did not believe that every statement in the Bible was literally true, and they questioned the divinity of Jesus. They defended free speech and opposed religious coercion.

UNITARIANISM AND UNIVERSALISM The ideals of Enlightenment rationalism that excited Deists soon began to make deep inroads into American Protestantism. The old churches in and around Boston proved especially vulnerable to the appeal of anti-Puritan (anti-Calvinist) religious liberalism. By the end of the eighteenth century, well-educated New Englanders, most of them Congregationalists, were embracing Unitarianism, a "liberal" faith that emphasized the compassion of a loving God, the natural goodness of humankind, the superiority of calm reason over emotional forms of worship, the rejection of the Calvinist belief in predestination, and a general rather than literal reading of the Bible.

Unitarians abandoned the concept of the Trinity (God the Father, the Son, and the Holy Ghost) that had long been central to the Christian faith, believing instead that God and Jesus were separate. Jesus was a saintly man (but not divine) who set a shining example.

Unitarians also stressed that people were not inherently sinful. By following the teachings of Jesus and trusting their own consciences, *all* people were eligible for salvation from a God blessed with boundless love.

Boston became the center of the Unitarian movement. During the early nineteenth century, "liberal" churches adopted the name *Unitarian*, a spiritual outlook especially popular with the educated elite in major cities. A parallel anti-Calvinist religious movement, Universalism, attracted a different—and much larger—social group: the working poor. In 1779, John Murray, a British clergyman, founded the first Universalist church, in Gloucester, Massachusetts. Like the Unitarians, **Universalists** proclaimed the dignity and worth of all people. They stressed that believers must liberate themselves from the rule of priests and ministers and use their capacity to reason to explore the mysteries of existence.

To Universalists and Unitarians, hell did not exist. Salvation was "universal," available to everyone through the sacrifice of Jesus. In essence, Universalists thought God was too caring to damn people to hell, while Unitarians thought themselves too good to be damned. (The two denominations would combine in 1961, becoming the Unitarian Universalist faith.)

THE SECOND GREAT AWAKENING The rise of Universalism and Unitarianism did not mean that traditional religious beliefs were waning. In fact, evangelism remained widespread. During the first Great Awakening in the early 1700s, traveling revivalists had promoted a more intense and personal relationship with God. In addition, Anglicanism suffered from being aligned with the Church of England; it lost its status as the official religion in most states after the American Revolution. To help erase their pro-British image, Virginia Anglicans renamed themselves *Episcopalians*.

Yet the new name did not prevent the Episcopal Church from losing its leadership position in the South. Newer denominations, especially Baptists and Methodists, 20 percent of whom were African American, attracted excited followers. These Christian sects promoted more-democratic principles and allowed individual congregations to exercise more power than did the Anglican Church.

Around 1800, the United States experienced a massive wave of religious revivals called the Great Revival or the **Second Great Awakening**. Without religion, revivalists warned, the American republic would give way to "unbridled appetites and lust." By 1830, the percentage of churchgoers had doubled.

While all denominations grew as a result of the Second Great Awakening, the evangelical sects—Baptists, Methodists, and Presbyterians—experienced explosive popularity. In 1780, the nation had only 50 Methodist churches; by 1860, there were 20,000, far more than any other denomination. The percentage of Americans who joined Protestant churches increased sixfold between 1800 and 1860.

The Second Great Awakening involved two centers of activity. One developed among the New England colleges that were founded as religious centers of learning, then spread across western New York into Pennsylvania and Ohio, Indiana, and Illinois. The other emerged in the backwoods of Tennessee and Kentucky and spread across rural America. Both phases of Protestant revivalism shared a simple message: salvation is available not just to a select few, but to *anyone* who repents and embraces Christ.

Religious revivalism Frontier revivals and prayer meetings ignited religious fervor within both ministers and participants. In this 1830s camp meeting, the women are so intensely moved by the sermon that they shed their bonnets and fall to their knees.

FRONTIER REVIVALS In its frontier phase, the Second Great Awakening, like the first, generated tremendous excitement and emotional excesses. It gave birth to two religious phenomena—the traveling backwoods evangelist and the frontier camp meeting.

People in the early nineteenth century found the supernatural inside as well as outside of churches; they readily believed in magic, dreams, visions, miraculous healings, and speaking in tongues (a spontaneous babbling precipitated by the workings of the Holy Spirit). Evangelists and "exhorters" (spiritual speakers who were not formal ministers) with colorful nicknames such as Jumpin' Jesus, Crazy Dow, and Mad Isaac found ready audiences among lonely frontier folk hungry for spiritual intensity and a more authentic sense of community.

Mass revivals along the western frontier were family-oriented, community-building events that bridged social, economic, political, and even racial divisions. Women, especially, flocked to the revivals and served as the backbone of religious life on the frontier.

At the end of the eighteenth century, ministers visiting the western territories reported that there were few frontier churches and few people attending them. To remedy the situation, traveling evangelists emerged to organize "camp meetings."

The first large camp meeting occurred in August 1801 on a Kentucky hillside called Cane Ridge, east of Lexington. A Scots-Irish Presbyterian minister named James McGready invited Protestants in the region to attend, and as many as 20,000 camped in tents for nine days at what came to be called the Great Revival.

McGready sought to help his parishioners see heaven's "glories and long to be there" while reminding them of "hell and its horrors." To him, the purpose of Christianity was simple: to convince sinners to convert themselves to saints assured of eternal bliss. His sermons left his listeners "powerless, groaning, praying, and crying for mercy."

The **frontier revivals** generated intense emotions as people experienced on-the-spot conversions. As news of the unscrubbed energy of the Cane Ridge gathering spread, Protestant evangelists, especially Methodists, organized similar revivals in other states. One participant reported that the revivals created "such a gust of the power of God" that it seemed "the very gates of hell would give way."

Not all were swept up in the overwrought religious emotionalism, however. Frances Trollope, an English writer who toured the United States in 1827, attended a frontier revival and thought the participants behaved like raving lunatics. Similarly, a Catholic priest in Kentucky scoffed at the absurd "mob fanaticism" of the camp meetings.

The revivals, however, were quite popular with many Americans. "Hell is trembling, and Satan's kingdom falling," reported a South Carolinian in 1802. "The sacred flame" of religious revival is "extending far and wide." In 1776, about one in six Americans belonged to a church; by 1850, it was one in three.

DENOMINATIONAL GROWTH   Among the established denominations, Presbyterianism was entrenched among those with Scots-Irish backgrounds, from Pennsylvania to Georgia. Presbyterians gained further from the Plan of Union with the Congregationalists. Since the Presbyterians and the Congregationalists agreed on theology, they were able to form unified congregations and "call" (recruit) a minister from either denomination. The result through much of the Old Northwest (Ohio, Michigan, Indiana, and Illinois) was that New Englanders became Presbyterians by way of the "Presbygational" churches.

Frontier revivals were dominated by Baptist and Methodist factions. There were Primitive Baptists, Hardshell Baptists, Freewill Baptists and Methodists, Particular Baptists, and many others.

The Baptist theology was grounded in biblical fundamentalism—a certainty that every word and story in the Bible were divinely inspired and literally true. Unlike the earlier Puritans, however, Baptists believed that *everyone* could gain salvation by choosing (via "free will") to receive God's grace and being baptized as adults. Baptists also stressed the social equality of all before God, regardless of wealth, status, or education.

Methodists, who also believed in free will, developed the most effective evangelical method: the "circuit rider," a traveling evangelist ("itinerant") on horseback who sought converts in remote frontier settlements. The itinerant system began with Francis Asbury, a British-born revivalist who traveled across fifteen states and preached thousands of sermons.

After Asbury, Peter Cartwright emerged as the most successful circuit rider. Cartwright grew up in one of the most violent and lawless regions of Kentucky. His brother was hanged as a murderer, and his sister was said to be a prostitute. Cartwright himself had been a hellion until, at age fifteen, he attended a frontier revival meeting:

> Divine light flashed all around me, unspeakable joy sprung up in my soul. I rose to my feet, opened my eyes, and it really seemed as if I was in heaven. . . . My mother raised the shout, my Christian friends crowded around me and joined me in praising God; and though I have been since then, in many instances, unfaithful, yet I have never for one moment, doubted that the Lord did, then and there, forgive my sins and give me religion.

The following year, Cartwright became a religious exhorter, preaching the faith even though he was not yet an ordained minister. At age eighteen, he began working as a Methodist circuit rider. For more than twenty years, he preached a sermon a day, three hours at a time. Crowds flocked to hear his message: Salvation is free for all to embrace.

Cartwright moved to Illinois in 1824 because of his opposition to slavery and a desire to live on "free soil." In Illinois, where clergymen were not prohibited from running for elective office, Cartwright was the first to inject evangelical preaching into politics. At one meeting, Cartwright, then running for Congress as an anti-slavery Jacksonian Democrat, asked those who thought they were going to heaven to stand. He then asked those who did not desire to go to hell to do the same.

The only person who did not stand for either choice was a thirty-seven-year-old Whig attorney named Abraham Lincoln—Cartwright's opponent in the election. "May I inquire of you, Mr. Lincoln," asked Cartwright, "where are you going?" Lincoln replied that he was "going to Congress." He wound up defeating Cartwright, who thereafter called Lincoln an "infidel."

REVIVALISM AND AFRICAN AMERICANS The revivals broke down conventional social barriers. Free African Americans were especially attracted to the emotional energies of the Methodist and Baptist churches, in part because many white circuit riders opposed slavery.

***Black Methodists Holding a Prayer Meeting* (1811)** This caricature of an African American Methodist meeting in Philadelphia shows a preacher in the church doorway, while his congregation engages in exuberant prayer.

African American Richard Allen, a freed slave in Philadelphia, claimed in 1787 that "there was no religious sect or denomination that would suit the capacity of the colored people as well as the Methodist." He decided that the "plain and simple gospel suits best for any people; for the unlearned can understand [it]." Even more important, the Methodists actively recruited blacks. They were "the first people," Allen noted, "that brought glad tidings to the colored people." In 1816, Allen helped found the African Methodist Episcopal (AME) Church, the first black denomination in America.

Yet racial tensions increased as mostly-white Methodist congregations required blacks to sit in designated pews. Such discrimination led Allen and others to found the Bethel African Methodist Episcopal Church in 1793. In 1816, as the racial discrimination continued, Allen helped found a new denomination: the African Methodist Episcopal (AME) Church.

The denomination grew quickly. By 1846, it boasted 296 churches, almost 200 ministers, and 17,375 members. During the nineteenth century, AME extended its outreach, initiating the first civil rights movement and promoting economic and educational opportunities for people of color. (Allen University in South Carolina is named in honor of Richard Allen.)

CAMP MEETINGS AND WOMEN The energies of the Second Great Awakening spread through the western states and into more-settled regions back East. The fastest growth was in rural areas, where camp meetings were an expression of the frontier's democratic spirit.

Baptist, Methodist, and Presbyterian ministers often worked as a team at revivals, and crowds would frequently number in the thousands. Infusions of the spirit sparked strange behavior. Some people went into trances; others contracted the "jerks," a spasmodic twitching. Still others babbled in unknown tongues or got down on all fours and barked like dogs to "tree the devil."

The camp meetings also offered a social outlet to isolated rural folk, especially women. Evangelical ministers repeatedly applauded the spiritual energies of women and affirmed their right to give public witness to their faith and to play a leading role in efforts at social reform.

At a time when women were banned from preaching, Jarena Lee, a free black who lived near Philadelphia, was the first African American woman to become a minister in the AME. As she wrote, "If the man may preach, because the Saviour died for him, why not the woman? Seeing [as] he died for her also." Lee became a tireless revivalist; according to her records, she "traveled 2,325 miles and preached 178 sermons."

The organizational needs of large revivals offered ample opportunities for women. Phoebe Worrall Palmer, for example, hosted prayer meetings in her

New York City home and eventually traveled across the country as a camp-meeting exhorter, assuring listeners that they could gain a life without sin.

Women found public roles within evangelical denominations because of their emphasis on individual religious experiences rather than conventional, male-dominated church structures. Palmer claimed a woman's right to preach by citing the biblical emphasis on obeying God rather than man. "It is always right to obey the Holy Spirit's command," she stressed, "and if that is laid upon a woman to preach the Gospel, then it is right for her to do so; it is a duty she cannot neglect without falling into condemnation." Such religious enthusiasm often inspired women to pursue social reforms for their benefit, including greater educational opportunities and the right to vote.

RELIGION AND REFORM Regions roiled by revival fever were compared to forests devastated by fire. Western New York, in fact, experienced so much evangelical activity that people labeled it the *burned-over district*. One reason the area was such a hotbed was the Erie Canal, which opened in 1825. Both the construction of and traffic on the canal turned many towns into rollicking scenes of lawlessness: gambling, prostitution, public drunkenness, and crime. Such widespread sinfulness made the region ripe for revivalism.

CHARLES G. FINNEY The most successful evangelist in the burned-over district was a former attorney turned Presbyterian minister named Charles Grandison Finney. In the winter of 1830–1831, he preached for six months in Rochester, at the time a canal boomtown in upstate New York. In the process, he became the most celebrated minister in the country and perfected religious revivals as orchestrated spectacles.

While rural camp-meeting revivals attracted farm families and other working-class groups, Finney's Northeast audiences attracted more-prosperous seekers. "The Lord," Finney declared, "was aiming at the conversion of the highest classes of society." In 1836, he built a huge church in New York City to accommodate his rapidly growing congregation.

Finney focused on one question: What role can the individual play in earning salvation? He and other free-will evangelists insisted that everyone, rich or poor, black or white, could *choose* to be "saved."

"The great business of the church," Finney asserted, is "to reform the world." By choosing Christ, a convert could thereafter be free of sin, but Christians also had an obligation to improve society by perfecting themselves. Christians should "aim to be holy and not rest satisfied until they are as perfect as God."

The revivals provided much of the energy behind the reform impulse that swept across America during the age of Jacksonian democracy. By the time the waves of reform crested at midcentury, the fabric of American society had been transformed. Catharine Beecher, a leading advocate for evangelical religion and social reform, stressed that the success of American democracy "depends upon the intellectual and moral character of the mass of people. If they are intelligent and virtuous, democracy is a blessing; but if they are ignorant and wicked, it is only a curse."

JOSEPH SMITH AND THE MORMONS

The Second Great Awakening also spawned new religious groups. The burned-over district in New York gave rise to several movements, the most important of which was Mormonism. Its founder, Joseph Smith Jr., was the child of intensely religious Vermont farm folk who settled in the village of Palmyra, in western New York.

In 1823, the eighteen-year-old Smith reported that an angel named Moroni had appeared by his bedside and announced that God needed Smith's help. The angel had led him to a hillside near his father's farm, where he had unearthed a box containing golden plates on which was etched, in an ancient language, a lost "gospel" explaining the history of ancient America. It described a group of Israelites ("Nephites") who crossed the Atlantic and settled America 2,100 years before Columbus.

Smith set about laboriously translating the "reformed Egyptian" inscriptions on the plates, which no one else ever saw. Much of the language he transcribed was in fact drawn from the Bible. In 1830, he convinced a friend to pay for the publication of the first 5,000 copies of the 500-page text he called *The Book of Mormon: An Account Written by the Hand of Mormon upon Plates Taken from the Plates of Nephi.*

Smith began gathering thousands of converts ("saints"). Eventually, convinced that his authority came directly from God, he formed what he called the Church of Jesus Christ of Latter-day Saints, more popularly known as the **Mormons**. Smith maintained that God, angels, and people were all members of the same flesh-and-blood species.

In his self-appointed role as the Mormon Prophet, Smith dismissed as frauds all Christian denominations (Protestant and Catholic), criticized the sins of the rich; preached universal salvation; denied that there was a hell; urged his followers to avoid liquor, tobacco, and caffeine; and asserted that the Second Coming of Christ was looming. He promised followers "a nation, a new Israel, a people bound as much by heritage and identity as by belief." Within a few years, he had gathered thousands of converts, most of them poor farmers.

YEARS OF PERSECUTION From the outset, the Mormon "saints" upset both their "gentile" neighbors and the civil authorities. Mormons stood out with their secret rituals, their refusal to abide by local laws and conventions, and their clannishness. Smith denied the legitimacy of civil governments and the U.S. Constitution. As a result, no community wanted to host him and his "peculiar people," a term taken from the New Testament.

In their search for a refuge from persecution and for the "promised land," the ever-growing contingent of Mormons moved from western New York to Ohio, then to Missouri, where the governor called for them to be "exterminated or driven from the state." Forced out, Smith and the Mormons moved in 1839 to the half-built town of Commerce, Illinois, on the Mississippi River. They renamed the town Nauvoo, a crude translation of a Hebrew word meaning "beautiful land."

Within five years, Nauvoo had become the second largest city in the state, and Joseph Smith, "the Prophet," was Nauvoo's religious dictator. He owned the hotel and general store; published the newspaper; and served as mayor, chief justice, and commander of the city's 2,000-strong army.

Smith's lust for power and for women grew. He began excommunicating dissidents, and in 1844 he announced his intention to become president of the United States. He proclaimed that the nation should peacefully acquire not only Texas and Oregon but also Mexico and Canada, and that slavery should be ended.

Smith's remarkable sexual energy and extramarital adventures led him to announce that God wanted men to have multiple wives—"plural marriage" (polygamy). He practiced what he preached, accumulating more than two dozen wives, many of them already married to other men. He encouraged other Mormon leaders to do the same. In 1844, Mormon dissenters, including Smith's first wife, Emma, denounced his polygamy. The result was not only a split in the church but also an attack on Nauvoo by non-Mormons. (The Mormon Church would ban polygamy in 1889.)

Brigham Young Young headed the Mormons from 1847 to 1877.

When Smith ordered Mormons to destroy an opposition newspaper, he and his brother Hyrum were arrested and charged with treason. On June 27, 1844, a mob stormed the jail and killed the Smith brothers.

BRIGHAM YOUNG In the charismatic Brigham Young, however, the Mormons found a new and, in many ways, better leader. Young would not only preserve the Mormon Church but create a new theocratic empire.

Because Nauvoo continued to arouse the suspicions of non-Mormons, Young began to look for another home for his flock. It turned out to be 1,300 miles away, near the Great Salt Lake in Utah, a vast, sparsely populated area that was then part of Mexico. The first 149 "saints" to arrive in July 1847 found "a broad and barren plain hemmed in by the mountains, blistering in the

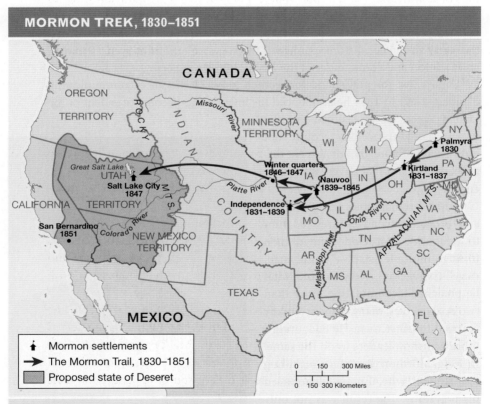

MORMON TREK, 1830–1851

Mormon settlements
The Mormon Trail, 1830–1851
Proposed state of Deseret

- Where were Mormon settlements established between 1830 and 1851?
- Why did Joseph Smith initially lead his congregation west?
- Why was the Utah Territory an ideal place for the Mormons to settle, at least initially?

burning rays of the mid-summer sun. No waving fields, no swaying forests, no verdant meadows." Young, however, declared that "this is the place" to settle.

By the end of 1848, the Mormons had developed an irrigation system for their farms, and over the next decade they brought about a spectacular greening of the Utah desert. At first they organized their own state, named Deseret (meaning "Land of the Honeybee"), and elected Young governor.

But their independence was short-lived. In 1848, Mexico signed the Treaty of Guadalupe Hidalgo, transferring to the United States what is now California, Nevada, Utah, Texas, and parts of Arizona, New Mexico, Colorado, and Wyoming. Two years later, Congress incorporated the Utah Territory into the United States. Nevertheless, when Young was named the territorial governor, the new arrangement gave the Mormons virtual independence.

For more than twenty years, Young ruled with an iron hand, allowing no dissent and defying federal authority. Not until 1896, after the Mormons disavowed polygamy, was Utah admitted as a state. Out of its secret beginnings and early struggles, Mormonism today is the fourth largest religious denomination in the world.

ROMANTICISM IN AMERICA

The revival of religious life during the early 1800s was one of many efforts to unleash the stirrings of the spirit throughout the United States and Europe. Another great cultural shift was the Romantic movement in thought, literature, and the arts.

The movement began in Europe as a rebellion against the well-ordered rational world promoted by scientific objectivity. Were there not, after all, more things in the world than reason, science, and logic could categorize and explain: spontaneous moods, impressions, and feelings; mysterious, unknown, and half-seen things?

In areas in which science could neither prove nor disprove concepts, the Romantics believed that people were justified in having faith. They preferred the stirrings of the heart over the calculations of the head, nonconformity over traditional behavior, and the mystical over the rational. Americans embraced this emphasis on individualism and the virtues of common people and civic democracy.

TRANSCENDENTALISM The most intense American advocates of Romantic ideals were the transcendentalists of New England. Transcendentalism was another of the diverse religious awakenings of the early nineteenth century, but it promoted a radical individualism and personal spirituality separate from organized religion. The word **transcendentalism** came from an emphasis on thoughts and behaviors that *transcend* (or rise above) the limits of reason and logic. To transcendentalists, the inner life of the spirit took priority over the hard facts of science and the rigidities of organized religion. Transcendentalism, said one of its champions, meant an interest in areas "a little beyond" the scope of reason.

Transcendentalism rejected both religious orthodoxy and the "corpse-cold" rationalism of Unitarianism. Reality was not simply what could be touched and seen and analyzed; it included the innate promptings of the mind and the spiritual world.

Above all, transcendentalists believed in "self-reliance" over conformity to social conventions and embraced a pure form of personal spirituality uncorrupted by theological dogma and denominational creeds. They wanted individuals to look *within* themselves for spiritual insights and to nurture a romantic spirituality in harmony with nature. Natural beauty, they assumed,

***The Indian's Vespers* (1847)** Asher B. Durand's painting of a Native American saluting the sun captures the Romantic ideals of personal spirituality and the uncorrupted natural world that swept America during the early nineteenth century.

had the power to startle people into self-awareness, and they believed that all people had the capacity to tap the divine "spark" present throughout God's creations. Ralph Waldo Emerson, the movement's leader, viewed nature as the "symbol of spirit."

In short, transcendentalists wanted everyone to think their *own* thoughts and develop their *own* beliefs. Self-discovery was essential to fulfilling potential. By the 1830s, New England transcendentalism had become the most influential force in American culture.

RALPH WALDO EMERSON   More than anyone, Ralph Waldo Emerson embodied the transcendentalist gospel. To Emerson, self-knowledge opened the doors to self-improvement and self-realization.

Emerson became the nation's most popular speaker during the 1840s. "We have listened too long to the courtly muses of Europe," he said. "We will walk on our own feet; we will work with our own hands; we will speak with our own minds." He exhorted the young republic to shed its cultural inferiority complex and create its own distinctive literature, art, and thought.

The son of the minister of Boston's First Unitarian Church and the descendant of eight generations of clergymen, Emerson graduated from Harvard College in 1821 and became a Unitarian parson in 1829. But three years later, following the death of his wife after only eighteen months of marriage, he turned away from organized religions because they stifled free thinking. He sought instead to cultivate a personal spirituality in communion with nature. As he explained, "I am more of a Quaker than anything else. I believe in the 'still, small voice,' and that voice is Christ within us."

After traveling in Europe, where he met England's greatest Romantic writers, Emerson settled in Concord, Massachusetts, to take up the life of an essayist, poet, and lecturer ("preacher to the world"). He found God in nature and came to believe in human perfectibility. He celebrated the virtues of self-reliance and the individual's unlimited potential—if people would only learn to think for themselves and defy traditional assumptions and beliefs.

In 1836, Emerson published the pathbreaking book *Nature*, which helped launch the transcendental movement. In it, he stressed that people could "transcend" the material world and discover the "spirit" animating the universe. Individuals, in other words, could exercise godlike powers to counter the emotional starvation of New England intellectual life. Every human being, said Emerson, should enjoy an "original relation to the universe."

Emerson's lectures and writings provided the energetic core of the transcendentalist outlook. His essay "Self-Reliance" (1841) expressed the transcendentalist ideal of intellectual independence: "Whoso would be a man," he declared, "must be a nonconformist. . . . Nothing is at last sacred but the integrity of your own mind. . . . It is easy in the world to live after the world's opinion; it is easy in solitude to live after our own; but the great man is he who in the midst of a crowd keeps with perfect sweetness the independence of solitude."

Emerson championed a self-reforming individualism that reinforced the democratic energies inspiring Jacksonian America, and he inspired others to follow his notion of perfectionism in which individuals could tap their divine potential and express their spiritual humanism.

THE TRANSCENDENTAL CLUB In 1836, a diverse, informal discussion group that came to be called the Transcendental Club began to meet in Boston and nearby Concord to discuss philosophy, literature, and religion. In describing life in Concord, writer Nathaniel Hawthorne said there "never was a poor, little country village infested with such a variety of queer, strangely dressed, oddly behaved mortals."

The club included cultural rebels; social critics; liberal clergymen; utopian reformers; militant abolitionists; innovative writers; and women such as Elizabeth Peabody, her sister Sophia (who married Hawthorne), and Margaret Fuller, the author of *Woman in the Nineteenth Century* (1845).

A brilliant conversationalist, the dynamic Fuller organized a transcendentalist discussion group that met in Elizabeth Peabody's Boston bookstore. Their "Conversations" were designed to embolden the city's brightest women to think and act for themselves. Fuller helped launch and edit the *Dial* (1840–1844), an experimental transcendentalist magazine that introduced European Romanticism to American readers. "A much greater range of occupations," Fuller asserted, must be made available to women to enable them to express their full potential.

HENRY DAVID THOREAU Ralph Waldo Emerson's friend, Henry David Thoreau, fourteen years younger, practiced the thoughtful self-reliance and pursuit of perfection that Emerson preached. "I like people who can do things," Emerson said, and Thoreau could do many things: carpentry, masonry, painting, surveying, sailing, gardening, lecturing.

Thoreau was America's original wild child. From an early age, he displayed a headstrong sense of uncompromising integrity, prickly individuality, and proud rebelliousness. He loved to unearth forbidden questions and lay bare everyday hypocrisies. "If a man does not keep pace with his companions," he wrote, "perhaps it is because he hears a different drummer."

And Thoreau always marched to a different drummer. He described himself as "a mystic, a transcendentalist, and a natural philosopher" who questioned tradition and challenged authority. Emerson delighted in Thoreau because he displayed "as free & erect a mind as any I have ever met." Thoreau, he added, was "stubborn and implacable; always manly and wise, but rarely sweet." A neighbor was more blunt. "I love Henry," said Elizabeth Hoar, "but I do not like him."

Born in Concord in 1817, Thoreau attended Harvard. After a brief stint as a teacher, he worked with his father, a celebrated pencil maker. Like Emerson, however, Thoreau frequently escaped to the woods to absorb nature's spiritual energies. He viewed "the indescribable innocence" of nature as a living bible; the earth to him was a form

Henry David Thoreau Thoreau was a social rebel, environmentalist, and lifelong abolitionist.

of poetry, full of hidden meanings. Daily rambles across the hills, forests, and meadows inspired him more than attending church. Christianity, he believed, was a dying institution. His priorities were inward.

Thoreau showed little interest in social life and no interest in wealth, which he believed made people slaves to materialism. "The mass of men," he wrote, "lead lives of quiet desperation" because they were preoccupied with making money and exploiting nature. Thoreau yearned to escape the constraints of stuffy traditions, unjust laws, "good behavior," or the opinions of his elders. He committed himself to leading what Emerson called a simple life centered on "plain living and high thinking." Thoreau rented a room at the Emersons' home, where he tended the garden, worked as a handyman, and took long walks with his host. In 1844, when Emerson bought fourteen acres along Walden Pond, Thoreau decided to embark upon an unusual experiment in self-reliance.

On July 4, 1845, just shy of his twenty-eighth birthday, Thoreau took to the woods to live in a tiny, one-room cabin he had built at Walden Pond, a mile outside of Concord. His hut featured three chairs: "one for solitude, two for friendship, and three for society."

Living at Walden Pond was Thoreau's personal declaration of independence. His goal was to lead a simple life in which he could discover what nature "had to teach" about those things that money can't buy. "I went to the woods because I wished to live deliberately," he wrote in *Walden, or Life in the Woods* (1854), " . . . and not, when I came to die, discover that I had not lived."

Thoreau ate only one meal a day and disdained coffee, alcohol, jam, tobacco, and salt ("the grossest of groceries"). He regarded sex with disgust and suspicion. His minimalist ethic led Emerson to observe that he "was never affectionate, but superior, didactic," forever scorning his neighbors and claiming that he was "more favored by the gods."

Walden continues to attract readers because it contains some of the most evocative nature writing in America. A first-rate naturalist, Thoreau was blessed with superhuman powers of observation. He urged readers to open their eyes and hearts to the infinite spontaneity of everyday sensory experiences. "We can never have enough of nature," he wrote. "We need to witness our own limits transgressed, and some life pasturing freely where we never wander."

Loving the earth was Thoreau's true romance, for to him there was something sacred and liberating about nature's beauty and sensuality. His ecstatic descriptions of the natural world have made him the patron saint of the environmental movement. (Nearly a million people visit his cabin site at Walden Pond each year.) "In wildness is the preservation of the world," he wrote, and his scriptural statement later became the motto of the Sierra Club.

During Thoreau's two years, two months, and two days at Walden Pond, his conscience was pricked by the abolitionist movement. He harbored a runaway slave and considered President James K. Polk's declaration of war against Mexico an unjust action pushed by southern cotton planters eager to add more slave territory. His disgust for the war led him to refuse to pay taxes, for which he was put in jail (for only one night; an aunt paid his overdue bill).

This incident inspired Thoreau to write his classic essay, "Civil Disobedience" (1849), which would influence Martin Luther King Jr. in shaping the civil rights movement 100 years later. "If the law is of such a nature that it requires you to be an agent of injustice to another," Thoreau wrote, "then, I say, break the law."

Until his death in 1862, Thoreau kept a meticulous journal of "close observations" and philosophical reflections. He also attacked slavery and applauded those who worked to undermine it. The continuing influence of his creed of individual action against injustice shows the impact that a thoughtful person can have on an imperfect world.

AN AMERICAN LITERATURE Henry David Thoreau and Ralph Waldo Emerson portrayed the transcendentalist movement as an expression of moral idealism; critics dismissed it as outrageous self-centeredness. Although the transcendentalists attracted only a small following in their time, they inspired a generation of writers that produced the first great age of American literature.

The half decade of 1850 to 1855 brought an outpouring of extraordinary writing for a nation that had long suffered an inferiority complex about the quality of its arts. Among the works produced were *Representative Men* by Emerson; *Walden, or Life in the Woods* by Thoreau; *The Scarlet Letter* and *The House of the Seven Gables* by Nathaniel Hawthorne; *Moby-Dick* by Herman Melville; *Leaves of Grass* by Walt Whitman; and hundreds of unpublished poems by Emily Dickinson.

LITERARY GIANTS

NATHANIEL HAWTHORNE

Nathaniel Hawthorne, the supreme writer of the New England group, never shared the sunny optimism of his neighbors or their perfectionist belief in reform. A native of Salem, Massachusetts, he was haunted by the knowledge of evil bequeathed to him by his Puritan forebears, one of whom (John Hathorne) had been a judge at the Salem witchcraft trials. After college, Hawthorne worked in obscurity in Salem before earning a degree of fame with *Twice-Told Tales* (1837). His central themes examined sin and its consequences: pride and selfishness, secret guilt, and the impossibility of rooting sin out of the human soul.

Emily Dickinson Dickinson offered the world of New England literature a fresh female voice.

EMILY DICKINSON

Emily Dickinson, the most original of the New England poets, never married. From her birth in 1830 to her death in 1886, she lived with her parents and sister in Amherst, Massachusetts. There, in a spartan corner bedroom on the second floor of the family house, the slim, red-haired Dickinson found self-expression in poetry, ever grateful that "one is one's self & not somebody else."

Dickinson lived what her niece called a life of "exquisite self-containment." Fired by "the light of insight and the fire of emotion," she wrote verse remarkable for its simplicity and brevity. Only ten or so of her almost 1,800 poems were published before her death at age fifty-five. As she famously wrote, "Success is counted sweetest / By those who ne'er succeed."

Whether her solitary existence was the result of severe eye trouble, aching despair generated by her love for a married minister, or fear of her possessive father, Dickinson's isolation and lifelong religious doubts led her, in the "solitude of space . . . that polar privacy," to probe the "white heat" of her heartbreak and disappointment in ways unusual for the time. Her often-abstract themes were elemental: life, death, fear, loneliness, nature, and above all, the withdrawal of God, "a distant, stately lover" who no longer could be found.

EDGAR ALLAN POE   Edgar Allan Poe was fascinated by the menace of death. Born in Boston in 1809 and orphaned as a child, he was raised by foster parents in Richmond, Virginia.

Poe led a stormy life. Although a top student and popular storyteller at the University of Virginia, he left the school after ten months, having racked up excessive gambling debts. After a two-year stint in the army, he enrolled at the U.S. Military Academy at West Point, where in 1831 he was expelled for disobedience and missing classes.

After spending time in New York City and Baltimore, Poe relocated in 1835 to Richmond, where he became an assistant editor of the *Southern Literary Messenger*. He secretly married Virginia Clemm, his thirteen-year-old cousin, claiming that she was twenty-one. They moved to Philadelphia in 1837, where he edited magazines and wrote scathing reviews and terrifying mystery stories. As the creator of the detective story, his influence on literature has been enormous.

In 1844, Poe moved to New York City. The following year, he published "The Raven," a poem about a man who, "once upon a midnight dreary," having lost his lover, a "sainted maiden" named Lenore, responds to a rapping at his door, only to find "darkness there and nothing more." Scanning the darkness, "dreaming dreams no mortal ever dared to dream before," he confronts a silence punctuated only by his mumbled query, "Lenore?" The man closes the door, only to hear the strange knocking again. Both angered and perplexed, he flings open the door and, "with many a flirt and flutter," in flies a raven, that "grim, ungainly, ghastly, gaunt, and ominous bird of yore." The raven utters but one haunting word: "Nevermore."

"The Raven" made Poe a household name across America. In 1847, however, tragedy struck when his young wife died of tuberculosis. Thereafter, he was seduced as much by alcohol and drug abuse as by writing. He died at age forty of mysterious causes.

Poe left behind an extraordinary collection of "unworldly" tales and haunting poems. He used horror to explore the darkest corners of human psychology and satisfy his lifelong obsession with death. To him, fear was the most powerful emotion, so he focused on making the grotesque and supernatural seem disturbingly real. Anyone who has read "The Tell-Tale Heart" or "The Pit and the Pendulum" can testify to his success.

HERMAN MELVILLE Herman Melville, the author of *Moby-Dick*, was a New Yorker who went to sea as a youth. After eighteen months aboard a whaler, he arrived in the Marquesas Islands, in the South Seas, and jumped ship. He spent several weeks with natives in "the valley of the Typees" before signing on with an Australian whaler. He joined a mutiny in Tahiti and finally returned home as a seaman aboard a U.S. Navy frigate. An account of his adventures, *Typee* (1846), became an instant success, which he repeated in *Omoo* (1847).

In 1851, the thirty-two-year-old Melville published *Moby-Dick*, one of the world's greatest novels. In the story of Captain Ahab's obsessive quest for an "accursed" white whale that had devoured his leg, Melville explored the darker recesses of the soul.

On one level, the book is a ripping good yarn of adventure on the high seas. On another level, however, it explores the unfathomable depths and darkness of human complexity, as Ahab's crazed obsession with finding and killing the white whale turns him into a monster who sacrifices his ship and his crew.

Walt Whitman This engraving of a thirty-seven-year-old Walt Whitman appeared in his acclaimed poetry collection *Leaves of Grass*.

WALT WHITMAN The most controversial writer during the nineteenth century was Walt Whitman, a New York journalist and poet. He was a self-promoting, robust personality. After meeting him, Henry David Thoreau wrote that Whitman "was not only eager to talk about himself but reluctant to have the conversation stray from the subject for long." Unlike Thoreau, Whitman wrote excitedly about industrial development, urban life, working men, sailors, and "simple humanity."

Born in 1819 on a farm in Long Island, New York, Whitman moved with his family to Brooklyn, where he worked as a carpenter, teacher, political activist, and editor of the *Brooklyn Eagle*. He frequently took the ferry across the East River to Manhattan, where the city's restless energy fascinated him.

By the time he met Ralph Waldo Emerson, Whitman had been "simmering, simmering." But Emerson "brought him to a boil" with his emphasis on defying tradition and celebrating the commonplaces of life, including sexuality and the body. These themes found their way into Whitman's controversial first book of unconventional, free verse poems, *Leaves of Grass* (1855). In its first year, it sold ten copies. One reviewer called it "an intensely vulgar, nay, absolutely *beastly* book." *Leaves of Grass*, however, became more influential with each passing year.

***Politics in an Oyster House* (1848)**
Commissioned by social activist John H. B. Latrobe, this painting captures the public debates that were fueled by newspapers and magazines.

Whitman introduced his book by declaring that "I celebrate myself, and sing myself." He was unapologetically "an American, one of the roughs . . . disorderly, fleshy, and sensual . . . eating, drinking, and breeding." Like Emerson, he was a self-proclaimed pioneer on behalf of "a new mightier world, a varied world," a bustling "world of labor" dignified by "common people." His poems, remarkable for their energy, exuberance, and intimacy, were seasoned with frank sexuality and homoerotic overtones. They expressed the color and texture of American democracy, "immense in passion, pulse, and power."

Although *Leaves of Grass* was banned in Boston because of its explicit sexuality, Emerson found it "the most extraordinary piece of wit and wisdom that America has yet contributed." More conventional literary critics, however, shuddered at the shocking "grossness" of Whitman's homosexual references ("manly love"; "the love of comrades"; "for the friend I love lay sleeping by my side"). Yet Whitman could never be truly honest about his sexuality (he identified as gay or bisexual in today's terms), for even discussing such perspectives was a felony in the nineteenth century.

NEWSPAPERS The flowering of American literature coincided with a massive expansion in newspaper readership sparked by rapid improvements in printing technology. The emerging availability of newspapers costing only a penny transformed daily reading into a form of popular entertainment. The "penny dailies," explained one editor, "are to be found in every street, lane, and alley; in every hotel, tavern, countinghouse, [and] shop."

By 1850, the United States had more newspapers than any other nation, and they forged a network of communications across the republic. As readership soared, the content of the papers expanded beyond political news and commentary to include society gossip, sports, and reports of sensational crimes and accidents. The proliferation of newspapers was largely a northern and western phenomenon, as literacy rates in the South lagged behind those of the rest of the country.

THE REFORM IMPULSE

In 1842, the United States was awash in reform movements led by dreamers and activists who saw social injustice or immorality and fought to correct them. Lyman Beecher, a prominent preacher and champion of evangelical Christian revivalism (and the father of writer Harriet Beecher Stowe), stressed that the Second Great Awakening was not focused simply on promoting individual conversions; it was also intended to "reform human society." In 1840, Ralph Waldo Emerson told an English friend that "we are all a little wild with numberless projects of social reform."

While an impulse to "perfect" people and society helped excite the reform movements, social and economic changes, including the Panic of 1837 and the ensuing depression, invigorated many reformers, most of whom were women. The rise of an urban middle class enabled growing numbers of women to hire cooks and maids, thus freeing them to devote more time to societal concerns. Many joined churches and charitable organizations, most of which were led by men.

Both women and men belonging to evangelical societies fanned out across America to organize Sunday schools, spread the gospel, and distribute Bibles to the children of the working poor. Other reformers tackled issues such as living conditions in prisons and workplaces, care of the disabled, temperance (reducing the consumption of alcoholic beverages), women's rights, and the abolition of slavery. Transcendentalists sought to improve the lot of the poor, the disenfranchised, and the enslaved.

That these reformers often met resistance, persecution, violence, and even death testified to the sincerity of their convictions and the power of their example. As Emerson said, "Never mind the ridicule, never mind the defeat, up again, old heart!" For there is "victory yet for all justice."

TEMPERANCE The **temperance** crusade was among the most widespread of the reform movements. Many people argued that most social problems were rooted in alcohol abuse. William Cobbett, an English reformer who traveled in the United States, noted in 1819 that one could "go into hardly any man's house without being asked to drink wine or spirits, even *in the morning.*"

In 1826, a group of ministers in Boston organized the American Society for the Promotion of Temperance, which sponsored lectures, press campaigns, and the formation of local and state societies. A favorite tactic was to ask each person who took the pledge to put by his or her signature a letter *T* for "total abstinence." With that, a new word entered the English language: *teetotaler.*

In 1833, the society formed the American Temperance Union. Like nearly every reform movement of the day, temperance had a wing of absolutists. They passed a resolution that liquor ought to be prohibited by law. The Temperance Union, at its spring convention in 1836, called for abstinence from all alcoholic beverages—which caused moderates to abstain from the temperance movement.

For men and women who feared Jacksonian democracy, who worried about the surge of poor immigrants from Ireland and Germany, and dreaded change itself, reform was a means of restoring social control. They were afraid of anything that upset the social status quo. As Lyman Beecher warned, Americans were fast becoming "another people" as the result of massive immigration and Jacksonian democracy. Fears that Americans were turning away from the Protestant faith led Beecher and other evangelicals to found societies such as the American Bible Society, the American Sunday School Union, and the American Tract Society—all designed to shore up the centrality of religion and churches in community life. Evangelical reformers sought to restrict freedom: no more Sunday mail service or Sunday recreation, no more families without Bibles, no communities without ministers, no more liquor.

PRISONS AND ASYLUMS The Romantic impulse differed from the evangelical outlook in that it often included the belief that people are innately good and capable of perfection. Such an optimistic view brought about major changes in the treatment of prisoners, the disabled, and orphans. Public institutions (often called asylums) emerged for the treatment of social ills. If removed from society, the theory went, the needy and deviant could be made whole again. Unhappily, however, the underfunded and understaffed asylums often became breeding grounds for brutality and neglect.

The idea of the penitentiary—a place where the guilty paid for their crimes but also underwent rehabilitation—developed as a new approach to reforming criminals. An early model of the system was the Auburn Penitentiary, which opened in New York in 1816.

The prisoners at Auburn had separate cells and gathered only for meals and group labor. Discipline was severe. The men marched in lockstep and were never put face-to-face or allowed to talk. But they were reasonably secure from abuse by their fellow prisoners. The system, its advocates argued, had a beneficial effect on the prisoners and saved money, since the facility's workshops supplied prison needs and produced goods for sale at a profit. By 1840, the nation had twelve Auburn-type penitentiaries.

The Romantic reform impulse also found an outlet in the care of the insane. Before 1800, the insane were usually confined at home, with hired keepers, or in jails or almshouses, where homeless debtors were housed. After 1815, however, asylums that separated the disturbed from the criminal began to appear.

The most important figure in boosting awareness of the plight of the mentally ill was Dorothea Lynde Dix. A pious Boston schoolteacher, she was asked to instruct a Sunday-school class at the East Cambridge House of Correction in 1841. There she found a roomful of insane people who had been completely neglected.

The scene so disturbed her that she began a two-year investigation of jails and almshouses in Massachusetts. In a report to the state legislature in 1843, Dix revealed that insane people were confined "in *cages, closets, cellars, stalls, pens! Chained, naked, beaten with rods,* and *lashed* into obedience." She won the support of leading reformers and proceeded to carry her campaign on behalf of "the miserable, the desolate, and the outcast" throughout the country and abroad. In the process, she helped to transform social attitudes toward mental illness.

WOMEN'S RIGHTS While countless middle-class women devoted themselves to improving the quality of life in America, some argued that women should focus on enhancing home life. In 1841, Harriet Beecher Stowe's sister, Catharine Beecher, published *A Treatise on Domestic Economy,* which promoted the **cult of domesticity,** a powerful ideology that called upon women to accept and celebrate their role as manager of the household and nurturer of the children, separate from the man's sphere of work outside the home. Catharine Beecher and many others argued that young women should be trained not for the workplace but in the domestic arts. Thus, the prospects for women remained much as they had been in the colonial era. They were barred from the ministry and most other professions. They could not vote or serve on juries. College was rarely an option. A wife often had no control over her property or her children. She could not make a will, sign a contract, or bring suit in court without her husband's permission.

Julia Ward Howe, known mostly as the poet who would provide the lyrics to the "Battle Hymn of the Republic," the anthem of the Union army during the Civil War, was living testimony to the deadening aspects of the cult of domesticity. Like most nineteenth-century women, she spent her time at home with her children while pregnant more often than not. Yet she was anything but happy. "My books are all that keeps me alive," she sighed in private frustration.

Howe's much older husband, Samuel Gridley Howe, lorded over her like a tyrant. During their honeymoon, Julia composed poems with ominous lines: "Hope died as I was led / Unto my marriage bed." Her husband belittled her writings and refused to let her have any pain killers during childbirth, despite her tearful pleas. Women, he asserted, needed discipline: "The pains of childbirth are meant by a beneficent creator to be the means of leading them back to lives of temperance, exercise, and reason."

In 1847, Howe confessed to her sister that her life had become unbearable: "You cannot, cannot know the history, the inner history of the last four years." Nathaniel Hawthorne observed that Howe's poetry "let out a whole history of domestic unhappiness."

After her husband's death in 1876, Howe would become a leader of the women's suffrage movement. A few years before her death in 1910, she wrote in her journal: "I do not desire ecstatic, disembodied sainthood. . . . I would be human, and American, and a woman."

SENECA FALLS Gradually, however, women began to protest their subordinate status, and some men began to listen. An organized push for women's rights emerged in 1840, when the anti-slavery movement split over the question of women's involvement. In 1848, two prominent women's rights advocates, abolitionists Lucretia Mott, a Philadelphia Quaker, and Elizabeth Cady Stanton of New York, called a convention of men and women to gather in Stanton's hometown of Seneca Falls, in western New York, to discuss "the social, civil, and religious condition and rights of women."

On July 19, 1848, when the **Seneca Falls Convention** convened, revolution was in the air. In Italy, Germany, and other European states, militant nationalists, including many women, rebelled against monarchies and promoted unification. In France, the Society for the Emancipation for Women demanded that women receive equal political rights. In April, the French government abolished slavery in its Caribbean colonies, and in June, European feminists called for "the complete, radical abolition of all the privileges of sex, of birth, of race, of rank, and of fortune."

The activists at Seneca Falls did not go that far, but they did issue a clever paraphrase of the Declaration of Independence. The **Declaration of Rights and Sentiments** proclaimed that "all men and women are created equal." All laws that placed women "in a position inferior to that of men, are contrary to the great precept of nature, and therefore of no force or authority." Its most controversial demand was the right to vote.

Such ambitious goals and strong language were too radical for most of the 300 delegates, and only about a third of them signed the Declaration of Rights and Sentiments. The *Philadelphia Public Ledger* sneeringly asked why women would want to climb down from their domestic pedestal and get involved with politics: "A woman is nothing. A wife is everything. A pretty girl is equal to ten thousand men, and a mother is, next to God, all powerful." Despite such

Elizabeth Cady Stanton and Susan B. Anthony Stanton (left, in 1856) was a young mother who organized the Seneca Falls Convention, while Anthony (right, in 1848) started as an anti-slavery and temperance activist in her twenties. The two would meet in 1851 and form a lifelong partnership in the fight for women's suffrage.

opposition, the Seneca Falls gathering represented an important first step in the campaign for women's rights.

From 1850 until the outbreak of the Civil War in 1861, women's rights advocates held conventions, delivered lectures, and circulated petitions. But the movement struggled in the face of meager funds and widespread opposition. A mother and housewife criticized the women reformers, claiming that the typical activist "struts and strides, and thinks that she proves herself superior to the rest of her sex." The movement eventually succeeded because of a few undaunted women who refused to cower in facing the odds against them.

SUSAN B. ANTHONY   Susan B. Anthony, already active in temperance and anti-slavery groups, joined the women's crusade in the 1850s. Unlike Elizabeth Cady Stanton and Lucretia Mott, she was unmarried and therefore able to devote most of her attention to the movement. As one observer put it, Stanton "forged the thunderbolts and Miss Anthony hurled them." Both lived into the twentieth century, focusing after the Civil War on women's suffrage (the right to vote).

Women nationwide did not gain the vote in the nineteenth century, but they did make legal gains. In 1839, Mississippi became the first state to grant married women control over their property; by the 1860s, eleven more states had done so. Still, the only jobs open to educated women in any number were nursing and teaching, both of which brought relatively lower status and pay than "men's work."

EARLY PUBLIC SCHOOLS   Early America, like most rural societies, offered few educational opportunities. That changed in the first half of the nineteenth century as reformers lobbied for **public schools** to serve all children. The working poor wanted free schools to give their children an equal chance to pursue the American dream. Education, people argued, would improve manners while reducing crime and poverty.

A well-informed, well-trained citizenry was considered one of the basic premises of a republic. If political power resided with the people, as the Constitution asserted, then the citizenry needed to be well educated. By 1830, however, no state had a public school system.

Horace Mann of Massachusetts, a state legislator and attorney, led the early drive for statewide, tax-supported public school systems. He proposed that the schools be free to all children regardless of class, race, or ethnicity—including immigrant children. He sponsored the creation of a state board of education and served as its leader. Universal access to education, Mann argued, "was the great equalizer of the conditions of men—the balance-wheel of the social machinery."

The George Barrell Emerson School, Boston (ca. 1850) Although higher education for women initially met with some resistance, "seminaries" like this one were established in the 1820s and 1830s to teach women mathematics, physics, and history, as well as music, art, and social graces.

Mann went on to promote the first state-supported "normal school" for the training of teachers, a state association of teachers, and a minimum school year of six months. He saw the public school system as a way not only to ensure that everyone had a basic level of knowledge and skills but also to reinforce values such as hard work and clean living. "If we do not prepare children to become good citizens, if we do not enrich their minds with knowledge," Mann warned, "then our republic must go down to destruction."

By the 1840s, most states in the North and Midwest (but not the South) had joined the public school movement. The initial conditions, however, were seldom ideal. Funds for buildings, books, and equipment were limited; teachers were poorly paid and often poorly prepared. Most students going beyond the elementary grades attended private academies, often organized by churches. Such schools, begun in colonial days, multiplied until there were more than 6,000 by 1850.

In 1821, Boston English High School opened as the nation's first free public *secondary* school. Beginning in 1827, Massachusetts required every town of 500 or more residents to have a high school. Other states were not as progressive, however. Public high schools flourished only after the Civil War. In 1860, there were barely 300 in the nation.

Yet by 1850, half the nation's white children between ages five and nineteen were enrolled in primary schools. Few were Southerners, however. With only a few exceptions, southern states did not establish public schools until after the Civil War. In most states, enslaved children were prohibited from learning to read and write or attend school. The South had some 500,000 illiterate whites, more than half the total in the country. In the South, North Carolina led the way in state-supported education, enrolling more than two thirds of its white school-age population by 1860. But the school year was only four months long because of the state's need for children to do farmwork.

The prolonged disparities between North and South in the number and quality of educational opportunities helped explain the growing economic and cultural differences between the two regions. Then, as now, undereducated people were more likely to remain economically deprived, less healthy, and less engaged in political life.

FOOD AND SEX The nation's widespread reform impulse excited causes and cranks of all sorts, including an array of health reformers, the most popular of whom was Sylvester Graham, a controversial preacher-turned-lecturer who blamed most of Americans' problems on bad eating and drinking habits.

Born in 1794 in West Suffield, Connecticut, Graham was the youngest of seventeen children. Soon after his minister father died, in 1796, his mother broke down, and Sylvester was sent to be raised by "strangers." As a young man he worked as a farmhand, clerk, and teacher before attending Amherst College in Massachusetts. He was expelled for his aggressive eccentricities, which did not prevent him from becoming a Presbyterian minister.

Religion inspired Graham less than nutrition did. He soon gave up preaching the Gospel of Christ to preach the gospel of bran and fiber. Although he had no medical training, Graham became the nation's leading health reformer after a massive cholera epidemic in 1832. Graham attributed cholera to people eating chicken pot pie and engaging in "excessive lewdness."

Thereafter, on the lecture circuit, in books, and in *Graham's Journal of Health and Longevity*, he preached convincingly against the dangers of alcohol and coffee, white flour, meat, gluttony, obesity, and body odor. Graham's "system" for a healthier America called for a diet of whole grains, fresh fruits, and nuts. The diet banned all meats and spices—including pepper and salt—as well as butter, cream, and soups. Alcohol and tobacco were also prohibited.

The centerpiece of Graham's celebrated vegetarian diet was the "Graham cracker," made of coarsely ground wheat bathed in molasses and baked. Graham stressed that daily meals of his crackers needed to be precisely six hours apart, with no snacking in between. The "Graham system" also prescribed fresh air, bathing in cold water, drinking only when thirsty (not with meals), and singing and dancing for exercise. He discouraged "excessive" sexual activity, meaning more than once a week for married couples, because it would cause indigestion, headache, feebleness of circulation, pulmonary consumption, spinal diseases, epilepsy, and insanity. He urged his followers to "avoid medicine and physicians—if you value your life."

Graham became one of the most famed and hated of the professional reformers. Butchers and bakers threatened to kill him, and many people laughed at his ideas. Yet others, called Grahamites, embraced his health system. There were Grahamite hotels in New York City, Boston, and Philadelphia, as well as stores, boarding houses, college dining halls, and a newspaper promoting his diet and ideas. One of Graham's followers called him an "eccentric and wayward genius."

UTOPIAN COMMUNITIES

Amid the climate of reform, the quest for everyday utopias—ideal communities with innovative social and economic relationships—flourished. Plans for creating heaven on earth had long been an American passion, at least since the Puritans set out to build a holy colony in New England.

In the nineteenth century, more than 100 **utopian communities** were created. Religious motives animated many of the ideal societies while others reflected faith in the Enlightenment ideal that every social problem had a solution discoverable by scientific study.

Some utopias were *communitarian* experiments emphasizing the welfare of the entire community rather than individual freedom and private profits. Others experimented with "free love," socialism, and special diets. What they shared was a profound belief that mainstream society was fundamentally flawed and irredeemable.

THE SHAKERS Communities founded by the Shakers (the United Society of Believers in Christ's Second Appearing) proved to be long lasting. Ann Lee (known as Mother Ann Lee) arrived in New York from England with eight followers in 1774. The illiterate daughter of a blacksmith and the wife of an abusive husband, she grew up with seven siblings. Early on she came to believe in the "depravity of human nature and the odiousness of sin." No sooner did she marry than she was constantly pregnant, bearing four children, none of whom lived beyond six years of age. The trauma of childbirth and the loss of her children convinced Ann Lee that sexual activity was "indecent" and sinful.

She eventually took shelter among a group of renegade Shaking Quakers who nurtured in her the dream of a celibate, spotlessly clean utopia devoted to the Second Coming of Christ in which she would play the role of Jesus's female counterpart. She also believed that God and Jesus spoke directly to her ("direct revelation").

As Ann Lee recounted her visions of Christ, listeners decided that "the candle of the Lord was in her hand." That is, she was both a prophet and a seer who equated cleanliness, hard work, and chastity with saintliness. Under her leadership, the Shakers publicly attacked the Anglican Church, adopted lives of strict celibacy, and developed eccentric forms of worship featuring loud singing, "inspired" dancing, shrieking, stamping feet, speaking in unknown tongues, and shaking, hence their name.

In 1774, having suffered constant harassment by the authorities in England, Ann Lee and her followers immigrated to upstate New York. They settled on 200 acres that they named New Lebanon, built a log cabin that housed men on the first floor and women on the second, and pursued Christian perfection by molding a "body of believers" isolated from a corrupt world. Six years later, they began recruiting others to their austere paradise.

Mother Ann died in 1784, but the Shakers found new leaders who spread the movement from New York into New England, Ohio, and Kentucky. By 1830, an estimated 4,000 Shakers lived in about twenty settlements. In these earnest communities, rules ruled. No pets, no rugs (favorite hiding places of the devil, they believed), no mixing of garden plants, no more than one rocking chair in a room, no "scuffing along, but lift your feet squarely and properly." All property was held in common. Life and labor were communal, as in a monastery, and men and women were equal. People of color were welcome. Shaker farms became leading sources of garden seed and medicinal herbs, and many Shaker products, especially furniture, came to be prized worldwide for their clean lines and simple beauty.

The Shakers took great pride in their ability to create stable colonies outside the mainstream of American life. As Mother Ann observed, "We are the people who turned the world upside down." They displayed their utopian faith in the perfectibility of life on earth. What they did not perfect was an ability to convince the orphaned children under their care to follow their example. Of the nearly 200 orphans raised at New Lebanon in New York, only one decided to become a Shaker. The lure of a glittering outside world was too powerful.

BROOK FARM Brook Farm in Massachusetts was the most celebrated utopian community because it grew out of the transcendental movement. George Ripley, a Unitarian minister and transcendentalist, conceived of Brook Farm as a kind of early-day think tank, combining plain living, high thinking, individual expression, and manual labor. In trying to convince Ralph Waldo Emerson to join his effort, Ripley explained: "I have a passion for being independent of the world, and of every man in it." His planned utopia would "insure a more natural union between intellectual and manual labor" by creating a community "of liberal, intelligent, and cultivated persons" leading "a more simple and wholesome life." In 1841, Ripley and several dozen like-minded utopians moved to the 175-acre farm eight miles southwest of Boston.

Brook Farm became America's first secular utopian community. One of its members, novelist Nathaniel Hawthorne, called it "our beautiful scheme of a noble and unselfish life." (He would satirize the community in his novel *The Blithedale Romance*.) Its residents maintained the buildings, tended the fields, and prepared the meals. They also organized picnics, dances, lectures, and discussions. Emerson, Thoreau, and Margaret Fuller were among the visiting lecturers.

In 1846, however, Brook Farm's main building burned, and the community spirit died in the ashes. In the end, such utopian communities had little impact on the outside world.

ONEIDA John Humphrey Noyes, founder of the Oneida Community in upstate New York, took keen interest in Brook Farm but developed a much different vision of the ideal community. The son of a Vermont congressman, Noyes attended Dartmouth College and Yale Divinity School. But in 1834 he was expelled from Yale and his license to preach was revoked after he announced that he was "perfect" and free of all sin, and that God had singled him out to be his divine instrument on earth. He would shepherd people to perfection. In 1836, Noyes gathered a group of "Perfectionists" in Putney, Vermont.

Ten years later, Noyes announced a new doctrine, "complex marriage," which meant that every man in the community was married to every woman, and vice versa. "In a holy community," he claimed, "there is no more reason why sexual intercourse should be restrained by law than why eating and drinking should be." Authorities thought otherwise. They charged Noyes with adultery for practicing his theology of "free love."

He fled to New York and in 1848 established the Oneida Community, which had more than 200 members by 1851 and became famous for producing fine silverware. Oneida would outlive Brook Farm, Noyes claimed, because the Massachusetts commune had "left God out of their tale and they came to nothing." He also told his followers that they would not make the mistake of

Oneida Community Known for its practice of "complex marriage," Oneida was a utopian community that disavowed private property and emphasized "free love." In this photo from 1870, members of the Oneida Community relax on the front lawn of the Oneida Mansion.

the Shakers. True, the Shakers had realized that "the law of marriage 'worketh wrath'" by putting men and women into competition with one another and creating a corrosive "egotism for two." But the Shakers were mistaken to center their lives on sexual abstinence.

Oneida would survive by promoting free sex. Adults would have multiple sexual partners and access to surprisingly effective birth control methods. Noyes separated couples that grew too fond of each other ("sticky love") and conveniently announced that it was his duty as "first husband" to initiate virgin women into sexual activity. Equally repellent were his experiments in scientific breeding, where he paired couples based on their positive attributes. Over ten years, Oneida produced sixty-two children from these pairings, ten of whom were fathered by Noyes. It was Noyes that Emerson had in mind when he wrote that many reformers "have their high origin in an ideal justice, but they do not retain the purity of an idea."

Like the Shakers, the Oneida Community banned private property. The various types of work were shared and rotated among the entire community. Everyone labored for the common good; selfishness would be eliminated on the road to perfection.

What none of the hundred or so utopian experiments resolved was the fundamental tension inherent in all perfectionist schemes: how to maintain solidarity when residents develop and display conflicting notions of paradise and perfection. As Adin Ballou of the Massachusetts Hopedale commune said after it closed, "few people are near enough right in heart, head, and habits to live in close social intimacy."

Although only a few of the utopian communities survived, they provided inspiration and hope for seekers who had given up on life as it was. In the end, utopianism also provided a dose of everyday reality sufficient to send them back to mainstream society. Idealists desperate enough to build a heaven on earth are usually destined for an unexpected hell of their own making.

THE ANTI-SLAVERY MOVEMENT

The collapse of perfectionist utopias created a vacuum in the reform movement that the anti-slavery crusade quickly filled. Many of those who participated in communitarian experiments ended up playing key roles in the abolitionist movement. Transcendentalist reformer Theodore Parker declared that slavery was "the blight of this nation, the curse of the North and the curse of the South."

The men who drafted the U.S. Constitution in 1787 hoped to keep the new nation from splitting apart over the question of slavery. To do so, they negotiated compromises to avoid dealing with the explosive issue. Still, most of the founders knew that eventually there would be a day of reckoning.

EARLY OPPOSITION TO SLAVERY The first organized emancipation movement appeared in 1816 with the formation of the **American Colonization Society** (ACS) in Washington, D.C., whose mission was to raise funds to "repatriate" free blacks back to Africa. Its supporters included James Madison, James Monroe, Andrew Jackson, Henry Clay, John Marshall, and Daniel Webster.

Some supported the colonization movement because they opposed slavery; others saw it as a way to get rid of free blacks. "We must save the Negro," one missionary explained, "or the Negro will ruin us." White supremacy remained a powerful assumption.

Leaders of the free black community denounced the colonization idea. The United States, they stressed, was their native land, and they had as valid a claim on U.S. citizenship as anyone else. "America is more our country than it is the whites," argued David Walker, an African American living in Boston. "We have enriched it with our blood and tears."

Nevertheless, the ACS acquired land on the Ivory Coast of West Africa, and on February 6, 1820, the *Elizabeth* sailed from New York with eighty-eight emigrants who formed the nucleus of a new nation, the Republic of Liberia.

Thereafter, however, the African colonization movement waned. During the 1830s, only 2,638 African Americans migrated to Liberia. In all, only about 15,000 resettled in Africa.

FROM GRADUALISM TO ABOLITIONISM The fight against slavery started in Great Britain in the late eighteenth century, and the movement's success in ending British involvement in the African slave trade helped spur the anti-slavery cause in America. British abolitionists lectured across the northern United States and often bought freedom for runaway slaves. Most of the leading American abolitionists visited Great Britain and came away inspired by the breadth and depth of anti-slavery organizations there.

The British example helped convince leaders of the cause in America to adopt an aggressive new strategy in the early 1830s. Equally important was the realization that slavery in the cotton states of the South was not dying out; it was rapidly growing.

This hard reality led to a change in tactics among anti-slavery organizations, many of which were energized by evangelical religions and the emerging social activism of transcendentalism. Their initial efforts to promote a *gradual* end to slavery by prohibiting it in the western territories and using moral persuasion to convince owners to free their slaves steadily gave way to demands for *immediate* **abolition** everywhere.

The reason for the shift was largely religious: to a new generation of reformers who came of age amid the Second Great Awakening, slavery was not simply evil, it was a sin, and Christians had an obligation to purge all sins, personal and societal. The abolitionists found in the goal of immediate emancipation a perfectionist formula for casting off the guilt of slavery. Theirs would be a moral crusade rather than a political movement. As the preamble to the American Anti-Slavery Society promised: "We shall send forth agents to lift up the voice of remonstrance, of warning, of entreaty, and of rebuke" to slaveholders everywhere.

By the 1820s, every northern state had abolished slavery. As the anti-slavery movement grew, it came to encompass a wide spectrum of attitudes. Some, like Abraham Lincoln, were gradualists. They focused on preventing the extension of slavery into the new western territories in the hope that slavery would eventually die out in the South. Others, known as immediatists, called for the immediate abolition of slavery everywhere.

WILLIAM LLOYD GARRISON A zealous white activist named William Lloyd Garrison drove the movement. Born in 1805 in Newburyport, Massachusetts, Garrison learned the printing trade and moved to Boston.

There he embraced the reform spirit of the era, writing anonymous letters and essays decrying alcohol abuse, Sabbath-breaking, and war.

But it was slavery that most excited his indignation. In 1831, free blacks helped convince Garrison to launch an anti-slavery newspaper, *The Liberator*, which became the voice of the nation's first civil rights movement. Of the first 500 subscribers, 450 were free blacks, leading Garrison to explain that *The Liberator* did not belong to whites—"They do not sustain it." Rather, people of color kept the newspaper afloat—"It is their organ."

William Lloyd Garrison A militant abolitionist and a committed pacifist.

In the first issue, Garrison condemned "the popular but pernicious doctrine of gradual emancipation." He dreamed of immediate equality in all spheres of American life, including the status of women. In pursuing that dream, he vowed to be "as harsh as truth, and as uncompromising as justice. . . . I am in earnest—I will not equivocate—I will not excuse—I will *not retreat a* single inch—and I WILL BE HEARD."

Garrison's courage in denouncing slavery as "the one great, distinctive, all-conquering sin in America" outraged slaveholders in the South, as well as some whites in the North. In 1835, a mob of angry whites dragged him through the streets of Boston. The South Carolina and Georgia legislatures promised a $5,000 reward to anyone who kidnapped Garrison and brought him south for trial. The intensity of the southern reaction wrecked the assumption of "Garrisonians" that moral righteousness would trump evil and that their fellow Americans would listen to reason.

Garrison's unflagging efforts helped make the impossible—abolition—seem possible to more and more people. Two wealthy New York City silk merchants, Arthur and Lewis Tappan, provided financial support, and in 1833, they joined with Garrison and a group of Quaker reformers, free blacks, and evangelicals to organize the American Anti-Slavery Society (AASS).

That same year, Parliament freed some 800,000 enslaved colonial peoples throughout the British Empire by passing the Emancipation Act, which paid slaveholders to give up their "human property." In 1835, the Tappans hired revivalist Charles G. Finney to head the anti-slavery faculty at Oberlin, a new college in northern Ohio that would be the first to admit black students.

In 1835, the group began flooding the South with anti-slavery pamphlets and newspapers. The materials so enraged southern slaveholders that a Louisiana community offered a $50,000 reward for the capture of the "notorious abolitionist, Arthur Tappan, of New York." Post offices throughout the South began destroying "anti-slavery propaganda."

By 1840, some 160,000 people belonged to the American Anti-Slavery Society, which stressed that "slaveholding is a heinous crime in the sight of God, and that the duty, safety, and best interests of all concerned, require its *immediate abandonment*." The AASS even argued that blacks should have full social and civil rights.

DAVID WALKER The most radical figure among the Garrisonians was David Walker, a free black who owned a used clothing store in Boston serving mostly seamen. In 1829, he published his *Appeal to the Colored Citizens of the World*, a pamphlet that denounced the hypocrisy of white Christians in the South for defending slavery, calling them "an unjust, jealous, unmerciful, avaricious, and bloodthirsty" people. Using religious imagery and spiritual fervor, he urged slaves to revolt. "The whites want slaves, and want us for their slaves," Walker warned, "but some of them will curse the day they ever saw us."

He challenged African Americans, slave and free, to use the "crushing arm of power" to gain their freedom. "Woe, woe will be to you," he threatened whites, "if we have to obtain our freedom by fighting."

Copies of Walker's *Appeal* were secretly carried to the South by black sailors who had frequented his shop, but whites in major cities seized the "vile" pamphlet. In 1830, the state of Mississippi outlawed efforts to "print, write, circulate, or put forth . . . any book, paper, magazine, pamphlet, handbill or circular" intended to arouse the "colored population" by "exciting riots and rebellion." By then, however, David Walker had been discovered dead near the doorway of his shop. His murderer was never found.

A SPLIT IN THE MOVEMENT As the abolitionist movement spread, debates over tactics intensified. The Garrisonians, who felt that slavery had corrupted all aspects of American life, embraced every important reform movement of the day: abolition, temperance, pacifism, vegetarianism, and women's rights. Garrison's unconventional religious ideas and social ideals led him to break with the established Protestant churches, which, to his mind, were in league with slavery, as was the federal government. The U.S. Constitution, he charged, was "a covenant with death and an agreement with hell."

Garrison was such a moral purist that he even refused to vote and encouraged others to do the same, arguing that the nation could not continue to proclaim the ideal of liberty while tolerating the reality of slavery. He believed that the South could be shamed into ending slavery.

Other reformers saw American society as fundamentally sound and concentrated on purging it of slavery. Garrison struck them as an unrealistic fanatic whose radicalism hurt the cause. Even Harriet Beecher Stowe, who would write *Uncle Tom's Cabin* (1852), called Garrisonians "moral monomaniacs." The Tappan brothers eventually broke with Garrison over religion. They argued that the anti-slavery movement should be led only by men of "evangelical piety" and declared that the Unitarians and Universalists in New England failed to meet that standard.

THE GRIMKÉ SISTERS A showdown between the rival anti-slavery camps erupted in 1840 over the issue of women's rights, with the scandalous activities of the Grimké sisters serving as the catalyst.

Sarah and Angelina Grimké, born to a wealthy South Carolina family, grew up being served by slaves. In 1821, soon after her father's death, Sarah moved

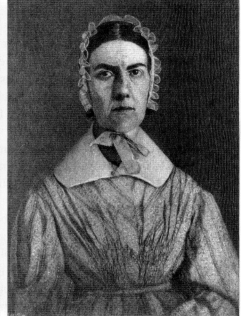

Sarah (left) and Angelina (right) Grimké After moving away from their South Carolina slaveholding family, the Grimké sisters devoted themselves to abolitionism and feminism.

from Charleston to Philadelphia, joined the Society of Friends (Quakers), and renounced slavery. Angelina soon followed her, and in 1835, the sisters joined the abolitionist movement, speaking to northern women's groups. After they appealed to southern Christian women to end slavery, the mayor of Charleston told their mother that they would be jailed if they returned home.

The Grimké sisters traveled widely, speaking first to audiences of women and eventually to groups of both sexes. Their unconventional ("promiscuous") behavior in speaking to mixed-gender audiences prompted sharp criticism from ministers in the anti-slavery movement. Catharine Beecher reminded the sisters that women occupied "a subordinate relation in society to the other sex" and that they should limit their activities to the "domestic and social circle."

Angelina Grimké firmly rejected such arguments: "The investigation of the rights of the slave has led me to a better understanding of my own [rights]." For centuries, she noted, women had been raised to view themselves as "inferior creatures." Now, she insisted, "It is a woman's right to have a voice in all laws and regulations by which she is to be governed, whether in church or in state." Soon, she and her sister began linking their efforts to free the slaves with their desire to free women from male domination. "Men and women are CREATED EQUAL!" Sarah Grimké said. "Whatever is right for man to do is right for woman."

THE ROLE OF WOMEN   The debate over the role of women in the anti-slavery movement exploded at the American Anti-Slavery Society's annual meeting in 1840, where the Garrisonians convinced a majority of delegates that women should participate equally in the organization. The Tappans and their supporters walked out and formed the American and Foreign Anti-Slavery Society.

A third faction of the American Anti-Slavery Society had grown skeptical that the nonviolent "moral suasion" promoted by Garrison would ever lead to abolition. They decided that political action was the most effective way to pursue their goal.

In 1840, activists formed the Liberty party in an effort to elect an American president who would restrict the spread of slavery. What had been a moral and religious crusade became a political movement. The Liberty party's presidential nominee, James Gillespie Birney, was a former Alabama slaveholder turned anti-slavery activist. His slogan was "vote as you pray, and pray as you vote." The platform called not for immediate abolition but for banning slavery in the western territories and the District of Columbia.

Yet the Liberty party found few supporters. In the 1840 election, Birney polled only 7,000 votes. In 1844, however, he would win 60,000. Thereafter, an anti-slavery party contested every national election until the Thirteenth Amendment officially ended slavery in 1865.

BLACK ANTI-SLAVERY ACTIVITY

Although many whites worked to end slavery, most of them, unlike William Lloyd Garrison, still insisted that blacks were socially inferior, and many expected free blacks to take a backseat in the movement.

Yet free African Americans were crucial in transforming the struggle against slavery into a more ambitious fight against racial discrimination, which remained widespread in most states. Even free blacks were barred from public places—churches, schools, hotels, railroad stations, and cemeteries. As Garrison reported from Boston, "Hardly any doors but those of our state prisons were open to our colored brethren."

WILLIAM WELLS BROWN Much of the energy and appeal of the abolitionist movement derived from the compelling testimonies provided by former slaves. Henry Bibb and William Wells Brown, both runaways from Kentucky, and Frederick Douglass, who had escaped from Maryland, and Sojourner Truth, a runaway from New York, became the most effective critics of the South's "peculiar institution."

Brown was just twenty years old when he escaped from his owner, a steamboat pilot on the Ohio River. An Ohio Quaker named Wells Brown provided shelter to the runaway, and Brown adopted the man's name while forging a new identity as a free man. He settled in Cleveland, Ohio, where he was a dockworker. He married, had three children, and helped runaway slaves cross the border into Canada. By 1842, he had learned to read and write, begun to publish columns in abolitionist newspapers, and was in great demand as a speaker at anti-slavery meetings. In 1847, he moved to Boston, where the Massachusetts Anti-Slavery Society hired him as a traveling lecturer.

That same year, the organization published Brown's autobiography, *Narrative of William W. Brown, A Fugitive Slave, Written by Himself,* which became a best seller. Brown gave thousands of speeches calling for an end to slavery and equality for both blacks and women. He stressed that African Americans were "endowed with those intellectual and amiable qualities which adorn and dignify human nature."

FREDERICK DOUGLASS Frederick Douglass was an even more effective spokesman for abolitionism. After escaping from Maryland, he made his way to Massachusetts, where he began speaking at anti-slavery meetings

Frederick Douglass and Sojourner Truth Both former slaves, Douglass and Truth were leading African American abolitionists and captivating orators.

in black churches. The Massachusetts Anti-Slavery Society recruited him as a traveling speaker, sending him across New England and west to Ohio and Indiana. He recounted his painful encounters with "the whip, the chain, the gag, the thumbscrew, the bloodhound, the stocks, and all the other bloody paraphernalia of the slave system."

Through his writings and dazzling presentations, Douglass became the best-known man of color in America. "I appear before the immense assembly this evening as a thief and a robber," he told a Massachusetts group in 1842. "I stole this head, these limbs, this body from my master, and ran off with them."

After publishing his *Narrative of the Life of Frederick Douglass, An American Slave* (1845), Douglass, fearing that his prominence would make him accessible to fugitive slave catchers, left for an extended lecture tour of the British Isles. He returned two years later with enough money to purchase his freedom. He then started an abolitionist newspaper for blacks, the *North Star*, in Rochester, New York. He named the newspaper after the star that runaway slaves used to guide them toward freedom.

SOJOURNER TRUTH African American women were immensely influential in the abolitionist movement. Sojourner Truth was born to enslaved parents in upstate New York in 1797. She was given the name Isabella "Bell" Hardenbergh but renamed herself in 1843 after experiencing a conversation with God, who told her "to travel up and down the land" preaching "the truth" against slavery. A slave until she was freed in 1827, Truth spoke with conviction about the evils of the "peculiar institution" as well as the inequality of women.

She traveled throughout the North during the 1840s and 1850s. As she told the Ohio Women's Rights Convention in 1851, "I have plowed, and planted, and gathered into barns, and no man could head me—and ar'n't I a woman? I have borne thirteen children, and seen 'em mos' all sold off into slavery, and when I cried out with a mother's grief, none but Jesus heard—and ar'n't I a woman?"

Through such compelling testimony, Sojourner Truth tapped the distinctive energies that women brought to reformist causes. "If the first woman God ever made was strong enough to turn the world upside down all alone," she concluded in her address to the Ohio gathering, "these women together ought to be able to turn it back, and get it right side up again!"

THE UNDERGROUND RAILROAD Between 1810 and 1850, tens of thousands of southern slaves fled North. Runaways would make their way, usually at night, from one "station," or safe house, to the next. The organizations and the systems of safe houses and shelters in the border states such as Maryland and Kentucky (and farther north) were referred to as the **Underground Railroad**. The "conductors" helping the runaways included freeborn blacks, white abolitionists, former slaves, and Native Americans. Unitarians, Quakers, Presbyterians, Methodists, and Baptists participated in substantial ways.

In Philadelphia, William Still, a free black who was a clerk at the Pennsylvania Society for the Abolition of Slavery, sheltered runaway slaves as they made their way to Canada. In the fourteen years he worked as a conductor for the Underground Railroad, he helped almost 800 fugitive slaves make their way to freedom. He later published an account of his efforts, explaining that "It was my good fortune to lend a helping hand to the weary travelers flying from the land of bondage."

A few courageous runaway slaves returned to the South to organize more escapes. Harriet Tubman, the most celebrated member of the Underground Railroad, was born a slave on Maryland's Eastern Shore in 1820 but escaped to Philadelphia in 1849, traveling some 90 miles on foot across Delaware. "I was free," she recalled, "but there was no one to welcome me to the land of freedom. I was a stranger in a strange land." Dressed like a man, she would return to the South nineteen times to help some 300 fugitive slaves, including her parents and brothers. She "never lost a passenger" during her legendary acts of bravery. She carried a pistol with her, and when a fugitive slave would panic and have second thoughts about escaping, she would pull out her gun, point it at the ambivalent runaway, and say, "You'll be free or die a slave."

During the Civil War, Tubman worked as a northern spy and scout, leading Union gunboats in the Carolinas to liberate some 750 Confederate slaves. By then, slaveowners in Maryland were demanding her arrest, dead or alive, and placed a $40,000 bounty on her head. The fearless Tubman explained that "there was two things I had a right to, liberty or death: if I could not have one, I would have the other."

ELIJAH P. LOVEJOY Despite the growing efforts of anti-slavery organizations, racism remained widespread in the North, especially among the working poor. Abolitionist speakers confronted hostile white crowds who disliked blacks or found anti-slavery agitation bad for business. In 1837, a mob in Illinois killed Elijah P. Lovejoy, editor of an anti-slavery newspaper, giving the movement a martyr to the causes of both abolition and freedom of the press.

Lovejoy had begun his career as a Presbyterian minister in New England. After receiving a "sign by God" to focus his life on the "destruction of slavery," he moved to St. Louis, in slaveholding Missouri, where his newspaper denounced alcohol, Catholicism, and slavery. When a pro-slavery mob destroyed his printing office, he moved across the Mississippi River to a warehouse in Alton, Illinois, where he tried to start an anti-slavery society. There mobs twice more destroyed his printing press. When a new press arrived, Lovejoy and several supporters armed themselves and took up defensive positions.

On November 7, 1837, thugs began hurling stones and firing shots into the building. One of Lovejoy's allies fired back, killing a rioter. The mob then set fire to the warehouse. A shotgun blast killed Lovejoy, and his murder aroused a frenzy of indignation. John Quincy Adams said the murder "sent a shock as of any earthquake throughout this continent." In Illinois, young Abraham Lincoln felt those shockwaves. Lovejoy's murder, he noted, was an "ill omen," for the "mob violence" threatened America's core values: "liberty and equal rights."

ABIGAIL KELLEY The powerful appeal of abolitionism and the broader reform impulse is illustrated in the colorful life of Abigail "Abbie" Kelley. A teacher born in Pelham, Massachusetts, in 1811, she initially became a Grahamite, giving up coffee, alcohol, meat, and tea in favor of vegetables and Graham crackers. Soon thereafter, she attended a lecture by William Lloyd Garrison and embraced abolitionism, joining the Female Anti-Slavery Society. In 1837, she wrote her sister that she was supporting a variety of "moral enterprises—Grahamism, Abolition, and Peace."

Kelley was a compelling speaker. In 1840, she was the first woman to be elected an officer in the American Anti-Slavery Society. Many male abolitionists were furious. One of them described Kelley as being one of those "women of masculine minds and aggressive tendencies . . . who cannot be satisfied in domestic life." The prejudice she experienced among male officers revealed to her that she and other women "were manacled [chained] *ourselves*."

During the 1850s, Kelley, while still a passionate abolitionist, began to champion women's rights and temperance. She spoke at the fourth national woman's rights convention in Cleveland. Lucy Stone, one of the women's rights leaders, called Kelley a heroine who "stood in the thick of the fight for the slaves, and at the same time, she hewed out that path over which women are now walking toward their equal political rights."

THE DEFENSE OF SLAVERY

The growing strength and visibility of the abolitionist movement, coupled with the profitability of cotton, prompted Southerners to launch an aggressive defense of slavery. During the 1830s and after, pro-slavery leaders worked out an elaborate rationale for what they considered the benefits of slavery. The Bible was their favorite weapon. Had not the patriarchs of the Hebrew Bible held people in bondage? Had not Saint Paul advised servants to obey their masters and told a runaway servant to return to his master? And had not Jesus remained silent on slavery?

Soon, bolder arguments emerged. In February 1837, South Carolina's John C. Calhoun told the Senate that slavery was "good—a great good," rooted in the Bible. He asserted that the "savage" Africans brought to America "had never existed in so comfortable, so respectable, or so civilized a condition, as that which is now enjoyed in the Southern states." If slavery were abolished, Calhoun warned, the principle of white racial supremacy would be compromised.

Calhoun and others also claimed that blacks were too shiftless, and if freed, they would be a danger to themselves and to others. White workers, on the other hand, feared the competition for jobs if slaves were freed.

The increasingly heated debate over slavery drove a deep wedge between North and South. In 1831, William Lloyd Garrison predicted that an eventual "separation between the free and slave States" was "unavoidable." By midcentury, a large number of Americans had decided that southern slavery was an abomination that should not be allowed to expand into the western territories. The militant reformers who were determined to prevent slavery from expanding outside the South came to be called "free soilers." Their crusade would reach a fiery climax in the Civil War.

CHAPTER REVIEW

SUMMARY

- **Religious Developments** Starting in the late eighteenth century, *Unitarians* and *Universalists* in New England challenged the Christian notion of predestination by arguing that everyone (not just the select few) could receive salvation. The evangelical preachers of the *Second Great Awakening* generated widespread interest among Protestants in fiery *frontier revivals*. The more democratic sects, such as Baptists and Methodists, which promoted the idea of free-will salvation, gained huge numbers of converts, including women and people of color. Religion went hand in hand with reform in the "burned-over district" in western New York, which was also the birthplace of several religious movements, including the Church of Jesus Christ of Latter-day Saints (the *Mormons*).

- **Transcendentalists** A group of New England poets, philosophers, writers, ministers, and reformers embraced a moral and spiritual idealism (Romanticism) in reaction to scientific rationalism and Christian orthodoxy. They sought to "transcend" reason and the material world and encourage more-independent thought and reflection. At the same time, *transcendentalism* influenced novelists, essayists, and poets, who created a uniquely "American" literature.

- **Social-Reform Movements** The *cult of domesticity* celebrated a "woman's sphere" in the home and argued that young women should be trained not for the workplace but in the domestic arts—managing a kitchen, running a household, and nurturing children. However, the rise of an urban middle class offered growing numbers of women more time to devote to societal concerns. Social reformers—many of them women—sought to improve society and eradicate social evils. The most widespread reform movement focused on *temperance*—the elimination of excessive drinking. With the *Seneca Falls Convention* of 1848, social reformers launched the women's rights movement with the *Declaration of Rights and Sentiments*. In many parts of the country, reformers called for greater access to education through free *public schools*. Amid the pervasive climate of reform, more than 100 *utopian communities* were established, including the Shakers, Brook Farm, and the Oneida Community.

- **Anti-Slavery Movement** Northern opponents of slavery promoted several solutions, including the *American Colonization Society's* call for gradual emancipation and the deportation of African Americans to colonies in Africa. *Abolitionism* emerged in the 1830s, demanding an immediate end to slavery. Some abolitionists went even further, calling for full social and political equality among the races, although they disagreed over tactics. Abolitionist efforts in the North provoked fear and resentment among southern whites. Yet many Northerners shared the belief in the racial inferiority of Africans and were hostile to the tactics and message of the abolitionists. African Americans in the North joined with abolitionists to create an *Underground Railroad,* a network of courageous people, both white and black, which helped runaway slaves escape.

CHRONOLOGY

1826	Ministers organize the American Society for the Promotion of Temperance
1830	Percentage of American churchgoers has doubled since 1800
	Joseph Smith publishes the *Book of Mormon*
1831	Charles G. Finney begins preaching in upstate New York
	William Lloyd Garrison begins publishing *The Liberator*
1833	American Anti-Slavery Society is founded
1836	Transcendental Club holds its first meeting
1837	Abolitionist editor Elijah P. Lovejoy is murdered
1840	Abolitionists form the Liberty party
1845	*Narrative of the Life of Frederick Douglass* is published
1846–1847	Mormons, led by Brigham Young, make the difficult trek to Utah
1848	At the Seneca Falls Convention, feminists issue the Declaration of Rights and Sentiments
1851	Sojourner Truth delivers her famous "Ar'n't I a Woman?" speech
1854	Henry David Thoreau's *Walden, or Life in the Woods* is published

KEY TERMS

Unitarians p. 453

Universalists p. 453

Second Great Awakening p. 454

frontier revivals p. 455

Mormons p. 460

transcendentalism p. 464

temperance p. 474

cult of domesticity p. 475

Seneca Falls Convention (1848) p. 476

Declaration of Rights and Sentiments (1848) p. 477

public schools p. 478

utopian communities p. 481

American Colonization Society (ACS) p. 485

abolitionism p. 486

Underground Railroad p. 493

 INQUIZITIVE

Go to InQuizitive to see what you've learned—and learn what you've missed—with personalized feedback along the way.

A HOUSE DIVIDED AND REBUILT

part four

During the first half of the nineteenth century, Americans were optimistic about the future. The nation's population and its boundaries continued to grow rapidly; new roads, canals, and railroads overcame the barrier of distance; new inventions and labor-saving machinery increased dramatically; the economy grew; and tensions with Great Britain eased.

Above all, Americans continued to move westward in great numbers, where cheap land lured farmers, ranchers, miners,

and missionaries. By the end of the 1840s, the United States had again dramatically expanded its territory, from Texas west to California and the Pacific Northwest.

This extraordinary surge of territorial expansion was a mixed blessing, however. How to deal with slavery in the new western territories acquired from Mexico emerged as the nation's flashpoint issue.

A series of political compromises had glossed over the fundamental issue of slavery, but activists opposed efforts to extend slavery into the West, and an emerging generation of politicians proved less willing to compromise. The continuing debate led Abraham Lincoln and others to predict that the nation could not survive half-slave and half-free. Something had to give.

In a last-ditch effort to preserve the institution of slavery, eleven southern states seceded from the Union by 1861 and created a separate Confederate nation, igniting a civil war to restore the Union.

No one realized in 1861 how costly the war would be; some 750,000 soldiers and sailors would die in the struggle. Nor did anyone envision how sweeping the war's effects would be. The North's victory in 1865 restored the Union and helped accelerate America's transformation into a modern urban-industrial superpower. A national consciousness began to replace sectional divisions, and a Republican-led Congress passed legislation to promote industrial and commercial development and western expansion.

Although the Civil War ended slavery, the status of freed African Americans remained precarious during the Reconstruction era. Former slaves found themselves legally free, but few had property, homes, education, or training. Although the Fourteenth Amendment (1868) guaranteed the civil rights of African Americans and the Fifteenth Amendment (1870) declared that black men could vote, southern officials often ignored the new laws (as did some in northern states).

Bitterness and resistance grew among the defeated Southerners. Although Confederate leaders were stripped of voting rights, they continued to exercise considerable authority. In 1877, when the last federal troops were removed from the occupied South, former Confederates declared themselves "redeemed" from the supposed "stain" of northern military occupation and "black rule" during Reconstruction. By the end of the nineteenth century, most of the former Confederacy had developed a system of legal discrimination (the "Jim Crow" system) against blacks that re-created many aspects of slavery.

13 Western Expansion

1830–1848

***Emigrants Crossing the Plains, or the Oregon Trail* (1869)** German American painter Albert Bierstadt captures the majestic sights of the frontier, though the transcontinental trek was also often grueling, bleak, and deadly.

I n the first half of the nineteenth century, most white Americans viewed the westward march of settlement as a renewable source of energy, hope, and yearning. Henry David Thoreau exclaimed that Americans "go westward as into the future, with a spirit of enterprise and adventure"—and the hope of freedom.

The West—whether imagined as the enticing lands over the Allegheny Mountains that became Ohio and Kentucky or, later, the farmlands of the Old Southwest, the fertile prairies watered by the Mississippi River, or the spectacular area along the Pacific coast that became the states of California, Oregon, and Washington—served as a powerful magnet for those who dreamed of freedom, self-fulfillment, and economic gain.

During the 1840s and after, waves of people moved westward. "If hell lay to the west," one pioneer declared, "Americans would cross heaven to get there." People endured unrelenting hardships to fulfill what many viewed as their "manifest destiny" to subdue the entire continent, even if it meant displacing Indians in the process. By 1860, some 4.3 million people had traversed the mile-wide Mississippi River and streamed across the Great Plains and Rocky Mountains to the Pacific coast.

Pioneers moved West largely for economic reasons. Enterprising trappers, farmers, miners, merchants, clerks, hunters, ranchers, teachers, household servants, and prostitutes, among others, headed West to seek their fortunes. "To make money was their chief object," said a Texas woman. Others sought religious freedom or converts to Christianity.

Of course, the West was not empty land. Others had been there long before the American migration. The Native American and Hispanic inhabitants of

focus questions

1. Why did Americans move west of the Mississippi River during the 1830s and 1840s? How did they accomplish this, and where did they move to?

2. How did Texas become part of the United States? Why was the process so complicated, and how did it impact national politics?

3. What were the similarities and differences in how California and Texas were settled and how they became part of the United States?

4. How did opposition to the Mexican-American War complicate national politics?

the region, however, soon found themselves swept aside as U.S. presidents and congressmen encouraged the nation's continental expansion.

Westward expansion was especially important to Southerners, many of whom viewed the new territories as a source of cheap land on which to grow cotton using slave labor. Southerners wanted governments of new western states to ensure that Northerners in Congress could never abolish slavery. As a Mississippi senator said, "I would spread the blessings of slavery . . . to the uttermost ends of the earth." Such motives made the addition of western lands a flashpoint of sectional debate. Would the new western territories be slave or free?

Southerners had long enjoyed disproportionate political power because of the provision in the U.S. Constitution that counted slaves as part of the population in determining the number of congressional seats for each state. Most of the first sixteen presidents were from the South, and Southerners held most of the leadership positions in Congress. But as the industrializing Midwest and Northeast grew and increased their representation in Congress, southern influence began to wane. This raised the great fear in the South that they would soon be outnumbered in a Congress that could vote to eliminate slavery.

MOVING WEST

In 1845, New York newspaper editor John L. O'Sullivan gave a catchy name to the nation's aggressive expansion. "Our **manifest destiny**," he wrote, "is to overspread and to possess the whole of the continent which Providence has given us for the free development of our yearly multiplying millions . . . [and for the] great experiment of liberty." O'Sullivan spoke for many who wanted to take control of all of North America: "Yes, more, more, more . . . until our national destiny is fulfilled."

The idea of a "manifest destiny" assumed that the United States had a God-given mission to extend its Christian republic and capitalist civilization from the Atlantic to the Pacific—and beyond. It also took for granted the superiority of American ideals and institutions, including the opportunity to bring liberty and prosperity to native peoples. This notion of manifest ("self-evident") destiny offered a moral justification for territorial growth and the expansion of slavery. However idealized, though, manifest destiny was in essence a cluster of flimsy rationalizations and racist attitudes justifying the conquest of weaker peoples.

THE WESTERN FRONTIER   Most western pioneers were American-born whites from the Upper South and the Midwest. What spurred the massive migration was the population explosion in the United States and the

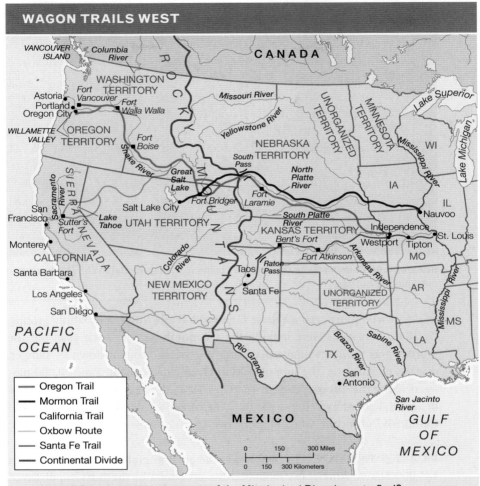

WAGON TRAILS WEST

VANCOUVER
ISLAND

Columbia
River

CANADA

WASHINGTON
TERRITORY

Astoria
Portland
Oregon City

Fort
Vancouver

Fort
Walla Walla

Missouri River

UNORGANIZED TERRITORY

MINNESOTA TERRITORY

Lake Superior

WILLAMETTE
VALLEY

OREGON
TERRITORY

Fort
Boise

Yellowstone River

NEBRASKA
TERRITORY

WI

Lake Michigan

Snake River

South
Pass

North
Platte
River

IA

Mississippi River

SIERRA NEVADA

Great
Salt
Lake

Fort Bridger

Fort
Laramie

IL

San
Francisco

Sutter's
Fort

Salt Lake City

Lake
Tahoe

UTAH TERRITORY

South Platte
River

KANSAS TERRITORY

Bent's Fort

Independence

Nauvoo

Westport   Tipton

St. Louis

Sacramento River

Monterey

CALIFORNIA

Santa Barbara

Los Angeles

San Diego

Colorado River

NEW MEXICO
TERRITORY

Taos

Santa Fe

Fort Atkinson

Arkansas River

Raton
Pass

UNORGANIZED
TERRITORY

MO

AR

Mississippi River

MS

PACIFIC
OCEAN

Rio Grande

TX

San
Antonio

Brazos River

Sabine River

LA

MEXICO

San Jacinto
River

GULF
OF
MEXICO

Legend	
—	Oregon Trail
—	Mormon Trail
—	California Trail
—	Oxbow Route
—	Santa Fe Trail
—	Continental Divide

0   150   300 Miles

0   150   300 Kilometers

- What did settlers migrating west of the Mississippi River hope to find?
- What were the perils of the Overland Trails?
- Describe the experience of a typical settler traveling on the Overland Trails.

widespread desire for land and wealth. California was an especially attractive destination, in part because gold was discovered there in 1848.

In the rush to the gold fields, some people traveled 13,000 miles by sea from Boston or New York City to reach California, sailing around the southern tip of South America and then up the Pacific coast. Most went overland, however. Between 1841 and 1867, some 350,000 men, women, and children made the difficult trek to California or Oregon, while many others settled in such areas as Colorado, Texas, and Arkansas.

***Buffalo Hunt, Chasing Back* (1860s)** This painting by George Catlin shows a hunter outrunning a buffalo.

Most who journeyed on these **Overland Trails** traveled in family groups. By 1845, thousands were making the six-month journey each year, but the journey was perilous: many died along the trails, brought down by hunger, disease, or violence. The lure of gold in California brought some 30,000 pioneers along the Oregon Trail in 1849. By 1850, the peak year along the trail, the annual count had risen to 55,000. "Any man who makes a trip by land to California," observed Alonzo Delano in 1849, "deserves to find a fortune."

PLAINS INDIANS In 1840, when the great migration began, more than 325,000 Native Americans inhabited the area west of the Mississippi River. They represented more than 200 nations, each with its own language, religion, cultural practices, and system of governance. Some were primarily farmers; others were nomadic hunters, following buffalo herds.

Native American life on the plains depended upon the abundance of buffalo, and the influx of white settlers and hunters posed a direct threat to the Indians' survival. When federal officials could not force Indian leaders to sell their lands, fighting ensued. After the discovery of gold in California, the wave of white expansion flowed all the way to the west coast, engulfing Native Americans and Mexicans in its wake.

MEXICO AND THE SPANISH WEST As American settlers trespassed across Indian lands, they also encountered Spanish-speaking peoples. Many whites were as prejudiced toward Hispanics as they were toward Indians and African Americans. Senator Lewis Cass from Michigan, who would be the Democratic candidate for president in 1848, expressed the common bias among white expansionists: "We do not want the people of Mexico, either as citizens or as subjects. All we want is their . . . territory."

The centuries-old Spanish efforts at colonization in the northernmost provinces of Mexico had been less successful in Arizona and Texas than in New Mexico and Florida. The Yuma and Apaches in Arizona and the Comanches and Apaches in Texas thwarted Spanish efforts to establish Catholic missions. By 1790, the Hispanic population in Texas numbered only 2,510, while in New Mexico it exceeded 20,000.

In 1807, French forces led by Napoléon had occupied Spain and imprisoned the king, creating confusion throughout Spain's colonial possessions in the Western Hemisphere, including Mexico. Miguel Hidalgo y Costilla, a creole priest (born in Mexico of European ancestry), took advantage of the fluid situation to convince Indians and Hispanics to revolt against Spanish rule in Mexico, but the poorly organized uprising failed.

In 1820, Mexican creoles again tried to liberate themselves. Facing a growing revolt, the last Spanish officials withdrew in 1821, and Mexico became an independent nation. However, it struggled to develop a stable government and an effective economy. Americans eagerly took advantage of Mexico's instability, especially in its northern provinces—areas that included present-day Texas, New Mexico, Arizona, Nevada, California, and portions of Colorado, Oklahoma, Kansas, and Wyoming.

Fur traders streamed into New Mexico and Arizona, developing a profitable commerce along the Santa Fe Trail to St. Louis. During the 1830s and 1840s, thousands of Americans made the journey in wagons on the Santa Fe Trail from Missouri to New Mexico. The trek was not for the fainthearted. In 1847 alone, marauding Indians, determined to stem the flow of the westward movement, killed forty-seven Americans, destroyed 330 wagons, and stole 6,500 horses, cattle, and oxen along the trail.

THE OVERLAND TRAILS During the early nineteenth century, the Far Northwest consisted of the Nebraska, Washington, and Oregon Territories. The Oregon Country included what became the states of Oregon, Idaho, and Washington, parts of Montana and Wyoming, and the Canadian province of British Columbia. It was an unsettled region claimed by both Great Britain and the United States. By the Convention of 1818, the two nations agreed to "joint occupation" of the Oregon Country, each drawn there initially by the profitable trade in fur pelts.

During the 1820s and 1830s, the fur trade inspired a reckless breed of "mountain men" to embrace a rough-hewn, solitary existence in the wilderness.

***Fur Traders Descending the Missouri* (1845)** Originally titled "French-Trader, Half-Breed Son," this oil painting depicts a white settler sailing down the river with his half–Native American son—not an uncommon sight in western America.

Among the most rugged and adventurous of the fur trappers was Jedediah Smith, who in 1826 left the Great Salt Lake in Utah, crossed the Mojave Desert, and entered southern California, thereby becoming the first white American to enter California from the east.

THE GREAT MIGRATION   Word of Oregon's fertile soil, plentiful rainfall, and magnificent forests gradually spread eastward. By 1840, a trickle of farmers, missionaries, teachers, fur traders, and shopkeepers was flowing along the Oregon Trail, a 2,000-mile footpath that connected the Missouri River near St. Louis with the Columbia River valley in Oregon, slicing across the ancestral lands of Plains Indians.

Soon, "**Oregon fever**" swept the nation, especially after the federal government promised 160 acres of free land to any settler who worked the property for four years. Some pioneers desperately sought to escape debts, or dull lives, or bad marriages. "We had nothing to lose," wrote one woman, "and we might gain a fortune." Tens of thousands began moving their families West. Many never made it to Oregon.

In 1841 and 1842, the first sizable wagon trains made the long trip across half the continent, and in 1843 the movement became a mass migration. Most of the pioneers walked the 2,000 miles. All their food and worldly goods were packed in wagons called prairie schooners, or Conestogas, after the valley in Pennsylvania where they were first built. Teams of mules or oxen pulled the sturdy, canvas-covered wagons, whose ends were higher than the sides to keep cargo from falling out when traveling up mountain ridges. The wheels were especially wide to enable the wagons to traverse mud or sand, and they could be removed to float the wagons across streams and rivers.

One pioneer remembered that the wagon trains were like mobile communities. "Everybody was supposed to rise at daylight, and while the women were preparing breakfast, the men rounded up the cattle, took down the tents, yoked the oxen to the wagons, and made everything ready to start." They found Oregon in a "primitive state" requiring backbreaking work to create self-sustaining homesteads. Women worked as hard as men, day and night. "I am a very old woman," reported twenty-nine-year-old Sarah Everett. "My face is thin, sunken, and wrinkled, my hands bony, withered, and hard." One Oregon pioneer warned that a "woman that cannot endure almost as much as a horse has no business here."

The wagon trains followed the Oregon Trail west from Independence, Missouri, along the winding North Platte River into what is now Wyoming, through South Pass to Fort Bridger, then down the Snake River through what is now Idaho to the salmon-filled Columbia River. From there, they moved through the Cascade Mountains to Oregon.

As the numbers of migrants along the Oregon Trail grew, they tore through Native American lands and culture. Buffalo disappeared, and nations like the Cheyenne and the Arapaho were forced to split into northern and southern branches. In negotiating treaties with the Native Americans, the federal government insisted that they be relocated onto reservations far from the Oregon Trail, which eventually served as the route for the Union Pacific Railroad.

LIFE ON THE TRAIL Traveling in prairie schooners, the sunburned settlers bumped and jostled their way across rugged trails, mountains, and plains blackened by vast herds of buffaloes.

Indians rarely attacked the wagon trains on the Oregon Trail; in fact, many served as guides, advisers, or traders. To be sure, as the number of pioneers grew during the 1850s, disputes with Indians over land and water increased, but never to the degree portrayed in novels, films, and television shows.

Still, the long journey west, usually five to six months, was an exodus of grinding hardship during broiling summers; fierce thunderstorms; and snowy, bitterly cold winters. Wagons broke down, oxen died, and diseases like cholera and dysentery took their toll. "The cowards never started," a popular saying went, "and the weak died on the way."

WOMEN PIONEERS The diary of Amelia Knight, who set out for Oregon in 1853 with her husband and seven children, reveals the threats along the trail: "Chatfield quite sick with scarlet fever. A calf took sick and died before breakfast. Lost one of our oxen; he dropped dead in the yoke. I could hardly help shedding tears. Yesterday my eighth child was born."

Cholera claimed many lives because of tainted water and contaminated food. On average, there was one grave every eighty yards along the trail. Each step "of the slow, plodding cattle," wrote a woman emigrant, "carried us farther and farther from civilization into a desolate, barbarous country."

Initially, the pioneers adopted the same division of labor used back East. Women cooked, washed, sewed, and monitored the children, while men drove the wagons, tended the horses and cattle, and did the heavy labor. But the demands of the western trails soon dissolved such neat distinctions. Women found themselves gathering buffalo dung for fuel, driving wagons, working to dislodge wagons mired in mud, helping to construct makeshift bridges, pitching tents, or participating in other "unladylike" tasks.

Southerner Lavinia Porter described the trip along the California Trail as so difficult that it was still "a source of wonder to me how we [women] were able to endure it." She became convinced that the American woman was "endowed with the courage of her brave pioneer ancestors, and no matter what the environment she can adapt herself to all situations, even the perilous trip across the western half of this great continent."

The hard labor of the trail strained relationships and provoked social tensions. Divorces soared in the West. Many a tired pioneer could identify with the following comment in a girl's journal: "Poor Ma said only this morning, 'Oh, I wish we had never started.' She looks so sorrowful and dejected." Another woman wondered "what had possessed my husband, anyway, that he should have thought of bringing us away out through this God forsaken country."

Some of the emigrants turned back, but most continued on, and once in Oregon or California, they set about establishing stable communities. Noted one settler: "Friday, October 27. Arrived at Oregon City at the falls of the Willamette River. Saturday, October 28. Went to work."

The struggle to establish new lives devastated many migrants. The Malick family, for example, left Illinois in 1848 and started a farm in the Oregon Territory. George Malick, the father, died soon thereafter, as did three of the older children. "We are all well," widow Abigail Malick wrote in 1855 to relatives in Illinois. "All that are left of us."

THE SETTLEMENT OF CALIFORNIA   California was also a powerful magnet. It had first felt the influence of European culture in 1769, when Spain, concerned about Russian seal traders moving south along the Pacific coast from Alaska, sent a naval expedition to settle the region. The Spanish discovered San Francisco Bay and constructed *presidios* (military garrisons)

American pioneers This 1850 photograph captures some of the many pioneers who headed west for brighter futures.

at San Diego and Monterey. Even more important, Franciscan friars, led by Junípero Serra, established a Catholic mission at San Diego. Over the next fifty years, Franciscans built twenty more missions, from San Diego northward to San Francisco.

The mission-centered culture in California was quite different from those in Texas and New Mexico, where the original missions were converted into secular communities and the property was divided among the Indians. In California, the missions were much larger, more influential, and longer lasting.

By the nineteenth century, Spanish Catholic missionaries, aided by Spanish soldiers, controlled most of the Indians living along the California coast. The friars (priests) enticed the Indians into missions by offering gifts or impressing them with "magical" religious rituals. Once inside the missions, the Indians were baptized as Catholics, taught Spanish, and stripped of their cultural heritage.

CATHOLIC MISSIONS The California Catholic missions served as churches, villages, fortresses, homes, schools, shops, farms, and outposts of Spanish rule. They quickly became agricultural enterprises, producing crops, livestock, clothing, and household goods, both for profit and to supply the neighboring presidios. Indians provided most of the labor.

A mission's daily routine began at dawn with the ringing of a bell, which summoned the community to prayer. Work began an hour later and did not end until an hour before sunset. Most Indian men worked in the fields. Women handled domestic chores, but during harvest season, everyone was expected to help in the fields. Instead of wages, the Indians received clothing, food, housing, and religious instruction.

Rebellious Native Americans were whipped or imprisoned, and mission Indians died at an alarming rate. One friar reported that "of every four Indian children born, three die in their first or second year, while those who survive do not reach the age of twenty-five." Infectious disease was the primary threat, but the grueling labor regimen took a high toll as well. The Native American population along the California coast declined from 72,000 in 1769 to 18,000 by 1821. Saving souls cost many lives.

With Mexican independence in 1821, the Spanish missions slowly fell into disuse. By the time the first Americans began to trickle into California, they found a vast, beautiful province with only a small, scattered population of 6,000 Mexicans ruled by a few dominant *caballeros* or *rancheros*—"gentlemen" who owned the largest ranches in the province, much like the planters who lorded over the Lower South.

Among the white immigrants to California was John A. Sutter, a Swiss settler who had founded a colony of European emigrants. He had left behind his debts and family in Europe to make his fortune in America. At the junction of the Sacramento and American Rivers (later the site of the city of Sacramento), Sutter hired local Indians and whites from America and Europe to build a fort with walls eighteen feet tall to protect the settlers and their workshops. Completed in 1843, Sutter's Fort stood at the end of the California Trail, which forked southward off the Oregon Trail and led through the Sierra Nevada.

Sutter set about creating a wilderness empire. In addition to trading furs, he put Indians to work making wool blankets and hats; cultivating vast acres of wheat and corn; and raising huge herds of cattle, sheep, hogs, and horses.

By 1846, there were perhaps 800 Americans in California, along with approximately 10,000 *Californios* and some 150,000 Native Americans. While Sutter paid his Indian workers, he also whipped, jailed, and even executed those who disobeyed his orders. The American migrants learned to speak Spanish, often embraced Catholicism, won Mexican citizenship, found Spanish or Native American spouses, and participated in local politics.

THE DONNER PARTY The most tragic story of pioneers traveling to California involved the party headed by George Donner, a prosperous sixty-two-year-old farmer from Illinois.

In mid-April 1846, Donner led his family in a train of seventy-four other settlers and twenty-three wagons from Springfield, Illinois, to the Oregon Trail. Early on, Donner's wife's outlook was optimistic: "Indeed, if I do not experience something far worse than I have yet done, I shall say that the trouble all is in getting started."

But "the trouble" soon appeared, for the Donner party made several fatal mistakes: starting too late in the year, overloading their wagons, and taking a foolish shortcut to California southward across the Wasatch Mountains and toward the Great Salt Lake in the Utah Territory. The group had inadequate food, water, clothing, and experience. As their challenges mounted, discipline broke down. One settler was murdered for his gold; another was banished after killing a man in self-defense; and a third, unable to walk, was left behind to die.

In the Wasatch Range, the Donner party got lost and was forced to backtrack, losing three precious weeks in the process. An early September snow further slowed their progress. They eventually found their way into the desert leading to the Great Salt Lake, but crossing the parched desert exacted a terrible toll. They lost more than 100 oxen and had to abandon several wagons with their precious supplies. Yet their greatest loss was time as winter weather soon set in.

When the Donner party reached Truckee Pass in eastern California, the last barrier in the Sierra Nevada before they would reach the Sacramento Valley, a two-week-long blizzard trapped them in two separate camps. By December, the pioneers, half of them children, were marooned by twenty feet of snow, with only enough food to last through the end of the month. Seventeen of the strongest members, calling themselves the "Forlorn Hope," decided to cross the pass on their own, but they were trapped by more snow. Two turned back; eight more died of exposure and starvation.

Donner party This hand-colored engraving from the 1800s depicts these pioneers struggling in the snow on a trail leading over the Rocky Mountains.

Just before he died, Billy Graves urged his daughters to eat his corpse. The daughters were appalled at first, but soon saw no other choice. When two other members of the party died, they, too, were eaten. Only seven reached the Sacramento Valley.

Back at the main camps, the survivors had slaughtered and eaten the last of the livestock, then boiled hides and bones. They had also killed two Indian guides and eaten them. When a rescue party finally reached them two months later, they discovered that thirteen people had died, and cannibalism had become commonplace. One pioneer noted casually in his diary, "Mrs. Murphy said here yesterday that she thought she would commence on Milt and eat him." As the rescuers led the forty-seven survivors over the pass, George Donner, too weak and distressed to walk, stayed behind to die. His wife chose to remain with him.

THE PATHFINDER: JOHN FRÉMONT Despite the dangers of the overland crossing, the Far West proved an irresistible attraction for hundreds of thousands of pioneers. The most enthusiastic champion of American settlement in Mexican California and the Far West was John Charles Frémont, an impetuous junior army officer who during the 1840s became America's most famous explorer.

Born and raised in the South, Frémont developed a robust love of the outdoors. In 1838, after attending the College of Charleston, he was commissioned a second lieutenant in the U.S. Topographical Corps, an organization whose mission was to explore and map new western territories. Frémont soon excelled at surveying, mapmaking, and woodcraft while becoming versed in geology, botany, ornithology, and zoology.

In 1841, Frémont courted and married seventeen-year-old Jessie Benton, the daughter of Thomas Hart Benton, the powerful Missouri senator. Once Benton's anger at his daughter subsided, he became Frémont's foremost booster and helped arrange the explorations that would bring his son-in-law fame.

In 1842, Frémont, who believed he was a man of God-determined destiny, set out from present-day Kansas City with two dozen soldiers to map the eastern half of the Oregon Trail. They spent five months collecting plant and animal specimens and drawing maps.

With his wife's considerable help, Frémont published in newspapers across the nation excerpts from a rip-roaring account of his explorations titled *A Report on an Exploration of the Country Lying between the Missouri River and the Rocky Mountains on the Line of the Kansas and Great Platte Rivers*. In describing the Great Plains, the Frémonts wrote that the "Indians and buffalo were the poetry and life of the prairie, and our camp was full of exhilaration."

The stories made Frémont an instant celebrity and earned him a nickname: "the Pathfinder." After reading about the expedition, Henry Wadsworth Longfellow, the nation's most popular poet, announced that "Frémont has touched my imagination. What a wild life, and what a fresh kind of existence! But ah, the discomforts!"

Frémont's success quickly led to another expedition, this one to map the more difficult half of the Oregon Trail from the South Pass, a twenty-mile gap in the Rocky Mountains in present-day Wyoming. The expedition would then go down the Snake River to the Columbia River and into Oregon, eventually making its way south through the Sierra Nevada to Sutter's Fort, near what would become Sacramento, California.

Frémont's group was the first to cross the snow- and ice-covered Sierra Nevada in the winter, a spectacular feat. His report of the expedition and the maps it generated spurred massive migrations to Utah, Oregon, and California throughout the 1840s, including the trek of the Mormons from Illinois to Salt Lake City, Utah.

Rarely one to follow orders, keep promises, or admit mistakes, Frémont surprised his superior officers when he launched a "military" expedition on his own. In August 1845, Frémont, now a captain, headed west from St. Louis on another mysterious expedition, this time leading sixty-two heavily armed soldiers, sailors, scientists, hunters, and frontiersmen.

In December, the adventurers swept down the western slopes of the Sierra Nevada and headed southward through the Central Valley of Mexican-controlled California. Frémont told Mexican authorities that his mission was strictly scientific and that his men were civilians. In Monterey, in January 1846, Frémont received secret instructions from President James Knox Polk indicating that the United States intended to take control of California from Mexico. Frémont was ordered to encourage a "spontaneous" uprising among the Americans living there.

Suspicious Mexican officials ordered Frémont to leave. He did, but soon devised a way to return. To cover his efforts to spark a revolution among the English-speaking Californians, most of whom were Americans, he officially resigned from the army so that he thereafter would be acting as a private citizen.

Then Frémont and his band of soldiers began stirring unrest. On June 14, 1846, American settlers captured Sonoma in northern California and proclaimed the Republic of California. They hoisted a flag featuring a grizzly bear and star, a version of which would later become the California state flag. On June 25, Frémont and his soldiers marched into Sonoma. All of California was in American control when news arrived of the outbreak of the Mexican-American War along the Texas border.

AMERICAN SETTLEMENTS IN TEXAS The American passion for new western land focused largely on Texas, an area of rich soil, lush prairie grass, plentiful timber, and abundant wildlife. During the 1820s, the United States had twice offered to buy Texas, but the Mexican government refused to sell. Mexicans were frightened and infuriated by the idea of Yankees taking their "sacred soil"—but that is what happened. By 1823, some 3,000 Americans or "*Texians*," called Anglos, were living in Texas illegally.

The leading promoter of American settlement in Mexican Texas was Stephen Fuller Austin, a visionary land developer (*empresario*) who convinced the Mexican government in 1824–1825 that he could recruit 300 American families to settle between the Colorado and Brazos Rivers along the Gulf coast of Texas and create a "buffer" on the northern frontier between the feared Comanche Indians and the Mexican settlements to the south. The Mexican government agreed to "legalize" American immigration as long as the settlers converted to Catholicism and did not bring slaves.

Americans who rushed to settle in Austin's Anglo "colony" each received 177 free acres and had access to thousands of acres of common pasture for ranching. Most of the Anglos were ranchers or farmers drawn to the fertile, inexpensive lands in the river valleys. A few were wealthy planters who brought slaves with them in spite of the law against it. The settlers marveled at the abundance of food sources. An American reported that eastern Texas was "literally alive with all kinds of game. We have only to go out a few miles into a swamp . . . to find as many wild cattle as one could wish." There were as many buffalo as cattle.

By 1830, coastal Texas had far more Americans than Tejanos (Spanish-speaking Texans) or Indians—about 20,000 white settlers and 1,000 enslaved blacks, brought to grow and harvest cotton. By 1835, there were 35,000 *Texians*, 3,000 African American slaves, and a booming cotton economy.

The flood of Americans into Texas led to numerous clashes with Indians as well as with Mexican officials, who began having second thoughts about their "tolerated guests." A Mexican congressman issued an accurate warning in 1830: "Mexicans! Watch closely, for you know all too well the Anglo-Saxon greed for territory. We have generously granted land to these Nordics; they have made their homes with us, but their hearts are with their native land. We are continually in civil wars and revolutions; we are weak, and know it—and they know it also. They may conspire with the United States to take Texas from us. From this time, be on your guard!"

THE TEXAS WAR FOR INDEPENDENCE Mexican officials were so worried about the intentions of the Texians that in April 1830 they outlawed further emigration from the United States. Americans, who viewed the

Mexicans with contempt, kept coming anyway—as illegal immigrants. By 1835, the *Texians* and their enslaved blacks outnumbered the Tejanos 10 to 1. In a letter to his cousin in 1835, Stephen F. Austin left no doubt about his plans: "It is very evident that Texas should be effectually, and fully, *Americanized*—that is— settled by a population that will harmonize with their neighbors on the *East*, in language, political principles, common origin, sympathy, and even interest. *Texas must be a slave country. It is no longer a matter of doubt*."

A changing political situation aggravated the growing tensions between the Mexican government and the Texians. In 1834, General Antonio López de Santa Anna, the Mexican president, suspended the national congress and became a dictator, calling himself the "Napoleon of the West." Texans feared that Santa Anna planned to free "our slaves and to make slaves of us."

When Santa Anna imprisoned Austin in 1834 for inciting rebelliousness among the Texians, American settlers decided that the Mexican ruler had to go. Upon his release from jail eighteen months later, Austin called for Texans to revolt: "War is our only resource. There is no other remedy." He urged that Texas become a fully American territory promoting slavery, and then officially become a new state.

In the fall of 1835, Texans rebelled against Santa Anna's "despotism." The Mexican leader ordered all Americans expelled, all Texans disarmed, and all

The Alamo David Crockett, pictured fighting with his rifle over his head, joined the legendary effort to defend the Alamo against the Mexican army's repeated assaults.

rebels arrested and executed as "pirates." As sporadic fighting erupted, hundreds of armed volunteers from southern states rushed to assist the 30,000 *Texians* and Tejanos fighting against a Mexican nation of 7 million people. "The sword is drawn!" Austin proclaimed.

THE ALAMO At San Antonio, the provincial capital in southern Texas, General Santa Anna's 3,000-man army assaulted a group of fewer than 200 *Texians*, Tejanos, and members of the Texas volunteer army holed up in an abandoned Catholic mission called the Alamo. The outnumbered and outgunned Texas rebels were led by three colorful adventurers with checkered pasts: James "Jim" Bowie, William Barret Travis, and David Crockett.

Bowie, a ruthless slave trader and deceitful land speculator, was most famous for the "bowie knife" he used to wound and kill. He claimed he had never started a fight—nor lost one. In his most famous brawl, he was shot twice, stabbed, and impaled by a sword before he killed his opponent with his knife.

Bowie, who migrated from Louisiana to Texas in 1828, settled near San Antonio and came to own about a million acres of land. He married a prominent Mexican woman, became a Mexican citizen, and learned Spanish, but a cholera epidemic killed his wife and two children, as well as his in-laws.

Upon learning of the Texas Revolution, Bowie joined the volunteer army and commanded the Texas volunteers in the Alamo. William Travis, a hot-tempered, twenty-six-year-old lawyer and teacher, led the "regular army" soldiers.

Travis had come to Texas by way of Alabama, leaving a failed marriage; a pregnant wife; a two-year-old son; considerable debts; and, rumors claimed, a man he had killed. Travis pledged that he would redeem himself by doing something great and honorable in Texas—or die trying. His determination led him to refuse orders to retreat from the Alamo.

The most famous American at the Alamo was David Crockett, the Tennessee frontiersman, sharpshooter, bear hunter, and storyteller who had fought under Andrew Jackson and served in Congress as an anti-Jackson Whig. In his last speech before Congress after being defeated for reelection, Crockett, who was not called "Davy" until long after his death, told his colleagues that he "was done with politics for the present, and that they might go to hell, and I would go to Texas," where he planned to make "a fortune."

Soon after arriving with his trusty rifle, "Old Betsy," Crockett learned that he would receive 4,000 acres for his service as a fighter. He then was assigned to the garrison at the Alamo. Full of bounce and brag, the forty-nine-year-old Crockett was thoroughly expert at killing. As he once told his men, "Pierce the heart of the enemy as you would a feller that spit in your face, knocked down your wife, burnt up your houses, and called your dog a skunk!"

The defenders of the Alamo shared a commitment to liberty in the face of Santa Anna's growing despotism. In late February 1836, Santa Anna demanded that the Alamo surrender. By then, Bowie had fallen seriously ill and turned over command to Travis, who answered the Mexican ultimatum with cannon fire. He then sent appeals to Texian towns for supplies and more men, while promising that "*I shall never surrender or retreat . . .* VICTORY OR DEATH!"

Help did not come, however, and the Mexicans launched a series of assaults against the outnumbered defenders. For twelve days, however, the Mexicans suffered heavy losses.

The ferocious fighting at the Alamo turned the rebellion into a war for Texan independence. On March 2, 1836, delegates from all fifty-nine Texas towns met in the tiny village of Washington-on-the-Brazos, some 150 miles northeast of San Antonio. There they signed a declaration of independence and drafted a constitution for the new Republic of Texas. They then named Sam Houston commander-in-chief of their disorganized but growing "army."

Four days later, the defenders of the Alamo were awakened at four o'clock in the morning by the sound of Mexican bugles playing the dreaded "Degüello" ("Slashing of the Throat," symbolizing no mercy). Colonel Travis shouted: "The Mexicans are upon us—give 'em Hell!"

The climactic Battle of the Alamo was fought in the predawn dark. Santa Anna's men attacked from every direction. They were twice forced back, but on the third try they broke through the battered north wall. Travis was killed by a bullet between the eyes. In the end, virtually all of the Texans were killed or wounded.

Seven Alamo defenders, perhaps including Crockett, survived and were captured. Santa Anna ordered them hacked to death with swords. A Mexican officer wrote that the captives "died without complaining and without humiliating themselves before their torturers."

By dawn, the battle was over. The only survivors were a handful of women and children, and Joe, Travis's slave. It was a costly victory, however, as more than 600 Mexicans died. The Battle of the Alamo also provided a rallying cry for vengeful Texians. While Santa Anna proclaimed a "glorious victory," his aide wrote ominously in his diary, "One more such 'glorious victory' and we are finished."

GOLIAD Two weeks later, at the Battle of Coleto Creek, a Mexican force again defeated a smaller Texian army, then marched the 465 captured Texians to a fort in the nearby town of Goliad. Despite pleas from his men to show mercy, Santa Anna ordered the captives killed as "pirates and outlaws." On

Palm Sunday, March 27, 1836, more than 300 Texians were marched out and murdered. The massacres at the Alamo and Goliad fueled a burning desire for revenge among Texians.

SAM HOUSTON   The fate of the **Texas Revolution** was now in the hands of the already legendary Sam Houston, a rowdy, larger-than-life frontier statesman born in Virginia to Scots-Irish immigrants. At age fourteen, after his father died, Houston had moved with his mother and siblings to eastern Tennessee. Two years later, he ran away from home and lived among the Cherokees, earning the nickname "The Raven." Like David Crockett, Houston had served under General Andrew Jackson during the War of 1812. Thereafter, he returned to Tennessee and became a federal Indian agent, an attorney, a U.S. congressman, commanding general of the Tennessee militia, and, in 1827, at the ripe age of thirty-four, governor.

Unlike Crockett, however, Houston adored Jackson and became his devoted disciple and surrogate son, leading many to speculate that he might become the next president. Like Jackson, however, Houston was at heart an oddball ruffian: he had an untamed yet gallant personality with a charming brashness that cloaked a violent temper. A friend called him a "magnificent barbarian."

Controversy dogged Houston. In 1829, he suddenly resigned the governorship of Tennessee because Eliza Allen, his beautiful, aristocratic, and much younger wife, had left him soon after their wedding and returned to her father's plantation near Nashville.

Houston never revealed the cause of the dispute, but Eliza's family accused him of "dishonoring" her. He, in turn, kept silent because, he explained to President Jackson, doing so reinforced his "notion of honor." If his character could not stand the "shock" of mean-spirited gossip, he said, then "let me lose it."

For years, wild rumors circulated about what had happened on Houston's wedding night. Some claimed that Eliza had discovered that Houston had sustained a "dreadful injury" (true, a wound in the groin from an Indian arrowhead) in the Creek War that had left him scarred and impotent (a falsehood). Others reported that his bride had confessed she was in love with someone else and had only married him to please her family. Whatever the cause, Houston later wrote that his ugly divorce threw him into an "agony of despair" over his "private afflictions" that had ruined his political career and exiled him from Nashville society.

The disconsolate Houston decided that suicide was his only option. As he was preparing to kill himself, however, an eagle suddenly swooped toward him and then soared upward into the sunset. Then and there, Houston later wrote, "I knew that a great destiny waited for me in the West."

In 1829, Houston boarded a steamboat and headed West, where he eventually joined the Cherokee; adopted their clothing, customs, and language; and changed his name. He married a Cherokee woman and was formally "adopted" by the Cherokee Nation.

Houston proved adept at helping rival Indian tribes—Cherokee, Creek, Osage, and Choctaws—negotiate among themselves and with the federal government. He also grew addicted to alcohol; the Cherokees called him "Big Drunk." In December 1832, he moved from the Arkansas Territory to Texas at Jackson's behest. Two months later, he sent a secret report to the president, indicating that Texas was ripe for revolt from Mexico, which was then embroiled in a civil war. Houston joined the rebellion.

THE BATTLE OF SAN JACINTO   After learning of the Mexican victory at the Alamo, Sam Houston led his outnumbered troops on a long strategic retreat to buy time while hoping that Santa Anna's pursuing army would make a mistake. On April 21, 1836, the cocky Mexican general let his guard down. Houston's army of 900 fighters caught Santa Anna's 1,600 troops napping near the San Jacinto River, about twenty-five miles southeast of the modern city of Houston. The Texians and Tejanos charged, yelling "Remember the Alamo, Remember Goliad!" They overwhelmed the Mexicans. General

Austin, Texas, in 1840 A view of the capital of the newly formed Republic of Texas— the town's population at the time numbered less than a thousand.

Santa Anna left his army leaderless that afternoon while he retreated to his tent, accompanied, some said, by his mistress.

The battle lasted only eighteen minutes, but Houston's troops spent the next two hours slaughtering fleeing Mexican soldiers. Some 650 Mexicans were killed and 300 captured. The Texians lost only eleven men. Santa Anna escaped but was captured the next day. He bought his freedom by signing a treaty recognizing the independence of the Republic of Texas, with the Rio Grande as its southern boundary with Mexico. The Texas Revolution had been accomplished in just seven weeks.

THE LONE STAR REPUBLIC   In 1836, the Lone Star Republic, as Texians called their new nation, legalized slavery, banned free blacks, elected Sam Houston as its first president, and voted overwhelmingly for annexation to the United States. But statehood for Texas soon became embroiled in the sectional dispute over slavery.

John C. Calhoun told the Senate that "there were powerful reasons why Texas should be part of this Union. The southern states, owning a slave population, were deeply interested in preventing that country from having the power to annoy them." Anti-slavery Northerners disagreed. In 1837, the Vermont legislature "solemnly protested" against the admission "of any state whose constitution tolerates domestic slavery."

President Andrew Jackson eagerly wanted Texas to join the Union. He knew, however, that adding Texas as a slave state would ignite an explosive quarrel between North and South that would fracture the Democratic party and endanger the election of New Yorker Martin Van Buren, his handpicked successor. Worse, any effort to add Texas to the Union would likely mean a war with Mexico, which refused to recognize Texan independence.

So, Jackson delayed official recognition of the Republic of Texas until his last day in office, early in 1837. Van Buren, Jackson's successor, did as predicted: he avoided all talk of Texas annexation during his single term as president.

WHIGS AND DEMOCRATS   When sixty-eight-year-old William Henry Harrison succeeded Martin Van Buren as president in 1841, he was the oldest man and the first Whig to win the office. The Whigs, who now controlled both houses of Congress, continued to promote federal government support for industrial development and economic growth, high tariffs to deter foreign imports, and federal funding for roads, bridges, and canals.

Yet Harrison won election primarily because of his prominence as a military hero. During the campaign he had avoided taking public stances on controversial issues. In the end, it mattered little, as he served the shortest term of any president. On April 4, 1841, exactly one month after his inauguration, he died of pneumonia. Vice President John Tyler became president.

Henry Clay, the formidable Kentucky senator, hoped to dominate the mild-mannered new president. Tyler "dares not resist," Clay threatened, or "I will drive him before me." Tyler, however, was not willing to be dominated.

JOHN TYLER The tall, thin, slave-owning Virginian was a political maverick and, at fifty-one, the youngest president to date. But he had lots of political experience, having served as a state legislator, governor, congressman, and senator. Perhaps most important, he was a man of stubborn independence and considerable charm. An acquaintance said Tyler was "approachable, courteous, always willing to do a kindly action, or to speak a kindly word."

Originally a Democrat, Tyler had endorsed the Jeffersonian commitment to states' rights, strict construction of the Constitution, and opposition to national banks. He joined the Whigs after President Jackson's "condemnation" of South Carolina's attempt to nullify federal laws. Tyler believed that South Carolina had a constitutional right to secede from the nation. Yet he never truly embraced the Whigs. As president, he opposed everything associated with Henry Clay's celebrated program of economic nationalism (the American System), which called for high tariffs, a national bank, and internal improvements.

When Congress met in a special session in 1841, Clay introduced a series of controversial resolutions. He called for the repeal of the Independent Treasury Act and the creation of another Bank of the United States; he proposed to revive the distribution program whereby the money generated by federal land sales was given to the states, and urged that tariffs be raised on imported goods to hamper foreign competitors.

Clay might have avoided a nasty dispute with Tyler over financial issues, but for once, driven by his compulsive quest to be president, the Great Compromiser lost his instinct for compromise. Although Tyler agreed to the repeal of the Independent Treasury Act and signed a higher tariff bill, he vetoed Clay's pet project: the new national bank.

An incensed Clay responded by calling Tyler a traitor who had disgraced his party. He claimed that the president was left "solitary and alone, shivering by the pitiless storm" against his veto. Clay then convinced Tyler's entire cabinet to resign, with the exception of Secretary of State Daniel Webster. A three-year-long war between Clay and Tyler had begun.

Tyler replaced the defectors in his cabinet with anti-Jackson Democrats who, like him, had become Whigs. The Whigs then expelled Tyler from the party, calling him "His Accidency" and the "Executive Ass." By 1842, Tyler had become a president without a party, shunned by both Whigs and Democrats.

The political turmoil coincided with the economic depression that had begun in the late 1830s. Yet Tyler refused to let either the sputtering economy or an international crisis with Great Britain deter him from annexing more territory into the United States.

TENSIONS WITH BRITAIN In late 1841, slaves being transported from Virginia to Louisiana on the American ship *Creole* revolted and took charge of the ship. They sailed into Nassau, in the Bahamas, where British authorities set 128 of them free. (Great Britain had abolished slavery throughout its empire in 1834.)

It was the most successful slave revolt in American history. Southerners were infuriated, and the incident mushroomed into an international crisis. Secretary of State Daniel Webster demanded that the slaves be returned as American property, but the British refused.

Rather than risk a war that the United States might lose, Tyler and Webster acquiesced to the British. This enraged southern slaveholders. James Henry Hammond, the South Carolina planter, lashed out: "With such a stupid imbecile as Tyler at the head of affairs and such an unprincipled and cowardly Sec. of State as Webster, we should fare badly for a time. They are bent on peace."

At this point, the British government decided to send Alexander Baring, Lord Ashburton, to meet with Webster, who viewed good relations with Britain as essential for the American economy. The meetings produced the Webster-Ashburton Treaty (1842), which provided for joint naval patrols off Africa to police the outlawed slave trade. The treaty also resolved a long-standing dispute over the northeastern U.S. boundary with British Canada. But it did nothing about returning the freed slaves. The dispute was not settled until 1853, when England paid $110,000 to the slaves' former owners. In May 1843, Webster resigned as secretary of state.

THE "EXTENSION OF OUR EMPIRE": TEXAS From the moment he became president, John Tyler had his eyes on annexing the Republic of Texas. In his first address to Congress, he pledged to do so, explaining that there was nothing to fear from "the extension of our Empire."

Tyler's efforts to recruit senators to approve an annexation treaty exhilarated Texas leaders who were long frustrated that they had not been welcomed into the United States. Sam Houston threatened to expand the Republic of Texas to the Pacific coast. But with little money, a rising debt, and continuing tensions with Mexico, this was mostly talk.

The Lone Star Republic had no infrastructure—no banks, no schools, no industries. Houston decided that the rickety republic had two choices: annexation to the United States or closer economic ties to Great Britain, which had extended formal diplomatic recognition to the republic and then began buying cotton from Texas planters.

Meanwhile, thousands more Americans poured into Texas, enticed by its offer of 1,280 acres of land to each white family. The population more than tripled between 1836 and 1845, from 40,000 to 150,000; the enslaved black population grew even faster than the white population.

A TRAGIC CRUISE On February 28, 1844, President Tyler and a group of 300 dignitaries boarded the U.S.S. *Princeton*, a new warship, for an excursion on the Potomac River. As sailors fired the ship's fifteen-foot-long cannons, one of them, "the Peacemaker," exploded, killing eight people, including the secretary of state and secretary of the navy. More than a dozen others were seriously wounded. Tyler, who was below deck at the time of the accident, rushed to see what had happened: "A more heart-rending scene scarcely ever occurred," he wrote. "What a loss I have sustained . . . "

After the funerals, Tyler seized the opportunity created by the accident to reorganize his cabinet by naming southern Democrats to key positions. He appointed John C. Calhoun secretary of state, primarily because he wanted the South Carolinian to complete the annexation of Texas as a slave state. On April 12, 1844, Calhoun signed a treaty of annexation, and Tyler submitted it to the Senate for approval. Texas would become an American territory in exchange for the United States assuming all of its debts. Tyler explained that the addition of Texas would "add to national greatness and wealth" and "strengthen rather than weaken the Union."

Calhoun, however, unwittingly undermined the treaty by writing the British ambassador what he thought was a confidential letter in which he declared that blacks were inferior to whites and better off enslaved than free. Slavery, Calhoun insisted, was "essential to the peace, safety, and prosperity" of the South. Adding Texas, he concluded, was necessary to keep the South in the Union. On June 8, 1844, outraged Northerners in the Senate voted down Calhoun's annexation treaty 35 to 16.

THE ELECTION OF 1844 Both political parties hoped to keep the divisive Texas issue out of the 1844 presidential campaign. Whig Henry Clay and Democrat Martin Van Buren, the leading candidates for each party's nomination, agreed that adding Texas to the Union would be a mistake, for it would aggravate tensions between North and South over slavery.

For his part, Tyler, having alienated both parties, initially announced that he would run for reelection as an independent, using the campaign slogan, "Tyler and Texas." Within a few weeks, however, he realized he had little support and dropped out of the race.

Van Buren's southern supporters, including former president Andrew Jackson, abandoned him because he opposed the annexation of Texas. They instead nominated James K. Polk, former Speaker of the House and former governor of Tennessee. Like Tyler, Polk was an enthusiastic expansionist. Unlike Tyler, he was a loyal Democrat who hated Whigs. On the ninth ballot, he became the first "dark horse" (unexpected) candidate to win a major-party nomination. The Democrats' platform called for the annexation of Texas and declared that the United States had a "clear and unquestionable claim" to all the Oregon Country.

The 1844 election proved to be one of the most significant in history. By promoting southern and western expansionism, the Democrats offered a winning strategy that forced Clay, the Whig candidate, to alter his position on Texas at the last minute. He now claimed that he had "no personal objection to the annexation" if it could be achieved "without dishonor, without war, with the common consent of the Union, and upon just and fair terms."

Clay's waffling shifted more anti-slavery votes to the new Liberty party (the anti-slavery party formed in 1840), which increased its count in the presidential election from about 7,000 in 1840 to more than 62,000 in 1844. In the western counties of New York, the Liberty party drew enough votes from Clay and the Whigs to give the crucial state to Polk.

Had Clay carried New York, he would have won the election by 7 electoral votes. Instead, Polk won a narrow national plurality of 38,000 popular votes—the first president since John Quincy Adams to win without a majority—but with a clear majority of the electoral college, 170 to 105. A devastated Clay had lost his third and last presidential election. He could not understand how he had lost to Polk, whom he considered a "third-rate" politician.

JAMES K. POLK James K. Polk had been surprising people his whole career. Born near Charlotte, North Carolina, the oldest of ten children, he graduated first in his class at the University of North Carolina. Polk then moved to Tennessee, where he became a successful lawyer and planter. He then entered politics, serving fourteen years in Congress (four as Speaker of the House) and two years as governor.

At forty-nine, Polk was America's youngest president. Short, thin, and humorless, he was called "Young Hickory" because of his admiration for "Old

Hickory," Andrew Jackson. Like Jackson, he believed that any efforts by the federal government to promote economic growth necessarily helped some people and regions and hurt others. He thus opposed tariffs, a national bank, and federally funded roads.

Polk's greatest virtue was his work ethic. He often labored from dawn to midnight and rarely took a vacation. Such unrelenting intensity eventually wore him out, however. Polk would die in 1849, at fifty-three years old, just three months after leaving office.

THE STATE OF TEXAS   Texas joined the Union just *before* Polk was sworn in as president. In his final months in office, President John Tyler had asked Congress to annex Texas by joint resolution, which required only a simple majority in each house rather than the two-thirds Senate vote needed to ratify a *treaty* of annexation.

The resolution narrowly passed, with most Whigs opposed. In his final presidential action, Tyler admitted Texas as the twenty-eighth state, and fifteenth slave state, on December 29, 1845. On February 16, 1846, the Lone Star flag of the Republic of Texas was lowered, and the flag of the United States was raised over the largest state in the nation.

At the time, Texas had a population of 100,000 whites and 38,000 enslaved African Americans. By 1850, the population—both white and black—had soared by almost 50 percent. (The census then did not include Native Americans.) By 1860, Texas had 600,000 people, most of them from southern states focused on growing cotton.

POLK'S GOALS   Perhaps because he pledged to serve only one term, Polk was a president in a hurry. He focused on four major objectives, all of which he accomplished. He managed to (1) reduce tariffs on imports; (2) reestablish the Independent Treasury ("We need no national banks!"); (3) settle the Oregon boundary dispute with Britain; and (4) acquire California from Mexico.

Polk wanted lower tariffs to allow more foreign goods to compete in the American marketplace and thereby help drive consumer prices down. Congress agreed by approving the Walker Tariff of 1846, named after Robert J. Walker, the secretary of the Treasury.

The same year, Polk persuaded Congress to restore the Independent Treasury Act that Martin Van Buren had signed into law in 1840 and the Whig-dominated Congress had repealed the next year. The act established Independent Treasury deposit offices to receive all federal government funds. The system was intended to replace the Second Bank of the United States,

Tariff of 1846 This political cartoon illustrates the public outcry—represented by a Quaker woman ready to whip Polk—against the Tariff of 1846, one of the lowest in the nation's history.

which Jackson had "killed," so as to offset the chaotic growth of unregulated state banks whose reckless lending practices had helped cause the depression of the late 1830s.

The new Independent Treasury entrusted the federal government, rather than state banks, with the exclusive management of government funds and required that all disbursements be made in gold or silver, or paper currency backed by gold or silver.

Polk also twice vetoed Whig-passed bills for federally funded infrastructure projects. His efforts to reverse Whig economic policies satisfied the slave-holding South but angered Northerners, who wanted higher tariffs to protect their industries from British competition, and westerners, who wanted federally financed roads and harbors.

OREGON Meanwhile, the dispute with Great Britain over the Oregon Country boundary heated up as expansionists insisted that Polk take the whole region rather than split it with the British. Polk was willing to go to the brink of war to achieve his goals. "If we do have war," the president blustered, "it will not be our fault."

Fortunately, the British were not willing to risk war. On June 15, 1846, James Buchanan, Polk's secretary of state, signed the Buchanan-Pakenham Treaty, which extended the border between the United States and British Canada westward to the Pacific coast along the 49th parallel. Once the treaty was approved by both nations, the *New York Herald* announced: "Now, we can thrash Mexico into decency at our leisure."

THE MEXICAN-AMERICAN WAR

On March 6, 1845, two days after James Polk became president, the Mexican government broke off relations with the United States to protest the annexation of Texas. Polk was willing to wage war against Mexico to acquire California and New Mexico, but he did not want Americans to fire the first shot.

Nor did he want a war that might produce a military hero who would become a Whig candidate for the presidency. Senator Thomas Hart Benton of Missouri, a powerful Democrat, disclosed that Polk "wanted a small war, just large enough to require a treaty for peace, and not large enough to create military reputations" that might pose a political challenge after the war.

Polk ordered several thousand U.S. troops under General Zachary Taylor to take up positions around Corpus Christi, Texas, at the mouth of the Nueces River, which Mexico claimed as its border with the United States. In March, Polk ordered Taylor to move his force to the north bank of the Rio Grande, where they built Fort Brown opposite the Mexican town of Matamoros, a provocative move that the Mexican government viewed as an invasion.

On the evening of May 9, 1845, Polk learned that Mexican troops had attacked U.S. soldiers north of the Rio Grande. Eleven Americans were killed, five wounded, and the rest taken prisoner. Polk's scheme to provoke an attack had worked. On May 13, Congress declared war and authorized the recruitment of 50,000 soldiers.

Some congressmen, however, were skeptical of Polk's explanation. Whig Garret Davis of Kentucky asserted, "It is our own President who began this war." Even Democrats were concerned about the president's story. A New York senator, John Dix, said he would not be "surprised if the next accounts should show that there is no Mexican invasion of our soil." The war, he later added, "was begun in fraud . . . and I think will end in disgrace."

President Polk steadfastly denied that the war had anything to do with the expansion of slavery. He argued that his efforts to extend America's boundaries to the Pacific were intended to replace sectional tensions with national unity.

After all, he stressed, slavery could not flourish in places like New Mexico and California because cotton could not be grown there because of the climate.

Most Americans accepted the president's account and rushed to support the military. "LET US GO TO WAR," screamed a New York newspaper. Another headline blared: "MEXICO OR DEATH!" The South was especially excited because of the possibility of acquiring more territory. So many Southerners ("wild, reckless young fellows") rushed to volunteer that thousands had to be turned away.

Eventually, 112,000 whites served in the war. (Blacks were banned.) Among the warriors were young army officers who would later distinguish themselves as opposing leaders in the Civil War: Ulysses S. Grant, Joseph Hooker, Thomas Jackson, James Longstreet, Robert E. Lee, George McClellan, George Meade, and William T. Sherman.

OPPOSITION TO THE WAR In New England and among northern abolitionists, there was much less enthusiasm for "Mr. Polk's War." Congressman John Quincy Adams, the former president who was now nearly eighty years old, called it "a most unrighteous war." He saw "Polk's War" as a southern scheme to extend slavery into new territories taken from Mexico.

William Lloyd Garrison, the fiery Boston abolitionist, charged that the war was one of "aggression, of invasion, of conquest." Henry David Thoreau spent a night in jail rather than pay taxes that might help fund the war. Thoreau's mentor, Ralph Waldo Emerson, predicted that the "United States will conquer Mexico, but it will be as the man who swallows arsenic, which brings him down in turn. Mexico will poison us."

Most northern Whigs, including a young Illinois congressman named Abraham Lincoln, opposed the war, arguing that Polk had maneuvered the Mexicans into attacking. The United States, many insisted, had no reason to place its army in the disputed border region between Texas and Mexico. In what came to be called "Spot Resolutions," Lincoln repeatedly asked the president to locate the precise "spot" where the American troops were fired upon, implying that they may have illegally crossed into Mexican territory.

Whig leader Henry Clay expressed concern that the nation was "becoming a warlike and conquering power," while Daniel Webster charged that the war's disputed origins were "unconstitutional." (Both Clay and Webster would lose sons in the war.)

PREPARING FOR BATTLE The United States was again ill prepared for a major war. At the outset, the regular army numbered barely more than 7,000, in contrast to the Mexican force of 32,000. Before the war ended, however, the U.S. military had grown to almost 79,000 troops, many of whom were frontier toughs who lacked uniforms, equipment, and discipline. Repeatedly, some of these soldiers engaged in plunder, rape, and murder. Yet they outfought the larger Mexican forces.

The Mexican-American War would last from May 1846 to April 1848 and would be fought on four fronts: southern Texas/northern Mexico, central Mexico, New Mexico, and California. Early on, the U.S. Army scored victories north of the Rio Grande, at Palo Alto (May 8) and Resaca de la Palma (May 9).

On May 18, General Zachary Taylor's army crossed the Rio Grande and occupied Matamoros. Those quick victories brought Taylor, a Whig, instant popularity; Polk agreed to public demand that Taylor be made overall commander. It was an excellent choice, since Taylor, "Old Rough and Ready," had spent thirty-eight years in the army and had earned the respect and affection of his men.

THE ANNEXATION OF CALIFORNIA President Polk's foremost objective was the acquisition of California. Not only did it have wonderful harbors (San Francisco, Monterey, and San Diego), but the president also feared that Great Britain or France would take control of California if the United States did not.

Polk had secretly instructed Commodore John D. Sloat, commander of the Pacific naval squadron, that if war erupted with Mexico, he was to use his warships to gain control "of the port of San Francisco, and blockade or occupy such other ports as your force may permit."

In May 1846, Sloat, having heard of the outbreak of hostilities along the Rio Grande, set sail for California. In early July, U.S. sailors and troops went ashore in San Francisco, took down the flag of the Republic of California, raised the American flag, and claimed California as part of the United States.

Soon thereafter, Sloat turned his command over to Commodore Robert F. Stockton, who sailed south to capture San Diego and Los Angeles. By mid-August, Mexican resistance had evaporated.

At the same time, another American military expedition headed for California. On August 18, General Stephen Kearny's army captured Santa Fe, the capital of New Mexico, then joined Stockton's forces in California. They took control of Los Angeles on January 10, 1847. The remaining Mexican forces surrendered three days later. Stockton and Kearny then quarreled over who was in command, since each carried orders to conquer and govern California.

In the meantime, the unpredictable John C. Frémont arrived from Sonoma with 400 newly recruited troops and claimed that Stockton was in charge.

Stockton responded by naming Frémont governor of California, and Frémont immediately set about giving orders, making proclamations, and appointing officials. This left Kearny in a bind; President Polk had ordered *him* to be the governor.

By June of 1847, Kearny had seen enough. He had Frémont arrested and transported him across the country for a court-martial. In the most celebrated

MAJOR CAMPAIGNS OF THE MEXICAN-AMERICAN WAR

- Why did John C. Frémont and his troops initially march north, only to turn around and march south to San Francisco?
- How did Polk's fear of Zachary Taylor's popularity undermine the Americans' military strategy?

trial since that of Vice President Aaron Burr in 1807, Frémont was found guilty of mutiny and insubordination and dismissed from the army. President Polk, however, quickly reversed the sentence in light of Frémont's "meritorious and valuable services." He urged Frémont to remain in the army and "resume the sword," but "the Pathfinder" was so angry at his treatment that he resigned his commission and settled in California, where he would become the state's first U.S. senator.

WAR IN NORTHERN MEXICO Both California and New Mexico had been taken before General Zachary Taylor fought his first major battle in northern Mexico. In September 1846, Taylor's army assaulted the fortified city of Monterrey, which surrendered after a five-day siege. Then, General Antonio López de Santa Anna, who had been forced out of power in 1845, sent word to Polk from his exile in Cuba that he would end the war if he were allowed to return to Mexico. Polk assured the exiled Mexican leader that the U.S. government would pay well for any territory taken from Mexico. In August 1846, on Polk's orders, Santa Anna was permitted to return to Mexico.

But Santa Anna had lied. Soon he was again president of Mexico and in command of the Mexican army. As it turned out, however, he was much more talented at raising armies than leading them in battle.

In October 1846, Santa Anna invited the outnumbered Americans to surrender. Taylor responded, "Tell him to go to hell." That launched the hard-fought Battle of Buena Vista (February 22–23, 1847), in northern Mexico. Both sides claimed victory, but the Mexicans suffered five times as many casualties as the Americans. Thereafter, the Mexicans continued to lose battles, but they refused to accept Polk's terms for surrender.

Frustrated by Taylor's inability to win a decisive victory, Polk authorized an assault on Mexico City, the nation's capital. On March 9, 1847, a large American force led by Winfield Scott, the general-in-chief of the U.S. Army, landed on the beaches south of Veracruz,the site of what was considered the strongest fortress in North America.

The American assault on Veracruz, the largest amphibious operation ever attempted by U.S. military forces, was carried out without loss. Veracruz surrendered on March 29, and the news made General Scott a national hero. The American troops then rested, accumulating supplies and awaiting reinforcements to replace the many volunteers whose enlistments had run out and who were eager to go home.

In August, Scott's formidable invasion force marched toward heavily defended Mexico City, 200 miles away. In England, the Duke of Wellington, who had defeated Napoléon at the Battle of Waterloo more than thirty years before, predicted that "Scott is lost—he cannot capture the city, and he cannot fall back upon his base."

Yet the Englishman was wrong. After four brilliantly orchestrated battles in which they overwhelmed the Mexican defenders, U.S. forces arrived at the gates of Mexico City in early September 1847. The Duke of Wellington now changed his tune, calling Scott the world's "greatest living soldier."

THE SAINT PATRICK'S BATTALION General Winfield Scott's triumphant assault on Mexico City was not without problems, however. Since the start of the war, some 7,000 soldiers had deserted. Several hundred of them, mostly poor Irish and German Catholic immigrants, crossed over to form the Saint Patrick's Battalion in the Mexican army, which included many foreign fighters.

Why the American soldiers, called *San Patricios* in Spanish, chose to switch sides remains in dispute, but several factors were at work. Many of the Catholic defectors resented the abuse ("harsh and cruel handling") they received from native U.S. Protestant officers and the atrocities they saw committed against Catholic Mexicans. Some were also attracted by the higher wages, land grants, and

St. Patrick's Battalion The men of St. Patrick's Battalion continue to be celebrated in Mexico as martyrs, with numerous cities, schools, and streets bearing the name *San Patricio.*

promises of citizenship by the Mexican government. The Mexican army circulated leaflets to American soldiers urging the foreign-born to switch sides and fight for their shared "sacred imperiled religion. If you are Catholic, the same as we, if you follow the doctrines of Our Savior, why are you murdering your brethren? Why are you antagonistic to those who defend their country and your own God?"

Whatever their motives, the *San Patricios* fought tenaciously. During one of the battles for Mexico City, the Americans captured seventy-two defectors. They were quickly tried, and most were sentenced to death. Although military law at the time called for traitors to be shot by a firing squad, General Scott ordered that about fifty of the deserters be hanged. The others were whipped and branded with a "D" on each cheek.

At dawn on September 13, 1847, twenty-nine of the captured *San Patricios*, their hands and feet bound, were made to stand in the hot sun under a gallows in sight of Chapultepec, the last Mexican fortress protecting Mexico City. There they were forced to watch the battle unfold over four hours. When the American troops finally scaled the walls of the fortress and raised the U.S. flag, the *San Patricios* were all hanged simultaneously.

Just before the mass execution, the army surgeon reported to Colonel William Harney, an officer infamous for his brutality, that one of the *San Patricios*, Francis O'Connor, had lost both legs in the fighting. The doctor asked what should be done with the man. Harney yelled: "Bring the damned son of a bitch out! My order was to hang thirty, and by God I'll do it." The Mexican government, which erected a monument to the *San Patricios,* described the executions as "improper in a civilized age, and [ironic] for a people who aspire to the title of illustrious and humane."

THE TREATY OF GUADALUPE HIDALGO After the fall of Mexico City, Santa Anna resigned and fled the country. The Mexican government was left in turmoil. Peace talks began on January 2, 1848, at the village of Guadalupe Hidalgo, just outside the capital, but dragged on for weeks, in part because different men claimed to have authority to speak for the Mexican government.

When the **Treaty of Guadalupe Hidalgo** was signed on February 2, a humiliated Mexico was forced to transfer the territories that would eventually become the states of Texas, California, Arizona, New Mexico—and significant parts of what would become Colorado, Utah, Wyoming and Nevada. This represented more than half the entire nation of Mexico.

With the addition of 30,000 square miles in southern Arizona and New Mexico through the Gadsden Purchase of 1853, these annexations rounded out the continental United States, doubled its size, and provided routes for eventual transcontinental rail lines. In return for what Polk called "an immense empire" that encompassed more than a half million square miles, the United States agreed to pay $15 million.

The Senate ratified the treaty ending the war on March 10, 1848. By the end of July, the last remaining U.S. soldiers had left Mexico. Ulysses S. Grant, who fought in the conflict, later called it "one of the most unjust wars ever waged by a stronger against a weaker nation."

THE WAR'S LEGACIES The Mexican-American War was America's first major military intervention outside the United States and the first time that U.S. military forces had conquered and occupied another country. More than 13,000 Americans died, 11,550 of them from disease, especially measles and dysentery. The war remains the deadliest in American history in terms of the percentage who died. Out of every 1,000 soldiers in Mexico, some 110 died.

The victory also helped end America's prolonged economic depression. As the years passed, however, the Mexican-American War was increasingly seen as a shameful war of conquest directed by a president bent on territorial expansion for the sake of slavery. Even General Zachary Taylor called it an "unnecessary and senseless" war.

News of the victory thrilled American expansionists, however. John O'Sullivan, who had coined the term *manifest destiny*, shouted, "More, More, More! Why not take all of Mexico?" Treasury Secretary Robert Walker was equally giddy about the addition of California and the Oregon Country. "Asia has suddenly become our neighbour . . . inviting our steamships upon the trade of a commerce greater than all of Europe combined."

John C. Calhoun spoke for many Southerners when he opposed the idea of taking more than the northernmost Mexican territories: "We have never dreamt of incorporating into our Union any but the Caucasian race—the free white race. To incorporate [all of] Mexico would be the very first instance of the kind of incorporating an Indian race . . . I protest against such a union as that! Ours, sir, is the government of the White race. The greatest misfortunes of Spanish America are to be traced to the fatal error of placing these colored races on equality with the white race."

Calhoun won the argument. The acquisition of the northern Mexican provinces made the United States a transcontinental nation and led to a dramatic expansion of the federal government. In 1849, Congress created the Department of the Interior to supervise the distribution of land, the creation of new territories and states, and the "protection" of the Indians and their reservations. Americans now had their long coveted western empire. But what were they to do with it?

President Polk had naively assumed that the expansion of American territory to the Pacific would strengthen "the bonds of Union." He was wrong. No sooner was Texas annexed and gold discovered in California than a violent debate erupted over the extension of slavery into the territories acquired from Mexico. That debate so enflamed sectional rivalries that it let to secession and civil war.

CHAPTER REVIEW

SUMMARY

- **Westward Migration**   In the 1830s, Americans came to believe in *manifest destiny*—that the West was divinely ordained to be part of the United States. Although populated by Native Americans and Hispanics, the West was portrayed as an empty land. But a population explosion and the lure of cheap, fertile land prompted Americans to move along the *Overland Trails*, enduring great physical hardships, to settle in Oregon (*Oregon fever*) and California. Traders and trappers were the first Americans to move into California during the 1830s. The discovery of gold there in 1848 brought a flood of people from across the world. At the same time, many Southerners also moved to the Mexican province of Texas to grow cotton, taking their slaves with them. The Mexican government, however, outlawed slavery, and in 1830 forbade further immigration. *Texians* rebelled, winning their independence in the *Texas Revolution (1835–1836)*, but statehood would not come for another decade because political leaders were determined to avoid war with Mexico over the territory and the issue of adding another slave state to the Union.

- **Mexican-American War**   When the United States finally annexed Texas in 1845, Mexico was furious. The newly elected U.S. president, James K. Polk, sought to acquire California and New Mexico as well, but negotiations soon failed. When Mexican troops crossed the Rio Grande, Polk urged Congress to declare war. American forces eventually won the war, despite high casualties. In 1848, in the *Treaty of Guadalupe Hidalgo*, Mexico ceded California and New Mexico to the United States and gave up claims to disputed land north of the Rio Grande. The vast acquisition did not strengthen the Union, however. Instead, it ignited a fierce dispute over the role of slavery in the new territories.

CHRONOLOGY

1821	Mexico gains independence from Spain
1836	Americans are defeated at the Alamo
1841	John Tyler becomes president
1842	Americans and British agree to the Webster-Ashburton Treaty
1845	United States annexes Texas
1846	Mexican-American War begins
1848	Treaty of Guadalupe Hidalgo ends the Mexican-American War
1853	With the Gadsden Purchase, the United States acquires an additional 30,000 square miles from Mexico needed for a transcontinental railroad route

Key Terms

manifest destiny p. 504

Overland Trails p. 506

Oregon fever p. 508

Texas Revolution (1835–1836) p. 520

Treaty of Guadalupe Hidalgo
(1848) p. 535

 INQUIZITIVE

Go to InQuizitive to see what you've learned—and learn what you've missed—with personalized feedback along the way.

14 The Gathering Storm

1848–1860

"Bleeding Kansas" (1856) This engraving depicts the sack of Lawrence, Kansas, in May 1856 by pro-slavery "border ruffians." The violence sparked by these slave-holding Missourians proved to be a foreboding sign of the destruction that would engulf the nation in the coming decade.

At midcentury, political storm clouds were forming over the fate of slavery. The United States, as Henry Clay said, was an "unhappy country" torn by the "uproar, confusion, and menace" caused by the deepening agony of slavery.

Without intending to, the United States had developed two different societies, one in the North and the other in the South. Those regions increasingly disagreed over the nation's future. In 1833, Andrew Jackson had predicted that pro-slavery militants ("fire-eaters") like John C. Calhoun "would do any act to destroy this union and form a southern confederacy bounded, north, by the Potomac River." By 1848, Jackson's prediction was coming true.

At midcentury, the sectional tensions over slavery generated constant political conflict. The tortuous Compromise of 1850 provided a short-term resolution, but new controversies such as the fate of slavery in the Kansas Territory, the creation of the anti-slavery Republican party, and the growing militancy of abolitionists led more and more people to decide that the United States, as Abraham Lincoln stressed, could not continue to be "half slave and half free." The result was first the secession of eleven southern states and then a bloody civil war to force them back into the Union. In the process, the "peculiar institution" of slavery ended.

SLAVERY IN THE TERRITORIES

THE WILMOT PROVISO On August 8, 1846, soon after the Mexican-American War erupted, David Wilmot, a first-term Democratic congressman from Pennsylvania, rose in the House of Representatives to endorse the annexation of Texas as a slave state. Yet he added that if any *new* territory should be acquired as a result of war with Mexico, "God forbid" that slavery would be allowed there. He proposed a bill ("proviso") doing just that.

focus questions

1. How did the federal government try to resolve the issue of slavery in the western territories during the 1850s?

2. Analyze the appeal of the Republican party to northern voters; how did it lead to Abraham Lincoln's victory in the 1860 presidential contest?

3. Why did seven southern states secede from the Union shortly after Lincoln's election in 1860?

SECTION OF THE PANORAMA OF THE MISSISSIPPI

Taylor

For sale at White & Potters 15 State St   *Mississippi River*

The Wilmot Proviso President Zachary Taylor would refuse to veto the proviso, even though he was a slave owner. This political cartoon, "Old Zack at Home," highlights his seeming hypocrisy.

President James K. Polk dismissed the **Wilmot Proviso** as a "mischievous and foolish amendment." The House approved it, but the Senate balked. When Congress reconvened in December 1846, Polk convinced Wilmot to withhold his amendment. By then, however, others were ready to take up the cause. In one form or another, Wilmot's idea would frame the debate over the westward expansion of slavery for the next fifteen years.

POPULAR SOVEREIGNTY Democrat Lewis Cass, the territorial governor of Michigan, tried to remove the controversy over slavery from national politics by proposing that voters in each *territory* be given the right to "regulate their own internal concerns in their own way," like the citizens of a state.

Popular sovereignty, as Cass's idea was called, appealed to many eager to protect states' rights because it seemed the most democratic solution to the debate over slavery. Its moral defects, however, were obvious. It did not allow African Americans to vote on their fate, and it allowed whites to strip blacks of the most basic human right: freedom.

When President Polk reaffirmed his pledge to serve only one term, Cass won the Democratic presidential nomination in 1848. But the party refused to endorse Cass's popular sovereignty plan. Instead, it claimed that Congress could not interfere with slavery in the states or territories.

The Whigs again passed over their leader, Henry Clay (three times a losing presidential nominee), and chose General Zachary Taylor, a hero of the Mexican-American War. Taylor owned a Louisiana plantation with 145 slaves, yet he opposed the extension of slavery into new western territories.

Taylor was a reluctant candidate. He had no political experience, claimed no party affiliation, and had never voted in a presidential election. No "sane person," he told his brother, would want to be president. In the end, however, he agreed to campaign "more from a sense of duty than from inclination."

THE FREE-SOIL MOVEMENT Some Americans who worried about the evils of slavery but did not endorse abolition supported banning slavery from the western territories. As a result, "free soil" in the new territories became the rallying cry for the Free-Soil party, a new political organization focused solely on stopping the spread of slavery.

The **Free-Soil party** attracted northern Democrats, anti-slavery Whigs, and members of the abolitionist Liberty party. In 1848, Free-Soilers nominated former president Martin Van Buren as their candidate. Their campaign slogan shouted, "Free Soil, Free Speech, Free Labor, and Free Men."

In the election, the Free-Soilers split the Democratic vote enough to throw New York to Zachary Taylor; they split the Whig vote enough to give Ohio to Democrat Lewis Cass. Nationwide, however, Van Buren's 291,000 votes lagged well behind the 1,361,000 for Taylor and 1,222,000 for Cass. Taylor won the presidency with 163 to 127 electoral votes.

THE CALIFORNIA GOLD RUSH Meanwhile, a new issue had emerged to complicate the debate over territorial expansion and slavery. On January 24, 1848, a group of workers building a sawmill discovered gold nuggets on the property of John A. Sutter, along the south fork of the American River in the Mexican province of California. Nine days later, California would be identified as the "great prize" transferred to the United States through the treaty ending the Mexican-American War.

News of the gold strike spread like wildfire, especially after President Polk told Congress that there was an "extraordinary abundance of gold." Within a year, nearly 100,000 Americans had set off for California. By 1854, the number would top 300,000, making it the greatest mass migration in American history to that point. The "forty-niners" included people from every social class and

Gold miners Chinese immigrants and white settlers mine for gold in the Auburn Ravine of California in 1856.

every state and territory, as well as local Indians and slaves brought by their owners. Thousands more came from Central and South America, Canada, Australia, Asia, and Europe. "Never was there such a gold-thirsty-race of men brought together," a Californian observed. "The principle is to get all of the wealth of the land possible in the shortest possible time, and then go *elsewhere to enjoy it.*"

Those infected with gold fever were fed by hope and fueled by greed. They quit jobs, left farms, sold businesses and belongings, borrowed money, and deserted families in the frantic pursuit of instant riches. So many men ("forty-niners") left New England as part of the **California gold rush** that it would be years before the region's gender ratio evened out again.

Between 1851 and 1855, California produced almost half the world's output of gold, and its infusion into the U.S. economy led to prolonged national prosperity. In addition, it shifted the nation's focus westward, spurred the construction of transcontinental railroads and telegraph lines, and excited dreams of an American commercial empire on the Pacific Coast linked to Asia.

At the same time, the influx of Americans into California proved disastrous for Native Americans and their ancestral lands. In 1850, the new California state legislature allowed whites to force "unemployed" Indians to work for them in exchange for food and clothing. Miners pushed them out of the gold diggings; those who resisted were killed. During the early 1850s, the Indian population in California plummeted by more than 80 percent. If infectious disease did not kill them, white settlers did.

The gold rush transformed the sleepy coastal village of San Francisco into the nation's largest city west of Chicago. In just two years, San Francisco grew from 800 residents to 20,000, its spacious harbor clogged by a forest of ship masts. Half the ships that arrived in the city never left, as their crews deserted and rushed to the mining towns in search of gold.

Fast-growing Sacramento became the staging area for the northern mines. New enterprises—saloons, taverns, restaurants, laundries, general stores— emerged to serve the burgeoning population of miners. The German-Jewish immigrant Levi Strauss supplied gold prospectors with trousers made of denim sailcloth. The rugged blue jeans, sewn to stand up to the physical labor of mining, included copper-rivet-reinforced pockets. "Levi's" are still sold today.

California quickly became a masculine society. At one point during the height of the gold rush, men outnumbered women in San Francisco 50 to 1, while across the state, it was 8 to 1. The few women who dared to live in the camps could demand a premium for their work as cooks, laundresses, entertainers, and prostitutes. One published a brutally candid ad for a husband in a local newspaper: "Her age is none of your business. She is neither handsome nor a fright, yet an *old* man need *not* apply, nor any who have not a little more education than she has, and a great deal more gold, for there must be $20,000 settled on her [paid] before she will" marry.

MINING LIFE California miners were mostly unmarried young men of varied ethnic and cultural backgrounds, including some 20,000 Chinese. Few were interested in staying in California; they wanted to strike it rich and return home. Mining camps sprang up like mushrooms and disappeared almost as rapidly. As soon as rumors of a new strike surfaced, miners converged on the area; when no more gold could be found, they moved on.

The mining camps and shantytowns were dirty, lawless, and dangerous places. In Calaveras County, there were fourteen murders in a single week. Vigilante justice prevailed; one newcomer reported that "in the short space of twenty-four days, we have had murders, fearful accidents, bloody deaths, a mob, whippings, a hanging, an attempt at suicide, and a fatal duel." Murderers who were caught were often lynched on the spot. Within six months of arriving in California in 1849, one gold seeker in every five was dead. The gold-fields and mining towns were so dangerous that insurance companies refused to provide coverage. Suicides were common, and disease was rampant.

In the camps, whites often looked with disdain upon the Hawaiians, Hispanics, African Americans, and Chinese, who were usually employed as wage laborers to help in the panning process, separating gold from sand and gravel. Whites, however, focused their contempt on the Indians; it was not a crime to kill Indians or to work them to death.

CALIFORNIA STATEHOOD

California was important for reasons other than gold. New president Zachary Taylor decided in 1849 to use California's request for statehood to end the stalemate in Congress over slavery. Why not make California and New Mexico free states immediately, he argued, and bypass the volatile issue of slavery?

Californians, however, were ahead of him. By December 1849, without consulting Congress, they had put a free-state (no slavery) government into operation. New Mexico responded more slowly, but by 1850 Americans there had also adopted a free-state constitution.

THE COMPROMISE OF 1850 On December 4, 1849, President Taylor endorsed immediate statehood for California and urged Congress to avoid injecting slavery into the issue. The new Congress, however, was in no mood for simple solutions.

Jefferson Davis, Taylor's son-in-law, dismissed the president's plan as being anti-southern, and irate Southerners threatened to leave the Union if Taylor brought California and New Mexico in as free states. "I avow before this House and country, and in the presence of the living God," shouted Robert Toombs, a Georgia congressman, "that if by your legislation you seek to drive us [slave-holders] from the territories of California and New Mexico . . . and to abolish slavery in this District [of Columbia] . . . *I am for disunion.*"

Americans began to worry for the fate of the republic. "Madness rules the hour," wrote Philip Hone, a New York Whig, in his diary. "Faction, personal recrimination, and denunciation prevail, and men for the first time in our history do not hesitate openly to threaten a dissolution of the Union."

As the controversy over the future of slavery unfolded, an all-star cast of outsized personalities with swollen egos resolved to find a way to preserve the Union. The "lions" of the Senate—Henry Clay, John C. Calhoun, and Daniel Webster (all of whom would die within two years)—took center stage, with William H. Seward, Stephen A. Douglas, and Jefferson Davis in supporting roles.

Together, they staged one of the great dramas of American politics: the **Compromise of 1850**, a ten-month-long debate over a series of resolutions intended to end the crisis between North and South.

IN SEARCH OF COMPROMISE With southern extremists threatening secession, congressional leaders again turned to an aging Henry Clay. As Abraham Lincoln acknowledged, Clay was "regarded by all, as *the* man for the crisis." No man had amassed a more distinguished political career. Clay had

Clay's compromise (1850) Warning against an impending sectional conflict, Henry Clay outlines his plan for "compromise and harmony" on the Senate floor.

gained every position he had sought except the presidency: senator, congressman, Speaker of the House, secretary of state.

Now, as his career was winding down, the seventy-two-year-old Clay hoped to save the Union by presenting his own plan to end another sectional crisis. On December 3, 1849, as the Thirty-First Congress assembled, Clay strode into the Senate to waves of applause and kisses from female followers. He asked to be relieved of all committee responsibilities so that he could focus on the crisis. Unless some compromise could be found, the slaveholding Clay warned, a "furious" civil war would fracture the Union.

Southerners mobilized to oppose President Taylor's proposal to admit California as a free state, for doing so would tip the political balance against slavery, with sixteen free states to fifteen slave states. The slaveholding states would become a permanent minority. As Jefferson Davis argued, the South could not allow that to happen.

On January 29, 1850, having gained the wholehearted support of Daniel Webster, the senior senator from Massachusetts whom he had known for thirty-six years, Henry Clay presented his "amicable" plan for "compromise and harmony."

Using all his wit, charm, and passion, Clay pleaded with the Senate to pass eight resolutions, six of which were paired as compromises between North and South, and all of which were designed to settle the "controversy between the free and slave states, growing out of the subject of slavery." Clay proposed to (1) admit California as a free state; (2) let the residents of the territories of New Mexico and Utah decide whether to allow slavery; (3) deny Texas its claim to much of New Mexico; (4) compensate Texas by having the federal government pay the pre-annexation Texas debts; (5) retain slavery in the District of Columbia but abolish the sale of slaves there; (6) adopt a more effective federal law designed to recapture fugitive slaves; and (7) deny Congress the authority to interfere with the interstate slave trade. His complex cluster of proposals, called the Omnibus bill, became in substance the Compromise of 1850, but only after seven months of negotiations punctuated by the greatest debate in congressional history.

THE GREAT DEBATE On March 4, a feeble Senator John C. Calhoun of South Carolina, desperately ill with tuberculosis, arrived in the Senate chamber. The uncompromising defender of slavery was so sick that a colleague had to read his defiant rejection of Clay's compromise.

The South, Calhoun explained, needed Congress to protect the rights of slave owners to take their "property" into the new territories. Otherwise, he warned, the "cords which bind" the Union would be severed. If California were admitted as a free state, the South could no longer "remain honorably and safely in the Union" because the free states would increasingly outnumber the slave states in Congress and in the Electoral College. Calhoun asserted that the only solution to the growing sectional divide was for the North to allow slavery in California and the other western territories. Otherwise, he threatened, the southern states would leave the Union (secede) and form their own national government.

Three days later, on March 7, Calhoun hobbled into the Senate to hear the "golden-throated" Daniel Webster speak. Widely recognized as the most eloquent orator in an age devoted to oratory, Webster, broad-shouldered and deep-chested, was resplendent in an indigo blue coat with shiny brass buttons.

"I wish to speak today," Webster began, "not as a Massachusetts man, not as a Northern man, but as an American . . . I speak today for the preservation of the Union." He blamed both Northerners and Southerners for the crisis but acknowledged that both regions had legitimate grievances: The South understandably objected to the excesses of "infernal fanatics and abolitionists" in the

North, and the North resented southern efforts to expand slavery into the new western territories.

With respect to escaped slaves, Webster reminded everyone that the Constitution of 1787 already required that every state cooperate in the recapture of runaways. He then shocked his fellow New Englanders and outraged abolitionists by declaring that "the South, in my judgment, is right, and the North is wrong." Fugitive slaves must be returned to their owners.

Webster, however, dismissed the notion of secession. Turning his withering gaze upon Calhoun, he said that he had no patience with men for whom "everything is absolute," who lack the capacity for compromise. Southern threats to leave the Union would bring civil war. "Secession! Peaceable secession! Sir, your eyes and mine are never destined to see that miracle." Instead of looking into such "caverns of darkness," let "men enjoy the fresh air of liberty and union. Let them look to a more hopeful future." For almost four hours, Webster, bathed in sweat, pleaded with his colleagues to rise above absolutism and become compromising statesmen.

Webster's evenhanded speech angered extremists on both sides. No sooner had he finished than someone in the overflowing gallery yelled, "Traitor!" Calhoun then stood to assert that the Union could indeed "be broken. Great moral causes will break it." Northern abolitionists savaged Webster for calling them fanatics and for his defense of the fugitive slave law.

On March 11, William Seward, the former New York governor who was now a first-year Whig senator, gave a provocative three-hour speech in which he declared that *any* compromise with slavery was "radically wrong and essentially vicious." There was, he insisted, "a *higher law* than the Constitution," and it demanded the abolition of slavery through acts of civil disobedience. Seward encouraged his fellow New Yorkers to defy the federal fugitive slave law by extending a "cordial welcome" to escaped slaves and defending them from efforts to return them south. The southern supporters of slavery, he concluded, must give way to the inevitable "progress of emancipation."

Seward's speech outraged Southerners, who repudiated his implication that the godly abolitionists were somehow above the law. Clay dismissed Seward's "wild, reckless, and abominable theories," and a Georgia newspaper said that Seward was a lunatic who should be ushered out of the Capitol in a straitjacket. The senator from New York, however, was unapologetic. He had sought to speak for the enslaved as well as all humankind.

COMPROMISE EFFORTS For his part, Henry Clay confessed that he was "angry at everybody." The extremists were postponing a vote on his compromise proposal. He got little help from President Taylor, who continued to focus solely on the admission of California as a new state. In a letter to his son, Clay reported that the "Administration, the Abolitionists, the Ultra Southern men, and the timid Whigs of the North are all combined against" his plan. He had given his all for the Great Compromise, but despite his herculean efforts, the Omnibus Bill was dead in the water.

On July 4, 1850, Congress celebrated Independence Day by gathering beneath a broiling summer sun at the base of the unfinished Washington Monument. President Taylor suffered a mild sunstroke while listening to three hours of patriotic speeches. At the White House, he tried to recover by gorging himself on iced milk, cherries, and raw vegetables. That night, he developed a violent stomach disorder. Five days later, he prayed and asked for water. "I am about to die," he said. "I expect the summons soon. I have endeavored to discharge all of my duties faithfully." A few minutes later, he died.

Taylor's shocking death bolstered the chances of a compromise in Congress because his successor, Vice President Millard Fillmore, supported Clay's proposals. It was a striking reversal: Taylor, the Louisiana slaveholder, had been ready to make war on his native South to save the Union; Fillmore, whom Southerners thought opposed slavery, was ready to make peace. Fillmore asserted his control by asking the entire Taylor-appointed cabinet to resign. He then named Daniel Webster as secretary of state, signaling that he joined Webster in supporting compromise.

Fillmore benefited from the support of Illinois senator Stephen A. Douglas, a rising star in the Democratic party, the youngest man in the Senate, and a friend of the South. Pragmatic, brash, and brilliant, Douglas, the clever "Little Giant" (he stood just five feet four), suggested that the best way to salvage Clay's "comprehensive scheme" was to break it into separate proposals and vote on them one at a time. President Fillmore endorsed the idea.

The plan worked miraculously, in part because John C. Calhoun had died and was no longer in the Senate to obstruct efforts at conciliation. Each component of Clay's plan passed in the Senate and the House, several of them by the narrowest of margins. (Only five senators voted for all the items of the compromise.)

On September 7, 1850, when it became apparent that the Compromise of 1850 would become law, senators and congressmen burst into tears. That night, celebrants in the streets of Washington lit bonfires, rang church bells, chanted "the Union is saved," and applauded as soldiers fired cannons to salute the compromise. "The long agony is over," sighed President Fillmore.

In its final version, the Compromise of 1850 included the following elements: (1) California entered the Union as a free state, ending forever the old balance of free and slave states; (2) the Texas–New Mexico Act made New Mexico a separate territory and set the Texas state boundary at its present location. In return for relinquishing its claims to much of New Mexico, Texas received $10 million, which secured payment of the state's debt; (3) the Utah Act set up the Utah Territory and gave the territorial legislature authority over "all rightful subjects of legislation," including slavery; (4) a Fugitive Slave Act required the federal government and northern states to help capture and return runaway slaves to the South; and (5) as a gesture to anti-slavery groups, the public sale of slaves (but not slavery itself) was abolished in the District of Columbia.

As President Fillmore signed the last of the measures into law, he claimed that they represented a "final settlement" to the sectional tensions over slavery. Many Americans agreed. "Harmony is secured. Patriots rejoice!" trumpeted one newspaper. Henry Clay predicted that his solution would "pacify, tranquilize, and harmonize the country."

The Compromise of 1850, however, was not so much an example of warring people making concessions as it was a temporary and imperfect truce over the future of slavery. Extremists on both sides vowed to defy it. As Salmon P. Chase, an Ohio Free-Soiler, stressed, "the question of slavery in the territories has been avoided. It has not been settled." In the Lower South, proslavery zealots dismissed Clay's compromise as a surrender to the fanatical abolitionists. John Quitman of Mississippi announced that the only option for the South was secession, while northern abolitionists called the compromise an "enactment of hell" because of the fugitive slave provision.

In the end, the Compromise of 1850 only postponed secession and civil war for ten years. Soon, aspects of the compromise would reignite sectional tensions.

THE FUGITIVE SLAVE ACT Within two months of the passage of the Compromise of 1850, the squabbling between North and South resumed.

The **Fugitive Slave Act** was the most controversial element of the Compromise of 1850. It did more than strengthen the hand of slave catchers; it sought to recover slaves who had already escaped months or years before and considered themselves safe. It also inspired unscrupulous slave traders to kidnap free blacks in northern free states, claiming that they were runaway slaves. The law denied fugitives a jury trial and forced citizens to help locate and capture runaways.

Abolitionists fumed. "This filthy enactment was made in the nineteenth century, by people who could read and write," Ralph Waldo Emerson marveled in his diary. He urged people to break the new law "on the earliest occasion."

The mere existence of the Fugitive Slave Act was intolerable to many northern abolitionists, several of whom advocated violence. "The only way to make the Fugitive Slave Law a dead letter," Frederick Douglass threatened, "is to make half-a-dozen or more dead kidnappers." In Springfield, Massachusetts, fiery abolitionist John Brown formed an armed band of African Americans, called the League of Gileadites, to attack slave catchers. Such efforts led Horace Greeley, a prominent New York newspaper editor, to write that the Fugitive Slave Act was "a very bad investment for slaveholders" because it was creating such a backlash against slavery throughout the northern states.

UNCLE TOM'S CABIN   During the 1850s, anti-slavery advocates gained a powerful new weapon in the form of Harriet Beecher Stowe's best-selling novel, *Uncle Tom's Cabin; or Life among the Lowly* (1852). Stowe, the daughter and sister of ministers, epitomized the deep religious underpinnings of the abolitionist movement. While raising six children in Cincinnati, Ohio, during the 1830s and 1840s, she helped runaway slaves who had crossed the Ohio River from Kentucky.

Like many anti-slavery activists, Stowe despised the Fugitive Slave Act. In the spring of 1850, having moved to Maine, she began writing *Uncle Tom's Cabin* "with her *heart's blood*." She intended the book to energize the abolitionist movement. "The time has come," she said, "when even a woman or a child who can speak a word for freedom and humanity is bound to speak."

Uncle Tom's Cabin was a smashing success. Within two days, the first printing had sold out, and by the end of its first year, it had sold 300,000 copies in the United States and more than a million in Great Britain. Soon there was a children's version and a traveling theater production. By 1855, it was called "the most popular novel of our day."

Uncle Tom's Cabin depicts improbable saints and sinners, crude stereotypes, impossibly virtuous black victims, and melodramatic escapes involving fugitive slaves. The persecuted Uncle Tom, whose gentleness and generosity grow even as he is sold

135,000 SETS, 270,000 VOLUMES SOLD.

UNCLE TOM'S CABIN

FOR SALE HERE.

AN EDITION FOR THE MILLION, COMPLETE IN 1 Vol. PRICE 37 1-2 CENTS.
" " IN GERMAN, IN 1 Vol. PRICE 50 CENTS.
" " IN 2 Vols. CLOTH, 6 PLATES, PRICE $1.50.
SUPERB ILLUSTRATED EDITION, IN 1 Vol. WITH 153 ENGRAVINGS,
PRICES FROM $2.50 TO $5.00.

The Greatest Book of the Age.

"The Greatest Book of the Age" *Uncle Tom's Cabin*, as this advertisement indicated, was an influential best seller.

as a slave and taken south; the villainous white planter Simon Legree, who torments and tortures Tom before ordering his death; the angelic Little Eva, a white girl who dies after befriending Tom; and the beautiful but desperate Eliza, who escapes from slave catchers by carrying her baby to freedom across the icy Ohio River—all became stock characters in American folklore.

The novel reveals how the brutal realities of slavery harmed everyone associated with it. It ends with Stowe predicting that Almighty God's wrath would destroy America if slavery were not abolished.

Abolitionist leader Frederick Douglass said that *Uncle Tom's Cabin* was like "a flash" that lit "a million camp fires in front of the embattled host of slavery." The book incensed slaveholders, one of whom called Stowe that "wretch in petticoats." Another mailed her a parcel containing the severed ear of a disobedient slave.

THE ELECTION OF 1852 In 1852, it took the Democrats forty-nine ballots before they chose Franklin Pierce of New Hampshire as their presidential candidate. When Pierce heard the results, he was stunned: "You are looking at the most surprised man who ever lived!" When his wife Jane learned of the nomination, she fainted. Their concerns were well-founded, for Pierce had few presidential qualities.

The Democrats' platform endorsed the Compromise of 1850, including enforcement of the Fugitive Slave Act. For their part, the Whigs repudiated Millard Fillmore, who had faithfully supported the Compromise of 1850, and chose General Winfield Scott, another hero of the Mexican-American War.

At six feet five and 300 pounds, Scott was a physically imposing leader and accomplished general. Yet he proved to be an inept campaigner—so conceited, short-tempered, and arrogant that he earned the nickname "Old Fuss and Feathers." He carried only the states of Tennessee, Kentucky, Massachusetts, and Vermont.

The Whigs, now without their greatest leaders, Henry Clay and Daniel Webster, had lost virtually all their support in the Lower South. Pierce overwhelmed Scott in the electoral college, 254 to 42, although the popular vote was close: 1.6 million to 1.4 million.

The forty-eight-year-old Pierce, a mediocre congressman and senator who had served as a general in the Mexican-American War, was, like James K. Polk, touted as another Andrew Jackson. Pierce promoted western expansion and the conversion of more territories into states, even if it meant adding more slave states to the Union. However, he also acknowledged that the Compromise of 1850 had defused a "perilous crisis." He urged North and South to avoid aggravating the other.

Pierce was burdened by the recent death of his eleven-year-old son, Benjamin. The president-elect and his wife had witnessed their son's death in a train accident just days before the inaugural ceremony. Benjamin was the third son that the Pierces had lost. Still in mourning, Jane Pierce refused to attend her husband's swearing in; she thereafter lived in seclusion, writing letters to her dead children, cursing politics, and blaming her husband for her troubles.

Pierce was an intelligent man capable of eloquent speechmaking, but he had tragic flaws and private demons. Blinded by a desire to be liked and cursed with raging ambition, he was a timid, indecisive leader who was often drunk. (He would die in 1869 of alcoholism.)

As president, Pierce sought—and failed—to acquire Cuba as a slave state and proved unable to unite the warring factions of his party. By the end of his first year in office, Democratic leaders had decided that he was a failure. James W. Forney, a political friend, confessed that the presidency "overshadows him [Pierce]. He is crushed by its great duties and seeks refuge in [alcohol]." Pierce was labeled a "doughface" by his opponents, meaning a Northern man with Southern principles who hated abolitionists for causing the tensions over slavery. His closest friend in the cabinet was Secretary of War Jefferson Davis, the future president of the Confederacy. Friendships such as this one led Harriet Beecher Stowe to call Pierce an "arch-traitor."

KANSAS-NEBRASKA CRISIS

During the mid–nineteenth century, Americans discovered the vast markets of Asia. As trade with China and Japan grew, merchants and manufacturers called for a transcontinental railroad connecting the Eastern Seaboard with the Pacific coast to facilitate both the flow of commerce with Asia and the settlement of the western territories. Those promoting the railroad did not realize that the issue would renew sectional rivalries and reignite the debate over the westward extension of slavery.

Stephen A. Douglas, ca. 1852
The Illinois Democratic senator authored the Kansas-Nebraska Act.

In 1852 and 1853, Congress considered several proposals for a transcontinental rail line. Secretary of War Jefferson Davis of Mississippi favored a southern route across the territories acquired from Mexico. Senator Stephen A. Douglas of Illinois insisted that Chicago be the Midwest hub for the new rail line and urged Congress to pass the **Kansas-Nebraska Act** so that the territory west of Missouri and Iowa could be settled.

To win the support of southern legislators, Douglas championed popular sovereignty, whereby voters in each new territory would decide whether to allow slavery. It was a clever way to get around the 1820 Missouri Compromise, which banned slavery north of the 36th parallel, where Kansas and Nebraska were located.

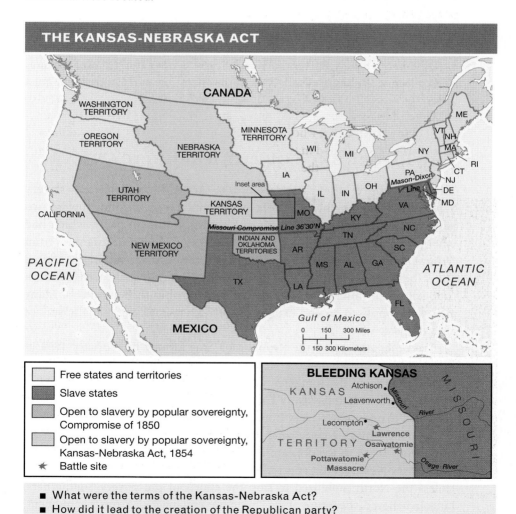

THE KANSAS-NEBRASKA ACT

Free states and territories

Slave states

Open to slavery by popular sovereignty, Compromise of 1850

Open to slavery by popular sovereignty, Kansas-Nebraska Act, 1854

★ Battle site

BLEEDING KANSAS

- ■ What were the terms of the Kansas-Nebraska Act?
- ■ How did it lead to the creation of the Republican party?
- ■ What happened at Pottawatomie and Osawatomie?

Southerners demanded more, however, and Douglas complied, in part because he would make a fortune if the bill passed; he owned property needed by a transcontinental railroad. He supported the South in recommending the formal repeal of the Missouri Compromise and the creation of *two* territorial governments rather than one: Kansas, west of Missouri, and Nebraska, west of Iowa and Minnesota. This meant that millions of fertile acres would be opened to slaveholders.

In May 1854, Douglas convinced both Democrats and southern Whigs to pass the Kansas-Nebraska Act. The measure was approved by a vote of 37 to 14 in the Senate and 113 to 100 in the House.

The anti-slavery faction in Congress, mostly Whigs, had been crushed, and the national Whig party essentially died with them. Out of its ashes would emerge a new party: the Republicans. As Senator Charles Sumner told colleague William Seward, "Out of the chaos, the party of freedom must arise."

The Emergence of the Republican Party

The dispute over the Kansas-Nebraska Act led northern anti-slavery Whigs and some northern anti-slavery Democrats to gravitate toward two new parties. One was the American ("Know-Nothing") party, which had emerged in opposition to the surge of mostly Catholic immigrants from Ireland and Germany, nearly 3 million of whom had arrived in the United States between 1845 and 1854. The Know-Nothings embraced *nativism* (opposition to immigrants) by denying citizenship to newcomers. Many also were opposed to the expansion of slavery and the "fanaticism" of abolitionists.

The other new party, the Republicans, was formed in February 1854 in Ripon, Wisconsin, when the so-called "conscience Whigs" (those opposed to slavery) split from the southern pro-slavery "cotton Whigs." The conscience Whigs joined with anti-slavery Democrats and Free-Soilers to form a party dedicated to excluding slavery from the western territories.

A young Illinois congressman named Abraham Lincoln made the transition from Whig to Republican. He said that the passage of Stephen Douglas's Kansas-Nebraska Act angered him and transformed his views on slavery. Unless the North mobilized to stop the efforts of pro-slavery Southerners, Lincoln believed, the future of the Union was endangered. From that moment, he focused on reversing the Kansas-Nebraska Act and preventing the extension of slavery into new territories.

"**BLEEDING KANSAS**" The passage of the Kansas-Nebraska Act soon placed Kansas at the center of the increasingly violent debate over slavery. While Nebraska would become a free state, Kansas was up for grabs. According to the Kansas-Nebraska Act, the residents of the Kansas Territory were "perfectly free to form and regulate their domestic institutions [slavery] in their own way."

The law, however, said nothing about *when* Kansans could decide about slavery, so each side tried to gain political control of the vast territory. "Come on then, Gentlemen of the Slave States," New York senator William Seward taunted. "We will engage in competition for the virgin soil of Kansas, and God give the victory to the side which is stronger in numbers as it is in the right." South Carolina congressman Preston Brooks accepted the challenge, announcing that "the fate of the South is to be decided in Kansas."

Groups for and against slavery recruited armed emigrants to move to Kansas. When Kansas's first federal governor arrived in 1854, he reported to President Pierce that Southerners were arriving with a "dogged determination to force slavery into this Territory" in advance of the election of a territorial legislature in March 1855.

On Election Day, thousands of heavily armed border ruffians from Missouri traveled to Kansas, illegally elected pro-slavery legislators, and vowed to kill every "God-damned abolitionist in the Territory," as militia leader David Atchison urged. As soon as it convened, the territorial legislature expelled its few anti-slavery members and declared that the territory would be open to slavery. The governor then rushed to Washington, D.C., to plead with Pierce to intervene with federal troops. Pierce's spineless solution was to replace the governor with a man who would support the pro-slavery faction.

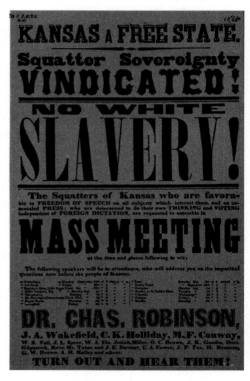

Kansas a Free State This broadside advertises a series of mass meetings in Kansas in support of the free-state cause, based on the principle of "squatter" or popular sovereignty, letting the residents decide the issue of slavery.

Outraged free-state advocates in Kansas, now a majority, spurned this "bogus" pro-slavery government and elected their own delegates to a constitutional convention that met in Topeka in 1855. There they applied for statehood and drafted a state constitution that excluded slavery. By 1856, a free-state "governor" and "legislature" were operating in Topeka. There were now two competing governments claiming to rule the Kansas Territory. Soon there was a territorial civil war, which journalists called "**Bleeding Kansas**."

In May 1856, a pro-slavery force of more than 500 Missourians, Alabamans, and South Carolinians invaded the free-state town of Lawrence, Kansas, just twenty-five miles from the Missouri border. The mob rampaged through the town, destroying the newspaper printing presses, burning homes, and ransacking shops.

The "Sack of Lawrence" ignited the passions of abolitionist John Brown. The son of fervent Ohio Calvinists who taught their children that life was a crusade against sin, Brown believed that Christians must "break the jaws of the wicked" and that the wickedest Americans were those who owned and traded slaves. Upon meeting Brown, many declared him crazy; those who supported his efforts thought he was a saint. He was some of both.

By the mid-1850s, the fifty-five-year-old Brown had left his home in Springfield, Massachusetts, to become a holy warrior against slavery. In his view, blacks deserved liberty and full social equality. A newspaper reporter said that Brown was a "strange" and "iron-willed" old man with a "fiery nature and a cold temper, and a cool head—a volcano beneath a covering of snow."

Two days after the attack on Lawrence, Brown led four of his sons and a son-in-law to Pottawatomie, Kansas, a pro-slavery settlement near the Missouri border. On the night of May 24, the group dragged five men from their houses and hacked them to death with swords. "God is my judge," Brown told one of his sons. "We were justified under the circumstances." Without "the shedding of blood," he added, "there is no remission of sins."

The Pottawatomie Massacre launched a brutal guerrilla war in the Kansas Territory. On August 30, pro-slavery Missourians raided a free-state settlement at Osawatomie. They looted and burned houses and shot Frederick Brown, John's son, through the heart. By the end of 1856, about 200 settlers had been killed in "Bleeding Kansas."

SENATE BLOODSHED On May 22, 1856, an ugly incident in the U.S. Senate shocked the nation. Two days before, Republican senator Charles Sumner of Massachusetts, a passionate abolitionist, had delivered a scalding speech in which he showered slave owners with insults and charged them with unleashing vigilantes and assassins in Kansas. His most savage attack was directed at

Andrew Pickens Butler, an elderly senator from South Carolina. Butler, Sumner charged, was a fumbling old man who had "chosen a mistress . . . who . . . though polluted in the sight of the world, is chaste [pure] in his sight—I mean the harlot [prostitute], Slavery."

Sumner's speech enraged Butler's cousin, South Carolina congressman Preston S. Brooks. On May 22, Brooks confronted Sumner as he sat at his Senate desk, shouting that Sumner had slandered Butler and the state of South Carolina. He then began beating Sumner with a gold-knobbed cane. Sumner, his head gushing blood, nearly died; he would not return to the Senate for almost four years.

Southerners celebrated Brooks as a hero. The *Richmond Enquirer* described his attack as "good in conception, better in execution, and best of all in consequences." In satisfying his rage, though, Brooks had created a martyr—"Bloodied Sumner"—for the anti-slavery cause. Sumner's brutal beating also had an unintended political effect: it drove more Northerners into the Republican party.

SECTIONAL SQUABBLES The violence of "Bleeding Kansas" and "Bloodied Sumner" spilled over into the 1856 presidential election. At its first national convention, the Republicans fastened on the eccentric, shameless self-promoter, John C. Frémont, who had led the conquest of Mexican California.

The Republican platform borrowed heavily from the former Whigs. It endorsed federal funding for a transcontinental railroad and other transportation improvements. It denounced the repeal of the Missouri Compromise, the Democratic party's policy of territorial expansion, and the "barbarism" of slavery. For the first time, a major-party platform had taken a stand against slavery.

The southern-dominated Democrats dumped President Franklin Pierce, who remains the only elected president to be denied renomination by his party. Instead, they chose sixty-five-year-old James Buchanan of Pennsylvania, a mild-mannered former senator and secretary of state. Their platform endorsed the Kansas-Nebraska Act, called for vigorous enforcement of the Fugitive Slave Act, and stressed that Congress should not interfere with slavery in states or territories.

In the campaign of 1856, the Republicans had few southern supporters and only a handful in the border slave states of Delaware, Maryland, Kentucky, and Missouri. Frémont swept the northernmost states with 114 electoral votes, but Buchanan added five free states—Pennsylvania, New Jersey, Illinois, Indiana, and California—to his southern majority for a total of 174. The Democrats now would control the White House, the Congress, and the Supreme Court.

THE ELECTION OF 1856

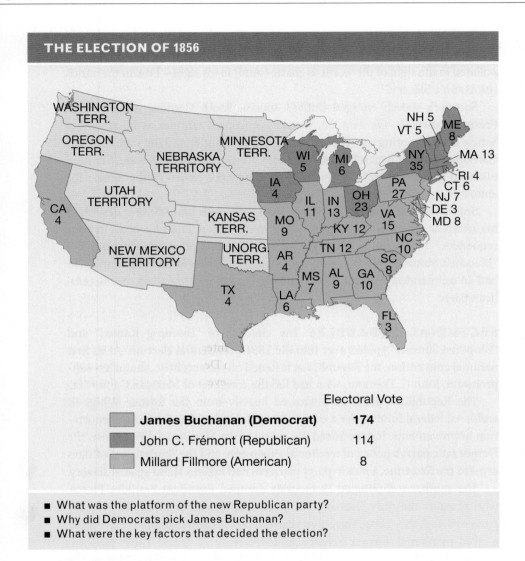

Electoral Vote

	James Buchanan (Democrat)	174
	John C. Frémont (Republican)	114
	Millard Fillmore (American)	8

- What was the platform of the new Republican party?
- Why did Democrats pick James Buchanan?
- What were the key factors that decided the election?

PRESIDENT BUCHANAN James Buchanan, America's first unmarried president, looked the part of a statesman. Blessed with a fine physique, he was handsome and had elegant manners. He had built an impressive political career on his commitment to states' rights and his aggressive promotion of territorial expansion. He believed that saving the Union depended upon ignoring abolitionists and making concessions to the South. Republicans charged that he lacked the backbone to stand up to the southern slaveholders who dominated the Democratic majorities in Congress.

Buchanan was one of the most experienced presidents of the nineteenth century. As it turned out, he had limited ability as a leader—and lots of bad luck. During his first six months in office, three major events caused his undoing: (1) a sharp downturn in the economy; (2) the Supreme Court decision in the *Dred Scott* case; and, (3) new troubles in strife-torn Kansas.

THE PANIC OF 1857   By the summer of 1857, the economy was growing too fast. Too many railroads and factories were being built, and European demand for American corn and wheat was declining. The result was a financial panic triggered by the failure of the Ohio Life Insurance and Trust Company on August 24, 1857. If such a prestigious institution could close its doors, people worried, the entire economy might collapse.

Upon hearing the news, worried customers began withdrawing their money from banks. This forced the banks to call in loans, causing many businesses to go bankrupt. By the fall, tens of thousands had lost their jobs, and banks had started foreclosing on homes, farms, and businesses. Virtually every bank closed in New York City, where federal troops had to disperse angry mobs.

Buchanan and his administration refused to intervene in what came to be called the Panic of 1857. In his annual message in December 1857, he pledged that the government would do nothing to relieve the individual suffering caused by the financial panic. Most of those complaining the loudest, he maintained, were speculators who "deserved a gambler's fate."

Planters in the South, whose agricultural economy suffered the least during the panic, took great delight in the problems plaguing the northern economy. Senator James Henry Hammond of South Carolina gave a speech in early 1858 in which he told northern businessmen:

> Your slaves are white, of your own race; you are brothers of one blood. They are your equals in natural endowment of intellect, and they feel galled by your degradation. Our slaves do not vote. We give them no political power. Yours do vote, and being the majority, they are the depositories of all your political power.

Hammond suggested that the North adopt race-based slavery to prevent working-class whites from taking control of the social and political order. He added that southern slaves were happier, healthier, and better cared for than their "free" working-class counterparts in the North. Northern states needed to "enslave" their white workers so as to enjoy the social stability that slavery brought to the southern states.

THE *DRED SCOTT* CASE In his inaugural address, President Buchanan asserted that the issue of slavery should be decided in the Supreme Court. Two days later, on March 6, 1857, the Court delivered a decision in the long-awaited case of ***Dred Scott v. Sandford,*** which had taken eleven years to work its way through the judicial process.

Scott, born a slave in Virginia, had been taken to St. Louis in 1830 and sold to an army surgeon, who took him to Illinois, then to the Wisconsin Territory (later Minnesota), and finally back to St. Louis in 1842. While in the Wisconsin Territory, Scott had married Harriet Robinson, and they eventually had two daughters.

In 1846, Scott, with the aid of abolitionist attorneys, filed suit in Missouri, claiming that his residence in Illinois and the Wisconsin Territory had made him free because slavery was outlawed in those areas. A Missouri jury decided in his favor, but the state Supreme Court ruled against him. When the case was appealed to the U.S. Supreme Court, the nation anxiously awaited its opinion.

Seven of the nine justices were Democrats, and five were Southerners. The vote was 7 to 2 against Scott, and five of the seven who voted against Scott were slaveholders. Seventy-nine-year-old Chief Justice Roger B. Taney

Dred Scott The Supreme Court's refusal to give Scott and his family their freedom fanned the flames of the intense debate over slavery.

of Maryland, a supporter of the South and of slavery, ruled that Scott lacked legal standing because he was not a U.S. citizen and could never become one. When the Constitution was drafted in 1787, Taney claimed, African Americans were deemed "an inferior and subject race" and had been implicitly excluded from citizenship. On the issue of Scott's residency, Taney argued that the now-defunct Missouri Compromise of 1820 had deprived citizens of property by prohibiting slavery in selected states, an action "not warranted by the Constitution."

The notorious *Dred Scott* decision thus declared an act of Congress (the Missouri Compromise) unconstitutional for the first time since *Marbury v. Madison* (1803). Even more important, the decision challenged the concept of popular sovereignty. If Congress could not exclude slavery from a territory, as Taney argued, then neither could a territorial government created by an act of Congress. Suddenly, all of the West—and the North—was open to slavery.

Pro-slavery advocates loved the Court's decision. Even President Buchanan approved. Republicans and abolitionists, on the other hand, protested the *Dred Scott* decision because it nullified their anti-slavery program.

THE LECOMPTON CONSTITUTION Meanwhile, in the Kansas Territory, the fight over slavery continued, with both sides resorting to trickery and violence. Just before James Buchanan's inauguration, in early 1857, the pro-slavery territorial legislature scheduled a constitutional convention. The governor vetoed the measure, but the legislature overrode his veto. The governor resigned in protest, and Buchanan replaced him with Robert J. Walker.

With Buchanan's approval, Walker pledged to free-state Kansans (who made up an overwhelming majority of the residents) that the new constitution would be submitted to a fair vote. But when the pro-slavery constitutional convention, meeting at Lecompton, drafted a constitution under which Kansas would become a slave state and exclude free blacks, opponents of slavery boycotted the referendum on the constitution, enabling the pro-slavery constitution to be approved. It was then sent to Congress for endorsement.

At that point, Buchanan took a critical step. Influenced by southern advisers, he urged Congress to approve the Lecompton Constitution. A new wave of outrage swept across the northern states. Stephen A. Douglas, the most prominent midwestern Democrat, sided with anti-slavery Republicans because Buchanan's action would deny the majority of Kansas voters the right to decide the issue in a general election. Douglas told a newspaper reporter that "I made Mr. James Buchanan, and by God, sir, I will unmake him."

Meanwhile, in Kansas, a new acting governor scheduled another referendum on the proposed pro-slavery Lecompton constitution. On January 4, 1858, voters overwhelmingly rejected it, 10,226 to 138. In April 1858, Congress ordered that Kansans vote yet again. On August 2, 1858, they rejected the Lecompton constitution, 11,300 to 1,788. With that vote, Kansas cleared the way for its eventual admission as a free state.

DOUGLAS VERSUS LINCOLN The controversy over slavery in Kansas fractured the Democratic party. Stephen A. Douglas, one of the few remaining Democrats with support in both the North and the South, struggled to keep the party from fragmenting. First, however, he had to secure his home base in Illinois, where in 1858 he faced reelection to the Senate.

To challenge Douglas, Illinois Republicans selected a respected lawyer, Abraham Lincoln. Lincoln was born in Kentucky in 1809, the son of a farmer/carpenter so poor that he rented out his hardworking son to neighbors.

When Abraham was seven, the family moved to Indiana. Two years later, his "angel mother" Nancy died, and his father remarried. In March 1830, the Lincolns moved to Illinois. In Springfield, Lincoln worked as a farmer, rail-splitter, and surveyor. He later became an attorney and married Mary Todd, who was from a wealthy, slave-owning family in Lexington, Kentucky.

In 1834, Lincoln was elected to the Illinois legislature and served four terms as a Whig. He supported Henry Clay's leadership and Clay's promotion of the American System. "My politics are short and sweet," Lincoln said. "I am in favor of a national bank. I am in favor of the internal improvement system and a high protective tariff." He opposed the expansion of slavery, although he was no abolitionist. He did not believe that the nation should force the South to end what he referred to as "the monstrous injustice," but did insist that slavery not be expanded into new western territories.

In 1846, Lincoln won a seat in the U.S. Congress while pledging to serve only one term. After his single term, he returned to Springfield. In 1854, however, the Kansas-Nebraska Act drew him back into the political arena.

In 1856, Lincoln joined the Republican party, and two years later he emerged as the obvious choice to oppose Stephen A. Douglas. Lincoln sought to raise his profile by challenging Douglas to a series of debates across Illinois. The seven **Lincoln-Douglas debates** took place between August 21 and October 15, 1858. They attracted tens of thousands of spectators and transformed the Senate race into a battle for the future of the republic.

The two men differed as much physically as they did politically. Lincoln was tall and gangly, sinewy and craggy-featured, with a long neck, big ears, and deep-set, brooding gray eyes. Unassuming in manner and attire, he lightened his speeches with folksy humor and entertaining stories. To sympathetic observers, he conveyed an air of simplicity, sincerity, and common sense.

The short, stocky Douglas, on the other hand, was quite the dandy. He wore custom-tailored suits, traveled to the debate sites in a luxurious private railroad car, and strutted with the pugnacious air of a predestined champion. Yet he knew Lincoln was a formidable opponent, describing him as "the strong man of the party—full of wit, facts, dates, and the best stump speaker. . . in the West."

The basic dispute between the two candidates, Lincoln insisted, lay in Douglas's indifference to the immorality of slavery. Douglas, he said, was preoccupied with process (popular sovereignty); in contrast, Lincoln claimed to be focused on principle. "I have always hated slavery as much as any abolitionist," he stressed. The American government, he predicted, could not "endure, permanently half *slave* and half *free*. . . . It will become *all* one thing, or *all* the other."

Douglas disagreed, asking what was to keep the United States from tolerating both slavery for blacks and freedom for whites? Lincoln responded by displaying his own racism. "I am not nor ever have been," he maintained, "in favor of bringing about in any way the social and political equality of the white and black races." He did not endorse giving blacks the vote or allowing them to run for office, serve on juries, or marry whites. The white race, he concluded, must always remain in "the superior position."

At one point, Douglas accused his opponent of being "two-faced." Lincoln replied: "I leave it to my audience. If I had another face, do you think I would wear this one?"

Although Lincoln won the popular vote, Douglas was elected because he won the support of the Democratic-controlled state legislature. Lincoln's energetic campaign, however, had made him a national figure. And across the northern states, the Republicans won so many congressional seats in 1858 that they seized control of the House of Representatives.

AN OUTNUMBERED SOUTH In May 1858, the free state of Minnesota entered the Union; in February 1859, another nonslave territory, Oregon, gained statehood. The slave states of the South were quickly becoming a besieged minority, and their insecurity deepened.

At the same time, tensions over slavery were becoming more violent. In 1858, more than fifty members of Congress engaged in the largest brawl ever staged on the floor of the House of Representatives. The fracas ended when John "Bowie Knife" Potter of Wisconsin yanked off the hairpiece of a Mississippi congressman and shouted, "I've scalped him."

Like the scuffling congressmen, more and more Americans began to feel that compromise was impossible, and that slavery could be ended or defended only with violence. The editor of a pro-slavery Kansas newspaper wanted to kill abolitionists: "If I can't kill a man, I'll kill a woman; and if I can't kill a woman, I'll kill a child." Some Southerners were already talking of secession again. In 1858, former Alabama congressman William L. Yancey, the leader of the hot-tempered southern "fire-eaters," said that it would be easy "to precipitate the Cotton States into a revolution."

In the North, Frederick Douglass spoke for many when he claimed that the "pure slavery party" was determined to suppress abolitionists and increase its political power by launching a "murderous onslaught" against basic American rights. Yet Douglass saw in the pro-slavery party the irony of self-destruction.

"While crushing its millions [of enslaved blacks], it is also crushing itself" by leading more Northerners to embrace abolitionism.

JOHN BROWN'S RAID In October 1859, militant abolitionist John Brown surfaced again, this time in the East. Since the Pottawatomie Massacre in Kansas in 1856, he had kept a low profile while acquiring money and weapons from New England sympathizers, but his heartfelt commitment to abolishing slavery and promoting racial equality had intensified.

Brown was convinced that he was carrying out a divine mission. A moral absolutist who disdained compromise, he was one of the few whites willing to live among black people and die for them, and he was a brilliant propagandist for the abolitionist cause.

In 1859, Brown hatched a plan to steal federal weapons and give them to rebellious slaves in western Virginia and Maryland in the hope of triggering mass uprisings across the South. "I want to free all the negroes in this state," he said. "If the citizens interfere with me, I must burn the town and have blood."

On the cool, rainy night of October 16, 1859, Brown left a Maryland farm and crossed the Potomac River with about twenty men, including three of his sons and five African Americans. Under cover of darkness, they walked five miles to the federal rifle arsenal in Harpers Ferry, Virginia (now West Virginia), where they took the sleeping town by surprise, cut the telegraph lines, and occupied the arsenal with its 100,000 rifles. Brown then dispatched several men to kidnap prominent slave owners and sound the alarm for local slaves to join the rebellion.

Only a few heeded the call, however, and by dawn, armed townsmen had surrounded the raiders. Brown and a dozen of his men, along with eleven white hostages and two of their slaves, holed up in a firehouse. Meanwhile, hundreds of armed whites poured into Harpers, Ferry, and Lieutenant Colonel Robert E. Lee arrived with a force of U.S. Marines.

On the morning of October 18, the marines ordered the abolitionists to surrender. Brown replied that he preferred to die fighting, warning that he "would sell his life as dearly as possible." Twelve marines then broke open the barricaded doors. Lieutenant Israel Green reported that he found himself face to face with "an old man kneeling with a carbine in his hand, with a long gray beard falling away from his face." Green would have killed Brown had his sword not bent back double when he plunged it into the abolitionist's chest. He then beat Brown until he passed out.

Brown's men had killed four townspeople and one marine while wounding another dozen. Of their own force, ten were killed (including two of Brown's sons) and five were captured; another five escaped.

A week later, Brown and his accomplices were put on trial for treason, murder, and "conspiring with Negroes to produce insurrection." The jury found him guilty. At his sentencing, Brown delivered a powerful speech in which he expressed pride in his effort to "mingle my blood further with the blood of my children and with the blood of millions in this slave country whose rights are disregarded by wicked, cruel, and unjust enactments." Though Virginia may execute him, he said, the question of slavery "is still to be settled."

On December 2, 1859, some 1,500 Virginia militiamen, including a young actor named John Wilkes Booth, who would later assassinate Abraham Lincoln, assembled for Brown's execution. Just before being placed atop his coffin in a wagon to take him to the scaffold, Brown wrote a final message,

John Brown   On his way to the gallows, Brown predicted that slavery would end only "after much bloodshed."

predicting that the "crimes of this *guilty* land will never be purged away, but with Blood."

Ralph Waldo Emerson called Brown a "saint" who had made "the gallows glorious like a cross." Frederick Douglass proclaimed him "our noblest American hero" whose commitment to ending slavery "was far greater than mine."

Caught up in a frenzy of fear after Brown's assault at Harper's Ferry, Southerners circulated wild rumors about slave rebellions. They "have declared war on us," warned Jefferson Davis. "Thank God there is no point left on which compromise can arise!"

Southern states strengthened their militia units and passed new restrictions on the movements of slaves. "We regard every man in our midst an enemy to the institutions of the South," said the *Atlanta Confederacy*, "who does not boldly declare that he believes African slavery to be a social, moral, and political blessing."

THE DEMOCRATS DIVIDE   Amid such hysteria, the nation mobilized for another presidential election, destined to be the most fateful in its history.

In April 1860, the Democrats gathered for what would become a disastrous nominating convention in Charleston, South Carolina.

President Buchanan had chosen not to seek a second term, leaving Stephen A. Douglas as the frontrunner. Douglas's northern supporters tried to straddle the slavery issue by promising to defend the institution in the South while assuring Northerners that it would not spread to new states. Southern firebrands, however, demanded federal protection for slavery in the territories as well as the states.

When the pro-slavery advocates lost, delegates from eight southern states walked out of the convention. "We say, go your way," exclaimed a Mississippi delegate to Douglas's supporters, "and we will go ours." Alabama's William Yancey declared that "we shall go to the wall" in the effort to spread slavery into the western territories. Planter William Preston left no doubt about the reason for the split: "Slavery is our King; Slavery is our truth; Slavery is our divine right."

The Democratic Convention then disintegrated into warring factions. Douglas's supporters reassembled at the Front Street Theater in Baltimore on June 18 and nominated him for president. Southern Democrats met first in Richmond and then in Baltimore, where they adopted the pro-slavery platform that had been defeated in Charleston. They named John C. Breckinridge, vice president under Buchanan, as their candidate because he promised to ensure that Congress would protect the right of emigrants to take their slaves to the western territories. Thus, another cord binding the nation together had snapped. The fracturing of the Democratic party into northern and southern factions made a Republican victory in 1860 almost certain.

LINCOLN'S ELECTION The Republican convention was held in May in Chicago, where everything came together for Abraham Lincoln. When he won the nomination over New York senator William H. Seward, the resulting cheer, wrote one journalist, was "like the rush of a great wind." The party reaffirmed its opposition to the extension of slavery and, to gain broader support, endorsed a series of traditional Whig policies promoting national economic expansion: a higher protective tariff, free farms ("homesteads") on federal lands out West, and federally financed internal improvements, including a transcontinental railroad.

The presidential nominating conventions revealed that opinions tended to be more radical in the Northeast and the Lower South. Attitude followed latitude. In the border states of Maryland, Delaware, Kentucky, and Missouri, a sense of moderation aroused former Whigs to make one more try at reconciliation. Meeting in Baltimore a week before the Republicans met in Chicago, they reorganized as the Constitutional Union party and nominated John Bell of Tennessee for president. Their platform centered on a vague statement promoting "the Constitution of the Country, the Union of the States, and the Enforcement of the Laws."

The bitterly contested campaign became a choice between Lincoln and Douglas in the North, and Breckinridge and Bell in the South. (Lincoln was not even on the ballot in the South.) Douglas, the only candidate to mount a nationwide campaign, promised that he would "make war boldly against Northern abolitionists and Southern disunionists." His heroic effort did little good, however.

At midnight on November 6, Lincoln's victory was announced. He had won 39 percent of the popular vote, the smallest plurality ever, but garnered a clear majority (180 votes) in the electoral college. He carried all eighteen free states but none of the slave states.

Abraham Lincoln A lanky and rawboned small-town lawyer, Lincoln won the presidential election in 1860.

Douglas came in second, with 29 percent of the popular vote. (He would die seven months later.)

Lincoln's political experience was meager, his learning limited, and his popular support shallow. "Never did a President enter upon office with less means at his command," poet James Russell Lowell remarked.

Yet the unassuming prairie lawyer from Springfield, Illinois, would earn the respect of colleagues and opponents who had originally scorned him. He would become, as poet Walt Whitman wrote, "the grandest figure yet, on all the crowded canvas of the Nineteenth Century."

THE RESPONSE IN THE SOUTH

Between November 8, 1860, when Lincoln was named president-elect, and March 4, 1861, when he was inaugurated, the United States of America disintegrated. Lincoln's election panicked Southerners who believed that the Republican party, as a Richmond newspaper asserted, was founded for one reason: "hatred of African slavery."

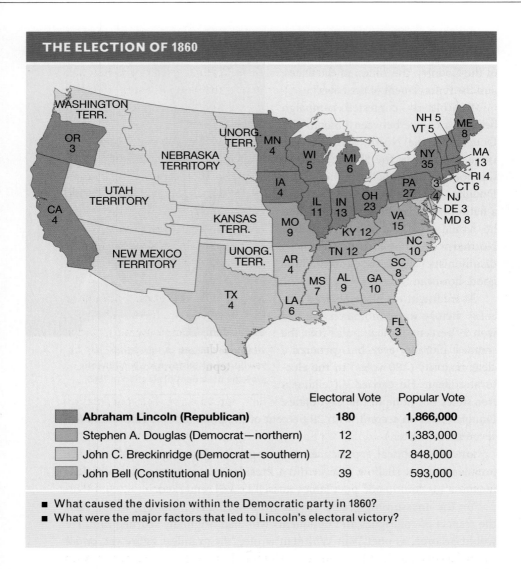

THE ELECTION OF 1860

	Electoral Vote	Popular Vote
Abraham Lincoln (Republican)	**180**	**1,866,000**
Stephen A. Douglas (Democrat—northern)	12	1,383,000
John C. Breckinridge (Democrat—southern)	72	848,000
John Bell (Constitutional Union)	39	593,000

■ What caused the division within the Democratic party in 1860?
■ What were the major factors that led to Lincoln's electoral victory?

Southerners especially feared that Lincoln was determined to prevent the expansion of a cotton economy that in 1860 had produced four million 500-pound bales—a record crop that made up nearly 60 percent of *all* American exports. Former president John Tyler wrote that the nation "had fallen on evil times" and that the "day of doom for the great model Republic is at hand."

False rumors that Lincoln planned to free the slaves raced across the South. One newspaper editorial called the president-elect a "bigoted, unscrupulous, and cold-blooded enemy of peace and equality of the slaveholding states."

Lincoln responded that southern fears were misguided. He stressed in a letter to a Georgia congressman that he was not a radical abolitionist and that his administration would not interfere with slavery. Yet he refused to provide such assurances in public, in part because he misread the depth of southern anger and concern over his election.

SOUTH CAROLINA SECEDES Pro-slavery fire-eaters in South Carolina viewed Lincoln's election as the final signal to abandon the Union. After Lincoln's victory, the state's entire congressional delegation resigned and left Washington, D.C. The state legislature then appointed a convention to decide whether it should remain in the Union.

Meeting in Charleston on December 20, 1860, the special convention focused on a single question: "How shall we sustain African slavery in South Carolina from a series of annoying attacks?" The delegates responded by unanimously voting to secede from the Union.

David Jamison Rutledge, who presided over the convention, announced that "the Ordinance of Secession has been signed and ratified, and I proclaim the State of South Carolina an Independent Commonwealth." Judge James L. Petigru, one of the few South Carolina Unionists, quipped that his newly independent state was "too small to be a Republic but too large to be an insane asylum."

As the news of South Carolina's secession spread across the state, church bells rang and shops closed. "THE UNION IS DISSOLVED!" screamed the *Charleston Mercury*. One Unionist kept a copy of the newspaper, scribbling on the bottom of it: "You'll regret the day you ever done this. I preserve this to see how it ends." Georgian Alexander Stephens, who would become the Confederacy's vice president, warned that "revolutions are much easier started than controlled."

PRESIDENT BUCHANAN BALKS The imploding nation needed a bold, decisive president, but instead it suffered under James Buchanan, who blamed the crisis on the "agitation" of fanatical abolitionists. He declared secession illegal, then claimed that he lacked the constitutional authority to force a state to rejoin the Union. "I can do nothing," he sighed. In the face of the president's clueless inaction, Southerners seized federal forts in the seceded states.

Amid the crisis, a Louisville, Kentucky, newspaper asked: "Will James Buchanan, who occupies the chair of Andrew Jackson, emulate the energy of the great Tennessean, or will he like a craven, cower before . . . the mad antics of those overexcited fanatics [who engineered secession]?" It was a timely question. Buchanan's secretary of state, Lewis Cass, who had served as Jackson's

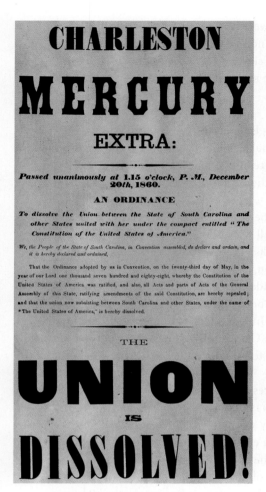

CHARLESTON

MERCURY

EXTRA:

Passed unanimously at 1.15 o'clock, P. M., December 20th, 1860.

AN ORDINANCE

To dissolve the Union between the State of South Carolina and other States united with her under the compact entitled " The Constitution of the United States of America."

We, the People of the State of South Carolina, in Convention assembled, do declare and ordain, and it is hereby declared and ordained,

That the Ordinance adopted by us in Convention, on the twenty-third day of May, in the year of our Lord one thousand seven hundred and eighty-eight, whereby the Constitution of the United States of America was ratified, and also, all Acts and parts of Acts of the General Assembly of this State, ratifying amendments of the said Constitution, are hereby repealed; and that the union now subsisting between South Carolina and other States, under the name of "The United States of America," is hereby dissolved.

THE

UNION

IS

DISSOLVED!

"The Union Is Dissolved!" An 1860 newspaper headline announcing South Carolina's secession from the Union.

secretary of war during the nullification crisis, urged the president to mimic Jackson and send federal troops and warships to the seceded states to show them that the Union would be preserved at all costs. Buchanan rejected the advice, prompting Cass to resign.

Among the federal facilities in the seceding states was Fort Sumter, nestled on a tiny man-made island at the mouth of Charleston Harbor. When South Carolina secessionists demanded that Major Robert Anderson, a Kentucky Unionist, surrender the fort, he refused. On January 5, 1861, Buchanan sent an unarmed ship, the *Star of the West*, to resupply Fort Sumter.

As the supply ship approached Charleston Harbor on January 9, Confederate cannons opened fire and drove it away. It was an act of war, but Buchanan chose to ignore the challenge, hoping that a compromise would be reached to avoid civil war. Many Southerners, however, were not in a compromising mood.

SECESSION OF THE LOWER SOUTH By February 1, 1861, the states of the Lower South—South Carolina, Mississippi, Florida, Alabama, Georgia, Louisiana, and Texas—had seceded. Although their secession ordinances mentioned various grievances against the federal government, they made it clear that their primary reason for leaving the Union was the preservation of slavery.

Texas's ordinance explained that the purpose of secession and the formation of the Confederacy was to *"secure the rights of the slave-holding States in their domestic institutions."* The Texas convention displayed the racism underlying secession, calling Africans "an inferior and dependent race" for whom slavery was "beneficial."

In Mississippi, William Harris, the state's secession commissioner, argued that Republicans "now demand equality between the white and negro races, under our constitution; equality in representation, equality in the right of suffrage . . . equality in the social circle, equality in the rights of matrimony." Such a future could not be tolerated. The South, in his view, faced a stark choice: "Sink or swim, live or die, survive or perish." Mississippi, he vowed, "will never submit to the principles and policy of this black Republican administration."

On February 4, 1861, fifty representatives of the seceding states, all but one of them slave owners, met in Montgomery, Alabama, where they adopted a constitution for the Confederate States of America. It mandated that "the institution of negro slavery, as it now exists in the Confederate States, shall be recognized and protected."

The delegates elected as the Confederacy's first president Mississippi's Jefferson Davis, a West Point graduate who had served as a Democrat in the House of Representatives and the Senate and had been secretary of war under Franklin Pierce.

Alexander H. Stephens of Georgia was named vice president. The sickly, baby-faced Stephens, weighing no more than ninety pounds, declared, "Our new government is founded upon . . . the great truth that the negro is not equal to the white man; that slavery, subordination to the superior [white] race, is his natural and normal condition."

In mid-February, Davis, cheered by jubilant crowds, traveled from Mississippi to Montgomery, Alabama, the Confederate capital, for his installation. On February 18, Alabama fire-eater William Yancey introduced Davis to the crowd by announcing that the "man and the hour have met." In his remarks, Davis claimed that "the time for compromise is now passed."

FINAL EFFORTS AT COMPROMISE President-elect Lincoln still assumed that the southern states were bluffing. Members of Congress, however, desperately sought a compromise to avoid a civil war. On December 18, 1860, John J. Crittenden of Kentucky offered a series of resolutions that would allow the extension of slavery into the new western territories *south* of the Missouri Compromise line (36°30′ parallel) and guarantee the preservation of slavery where it already existed. Lincoln, however, opposed any plan that would expand slavery westward, and the Senate defeated the Crittenden Compromise, 25–23.

Several weeks later, in February 1861, twenty-one states sent delegates to a peace conference in Washington, D.C. Former president John Tyler presided, but the conference's proposal, substantially the same as the Crittenden Compromise, won little support. (Tyler himself voted against it and urged Virginia to secede at once.) The only proposal that generated much interest was a constitutional amendment guaranteeing slavery where it existed. Many Republicans, including Lincoln, were prepared to go that far, but no further.

After passing the House, the slavery amendment passed the Senate 24 to 12 on the morning of March 4, 1861, Lincoln's inauguration day. It would have become the Thirteenth Amendment and would have been the first time the word *slavery* had appeared in the Constitution, but the states never ratified it. When the states eventually ratified the Thirteenth Amendment in 1865, it did not protect slavery—it ended it.

LINCOLN'S INAUGURATION In mid-February 1861, Abraham Lincoln boarded a train in Springfield, Illinois, headed to Washington, D.C., for his inauguration. Alerted to a plot to assassinate him when he changed trains in Baltimore, federal officials had Lincoln wear a disguise and board a secret train in Harrisburg, Pennsylvania. The train carrying Lincoln slipped through Baltimore unnoticed. On March 4, 1861—Inauguration Day—Lincoln and James Buchanan rode together in a carriage down Pennsylvania Avenue beneath the careful gaze of rooftop sharpshooters there to protect them.

In his inaugural address, the fifty-two-year-old Lincoln repeated his pledge not "to interfere with the institution of slavery in the states where it exists." Yet the immediate question had shifted from slavery to secession. Lincoln insisted that "the Union of these States is perpetual." No state, he stressed, "can lawfully get out of the Union." He pledged to defend "federal forts in the South," but beyond that "there [would] be no invasion, no using of force against or among the people anywhere." In closing, he appealed for the Union:

> We are not enemies, but friends. We must not be enemies. Though passion may have strained, it must not break our bonds of affection. The mystic chords of memory, stretching from every battlefield and patriot grave to every living heart and hearthstone all over this broad land, will yet swell the chorus of the Union, when again touched, as surely they will be, by the better angels of our nature.

Southerners were not impressed. A North Carolina newspaper warned that Lincoln's speech made civil war "inevitable." On both sides, however, people assumed that any war would be over quickly and that their lives would go on as usual.

THE END OF THE WAITING GAME On March 5, 1861, his first day in office, President Lincoln found a letter on his desk from Major Robert Anderson at Fort Sumter. Anderson reported that his men had enough food for only a few weeks, and that the Confederates were encircling the fort with a "ring of fire." It would take thousands of federal soldiers to rescue them.

On April 4, 1861, Lincoln ordered unarmed ships to take food and supplies to the sixty-nine soldiers at Fort Sumter. Jefferson Davis was equally determined to stop any effort to supply the fort, even if it meant using military force. The secretary of state for the Confederacy, Richard Lathers, warned Davis that if the South fired first, "There will be no compromise with Secession if war is forced upon the north." Davis ignored the warning.

On April 11, Confederate general Pierre G.T. Beauregard, who had studied under Anderson at West Point, urged his former professor to surrender and sent him cases of whiskey and boxes of cigars to help convince him. Anderson refused the gifts and the request. At four-thirty on the morning of April 12, Confederate cannons began firing on Fort Sumter.

The bright flashes and thundering booms awakened the city. Thousands rushed out to watch the shelling. Finally, the outgunned Anderson, his ammunition and food gone, lowered the "stars and stripes."

The attack on Fort Sumter "has made the North a unit," New York Democratic Congressman Daniel Sickles wrote Lincoln's secretary of war. "We are at war with a foreign power." A Kentucky man told a reporter that the assault on Fort Sumter changed everything: "I was a Kentuckian, but now I am an American." A civil war of unimagined horrors had begun. "War begins where reason ends," said Frederick Douglass, and the South's irrational fears confirmed the logic of his statement.

CHAPTER REVIEW

SUMMARY

- **Slavery in the Territories**   Representative David *Wilmot's Proviso*, although it never became law, declared that since Mexican territories acquired by the United States had been free, they should remain so. Like the Wilmot Proviso, the new *Free-Soil party* demanded that slavery not be expanded to the territories. But it was the discovery of gold in California and the ensuing *California gold rush (1849)* that escalated tensions. Californians wanted to enter the Union as a free state. Southerners feared that they would lose federal protection of their "peculiar institution" if there were more free states than slave states. It had been agreed that *popular sovereignty* would settle the status of the territories, but when the territories applied for statehood, the debate over slavery was renewed. Through the wildly celebrated *Compromise of 1850*, California entered the Union as a free state; the territories of Texas, New Mexico, and Utah were established without direct reference to slavery; the slave trade (but not slavery) was banned in Washington, D.C.; and a new *Fugitive Slave Act (1850)* was passed. Tensions turned violent with the passage of the *Kansas-Nebraska Act (1854)*, which overturned the Missouri Compromise by allowing slavery in the territories where the institution had been banned in 1821.

- **The Republican Party's Appeal**   The efforts of pro-slavery advocates in Kansas to force slavery on the territory enraged northern opinion, even though anti-slavery settlers such as John Brown were equally violent in the events known as *Bleeding Kansas (1856)*. The Supreme Court's *Dred Scott v. Sandford (1857)* decision, which ruled that Congress could not interfere with slavery in the territories, further fueled sectional conflict. Northern voters gravitated toward the Republican party as events unfolded. Republicans also advocated raising protective tariffs and funding the development of the nation's infrastructure, which appealed to northern manufacturers and commercial farmers. Abraham Lincoln's narrow failure to unseat Democrat Stephen A. Douglas in the 1858 Illinois Senate election, which included the famous *Lincoln-Douglas debates (1858)*, revealed the Republican party's growing appeal. In 1860, Lincoln carried every free state and won a clear electoral college victory.

- **The Secession of the Lower South and Civil War**   Following Lincoln's election, South Carolina seceded. Six other Lower South states quickly followed. Together they formed the Confederate States of America, citing their belief that secession was necessary for the preservation of slavery. In his inaugural address, Lincoln made it clear that secession was unconstitutional but that the North would not invade the South. However, the Confederate states stood by their declarations of secession, and war came when South Carolinians fired on the "stars and stripes" at Fort Sumter.

CHRONOLOGY

1848	Free-Soil party is organized
1849	California gold rush begins
1854	Congress passes the Kansas-Nebraska Act
	The Republican party is founded
1856	A pro-slavery mob sacks Lawrence, Kansas; John Brown stages the Pottawatomie Massacre in retaliation
	Charles Sumner of Massachusetts is caned and seriously injured by a pro-slavery congressman in the U.S. Senate
1857	U.S. Supreme Court issues the *Dred Scott* decision
	Lecompton Constitution declares that slavery will be allowed in Kansas
1858	Abraham Lincoln debates Stephen A. Douglas during the 1858 Illinois Senate race
1859	John Brown and his followers stage a failed raid at Harpers Ferry, Virginia, in an attempt to incite a slave insurrection
1860–1861	South Carolina and six other southern states secede from the Union
	Crittenden Compromise is proposed but fails
March 4, 1861	Abraham Lincoln is inaugurated president
April 1861	Fort Sumter falls to Confederate forces, triggers Civil War

KEY TERMS

Wilmot Proviso (1846) p. 542

popular sovereignty p. 542

Free-Soil party p. 543

California gold rush (1849) p. 544

Compromise of 1850 p. 546

Fugitive Slave Act (1850) p. 551

Kansas-Nebraska Act (1854) p. 555

Bleeding Kansas (1856) p. 558

Dred Scott v. Sandford (1857) p. 562

Lincoln-Douglas debates (1858) p. 564

 INQUIZITIVE

Go to InQuizitive to see what you've learned—and learn what you've missed—with personalized feedback along the way.

15 The War of the Union

1861–1865

***Lincoln's Drive through Richmond* (1866)** Shortly after the Confederate capital of Richmond, Virginia, fell to Union forces in April 1865, President Abraham Lincoln visited the war-torn city. His carriage was swarmed by enslaved blacks who were freed by the war, as well as whites whose loyalties were with the Union.

The fall of Fort Sumter started the Civil War and triggered a wave of patriotic bluster on both sides. A southern woman prayed that God would "give us strength to conquer the Yankees, to exterminate *them*, to lay waste every Northern city, town and village, to destroy them utterly." Northern sentiment was not much different. Writer Nathaniel Hawthorne reported from Massachusetts that his transcendentalist friend Ralph Waldo Emerson was "breathing slaughter" as the Union army prepared for its first battle. Emerson, a pacifist, now said that "sometimes gunpowder smells good."

Many Southerners, then and since, argued that the Civil War was not about slavery but about the South's effort to defend states' rights. Confederate president Jefferson Davis, for example, claimed that the Rebels fought for the South's right to secede from the Union and its need to defend itself against a "tyrannical majority"—meaning those who had elected President Abraham Lincoln, the anti-slavery Republican.

For his part, Lincoln stressed repeatedly that the "paramount object in this struggle *is* to save the Union, and is *not* either to save or to destroy slavery. If I could save the Union without freeing *any* slave I would do it, and if I could save it by freeing *all* the slaves I would do it; and if I could save it by freeing some and leaving others alone I would also do that." If the southern states returned to the Union, he promised, they could retain their slaves. None of the Confederate states accepted Lincoln's offer, in large part because most white Southerners were convinced that he was lying. They believed the "Black Republican," as they called the president, was determined to end slavery.

focus questions

1. What were the respective advantages of the North and South as the Civil War began? How did those advantages affect the military strategies of the Union and the Confederacy?

2. Why did Abraham Lincoln decide to issue the Emancipation Proclamation? How did it impact the war?

3. In what ways did the war affect social and economic life in the North and South?

4. What were the military turning points in 1863 and 1864 that ultimately led to the Confederacy's defeat?

5. How did the Civil War change the nation?

Southerners claimed their *right* to secede from the Union, but protecting slavery was the *reason* Confederate leaders repeatedly used to justify secession and war. The South Carolina Declaration on the Immediate Causes of Secession, for example, explained that the state left the Union because of the "increasing hostility on the part of the non-slaveholding states to the institution of slavery." Mississippi mentioned only one reason: preserving slavery. Georgian Alexander Stephens, vice president of the Confederate States of America, said that slavery was the "immediate cause" of secession and war and that white supremacy was the "cornerstone" of the Confederacy.

On April 15, three days after the Confederate attack on Fort Sumter, Lincoln directed the "loyal" states to supply 75,000 militiamen for ninety days to suppress the rebellion. The Civil War would force everyone—men and women, white and black, immigrants and Native Americans, free and enslaved—to choose sides. Neither the Union nor the Confederacy enjoyed unanimous support. Some 100,000 Southerners fought for the Union; thousands of Northerners fought for the Confederacy. Thousands of European volunteers fought on each side.

CHOOSING SIDES

Of the slaveholding states along the border between North and South, Delaware remained firmly in the Union, but Maryland, Kentucky, and Missouri went through bitter struggles to decide which side to support. "I think to lose Kentucky is nearly the same as to lose the whole game," Lincoln told a friend. If Kentucky were to join the Confederacy, "we cannot hold Missouri, nor, as I think, Maryland." Lincoln was so determined to keep slaveholding Kentucky on the Union side that he muffled all talk of abolition.

If Maryland had seceded, Confederates would have surrounded Washington, D.C. To keep Maryland in the Union, Lincoln had pro-Confederate leaders there arrested, including Baltimore's mayor and chief of police. The fragile neutrality of Kentucky lasted until September 3, when Confederate and Union armies moved into the divided state. Kentucky voters elected a secessionist governor and a Unionist majority in the state legislature, as did Missouri, a state with many European immigrants, especially Germans.

When a pro-Confederate militia gathered in St. Louis, hoping to take control of the federal arsenal, it was surprised and disarmed by German immigrants "eager to teach the German-haters a never-to-be-forgotten lesson." The German militiamen then chased the pro-Confederate governor across the border to Arkansas. When news of the Civil War reached Missouri, 4,200 men volunteered to join the Union army; all but 100 were German Americans.

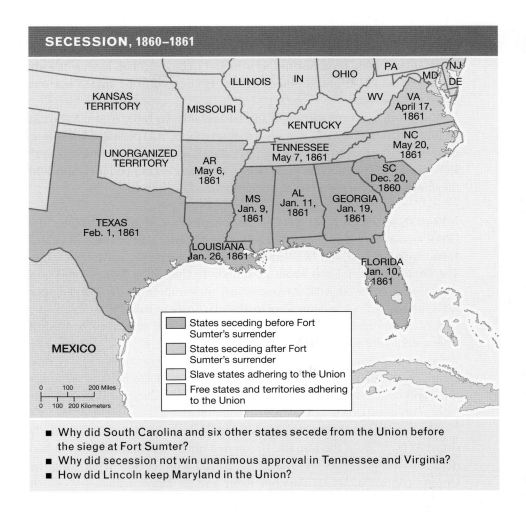

SECESSION, 1860–1861

ILLINOIS   IN   OHIO   PA   NJ   MD   DE

KANSAS TERRITORY   MISSOURI   WV   VA April 17, 1861

KENTUCKY

UNORGANIZED TERRITORY   AR May 6, 1861   TENNESSEE May 7, 1861   NC May 20, 1861

SC Dec. 20, 1860

MS Jan. 9, 1861   AL Jan. 11, 1861   GEORGIA Jan. 19, 1861

TEXAS Feb. 1, 1861

LOUISIANA Jan. 26, 1861

FLORIDA Jan. 10, 1861

MEXICO

States seceding before Fort Sumter's surrender

States seceding after Fort Sumter's surrender

Slave states adhering to the Union

Free states and territories adhering to the Union

0   100   200 Miles

0   100   200 Kilometers

- Why did South Carolina and six other states secede from the Union before the siege at Fort Sumter?
- Why did secession not win unanimous approval in Tennessee and Virginia?
- How did Lincoln keep Maryland in the Union?

German immigrants overwhelmingly supported the Union. Having fled from German states where aristocratic elites and military officers suppressed democracy, they viewed the Confederacy as a similarly undemocratic society. New Yorker August Willich, a German immigrant who had been an army officer, wrote after the attack on Fort Sumter that German Americans needed to "protect their new republican homeland against the aristocracy of the South." Willich would become a Union army general.

In areas of the South where Union sentiment remained strong, the Civil War was brutally uncivil. In January 1863, a detachment of Confederate soldiers in Madison County, North Carolina, captured thirteen men and boys and began marching them to Knoxville, Tennessee, to be tried for desertion and treason. The prisoners never made it to Knoxville, however. Along the way, the detachment stopped, lined up the captives, and killed them. Thirteen-year-old David Shelton was the last to be executed, having already witnessed his father and brother's deaths. He begged to be spared but was killed like the rest.

The northern states witnessed similar brutality. In 1863, Anson Babcock, an Illinois farmer, reported that his "rebel neighbors" had poisoned his horses, destroyed his orchards, wrecked his fences, and "annoyed me in various ways," all because "'my politics don't suit'" them, for "I am 'a damned Lincolnite,' and they intend to drive me out of the neighborhood."

REGIONAL ADVANTAGES   Once battle lines were finally drawn, the Union had twenty-three states, including four border slave states—Missouri, Kentucky, Maryland, and Delaware—while the Confederacy had eleven states. The population count was about 22 million in the Union (some 400,000 of whom were enslaved African Americans) to 9 million in the Confederacy (of whom about 3.5 million were enslaved). To help balance the odds, the Confederacy mobilized 80 percent of its military-age white men, a third of whom would die during the four-year war.

An even greater asset for the North was its superior industrial development. The southern states produced just 7 percent of the nation's manufactured goods on the eve of the war. The Union states produced 97 percent of the firearms and 96 percent of the railroad equipment.

The North also had a huge advantage in transportation, particularly ships. At the start of the war, the Union had ninety warships; the South had none. Federal gunboats and transports played a direct role in securing the Union's control of the Mississippi River and its larger tributaries, which provided easy invasion routes into the center of the Confederacy. Early on, the Union navy's blockade of the major southern ports sharply reduced the amount of cotton that could be exported to Britain and France as well as the flow of goods (including military weapons) imported from Europe. In addition, the Union had more wagons and horses and an impressive edge in railroad locomotives.

The Confederates, however, had major geographic and emotional advantages: they could fight on their own territory in defense of their homeland. "For our people," Confederate general Stonewall Jackson said, "the war was a struggle for life and death." In warfare, it is usually easier to defend than to attack, since defending troops have the opportunity to dig protective trenches and fortifications. In the Civil War, armies that assaulted well-defended positions were mauled 90 percent of the time. Many Confederate leaders thought that if they could hold out long enough, disgruntled northern voters might convince Lincoln and Congress to end the war.

THE WAR'S EARLY STRATEGIES

The two sides initially had different goals. The Confederacy sought to convince the Union and the world to recognize its independence. The United States, on the other hand, fought to restore the Union. The future of slavery was not yet an issue as the war started.

After the fall of Fort Sumter, excited newspaper editors and politicians on both sides pressured the generals to strike quickly. "Forward to Richmond!" screamed a New York newspaper headline. Most people thought the war would be, in President Lincoln's words, "a short and decisive one." They were sorely wrong.

In the summer of 1861, Jefferson Davis told General Pierre G. T. Beauregard to rush the main Confederate army to Manassas Junction, a railroad crossing in northern Virginia, about twenty-five miles west of Washington. Lincoln hoped that the Union army (often called *Federals*) would overrun the outnumbered Confederates (often called *Rebels*) and quickly push on to Richmond, only 107 miles to the south.

FIRST BULL RUN   When word reached Washington, D.C., that the two armies were converging for battle, hundreds of civilians packed picnic lunches and rode out to watch, assuming that the first clash of arms would be short, glorious, and bloodless.

It was a hot, dry day on July 21, 1861, when 37,000 untested Union recruits marched to battle, some of them breaking ranks to eat blackberries or drink water from streams along the way. Many of them died with the berry juice still on their lips as they engaged the Confederates dug in behind a tree-choked branch of the Potomac River called Bull Run.

For most of the soldiers, the battle provided their first taste of the chaos and confusion of combat. Many were disoriented by the smoke from gunpowder and saltpeter, the roar of cannon fire, the screaming of fallen comrades, and the sound of bullets whizzing past. Because neither side yet wore standard-colored uniforms, the soldiers had trouble deciding friend from foe.

The Union troops almost won the battle early in the afternoon. "We fired a volley," wrote a Massachusetts private, "and saw the Rebels running. . . . The boys were saying constantly, in great glee, 'We've whipped them.' 'We'll hang Jeff Davis from a sour apple tree.' 'They're running.' 'The war is over.'"

But Confederate reinforcements poured in. Amid the furious fighting, a South Carolina officer rallied his troops by pointing to the courageous example of Thomas Jackson: "Look! There is General Jackson with his Virginians, standing like a stone wall!" Jackson ordered his men to charge, urging them to "yell like furies!" From that day forward, "Stonewall" became Jackson's popular nickname, and he would be the most celebrated—and feared—Confederate field commander.

The Union army panicked, and fleeing soldiers and terrified civilians clogged the road to Washington, D.C. The victorious Confederates, however, were so disorganized and exhausted that they failed to give chase.

Left behind was a battlefield strewn with the dead and dying—mangled men and bloated horses and mules scattered among discarded knapsacks, canteens, blankets, rifles, wagons, and cannons. Jackson wrote his wife that "we fought a great battle and gained a great victory, for which all the glory is due to God alone."

The news of the Confederate victory triggered sharp criticism of President Lincoln. Michigan senator Zachariah Chandler, a Republican, dismissed the president as "timid, vacillating & inefficient." An Ohio Republican was even more critical, denouncing Lincoln as "an admitted failure" who "has no will, no courage, no executive capacity."

The hallmark of Lincoln's presidency, however, was his ability to acknowledge mistakes and move forward. With each passing year, he would grow surer of himself as a wartime leader. As Stonewall Jackson later observed, the Confederacy emerged from the first major battle assuming that a quick and total victory was in its grasp. The North, while "mortified by defeat and stunned by ridicule, pulled itself together, raised armies, stirred up its people, and prepared for war in earnest."

THE UNION'S "ANACONDA" PLAN   The Battle of Bull Run demonstrated that the war would not be decided with one sudden stroke, as many had assumed. General Winfield Scott, the seventy-five-year-old commander of the Union war effort, devised a three-pronged strategy. First, the Army of the Potomac, the main Union army, would defend Washington, D.C., and exert constant pressure on the Confederate capital at Richmond.

Second, the Federal navy's blockade of southern ports would cut off the Confederacy's access to foreign goods and weapons. The third component of the plan called for other Union armies to divide the Confederacy by pushing south along the crucial inland water routes: the Mississippi, Tennessee, and Cumberland Rivers. This so-called **Anaconda Plan** was intended to slowly trap and crush the southern resistance, like an anaconda snake strangling its prey.

CONFEDERATE STRATEGY The Confederate plan was simpler. If the Union forces could be stalemated and the war prolonged, as Jefferson Davis and others hoped, then the British or French, desperate for southern cotton, might be persuaded to join the cause. Or perhaps a long war would change public sentiment in the North and force Lincoln to seek a negotiated settlement. So, while armies were forming in the South, Confederate diplomats were seeking military and financial assistance in London and Paris, and Confederate sympathizers in the North were urging an end to the Union's war effort.

The Confederate representatives in Paris won a promise from France to recognize the Confederacy as a new nation *if* Great Britain would do the same. But the British refused, partly in response to pressure from President Lincoln and partly out of their desire to maintain trade with the United States.

Confederate leaders had assumed that Britain would support the South in order to get its cotton. As it turned out, however, the British were able to import enough cotton from India to maintain production. In the end, Confederate diplomacy in Europe was more successful in purchasing military supplies than in gaining official recognition as an independent nation.

FORMING ARMIES Once fighting began, President Lincoln called for 500,000 more men, a staggering number and one that the Confederacy struggled to match.

In Illinois, Ulysses S. Grant, the Ohio-born West Point graduate who had distinguished himself in the Mexican-American War, rejoined the army in 1861. He had been ushered out of the peacetime military seven years earlier because of binge drinking. Thereafter, as a civilian, he pursued several business ventures in Missouri and Illinois, all of which were dismal failures. By 1861, he was virtually a pauper, forced to walk the streets of St. Louis hawking firewood out of a handcart.

The outbreak of war gave Grant renewed hope and purpose. Back in uniform and mobilizing an Illinois regiment, he explained that there "are but two parties now—traitors and patriots—and I want hereafter to be ranked with the latter."

Confederates were equally committed to their cause. Charleston, wrote Mary Chesnut, the literary wife of a prominent planter, was "crowded with soldiers" who feared "the war will be over before they get a sight of the fun." Sam Watkins of Tennessee reported that everyone "was eager for the war."

Although the average age of soldiers in the Civil War was twenty-six, the Union armies included more than 100,000 soldiers younger than fifteen. Almost a fifth of Union soldiers and sailors were immigrants—French, Germans, Poles, Italians, and other Europeans—and many could not speak

The U.S. Army recruiting office in City Hall Park, New York City The sign advertises the money offered to those willing to serve: $677 to new recruits, $777 to veteran soldiers, and $15 to anyone who brought in a recruit.

English. The Union army also included 50,000 Canadians and an equal number of Englishmen. Some 210,000 Irish-born men served in the war, 170,000 of them on the Union side.

Immigrants fought for many reasons: a strong belief in the Union cause, cash bonuses, extra food, regular pay, the need for a steady job. Whatever the reason, the high proportion of immigrants in the Union army gave it an ethnic diversity absent in the Confederate ranks.

Because the Confederacy had a smaller male population, Jefferson Davis was forced to enact a conscription law (mandatory military draft). On April 16, 1862, all white males between eighteen and thirty-five were required to serve in the army for three years. "From this time until the end of the war," a Tennessee soldier wrote, "a soldier was simply a machine, a conscript . . . All our pride and valor had gone, and we were sick of war and cursed the Southern Confederacy."

The conscription law included controversial loopholes. A draftee might avoid service either by paying a "substitute" who was not of draft age or by paying $500 to the government. Elected officials and key civilian workers, as well as planters with twenty or more slaves, were exempted from military service.

The Union waited nearly a year before forcing men into service. In 1863, with the war going badly, the U.S. government began to draft men. As in the South, Northerners found ways to avoid military service. A draftee might pay $300 to avoid service, and exemptions were granted to selected federal and state officeholders and to others on medical or compassionate grounds. Such exemptions led to bitter complaints on both sides about the conflict being "a rich man's war and a poor man's fight."

WHY THEY FOUGHT Most of those who fought on both sides were volunteers. Why did they risk their lives? The reasons varied, but many felt compelled by duty, honor, and patriotism. Their duties as *men* drove many combatants. As an Alabama planter who joined the Confederate army as a cavalryman explained to his wife, "My honor, my duty, your reputation & that of my darling little boy" forced him to don a uniform "when our bleeding country needs the services of every man." Likewise, an Illinois officer felt that Union soldiers were guided by "a high and noble sentiment, but after all a sentiment [preserving the Union and ending slavery]. They [Confederates] are fighting for independence and are animated by passion and hatred against invaders [Yankees]."

A NEW YORK PRIVATE
Nineteen-year-old Lyons Wakeman, the eldest of nine children in an upstate New York farm family, enlisted in the Union army in 1862. In exchange for a $152 cash bonus, the five-foot-tall, blue-eyed Wakeman signed up for three years. The pay was $13 a month, some of which went home to help the family. Initially, at least, army life was tolerable, and the prospect of death in combat did not faze Wakeman: "I don't fear the rebel bullets, nor do I fear the cannon. If it is God's will for me to be killed here, it is my will to die." In letters home, first from Virginia and later from Louisiana,

Private Wakeman Sarah Rosetta Wakeman, alias Lyons Wakeman, served in the Union Army.

Private Wakeman asked about the family farm, how many hogs were slaughtered, what the new barn looked like, and how much it might cost to buy a farm on the Wisconsin prairie.

Yet Wakeman never became a farmer. In a fierce battle, the New Yorker faced "enemy bullets with my regiment. I was under fire about four hours and lay on the field of battle all night." Wakeman did not die from wounds but did succumb a few weeks later to dysentery (chronic diarrhea), after drinking from a stream contaminated with the carcasses of dead horses. The private was buried in a New Orleans cemetery, under a headstone that simply read: "Lyons Wakeman—N.Y."

What might have been added was that Lyons Wakeman was a woman. Born Sarah Rosetta Wakeman, she, like hundreds of women on both sides, had disguised her gender to serve in the war. Why she did so remains a mystery. Was it simply patriotism? Or did it also involve seizing the opportunity afforded by the war to explore alternative modes of gender identity?

WHAT WAS AT STAKE Many Confederates were convinced that defeat would enslave southern whites. "If we was to lose," a Mississippi private wrote his wife in 1862, "we would be slaves to the Yanks and our children would have a yoke of bondage thrown around their necks."

Most Confederates could not imagine life without black slavery. "This country without slave labor would be completely worthless," wrote a Mississippi lieutenant. "We can only live & exist by that species of labor: hence I am willing to fight to the last."

Many Union soldiers were fighting to preserve the Union rather than free the slaves, but a surprising number insisted that winning the war meant ending slavery. A private from Minnesota felt that the war "will never end until we end slavery."

Despite the patriotic fervor, people remained ambivalent about their loyalties. In Virginia, for example, Confederate Joseph Waddill admitted in his diary in 1863 that he actually regretted secession. "I never ceased to deplore the disruption [of the Union], and never could have loved my country and government as I loved the old United States."

DIVIDED FAMILIES The Civil War divided families. President Lincoln's wife, Mary Todd of Kentucky, for example, saw her youngest brother join the Confederate army, as did three of her half-brothers and a brother-in-law. At the same time, Varina Davis, the Confederate First Lady, had divided loyalties. While pro-slavery, she was privately pro-Union.

In June 1862, two brothers, Alexander and James Campbell, fought against each other at the Battle of Secessionville on James Island, South Carolina. Alexander joined the Union forces in assaulting a Confederate fort, where his brother served. Afterward, James wrote his brother, expressing astonishment that Alexander had been among the Union attackers. "I was . . . doing my best to Beat you, but I hope that you and I will never again meet face to face." If they should meet again in combat, he urged his brother to "do your duty to your cause, for I can assure you I will strive to discharge my duty to my country & my cause."

THE LIFE OF A SOLDIER The average Civil War soldier stood five feet eight inches tall and weighed 143 pounds. A third of the southern soldiers could neither read nor write. Half of the Union soldiers and two-thirds of the Confederates were farmers.

Army camps featured their own libraries, theatrical stages, churches, numerous "mascot" pets—and monotonous routine. Because most of the fighting occurred in the spring and summer, soldiers spent far more time preparing for war than actually fighting. A Pennsylvania private wrote home that "the first thing in the morning is drill. Then drill, then drill again. Then drill, drill, a little more drill, then drill, lastly drill."

When not training, soldiers spent time outdoors in makeshift shelters or small tents—talking, reading, playing cards or checkers, singing songs, smoking pipes, washing and mending clothes, and fighting swarms of lice, ticks, chiggers, and mosquitoes. Their diet was plain and dull: baked bread crackers (called hardtack), salted meat (pork or beef), and coffee.

Some soldiers on both sides were so overwhelmed by the rigors of combat and camp life or so concerned about their families and farms that they deserted, even though they risked execution if caught. Desertions soared with each passing year, as did incidents of drunkenness, thievery, and insubordination.

Punishments varied. Some deserters were shot or hanged. Others were tied to a ball and chain, forced to bury dead horses or tend to animals, or drummed out of the service. Most soldiers on both sides, however, came to view their military experience as beneficial.

BECOMING WARRIORS Sullivan Ballou, a thirty-two-year-old Rhode Island lawyer and legislator who enlisted in the Union army, wrote his wife that he would have loved nothing more than to have stayed and seen their sons grow to "honorable manhood," but his ultimate priority was serving his country. He felt a great debt to "those who went before us through the blood and sufferings of the Revolution." A week later, Ballou was killed in the first Battle of Bull Run. In his last letter to his wife, he had expressed a premonition of death: "do not mourn me dead . . . wait for me, for we shall meet again."

Southerners felt the same sense of patriotism and manly honor. As the months passed, however, enthusiasm faded for many combatants on both sides. Charles Biddlecom, a farmer from upstate New York, volunteered in May 1861 for the Union army. He was eager to whip the "Southern whelps." By 1863, however, Biddlecom had had enough. Sick with dysentery, overrun with lice, and miserably lonesome, he and three comrades were forced to live in a "little dog kennel" just four feet high. Although he hated slaveholders, he now felt it might have been "better in the end to have let the South go out peaceably and tried her hand at making a nation."

Like many other soldiers and sailors, Biddlecom's moods and motives fluctuated depending upon the course of the war. In 1864, he confessed that the Union army was "worn out, discouraged, [and] demoralized." He stuck it out, but "as for men fighting from pure love of country, I think them as few as white blackbirds." He declared that he was neither a "Union saver" nor a "freedom shrieker." At war's end, however, Biddlecom celebrated the defeat of the Confederacy, since it affirmed that "freedom shall extend over the whole nation." The "greatest nation of Earth" showed that it would not surrender to "traitors in arms."

BLACKS IN THE SOUTH   As had happened during the Revolutionary War and the War of 1812, enslaved African Americans took advantage of the confusion created by the war to run away, engage in sabotage, join the fighting, or pursue their own interests.

Perhaps the most dramatic instance of slave rebelliousness occurred in Charleston Harbor. On May 13, 1862, twenty-three-year-old Robert Smalls, an enslaved black harbor pilot aboard the C.S.S. *Planter,* stole the ship and headed out to sea in a desperate quest for freedom. Sneaking past Confederate forts and cannons, he guided the *Planter* up the Cooper River and docked at a wharf where his wife, child, and the families of his crew were waiting.

Once they had boarded, the *Planter* and its seventeen passengers (nine men, five women, and three children) crept out of the harbor. As the sun rose, Smalls had a crew member hoist a white bed sheet to signal their intention to surrender, and they headed for the Union fleet blockading Charleston Harbor. A warship summoned Smalls onboard, whereupon he announced: "I am delivering this war material, including these cannons, and I think Uncle Abraham Lincoln can put them to good use."

Union soldiers Smoking their pipes, these soldiers share a moment of rest and a bottle of whiskey.

Smalls was hailed as a hero in the North. He met with President Lincoln at the White House, toured northern cities urging that blacks be allowed to serve in the Union army and navy, and became a ship pilot for the Union navy. After the war, he would become a South Carolina legislator and U.S. congressman.

FIGHTING IN THE WEST

During the Civil War, fighting spilled across the Mississippi River into the Great Plains and all the way to California. In 1862, a small Confederate army tried to conquer the New Mexico territory but was repelled.

Amid the sporadic fighting, western settlement slowed but did not stop. New discoveries of gold and silver in eastern California and in Montana and Colorado lured more prospectors. Dakota, Colorado, and Nevada gained territorial status in 1861, Idaho and Arizona in 1863. Both Montana and silver-rich Nevada gained statehood in 1864.

WAR IN THE WEST The most intense fighting west of the Mississippi occurred along the Kansas-Missouri border, where the disputes that had developed between pro-slavery and anti-slavery settlers in the 1850s turned into brutal guerrilla warfare.

The most prominent pro-Confederate leader in the area was William Quantrill. He and his followers, mostly teenagers, fought under a black flag, meaning that they would kill anyone who surrendered. In destroying Lawrence, Kansas, in 1863, Quantrill ordered his men to "kill every male and burn every house." By the end of the day, they had massacred 182 men and boys. Their opponents, the Jayhawkers (originally slang for thieves), responded by torturing and hanging pro-Confederate prisoners, burning houses, and destroying livestock.

Many Indian nations were caught up in the war. Some 20,000 Native Americans allied with one side or the other. Several Indian tribes owned African American slaves and felt a bond with southern whites. Stand Watie, an Oklahoma Cherokee leader, chose the Confederacy in 1861 and raised a volunteer regiment called the Cherokee Mounted Rifles. By the end of the war, he had been promoted to brigadier general and was the principal chief of the Confederate Cherokees.

Oklahoma's proximity to Texas influenced the Choctaws and Chickasaws to support the Confederacy. The Cherokees, Creeks, and Seminoles were more divided in their loyalties. The Cherokees, for example, split in two, some supporting the Union and others the Confederacy. Caught in the crossfire of battle, one-third of Cherokee women ended up widows.

KENTUCKY AND TENNESSEE Little happened of military significance east of the Appalachian Mountains before May 1862. On the other hand, important battles occurred in the West (from the Appalachians to the Mississippi River).

Early in 1862, General Ulysses S. Grant made the first Union thrust against the Confederate army that was defending Kentucky and Tennessee. To combat his weakness for liquor, he looked to his chief of staff, John A. Rawlins, a teetotaler, to keep him sober. Rawlins took his role seriously, for when Grant was sober, he had only one equal as a military commander: Robert E. Lee.

Moving on boats out of Cairo, Illinois, and Paducah, Kentucky, the Union army captured two hastily built Confederate strongholds: Fort Henry on the east bank of the Tennessee River on February 6, 1862, and nearby Fort Donelson, perched on a hill overlooking the Cumberland River, where, on February 16, some 12,000 Confederates surrendered. Eight days later, Union forces took control of Nashville, then serving as Tennessee's capital.

These first major victories ignited wild celebrations throughout the North. They helped ensure that Kentucky would stay within the Union and gave the North access to the Cumberland and Tennessee Rivers. At the same time, the victory at Fort Donelson gave Grant a catchy nickname matching his initials:

"Unconditional Surrender" Grant. The *New York Times* reported that Grant's "prestige is second now to that of no general in the army." Admirers rushed him 10,000 cigars, and he soon began smoking twenty a day. (He would die in 1885 of throat cancer.)

President Lincoln's delight with the Union army's success, however, was tempered by the death of his eleven-year-old son Willie, of typhoid fever. The tragedy "overwhelmed" the president. A White House staff member said she had never seen "a man so bowed down in grief."

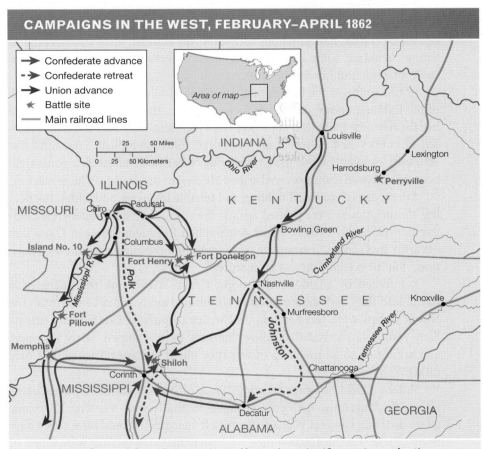

CAMPAIGNS IN THE WEST, FEBRUARY–APRIL 1862

- Why was General Grant's campaign in Kentucky a significant victory for the Union army?
- Describe the events at Shiloh. What were the costs to the Union as a result of the battle?

SHILOH   After the defeats in Kentucky and Tennessee, the Confederate forces fled southward before regrouping under General Albert Sydney Johnston at Corinth, in northern Mississippi, near the Tennessee border. Their goal was to protect the Memphis and Charleston Railroad linking the lower Mississippi Valley and the Atlantic coast.

While planning his attack on Corinth, General Grant made a costly mistake when he exposed his 42,000 troops on a rolling plateau between Lick and Snake Creeks flowing into the Tennessee River. He also failed to have his men dig defensive trenches. Johnston recognized Grant's blunder, and at dawn on Sunday, April 6, he launched a surprise attack.

The screaming Confederates struck the Union lines near Shiloh, a Methodist church in the center of the Union camp in southwestern Tennessee. Many of Grant's troops, half of whom had yet to see combat, were still sleeping or eating breakfast; some died in their tents. Panic-stricken soldiers dropped their weapons and ran for the river.

At one point on the battle's first day, General Johnston rode into the thick of the fighting, urging the Rebels forward: "Men, they are stubborn; we must use the bayonet. I will lead you!" Johnston led them well, only to be shot himself. His aide yelled, "General, are you hurt?" Johnston replied, "Yes, and I fear seriously." Soldiers helped the Confederate commander off his horse, his right boot full of blood from a severed artery. He died in the shade of a large oak tree.

After a day of confused fighting and terrible losses on both sides, the fleeing Union soldiers were pinned against the river. The new Confederate commander, Pierre G. T. Beauregard, telegraphed President Jefferson Davis that his army had scored "a complete victory, driving the enemy from every position." But his celebration was premature.

Reinforced by 25,000 fresh troops, Grant's army took the offensive at dawn, and the Confederates glumly withdrew twenty miles to Corinth. The Union troops were too battered and weary to pursue. Confederate private Sam Watkins observed that "those Yankees were whipped, fairly whipped, and according to all the rules of war they ought to have retreated. But they didn't."

Shiloh, a Hebrew word meaning "Place of Peace," was the costliest battle in which Americans had ever engaged to that point. Viewing the scene afterward, said General William Tecumseh Sherman, "would have cured anybody of war." Of the 100,000 men who participated, a quarter were killed or wounded, seven times the casualties at the Battle of Bull Run. And like Bull Run earlier and so many battles to come, Shiloh was a story of missed opportunities and lucky accidents. Throughout the war, winning armies would fail to pursue their retreating foes, allowing the wounded opponent to slip away, recover, and fight again.

After Shiloh, Union general Henry Halleck, a military bureaucrat jealous of Grant's success, spread a false rumor that Grant had been drinking during the battle. Grant stressed in a letter to his wife that he had been "sober as a deacon." Some urged Abraham Lincoln to fire the "unmilitary" Grant, but the president refused: "I can't spare this man; he fights." Halleck, however, took Grant's place as field commander, and soon thereafter the Union thrust in the Mississippi Valley ground to a halt. Lincoln quickly realized that Halleck was a paper-pusher who "shirked responsibility" and was a "moral coward."

NEW ORLEANS Just three weeks after the Battle of Shiloh, the Union won a great naval victory at New Orleans, as David G. Farragut's warships blasted their way past Confederate forts to take control of the largest city in the Confederacy. Union general Benjamin F. Butler thereafter served as the military governor of New Orleans.

When a Confederate sympathizer ripped down a Union flag, Butler had him hanged. After a Rebel woman leaned out her window and emptied her chamber pot on Farragut's head, Butler decreed that any woman who was disrespectful of Union soldiers would be treated as a "woman of the town plying her avocation"—that is, as a prostitute. Residents thereafter referred to Butler as "the Beast," but they quit harassing Union soldiers and sailors.

The loss of New Orleans was a devastating blow to the Confederate economy. The Union army gained control of 1,500 cotton plantations and liberated 50,000 slaves in the Mississippi Valley. As a result, the slave system in Louisiana was "forever destroyed and worthless," reported a northern journalist.

PERRYVILLE In the late summer of 1862, General Braxton Bragg's Army of Mississippi, 30,000 strong, used railroads to link up with General Edmund Kirby Smith's Army of East Tennessee. Their goal was to invade the North by taking control of the border state of Kentucky.

The Confederates met the Union Army of Ohio, led by General Don Carlos Buell, at the central Kentucky village of Perryville in October 1862. The outnumbered Confederates attacked the Union lines, pushing them back more than a mile. When Bragg learned that Union reinforcements were approaching, however, he ordered his army to withdraw south toward Tennessee. The Union retained control of Kentucky for the rest of the war.

FIGHTING IN THE EAST

The fighting in the East remained fairly quiet for nine months after Bull Run. In the wake of the Union defeat there, Lincoln had appointed General George B. McClellan as head of the Army of the Potomac. The thirty-four-year-old McClellan, who encouraged journalists to call him "Little Napoleon," set about building the Union's most powerful, best-trained army.

Yet for all his boundless self-confidence and organizational ability, McClellan was afraid to attack. Months passed while he trained his massive army

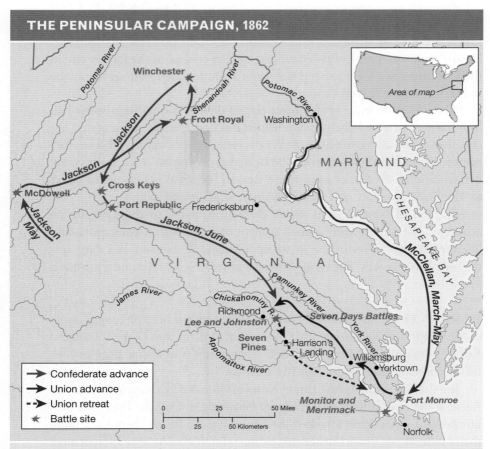

THE PENINSULAR CAMPAIGN, 1862

Legend:
→ Confederate advance
→ Union advance
- -▶ Union retreat
★ Battle site

0   25   50 Miles
0   25   50 Kilometers

- What was General McClellan's strategy for attacking Richmond?
- How did General Jackson divert the attention of the Union army?
- Why did President Lincoln demote McClellan after the Peninsular campaign?

to meet the superior numbers of Confederates he mistakenly believed were facing him. Lincoln finally lost his patience and ordered McClellan to attack.

MCCLELLAN'S PENINSULAR CAMPAIGN   In mid-March 1862, McClellan moved his army of 122,000 men on 400 ships and barges down the Potomac River and through the Chesapeake Bay to the mouth of the James River at the tip of the Yorktown peninsula, within sixty miles of the Confederate capital of Richmond, Virginia. Thousands of residents fled the city in panic, but McClellan waited too long to strike. A frustrated Lincoln told McClellan that the war could be won only by *engaging* the Rebel army. "Once more," Lincoln telegraphed, "it is indispensable that you strike a blow."

On May 31, 1862, Confederate general Joseph E. Johnston struck at McClellan's army along the Chickahominy River, six miles east of Richmond. In the Battle of Seven Pines (Fair Oaks), only the arrival of Federal reinforcements prevented a disastrous Union defeat. Both sides took heavy casualties, and Johnston was severely wounded.

At this point, Robert E. Lee assumed command of the main Confederate army, the Army of Northern Virginia, a development that changed the course of the war. Lee, a slave-owning planter whose father was a celebrated cavalry officer during the Revolutionary War, had graduated second in his class at West Point. During the Mexican-American War, he had impressed General Winfield Scott as the "very best soldier I ever saw in the field." Lee would prove to be a daring strategist who was as aggressive as McClellan was timid. "He is silent, inscrutable, strong, like a God," said a Confederate officer.

On July 9, when Lincoln visited McClellan's headquarters on the coast of Virginia, the general complained that the administration had failed to support him and lectured the president on military strategy. Such insubordination was ample reason to relieve McClellan of his overall command. After returning to Washington, Lincoln called Henry Halleck from the West to take charge.

Robert E. Lee Military adviser to President Jefferson Davis and later commander of the Army of Northern Virginia.

SECOND BULL RUN Lincoln and Halleck ordered McClellan to move his Army of the Potomac back to Washington, D.C., and join General John Pope, commander of the Union Army of Virginia, in a new assault on Richmond. In a letter to his wife, a jealous McClellan predicted—accurately— that "Pope will be thrashed and disposed of" by General Lee's army. He also dismissed Lincoln "as an idiot" and a "baboon."

Lee, aware that his only chance was to drive a wedge between the two larger Union armies so that he could deal with them one at a time, moved northward to strike Pope's army before McClellan's troops could arrive. Lee boldly divided his forces, sending Stonewall Jackson's "foot cavalry" around Pope's flank to attack the supply lines in the rear. At the Second Battle of Bull Run (or Manassas), fought on almost the same site as the earlier battle, a confused Pope assumed that he faced only Jackson, but Lee's main army by that time had joined in.

On August 30, 1862, a crushing Confederate attack drove the larger Union army from the field, giving the Confederates a sensational victory and leading a disheartened Union officer to confess from his deathbed that "General Pope had been outwitted . . . Our generals have defeated us." Pope was relieved of command on September 12. A Rebel soldier wrote home that "General Lee stands now above all generals in modern history. Our men will follow him to the end."

EMANCIPATION

The Confederate victories in 1862 devastated morale in the North and convinced Lincoln that he had to take bolder steps. When fighting began in 1861, the need to keep the border slave states (Delaware, Kentucky, Maryland, and Missouri) in the Union dictated caution on the volatile issue of emancipation. In August 1862, Lincoln worried that "to arm the negroes would turn 50,000 bayonets from the loyal Border states *against* us that were *for* us." Beyond that, Lincoln had to contend with a deep-seated racial prejudice among most Northerners, who were willing to allow slavery to continue in the South as long as it was not allowed to expand into the West. Lincoln himself harbored doubts about his constitutional authority to end slavery, and he did not believe that blacks, if freed, could coexist with whites.

SLAVES IN THE WAR The expanding war forced the issue. As Federal forces pushed into the Confederacy, fugitive slaves began to arrive in Union army camps, and the commanders did not know what to do with them. One general designated them as "contraband of war," and thereafter the thousands of slaves who sought protection and freedom were known as **contrabands.** Some Union officers put the refugees to work digging trenches, building fortifications, tending livestock, and burying the dead; others simply set them free.

Lincoln, meanwhile, began to edge toward ending slavery. On April 16, 1862, he signed an act that abolished slavery in the District of Columbia; on June 19, he signed another bill that excluded slavery from the western territories. Still, he insisted that the war was about restoring the Union and ending secession, not freeing the slaves in the South.

Circumstances, however, changed Lincoln's outlook. In March 1862, he urged representatives of the four border states to begin gradually to emancipate their slaves. The next month, the Republican-controlled Congress passed the Second Confiscation Act, which declared that contrabands who had made it to Union army camps were "forever free." That summer, Lincoln decided that emancipation of all slaves in the Confederate states was necessary to win the war. In July 1862, he confided to his cabinet that "decisive and extreme measures must be adopted." Emancipation, he said, had become "a military necessity, absolutely necessary to the preservation of the Union. We must free the slaves or be ourselves subdued." Secretary of State William H. Seward agreed but advised Lincoln to delay the announcement until after a Union battlefield victory, to avoid being viewed as desperate.

Contrabands Former slaves on a farm in Cumberland Landing, Virginia, 1862.

ANTIETAM: A TURNING POINT   Robert E. Lee made his own momentous decision in the summer of 1862: He would invade Maryland and force the "much weakened and demoralized" Army of the Potomac and its "timid" commander George McClellan to leave northern Virginia and thereby relieve the pressure on Richmond, the Confederate capital. "The idea of waiting for blows, instead of inflicting them, is altogether unsuited to the genius of our people," explained the *Richmond Examiner*.

Lee also hoped a northern invasion would influence the upcoming elections in the North. He also wanted to gain official British and French recognition of the Confederacy, which would bring his troops desperately needed supplies. In addition, Lee and Jefferson Davis planned to capture Maryland (with its many Confederate supporters), separate it from the Union, and gain control of its farms, crops, and livestock.

In September 1862, Lee and his 40,000 troops, many of them barefoot and underfed, pushed north across the Potomac River into western Maryland. "I have never seen such a mass of filthy, strong-smelling men," said a Marylander. "They are the roughest looking set of creatures I ever saw, their features, hair, and clothing matted with dirt and filth."

On September 17 the Union and Confederate armies clashed in the furious **Battle of Antietam** (Sharpsburg). Had not Union soldiers discovered Lee's detailed battle plans wrapped around three cigars that a Rebel soldier had carelessly dropped on the ground, the Confederates might have won.

And, had McClellan acted preemptively and moved his 100,000 men more quickly, he could have destroyed Lee's Army of Northern Virginia while it was scattered and still on the march. As always, however, McClellan mobilized slowly, enabling Lee and his troops to regroup at Sharpsburg, Maryland, between Antietam Creek and the Potomac River.

There, over the course of fourteen hours, the poorly coordinated Union army launched repeated attacks. The fighting was savage; a Union officer counted "hundreds of dead bodies lying in rows and in piles." The scene after "five hours of continuous slaughter" was "sickening, harrowing, horrible. O what a terrible sight!"

The next day, Lee braced for another Union attack that never came. That night, cloaked by fog and drizzling rain, the battered Confederates slipped back across the Potomac River to the safety of Virginia. "The 'barefoot boys' have done some terrible fighting," a Georgian wrote his parents. "We are a dirty, ragged set [of soldiers], mother, but courage & heroism find many a true disciple among us."

Although the battle was technically a draw, Lee's northern invasion had failed. One Rebel general called it the "hardest fought battle of the war."

McClellan, never known for his modesty, told his wife that he "had fought the battle splendidly" against great odds. To him, the Battle of Antietam was "the most terrible battle of the age." Indeed, it was the bloodiest day in American history. Some 6,400 soldiers on both sides were killed, twice as many as at Shiloh, and another 17,000 were wounded or listed as missing.

President Lincoln was pleased that Lee's army had been forced to retreat, but he was disgusted by McClellan's failure to pursue the Confederates and win the war. The exasperated president sent a sarcastic message to the general: "I have just read your dispatch about sore-tongued and fatigued horses. Will you pardon me for asking what the horses of your army have done . . . that fatigues anything?" Failing to receive a satisfactory answer, Lincoln sacked McClellan as commander of the Army of the Potomac and assigned him to recruiting duty in New Jersey. Never again would McClellan command troops, but he would challenge Lincoln for the presidency in 1864.

The Battle of Antietam revived sagging northern morale and dashed the Confederacy's hopes of forging alliances with Great Britain and France. It also convinced Lincoln to transform the war from an effort to restore the Union to a crusade to end slavery.

Union view of the Emancipation Proclamation A thoughtful Lincoln composes the proclamation with the Constitution and the Bible in his lap. The scales of justice hang on the wall behind him.

EMANCIPATION PROCLAMATION On September 22, 1862, five days after the Battle of Antietam, President Lincoln issued the preliminary **Emancipation Proclamation**, which warned the Confederacy that if it did not stop fighting, all slaves still under its control were to be made "forever free" in exactly 100 days, on January 1, 1863.

The Emancipation Proclamation was not based on ideas of racial equality or abstract ideals of human dignity. It was, according to Lincoln, a "military necessity" and therefore an act of war. The proclamation would free only those slaves in areas still controlled by the Confederacy; it had no bearing on slaves in the four border states because they remained in the Union, and Lincoln had no constitutional authority to free them.

Lincoln believed that the Constitution allowed each state to decide the fate of slavery, so his only legal avenue was to act as commander in chief of the armed forces rather than as president. He would declare the end of slavery in Confederate-controlled areas as a "fit and necessary war measure" to save the Union.

When he signed the actual Emancipation Proclamation in January, however, Lincoln amended his original message, adding that the proclamation was "an act of justice" as well as a military necessity. His constitutional concerns

Confederate view of the Emancipation Proclamation Surrounded by demonic faces hidden in his furnishings, Lincoln pens the proclamation with a foot trampling the Constitution. The devil holds the inkwell before him.

about abolishing slavery would lead him to promote the Thirteenth Amendment ending slavery across the nation. As Lincoln signed the Emancipation Proclamation, he said, "I never, in my life, felt more certain that I was doing the right thing than I do in signing this paper." Simply restoring the Union was no longer the purpose of the war; the transformation of the South and the slave system was now the goal.

REACTIONS TO EMANCIPATION   Abraham Lincoln's threat to free slaves under Confederate control triggered emotional reactions. The *Illinois State Register* savaged the president for violating the Constitution and causing "the permanent disruption of the republic." Democrats called his decision dictatorial, unconstitutional, and catastrophic. "We Won't Fight to Free the Nigger," proclaimed one popular banner. Many others felt likewise. In the months following the proclamation, thousands of Union troops deserted, explaining that they did not enlist to free slaves, much less to provide racial equality. In the November elections, Democrats, scolding Republicans as "Nigger Worshippers," took twenty-eight Republican seats.

Lincoln forcefully responded to his critics. "You say you will not fight to free negroes," he wrote. "Some of them seem willing to fight for you; but, no matter. Fight you, then, exclusively to save the Union. I issued the [emancipation] proclamation on purpose to aid you in saving the Union."

Although Lincoln's proclamation technically would free only the slaves where Confederates remained in control, many slaves in the northern border states and the South claimed their freedom anyway. As Lincoln had hoped, word spread rapidly among slave communities in the Confederacy, creating general confusion in the cities and encouraging hundreds of thousands to escape. A Union general said that emancipation "was like an earthquake. It shook and shattered the whole previously existing social system."

George Washington Albright, an enslaved teen in Mississippi, recalled that although white planters tried to prevent slaves from learning about the proclamation, word slipped through the "grapevine." His father was inspired to escape and join the Union army, and the younger Albright served as a "runner" for the 4Ls ("Lincoln's Legal Loyal League"), a secret group created to spread the news to slaves throughout the region.

Lincoln's proclamation incensed Confederate leaders, who predicted it would ignite a race war. By contrast, Frederick Douglass, the African American abolitionist leader, loved the "righteous decree"; he knew it would inspire abolitionists in the North and set in motion the eventual end of slavery everywhere.

As Lincoln had hoped, the Emancipation Proclamation boosted the Union war effort. It enabled African Americans to enlist in the Union army and navy, and it undermined support for the Confederacy in Europe. The conversion of the Civil War from a conflict to restore the Union into a crusade to end slavery gave the Federal war effort moral legitimacy in the eyes of Europeans.

As Union armies advanced deeper into the southern states, they became forces of liberation, freeing slaves and circulating thousands of copies of the Emancipation Proclamation. At Camp Saxton, a former plantation on the coast of South Carolina, the First South Carolina Volunteers, a Union regiment made up of former slaves, gathered on January 1, 1863, to celebrate Lincoln's signing of the Emancipation Proclamation.

After the proclamation was read aloud, it was "cheered to the skies." As Colonel Thomas W. Higginson, the unit's commander, unfurled an American flag, the black troops spontaneously began singing "My Country 'Tis of Thee / Sweet land of liberty / Of thee I sing!" "I never saw anything so electric," Higginson reported; "it made all other words cheap; it seemed the choked voice of a race at last unloosed."

FREDERICKSBURG Meanwhile, the war was growing in scope and destruction. In Richmond, Mary Chesnut reported that everyone she encountered seemed shell-shocked: "They press your hand, tears stand in their eyes or roll down their cheeks . . . They have brothers, fathers, or sons—as the case may be—in the battle. And this thing now never seems to stop."

In his search for an effective commanding general, Lincoln turned in the fall of 1862 to Ambrose E. Burnside, whose greatest attribute was that he looked the part of a general: tall and imposing, with massive facial hair that gave rise to the term "sideburns." Twice before, Burnside had turned down the job, saying he was unfit for such responsibility. Now he accepted, although he remained full of self-doubts.

Burnside decided to try again to capture Richmond, the Confederate capital. To that end, in mid-November 1862, he positioned most of the 122,000 men in the Army of the Potomac east of the icy Rappahannock River overlooking the town of Fredericksburg, Virginia. Robert E. Lee rushed his Army of Northern Virginia to defend the town.

As the days passed, Lee's outnumbered forces established heavily fortified positions along a line of ridges and behind stone walls at the base of Marye's Heights, west of Fredericksburg. A Union soldier wrote home before the battle, predicting what was to happen: "It looks to me as if we are going over there to get murdered."

On December 13, the Union soldiers formed ranks south of town and began to assault Lee's entrenched positions. Confederate cannons and muskets chewed up the advancing Federals as they crossed a half mile of open

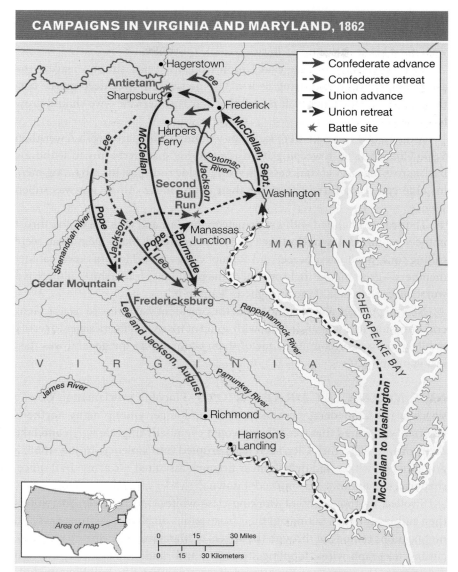

CAMPAIGNS IN VIRGINIA AND MARYLAND, 1862

- → Confederate advance
- --→ Confederate retreat
- → Union advance
- --→ Union retreat
- ✳ Battle site

Hagerstown

Antietam
Sharpsburg

Frederick

Harpers
Ferry

McClellan, Sept.

Potomac
River

Jackson

McClellan

Lee

Second
Bull
Run

Washington

Manassas
Junction

Pope

Jackson

Pope

Burnside

Lee

MARYLAND

Shenandoah River

Cedar Mountain

Fredericksburg

Rappahannock River

CHESAPEAKE BAY

Lee and Jackson, August

VIRGINIA

Pamunkey River

James River

Richmond

Harrison's
Landing

McClellan to Washington

Area of map

0   15   30 Miles

0   15   30 Kilometers

- How did the Confederate army defeat General Pope at the Second Battle of Bull Run?
- Why was General Burnside's decision to attack at Fredericksburg a mistake?

land. The assault was, a Union general regretted, "a great slaughter-pen." The Pennsylvania governor, on hand to observe, later told President Lincoln that it was "not a battle, it was a butchery."

Wave after wave of blue-clad Union troops fell like autumn leaves. The awful scene of dead and dying Federals, some stacked three deep on the battlefield, led Lee to remark: "It is well that war is so terrible—we should grow too fond of it."

After 12,600 Federals were killed or wounded, compared with fewer than 5,300 Confederates, a weeping Burnside told his shattered army to withdraw back across the river as darkness fell. As Burnside rode past his retreating men, his aide called for three cheers for their commander. All he got was sullen silence.

The year 1862 ended with a stalemate in the East and with the Union thrust in the West mired down. Northern morale plummeted. Many Democrats were calling for a negotiated peace, and Republicans—even Lincoln's own cabinet members—grew increasingly critical of the president's leadership. "If there is a worse place than hell," Lincoln sighed, "I am in it."

Newspapers circulated rumors that the president was going to resign. General Burnside, too, was under fire, with some of his own officers eager to testify publicly to his shortcomings. One of them claimed that the general was "fast losing his mind."

NEW YORK CITY DRAFT RIOTS Lincoln's proclamation freeing slaves in the Confederacy created anxiety and anger among many northern laborers who feared that freed slaves would eventually migrate north and take their jobs. In New York City, such fears erupted into violence. In July 1863, a group of 500 whites, led by volunteer firemen, assaulted the army draft office, shattered its windows, and burned it down.

Swollen by thousands of working-class whites, mostly Irish, the rioters then ruthlessly began taking out their frustrations on blacks. For four days and nights, mobs rampaged through the streets of Manhattan, tearing up rail lines, cutting telegraph wires, toppling streetcars, and randomly attacking African Americans. The protesters also burned down more than fifty buildings, including the mayor's home, police stations, two Protestant churches, and the Colored Orphan Asylum, forcing 233 children to flee.

The violence killed 120 people and injured thousands. Only the arrival of Federal soldiers ended it.

BLACK SOLDIERS AND SAILORS In July 1862, in an effort to strengthen the Union war effort, the U.S. Congress had passed the **Militia Act**, which authorized the army to use freed slaves as laborers or soldiers. (They were already eligible to serve in the navy.) Lincoln, however, did not encourage their use as soldiers because he feared the reaction in the border states, where slavery remained in place. Only after the formal signing of the Emancipation Proclamation in January 1863 did the Union army recruit black soldiers in large numbers.

On May 22, 1863, the U.S. War Department created the Bureau of Colored Troops to recruit free blacks and freed slaves. More than 180,000 blacks enlisted. Some 80 percent of them were from southern states, and 38,000 of them gave their lives. In the navy, African Americans accounted for about a fourth of all enlistments; more than 2,800 of them died. Initially, blacks were not allowed in combat, but the need to win the war changed that. A white Union army private reported in the late spring of 1863 that the black troops "fight like the Devil."

To be sure, racism in the North influenced the status of African Americans in the military. Black soldiers and sailors served in all-black units led by white officers. They were paid less than whites ($7 per month versus $16 for white recruits) and were ineligible for the enlistment bonus paid to

Black Union army sergeant Wearing his uniform and sword, he poses with a copy of J. T. Headley's *The Great Rebellion* in his hand.

whites. Still, as Frederick Douglass declared, "this is no time for hesitation . . . This is our chance, and woe betide us if we fail to embrace it."

Service in the Union army or navy provided former slaves a unique opportunity to grow in confidence, awareness, and maturity. A northern social worker in the South Carolina Sea Islands was "astonished" at the positive effects of "soldiering" on ex-slaves: "Some who left here a month ago to join [the army were] cringing, dumpish, slow," but now they "are ready to look you in the eye—are wide awake and active." Commenting on Union victories at Port Hudson and Milliken's Bend, Louisiana, Lincoln reported that "some of our commanders . . . believe that . . . the use of colored troops constitutes the heaviest blow yet dealt to the rebels." One African American soldier who recognized his former owner among a group of Confederate prisoners called out: "Hello master. Bottom rail on top this time!"

THE WAR BEHIND THE LINES

Feeding, clothing, supplying, and nursing the vast armies required tremendous sacrifices. Farms and villages were transformed into battlefields, churches became makeshift hospitals, civilian life was disrupted, and families grieved for those who would not be coming home.

CIVIL WAR MEDICINE Medical knowledge lagged behind the development of military weapons during the war. Antibiotics had yet to be developed, and pain-killing medicines were in short supply. Amputation was the common treatment for gunshot wounds to the arm or leg, and stomach wounds were usually fatal because the resulting infection (peritonitis) could not be prevented. Of those killed by combat, some 60 percent died in battle, and 40 percent succumbed later to their wounds. Some 50,000 soldiers died in prisoner-of-war camps where infectious diseases—typhoid, typhus, malaria, pneumonia, smallpox, and measles—ran rampant.

WOMEN AND THE WAR While breaking the bonds of slavery, the Civil War also loosened traditional restraints on female activity. "No conflict in history," a journalist wrote, "was such a woman's war as the Civil War."

Women played prominent roles in both the North and South. They went to work in mills and factories, sewed uniforms, raised money and supplies, and volunteered as nurses. In Greenville, South Carolina, when T. G. Gower went off to fight, his wife Elizabeth took over the family business, converting production in their carriage factory to military wagons and ambulances. Three thousand northern women worked as nurses with the U.S. Sanitary Commission, a civilian agency that provided medical relief and other services for soldiers. Countless women, black and white, supported the freedmen's aid movement to help freed slaves.

In the North thousands of women served as nurses and health-related volunteers. The most famous were Clara Barton and Dorothea Lynde Dix. Barton explained that her place was "anywhere between the bullet and the battlefield." For her part, Dix, who was appointed superintendent of Union nurses in 1861, issued an appeal for "plain looking" women between the ages of thirty-five and

fifty who wore no jewelry and could
"bear the presence of suffering and
exercise entire self-control."

Barton, who later founded the
American Red Cross, decided to go to
the killing fields on her own, delivering
medical supplies and food to the sick
and wounded. At Fredericksburg, she
nursed some 1,200 wounded in a single
building. "I wrung the blood from the
bottom of my clothing before I could
step," she reported, "for the weight
about my feet" kept her from moving. "I am singularly free," she said,
"—there are few to mourn for me, and
I take my life in my hand and go where
men fall and die, to see if perchance
I can render some little comfort."

Clara Barton She oversaw the
distribution of medicines to Union
troops and would later help found the
American Red Cross.

In many southern towns and counties, the home front became a world of
white women and children and African
American slaves. A resident of Lexing-
ton, Virginia, reported that there were "no men left" in town by mid-1862.
Women suddenly found themselves full-time farmers or plantation managers,
clerks, and schoolteachers.

Other women traveled with the armies as camp followers, cooking meals,
writing letters, and assisting with amputations. Several dozen served as spies.
New Yorker Mary Edwards Walker, a Union battlefield surgeon, was captured
and imprisoned by the Confederates for spying, but later released in a prisoner
exchange. She was the only woman in the war (and since) to be awarded the Congressional Medal of Honor, the nation's highest military award, which Lincoln
had authorized in 1861. In 1864, President Lincoln told a soldier that all the praise
of women over the centuries did not do justice "for their conduct during the war."

WARTIME GOVERNMENT While freeing the slaves in the Confederacy was a transformational development, a political revolution began as a
result of the shift in congressional power from the South to the North after
secession.

In 1862, the Republican-dominated Congress sought to promote the
"prosperity and happiness of the whole people" by passing a more comprehensive

Susie King Taylor Born into slavery, she served as a nurse in Union-occupied Georgia and operated a school for freed slaves.

tariff bill (called the Morrill Tariff in honor of its sponsor, Vermont Republican congressman Justin Smith Morrill) to raise government revenue and "protect" America's manufacturing, agricultural, mining, and fishing industries from foreign competition.

Republicans in Congress, with Lincoln's support, enacted legislation reflecting their belief (and that of the old Whig party) that the federal government should actively promote economic development. To that end, Congress approved the Pacific Railway Act (1862), which provided funding and grants of land for construction of a 1,900-mile-long transcontinental railroad line from Omaha, Nebraska, to Sacramento, California. In addition, a **Homestead Act** (1862) granted 160 acres of public land to each settler who agreed to work that land for five years. To help farmers become more productive, Congress created a new federal agency, the Department of Agriculture.

Two other key pieces of legislation were the **Morrill Land Grant College Act** (1862), which provided states with 30,000 acres of federal land to finance the establishment of public universities that would teach "agriculture and mechanic arts," and the National Banking Act (1863), which created national banks that could issue paper money that would be accepted across the country. These wartime measures had long-term significance for the growth of the national economy—and the expansion of the federal government.

UNION FINANCES In December 1860, as southern states announced plans to secede, the federal Treasury was virtually empty. To meet the war's huge expenses, Congress needed money fast—and lots of it. It focused on three options: raising taxes, printing paper money, and selling government bonds to investors. The taxes came chiefly in the form of the Morrill Tariff on imports and a 3 percent tax on manufactures and most professions.

In 1862, Congress created the Internal Revenue Service to collect the first income tax on citizens and corporations. The tax rate was 3 percent on those with annual incomes of more than $800 and went up to 5 percent on incomes of more than $10,000. Yet only 250,000 people out of a population of 39 million had income high enough to pay taxes.

In the end, the tax revenues fell short of what was needed, meeting only 21 percent of wartime expenditures. In 1862, Congress approved the printing of paper money to help finance the war. With the Legal Tender Act of 1862, the Treasury issued $450 million in new paper currency, called *greenbacks* because of the color of the ink used to print the bills.

The federal government also relied upon the sale of bonds. A Philadelphia banker named Jay Cooke (the "Financier of the Civil War") mobilized a nation-wide campaign to sell $2 billion in government bonds to private investors.

CONFEDERATE FINANCES In comparison to the Union, Confederate efforts to finance the war were a disaster. Jefferson Davis had to create a treasury and a revenue-collecting system from scratch. Moreover, the South's agrarian economy was land-rich but cash-poor. While the Confederacy owned 30 percent of America's assets (businesses, land, slaves) in 1861, its currency in circulation was only 12 percent of that in the North.

In its first year, the Confederacy created a property tax, which should have yielded a hefty amount of revenue. Collecting taxes was left to the states, however, and the result was chaos. In 1863, the desperate Confederate Congress began taxing nearly everything, but enforcement was poor and evasion easy. Altogether, taxes covered no more than 5 percent of Confederate war costs, and bond issues accounted for less than 33 percent. Treasury notes (paper money) accounted for more than 60 percent.

During the war, the Confederacy issued more than $1 billion in paper money, which, along with a shortage of consumer goods, caused prices to soar. By 1864, a turkey sold in the Richmond market for $100, and bacon was $10 a pound. Such rampant price increases caused great distress, and frustrations over the burdens of war erupted into rioting, looting, and mass protests.

By 1865, some 100,000 Confederate soldiers, hungry, weary and frustrated by delayed pay, were deserting the army and heading home. Some were upset that they were expected to risk their lives so that haughty planters could maintain their army of slaves. As one said, he and his comrades were "tired of fighting for this negro-owning aristockracy [sic]."

UNION POLITICS The North also had its share of dissension and factionalism. But President Lincoln proved to be a remarkable conflict manager, in part because he refused to nurse grudges. He loved the jockeying of backroom politics, and he excelled at fending off uprisings and attempts to subvert his leadership.

Led by Thaddeus Stevens in the House and Charles Sumner in the Senate, the so-called Radical Republicans wanted more than the Confederacy's defeat; they wanted to "reconstruct" it by having Union armies seize southern plantations and give the land to the former slaves. The majority of Republicans, however, continued to back Lincoln's more cautious approach.

The Democratic party was devastated by the loss of its long-dominant southern wing and the death of its nationalist spokesman, Stephen A. Douglas. Peace Democrats favored restoring the Union "as it was [before 1860] and the Constitution as it is." They reluctantly supported Lincoln's war policies but opposed Republican economic legislation. Those referred to as the War Democrats, such as Tennessee senator Andrew Johnson and Secretary of War Edwin M. Stanton, backed Lincoln's policies.

A few Peace Democrats verged on treason. The **Copperhead Democrats** (named for copper coins they wore as lapel pins) were strongest in states such as Ohio, Indiana, and Illinois, where substantial numbers of former Southerners resided. The Copperheads openly sympathized with the Confederacy and called for an immediate end to the war.

CIVIL LIBERTIES   Such support for the enemy led President Lincoln to crack down hard. Like all wartime leaders, his challenge was to balance the urgent needs of winning a war with the protection of civil liberties. Using his authority as commander in chief, Lincoln exercised emergency powers, including suspending the writ of *habeas corpus*, which guarantees arrested citizens a speedy hearing before a judge. The Constitution states that the government may suspend habeas corpus only in cases of foreign invasion, but Supreme Court justice Roger Taney and several congressional leaders argued that Congress alone had the authority to take such action.

By the Habeas Corpus Act of 1863, Congress allowed the president to have people arrested on the "suspicion" of treason. Thereafter, Union soldiers and local sheriffs arrested thousands of Confederate sympathizers in the northern states without using a writ of habeas corpus. Union general Henry Halleck jailed a Missourian for saying, "[I] wouldn't wipe my ass with the stars and stripes."

CONFEDERATE POLITICS AND STATES' RIGHTS   As the war dragged on, discontented Confederates directed much of their frustration toward their leaders. A Richmond newspaper reported in 1862 that the Confederacy had "reached a very dark hour" because of Jefferson Davis's faulty leadership. It described the Rebel leader as "cold, haughty, peevish, narrow-minded, pig-headed, [and] malignant."

Poor white Southerners resented the planter elite while food grew scarce and prices skyrocketed. A food riot erupted in Richmond on April 2, 1863, when an angry mob, mostly women armed with pistols or knives, marched to the governor's mansion to demand that bread in Confederate warehouses be shared with civilians. When the governor announced that nothing could be done, the protesters shouted, "Bread or blood!" They broke into stores, stealing shoes and clothing as well as food. The riot ended only when President Davis arrived and threatened to shoot the protesters. Over several days, police arrested forty-four women and twenty-nine men. "We had forgotten Yankees and were fighting each other," Mary Chesnut confessed.

Davis's greatest challenge came from southern politicians who criticized the "tyrannical" powers of the Confederate government. As a general reported, "The state of feeling between the President [Davis] and Congress is bad—could not be worse." Critics asserted states' rights against the Confederate government, just as they had against the Union. Georgia governor Joseph Brown explained that he had joined the Confederacy to "sustain the rights of the states and prevent the consolidation of the Government, and I am still a *rebel . . . no* matter who may be in power."

While Lincoln was a shrewd pragmatist, Davis was a brittle ideologue with a waspish temper. Once he made a decision, nothing could change his mind, and he could never admit a mistake. One southern politician said that Davis was "as stubborn as a mule."

Such a dogmatic personality was ill-suited to the chief executive of an infant—and fractious—nation. Cabinet members resigned almost as soon as they were appointed. During its four years, the Confederacy had three secretaries of state and six secretaries of war. Vice President Alexander Stephens found Davis so "timid, petulant, peevish, and obstinate" that in 1862 he left Richmond, the Confederate capital, to sulk at his Georgia home.

Jefferson Davis President of the Confederacy.

THE FALTERING CONFEDERACY

Amid the political infighting, the war ground on. The Confederate strategy of fighting largely a defensive war was working well, and President Lincoln was still searching for a general-in-chief comparable to Robert E. Lee.

CHANCELLORSVILLE After the Union disaster at Fredericksburg at the end of 1862, President Lincoln fired Ambrose Burnside and appointed General Joseph Hooker, a hard-drinking warrior known as "Fighting Joe," to lead the Army of the Potomac. With a force of 130,000 men, the largest Union army yet gathered, an overconfident Hooker attacked the Confederates at Chancellorsville, in eastern Virginia, during the first week of May 1863. "My plans are perfect," Hooker boasted. "May God have mercy on General Lee, for I will have none."

Hooker spoke too soon. Lee, with perhaps half as many troops, split his army in thirds and gave Hooker a painful lesson in the art of elusive mobility when Stonewall Jackson's 28,000 Confederates surprised the Union army by smashing into its exposed right flank. Jackson's surprise attack ultimately forced Hooker's army to retreat and resulted in a devastating defeat for the Union. "My God, my God," moaned Lincoln when he heard the news. "What will the country say?"

The Confederate victory was costly, however. As night fell during the second day of battle, Stonewall Jackson and several aides rode out beyond the skirmish line to locate the Union forces. Shooting erupted in the darkness, and nervous Confederates mistakenly opened fire on Jackson's group. Three bullets struck the celebrated commander, shattering his left arm and right hand. The next day, a surgeon amputated his arm. The indispensable Jackson seemed to be recovering, but he then contracted pneumonia and died. "I have lost my right arm," Lee lamented, and "I do not know how to replace him." The next day, Lee forced

Thomas "Stonewall" Jackson The celebrated Confederate commander, Jackson would die of friendly fire in the Battle of Chancellorsville.

Hooker's Union army to retreat. It was the peak of Lee's career, but Chancellorsville was his last significant victory.

VICKSBURG While General Lee frustrated the Federals in the East, General Grant had been inching his army down the Mississippi River toward the Confederate stronghold of Vicksburg, Mississippi, a busy commercial town situated on high bluffs overlooking a sharp, hairpin bend of the river. Capturing the Rebel stronghold, Grant stressed, "was of the first importance," because Vicksburg was the only rail and river junction between Memphis, Tennessee, and New Orleans. Yet he knew it would be difficult to conquer the "impregnable" Confederate defenses.

Meanwhile, Jefferson Davis stressed the importance of holding the Mississippi River open: "Vicksburg must not be lost!" If Union forces gained control of the river, they could split the Confederacy in two and prevent food and livestock from reaching Confederate armies in the East.

While Union warships sneaked past the Confederate cannons overlooking the river, Grant moved his army eastward across Mississippi on a campaign that President Lincoln later called "one of the most brilliant in the world." Grant's forces captured Jackson, Mississippi, the state capital, and won a half dozen battles before pinning 31,000 Rebel soldiers inside Vicksburg so tightly that "not a cat could have crept out . . . without being discovered." In late May and early June 1863, the Union forces dug twelve miles of interconnected trenches around the besieged city.

In the **Battle of Vicksburg**, Grant decided to use constant bombardment from gunboats and cannons to starve and gradually wear down the trapped Confederates. Many civilians were forced to live in cellars or caves dug as protection from the unending shelling. The Rebel soldiers and the city's residents could neither escape nor be reinforced nor resupplied with food and ammunition. As the weeks passed, they ate their horses and mules, then dogs and cats, and, finally, rats, which sold for a dollar each. One starving girl ate her pet bird.

General John C. Pemberton, the Confederate commander at Vicksburg, wrote Jefferson Davis that the situation was "hopeless." A group of ragged soldiers pleaded with their commander: "If you can't feed us, you had better surrender us, horrible as that idea is." Yet Pemberton, a Pennsylvanian whose Virginia-born wife convinced him to fight for the Confederacy, was determined to outlast Grant's troops.

GETTYSBURG Vicksburg's dilemma led Jefferson Davis to ask General Lee to send troops from Virginia to Mississippi to break the Union siege. Lee, however, thought he had a better plan. He would make another daring strike into the North in hopes of forcing the Union army surrounding Vicksburg to rush home to defend the northern heartland. He also wagered that a bold northern offensive would persuade peace-seeking Copperhead Democrats to try again to end the war on terms favorable to the Confederacy. The stakes were high. A Confederate general said the invasion across Maryland and into Pennsylvania would "either destroy the Yankees or bring them to terms." Or be a disaster for Lee.

In June 1863, the fabled Army of Northern Virginia, which Lee said was made up of "invincible troops" who would "go anywhere and do anything if properly led," moved northward, taking thousands of animals and wagons as well as throngs of slaves for support.

One reason Lee moved into the North was to find food for his men and horses. The Union armies had spent so much time in northern Virginia that there were not enough rations to go around. So as Lee's army moved north, his soldiers and slaves confiscated thousands of horses, cattle, and hogs, as well as tons of wheat and corn. They also captured free blacks in Maryland and Pennsylvania, returning them to slavery in Virginia.

Once the Union commander, General George Meade, realized the Confederates were again moving north, he gave chase, knowing that the next battle would "decide the fate of our country and our cause." As Lee's army moved into Pennsylvania, he lost track of the Federals following him because of the unexplained absence of General J. E. B. Stuart's 5,000 horse soldiers, who were Lee's "eyes and ears." Stuart, it turned out, had decided on his own to create a panic in the Union capital by threatening an attack on Washington, D.C. On June 28, an exasperated Lee exploded: "I cannot think what has become of Stuart. I ought to have heard from him long before now."

Neither side expected Gettysburg, a hilly farming town in southeastern Pennsylvania to be the site of the largest battle ever fought in North America. Unsuspecting Confederate troops entered the town at dawn on June 30 and collided with Union cavalry units that had been tracking their movements.

The main forces of both sides—65,000 Confederates and 85,000 Federals—then raced to the scene, and on July 1, the armies clashed in what came to be called the **Battle of Gettysburg**, the most dramatic contest of the war. While preparing to fight, a Union cavalryman yelled at soldiers from New York and Pennsylvania: "You stand alone, between the Rebel army and your homes. Fight like hell!"

Initially, the Confederates forced the Federals to retreat, but the Union troops regrouped to stronger positions on high ridges overlooking the town. General Meade rushed in reinforcements. That night he wrote his wife that both armies had been "shattered" by the first day's combat.

"A Harvest of Death" Timothy H. O'Sullivan's grim photograph of the dead at Gettysburg.

On July 2, wave after wave of screaming Confederates assaulted Meade's army, pushing the Federals back across blood-soaked wheat fields and through peach orchards, but never breaking through. A wounded Confederate officer scrawled a note before he died: "Tell my father I died with my face to the enemy." Some 16,000 were killed or wounded on both sides during the second day of fighting. Worse was to come.

The next day, July 3, against the objections of his senior general, Georgian James Longstreet, Robert E. Lee risked all on a gallant but doomed assault against the well-defended Union lines along Cemetery Ridge. For two hours, both sides bombarded the other, leading a Union soldier to write that it felt "as if the heavens and earth were crashing together."

Then, the cannons stopped. At about two o'clock on the broiling summer afternoon, three Confederate infantry divisions—about 12,500 men—emerged from the woods and prepared to attack in the 90-degree heat. General George Pickett, commander of the lead division, told his men to "Charge the enemy and remember Old Virginia!"

With drums pounding and bugles blaring, a gray wave of sweating Rebels began a mile-long dash up a grassy slope of newly mown hay crisscrossed with split-rail fences. Awaiting them behind a low stone wall at the top of Cemetery Ridge were 120 Union cannons and thousands of riflemen. It was as hopeless as the Union charge at Fredericksburg.

When the Federals opened fire, the Confederates were "enveloped in a dense cloud of dust. Arms, heads, blankets, guns, and knapsacks were tossed into the clear air." Only a few Rebels made it to the top, where they grappled in hand-to-hand combat. A Confederate general climbed atop the stone wall and shouted: "Come on, boys! Give them the cold steel! Who will follow me?" Two minutes later, he was dead—as was the Confederate attack—when Union soldiers held in reserve rushed to close the gap in their lines.

With stunning suddenness, the carnage was over. The surviving Confederates retreated to the woods, and the once roaring battlefield was now covered with the corpses of men and horses, a scene made ghastlier by the "moanings and groanings" of thousands of wounded. Each corpse told a poignant story. Scattered beside a dead Federal officer were papers granting him leave to go home and be married, and a letter from his soon-to-be bride expressing her "happiness at the approaching event." Five men from the Coffey family in North Carolina died on that battlefield, including twin brothers.

What General Lee had called the "grand charge" was, in the end, a grand failure. As he watched the survivors straggle back across the bloody field, he muttered, "All this has been my fault. It is I who have lost this fight." He ordered General Pickett to prepare his battered division for another attack, only to have Pickett reply: "General Lee, I have no division now." Half his men lay dead or wounded.

Lee sought to console Pickett by assuring him that he and his troops "have covered yourselves with glory." Pickett would have none of it. "Not all the glory in the world, General Lee, can atone for the widows and orphans this day has made."

Some 42,000 were dead, wounded, or missing after three days at Gettysburg. Thousands of horses were also killed and left to rot in the summer heat. A Union soldier wrote home: "Great God! When will this horrid war stop?"

Others asked the same question. John Futch, a Confederate private from North Carolina, had seen his brother Charley shot in the head. He wrote his wife that the slaughter had left him "half crazy." A few weeks after the battle, he quit his post and headed home, only to be captured, tried as a deserter, and executed.

LEE'S RETREAT   Again, as after Antietam, Robert E. Lee's mangled army retreated to Virginia—and again, the Federals were slow to give chase. Had General Meade quickly pursued Lee's battered army, he might have ended the war. President Lincoln was outraged: "We had them within our grasp! Your golden opportunity is gone."

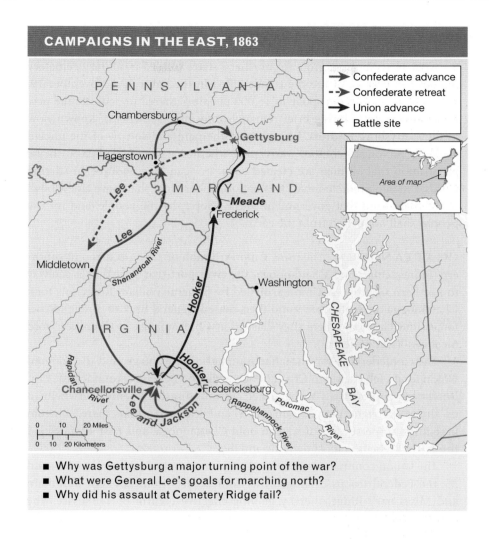

CAMPAIGNS IN THE EAST, 1863

→ Confederate advance
--▸ Confederate retreat
→ Union advance
✶ Battle site

PENNSYLVANIA

Chambersburg

Gettysburg

Hagerstown

MARYLAND

Meade

Frederick

Middletown

Shenandoah River

Washington

Lee

Lee

VIRGINIA

Rapidan River

Chancellorsville

River

Hooker

Hooker

Fredericksburg

Lee and Jackson

Rappahannock River

Potomac

CHESAPEAKE BAY

River

Area of map

0   10   20 Miles
0   10   20 Kilometers

- Why was Gettysburg a major turning point of the war?
- What were General Lee's goals for marching north?
- Why did his assault at Cemetery Ridge fail?

The war would grind on for another twenty-one months. Still, Rebel morale plummeted. A barely literate Georgia soldier wrote his mother that "the Armey is broken harted" and "don't care which way the war closes, for we have suffered very much."

Lee's desperate gamble had failed in every way, not the least being its inability to relieve the pressure on Vicksburg, Mississippi. On July 4, as Lee's defeated army left Pennsylvania, General John Pemberton, the Confederate commander at Vicksburg, surrendered his starving 31,000-man army, ending the forty-seven-day siege. Union vessels now controlled the Mississippi River and the Confederacy was effectively split in two, with Louisiana, Texas, and

Arkansas cut off from the other Rebel states. Jefferson Davis said that it was the Confederacy's "period of disaster."

After Gettysburg, a group of northern states funded a military cemetery in commemoration of the thousands killed in the battle. On November 19, 1863, President Lincoln spoke to 15,000 people gathered to dedicate the new national cemetery. In his brief remarks (only nine sentences), known now as the Gettysburg Address, he expressed the pain and sorrow of the uncivil war. The prolonged conflict was testing whether a nation "dedicated to the proposition that all men are created equal . . . can long endure." In stirring words, Lincoln predicted that "this nation, under God, shall have a new birth of freedom—and that government of the people, by the people, and for the people, shall not perish from the earth."

CHATTANOOGA   The third Union triumph of 1863 occurred in southern Tennessee around Chattanooga, the river port that served as a gateway to northern Georgia. A Union army led by General William Rosecrans took Chattanooga on September 9 and then chased General Braxton Bragg's Rebel forces into Georgia, where they clashed at Chickamauga (a Cherokee word meaning "river of death").

The Confederates, for once, had a numerical advantage, and the battered Union forces fell back into Chattanooga while the Rebels surrounded the city. Rosecrans reported that "we have met a serious disaster. Enemy overwhelmed us, drove our right, pierced our center, and scattered troops there." Lincoln urged him to persevere: "If we can hold Chattanooga, and East Tennessee, I think [the] rebellion must dwindle and die."

The Union command rushed in reinforcements, and on November 24 and 25, the Federal troops dislodged the Confederates from Lookout Mountain and Missionary Ridge, thereby gaining effective control of Tennessee. The South had lost the war in the West.

THE CONFEDERACY AT RISK   The dramatic Union victories at Vicksburg, Gettysburg, and Chattanooga seemed to turn the tide against the Confederacy. During the summer and fall of 1863, however, Union generals in the East lost the momentum Gettysburg had provided, thereby allowing the Army of Northern Virginia to nurse its wounds and continue fighting.

By 1864, Robert E. Lee, whose offer to resign after Gettysburg was refused by Jefferson Davis, was ready to renew the war. His men were "in fine spirits and anxious for a fight." Still, the tone had changed. Confederate leaders had long assumed they could win the war. Now, they began to worry about defeat. A Confederate officer in Richmond noted in his diary after the defeat at Gettysburg that "today absolute ruin seems to be our fortune. The Confederacy totters to its destruction."

A WARTIME ELECTION War or no war, 1864 was a presidential election year, and by autumn the contest would become a referendum on the war itself. No president since Andrew Jackson had won reelection, and Abraham Lincoln became convinced that he would lose without a dramatic change in the course of the war.

Radical Republicans, frustrated that the war had not been won, tried to prevent Lincoln's nomination for a second term, but he consistently outmaneuvered them. Once Lincoln was assured of the nomination, he selected Andrew Johnson, a War Democrat from Tennessee, as his running mate on the "National Union" ticket.

The War Democrats had indiscreetly asked General Grant to be their candidate. He firmly declined, explaining that "I am not a politician, never was, and hope never to be." Becoming president, he said, "is the last thing in the world I desire."

Spurned by Grant, the Democrats called for an immediate end to the fighting. They nominated General George B. McClellan, the former Union commander who had clashed with Lincoln. McClellan pledged to stop the war and, if the Rebels refused to return to the Union, he would allow the Confederacy to "go in peace."

Lincoln knew that the election would be decided on the battlefields. To save the Union, the president had brought Grant, his best commander, to Washington, D.C., in March 1864; promoted him to general in chief; and given him overall command of the war effort, promising all the troops and supplies he needed.

A New York newspaper reported that Lincoln's presidency was now "in the hands of General Grant, and the failure of the General will be the overthrow of the president." When a delegation visited the White House to complain about Grant's reputation as a heavy drinker, Lincoln told the visitors

Ulysses S. Grant At his headquarters in City Point (now Hopewell), Virginia.

that if he could find the brand of whiskey Grant used, he would distribute it to the rest of his generals.

GRANT'S STRATEGY   General Grant was a hard-nosed warrior with unflagging energy and persistence. One soldier said that Grant always looked like he was "determined to drive his head through a brick wall and was about to do it." Yet the Union commander hated war. "I never went into battle willingly or with enthusiasm," he admitted. Nevertheless, he was a brilliant military strategist driven by a simple concept: "Find out where your enemy is, get to him as soon as you can, and strike him as hard as you can, and keep moving on"—regardless of the number of dead and wounded.

Grant's predecessors had focused on trying to capture Richmond; his purpose was to defeat Confederate armies. To do so, he would wage a relentless war of attrition, one in which victory would favor the side that could absorb the most punishment and keep fighting. He would pressure the shrinking Confederate armies wherever they were. Grant, as Abraham Lincoln noted, understood that winning the war was a matter of "awful arithmetic." The Union had the greater numbers, so victory was "only a matter of time."

To that end, Grant ordered the three largest Union armies, one in Virginia, one in Tennessee, and one in Louisiana, to launch offensives in the spring of 1864. No more short battles followed by long pauses. They would force the outnumbered Confederates to keep fighting, day after day, week after week, until they were worn out.

Grant assigned his trusted friend, General William Tecumseh Sherman, a rail-thin, red-haired Ohioan, to lead the Union army in Tennessee southward and apply a strategy of "complete conquest." Sherman, cool under pressure and obsessed with winning at all costs, owed much of his success to Grant's support. "He stood by me when I was crazy, and I stood by him when he was drunk," Sherman said.

William Tecumseh Sherman Sherman's campaign through Georgia hastened the end of the war.

Grant and Sherman would now wage total war, confiscating or destroying any civilian property that might be of use to the military. It was a ruthless and costly plan, but in the end, it would prove effective.

FORT PILLOW MASSACRE As the war ground on, the fighting grew more brutal. On April 12, 1864, at Fort Pillow, perched on a bluff overlooking the Mississippi River forty miles north of Memphis, Tennessee, Confederate troops under General Nathan Bedford Forrest, who would help found the Ku Klux Klan after the war, murdered some 300 Union soldiers who had surrendered. Most of them were African Americans. A Confederate sergeant reported that "the poor, deluded negroes would run up to our men, fall upon their knees, and with uplifted hand scream for mercy, but were ordered to their feet and then shot down."

Word of the Fort Pillow Massacre spread across the nation. Violence begat violence. A few weeks later, a Union soldier from Wisconsin fighting in north Georgia wrote to his future wife about a recent battle. "Twenty-three of the Rebs surrendered but our boys asked if they remembered Fort Pillow and killed all of them. Where there is no officer with us, we take no prisoners . . . We want revenge for our brother soldiers and will have it."

CHASING LEE In May 1864, General Grant's massive Army of the Potomac, numbering about 115,000 (nearly twice the size of General Lee's Army of Northern Virginia), moved south across the Rappahannock and Rapidan Rivers in eastern Virginia. In the nightmarish Battle of the Wilderness (May 5–6), the armies clashed in an impenetrable tangle of dense forest and thickets. Cannons set off brushfires that burned many wounded soldiers to death.

At one point in the intense battle, the Union forces threatened to overrun Lee's headquarters. Lee himself helped organize a counterattack, lining up soldiers from Texas to lead the effort. Spurred by a rush of adrenaline, he stood high in his stirrups, waved his hat, and yelled: "Texans always move them!" He then turned his horse toward the enemy to lead the charge. The soldiers shouted, "Go back, General Lee, go back!" But he kept moving forward. Finally, an officer pulled ahead of Lee, grabbed the reins of his horse, and prevented him from moving. "Can't I, too, die for my country?" the general muttered. His mood brightened as the Confederates swept the Federals from the field and broke the Union advance.

Grant's men suffered more casualties than the Confederates, but the Rebels struggled to find replacements. Always before, when bloodied by Lee's troops, Union armies had quit fighting to rest and nurse their wounds, but now Grant refused to halt. Instead, he continued to push southward, forcing the Rebels to keep fighting.

Lee knew what he was up against. As he told aides, the "great thing about Grant is his perfect coolness and persistency of purpose . . . he is not easily excited . . . and he has the grit of a bull-dog! Once let him get his 'teeth' in, and nothing can shake him off." When General John B. Gordon boasted after the Battle of the Wilderness that Grant was retreating, Lee corrected him: "You are mistaken, quite mistaken. Grant is not retreating; he is not a *retreating* man."

Lee predicted that Grant's army would head for Spotsylvania, which it did. There, it engaged Lee's men near Spotsylvania Court House, eleven miles southwest of Fredericksburg, on the road to Richmond. For twelve brutally hot days in May, the opposing armies were locked in some of the fiercest combat of the war. Grant's troops kept the pressure on.

In the first days of June, just as Republican leaders were gathering to renominate Abraham Lincoln as their presidential candidate, Grant foolishly ordered a poorly coordinated frontal assault on Lee's entrenched Rebels at Cold Harbor, near the Chickahominy River, just ten miles east of Richmond. In twenty minutes, almost 4,000 Federals, caught in a blistering cross fire, were killed or wounded. It was, according to a Union general, "one of the most disastrous days the Army of the Potomac has ever seen." A Confederate commander reported that "it was not war; it was murder."

The frightful losses nearly unhinged Grant, who later admitted that the botched attack was his greatest mistake as a commander. Critics, including Lincoln's wife Mary, called Grant "a butcher" who was "not fit to be at the head of an army." In just two months, Grant's massive offensive across Virginia, labeled the Overland Campaign, had cost some 65,000 killed, wounded, or missing Union soldiers and 33,000 Rebel casualties.

Criticism of Grant's campaign skyrocketed. Even Horace Greeley, the powerful Unionist publisher of the *New York Tribune*, urged Lincoln to negotiate with Confederate leaders to save the "bleeding, bankrupt, almost dying country." The Union war effort came close to ending.

Yet Grant, for all his mistakes, knew that his army could replace its dead and wounded; the Rebels could not. And, Grant reminded Lincoln, he was slowly pushing Lee's army toward Richmond, backing the Confederates into a corner from which they could not escape. Lincoln stood in awe of Grant's tenacity. So, too, did many of his soldiers. "Grant is striking out boldly in every possible direction," a Union officer wrote, "like a mad dog in a meat house."

In June 1864, Grant brilliantly maneuvered his battered forces around Lee's army and headed for Petersburg, a major supply center and railroad hub twenty-five miles south of Richmond. The opposing armies dug in above and

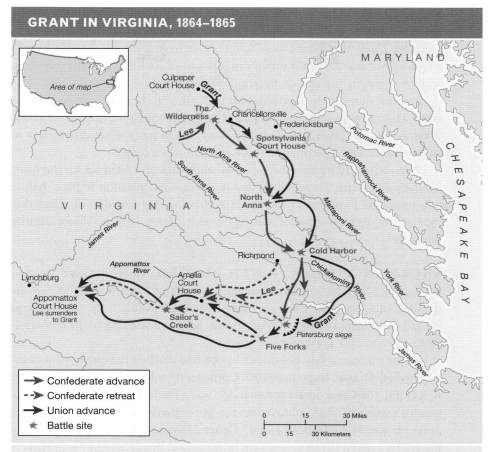

GRANT IN VIRGINIA, 1864–1865

Confederate advance
Confederate retreat
Union advance
Battle site

0   15   30 Miles
0   15   30 Kilometers

■ How were General Grant's tactics in the Battle of the Wilderness different from the Union's previous encounters with General Lee's army?
■ Why did Grant have the advantage at Petersburg?

below Petersburg. Grant began a long siege of the trapped Confederate army, tightening the noose as he had done at Vicksburg.

To cut off supplies to the Rebel troops, Grant sent an army commanded by General Philip Sheridan to destroy the farms in the fertile Shenandoah Valley that kept Lee's army and its horses alive. Sheridan was pleased, for he believed that reducing Confederate farmers to poverty would shorten the war, which placed him "on the side of humanity."

Within weeks, residents of the Shenandoah Valley saw "columns of smoke . . . rising in every direction from burning houses and burning barns." Union troops burned stored grain and rounded up sheep, cattle, and horses to be sent to Grant's army. At the end of August, Lee reported to Jefferson Davis that Grant was "reducing us by starvation." Mary Chesnut wrote in her diary that Grant's strangulation of Richmond and Petersburg was "very disgusting and depressing to the spirits."

For nine months, the two sides held each other in check around Petersburg. Grant's troops were generously supplied by Union vessels moving up the James River, while the Confederates wasted away. The number of deserters grew so large that Lee asked permission to shoot them when caught.

Petersburg had become Lee's prison while disasters piled up for the Confederacy elsewhere. He admitted that it was "a mere question of time" before he would have to retreat or surrender. A Rebel soldier noted in his diary that "our affairs do look gloomy." Grant, he added later, "will no doubt capture the place."

SHERMAN PUSHES SOUTH Meanwhile, General Grant ordered William T. Sherman to drive through the heart of Dixie and inflict "all the damage you can." As Sherman moved his army south from Chattanooga toward the crucial railroad hub of Atlanta, he sent a warning to the city's residents: "Prepare for my coming."

By the middle of July, Sherman's troops had reached the outskirts of heavily fortified Atlanta, trapping 40,000 Confederate soldiers there. General John Bell Hood, the Confederate commander, was a fearless fighter. A Confederate senator's wife said that "a braver man, a purer patriot, a more gallant soldier never breathed than General Hood." General Grant's opinion of him was more mixed. He viewed Hood as "a gallant brave fellow" but believed he would likely "dash out and fight every time you raised a [Union] flag before him." And that is just what Grant and Sherman wanted him to do.

Hood's arm had been shattered at Gettysburg, and he had lost a leg at Chickamauga. Strapped to his saddle, he refused simply to "defend" Atlanta; instead, he attacked. Three times in eight days, the Confederates lashed out at the Union lines encircling the city. Each time they were repulsed, suffering *seven* times as many casualties as the Federals. The Battle of Atlanta left Hood's army wounded, surrounded, and outnumbered. "All lion," Robert E. Lee called Hood, "none of the fox."

Finally, on September 1, the Confederates evacuated the city. Sherman then moved in, gleefully telegraphing Lincoln in September 1864, "Atlanta is ours and fairly won."

Sherman's soldiers stayed in Atlanta until November, resting and resupplying themselves. The 20,000 residents were told to leave before he destroyed much of the city. When they protested, the Union commander replied: "War is cruelty." His men then set fire to the city's railroad station, iron foundries, shops, mills, hotels, and businesses. After Grant congratulated Sherman, he ordered him to commence another campaign, for "We want to keep the enemy constantly pressed to the end of the war."

LINCOLN REELECTED William Tecumseh Sherman's conquest of Atlanta turned the tide of the **election of 1864**. As a Republican senator said, the Union victory in Georgia "created the most extraordinary change in public opinion here [in the North] that ever was known." The capture of Mobile, Alabama, by Union naval forces in August, and Confederate defeats in Virginia's Shenandoah Valley in October, also spurred a dramatic revival of Abraham Lincoln's political support in the North. A Union newspaper editor reported that the fall of Atlanta "has secured a sudden unanimity for Mr. Lincoln." The South's hope that northern discontent would lead to a negotiated peace vanished.

In the 1864 election, the Democratic candidate, George McClellan, the former Union army commander, carried only New Jersey, Delaware, and Kentucky, winning just 21 electoral votes to Lincoln's 212 and 1.8 million popular votes (45 percent) to Lincoln's 2.2 million (55 percent). Union soldiers and sailors voted in large numbers, and almost 80 percent voted for Lincoln. The president's victory sealed the fate of the Confederacy, for it ensured that Union armies would keep the pressure on the Rebels.

SHERMAN'S "MARCH TO THE SEA" In November 1864, General Sherman led 60,000 soldiers out of Atlanta on their famous 300-mile **March to the Sea**. Sherman was eager to "make Georgia howl" by making every Rebel, soldier or civilian "feel the hard hand of war." Why? Because "we are not only fighting hostile armies, but a hostile people" who must be made "so sick of war" that they would never support a civil war again. Sherman pledged to break the will of Georgians.

John Bell Hood's Confederate Army of Tennessee, meanwhile, tried a desperate gamble by heading in the opposite direction from the Union forces, pushing northward into Alabama and then Tennessee. Hood hoped to trick Sherman into chasing him. Sherman refused to take the bait, however. He was determined to keep his main army moving southward to the Georgia coast and then into South Carolina, the seedbed of secession.

Sherman, however, did send General George Thomas and 30,000 soldiers to shadow Hood's Confederates. The two forces clashed in Tennessee. In the Battle of Franklin (November 30, 1864), near Nashville, Hood's 18,000 soldiers

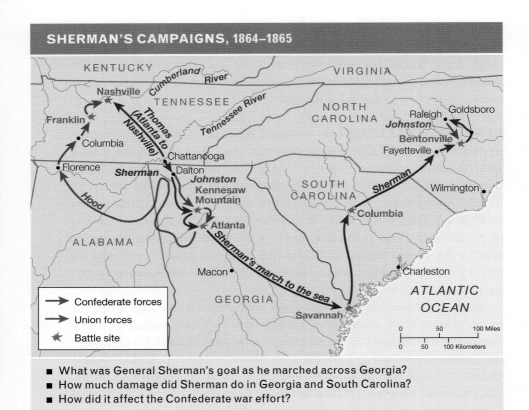

SHERMAN'S CAMPAIGNS, 1864–1865

KENTUCKY
Cumberland River
VIRGINIA
Nashville
TENNESSEE
Tennessee River
NORTH CAROLINA
Raleigh
Goldsboro
Franklin
Thomas (Atlanta to Nashville)
Johnston
Columbia
Bentonville
Florence
Sherman
Chattanooga
Fayetteville
Dalton
Johnston
Kennesaw Mountain
SOUTH CAROLINA
Sherman
Wilmington
Hood
Atlanta
Columbia
ALABAMA
Sherman's march to the sea
Macon
Charleston
GEORGIA
ATLANTIC OCEAN
Savannah

→ Confederate forces
→ Union forces
✳ Battle site

0   50   100 Miles
0   50   100 Kilometers

■ What was General Sherman's goal as he marched across Georgia?
■ How much damage did Sherman do in Georgia and South Carolina?
■ How did it affect the Confederate war effort?

launched a hopeless frontal assault against well-fortified Union troops. In a few hours, Hood lost six generals and saw 6,252 of his men killed or wounded, a casualty figure higher than "Pickett's Charge" at Gettysburg. A Confederate captain wrote that the "wails and cries of the widows and orphans made at Franklin, Tennessee, will heat up the fires of the bottomless pit to burn the soul of General J. B. Hood for murdering their husbands and fathers." Two weeks later, in the Battle of Nashville, the Federals scattered what was left of Hood's bloodied army.

Meanwhile, Sherman's Union army raced southward across Georgia, living off the land while destroying plantations, barns, crops, warehouses, bridges, and rail lines. An Ohio sergeant said, "Every house, barn, fence, and cotton gin gets an application of the torch. That prospect is revolting, but war is an uncivil game, and can't be civilized."

Sherman's March through Georgia became infamous among Southerners as a supposed example of Union tyranny. After the war, however, a

Confederate officer acknowledged that the campaign was well-conceived and well-managed. "I don't think there was ever an army in the world that would have behaved better, in a similar expedition, in an enemy country. Our army certainly wouldn't have."

On December 24, 1864, Sherman sent a whimsical telegram to President Lincoln offering him the coastal city of Savannah as a Christmas present. By the time Union troops arrived in Savannah, they had freed more than 40,000 slaves, burned scores of plantations, and destroyed the railroads. "God bless you, Yanks!" shouted a freed slave. "Come at last! God knows how long I been waitin'."

SOUTH CAROLINA   On February 1, 1865, Sherman's army headed north across the Savannah River into South Carolina, the "hell-hole of secession" in the eyes of Union troops. Sherman reported that his "whole army is burning with an insatiable desire to wreak vengeance upon South Carolina. I almost tremble at her fate, but feel she deserves all that seems in store for her."

South Carolina paid a high price for having led the southern states out of the Union. Sherman's men burned more than a dozen towns, including Barnwell, which they called "Burnwell." On February 17, 1865, they captured the state capital of Columbia. Soon thereafter, Charleston surrendered after Confederate soldiers torched to buildings containing material that would be valuable to the Yankees.

It was no accident that Sherman ordered two all-black regiments to lead the Union advance into the city that launched secession and war. On April 14, the Union general gave Major Robert Anderson the honor of raising the U.S. flag once again over Fort Sumter.

A LOSING CAUSE   During late 1864 and early 1865, the Confederacy found itself besieged on all sides. Defeat was in the air. Some Rebel leaders, including Secretary of War John C. Breckinridge, wanted to negotiate a peace settlement. Breckinridge, who had been vice president under James Buchanan and had run for president in 1860, urged Robert E. Lee to pursue an honorable end to the war. "This has been a magnificent epic," he said. "In God's name, let it not terminate in a farce."

By December 1864, Grant had tightened the vice around Richmond, cutting off rail service "until the rebellion is crushed or strangled." His ruthless strategy slowly proved its worth.

Jefferson Davis stubbornly rejected any talk of surrender, however. If his armies should be defeated, he wanted soldiers to scatter and fight an unending guerrilla war. "The war came and now it must go on," he stubbornly insisted, "till the last man of this generation falls in his tracks, and his children seize his musket and fight our battle."

Davis, Lee, and others finally became so desperate that they did the unthinkable: On March 13, 1865, Davis signed a bill calling for the immediate recruitment of slaves into the army—with the permission of their owners. Most Confederates were not happy about this desperate step. Before African Americans could be enlisted and trained, however, the war came to an end.

A SECOND TERM While Confederate forces made their last stands, Abraham Lincoln prepared for his second term as president. The weary commander in chief had weathered constant criticism during his first term, but he now garnered deserved praise. The *Chicago Tribune* observed that Lincoln "has slowly and steadily risen in the respect, confidence, and admiration of the people."

On March 4, 1865, amid rumors of a Confederate attempt to abduct or assassinate the president, some 30,000 people defied frigid weather to attend his second inauguration. Half of them were people of color. Lincoln, dressed in a black suit and stovepipe hat, delivered his address on the East Portico of the Capitol. Not 100 feet away, looking down from the Capitol porch, twenty-six-year-old John Wilkes Booth, who five weeks later would kill the president in a desperate attempt to do something "heroic" for his beloved South.

Lincoln's second inaugural address was more sermon than speech. Slavery, he said, had "somehow" caused the war, and everyone bore some guilt for the national shame of racial injustice and the awful war to end it. Both sides had known that war should be avoided at all costs, but "one of them would *make* war rather than let the nation survive; and the other would *accept* war rather than let it perish."

Lincoln longed for peace. "Fondly do we hope—fervently do we pray—that this mighty scourge of war may speedily pass away." He noted the paradoxical irony of both Unionists and Confederates reading the same Bible, praying to the same God, and appealing for divine support in their fight. Now the president urged the Union forces "to finish the work we are in," bolstered with "firmness in the right insofar as God gives us to see the right."

As Lincoln looked ahead to a "just and lasting peace," he stressed that vengeance must be avoided at all costs. Reconciliation must be pursued "with malice toward none; with charity for all." Those eight words captured his hopes for a restored Union. Redemption and reunion were his goals, not reprisals.

APPOMATTOX During the spring of 1865, General Grant's army kept pounding the Rebels defending Petersburg, Virginia. Robert E. Lee had no way to replace the men he was losing, and his dwindling army couldn't kill enough Yankees to make Grant quit. On April 2, 1865, after General Philip Sheridan's horse soldiers cut off the last railroad serving the Confederate army in Petersburg, a desperate Lee made a desperate decision: the badly outnumbered Confederates abandoned Petersburg and headed west, with the Union army in hot pursuit. At the same time, the Confederate government fled Richmond, but not before burning anything of value.

The Confederacy was in chaos. "Women were weeping, children crying," noted a reporter in Richmond. "Men stood speechless, haggard, woebegone." Five days later, on April 7, Grant sent a note urging the trapped Lee to surrender. With the remnants of his army virtually surrounded and no food, Lee recognized that "there is nothing left for me to do but go and see General Grant, and I would rather die a thousand deaths."

On April 9 (Palm Sunday), four years to the day since the Confederate attack on Fort Sumter, the tall, dignified Lee, stiff and formal in his impeccable dress uniform, ceremonial sword, and shiny boots, met the short, mud-spattered Grant in a small brick house in the village of **Appomattox Court House**. Grant apologized for his "rough" appearance, explaining that he had left behind his dress uniform. Lee, in turn, stressed that he was in a new uniform because it was the only one he had left.

After some awkward exchanges about their service in the Mexican-American War, Lee asked Grant about the terms of surrender. In keeping with Lincoln's desire for a gracious peace with "malice toward none," Grant let the Confederates keep their pistols, horses, and mules, and he ensured that none of them would be tried for treason. Lee replied that "this would have a most happy effect" upon his men and accepted the terms as "more than he expected." He then confessed that his men were starving, and Grant ordered that they be provided food.

After drafting and signing the surrender documents, Lee mounted his horse. Grant and his men saluted him, raising their hats, and Lee responded in kind before returning to his defeated army. Grant ordered that there be no cheering or gloating. "The war is over," he said, adding that "the rebels are our countrymen again, and the best sign of rejoicing after the victory will be to abstain from all demonstrations in the field."

The next day, as the gaunt Confederates formed ranks for the last time, Joshua Chamberlain, the Union general in charge of the surrender ceremony, told his men to salute the Rebel soldiers as they paraded past to give up their muskets. His Confederate counterpart signaled his men to do likewise. Chamberlain remembered that there was not a sound, simply an "awed stillness . . . as if it were the passing of the dead." The remaining Confederate forces in Texas and North Carolina surrendered in May. Jefferson Davis, who had fled Richmond ahead of the advancing Federal troops, was captured in Georgia on May 10. He was eventually imprisoned in Virginia for two years.

The brutal war was at last over. Upon learning of the Union victory, John Wilkes Booth wrote in his diary that "something *decisive* and great must be done" to avenge the Confederate defeat. He began plotting to kill President Lincoln and members of his cabinet.

Two days after Lee surrendered, Lincoln gave a speech on the White House lawn in which he said he looked forward to "reconstructing" the Confederate states. He also hoped that literate freed blacks and those who had served in the Union military would be able to vote. Booth, who was in the audience, noted that Lincoln's pledge "meant nigger citizenship. Now, by God, I'll put him through [kill him]. That is the last speech he will ever make."

A Transformational War

The Civil War was the most traumatic event in American history. "We have shared the incommunicable experience of war," reflected Oliver Wendell Holmes Jr., a twice-wounded Union officer who would become chief justice of the Supreme Court. "We have felt, we still feel, the passion of life to its top . . . In our youth, our hearts were touched by fire."

In Virginia, elderly Edmund Ruffin, the arch secessionist who had been given the honor of firing the first shots at Fort Sumter, was so devastated by the Confederate surrender that he put his musket barrel in his mouth and blew off the top of his head.

The nation had been transformed. A *New York Times* editorial reflected that the war had left "nothing as it found it . . . It leaves us a different people in everything." The war destroyed the South's economy, many of its railroads and factories, much of its livestock, and several of its cities. In 1860, the northern and southern economies had been essentially equal in size. By 1865, the southern economy's productivity had been halved.

THE UNION PRESERVED The war ended the Confederacy and preserved the Union; shifted the political balance of power in Congress, the U.S. Supreme Court, and the presidency from South to North; strengthened the Republican party; and boosted the northern economy's industrial development, commercial agriculture, and western settlement. The Homestead Act (1862) made more than a billion acres in the West available to the landless. The power and scope of the federal government were expanded at the expense of states' rights. In 1860, the annual federal budget was $63 million; by 1865, it was more than $1 billion. In winning the war, the federal government had become the nation's largest employer.

By the end of the war, the Union was spending $2.5 million per day on the military effort, and whole new industries had been established to meet its needs for weapons, uniforms, food, equipment, and supplies. The massive amounts of preserved food required by the Union armies, for example, helped create the canning industry and transformed Chicago into the meatpacking capital of the world.

Federal contracts also provided money needed to accelerate the growth of new industries, such as the production of iron, steel, and petroleum, thus laying the groundwork for a postwar economic boom. Ohio senator John Sherman, in a letter to his brother, General William T. Sherman, said the war had dramatically expanded the vision "of leading capitalists" who now talked of earning "millions as confidently as formerly of thousands."

The war also influenced world events. Southern cotton had fed national prosperity during the first half of the nineteenth century, but the onset of war in 1861 changed that. In 1860, the South had sent nearly 4 million bales of cotton to Europe. By 1862, hardly any arrived in Europe. By cutting off the supply of southern cotton to Great Britain and Europe, the war fueled global colonialism, as European nations looked for other sources of cotton in India, Egypt, and West Africa.

THE FIRST "MODERN" WAR   In many respects, the Civil War was the first modern war. Its scope and scale were unprecedented, as it was fought across the entire continent. For the first time, armies used railroads and steamboats to move around.

One of every twelve men served in the war, and few families were unaffected. More than 750,000 soldiers and sailors (37,000 of whom were blacks fighting for the Union) died, 50 percent more than would die in the Second World War. The comparable number of deaths relative to today's population would be almost 7.5 million. Of the surviving combatants, 50,000 returned home with one or more limbs amputated. Disease, however, was the greatest threat to soldiers, killing twice as many as were lost in battle. Some 50,000 civilians died as well, and virtually every community had uncounted widows and orphans.

The Civil War also accelerated the American love affair with guns. Hundreds of thousands of men who had never owned or used a pistol or rifle now believed that the "right to own and use weapons" was an essential constitutional principle.

Unlike previous conflicts, much of the fighting in the Civil War was distant and impersonal, in part because of improvements in the effectiveness of muskets, rifles, and cannons. Men were killed at long distance, without knowing who had fired the shots that felled them. Among the array of new weapons and instruments were cannons with "rifled," or grooved, barrels for greater accuracy; repeating rifles; ironclad ships; railroad artillery; the first military telegraph; observation balloons; and wire entanglements. Civilians could also follow the war by reading the newspapers that sent reporters to the front lines, or by visiting exhibitions of photographs taken at the battlefields and camps.

THIRTEENTH AMENDMENT The most important result of the war was the liberation of almost 4 million slaves. The Emancipation Proclamation had technically freed only those slaves in areas still controlled by the Confederacy. As the war entered its final months, however, freedom for all slaves emerged as a legal reality, as President Lincoln moved from viewing emancipation as a military weapon to seeing it as the mainspring of the conflict itself.

Three major steps occurred in January 1865. Missouri and then Tennessee abolished slavery, and, at Lincoln's insistence, the U.S. House of Representatives passed an amendment to the Constitution that banned slavery everywhere. Upon ratification by three-fourths of the reunited states, the **Thirteenth Amendment** became law eight months after the war ended, on December 18, 1865. It removed any lingering doubts about the legality of emancipation. By then, slavery remained only in the border states of Kentucky and Delaware.

THE DEBATE CONTINUES Historians continue to debate the reasons for the Union victory. Some have focused on the weaknesses of the Confederacy: its lack of industry and railroads, the tensions between the states and the central government in Richmond, poor political leadership, faulty coordination and communication, the expense of preventing slave rebellions and runaways, and the advantages in population and resources enjoyed by the North. Still others have highlighted the erosion of Confederate morale in the face of terrible food shortages and unimaginable human losses.

The debate about why the North won and the South lost will probably never end, but Robert E. Lee's explanation remains accurate: "After four years of arduous service marked by unsurpassed courage and fortitude, the Army of Northern Virginia has been compelled to yield to overwhelming numbers and resources." General George Pickett had a similar view. When asked after the Battle of Gettysburg why the Confederates lost, he replied: "I've always thought the Yankees had something to do with it."

Whatever the reasons, the North's victory resolved a key issue: no state could divorce itself from the Union. The Union, as Lincoln had always maintained, was indissoluble. At the same time, the war led to the Constitution being permanently amended to eliminate slavery. The terrible war thus served to clarify the meaning of the ideals ("All men are created equal") on which the United States had been established. The largest slaveholding nation in the world had at last chosen liberty—for all.

In his first message to Congress in December 1861, Lincoln had recognized early on what was at stake: "The struggle of today is not altogether for today; it is for a vast future also." So it was. The "fiery trial" of a war both "fundamental and astounding" produced, as Lincoln said, not just a preserved Union but "a new birth of freedom."

CHAPTER REVIEW

SUMMARY

- **Civil War Strategies** The Confederacy had a geographic advantage of fighting a defensive war on its own territory. The Union, however, had a larger population and greater industrial capability, particularly in the production of weapons, ships, and railroad equipment. After suffering a defeat at the First Battle of Bull Run, the Union adopted the "*Anaconda Plan*," imposing a naval blockade on southern ports and slowly crushing resistance on all fronts. As Union armies penetrated the Confederacy, runaway slaves, called *contrabands*, fled to their camps. *The Militia Act (1862)* allowed African Americans to serve as laborers and soldiers.

- **Emancipation Proclamation** Initially, President Lincoln declared that the war's aim was to restore the Union and that slavery would be maintained where it existed. Gradually, however, he came to see that winning the war required ending slavery. He justified the *Emancipation Proclamation (1862)* as a military necessity because it would deprive the South of its captive labor force. After the *Battle of Antietam* in September 1862, he announced plans to free the slaves living in areas under Confederate control on January 1, 1863.

- **Wartime Home Fronts** The federal government proved much more capable with finances than did the Confederacy. Through tariffs, income taxes, bond sales, and banking reforms, the Union was better able to absorb the war's soaring costs. In the absence of the southern delegation in Congress, Republicans approved a higher tariff, a transcontinental railroad, and a *Homestead Act (1862)*, all of which accelerated settlement of the West and the growth of a national economy.

- **The Winning Union Strategy** Victories at the *Battles of Vicksburg and Gettysburg* in July 1863 turned the war in the Union's favor. With the capture of Vicksburg, the last Confederate-controlled city along the Mississippi River, Union forces cut the Confederacy in two, depriving armies in the East of supplies and manpower. In 1864, Lincoln placed General Ulysses S. Grant in charge of the Union's war efforts. For the next year, Grant's forces constantly attacked Robert E. Lee's forces in Virginia while, farther south, General William T. Sherman's "*March to the Sea*" destroyed plantations, railroads, and morale in Georgia and South Carolina. Their successes helped propel Lincoln to victory in the *election of 1864*. After that, southern resistance wilted. Lee surrendered to Grant at *Appomattox Court House* in April 1865.

- **The Significance of the Civil War** The Civil War involved the largest number of casualties of any American war, and the Union's victory changed the course of the nation's development. Most important, the war ended slavery, embodied in the adoption of the *Thirteenth Amendment* to the U.S. Constitution in late 1865. Not only did the power of the federal government increase, but the center of political and economic power shifted away from the South and the planter class. The

Republican-controlled Congress enacted legislation during the war to raise tariffs, fund the first transcontinental railroad, and introduce many financial reforms that would drive the nation's economic development for the rest of the century.

CHRONOLOGY

April 1861	Virginia, North Carolina, Tennessee, and Arkansas join Confederacy; West Virginia splits from Virginia to stay with Union
July 1861	First Battle of Bull Run (Manassas)
April–September 1862	Battles of Shiloh, Second Bull Run, and Antietam
September 1862	Lincoln issues Emancipation Proclamation
May–July 1863	New York City draft riots; siege of Vicksburg; Battle of Gettysburg
March 1864	Lincoln places General Ulysses S. Grant in charge of Union military operations
September 1864	General William T. Sherman seizes and burns Atlanta
November 1864	Lincoln is reelected
April 9, 1865	General Robert E. Lee surrenders at Appomattox Court House
December 1865	Thirteenth Amendment is ratified

KEY TERMS

Anaconda Plan p. 584

contrabands p. 599

Battle of Antietam (1862) p. 600

Emancipation Proclamation (1862) p. 602

Militia Act (1862) p. 606

Homestead Act (1862) p. 610

Morrill Land Grant College Act (1862) p. 610

Copperhead Democrats p. 612

Battle of Vicksburg (1863) p. 615

Battle of Gettysburg (1863) p. 616

election of 1864 p. 627

Sherman's March to the Sea p. 627

Appomattox Court House p. 631

Thirteenth Amendment (1865) p. 634

 INQUIZITIVE

Go to InQuizitive to see what you've learned—and learn what you've missed—with personalized feedback along the way.

16 The Era of Reconstruction

1865–1877

***A Visit from the Old Mistress* (1876)** This powerful painting by Winslow Homer depicts a plantation mistress visiting her former slaves in the postwar South. Although their living conditions are humble, these freedwomen stand firmly and eye-to-eye with the woman who had kept them in bondage.

I n the spring of 1865, the terrible conflict was finally over. The war to restore the Union transformed American life. The United States was a "new nation," said an Illinois congressman, because it was now "wholly free." At a cost of some 750,000 lives and the destruction of the southern economy, the Union had won the war, and almost 4 million enslaved Americans had seized their freedom. But the end of slavery did not bring the end of racism, nor did it bring equality to people of color.

The defeated Confederates had seen their world turned upside down. The abolition of slavery, the disruptions to the southern economy, and the horrifying human losses had destroyed the plantation system and upended racial relations in the South. "Change, change, indelibly stamped upon everything I meet, even upon the faces of the people!" marveled Alexander Stephens, vice president of the Confederacy. His native region now had to come to terms with a new era and a new order as the U.S. government set about "reconstructing" the South and policing defiant ex-Confederates. Diarist Mary Chesnut expressed the anger and frustration felt by the southern white elite when she wished that "they were *all* dead—all Yankees!"

Freed slaves felt just the opposite. Yankees were their saviors. No longer would enslaved workers be sold and separated from their families or prevented from learning to read and write or attending church. "I felt like a bird out of a cage," said former slave Houston Holloway of Georgia, who had been sold to three different owners during his first twenty years. "Amen. Amen. Amen. I could hardly ask to feel any better than I did that day."

Few owners, however, willingly freed their slaves until forced to by the arrival of Union soldiers. A North Carolina planter pledged that he and other whites "will never get along with the free negroes" because they were an "inferior race."

focus questions

1. What major challenges did the federal government face in reconstructing the South after the Civil War?

2. How and why did Reconstruction policies change over time?

3. In what ways did white and black Southerners react to Reconstruction?

4. What were the political and economic factors that helped end Reconstruction in 1877?

5. What was the significance of Reconstruction on the nation's future?

Similarly, a Mississippi planter predicted that "these niggers will all be slaves again in twelve months."

In South Carolina, violence against freedpeople was widespread. Union soldiers found "the bodies of murdered Negroes" strewn in the forest. When a South Carolina white man caught an enslaved mother and her children running toward freedom, he "drew his bowie-knife and cut her throat; also the throat of her boy, nine years old; also the throat of her girl, seven years of age; threw their bodies into the river, and the live baby after them."

Such brutal incidents illuminate the extraordinary challenges the nation faced in "reconstructing" a ravaged and resentful South while helping to transform ex-slaves into free workers and equal citizens. It would not be easy. The Rebels had been conquered, but they were far from being loyal Unionists.

Although the Reconstruction era lasted only twelve years, it was one of the most challenging and significant periods in U.S. history. At the center of the debate over how best to restore the Union were questions of continuing significance: Who is deserving of citizenship, and what does it entail? What rights should all Americans enjoy? What role should the federal government play in ensuring freedom and equality? Those questions are still shaping American life nearly 150 years later.

THE WAR'S AFTERMATH IN THE SOUTH

In the spring of 1865, Southerners were emotionally exhausted; fully a fifth of southern white males had died in the war, and many others had been maimed for life. In 1866, Mississippi spent 20 percent of the state's budget on artificial limbs for Confederate veterans.

Property values had collapsed. In the year after the war ended, eighty-one plantations in Mississippi were sold for less than a tenth of what they had been worth in 1860. Confederate money was worthless; personal savings had vanished; tens of thousands of horses and mules had been killed in the fighting; and countless farm buildings and agricultural equipment had been destroyed.

Many of the largest southern cities—Richmond, Atlanta, Columbia—were devastated. Most railroads and many bridges were damaged or destroyed, and Southerners, white and black, were homeless and hungry. Along the path that General William Tecumseh Sherman's Union army had blazed across Georgia and the Carolinas, one observer reported in 1866, the countryside "looked for many miles like a broad black streak of ruin and desolation." Burned-out Columbia, South Carolina, said another witness, was "a wilderness of ruins"; Charleston, the birthplace of secession, had become a place of "vacant

Richmond after the Civil War Before evacuating Richmond, Virginia, the capital of the Confederacy, Rebels set fire to warehouses and factories to prevent them from falling into Union hands. Pictured here is one of Richmond's burned districts in April 1865. Women in mourning attire walk among the shambles.

houses, of widowed women, of rotting wharves, of deserted warehouses, of weed-wild gardens, of miles of grass-grown streets, of acres of pitiful and voiceless barrenness."

Between 1860 and 1870, northern wealth grew by 50 percent while southern wealth dropped 60 percent. Emancipation wiped out $4 billion invested in slavery, which had enabled the explosive growth of the cotton culture. Not until 1879 would the cotton crop again equal the record harvest of 1860. Tobacco production did not regain its prewar level until 1880, the sugar crop of Louisiana did not recover until 1893, and the rice economy along the coasts of South Carolina and Georgia never regained its prewar levels of production or profit.

In 1860, just before the Civil War, the South had generated 30 percent of the nation's wealth; in 1870, it produced but 12 percent. Amanda Worthington, a planter's wife from Mississippi, assessed the damage in the fall of 1865: "None of us can realize that we are no longer wealthy—yet thanks to the Yankees, the cause of all unhappiness, such is the case."

Resentment boiled over. Union soldiers were cursed and spat upon. A Virginia woman expressed a spirited defiance common among her Confederate friends: "Every day, every hour, that I live increases my hatred and detestation, and loathing of that race. They [Yankees] disgrace our common humanity. As a people I consider them vastly inferior to the better classes of our slaves." Fervent southern nationalists implanted in their children a similar hatred of Yankees and a defiance of northern rule.

Rebuilding the former Confederate states would not be easy, and the issues related to Reconstruction were complicated and controversial. For example, the process of forming new state governments required first determining the official status of the states that had seceded: Were they now conquered territories? If so, then the Constitution assigned Congress authority to re-create their state governments. But what if, as Abraham Lincoln argued, the Confederate states had never officially left the Union because the act of secession was itself illegal? In that circumstance, the president would be responsible for re-forming state governments.

Whichever branch of government—Congress or the presidency—directed the reconstruction of the South, it would have to address the most difficult issue: What would be the political, social, and economic status of the freedpeople? Were they citizens? If not, what was their status?

What former slaves most wanted was to become self-reliant, to be compensated for their labor, to reunite with their family members, to gain education for their children, to enjoy full participation in political life, and to create their own community organizations and social life. Most southern whites were determined to prevent that from happening.

DEBATES OVER POLITICAL RECONSTRUCTION

Reconstruction of the former Confederate states actually began during the war and went through several phases, the first of which was called Presidential Reconstruction. In 1862, President Lincoln had named army generals to serve as temporary military governors for conquered Confederate areas. By the end of 1863, he had formulated a plan to reestablish governments in states liberated from Confederate rule.

LINCOLN'S PLAN In late 1863, President Lincoln issued a Proclamation of Amnesty and Reconstruction, under which former Confederate states could re-create a Union government once a number equal to 10 percent of those who had voted in 1860 swore allegiance to the Constitution. They also received a presidential pardon acquitting them of treason. Certain groups, however, were denied pardons: Confederate government officials; senior officers of the Confederate army and navy; judges, congressmen, and military officers of the United States who had left their posts to join the rebellion; and those who had abused captured African American soldiers.

CONGRESSIONAL PLANS A few conservative and most moderate Republicans supported President Lincoln's "10 percent" program that immediately restored pro-Union southern governments. *Radical Republicans*, however, argued that Congress, not the president, should supervise Reconstruction.

The **Radical Republicans** favored a drastic transformation of southern society that would grant ex-slaves full citizenship. Many Radicals believed that all people, regardless of race, were equal in God's eyes. They wanted no compromise with the "sin" of racism.

They also hoped to replace the white, Democratic planter elite with a new generation of small farmers. "The middling classes who own the soil, and work it with their own hands," explained Radical leader Thaddeus Stevens, "are the main support of every free government."

THE WADE-DAVIS BILL In 1864, with war still raging, the Radicals tried to take charge of Reconstruction by passing the Wade-Davis Bill, named for two leading Republicans. In contrast to Lincoln's 10 percent Reconstruction plan, the Wade-Davis Bill required that a *majority* of white male citizens declare their allegiance to the Union before a Confederate state could be readmitted.

The bill never became law, however, because Lincoln vetoed it. In retaliation, Radicals issued the Wade-Davis Manifesto, which accused Lincoln of exceeding his constitutional authority. Unfazed by the criticism, Lincoln continued his efforts to restore the Confederate states to the Union. He also rushed assistance to the freedpeople in the South.

THE FREEDMEN'S BUREAU In early 1865, Congress approved the Thirteenth Amendment to the Constitution, officially abolishing slavery in the United States. It became law in December. Yet what did freedom mean for the former slaves, most of whom had no land, no home, no food, no jobs, and no education? The debate over what freedom should entail became the central issue of Reconstruction. "Liberty has been won," Senator Charles Sumner noted. "The battle for Equality is still pending."

To address the complex issues raised by emancipation, Congress on March 3, 1865, created the **Freedmen's Bureau** to assist "freedmen and their wives and children." It was the first federal effort to provide help directly to people rather than to states. And its task was daunting. When General William T. Sherman learned that his friend, General Oliver O. Howard, had been appointed to lead the Freedmen's Bureau, he warned: "It is not . . . in your power to fulfill one-tenth of the expectations of those who framed the Bureau."

Undeterred by such realities, in May 1865, Howard declared that freed slaves "must be free to choose their own employers, and be paid for their labor." He sent agents to the South to negotiate labor contracts between freed people and white landowners, many of whom resisted. The Bureau provided former slaves with medical care and food and clothing, and helped set up schools. Northern missionary societies also established schools for the former slaves. As a Mississippi freedman explained, education "was the next best thing to liberty."

By 1870, the Freedmen's Bureau was supervising nearly 4,000 new schools serving almost 250,000 students. The Freedmen's Bureau also helped former slaves reestablish connections with their family members and legalize marriages that had been banned prior to the war.

SELF-SUSTAINING FREEDMEN In July 1865, hundreds of freed slaves gathered on St. Helena Island off the South Carolina coast. There, Virginia-born freeman Martin Delaney, the highest-ranking officer in the U.S. Colored Troops, addressed them. Before the Civil War, he had been a prominent abolitionist in the North. Now, Major Delaney assured the gathering that slavery had indeed been "absolutely abolished." But abolition, he stressed, was less the result of Abraham Lincoln's leadership than it was the outcome of former slaves and free blacks like him undermining the Confederacy. Slavery was dead, and freedom was now in their hands. "Yes, yes, yes," his listeners shouted.

Delaney then noted that many of the white planters in the area claimed that former slaves were lazy and "have not the intelligence to get on for yourselves without being guided and driven to the work by [white] overseers." Delaney dismissed such assumptions as lies intended to restore a system of forced labor for blacks. He then told the freed slaves that their best hope was to become self-sustaining farmers: "Get a community and get all the lands you can—if you cannot get any singly." He added that if they could not become economically self-reliant, they would find themselves slaves again.

Several white planters attended Delaney's talk, and an army officer at the scene reported that they "listened with horror depicted in their faces." The planters predicted that such speeches would incite "open rebellion" among southern blacks.

DEATH OF A PRESIDENT The possibility of a lenient federal Reconstruction of the Confederacy would die with Abraham Lincoln. The president who had yearned for a peace "with malice toward none, with charity for all" offered his last view of Reconstruction in the final speech of his life.

On April 11, 1865, Lincoln rejected calls for a vengeful peace. He wanted "no persecution, no bloody work," no hangings of Confederate leaders, and no extreme efforts to restructure southern social and economic life. Three days later, on April 14, he and his wife Mary Todd attended a play at Ford's Theatre in Washington, D.C.

With his trusted bodyguard called away to Richmond, Lincoln was defenseless as twenty-six-year-old John Wilkes Booth, an actor and rabid Confederate, slipped into the unguarded presidential box and shot the president in the head. As Lincoln slumped forward, Booth pulled out a knife, stabbed the president's military aide, and jumped from the box to the stage, breaking his leg in the process. He then mounted a waiting horse and fled the city. Lincoln died nine hours later.

The nation was suddenly leaderless. Vice President Andrew Johnson was sworn in as the new president, but for a time chaos reigned. Secretary of War Edwin Stanton, not knowing if the assassination was a prelude to a Confederate invasion, summoned Ulysses S. Grant to defend the government in Washington, D.C. Eleven days later, Union troops found Booth hiding in a northern Virginia tobacco barn, where he was shot and killed. Booth whispered as he lay dying, "Tell my mother I died for my country."

The nation extracted a full measure of vengeance from the conspirators. Three of Booth's collaborators were convicted by a military court and hanged, as was Mary Surratt, who owned the Washington boardinghouse where the assassination had been planned.

The outpouring of grief after Lincoln's death was overwhelming. Planned victory celebrations were canceled. Even a Richmond, Virginia, newspaper called the assassination the "heaviest blow which has fallen on the people of the South."

Andrew Johnson A pro-Union Democrat from Tennessee, Johnson became president after Abraham Lincoln was assassinated during his vice presidency.

Lincoln's body lay in state for several days in Washington, D.C., before being transported 1,600 miles by train for burial in Springfield, Illinois. In Philadelphia, 300,000 mourners paid their last respects; in New York City, 500,000 people viewed the president's body. On May 4, Lincoln was laid to rest.

JOHNSON'S PLAN   President Lincoln's shocking death propelled Andrew Johnson of Tennessee, a pro-Union Democrat, into the White House. Johnson had been added to Lincoln's National Union ticket in 1864 solely to help the president win reelection. Humorless, insecure, combative, and self-righteous, Johnson hated both the white southern elite and the idea of racial equality. He also had a weakness for liquor. At the inaugural ceremonies in 1865, he had delivered his vice-presidential address in a state of slurring drunkenness.

Like Lincoln, Johnson was a self-made man. Born in 1808 in a log cabin near Raleigh, North Carolina, he lost his father when he was three and never attended school. His illiterate mother apprenticed him to a tailor to learn a trade. He ran away from home at thirteen and eventually landed in Greeneville, in the mountains of East Tennessee, where he became a tailor. He taught himself to read, and his sixteen-year-old wife showed him how to write and do basic arithmetic.

Over time, Johnson prospered and acquired five slaves, which he sold in 1863. A natural leader, he eventually served as mayor, state legislator, governor, congressional representative, and U.S. senator. A friend described the trajectory of Johnson's life as "one intense, unceasing, desperate upward struggle" during which he identified with poor farmers and came to hate the "pampered, bloated, corrupted aristocracy" of wealthy planters.

During the Civil War, Johnson called himself a Jacksonian Democrat "in the strictest meaning of the term. I am for putting down the [Confederate] rebellion, because it is a war [of wealthy plantation owners] against democracy." Yet Johnson also shared the racist attitudes of most southern whites. "Damn the negroes," he exclaimed during the war. "I am fighting those traitorous aristocrats, their masters." Impoverished whites, Johnson maintained, were most hurt by the slave system, and he was an unapologetic white supremacist. "White men alone must manage the South," he declared.

As a states' rights Democrat, Johnson also insisted that the federal government be as small and inactive as possible. He strongly opposed Republican economic policies designed to spur industrial development.

In May 1865, Johnson issued a new Proclamation of Amnesty that excluded not only those ex-Confederates whom Lincoln had barred from a presidential pardon but also anyone with property worth more than $20,000. Johnson was determined to keep the wealthiest Southerners from regaining political power.

Surprisingly, however, by 1866 he had pardoned some 7,000 former Confederates, and he eventually pardoned most of the white "aristocrats" he claimed to despise. What brought about this change of heart? Johnson had decided that he could buy the political support of prominent Southerners by pardoning them, improving his chances of reelection.

Johnson's Restoration Plan mandated the appointment of a Unionist as provisional governor in each southern state. Each governor was given the authority to call a convention of men elected by "loyal" (not Confederate) voters. Johnson's plan required that each state convention ratify the Thirteenth Amendment. He also encouraged giving a few blacks voting rights, especially those who had some education or had served in the military, so as to "disarm" the "Radicals who are wild upon" giving *all* African Americans the right to vote. Except for Mississippi, each former Confederate state held a convention that met Johnson's requirements but ignored his suggestion about voting rights for blacks.

FREEDMEN'S CONVENTIONS Neither Abraham Lincoln nor Andrew Johnson saw fit to ask freedpeople in the South what they most needed. So the former slaves took matters into their own hands. They met and marched, demanding not just freedom but citizenship and full civil rights, land of their own, and voting rights. Especially in and around large cities such as New Orleans, Mobile, Norfolk, Wilmington, Nashville, Memphis, and Charleston, former slaves organized regular meetings, chose leaders, protested mistreatment, learned the workings of the federal bureaucracy, and sought economic opportunities.

During the summer and fall of 1865, liberated slaves and freepeople from the North ("missionaries") and South organized freedmen's conventions (sometimes called Equal Rights Associations). Often led by ministers, they met in state capitals "to impress upon the white men," as the Reverend James D. Lynch told the Tennessee freedmen's convention, "that we are part and parcel of the American republic." As such, they were eager to counter the whites-only state conventions organized under Johnson's Reconstruction plan.

The North Carolina freedmen's convention elected as its president James Walker Hood, a free black from Connecticut. In his acceptance speech, he emphasized their goals: "We and the white people have to live here together. Some people talk of emigration for the black race, some of expatriation, and some of colonization. I regard this as all nonsense. We have been living together for a hundred years and more, and we have got to live together still; and the best way is to harmonize our feelings as much as possible, and to treat all men respectfully." Hood then demanded three constitutional rights for

African Americans: the right to testify in courts, serve on juries, and "the right to carry [a] ballot to the ballot box."

In sum, the freedmen's conventions demanded that their voices be heard in Washington and southern state capitals. As the Virginia freedmen's convention asserted, "Any attempt to reconstruct the states . . . without giving to American citizens of African descent all the rights and immunities accorded to white citizens . . . is an act of gross injustice."

THE RADICALS REBEL President Johnson's initial assault on the southern planter elite pleased Radical Republicans, but not for long. The most extreme Radicals, led by Thaddeus Stevens of Pennsylvania and Charles Sumner of Massachusetts, wanted Reconstruction to provide social and political equality for blacks. They resented Johnson's efforts to bring the South back into the Union as quickly as possible.

Stevens argued that the Civil War had been fought to produce a "*radical revolution*" in southern life: The "whole fabric of southern society must be changed" to "revolutionize southern institutions, habits, and manners." The Confederate states were, in his view, "conquered provinces" to be readmitted to the Union by the U.S. Congress, not the president. Johnson, however, balked at such an expansion of federal authority. He was committed to the states' rights to control their affairs.

Former Confederates agreed with Johnson. After the war, most white Southerners resented and resisted the North's efforts to reconstruct their homeland. They wanted to rebuild the South as it had been before the war, and they were determined to do so in their own way and under their own leadership. As a white woman lamented, "Think of all our sacrifices—of broken hearts, and desolated homes—or our *noble, glorious* dead—and say for what? *Reconstruction!* How the very word galls."

So when the U.S. Congress met in December 1865 for the first time since the end of the war, the new southern state governments looked remarkably like the former Confederate governments. Southern voters had refused to extend voting rights to the newly freed slaves. Instead, they had elected former Confederate leaders as their new U.S. senators and congressmen. Georgia, for example, had elected Alexander Stephens, former vice president of the Confederacy.

Across the South, four Confederate generals, eight colonels, six Confederate cabinet members, and several Confederate legislators were also elected. Outraged Republicans denied seats to all such "Rebel" officials and appointed a Joint Committee on Reconstruction to develop a new plan to bring the former Confederate states back into the Union.

The Joint Committee discovered that white violence against blacks in the South was widespread. A former slave in Shreveport, Louisiana, testified that whites still bullwhipped blacks as if they were slaves. He estimated that 2,000 freedpeople had been killed in Shreveport in 1865.

In May and July of 1866, white mobs murdered African Americans in Memphis and New Orleans. General Grant reported that Memphis was "a scene of murder, arson, rape & robbery in which the victims were all help-less and unresisting negroes, stamping lasting disgrace upon the [white] civil authorities that permitted them." Memphis authorities arrested no one respon-sible for the mayhem.

The massacres, Radical Republicans argued, resulted from Andrew Johnson's lenient policy toward white supremacists. Senator Charles Sumner cried, "Who can doubt that the President is the author of these tragedies?" The race riots helped spur the Republican-controlled Congress to pass the Fourteenth Amendment (1868), extending federal civil rights protections to African Americans.

BLACK CODES The violence aga-inst southern blacks was triggered in part by black protests over restrictive laws passed by the new all-white south-ern state legislatures. These "**black codes**," as a white Southerner explained, would ensure "the ex-slave was not a free man; he was a free Negro." A North-erner visiting the South observed that the new black codes would guarantee that "the blacks at large belong to the whites at large."

Black codes varied from state to state. In South Carolina, African Americans were required to remain on their former plantations, forced to labor from dawn to dusk. Mississippi declared that blacks could not hunt or fish, making them even more depen-dent on their white employers.

Some black codes recognized black marriages but prohibited interra-cial marriage. The Mississippi codes

"(?) Slavery Is Dead (?)" (1867)
Thomas Nast's cartoon argues that southern blacks were still being treated as slaves despite the passage of the Fourteenth Amendment. This detail illustrates a case in Raleigh, North Carolina: a black man was whipped for a crime despite federal orders specifically prohibiting such forms of punishment.

stipulated that "no white person could intermarry with a freedman, free negro, or mulatto." Violators faced life imprisonment.

The codes also prohibited African Americans from voting, serving on juries, or testifying against whites. They could own property, but they could not own farmland in Mississippi or city property in South Carolina. In Mississippi, every black male over the age of eighteen had to be apprenticed to a white, preferably a former slave owner. Any blacks not apprenticed or employed by January 1866 would be jailed as "vagrants." If they could not pay the vagrancy fine—and most of them could not—they were jailed and forced to work for whites as convict laborers in "chain gangs."

In part, states employed this "convict lease" system as a means of increasing government revenue and cutting the expenses of housing prisoners. At its worst, however, convict leasing was one of the most exploitive labor systems in history, as people convicted of crimes, mostly African Americans often falsely accused, were hired out by county and state governments to work for individuals and businesses—coal mines, lumber camps, brickyards, railroads, quarries, mills, and plantations. Convict leasing, in other words, was a thinly disguised form of neo-slavery.

The black codes infuriated Republicans. "We [Republicans] must see to it," Senator William Stewart of Nevada resolved, "that the man made free by the Constitution of the United States is a freeman indeed." And that is what they set out to do.

JOHNSON'S BATTLE WITH CONGRESS Early in 1866, the Radical Republicans openly challenged Andrew Johnson over Reconstruction policies. Johnson started the fight when he vetoed a bill renewing funding for the Freedmen's Bureau. The Republicans could not overturn the veto. Then, on February 22, 1866, Johnson criticized the Radical Republicans for promoting black civil rights. Moderate Republicans thereafter deserted the president and supported the Radicals. Johnson had become "an alien enemy of a foreign state," Thaddeus Stevens declared.

In mid-March 1866, the Radical-led Congress passed the pathbreaking Civil Rights Act, which declared that "all persons born in the United States," including the children of immigrants, but excluding Native Americans, were citizens entitled to "full and equal benefit of all laws." The legislation infuriated Johnson. Congress, he fumed, could not grant citizenship to blacks, who did not deserve it. Claiming that the proposed Civil Rights Act discriminated against the "white race," Johnson vetoed it, but this time, on April 6, 1866, Republicans overrode the veto.

It was the first time in history that Congress had overturned a presidential veto of a major bill. From that point on, President Johnson steadily lost both public and political support. A New Yorker noted in his diary that "the feud between Johnson and the 'Radicals' grows more and more deadly every day." General Ulysses S. Grant told his wife that Johnson had become "a national disgrace."

FOURTEENTH AMENDMENT

To remove all doubt about the legality of the new Civil Rights Act, Congress passed the **Fourteenth Amendment** to the U.S. Constitution in 1866 (it gained ratification in 1868). It guaranteed citizenship not just to freemen but also to immigrant children born in the United States. Taking direct aim at the black codes, it also prohibited any efforts to violate the civil rights of "citizens," black or white; to deprive any person "of life, liberty, or property, without due process of law"; or to "deny any person…the equal protection of the laws."

A Man Knows A Man A black soldier for the Union with an amputated leg clasps hands with a white amputee in this 1865 cartoon. The caption reads: "Give me your hand, comrade! We have each lost a leg for the good cause; but, thank God, we never lost heart."

With the Fourteenth Amendment, Congress gave the federal government responsibility for protecting (and enforcing) civil rights. Not a single Democrat in the House or Senate voted for it. All states in the former Confederacy were required to ratify the amendment before they could be readmitted to the Union and to Congress.

President Johnson urged the southern states to refuse to ratify the amendment. He predicted that the Democrats would win the congressional elections in November and then nix the new amendment. But Johnson was steadily losing support in the North. New York newspaper editor Horace Greeley called Johnson "an aching tooth in the national jaw, a screeching infant in a crowded lecture room."

JOHNSON VERSUS RADICALS To win votes for Democratic candidates in the 1866 congressional elections, Andrew Johnson went on a speaking tour of the Midwest during which he denounced Radical Republicans as traitors who should be hanged. His partisan speeches backfired, however.

In Cleveland, Ohio, Johnson described the Radical Republicans as "factious, domineering, tyrannical" men and exchanged hot-tempered insults with a heckler. At another stop, while the president was speaking from the back of a railway car, the engineer mistakenly pulled the train out of the station, making the president appear quite the fool. Republicans charged that such unseemly incidents confirmed Johnson's image as a "ludicrous boor" and a "drunken imbecile."

Voters agreed. The 1866 congressional elections brought a devastating defeat for Johnson and the Democrats; in each house, Radical Republican candidates won more than a two-thirds majority, the margin required to override presidential vetoes. Congressional Republicans would now take over the process of reconstructing the former Confederacy.

CONGRESS TAKES CHARGE On March 2, 1867, Congress passed, over President Johnson's vetoes, the First Reconstruction Act, which included three laws creating what came to be called **Congressional Reconstruction**: the Military Reconstruction Act, the Command of the Army Act, and the Tenure of Office Act.

The Military Reconstruction Act was the capstone of the Congressional Reconstruction plan. It abolished the new governments "in the Rebel States" established under Johnson's lenient Reconstruction policies. In their place, Congress established military control over ten of the eleven former Confederate states. (Tennessee was exempted because it had already ratified the Fourteenth Amendment.) The other ten states were divided into five military districts, each commanded by an army general who acted as governor.

Yet only 10,000 federal troops, mostly African Americans, were expected to police those sprawling "military districts." There were never enough soldiers to enforce Congressional Reconstruction. The entire state of Mississippi, for instance, had fewer than 400 soldiers assigned to ensure compliance.

The Military Reconstruction Act required each former Confederate state to create a new constitution that guaranteed all adult males the right to vote—black or white, rich or poor, landless or property owners. Women—black or white—were still not allowed to vote.

The act also stipulated that the new constitutions were to be drafted by conventions elected by male citizens "of whatever race, color, or previous condition." Once a majority of voters ratified the new constitutions, the state legislatures had to ratify the Fourteenth Amendment; once the amendment became part of the Constitution, the former Confederate states would be entitled to representation in Congress. Several hundred African American delegates participated in the constitutional conventions.

The Command of the Army Act required that the president issue all army orders through General-in-Chief Ulysses S. Grant. (The Radicals feared that President Johnson would appoint anti-black generals to head the military districts who would be too lenient toward defiant whites.)

The Tenure of Office Act stipulated that the Senate must approve any presidential effort to remove federal officials whose appointments the Senate had confirmed. Radicals intended this act to prevent Johnson from firing Secretary of War Edwin Stanton, the president's most outspoken critic in the cabinet.

Congressional Reconstruction embodied the most sweeping peacetime legislation in American history to that point. It sought to ensure that freed slaves could participate in the creation of new state governments in the former Confederacy. As Thaddeus Stevens explained, the Congressional Reconstruction plan would create a "perfect republic" based on the principle of *equal rights* for all citizens. "This is the promise of America," he insisted. "No More. No Less."

IMPEACHING THE PRESIDENT The first two years of Congressional Reconstruction produced dramatic changes in the South, as new state legislatures rewrote their constitutions and ratified the Fourteenth Amendment. Radical Republicans now seemed fully in control of Reconstruction, but one person still stood in their way—Andrew Johnson. During 1867 and early 1868, more and more Radicals decided that the president must be removed from office.

Johnson himself opened the door to impeachment (the formal process by which Congress charges the president with "high crimes and misdemeanors") when, in violation of the Tenure of Office Act, he fired Secretary of War Edwin Stanton, who had refused to resign from the cabinet despite his harsh criticism of the president's Reconstruction policy. Johnson, who considered the Tenure of Office Act an illegal restriction of presidential power, fired Stanton on August 12, 1867, and replaced him with Ulysses S. Grant.

The Radicals now saw their chance. By removing Stanton without congressional approval, Johnson had violated the Tenure of Office Act.

On February 24, 1868, the Republican-dominated House passed eleven articles of impeachment (that is, specific charges against the president), most of which dealt with Stanton's firing—and all of which were flimsy. In reality, the essential grievance against the president was that he had opposed the policies of the Radical Republicans. According to Secretary of the Navy Gideon Welles, Radicals were so angry at Johnson that they "would have tried to remove him had he been accused of stepping on a dog's tail."

The first Senate trial of a sitting president began on March 5, 1868. It was a dramatic spectacle before a packed gallery of journalists, foreign dignitaries, and political officials. As it began, Stevens warned the president: "Unfortunate, unhappy man, behold your doom!"

The five-week trial came to a stunning end when the Senate voted 35–19 for conviction, only *one* vote short of the two-thirds needed for removal.

Senator Edmund G. Ross, a young Radical from Kansas, cast the deciding vote in favor of acquittal, knowing that his vote would ruin his political career. He had decided that the evidence against Johnson was both insufficient for conviction and overtly partisan. "I almost literally looked down into my open grave," Ross explained afterward. "Friendships, position, fortune, everything that makes life desirable . . . were about to be swept away by the breath of my mouth." Angry Radicals thereafter shunned Ross. He lost his reelection campaign and died in near poverty.

In the end, the effort to remove Johnson was a grave political mistake, for it weakened public support for Congressional Reconstruction. The Richmond *Daily Dispatch* stressed that Johnson's acquittal was "a terrible rebuke on the Radical party, and diminished its physical force (it never had any other)." Nevertheless, the Radical cause did gain Johnson's private agreement to stop obstructing Congressional Reconstruction. (He would later break his pledge by turning a deaf ear to pleas for federal support in suppressing Klan violence.)

General Grant urged Johnson to let him exert more federal force in the South. To that end, he forwarded to the president a letter from a Tennessee legislator that documented gangs of whites "scouring the country by night—causing dismay & terror to all—Our civil authorities are powerless." Johnson declared that it was a local issue. Federal troops should stay out of it.

Grant refused to take no for an answer. He continued to barrage Johnson with fresh evidence of white efforts to terrorize blacks. "If Civil Government fails to protect the Citizen," Grant argued, "Military government should supply its place."

REPUBLICAN RULE IN THE SOUTH In June 1868, congressional Republicans announced that eight southern states could again send delegates to Congress. The remaining former Confederate states—Virginia, Mississippi, and Texas—were readmitted in 1870, with the added requirement that they ratify the **Fifteenth Amendment**, which gave voting rights to African American men. As Frederick Douglass, himself a former slave, had declared in 1865, "slavery is not abolished until the black man has the ballot."

The Fifteenth Amendment prohibited states from denying a citizen's right to vote on grounds of "race, color, or previous condition of servitude." But Susan B. Anthony and Elizabeth Cady Stanton, leaders of the movement to secure voting rights for women, insisted that the amendment should have included women. As Anthony stressed in a famous speech, the U.S. Constitution refers to "We, the people; not we, the white male citizens; nor yet we, the male citizens; but we, the whole people, who formed the Union—women as well as men."

Most men, however, remained opposed to voting rights for women. Radical Republicans tried to deflect the issue by declaring that it was the "Negro's hour." Women seeking voting rights would have to wait—another fifty years, as it turned out.

BLACK SOCIETY UNDER RECONSTRUCTION

When a federal official asked Garrison Frazier, a former Georgia slave, if he and others wanted to live among whites, Frazier said that they preferred "to live by ourselves, for there is a prejudice against us in the South that will take years to get over." In forging new lives, Frazier and many other former slaves set about creating their own social institutions.

FREED BUT NOT EQUAL African Americans were active agents in affecting the course of Reconstruction. It was not an easy process, however, because whites, both northern and southern, still practiced racism. A northern journalist traveling in the South after the war reported that the "whites seem wholly unable to comprehend that freedom for the negro means the same thing as freedom for them."

Once the excitement of freedom wore off, most southern blacks realized that their best chance to make a living was by working for pay for their former owners. In fact, the Freedmen's Bureau and federal soldiers urged and even ordered them to sign labor contracts with local whites. Many planters, however, conspired to control the amount of wages paid to freedmen. "It seems humiliating to be compelled to bargain and haggle with our own servants about wages," complained a white planter's daughter.

White Southerners were also determined to suppress black efforts to gain social and economic equality. In many respects, the war had not ended, as armed men organized to thwart federal efforts to reconstruct the South. In July 1866, a black woman in Clinch County, Georgia, was arrested and given sixty-five lashes for "using abusive language" during an encounter with a white woman. The Civil War brought freedom to enslaved African Americans, but it did not bring them protection against exploitation or abuse.

After emancipation, Union soldiers and northern observers often expressed surprise that freed slaves did not leave the South. But why would they leave what they knew so well? As a group of African Americans explained, they did not want to abandon "land they had laid their fathers' bones upon." A Union officer noted that southern blacks seemed "more attached to familiar places" than any other group in the nation.

Participation in the Union army or navy had given many freedmen training in leadership. Indeed, black military veterans would form the core of the first generation of African American political leaders in the postwar South. Military service also gave many former slaves their first opportunities to learn to read and write and alerted them to new possibilities for economic advancement, social respectability, and civic leadership.

BLACK CHURCHES AND SCHOOLS African American religious life in the South was transformed during and after the war. Many former slaves identified with the biblical Hebrews, who were led out of slavery into the "promised land." Emancipation demonstrated that God was on *their* side. Before the war, slaves who attended white churches were forced to sit in the back. After the war, with the help of many northern Christian missionaries, both black and white, ex-slaves established their own churches that became the crossroads for black community life.

Ministers emerged as social and political leaders. One could not be a real minister, one of them claimed, without looking "out for the political interests of his people." Many African Americans became Baptists or Methodists, in

African American political figures of Reconstruction Blanche K. Bruce (left) and Hiram Revels (right) served in the U.S. Senate. Frederick Douglass (center) was a major figure in the abolitionist movement.

part because these were already the largest denominations in the South and in part because they reached out to the working poor. In 1866 alone, the African Methodist Episcopal (AME) Church gained 50,000 members. By 1890, more than 1.3 million African Americans in the South had become Baptists, nearly three times as many as had joined any other denomination.

African American communities also rushed to establish schools. Starting schools, said a former slave, was the "first proof" of freedom. Before the Civil War, most plantation owners had denied an education to their slaves to keep them from reading abolitionist literature and organizing uprisings. After the war, the white elite worried that education would distract poor whites and blacks from their work in the fields or encourage them to leave the South in search of better social and economic opportunities.

POLITICS AND AFRICAN AMERICANS With many ex-Confederates denied voting rights, new African American voters helped elect some 600 blacks—most of them former slaves—as state legislators under Congressional Reconstruction. In Louisiana, Pinckney Pinchback, a northern free black and former Union soldier, was elected lieutenant governor. Several other African Americans were elected to high state offices. There were two black senators in Congress, Hiram Revels and Blanche K. Bruce, both Mississippi natives who had been educated in the North, while fourteen blacks served in the U.S. House of Representatives.

The election of black politicians appalled southern whites. Democrats claimed that Radicals were trying to "organize a hell in the South" by putting "the Caucasian race" under the rule of "their own negroes." Southern whites complained that freed slaves were illiterate and had no civic experience or appreciation of political issues and processes. In this regard, however, blacks were no different from millions of poor or immigrant white males who had been voting and serving in office for years.

LAND, LABOR, AND DISAPPOINTMENT Many ex-slaves argued that what they needed most was land. A New Englander traveling in the post-war South noted that the "sole ambition of the freedman" was "to become the owner of a little piece of land, there to erect a humble home, and to dwell in peace and security at his own free will and pleasure."

In several southern states, former slaves had been given land by Union armies after they had taken control of Confederate areas during the war. But Andrew Johnson reversed such transfers of white-owned property to former slaves. In South Carolina, the Union general responsible for evicting former slaves urged them to "lay aside their bitter feelings, and become reconciled

Freedmen voting in New Orleans The Fifteenth Amendment, ratified in 1870, guaranteed at the federal level the right of citizens to vote regardless of "race, color, or previous condition of servitude." But former slaves had been registering to vote—and voting in large numbers—in some state elections since 1867, as in this scene.

to their old masters." But the assembled freedmen shouted "No, never!" and "Can't do it!" They knew that ownership of land was the foundation of their freedom. They may have had no deeds or titles for the land they now worked, but it had been "earned by the sweat of *our* brows," said a group of Alabama freedmen. "Our wives, our children, our husbands, has been sold over and over again to purchase the lands we now locate on," a Virginia freedman noted. "Didn't we clear the land and raise de crops? We have a right to [that] land."

Thousands of former slaves were forced to return their farms to white owners. In addition, it was virtually impossible for former slaves to get loans to buy farmland because few banks were willing to lend to blacks. Their sense of betrayal was profound. An ex-slave in Mississippi said that he and others were left with nothing: "no *land*, no *house*, not so much as a place to lay our head."

As former slaves were stripped of their land, they had little choice but to become farmworkers under a new system: **sharecropping**. White landowners would provide land, seed, and tools to poor laborers in exchange for a *share* of the crop. This essentially re-enslaved the workers because, as a federal army officer said, no matter "how much they are abused, they cannot leave without permission of the owner." If they left, they would forfeit their portion of the crop. Workers who violated the terms of the contract could be evicted from the plantation, leaving them jobless and homeless—and subject to arrest as "vagrants." Across the former Confederacy, the growth of sharecropping revealed that most white plantation owners and small farmers were determined to control African Americans as if they were still enslaved. And if bad weather or insects or disease stunted the harvest, it pushed the sharecropper only deeper in debt.

Sharecroppers A family is shown outside their Virginia home in this 1899 photograph, taken by Frances Benjamin Johnston, one of the earliest American female photojournalists.

Many freed blacks preferred sharecropping over working for wages, since it freed them from day-to-day supervision by white landowners. Over time, however, most sharecroppers, black and white, found themselves deep in debt to the landowner, with little choice but to remain tied to the same discouraging system of dependence that, over the years, felt much like slavery. As a former slave acknowledged, he and others had discovered that "freedom could make folks proud but it didn't make 'em rich."

TENSIONS AMONG SOUTHERN BLACKS African Americans in the postwar South were by no means a uniform community. They had their own differences and disputes, especially between the few who owned property and the many who did not. In North Carolina, for example, less than 7 percent of blacks owned land by 1870.

Affluent northern blacks and the southern free black elite, most of whom were city dwellers and "mulattos" (people of mixed racial parentage), often opposed efforts to redistribute land to the freedmen, and many insisted that political equality did not mean social equality. As an African American leader in Alabama stressed, "We do not ask that the ignorant and degraded shall be put on a social equality with the refined and intelligent." In general, however, unity prevailed, and African Americans focused on common concerns. "All we ask," said a black member of the state constitutional convention in Mississippi, "is justice, and to be treated like human beings."

BLACKS IN POLITICS Many African Americans served in state governments with distinction. Nonetheless, the scornful label "black Reconstruction," used by critics then and since, distorts African American political influence. Such criticism also overlooks the political clout of the large number of white Republicans, especially in the mountain areas of the Upper South, who favored the Radical plan for Reconstruction.

Only South Carolina's Republican state convention had a black majority. Louisiana's was evenly divided racially, and in only two other state conventions were more than 20 percent of the members black: Florida and Virginia. The Texas convention was only 10 percent black, and North Carolina's was 11 percent—which did not stop a white newspaper from calling it a group of "baboons, monkeys, mules . . . and other jackasses."

"CARPETBAGGERS" AND "SCALAWAGS" Unreconstructed white Southerners dismissed whites who served in the new Republican state governments as "carpetbaggers" or "scalawags." Carpetbaggers, critics argued, were the 30,000 scheming Northerners who rushed South with their belongings in cheap suitcases made of carpeting ("carpetbags") to grab political power or buy plantations.

Some of the Northerners who migrated south were corrupt opportunists. However, most were Union military veterans drawn to the South by the desire to rebuild the region's devastated economy. Many other so-called carpetbaggers were teachers, social workers, attorneys, physicians, editors, and ministers motivated by a genuine desire to help free blacks and poor whites improve their lives.

For example, Union general Adelbert Ames, who won the Medal of Honor, stayed in the South after the war because he felt a "sense of Mission with a large M" to help the former slaves develop healthy communities. He served as the military governor of Mississippi before being elected a Republican U.S. senator in 1870.

Southern Democrats especially hated the scalawags, or southern white Republicans, calling them traitors to their region. A Nashville newspaper editor described them as the "merest trash." Most scalawags had been Unionists opposed to secession. They were prominent in the mountain counties of Georgia and Alabama and especially in the hills of eastern Tennessee. What the scalawags had in common was a willingness to work with Republicans to rebuild the southern economy.

SOUTHERN RESISTANCE AND WHITE "REDEMPTION" Most southern whites viewed secession as a noble "lost cause." They used all means possible—legal and illegal—to "redeem" their beloved South from northern control, Republican rule, and black equality. An Alabama planter admitted that southern whites simply "can't learn to treat the freedmen like human beings."

RECONSTRUCTION, 1865–1877

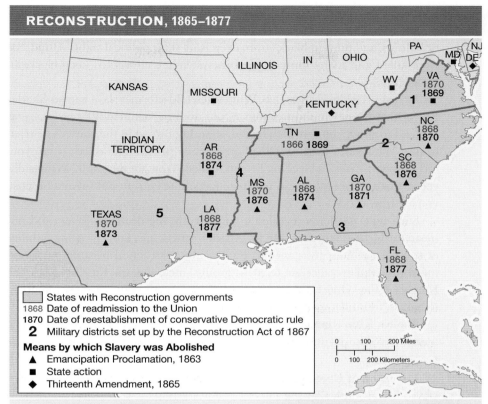

States with Reconstruction governments
1868 Date of readmission to the Union
1870 Date of reestablishment of conservative Democratic rule
2 Military districts set up by the Reconstruction Act of 1867
Means by which Slavery was Abolished
▲ Emancipation Proclamation, 1863
■ State action
◆ Thirteenth Amendment, 1865

- How did the Military Reconstruction Act reorganize governments in the South in the late 1860s and 1870s?
- What did the former Confederate states have to do to be readmitted to the Union?
- Why did "Conservative" white parties gradually regain control of the South from the Republicans in the 1870s?

White southern ministers assured their congregations that God endorsed white supremacy. In an attempt to reunite the Protestant denominations of the North and South, many northern religionists became "apostles of forgiveness" for their southern white brethren. Even abolitionists such as the Reverend Henry Ward Beecher, whose sister Harriet Beecher Stowe had written *Uncle Tom's Cabin* (1857), called for southern whites—rather than federal officials or African Americans themselves—to govern the South after the war.

With each passing year during Reconstruction, African Americans suffered increasing exploitation and abuse. The black codes created by white state governments in 1865 and 1866 were the first of many efforts to deny equality.

Southern whites used terror, intimidation, and violence to disrupt black Republican meetings, target black and white Republican leaders for beatings or killings, and prevent blacks from exercising their political rights. Hundreds were killed and many more injured in systematic efforts to "keep blacks in their place."

In Texas, a white farmer, D. B. Whitesides, told a former slave named Charles Brown that his newfound freedom would do him "damned little good . . . as I intend to shoot you"—which he did, shooting Brown in the chest as he tried to flee. Whitesides then rode his horse beside Brown and asked, "I got you, did I Brown?" "Yes," a bleeding Brown replied. "You got me good." Whitesides yelled that the wound would teach "niggers [like you] to put on airs because you are free."

Such ugly incidents revealed a harsh truth: the death of slavery did not mean the birth of true freedom for African Americans. For a growing number of southern whites, resistance to Radical Reconstruction became more and more violent. Several secret terrorist groups, including the Ku Klux Klan, the Knights of the White Camelia, the White Line, and the White League, emerged to harass, intimidate, and even kill African Americans.

The **Ku Klux Klan** (KKK) was formed in 1866 in Pulaski, Tennessee. The name *Ku Klux* was derived from the Greek word *kuklos*, meaning "circle" or "band"; *Klan* came from the English word *clan*, or family. The Klan, and other groups like it, began initially as a social club, with spooky costumes and secret rituals. But its members, most of them former Confederate soldiers, soon began harassing blacks and white Republicans. General Philip Sheridan, who supervised the district that included Louisiana and Texas, reported that Klansmen were "terrorists" intent on suppressing black political participation.

"Worse Than Slavery" This Thomas Nast cartoon condemns the Ku Klux Klan for promoting conditions "worse than slavery" for southern blacks after the Civil War.

These groups' motives varied—anger over the Confederate defeat, resentment against federal soldiers occupying the South, complaints about having to pay black workers, and an almost paranoid fear that former slaves might seek revenge against whites. Klansmen marauded at night on horseback, spreading rumors, issuing threats, and burning schools and churches. "We are going to kill all the Negroes," a white supremacist declared during one massacre.

THE LEGACY OF CONGRESSIONAL RECONSTRUCTION

One by one, the Republican state governments were gradually overturned. Yet they left behind an important accomplishment: The new constitutions they created remained in effect for years, and later constitutions incorporated many of their most progressive features.

Some of the significant innovations brought about by the Republican state governments protected black voting rights and restructured legislatures to reflect shifting populations. More state offices were changed from appointed to elective positions to weaken the "good old boy" tradition of rewarding political supporters with state government jobs. In South Carolina, former Confederate leaders opposed the Republican state legislature not simply because of its black members but because poor whites were also enjoying political clout for the first time, thereby threatening the dominance of wealthy white plantation owners and merchants.

Given the hostile circumstances under which Republican state governments operated in the South, their achievements were remarkable. They rebuilt an extensive railroad network and established public school systems funded by state governments and open to all children, although the buildings were segregated by race. Some 600,000 black pupils had enrolled in southern schools by 1877.

The Radicals also gave more attention to the poor and to orphanages, asylums, and institutions for the deaf and blind of both races. Much-needed infrastructure—roads, bridges, and buildings—was repaired or rebuilt. African Americans achieved rights and opportunities that would repeatedly be violated in coming decades but would never completely be taken away, at least in principle, such as equality before the law and the rights to own property, attend schools, learn to read and write, enter professions, and carry on business.

Yet government officials also engaged in corrupt practices. Bribes and kickbacks, whereby companies received government contracts in return for giving government officials cash or stock, were commonplace. In Louisiana, a twenty-six-year-old carpetbagger, Henry Clay Warmoth, somehow turned an annual salary of $8,000 into a million-dollar fortune during his four years as governor. (He was eventually impeached and removed from office.) "I don't pretend to be honest," he admitted. "I only pretend to be as honest as anybody in politics."

As was true in the North and the Midwest, southern state governments awarded money to corporations, notably railroads, under conditions that invited shady dealings and outright corruption. Some railroad corporations received state funds but never built railroads, and bribery was rampant. But the Radical Republican regimes did not invent such corruption, nor did it die with them. Governor Warmoth recognized as much: "Corruption is the fashion" in Louisiana, he explained.

THE GRANT ADMINISTRATION

Andrew Johnson's crippled presidency created an opportunity for Republicans to elect one of their own in 1868. Both parties wooed Ulysses S. Grant, the "Lion of Vicksburg" credited by most with the Union victory in the Civil War. His falling-out with President Johnson, however, had pushed him toward the Republicans, who unanimously nominated him as their presidential candidate.

THE ELECTION OF 1868 The Republican party platform endorsed Congressional Reconstruction. More important, however, were the public expectations driving the candidacy of Ulysses S. Grant, whose slogan was "Let us have peace." Grant promised that, if elected, he would enforce the laws and promote prosperity for all.

"This is a white man's country," the Democrats claimed, so "let white men rule." They charged that the Radical Republicans were subjecting the South "to military despotism and Negro supremacy." They nominated Horatio Seymour, the wartime governor of New York and a passionate critic of Congressional Reconstruction, who dismissed the Emancipation Proclamation as "a proposal for the butchery of women and children." His running mate, Francis P. Blair Jr., a former Union general from Missouri who had served in Congress, was an unapologetic racist who denounced Republicans for promoting equality for "a semi-barbarous race" who sought to "subject the white women to their unbridled lust." Blair attacked Grant for exercising military tyranny "over the eight millions of white people in the South, fixed to the earth with his bayonets."

A Democrat later said that Blair's "stupid and indefensible" remarks cost Seymour a close election. Grant won all but eight states and swept the electoral college, 214–80, but his popular majority was only 307,000 out of almost 6 million votes.

More than 500,000 African American voters, mostly in the South, accounted for Grant's margin of victory, and many risked their lives supporting him. Klan violence soared during the campaign, and hundreds of freedpeople paid with their lives. Still, the efforts of Radical Republicans to ensure voting rights for southern blacks had paid off. As Frederick Douglass explained, "the Republican party is the ship and all else is the sea" as far as black voters were concerned.

Grant, the youngest president (forty-six years old at the time of his inauguration), was a courageous defender of Congressional Reconstruction, but he was not a great president. He later admitted that he took office "without any previous experience either in civil or political life. I thought I could run the government of the United States as I did the staff of my army. It was my mistake, and it led me into other mistakes."

Grant passively followed the lead of Congress and was often blind to the political forces and self-serving influence peddlers around him. He showed poor judgment in his selection of cabinet members, often favoring friendship, family, loyalty, and military service over integrity and ability.

During his two terms in office, his seven cabinet positions changed twenty-four times. Some of the men betrayed his trust and engaged in criminal behavior. His former comrade in arms and close friend, General William T. Sherman, said he felt sorry for Grant because so many supposedly "loyal" Republicans used the president for their own selfish gains. Carl Schurz, a Union war hero who became a Republican senator from Missouri, expressed frustration that Grant was misled by cunning advisers who "prostituted" his administration.

Yet Grant excelled at bringing diversity to the federal government. During his two presidential terms, he appointed more African Americans, Native Americans, Jews, and women than any of his predecessors, and he fulfilled his campaign pledge to bring the nation "peace and prosperity."

THE FIFTEENTH AMENDMENT President Grant viewed Reconstruction of the South as the nation's top priority, and he doggedly insisted that freedpeople be allowed to exercise their civil rights without fear of violence. On March 30, 1870, Grant delivered a speech to Congress in which he celebrated the ratification of the Fifteenth Amendment, which gave voting rights to African American men nationwide. "It was," he declared, ". . . the most important event that has occurred since the nation came into life . . . the realization of the Declaration of Independence." Frederick Douglass appreciated Grant's efforts: "To Grant, more than any other man, the Negro owes his enfranchisement."

But the Fifteenth Amendment ignited a violent backlash in the South. The idea of the federal government guaranteeing the right of freedmen to vote deepened resentment of Reconstruction. In Georgia, white officials devised new ways to restrict black voting, such as poll taxes and onerous registration procedures. Other states followed suit.

Four months after the Fifteenth Amendment became the law of the land, Congress also passed the Naturalization Act of 1870. For the first time, it extended the process whereby immigrants had gained citizenship to include *"aliens of African nativity and to persons of African descent."* Efforts to include Asians and Native Americans in the new naturalization law were defeated, however.

THE UNION LEAGUE The Fifteenth Amendment had enormous political consequences. Southern whites feared nothing more than black voters, while Republicans were eager to recruit them. To do so, Republicans organized Union Leagues throughout the former Confederacy. Republicans had founded the Union League (also called Lincoln's Loyal League) in 1862 to rally voters behind Lincoln, the war, and the party. By late 1863, the leagues claimed more than 700,000 members in 4,554 councils across the nation.

In the South, the leagues operated like fraternities, with formal initiations and rituals and secret meetings to protect freedpeople from being persecuted by angry white Democrats. They met in churches, schools, homes, and fields, often hearing from northern speakers who traveled the South extolling the Republican party and encouraging blacks to register and vote. By the early 1870s, the Union League in the South had become one of the largest black social movements in history.

With the help of the Union Leagues, some 90 percent of southern freedmen registered to vote, almost all of them as Republicans, and they voted in record numbers (often as high as 80 to 90 percent). In Mississippi and South Carolina, black registered voters outnumbered whites.

Voting was not easy for freedmen, however, because most white Southerners were eager to deny them the vote. "All the blacks who vote against my ticket shall walk the plank," threatened former Georgia governor Howell Cobb, a Democrat who had been a Confederate general. Angry whites persecuted, evicted, or fired African American workers who "exercised their political rights," as a Union officer reported from Virginia.

Black Republicans were at times equally coercive. "The Negroes are as intolerant of opposition as the whites," a white South Carolina Democrat observed. They shunned, expelled, and even killed any "of their own" who "would turn democrats." He added that freedwomen were as partisan as men—and as intolerant of opposition: The "women are worse than the men, refusing to talk to or marry a renegade [black Democrat], and aiding [men] in mobbing him."

Yet the net result of the Union Leagues was the mobilization of African American voters, who enabled African American men to gain elected offices for the first time in the states of the former Confederacy. Francis Cardozo, a black minister who served as president of the South Carolina Council of Union Leagues, declared in 1870 that the state had "prospered in every respect" as a result of the enfranchisement of black voters enabled by the Union Leagues.

INDIAN POLICY President Grant was almost as progressive in his outlook toward Native Americans as he was toward African Americans. In 1869, he appointed General Ely Parker, a Seneca chief trained as an attorney and engineer, as the new Commissioner of Indian Affairs, the first Native American to hold the position. Parker had served as Grant's military secretary during the war. Now, as commissioner, Parker faced formidable challenges in creating policies for the 300,000 Indians across the nation, many of whom continued to be pressured by white settlers, miners, railroads, and telegraph companies to give up their ancestral lands.

Working with Parker, Grant created a new Peace Policy toward Native Americans. "The Indians," he observed, "require as much protection from the whites as the white does from the Indians." He did not want the army "shooting these poor savages; I want to conciliate them and make them peaceful citizens." His own experiences had shown that the "Indian problem" was in fact the result of "bad whites." Grant believed that lasting peace could only result from Indians abandoning their nomadic tradition and relocating to government reservations, where federal troops would provide them "absolute protection."

Grant also promised to end the chronic corruption whereby congressmen appointed cronies as licensed government traders with access to the Indian reservations. Many of the traders used their positions to swindle the Native Americans out of the federally supplied food, clothing, and other provisions intended solely for the reservations. One of the accused traders was the president's brother.

To clean up the so-called Indian Ring, Grant moved the Bureau of Indian Affairs out of the control of Congress and into the War Department. He also created a ten-man Board of Indian Commissioners, a new civilian agency whose mission was to oversee the operations of the Bureau of Indian Affairs to ensure that corruption was rooted out. Grant then appointed Quakers as reservation traders, assuming that their honesty, humility, and pacifism would improve the distribution of government resources. "If you can make Quakers out of the Indians," Grant told them, "it will take the fight out of them. Let us have peace." Yet Quakers proved no more able to manage Indian policy than government bureaucrats could.

Like other presidents, Grant discovered that there often emerged a gap between the policies he created and the implementation of them by others. Many of the officers and soldiers sent to the West to "pacify" Indian peoples in the Great Plains displayed an attitude toward Native Americans quite different from Grant's. For example, it was General Philip Sheridan who coined the infamous statement: "The only good Indians I know are dead." He also dismissed Indians as "the enemies of our race and of our civilization." Those "savages" who refused to move to government-mandated reservations should be killed, he argued. General William T. Sherman agreed. He stressed to Sheridan that "the more [Indians] we kill this year, the less we would have to kill next year."

Such attitudes led the abolitionist Wendell Phillips to ask why Indians were one of the only groups still denied citizenship. His answer was clear: "The great poison of the age is race hatred" directed at both African Americans and Native Americans. Most white Americans, however, did not care that racism was at work. "Wendell Phillips' new nigger," the editors of the *New York Herald* observed with disdain, "is the 'noble red man.'" Phillips responded, "We shall never be able to be just to other races . . . until we 'unlearn' contempt" for others different from us.

SCANDALS   President Grant's naive trust in people led his administration to stumble into a cesspool of scandal. Perhaps because of his own disastrous efforts as a storekeeper and farmer before the Civil War, Grant was awestruck by men of wealth. As they lavished gifts and attention on him, he was lured into their webs of self-serving deception.

In the summer of 1869, two unprincipled financial schemers, Jay Gould and James Fisk Jr., both infamous for bribing politicians and judges, plotted with Abel Corbin, the president's brother-in-law, to "corner" (manipulate) the nation's gold market. They intended to create a public craze for gold by purchasing massive quantities of the precious metal to drive up its value.

The only danger to the complicated scheme lay in the possibility that the federal Treasury would burst the bubble by selling large amounts of its gold, which would deflate its market value. When Grant was seen in public with Gould and Fisk, people assumed that he supported their scheme. As the false rumor spread in New York City's financial district that the president endorsed the run-up in gold, its value soared.

On September 24, 1869—soon to be remembered mournfully as Black Friday—the Gould-Fisk scheme worked, at least for a while. Starting at $150 an ounce, the price of gold rose, first to $160, then $165, leading more and more investors to join the stampede.

Then, around noon, Grant and his Treasury secretary realized what was happening and began selling government gold. Within fifteen minutes, the price plummeted to $138. Schemers lost fortunes amid the chaotic trading. Some ruined traders wept. One fainted. Another committed suicide. Soon the turmoil spread to the entire stock market, claiming thousands of victims. As Fisk noted, each man was left to "drag out his own corpse."

For weeks after the gold bubble collapsed, financial markets were paralyzed and business confidence was shaken. Congressman James Garfield wrote privately to a friend that President Grant had compromised his office by his "indiscreet acceptance" of gifts from Fisk and Gould and that any investigation of Black Friday would lead "into the parlor of the President." One critic announced that U.S. Grant's initials actually stood for "uniquely stupid."

The plot to corner the gold market was only the first of several scandals that rocked the Grant administration. The secretary of war, it turned out, had accepted bribes from merchants who traded with Indians at army posts in the West. And in St. Louis, whiskey distillers bribed federal Treasury agents in an effort to avoid paying excise taxes on alcohol. Grant's personal secretary participated in the scheme, taking secret payments in exchange for confidential information. Grant, spotlessly honest himself, urged Congress to investigate. "Let no guilty man escape," he stressed. "No personal considerations should stand in the way of performing a public duty."

Various congressional committees uncovered no evidence that Grant was personally involved. His poor choice of associates, however, earned him widespread criticism. Democrats scolded Republicans for their "monstrous corruption and extravagance" and reinforced public suspicion that elected officials were less servants of the people than they were self-serving bandits.

LIBERAL REPUBLICANS Disputes over political corruption and the fate of Reconstruction helped divide Republicans into two factions: Liberals (or Conscience Republicans) and Stalwarts (or Grant Republicans).

Liberal Republicans, led by Senator Carl Schurz, embraced free enterprise capitalism and opposed government regulation of business and industry while championing gold coins as the only reliable currency. They wanted to oust the "tyrannical" Grant from the presidency and end Reconstruction. They also sought to lower the tariffs lining the pockets of big corporations, and promote "civil service reforms" to end the "partisan tyranny" of the "patronage system," whereby new presidents rewarded the "selfish greed" of political supporters with federal government jobs.

Liberal Republicans charged that Grant and his cronies were pursuing policies and making decisions solely to benefit themselves. They also opposed Grant's efforts to suppress racism and Ku Klux Klan terrorism. As the *Nation* magazine stressed, "Everybody is heartily tired of discussing [the Negro's] rights." They believed there was no more need for federal intervention in the South. "The removal of white prejudice against the negro depends almost entirely on the negro himself" rather than the presence of federal troops.

THE 1872 ELECTION In 1872, the Liberal Republicans, many of whom were elitist newspaper editors suspicious of the "working classes," held their own national convention in Cincinnati, during which they accused the Grant administration of corruption, incompetence, and "despotism." They then committed political suicide by nominating Horace Greeley, the editor of the *New York Tribune* and a longtime champion of causes ranging from abolitionism to socialism, vegetarianism, and spiritualism (communicating with the dead).

E. L. Godkin, editor of the *Nation* and a Liberal Republican sympathizer, could not imagine voting for Greeley, whom he dismissed as "a conceited, ignorant, half-cracked, obstinate old creature." Greeley's image as an eccentric who repeatedly reversed his political positions was matched by his record of hostility toward Democrats, whose support the Liberal Republicans needed if they were to win.

Southern Democrats, however, liked Greeley's criticism of Reconstruction policies. His newspaper, for example, claimed that "ignorant, superstitious, semi-barbarian" former slaves were "extremely indolent, and will make no exertion beyond what is necessary to obtain food enough to satisfy their hunger." Moreover, Radical Republicans had given the vote to "ignorant" former slaves whose "Nigger Government" exercised "absolute political supremacy" in several states and was transferring wealth from the "most intelligent" and "influential" southern whites to themselves.

Most Northerners, however, were appalled at Greeley's candidacy. By nominating Greeley, said the *New York Times*, the Liberal Republicans and Democrats had killed any chance of electoral victory.

In the 1872 balloting, Greeley carried only six southern states and none in the North. Grant won thirty-one states and tallied 3,598,235 votes to Greeley's 2,834,761. An exhausted Greeley confessed that he was "the worst beaten man who ever ran for high office." His wife died six days before the election, and he died three weeks later.

Grant was delighted that the "soreheads and thieves who had deserted the Republican party" were defeated, and he promised to avoid the "mistakes" he had made in his first term.

THE MONEY SUPPLY Complex financial issues—especially monetary policy—dominated Ulysses S. Grant's second term. Prior to the Civil War, the economy operated on a gold standard; state banks issued paper money that could be exchanged for an equal value of gold coins. So, both gold coins and state bank notes circulated as currency. **Greenbacks** (so called because of the dye used on the printed dollars) were issued by the federal Treasury during the Civil War to help pay for the war.

When a nation's supply of money grows faster than the economy itself, prices for goods and services increase (inflation). This happened when the greenbacks were issued. After the war, the U.S. Treasury assumed that the greenbacks would be recalled from circulation so that consumer prices would decline and the nation could return to a "hard-money" currency—gold, silver, and copper coins—which had always been viewed as more reliable in value than paper currency.

The most vocal supporters of a return to hard money were eastern creditors (mostly bankers and merchants) who did not want their debtors to pay them in paper currency. Critics of the gold standard tended to be farmers and other debtors. These so-called soft-money advocates opposed taking greenbacks out of circulation because shrinking the supply of money would bring lower prices (deflation) for their crops and livestock, thereby reducing their income and making it harder for them to pay their long-term debts. In 1868, congressional supporters of such a soft-money policy—mostly Democrats—forced the Treasury to stop withdrawing greenbacks.

President Grant sided with the hard-money camp. On March 18, 1869, he signed the Public Credit Act, which said that investors who purchased government bonds to help finance the war effort must be paid back in gold. The act led to a decline in consumer prices that hurt debtors and helped creditors. It also ignited a ferocious political debate over the merits of hard and soft money that would last throughout the nineteenth century—and beyond.

FINANCIAL PANIC President Grant's effort to withdraw greenbacks from circulation unintentionally helped cause a major economic collapse. During 1873, two dozen overextended railroads stopped paying their bills, forcing Jay Cooke and Company, the nation's leading business lender, to go bankrupt and close its doors on September 18, 1873.

The shocking news created a snowball effect, as other hard-pressed banks began shutting down. A Republican senator sent Grant an urgent telegram from New York City: "Results of today indicate imminent danger of general national bank panic."

The resulting **Panic of 1873** triggered a deep depression. Tens of thousands of businesses closed, 3 million workers lost jobs, and those with jobs saw their wages slashed. In major cities, the unemployed and homeless roamed the streets and formed long lines at soup kitchens.

The depression led the U.S. Treasury to reverse course and begin printing more greenbacks. For a time, the supporters of paper money celebrated, but in 1874, Grant overruled his cabinet and vetoed a bill to issue even more greenbacks. His decision pleased the financial community but ignited a barrage of criticism. A Tennessee Republican congressman called the veto "cold-blooded murder," and a group of merchants in Indiana charged that Grant had sold his soul to those "whose god is the dollar."

In the end, Grant's decision only prolonged what was then the worst depression in the nation's history. It also brought about a catastrophe for Republicans in the 1874 congressional elections, as Democrats blamed them for the economic hard times. In the House, Republicans went from a 70 percent majority to a 37 percent minority. They maintained control of the Senate but were placed on the defensive.

WHITE TERROR President Grant initially fought to enforce federal efforts to reconstruct the postwar South, but southern resistance to "Radical rule" increased and turned brutally violent. In Grayson County, Texas, a white man and two friends murdered three former slaves because they wanted to "thin the niggers out and drive them to their holes."

Klansmen focused their program of murder, violence, and intimidation on prominent Republicans, black and white—elected officials, teachers in black schools, state militias. In Mississippi, they killed a black Republican leader in front of his family. Three white scalawag Republicans were murdered in Georgia in 1870, and that same year an armed mob of whites assaulted a Republican political rally in Alabama, killing four blacks and wounding fifty-four. An Alabama Republican pleaded with President Grant to intervene. "Give us poor people some guarantee of our lives," G. T. F. Boulding wrote. "We are hunted and shot down as if we were wild beasts."

In South Carolina, white supremacists were especially violent. In 1871, some 500 masked men laid siege to the Union County jail and eventually lynched eight black prisoners. In March 1871, Klansmen killed thirty African Americans in Meridian, Mississippi.

At Grant's urging, Republicans in Congress responded with three Enforcement Acts (1870–1871). The first imposed penalties on anyone who interfered with a citizen's right to vote. The second dispatched federal supervisors to monitor elections in southern districts where political terrorism flourished. The third, called the Ku Klux Klan Act (1871), outlawed the main activities of the KKK—forming conspiracies, wearing disguises, resisting officers, and intimidating officials. It also allowed the president to send federal troops to any community where voting rights were being violated.

Once the legislation was approved, Grant sent Attorney General Amos Akerman, a Georgian, to recruit prosecutors and marshals to enforce it. The Klan, Akerman reported, "was the most atrocious organization that the civilized part of the world has ever known." Its violent acts "amount to war." In South Carolina alone, Akerman and federal troops and prosecutors convinced local juries to convict 1,143 Klansmen. By 1872, Grant's stern actions had effectively killed the Klan. In general, however, the Enforcement Acts were not consistently enforced. As a result, the violent efforts of southern whites to thwart Reconstruction escalated.

On Easter Sunday 1873 in the black Republican township of Colfax, Louisiana, a mob of 140 white vigilantes, most of them ex-Confederate soldiers led by Klansmen, used a cannon, rifles, and pistols to attack a group of black Republicans holed up in the courthouse, slaughtering eighty-one and burning the building.

When federal troops arrived, an officer reported that they found heaps of black bodies being picked over by dogs and buzzards. "We were unable to find the body of a single white man," he said. Many of the dead "were shot in the back of the head and neck." Most had "three to a dozen wounds."

President Grant told the Senate that the Colfax Massacre was unprecedented in its "barbarity." He declared parts of Louisiana to be in a state of insurrection and imposed military rule. Federal prosecutors used the Enforcement Acts to indict seventy whites, but only nine were put on trial and just three were convicted—but of "conspiracy," not murder.

SOUTHERN "REDEEMERS" The Klan's impact on southern politics varied from state to state. In the Upper South, it played only a modest role in helping Democrats win local elections. In the Lower South, however, Klan violence had more serious effects. In overwhelmingly black Yazoo County, Mississippi, vengeful whites used terrorism to reverse the political balance of power. In the 1873 elections, for example, the Republicans cast 2,449 votes and the Democrats 638; two years later, the Democrats polled 4,049 votes, the Republicans 7. Once Democrats regained power, they ousted black legislators, closed public schools for black children, and instituted poll taxes to restrict black voting.

The activities of white supremacists disheartened black and white Republicans alike. "We are helpless and unable to organize," wrote a Mississippi scalawag. We "dare not attempt to canvass [campaign for candidates], or make public speeches." At the same time, Northerners displayed a growing weariness with using federal troops to reconstruct the South. "The plain truth is," noted the *New York Herald*, "the North has got tired of the Negro."

President Grant, however, desperately wanted to use more federal force to preserve peace. He asked Congress to pass new legislation that would "leave my duties perfectly clear." Congress responded with the Civil Rights Act of 1875, which said that people of all races must be granted equal access to hotels and restaurants, railroads and stagecoaches, theaters, and other "places of public amusement."

Unfortunately for Grant, the new anti-segregation law provided little enforcement authority. Those who felt their rights were being violated had to file suit in court, and the penalties for violators were modest. In 1883, the U.S. Supreme Court, in an opinion arising from five similar cases, struck down the Civil Rights Act on the grounds that the Fourteenth Amendment focused only on the actions of state governments; it did not have authority over the policies of private businesses or individuals. Chief Justice Joseph Bradley added that it was time for blacks to assume "the rank of a mere citizen" and stop being the "special favorite of the laws." As a result, the *Civil Rights Cases* (1883) opened the door for a wave of racial segregation that washed over the South during the late nineteenth century.

Republican political control in the South and public interest in protecting civil rights gradually loosened during the 1870s as all-white "Conservative" parties mobilized the anti-Reconstruction vote. They called themselves Conservatives to distinguish themselves from northern Democrats. Conservatives—the so-called **redeemers** who supposedly "saved" the South from Republican control and "black rule"—used the race issue to excite the white electorate and threaten black voters. Where persuasion failed to work, Conservatives used trickery to rig the voting. As one boasted, "The white and black Republicans may outvote us, but we can outcount them."

Republican political control ended in Virginia and Tennessee as early as 1869 and collapsed a year later in Georgia and North Carolina, although North Carolina had a Republican governor until 1876. Reconstruction lasted longest in the Lower South, where whites abandoned Klan robes for barefaced intimidation in paramilitary groups such as the Mississippi Rifle Club and the South Carolina Red Shirts. The last Radical Republican regimes ended, however, after the elections of 1876, and the return of the old white political elite further undermined the country's commitment to Congressional Reconstruction.

THE SUPREME COURT Key rulings by the U.S. Supreme Court further eroded Congressional Reconstruction. The *Slaughterhouse Cases* (1873) limited the "privileges or immunities" of U.S. citizenship as outlined in the Fourteenth Amendment.

In 1869, the Louisiana legislature had granted the New Orleans livestock slaughtering business to a single company for twenty-five years as a means of protecting public health. Competing butchers sued the state, arguing that the monopoly violated their "privileges" as U.S. citizens under the Fourteenth Amendment and deprived them of property without due process of law.

In a 5–4 decision, the Court ruled that the monopoly did not violate the Fourteenth Amendment because its "privileges and immunities" clause applied only to U.S. citizenship, not state citizenship. States, in other words, retained legal jurisdiction over their citizens, and federal protection of civil rights did not extend to the property rights of businesses.

Dissenting Justice Stephen J. Field argued that the Court's ruling rendered the Fourteenth Amendment a "vain and idle enactment" with little scope or authority. By designating the rights of state citizens as being beyond the jurisdiction of federal law, the *Slaughterhouse Cases* unwittingly opened the door for states to discriminate against African Americans.

Three years later, in *United States v. Cruikshank* (1876), the Supreme Court further eroded the protections of individuals by overturning the convictions of William Cruikshank and two other white men who had led the Colfax Massacre. In doing so, the Court argued that the equal protection and due process clauses in the Fourteenth Amendment governed only state actions, not the behavior of individuals. Furthermore, the prosecution's failure to prove racial intent placed the convictions outside the reach of the Equal Protection Clause of the Fourteenth Amendment.

In Chief Justice Morrison Waite's view, the duty to protect the "equality of the rights of citizens" had been "originally assumed by the States; and it still remains there." He and the other justices thus struck down the Enforcement Acts, ruling that the states, not the federal government, were responsible for protecting citizens from attack by other private citizens.

Taken together, the *Slaughterhouse* and *Cruikshank* cases so gutted the Fourteenth Amendment that freedpeople were left even more vulnerable to violence and discrimination. The federal government was effectively abandoning its role in enforcing Reconstruction.

THE CONTESTED ELECTION OF 1876 President Grant wanted to run for an unprecedented third term in 1876, but many Republicans had lost confidence in his leadership. In the summer of 1875, he acknowledged the inevitable and announced that he would retire. James Gillespie Blaine of Maine, former Speaker of the House, initially seemed the likeliest Republican to succeed Grant, but his candidacy crumbled when newspapers revealed that he had secretly promised political favors to railroad executives in exchange for shares of stock in the company.

The scandal led the Republican convention to select Ohio's favorite son, Rutherford B. Hayes. A former Union general who had been wounded five times during the Civil War, Hayes had served three terms as governor of Ohio. He was a civil service reformer eager to reduce the number of federal jobs subject to political appointment. But his chief virtue was that he offended neither Radicals nor reformers. As a journalist put it, he was "obnoxious to no one."

Hayes called for reforming the civil service to eliminate cronyism and corruption within his administration and promised to reject a second term for himself. The Republican platform criticized the "corrupt centralism" of the Grant administration that had infested the federal government with "incapacity, waste, and fraud."

The Democratic convention was uncharacteristically harmonious. On the second ballot, the nomination went to Samuel J. Tilden, a wealthy corporate lawyer and reform governor of New York.

The 1876 campaign avoided controversial issues. In the absence of strong ideological differences, Democrats highlighted the Republican scandals. Republicans responded by repeatedly waving "the bloody shirt," linking the Democrats to secession, civil war, and the violence committed against Republicans in the South. As Robert G. Ingersoll, the most celebrated Republican public speaker of the time, insisted: "The man that assassinated Abraham Lincoln was a Democrat . . . Soldiers, every scar you have on your heroic bodies was given you by a Democrat!"

Early election returns pointed to a victory for Tilden. Nationwide, he outpolled Hayes by almost 300,000 votes, and by midnight following Election Day, Tilden had won 184 electoral votes, just 1 short of the total needed for victory. Overnight, however, Republican activists realized that the election hinged on 19 disputed electoral votes from Florida, Louisiana, and South Carolina.

The Democrats needed only one of the challenged votes to claim victory; the Republicans needed all nineteen. Republicans in the three states had engaged in election fraud, while Democrats had used violence to keep black voters at home. All three states, however, were governed by Republicans who appointed the election boards, each of which reported narrow victories for Hayes. The Democrats immediately challenged the results.

In all three states, rival election boards submitted conflicting vote counts. Weeks passed with no solution. On January 29, 1877, Congress appointed an electoral commission to settle the dispute. Finally, on March 1, 1877, the commission voted 8–7 in favor of Hayes. The next day, the House of Representatives declared Hayes president by an electoral vote of 185–184.

Tilden decided not to protest the decision. His campaign manager explained that they preferred "four years of Hayes's administration to four years of civil war."

Hayes's victory hinged on the defection of key southern Democrats, who, it turned out, had made secret deals with the Republicans. On February 26, 1877, prominent Ohio Republicans and powerful southern Democrats had struck a private bargain—the **Compromise of 1877**—at Wormley's Hotel in Washington, D.C. The Republicans promised that if Hayes were named president, he would remove the last federal troops from the South.

For his part, President Grant was eager to leave the White House: "I never wanted to get out of a place as much as I did to get out of the Presidency." Others were sorry to see him leave. T. Jefferson Martin spoke for many African Americans when he wrote Grant upon his retirement: "As a colored man I feel in duty bound to return you my greatful [sic] and heartfelt thanks, for your firm, steadfast, and successful administrations of our country, both as military chieftain and civil ruler of this nation . . . My dear friend of humanity."

THE END OF RECONSTRUCTION In 1877, the Democrat-controlled House of Representatives refused to fund federal troops in the South after July, and President Hayes withdrew U.S. soldiers from Louisiana and South Carolina, whose Republican governments collapsed soon thereafter. In the Congressional elections of 1878, Hayes admitted that the balloting in southern states was corrupted by "violence of the most atrocious character," but he was not about to send federal troops again.

Over the next thirty years, federal protection of black civil rights in the South crumbled. As Henry Adams, a former Louisiana slave, observed in 1877, "The whole South—every state in the South—has got [back] into the hands of the very men that held us as slaves." New white state governments rewrote their constitutions, ousted the "carpetbaggers, scalawags, and blacks," and cut spending. "The Yankees helped free us, so they say," a former North Carolina slave named Thomas Hall remembered, "but [in 1877] they let us be put back in slavery again."

THE "LOST CAUSE" While white conservatives were reasserting control and reinforcing white supremacy, novelists, poets, and former Confederate leaders were fashioning what came to be called the Lost Cause narrative, a sanitized version of history in which a romanticized Confederacy could do no wrong during the "War of Northern Aggression."

Nostalgic apologists for secession glamorized the old plantation culture and insisted that the Civil War had little to do with slavery and everything to do with a noble defense of states' rights and the southern homeland against the aggressions of a tyrannical Republican party. As Jefferson Davis claimed in 1881, the loyal and faithful slaves in the South were "contented with their lot" in 1861. President Lincoln, however, hoodwinked them into believing they would be better off free and "sent them out to devastate their benefactors [owners]."

The Lost Cause myth also demonized abolitionists and idealized the leadership of Confederate generals Robert E. Lee ("the soldier who walked with God") and Stonewall Jackson, deifying them as chivalrous pillars of southern virtue who fought bravely and ethically against far larger Union armies led by ruthless outlaws such as Ulysses S. Grant and William T. Sherman.

To bolster this intentional reimagining of southern history, communities erected scores of monuments and memorials glorifying Confederate leaders. On Memorial Day 1890, for example, more than 100,000 people gathered in Richmond, Virginia, to celebrate the unveiling of a massive statue of General Lee seated on his celebrated warhorse, "Traveler." What the speakers at the event failed to mention was that Lee, before his death in 1871, had urged southerners *not* to create such memorials to a cause that was "lost" on the battlefields.

RECONSTRUCTION'S SIGNIFICANCE

The collapse of Congressional Reconstruction in 1877 had tragic consequences, as the white South aggressively renewed traditional patterns of discrimination against African Americans. Black activist W. E. B. DuBois called the effort to make slaves into citizens a "splendid failure."

Yet for all its unfulfilled promises, Congressional Reconstruction did leave an enduring legacy—the Thirteenth, Fourteenth, and Fifteenth Amendments. If Reconstruction's experiment in interracial democracy failed to provide true social equality or substantial economic opportunities for African Americans, it did create the essential constitutional foundation for future advances in the quest for equality and civil rights—and not just for African Americans, but for women and other minority groups.

Until the pivotal Reconstruction era, the states were responsible for protecting citizens' rights. Thereafter, thanks to the Fourteenth and Fifteenth Amendments, blacks had gained equal rights (in theory), and the federal government had assumed responsibility for ensuring that states treated blacks equally. A hundred years later, the cause of civil rights would be embraced again by the federal government—this time permanently.

CHAPTER REVIEW

SUMMARY

- **Reconstruction Challenges**   With the defeat of the Confederacy, the federal government had to develop policies and procedures to address a number of vexing questions: What was the status of the defeated states, and how would they be reintegrated into the nation's political life? What would be the political status of the former slaves, and what would the federal government do to integrate them into the nation's social and economic fabric?

- **Reconstruction over Time**   Abraham Lincoln and his successor, Southerner Andrew Johnson, wanted a lenient plan for Reconstruction. *Johnson's Restoration Plan (1865)*, like Lincoln's, said that when ten percent of a former Confederate state's voters swore a loyalty oath to the Union, that state could be readmitted. The *Freedmen's Bureau* helped to educate and aid freed slaves, negotiate labor contracts, and reunite families. Lincoln's assassination led many Northerners to favor the *Radical Republicans,* who wanted to end the grasp of the old plantation elite on the South's society and economy. Whites resisted and established *black codes* to restrict the freedom of former slaves. *Congressional Reconstruction* responded by stipulating that former Confederate states had to ratify the *Fourteenth (1868)* and *Fifteenth Amendments (1870)* to the U.S. Constitution to protect the rights of African Americans. Congress also passed the Military Reconstruction Act, which used federal troops to enforce the voting and civil rights of African Americans.

- **Views of Reconstruction**   After the war, land ownership reverted to the old white elite, reducing newly freed blacks to *sharecropping*. African Americans enthusiastically participated in politics, with many serving as elected officials. Along with white southern Republicans (scalawags) and northern carpetbaggers, they worked to rebuild the southern economy. Many white Southerners, however, supported the *Ku Klux Klan*'s violent intimidation and conservative control of southern state governments.

- **Political and Economic Developments and the End of Reconstruction**   Scandals during the Grant administration involving an attempt to corner the gold market, plus the *Panic of 1873* and disagreement over whether to continue the use of *greenbacks* or return to the gold standard, eroded northern support for the status quo in government and weakened Reconstruction. Southern white *redeemers* were elected in 1874, successfully reversing the political progress of Republicans and blacks. In the *Compromise of 1877,* Democrats agreed to the election of Republican Rutherford B. Hayes, who put an end to the Radical Republican administrations in the southern states.

- **The Significance of Reconstruction**   Southern state governments quickly renewed long-standing patterns of discrimination against African Americans, but the Fourteenth and Fifteenth Amendments remained enshrined in the Constitution, creating the essential constitutional foundation for future advances in civil rights.

CHRONOLOGY

1865	Congress sets up the Freedmen's Bureau
April 14, 1865	Lincoln assassinated
1865	Johnson issues Proclamation of Amnesty
	All-white southern state legislatures pass various black codes
1866	Ku Klux Klan organized
	Congress passes the Civil Rights Act
1867	Congress passes the Military Reconstruction Act
1868	Fourteenth Amendment is ratified
	The U.S. House of Representatives impeaches President Andrew Johnson; the Senate fails to convict him
	Grant elected president
	Eight former Confederate states readmitted to the Union
1870	Fifteenth Amendment ratified
	First Enforcement Acts passed in response to white terror in the South
1872	Grant wins reelection
1873	Panic of 1873 triggers depression
1877	Reconstruction ends; Hayes becomes president

KEY TERMS

 INQUIZITIVE

Go to InQuizitive to see what you've learned—and learn what you've missed—with personalized feedback along the way.

GLOSSARY

1968 Chicago Democratic National Convention Held August 26–29 in Chicago, Illinois, the event was infamously tumultuous. Inside the International Amphitheatre, the Democratic Party fought over its direction on Vietnam, while outside tens of thousands of Vietnam War protestors clashed with police.

36°30' According to the Missouri Compromise, any part of the Louisiana Purchase north of this line (Missouri's southern border) was to be excluded from slavery.

54th Massachusetts Regiment After President Abraham Lincoln's Emancipation Proclamation, the Union army organized all black military units, which white officers led. The 54th Massachusetts Regiment was one of the first of such units to be organized.

Abigail Adams (1744–1818) As the wife of John Adams, she endured long periods of separation from him while he served in many political roles. During these times apart, she wrote often to her husband, and their correspondence has provided a detailed portrait of life during the Revolutionary War.

abolition In the early 1830s, the anti-slavery movement shifted its goal from the gradual end of slavery to the immediate end or abolition of slavery.

John Adams (1735–1826) He was a signer of the Declaration of Independence and a delegate to the First and Second Continental Congresses. A member of the Federalist Party, he served as the first vice president and the second president of the United States. As president, he passed the Alien and Sedition Acts and endured a stormy relationship with France, which included the XYZ affair.

John Quincy Adams (1767–1848) As secretary of state, he urged President Monroe to issue the Monroe Doctrine, which incorporated his belief in an expanded use of federal powers. As the sixth president, Adams's nationalism and praise of European leaders caused a split in his party, causing some Republicans to leave and form the Democrat party.

Samuel Adams (1722–1803) A genius of revolutionary agitation, he believed that English Parliament had no right to legislate for the colonies. He organized the Sons of Liberty as well as protests in Boston against the British.

Jane Addams (1860–1935) She founded and ran of one of the best known settlement houses, the Hull House. Active in the peace and suffragist movements, she established child care for working mothers, health clinics, job training, and other social programs.

affirmative action Programs designed to give preferential treatment to women and people of color as compensation for past injustices.

Affordable Care Act (ACA) (2010) Vast health-care reform initiative signed into law and championed by President Obama, and widely criticized by Republicans, that aims to make health insurance more affordable and make health care accessible to everyone, regardless of income or prior medical conditions.

Agricultural Adjustment Act (1933) Legislation that paid farmers to produce less in order to raise crop prices for all; the AAA was later declared unconstitutional by the U.S. Supreme Court in the case of *United States v. Butler* (1936).

Emilio Aguinaldo (1869?–1964) He was a leader in the Filipino struggle for independence. During the war of 1898, Commodore George Dewey brought Aguinaldo back to the Philippines from exile to help fight the Spanish. However, after the Spanish surrendered to Americans, America annexed the Philippines and Aguinaldo fought against the American military until he was captured in 1901.

Battle of the Alamo Siege in the Texas War for Independence of 1836, in which the San Antonio mission fell to the Mexicans. Davy Crockett and Jim Bowie were among the courageous defenders.

Albany Plan of Union (1754) A failed proposal by the seven northern colonies in anticipation of the French and Indian War, urging the unification of the colonies under one Crown-appointed president.

Alien and Sedition Acts of 1798 Four measures passed during the undeclared war with France that limited the freedoms of speech and press and restricted the liberty of noncitizens.

alliance with France Critical diplomatic, military, and economic alliance between France and the newly independent United States, codified by the Treaty of Amity and Commerce and the Treaty of Alliance (1778).

Allied Powers The nations fighting the Central Powers during the First World War, including France, Great Britain, and Russia; later joined by Italy and, after Russia quit the war in 1917, the United States.

American Anti-Imperialist League Coalition of anti-imperialist groups united in 1899 to protest American territorial expansion, especially in the Philippine Islands; its membership included prominent politicians, industrialists, labor leaders, and social reformers.

American Colonization Society Established in 1817, an organization whose mission was to return freed slaves to Africa.

American Federation of Labor Founded in 1881 as a national federation of trade unions made up of skilled workers.

American Indian Movement (AIM) Fed up with the poor conditions on Indian reservations and the federal government's unwillingness to help, Native Americans founded the American Indian Movement (AIM) in 1963. In 1973, AIM led 200 Sioux in the occupation of Wounded Knee. After a ten-week standoff with the federal authorities, the government agreed to reexamine Indian treaty rights and the occupation ended.

American Recovery and Reinvestment Act Hoping to restart the weak economy, President Obama signed this $787-billion economic stimulus bill in February of 2009. The bill included cash distributions to states, funds for food stamps, unemployment benefits, construction projects to renew the nation's infrastructure, funds for renewable-energy systems, and tax reductions.

American System Economic plan championed by Henry Clay of Kentucky that called for federal tariffs on imports, a strong national bank, and federally financed internal improvements—roads, bridges, canals—all intended to strengthen the national economy and end American dependence on Great Britain.

American Tobacco Company Business founded in 1890 by North Carolina's James Buchanan Duke, who combined the major tobacco manufacturers of the time, ultimately controlling 90 percent of the country's cigarette production.

Anaconda Plan The Union's primary war strategy calling for a naval blockade of major southern seaports and then dividing the Confederacy by gaining control of the Tennessee, Cumberland, and Mississippi Rivers.

Annapolis Convention In 1786, all thirteen colonies were invited to a convention in Annapolis to discuss commercial problems, but only representatives from five states attended. However, the convention was not a complete failure because the delegates decided to have another convention in order to write the constitution.

Battle of Antietam (1862) Turning-point battle near Sharpsburg, Maryland, leaving over 20,000 soldiers dead or wounded, in which Union forces halted a Confederate invasion of the North.

anti-Federalists Opponents of the Constitution as an infringement on individual and states' rights, whose criticism led to the addition of a Bill of Rights to the document. Many anti-Federalists later joined Thomas Jefferson's Democratic-Republican party.

Anti-Masonic party This party grew out of popular hostility toward the Masonic fraternal order and entered the presidential election of 1832 as a third party. It was the first party to run as a third party in a presidential election as well as the first to hold a nomination convention and announce a party platform.

Appomattox Court House Virginia village where Confederate general Robert E. Lee surrendered to Union general Ulysses S. Grant on April 9, 1865.

Arab Awakening A wave of spontaneous democratic uprisings that spread throughout the Arab world beginning in 2011, in which long-oppressed peoples demanded basic liberties from generations-old authoritarian regimes.

Armory Show A divisive and sensational art exhibition in 1913 that introduced European-inspired modernism to American audiences.

Benedict Arnold (1741–1801) A traitorous American commander who planned to sell out the American garrison at West Point to the British; his plot was discovered before it could be executed and he joined the British army.

Articles of Confederation The first form of government for the United States, ratified by the original thirteen states in 1781; weak in central authority, it was replaced by the U.S. Constitution in 1789.

Atlanta Compromise (1895) A speech by Booker T. Washington that called for the black community to strive for economic prosperity before attempting political and social equality.

Atlantic Charter (1941) Joint statement crafted by Franklin D. Roosevelt and British prime minister Winston Churchill that listed the war goals of the Allied Powers.

Crispus Attucks (1723–1770) During the Boston Massacre, he was supposedly at the head of the crowd of hecklers who baited the British troops. He was killed when the British troops fired on the crowd.

Stephen F. Austin (1793–1836) He established the first colony of Americans in Texas, which eventually attracted 2,000 people.

Axis alliance Military alliance formed in 1937 by the three major fascist powers: Germany, Italy, and Japan.

Aztec Empire Mesoamerican people who were conquered by the Spanish under Hernando Cortés, 1519–1528.

baby boom Markedly high birth rate in the years following World War II, leading to the biggest demographic "bubble" in U.S. history.

Bacon's Rebellion Unsuccessful 1676 revolt led by planter Nathaniel Bacon against Virginia governor William Berkeley's administration, which, Bacon charged, had failed to protect settlers from Indian raids.

Bank of the United States (1791) National bank responsible for holding and transferring federal government funds, making business loans, and issuing a national currency.

Bank War Political struggle in the early 1830s between President Jackson and financier Nicholas Biddle over the renewing of the Second Bank's charter.

Barbary pirates North Africans who waged war (1801–1805) on the United States after President Thomas Jefferson refused to pay tribute (a bribe) to protect American ships.

Bay of Pigs Failed CIA operation that, in April 1961, deployed a band of Cuban rebels to overthrow Fidel Castro's Communist regime.

Battle of the Bulge On December 16, 1944, the German army launched a counterattack against the Allied forces, which pushed them back. However, the Allies were eventually able to recover and break through the German lines. This defeat was a great blow to the Nazi's morale and their army's strength. The battle used up the last of Hitler's reserve units and opened a route into Germany's heartland.

Bear Flag Republic On June 14, 1846, a group of Americans in California captured Sonoma from the Mexican army and declared it the Republic of California whose flag featured a grizzly bear. In July, the commodore of the U.S. Pacific Fleet landed troops on California's shores and declared it part of the United States.

Beats Group of bohemian, downtown New York writers, artists, and musicians who flouted convention in favor of liberated forms of self-expression.

beatnik A name referring to almost any young rebel who openly dissented from the middle-class life. The name itself stems from the Beats.

Berlin airlift (1948–1949) Effort by the United States and Great Britain to deliver massive amounts of food and supplies flown to West Berlin in response to the Soviet land blockade of the city.

Berlin Wall Twenty-seven-mile-long concrete wall constructed in 1961 by East German authorities to stop the flow of East Germans fleeing to West Berlin.

Bessemer converter Apparatus that blasts air through molten iron to produce steel in very large quantities.

Nicholas Biddle (1786–1844) He was the president of the second Bank of the United States. In response to President Andrew Jackson's attacks on the bank, Biddle curtailed the bank's loans and exchanged its paper currency for gold and silver. In response, state banks began printing paper without restraint and lent it to speculators, causing a binge in speculating and an enormous increase in debt.

Bill of Rights First ten amendments to the U.S. Constitution, adopted in 1791 to guarantee individual rights and to help secure ratification of the Constitution by the states.

Osama bin Laden (1957–2011) The Saudi-born leader of al Qaeda, whose members attacked America on September 11, 2001. Years before the attack, he had declared *jihad* (holy war) on the United States, Israel, and the Saudi monarchy. In Afghanistan, the Taliban leaders gave bin Laden a safe haven in exchange for aid in fighting the Northern Alliance, who were rebels opposed to the Taliban. Following the Taliban's refusal to turn over bin Laden to the United States, America and a multinational coalition invaded Afghanistan and overthrew the Taliban. In May 2011, bin Laden was shot and killed by American special forces during a covert operation in Pakistan.

birth rate Proportion of births per 1,000 of the total population.

black codes Laws passed in southern states to restrict the rights of former slaves; to combat the codes, Congress passed the Civil Rights Act of 1866 and the Fourteenth Amendment and set up military governments in southern states that refused to ratify the amendment.

Black nationalism A cultural and political movement in the 1920s spearheaded by Marcus Garvey that exalted blackness, black cultural expression, and black exclusiveness.

Black Power movement Militant form of civil rights protest focused on urban communities in the North and led by Malcolm X that grew as a response to impatience with the nonviolent tactics of Martin Luther King Jr.

James Gillespie Blaine (1830–1893) As a Republican congressman from Maine, he developed close ties with business leaders, which contributed to him losing the presidential election of 1884. He later opposed President Cleveland's efforts to reduce tariffs, which became a significant issue in the 1888 presidential election. Blaine served as secretary of state under President Benjamin Harrison.

Bleeding Kansas (1856) A series of violent conflicts in the Kansas Territory between anti-slavery and pro-slavery factions over the status of slavery.

blitzkrieg (1940) The German "lightning war" strategy characterized by swift, well-organized attacks using infantry, tanks, and warplanes.

Bolsheviks Under the leadership of Vladimir Lenin, this Marxist party led the November 1917 revolution against the newly formed provisional government in Russia. After seizing control, the Bolsheviks negotiated a peace treaty with Germany, the Treaty of Brest-Litovsk, and ended their participation in World War I.

Bonus Expeditionary Force (1932) Protest march in Washington, D.C., by thousands of World War I veterans and their families, calling for immediate payment of their service bonuses certificates; violence ensued when President Herbert Hoover ordered their tent villages cleared.

boomtown Town, often in the West, that developed rapidly due to the sudden influx of wealth and work opportunities; often male-dominated with a substantial immigrant population.

Daniel Boone (1734–1820) He found and expanded a trail into Kentucky, which pioneers used to reach and settle the area.

John Wilkes Booth (1838?–1865) He assassinated President Abraham Lincoln at the Ford's Theater on April 14, 1865. He was pursued and killed.

Boston Massacre Violent confrontation between British soldiers and a Boston mob on March 5, 1770, in which five colonists were killed.

Boston Tea Party Demonstration against the Tea Act of 1773 in which the Sons of Liberty, dressed as Indians, dumped hundreds of chests of British-owned tea into Boston Harbor.

Bourbons In post–Civil War southern politics, the opponents of the Redeemers were called Bourbons. They were known for having forgotten nothing and learned nothing from the ordeal of the Civil War.

bracero program (1942) System created in 1942 that permitted seasonal farm workers from Mexico to work in the United States on year-long contracts.

Joseph Brant (1742?–1807) Mohawk leader who led the Iroquois against the Americans in the Revolutionary War.

brinksmanship Secretary of State John Foster Dulles believed that communism could be contained by bringing America to the brink of war with an aggressive Communist nation. He believed that the aggressor would back down when confronted with the prospect of receiving a mass retaliation from a country with nuclear weapons.

John Brown (1800–1859) In response to a pro-slavery mob's sacking of the free-state town of Lawrence, Kansas, Brown went to the pro-slavery settlement of Pottawatomie, Kansas, which led to a guerrilla war in the Kansas territory. In 1859, he attempted to raid the federal arsenal at Harpers Ferry, hoping to use the stolen weapons to arm slaves, but he was captured and executed.

Brown v. Board of Education (1954) Landmark Supreme Court case that struck down racial segregation in public schools and declared "separate-but-equal" unconstitutional.

William Jennings Bryan (1860–1925) He delivered the pro-silver "cross of gold" speech at the 1896 Democratic Convention and won his party's nomination for president. Disappointed pro-gold Democrats chose to walk out of the convention and nominate their own candidate, which split the Democratic party and cost them the White House. Bryan's loss also crippled the Populist movement that had endorsed him.

"Bull Moose" Progressive party *See* Progressive party

Battles of (First and Second Manassas) Bull Run First land engagement of the Civil War took place on July 21, 1861, at Manassas Junction, Virginia, at which surprised Union troops quickly retreated; one year later, on August 29–30, Confederates captured the federal supply depot and forced Union troops back to Washington.

Martin Van Buren (1782–1862) During President Jackson's first term, he served as secretary of state and minister to London. In 1836, Van Buren was elected president, and he inherited a financial crisis. He believed that the government should not continue to keep its deposits in state banks and set up an independent Treasury, which was approved by Congress after several years of political maneuvering.

General John Burgoyne (1722–1792) He was the commander of Britain's northern forces during the Revolutionary War. He and most of his troops surrendered to the Americans at the Battle of Saratoga.

burial mounds A funeral tradition, practiced in the Mississippi and Ohio Valleys by the Adena-Hopewell cultures, of erecting massive mounds of earth over graves, often in the designs of serpents and other animals.

burned-over district Area of western New York strongly influenced by the revivalist fervor of the Second Great Awakening; Disciples of Christ and Mormons are among the many sects that trace their roots to the phenomenon.

Aaron Burr (1756–1836) Even though he was Thomas Jefferson's vice president, he lost favor with Jefferson's Republican supporters. He sought to work with the Federalists and run as their candidate for the governor of New York. Alexander Hamilton opposed Burr's candidacy and his stinging remarks on the subject led to Burr challenging him to duel in which Hamilton was killed.

George H. W. Bush (1924–) He served as vice president during the Reagan administration and then won the presidential election of 1988. His presidency was marked by raised taxes in the face of the federal deficit, the creation of the Office of National Drug Control Policy, and military activity abroad, including the invasion of Panama and Operation Desert Storm in Kuwait. He lost the 1992 presidential election to Bill Clinton.

George W. Bush (1946–) In the 2000 presidential election, Texas governor George W. Bush won as the Republican nominee against Democratic nominee Vice President Al Gore. After the September 11 terrorist attacks, he launched his "war on terrorism." President Bush adopted the Bush Doctrine, and United States invaded Afghanistan and Iraq with unclear outcomes leaving the countries divided. In September 2008, the nation's economy nose-dived as a credit crunch spiraled into a global economic meltdown. Bush signed into law the bank bailout fund called Troubled Asset Relief Program (TARP), but the economy did not improve.

Bush v. Gore (2000) The close 2000 presidential election came down to Florida's decisive twenty-five electoral votes. The final tally in Florida gave Bush a slight lead, but it was so small that a recount was required by state law. While the votes were being recounted, a legal battle was being waged to stop the recount. Finally, the case, *Bush v. Gore*, was presented to the Supreme Court who ruled 5–4 to stop the recount and Bush was declared the winner.

Bush Doctrine National security policy launched in 2002 by which the Bush administration claimed the right to launch preemptive military attacks against perceived enemies, particularly outlaw nations or terrorist organizations believed to possess weapons of mass destruction.

buying (stock) on margin The investment practice of making a small down payment (the "margin") on a stock and borrowing the rest of the money needed for the purchase from a broker who held the stock as security against a down market. If the stock's value declined and the buyer failed to meet a margin call for more funds, the broker could sell the stock to cover his loan.

Cahokia The largest chiefdom and city of the Mississippian Indian culture located in present-day Illinois, and the site of a sophisticated farming settlement that supported up to 15,000 inhabitants.

John C. Calhoun (1782–1850) He served in both the House of Representatives and the Senate for South Carolina before becoming secretary of war under President Monroe and then John Quincy Adams's vice president. Though he started his political career as an advocate of a strong national government, he eventually believed that states' rights, limited central government, and the power of nullification were necessary to preserve the Union.

California gold rush (1849) A massive migration of gold hunters, mostly men, who transformed the economy of California after gold was discovered in the foothills of northern California.

Camp David Accords (1978) Peace agreement between Prime Minister Menachem Begin of Israel and President Anwar Sadat of Egypt, the first Arab head of state to officially recognize the state of Israel.

"Scarface" Al Capone (1899–1947) The most successful gangster of the Prohibition era whose Chicago-based criminal empire included bootlegging, prostitution, and gambling.

Andrew Carnegie (1835–1919) A steel magnate who believed that the general public benefited from big business even if these companies employed harsh business practices. This philosophy became deeply ingrained in the conventional wisdom of some Americans. After retiring, he devoted himself to philanthropy in hopes of promoting social welfare and world peace.

Carnegie Steel Company Corporation under the leadership of Andrew Carnegie that came to dominate the American steel industry.

Carolina colonies English proprietary colonies comprised of North and South Carolina, whose semitropical climate made them profitable centers of rice, timber, and tar production.

carpetbaggers Northern emigrants who participated in the Republican governments of the reconstructed South.

Jimmy Carter (1924–) Elected president in 1976, Jimmy Carter was an outsider to Washington. He created the departments of Energy and Education and signed into law several environmental initiatives. In 1978, he successfully brokered a peace agreement between Israel and Egypt called the Camp David Accords. However, his unwillingness to make deals with legislators caused other bills to be either gutted or stalled in Congress. His administration was plagued with a series of crises: a recession and increased inflation, a fuel shortage, the Soviet invasion of Afghanistan, and the overthrow of the Shah of Iran, leading to the Iran Hostage Crisis. Carter struggled to get the hostages released and was unable to do so until after he lost the 1980 election to Ronald Reagan. He was awarded the Nobel Peace Prize in 2002 for his efforts to further peace and democratic elections around the world.

Jacques Cartier (1491–1557) He led the first French effort to colonize North America and explored the Gulf of St. Lawrence, reaching as far as present day Montreal on the St. Lawrence River.

Fidel Castro (1926–) In 1959, his Communist regime came to power in Cuba after two years of guerrilla warfare against the dictator Fulgenico Batista. He enacted land redistribution programs and nationalized all foreign-owned property. The latter action as well as his political trials and summary executions damaged relations between Cuba and America. Castro was turned down when he asked for loans from the United States. However, he did receive aid from the Soviet Union.

Central Intelligence Agency (CIA) Intelligence-gathering government agency founded in 1947; under President Eisenhower's orders, secretly undermined elected governments deemed susceptible to communism.

Central Powers One of the two sides during the First World War, including Germany, Austria-Hungary, the Ottoman Empire (Turkey), and Bulgaria.

Carrie Chapman Catt (1859–1947) She was a leader of a new generation of activists in the women's suffrage movement who carried on the work started by Elizabeth Cady Stanton and Susan B. Anthony.

Cesar Chavez (1927–1993) He founded the United Farm Workers (UFW) in 1962 and worked to organize migrant farm workers. In 1965, the UFW joined Filipino farm workers striking against corporate grape farmers in California's San Joaquin Valley. In 1970, the strike and a consumer boycott on grapes compelled the farmers to formally recognize the UFW. As the result of Chavez's efforts, wages and working conditions improved for migrant workers. In 1975, the California state legislature passed a bill that required growers to bargain collectively with representatives of the farm workers.

child labor The practice of sending children to work in mines, mills, and factories, often in unsafe conditions; widespread among poor families in the late nineteenth century.

Chinese Exclusion Act (1882) Federal law that barred Chinese laborers from immigrating to America.

Church of Jesus Christ of Latter-day Saints / Mormons Founded in 1830 by Joseph Smith, the sect was a product of the intense revivalism of the burned-over district of New York; Smith's successor Brigham Young led 15,000 followers to Utah in 1847 to escape persecution.

Winston Churchill (1874–1965) The British prime minister who led the country during the Second World War. Along with Roosevelt and Stalin, he helped shape the postwar world at the Yalta Conference. He also coined the term "iron curtain," which he used in his famous "The Sinews of Peace" speech.

citizen-soldiers Part-time nonprofessional soldiers, mostly poor farmers or recent immigrants who had been indentured servants, who played an important role in the Revolutionary War.

"city machines" Local political party officials used these organizations to dispense patronage and favoritism amongst voters and businesses to ensure their loyal support to the political party.

Civil Rights Act of 1957 First federal civil rights law since Reconstruction; established the Civil Rights Commission and the Civil Rights Division of the Department of Justice.

Civil Rights Act of 1964 Legislation that outlawed discrimination in public accommodations and employment, passed at the urging of President Lyndon B. Johnson.

civil service reform An extended effort led by political reformers to end the patronage system; led to the Pendleton Act (1883), which called for government positions to be awarded based on merit rather than party loyalty.

Henry Clay (1777–1852) In the first half of the nineteenth century, he was the foremost spokesman for the American system. As Speaker of the House in the 1820s, he promoted economic nationalism, "market revolution," and the rapid development of western states and territories. A broker of compromise, he formulated the "second" Missouri Compromise and the Compromise of 1850. In 1824, Clay supported John Quincy Adams, who won the presidency and appointed Clay to secretary of state. Andrew Jackson claimed that Clay had entered into a "corrupt bargain" with Adams for his own selfish gains.

Clayton Anti-Trust Act (1914) Legislation that served to enhance the Sherman Anti-Trust Act (1890) by clarifying what constituted "monopolistic" activities and declaring that labor unions were not to be viewed as "monopolies in restraint of trade."

Bill Clinton (1946–) The governor of Arkansas won the 1992 presidential election against President George H. W. Bush. In his first term, he pushed through Congress a tax increase, an economic stimulus package, the adoption of the North America Free Trade Agreement, welfare reform, a raise in the minimum wage, and improved public access to health insurance. His administration also negotiated the Oslo Accord and the Dayton Accords. After his re-election in 1996, he was involved in two high-profile scandals: his investment in the fraudulent Whitewater Development Corporation (but no evidence was found of him being involved in any wrong-doing) and his sexual affair with a White House intern. His attempt to cover up the affair led to a vote in Congress on whether or not to begin an impeachment inquiry. The House of Representatives voted to impeach Clinton, but the Senate found him not guilty.

Hillary Rodham Clinton (1947–) In the 2008 presidential election, Senator Hillary Clinton, the spouse of former President Bill Clinton, initially was the front-runner for the Democratic nomination, which made her the first woman with a serious chance to win the presidency. However, Senator Barack Obama's Internet-based and grassroots-orientated campaign garnered him enough delegates to win the nomination. After Obama became president, she was appointed secretary of state. In 2016, Clinton ran again and won the Democratic nomination for the presidency. Although she won the popular vote, she lost the election to Donald Trump.

clipper ships Tall, slender, mid-nineteenth-century sailing ships that were favored over older merchant ships for their speed, but ultimately gave way to steamships because they lacked cargo space.

Coercive Acts (1774) Four parliamentary measures that required the colonies to pay for the Boston Tea Party's damages, imposed a military government, disallowed colonial trials of British soldiers, and forced the quartering of troops in private homes.

coffin ships Irish immigrants fleeing the potato famine had to endure a six-week journey across the Atlantic to reach America. During these voyages, thousands of passengers died of disease and starvation, which led to the ships being called "coffin ships."

cold war A state of political and ideological conflict between nations, primarily the United States, representing western-democratic nations, and the Soviet Union, representing Marxist-communist nations, marked by propaganda, threats, and other hostilities falling short of direct open warfare between the United States and Soviet Union.

Columbian Exchange The transfer of biological and social elements, such as plants, animals, people, diseases, and cultural practices, among Europe, the Americas, and Africa in the wake of Christopher Columbus's voyages to the "New World."

Christopher Columbus (1451–1506) The Italian sailor who persuaded King Ferdinad and Queen Isabella of Spain to fund his expedition across the Atlantic to discover a new trade route to Asia. Instead of arriving at China or Japan, he reached the Bahamas in 1492.

James B. Comey (1960–) FBI director fired by President Donald Trump in 2017.

Committee of Correspondence Group organized by Samuel Adams in retaliation for the *Gaspée* incident to address American grievances, assert American rights, and form a network of rebellion.

Committee on Public Information During the First World War, this committee produced war propaganda that conveyed the Allies' war aims to Americans as well as attempted to weaken the enemy's morale.

Committee to Re-elect the President (CREEP) During Nixon's presidency, his administration engaged in a number of immoral acts, such as attempting to steal information and falsely accusing political appointments of sexual improprieties. These acts were funded by money illegally collected through CREEP.

***Common Sense* (1776)** Popular pamphlet written by Thomas Paine attacking British principles of hereditary rule and monarchical government, and advocating a declaration of American independence.

Compromise of 1850 A package of five bills presented to the Congress by Henry Clay intended to avoid secession or civil war by reducing tensions between North and South over the status of slavery.

Compromise of 1877 Deal made by a special congressional commission on March 2, 1877, to resolve the disputed presidential election of 1876; Republican Rutherford B. Hayes, who had lost the popular vote, was declared the winner in exchange for the withdrawal of federal troops from the South, marking the end of Reconstruction.

Comstock Lode Mine in eastern Nevada acquired by Canadian fur trapper Henry Comstock that between 1860 and 1880 yielded almost $1 billion worth of gold and silver.

Conestoga wagons These large horse-drawn wagons were used to carry people or heavy freight long distances, including from the East to the western frontier settlements.

Congressional Reconstruction Phase of Reconstruction directed by Radical Republicans through the passage of three laws: the Military Reconstruction Act, the Command of the Army Act, and the Tenure of Office Act.

conquistadores Spanish term for "conquerors," applied to Spanish and Portuguese soldiers who conquered lands held by indigenous peoples in central and southern America as well as the current states of Texas, New Mexico, Arizona, and California.

consumer culture A society in which mass production and consumption of nationally advertised products comes to dictate much of social life and status.

containment U.S. cold war strategy that sought to prevent global Soviet expansion and influence through political, economic, and, if necessary, military pressure as a means of combating the spread of communism.

Continental army Army authorized by the Continental Congress, 1775–1784, to fight the British; commanded by General George Washington.

Contract with America A list of conservative promises in response to the supposed liberalism of the Clinton administration, that was drafted by Speaker of the House Newt Gingrich and other congressional Republicans as the GOP platform for the 1994 midterm elections. More a campaign tactic than a practical program, few of its proposed items ever became law.

contrabands Slaves who sought refuge in Union military camps or who lived in areas of the Confederacy under Union control.

Contras The Reagan administration ordered the CIA to train and supply guerrilla bands of anti-Communist Nicaraguans called Contras. They were fighting the Sandinista government that had recently come to power in Nicaragua. The State Department believed that the Sandinista government was supplying the leftist Salvadoran rebels with Soviet and Cuban arms. A cease-fire agreement between the Contras and Sandinistas was signed in 1988.

Calvin Coolidge (1872–1933) After President Harding's death, his vice president, Calvin Coolidge, assumed the presidency. Coolidge believed that the nation's welfare was tied to the success of Big Business, and he worked to end government regulation of business and industry as well as reduce taxes. In particular, he focused on the nation's industrial development.

Copperhead Democrats Democrats in northern states who opposed the Civil War and argued for an immediate peace settlement with the Confederates; Republicans labeled them "Copperheads," because they wore copper coins on their lapels.

Hernán Cortés (1485–1547) The Spanish conquistador who conquered the Aztec Empire and set the precedent for other plundering conquistadores.

General Charles Cornwallis (1738–1805) He was in charge of British troops in the South during the Revolutionary War. His surrender to George Washington at the Battle of Yorktown ended the Revolutionary War.

Corps of Discovery Meriwether Lewis and William Clark led this group of men on an expedition of the newly purchased Louisiana territory, which took them from Missouri to Oregon. As they traveled, they kept detailed journals and drew maps of the previously unexplored territory. Their reports attracted traders and trappers to the region and gave the United States a claim to the Oregon country by right of discovery and exploration.

corrupt bargain Scandal in which presidential candidate and Speaker of the House Henry Clay secured John Quincy Adams's victory over Andrew Jackson in the 1824 election, supposedly in exchange for Clay being named secretary of state.

cotton White fibers harvested from cotton plants, spun into yarn, and woven into textiles that made comfortable, easy-to-clean products, especially clothing; the most valuable cash crop driving the economy in the United States and Great Britain during the nineteenth century.

cotton gin Hand-operated machine invented by Eli Whitney in the late eighteenth century that quickly removed seeds from cotton bolls, enabling the mass production of cotton in nineteenth-century America.

Cotton Kingdom Cotton-producing region, relying predominantly on slave labor, that spanned from North Carolina west to Louisiana and reached as far north as southern Illinois.

counterculture Unorganized youth rebellion against mainstream institutions, values, and behavior that more often focused on cultural rather than political activism.

Court-packing scheme President Franklin D. Roosevelt's failed 1937 attempt to increase the number of U.S. Supreme Court justices from nine to fifteen in order to save his Second New Deal programs from constitutional challenges.

covenant theory A Puritan concept that believed true Christians could enter a voluntary union for the common worship of God. Taking the idea one step further, the union could also be used for the purposes of establishing governments.

crop-lien system Credit system used by sharecroppers and share tenants who pledged a portion ("share") of their future crop to local merchants or land owners in exchange for farming supplies and food.

"Cross of Gold" Speech In the 1896 election, the Democratic Party split over the issue of whether to use gold or silver to back American currency. Significant to this division was the pro-silver "Cross of Gold" speech that William Jennings Bryan delivered at the Democratic convention, which was so well received that Bryan won the nomination to be their presidential candidate. Disappointed pro-gold Democrats chose to walk out of the convention and nominate their own candidate.

Cuban missile crisis Thirteen-day U.S.-Soviet standoff in October 1962, sparked by the discovery of Soviet missile sites in Cuba; the crisis was the closest the world has come to nuclear war since 1945.

cult of domesticity A pervasive nineteenth-century ideology that urged women to celebrate their role as manager of the household and nurturer of the children.

George A. Custer (1839–1876) He was a reckless and glory-seeking Lieutenant Colonel of the U.S. Army who fought the Sioux Indians in the Great Sioux War. In 1876, he and his detachment of soldiers were entirely wiped out in the Battle of Little Bighorn.

Dartmouth College v. Woodward **(1819)** Supreme Court ruling that enlarged the definition of *contract* to put corporations beyond the reach of the states that chartered them.

Daughters of Liberty Colonial women who protested the British government's tax policies by boycotting British products, such as clothing, and who wove their own fabric, or "homespun."

Dawes Severalty Act (1887) Federal legislation that divided ancestral Native American lands among the heads of each Indian family in an attempt to "Americanize" Indians by forcing them to become farmers working individual plots of land.

D-day June 6, 1944, when an Allied amphibious assault landed on the Normandy coast and established a foothold in Europe from which Hitler's defenses could not recover.

Jefferson Davis (1808–1889) He was the president of the Confederacy during the Civil War. When the Confederacy's defeat seemed invitable in early 1865, he refused to surrender. Union forces captured him in May of that year.

Bartolomé de Las Casas (1484–1566) A Catholic missionary who renounced the Spanish practice of coercively converting Indians and advocated their better treatment. In 1552, he wrote *A Brief Relation of the Destruction of the Indies*, which described the Spanish's cruel treatment of the Indians.

death rate Proportion of deaths per 1,000 of the total population; also called *mortality rate*.

Eugene V. Debs (1855–1926) Founder of the American Railway Union, which he organized against the Pullman Palace Car Company during the Pullman strike. Later he organized the Social Democratic party, which eventually became the Socialist Party of America. In the 1912 presidential election, he ran as the Socialist party's candidate and received more than 900,000 votes.

Declaration of Independence Formal statement, principally drafted by Thomas Jefferson and adopted by the Second Continental Congress on July 4, 1776, that officially announced the thirteen colonies' break with Great Britain.

Declaration of Rights and Sentiments Document based on the Declaration of Independence that called for gender equality, written primarily by Elizabeth Cady Stanton and signed by Seneca Falls Convention delegates in 1848.

Declaratory Act Following the repeal of the Stamp Act in 1766, Parliament passed this act which asserted Parliament's full power to make laws binding the colonies "in all cases whatsoever."

Deism Enlightenment thought applied to religion, emphasizing reason, morality, and natural law rather than scriptural authority or an ever-present God intervening in human life.

détente Period of improving relations between the United States and Communist nations, particularly China and the Soviet Union, during the Nixon administration.

George Dewey (1837–1917) On April 30, 1898, Commodore George Dewey's small U.S. naval squadron defeated the Spanish warships in Manila Bay in the Philippines. This quick victory aroused expansionist fever in the United States.

John Dewey (1859–1952) He is an important philosopher of pragmatism. However, he preferred to use the term *instrumentalism*, because he saw ideas as instruments of action.

Ngo Dinh Diem (1901–1963) Following the Geneva Accords, the French, with the support of America, forced the Vietnamese emperor to accept Dinh Diem as the new premier of South Vietnam. President Eisenhower sent advisors to train Diem's police and army. In return, the United States expected Diem to enact democratic reforms and distribute land to the peasants. Instead, he suppressed his political opponents, did little or no land distribution, and let corruption grow. In 1956, he refused to participate in elections to reunify Vietnam. Eventually, he ousted the emperor and declared himself president.

Distribution Act (1836) Law requiring the distribution of the federal budget surplus to the states, creating chaos among state banks that had become dependent on such federal funds.

Dorothea Lynde Dix (1802–1887) She was an important figure in increasing the public's awareness of the plight of the mentally ill. After a two-year investigation of the treatment of the mentally ill in Massachusetts, she presented her findings and won the support of leading reformers. She eventually convinced twenty states to reform their treatment of the mentally ill.

Dixiecrats Breakaway faction of southern Democrats who defected from the national Democratic party in 1948 to protest the party's increased support for civil rights and to nominate their own segregationist candidates for elective office.

dollar diplomacy Practice advocated by President Theodore Roosevelt in which the U.S. government fostered American investments in less developed nations and then used U.S. military force to protect those investments

Donner party Forty-seven surviving members of a group of migrants to California were forced to resort to cannibalism to survive a brutal winter trapped in the Sierra Nevadas, 1846–1847; highest death toll of any group traveling the Overland Trail.

Stephen A. Douglas (1812–1861) As a senator from Illinois, he authored the Kansas-Nebraska Act. Running for senatorial reelection in 1858, he engaged Abraham Lincoln in a series of public debates about slavery in the territories. Even though Douglas won the election, the debates gave Lincoln a national reputation.

Frederick Douglass (1818–1895) He escaped from slavery and become an eloquent speaker and writer against the institution. In 1845, he published his autobiography entitled *Narrative of the Life of Frederick Douglass* and two years later he founded an abolitionist newspaper for blacks called the *North Star*.

dot-coms In the late 1990s, the stock market soared to new heights and defied the predictions of experts that the economy could not sustain such a performance. Much of the economic success was based on dot-com enterprises, which were firms specializing in computers, software, telecommunications, and the internet. However, many of the companies' stock market values were driven higher and higher by speculation instead of financial success. Eventually the stock market bubble burst.

***Dred Scott v. Sandford* (1857)** U.S. Supreme Court ruling that slaves were not U.S. citizens and therefore could not sue for their freedom and that Congress could not prohibit slavery in the western territories.

W. E. B. Du Bois (1868–1963) He criticized Booker T. Washington's views on civil rights as being accommodationist. He advocated "ceaseless agitation" for civil rights and the immediate end to segregation and an enforcement of laws to protect civil rights and equality. He promoted an education for African Americans that would nurture bold leaders who were willing to challenge discrimination in politics.

John Foster Dulles (1888–1959) As President Eisenhower's secretary of state, he institutionalized the policy of containment and introduced the strategy of deterrence.

He believed in using brinkmanship to halt the spread of communism. He attempted to employ it in Indochina, which led to the United States' involvement in Vietnam.

Dust Bowl Vast area of the Midwest where windstorms blew away millions of tons of top-soil from parched farmland after a long drought in the 1930s, causing great social distress and a massive migration of farm families.

Eastern Woodlands Peoples Various Native American peoples, particularly the Algonquian, Iroquoian, and Muskogean regional groups, who once dominated the Atlantic seaboard from Maine to Louisiana.

Peggy Eaton (1796–1879) The wife of John Eaton, President Jackson's secretary of war, was the daughter of a tavern owner with an unsavory past. Supposedly her first husband had committed suicide after learning that she was having an affair with John Eaton. The wives of members of Jackson's cabinet snubbed her because of her lowly origins and past, resulting in a scandal known as the Eaton Affair.

Economic Opportunity Act (1964) Key legislation in President Johnson's "War on Poverty" which created the Office of Economic Opportunity and programs like Head Start and work-study.

Jonathan Edwards (1703–1758) New England Congregationalist minister who began a religious revival in his Northampton church and was an important figure in the Great Awakening.

election of 1800 Presidential election between Thomas Jefferson and John Adams; resulted in the first Democratic-Republican party victory after the Federalist administrations of George Washington and John Adams.

election campaign of 1828 Bitter presidential contest between Democrat Andrew Jackson and National Republican John Quincy Adams (running for reelection), resulting in Jackson's victory.

election of 1864 Abraham Lincoln's successful reelection campaign, capitalizing on Union military successes in Georgia, to defeat Democratic opponent, former general George B. McClellan, who ran on a peace platform.

election of 1912 The presidential election of 1912 featured four candidates: Wilson, Taft, Roosevelt, and Debs. Each candidate believed in the basic assumptions of progressive politics, but each had a different view on how progressive ideals should be implemented through policy. In the end, Taft and Roosevelt split the Republican party votes and Wilson emerged as the winner.

Queen Elizabeth I of England (1533–1603) The protestant daughter of Henry VIII, she was Queen of England from 1558–1603 and played a major role in the Protestant Reformation. During her long reign, the doctrines and services of the Church of England were defined and the Spanish Armada was defeated.

General Dwight D. Eisenhower (1890–1969) During the Second World War, he commanded the Allied Forces landing in Africa and was the supreme Allied commander as well as planner for Operation Overlord. In 1952, he was elected president on his popularity as a war hero and his promises to clean up Washington. His administration sought to cut the nation's domestic programs and budget, ended the fighting in Korea, and institutionalized the policies of containment and deterrence. He established the Eisenhower doctrine, which promised to aid any nation against aggression by a Communist nation.

Ellis Island Reception center in New York Harbor through which most European immigrants to America were processed from 1892 to 1954.

Emancipation Proclamation (1862) Military order issued by President Abraham Lincoln that freed slaves in areas still controlled by the Confederacy but did not free the 500,000 slaves in the four border states that remained in the Union.

Embargo Act (1807) A law promoted by President Thomas Jefferson prohibiting American ships from leaving for foreign ports, in order to safeguard them from British and French attacks. This ban on American exports proved disastrous to the U.S. economy.

Ralph Waldo Emerson (1803–1882) As a leader of the transcendentalist movement, he wrote poems, essays, and speeches that discussed the sacredness of nature, optimism, self-reliance, and the unlimited potential of the individual. He wanted to transcend the limitations of inherited conventions and rationalism to reach the inner recesses of the self.

encomienda A land-grant system under which Spanish army officers (*conquistadores*) were awarded large parcels of land taken from Native Americans.

Enlightenment A revolution in thought begun in Europe in the seventeenth century that emphasized reason and science over the authority and myths of traditional religion.

enumerated goods According to the Navigation Act, these particular goods, like tobacco or cotton, could only be shipped to England or other English colonies.

Environmental Protection Agency (EPA) (1970) Federal environmental agency created by Nixon to appease the demands of congressional Democrats for a federal environmental watchdog agency.

Erie Canal (1825) Most important and profitable of the barge canals of the 1820s and 1830s; stretched from Buffalo to Albany, New York, connecting the Great Lakes to the East Coast and making New York City the nation's largest port.

ethnic cleansing The systematic removal of an ethnic group from a territory through violence or intimidation in order to create a homogenous society; the term was popularized by the Yugoslav policy brutally targeting Albanian Muslims in Kosovo.

Exodusters African Americans who migrated west from the South in search of a haven from racism and poverty after the collapse of Radical Republican rule.

Fair Deal (1949) President Truman's proposals to build upon the New Deal with national health insurance, the repeal of the Taft-Hartley Act, new civil rights legislation, and other initiatives; most were rejected by the Republican-controlled Congress.

Fair Employment Practices Commission Created in 1941 by executive order, the FEPC sought to eliminate racial discrimination in jobs; it possessed little power but represented a step toward civil rights for African Americans.

falling-domino theory Theory that if one country fell to communism, its neighboring countries would follow suit.

Farmers' Alliances Like the Granger movement, these organizations sought to address the issues of small farming communities; however Alliances emphasized more political action and called for the creation of a Third Party to advocate their concerns.

fascism A radical form of totalitarian government that emerged in Italy and Germany in the 1920s in which a dictator uses propaganda and brute force to seize control of all aspects of national life.

Federal-Aid Highway Act (1956) Largest federal project in U.S. history that created a national network of interstate highways and was the largest federal project in history.

Federal Deposit Insurance Corporation (1933) Independent government agency, established to prevent bank panics, which guarantees the safety of deposits in citizens' savings accounts.

Federal Reserve Act (1913) Legislation passed by Congress to create a new national banking system in order to regulate the nation's currency supply and ensure the stability and integrity of member banks who made up the Federal Reserve System across the nation.

Federal Trade Commission (1914) Independent agency created by the Wilson administration that replaced the Bureau of Corporations as an even more powerful tool to combat unfair trade practices and monopolies.

Federal Writers' Project During the Great Depression, this project provided writers, such as Ralph Ellison, Richard Wright, and Saul Bellow, with work, which gave them employment and a chance to develop as artists.

federalism Concept of dividing governmental authority between the national government and the states.

The Federalist Papers Collection of eighty-five essays, published widely in newspapers in 1787 and 1788, written by Alexander Hamilton, James Madison, and John Jay in support of adopting the proposed U.S. Constitution.

Federalists Proponents of a centralized federal system and the ratification of the Constitution. Most Federalists were relatively young, educated men who supported a broad interpretation of the Constitution whenever national interest dictated such flexibility. Notable Federalists included Alexander Hamilton and John Jay.

Geraldine Ferraro (1935–) In the 1984 presidential election, Democratic nominee, Walter Mondale, chose her as his running mate. As a member of the U.S. House of Representatives from New York, she was the first woman to be a vice-presidential nominee for a major political party. However, she was placed on the defensive because of her husband's complicated business dealings.

field hands Slaves who toiled in the cotton or cane fields in organized work gangs.

Fifteenth Amendment (1870) This amendment forbids states to deny any person the right to vote on grounds of "race, color or pervious condition of servitude." Former Confederate states were required to ratify this amendment before they could be readmitted to the Union.

"final solution" The Nazi party's systematic murder of some 6 million Jews along with more than a million other people including, but not limited to, gypsies, homosexuals, and handicap individuals.

First New Deal (1933–1935) Franklin D. Roosevelt's ambitious first-term cluster of economic and social programs designed to combat the Great Depression.

First Red Scare (1919–1920) Outbreak of anti-Communist hysteria that included the arrest without warrants of thousands of suspected radicals, most of whom (mainly Russian immigrants) were deported.

flappers Young women of the 1920s whose rebellion against prewar standards of femininity included wearing shorter dresses, bobbing their hair, dancing to jazz music, driving cars, smoking cigarettes, and indulging in illegal drinking and gambling.

Food Administration After America's entry into World War I, the economy of the home front needed to be reorganized to provide the most efficient means of conducting the war. The Food Administration was a part of this effort. Under the leadership of Herbert Hoover, the organization sought to increase agricultural production while reducing civilian consumption of foodstuffs.

Force Bill (1833) Legislation, sparked by the Nullification Crisis in South Carolina, that authorized the president's use of the army to compel states to comply with federal law.

Gerald Ford (1913–2006) He was appointed to the vice presidency under President Nixon after the resignation of Spiro Agnew, and assumed the presidency after President Nixon's resignation. He resisted congressional pressure to both reduce taxes and increase federal spending, which sent the American economy into the deepest recession since the Great Depression. Ford retained Kissinger as his secretary of state and continued Nixon's foreign policy goals. He was heavily criticized following the collapse of South Vietnam.

Fort Laramie Treaty (1851) Restricted the Plains Indians from using the Overland Trail and permitted the building of government forts.

Fort Necessity After attacking a group of French soldiers, George Washington constructed and took shelter in this fort from vengeful French troops. Washington eventually surrendered to them after a day-long battle. This conflict was a significant event in igniting the French and Indian War.

Fort Sumter First battle of the Civil War, in which the federal fort in Charleston (South Carolina) Harbor was captured by the Confederates on April 14, 1861, after two days of shelling.

"forty-niners" Speculators who went to northern California following the discovery of gold in 1848; the first of several years of large-scale migration was 1849.

Fourteen Points (1918) President Woodrow Wilson's proposed plan for the peace agreement after the First World War that included the creation of a "league of nations" intended to keep the peace.

Fourteenth Amendment (1866) Guaranteed rights of citizenship to former slaves, in words similar to those of the Civil Rights Act of 1866.

Franciscan Missions In 1769, Franciscan missioners accompanied Spanish soldiers to California and over the next fifty years established a chain of missions from San Diego to San Francisco. At these missions, friars sought to convert Indians to Catholicism and make them members of the Spanish empire. The friars stripped the Indians of their native heritage and used soldiers to enforce their will.

Benjamin Franklin (1706–1790) A Boston-born American, who epitomized the Enlightenment for many Americans and Europeans, Franklin's wide range of interests led him to become a publisher, inventor, and statesman. As the latter, he contributed to the writing of the Declaration of Independence, served as the minister to France during the Revolutionary War, and was a delegate to the Constitutional Convention.

Free-Soil party A political coalition created in 1848 that opposed the expansion of slavery into the new western territories.

Freedmen's Bureau Reconstruction agency established in 1865 to protect the legal rights of former slaves and to assist with their education, jobs, health care, and landowning.

Freedom Riders Activists who, beginning in 1961, traveled by bus through the South to test federal court rulings that banned segregation on buses and trains.

John C. Frémont "the Pathfinder" (1813–1890) He was an explorer and surveyor who helped inspire Americans living in California to rebel against the Mexican government and declare independence.

French and Indian War (Seven Years' War) (1756–1763) The last—and the most important—of four colonial wars fought between England and France for control of North America east of the Mississippi River.

French Revolution Revolutionary movement beginning in 1789 that overthrew the monarchy and transformed France into an unstable republic before Napoleon Bonaparte assumed power in 1799.

Sigmund Freud (1865–1939) He was the founder of psychoanalysis, which suggested that human behavior was motivated by unconscious and irrational forces. By the 1920s, his ideas were being discussed more openly in America.

frontier revivals Religious revival movement within the Second Great Awakening, that took place in frontier churches in western territories and states in the early nineteenth century.

Fugitive Slave Act (1850) Part of the Compromise of 1850, a provision that authorized federal officials to help capture and then return escaped slaves to their owners without trials.

fundamentalism Anti-modernist Protestant movement started in the early twentieth century that proclaimed the literal truth of the Bible; the name came from *The Fundamentals*, published by conservative leaders.

William Lloyd Garrison (1805–1879) In 1831, he started the anti-slavery newspaper *Liberator* and helped start the New England Anti-Slavery Society. Two years later, he assisted Arthur and Lewis Tappan in the founding of the American Anti-Slavery Society. He and his followers believed that America had been thoroughly corrupted and needed a wide range of reforms, embracing abolition, temperance, pacifism, and women's rights.

Marcus Garvey (1887–1940) He was the leading spokesman for Negro Nationalism, which exalted blackness, black cultural expression, and black exclusiveness. He called upon African Americans to liberate themselves from the surrounding white culture and create their own businesses, cultural centers, and newspapers. He was also the founder of the Universal Negro Improvement Association.

Citizen Genet (1763–1834) As the ambassador to the United States from the new French Republic, he engaged American privateers to attack British ships and conspired with frontiersmen and land speculators to organize an attack on Spanish Florida and Louisiana. His actions and the French radicals excessive actions against their enemies in the new French Republic caused the French Revolution to lose support among Americans.

Geneva Accords In 1954, the Geneva Accords were signed, which ended French colonial rule in Indochina. The agreement created the independent nations of Laos and Cambodia and divided Vietnam along the 17th parallel until an election in 1956 would reunify the country.

Battle of Gettysburg (1863) A monumental three-day battle in southern Pennsylvania, widely considered a turning point in the war, in which Union forces successfully countered a second Confederate invasion of the North.

Ghost Dance movement A spiritual and political movement among Native Americans whose followers performed a ceremonial "ghost dance" intended to connect the living with the dead and make the Indians bulletproof in battles to restore their homelands.

GI Bill of Rights (1944) Provided unemployment, education, and financial benefits for World War II veterans to ease their transition back to the civilian world.

***Gibbons v. Ogden* (1824)** Supreme Court case that gave the federal government the power to regulate interstate commerce.

Newt Gingrich (1943–) He led the Republican insurgency in Congress in the mid 1990s through mobilizing religious and social conservatives. Along with other Republican congressmen, he created the Contract with America, which was a ten-point anti-big government program. However, the program fizzled out after many of its bills were not passed by Congress.

Gilded Age (1860–1896) An era of dramatic industrial and urban growth characterized by widespread political corruption and loose government oversight of corporations.

The Gilded Age Mark Twain and Charles Dudley Warner's 1873 novel, the title of which became the popular name for the period from the end of the Civil War to the turn of the century.

glasnost Russian term for "openness"; applied to the loosening of censorship in the Soviet Union under Mikhail Gorbachev.

globalization An important, and controversial, transformation of the world economy whereby the Internet helped revolutionize global commerce by creating an international marketplace for goods and services. Led by the growing number of multinational companies and the Americanization of many foreign consumer cultures, with companies like McDonald's and Starbucks appearing in all of the major cities of the world.

Glorious Revolution (1688) Successful coup, instigated by a group of English aristocrats, which overthrew King James II and instated William of Orange and Mary, his English wife, to the British throne.

Barry Goldwater (1909–1998) A leader of the Republican right whose book, *The Conscience of a Conservative*, was highly influential to that segment of the party. He proposed eliminating the income tax and overhauling Social Security. In 1964, he ran as the Republican presidential candidate and lost to President Johnson. He campaigned against Johnson's war on poverty, the tradition of New Deal, the nuclear test ban and the Civil Rights Act of 1964 and advocated the wholesale bombing of North Vietnam.

Samuel Gompers (1850–1924) He served as the president of the American Federation of Labor from its inception until his death. He focused on achieving concrete economic gains such as higher wages, shorter hours, and better working conditions.

"good neighbor" policy Proclaimed by President Franklin D. Roosevelt in his first inaugural address in 1933, it sought improved diplomatic relations between the United States and its Latin American neighbors.

Mikhail Gorbachev (1931–) In the late 1980s, Soviet leader Mikhail Gorbachev attempted to reform the Soviet Union through his programs of *perestroika* and *glasnost* and pursued a renewal of détente with America, signing new arms-control agreements with President Reagan. Gorbachev allowed the velvet revolutions of Eastern Europe to occur without outside interference. Eventually the political, social, and economic upheaval he had unleashed would lead to the break-up of the Soviet Union.

Albert Gore Jr. (1948–) He served as a senator of Tennessee and then as President Clinton's vice president. In the 2000 presidential election, he was the Democratic candidate against Governor George W. Bush. The close election came down to Florida's electoral votes. While the votes were being recounted as required by state law, a legal battle was being waged to stop the recount. Finally, the case, *Bush v. Gore*, was presented to the Supreme Court who ruled 5–4 to stop the recount and Bush was declared the winner.

Jay Gould (1836–1892) As one of the biggest railroad robber barons, he was infamous for buying rundown railroads, making cosmetic improvements and then reselling them for a profit. He used corporate funds for personal investments and to bribe politicians and judges.

gradualism This strategy for ending slavery involved promoting the banning of slavery in the new western territories and encouraging the release of slaves from slavery. Supporters of this method believed that it would bring about the gradual end of slavery.

Granger movement Began by offering social and educational activities for isolated farmers and their families and later started to promote "cooperatives" where farmers could join together to buy, store, and sell their crops to avoid the high fees charged by brokers and other middle-men.

Ulysses S. Grant (1822–1885) After distinguishing himself in the western theater of the Civil War, he was appointed general in chief of the Union army in 1864. Afterward, he defeated General Robert E. Lee through a policy of aggressive attrition. Lee surrendered to Grant on April 9th, 1865 at the Appomattox Court House. His presidential tenure suffered from scandals and fiscal problems, including the debate on whether or not greenbacks, paper money, should be removed from circulation.

Great Awakening Fervent religious revival movement that swept the thirteen colonies from the 1720s through the 1740s.

Great Compromise (Connecticut Compromise) Mediated the differences between the New Jersey and Virginia delegations to the Constitutional Convention by providing for a bicameral legislature, the upper house of which would have equal representation and the lower house of which would be apportioned by population.

Great Depression (1929–1941) Worst economic downturn in American history; it was spurred by the stock market crash in the fall of 1929 and lasted until the Second World War.

Great Migration Mass exodus of African Americans from the rural South to the Northeast and Midwest during and after the First World War.

Great Railroad Strike of 1877 A series of demonstrations, some violent, held nationwide in support of striking railroad workers in Martinsburg, West Virginia, who refused to work due to wage cuts.

Great Recession (2007–2009) Massive, prolonged economic downturn sparked by the collapse of the housing market and the financial institutions holding unpaid mortgages; it lasted from December 2007 to January 2009 and resulted in 9 million Americans losing their jobs.

Great Sioux War Conflict between Sioux and Cheyenne Indians and federal troops over lands in the Dakotas in the mid-1870s.

Great Society Term coined by President Lyndon B. Johnson in his 1965 State of the Union address, in which he proposed legislation to address problems of voting rights, poverty, diseases, education, immigration, and the environment.

Horace Greeley (1811–1872) In reaction to Radical Reconstruction and corruption in President Ulysses S. Grant's administration, a group of Republicans broke from the party to form the Liberal Republicans. In 1872, the Liberal Republicans chose Horace Greeley as their presidential candidate who ran on a platform of favoring civil service reform and condemning the Republican's Reconstruction policy.

greenbacks Paper money issued during the Civil War. After the war ended, a debate emerged on whether or not to remove the paper currency from circulation and revert back to hard-money currency (gold coins). Opponents of hard-money feared that eliminating the greenbacks would shrink the money supply, which would lower crop prices and make it more difficult to repay long-term debts. President Ulysses S. Grant, as well as hard-currency advocates, believed that gold coins were morally preferable to paper currency.

Greenback party Formed in 1876 in reaction to economic depression, the party favored issuance of unsecured paper money to help farmers repay debts; the movement for free coinage of silver took the place of the greenback movement by the 1880s.

General Nathanael Greene (1742–1786) He was appointed by Congress to command the American army fighting in the South during the Revolutionary War. Using his patience and his skills of managing men, saving supplies, and avoiding needless risks, he waged a successful war of attrition against the British.

Sarah Grimké (1792–1873) and **Angelina Grimké (1805–1879)** These two sisters gave anti-slavery speeches to crowds of mixed gender that caused some people to condemn them for engaging in unfeminine activities. In 1840, William Lloyd Garrison convinced the Anti-Slavery Society to allow women equal participation in the organization.

Half-Way Covenant Allowed baptized children of church members to be admitted to a "halfway" membership in the church and secure baptism for their own children in turn, but allowed them neither a vote in the church, nor communion.

Alexander Hamilton (1755–1804) His belief in a strong federal government led him to become a leader of the Federalists. As the first secretary of the Treasury, he laid the foundation for American capitalism through his creation of a federal budget, funded debt, a federal tax system, a national bank, a customs service, and a coast guard. His "Reports on Public Credit" and "Reports on Manufactures" outlined his vision for economic development and government finances. He died in a duel against Aaron Burr.

Alexander Hamilton's economic reforms Various measures designed to strengthen the nation's economy and generate federal revenue through the promotion of new industries, the adoption of new tax policies, the payment of war debts, and the establishment of a national bank.

Warren G. Harding (1865–1923) In the 1920 presidential election, he was the Republican nominee who promised Americans a "return to normalcy." Once in office, Harding's administration dismantled many of the social and economic components of progressivism and pursued a pro-business agenda. Harding appointed four pro-business Supreme Court Justices, cut taxes, increased tariffs, and promoted a lenient attitude towards regulation of corporations. However, he did speak out against racism and ended the exclusion of African Americans from federal positions.

Harlem Renaissance The nation's first self-conscious black literary and artistic movement; it was centered in New York City's Harlem district, which had a largely black population in the wake of the Great Migration from the South.

Hartford Convention A series of secret meetings in December 1814 and January 1815 at which New England Federalists protested American involvement in the War of 1812 and discussed several constitutional amendments, including limiting each president to one term, designed to weaken the dominant Republican party.

Haymarket riot (1886) Violent uprising in Haymarket Square, Chicago, where police clashed with labor demonstrators in the aftermath of a bombing.

headright A land-grant policy that promised fifty acres to any colonist who could afford passage to Virginia, as well as fifty more for any accompanying servants. The headright policy was eventually expanded to include any colonists—and was also adopted in other colonies.

Patrick Henry (1736–1799) He inspired the Virginia Resolves, which declared that Englishmen could only be taxed by their elected representatives. In March of 1775, he met with other colonial leaders to discuss the goals of the upcoming Continental Congress and famously declared "Give me liberty or give me death." During the ratification process of the U.S. Constitution, he became one of the leaders of the anti-federalists.

Hessians German mercenary soldiers who are paid by the royal government to fight alongside the British army.

Hiroshima (1945) Japanese port city that was the first target of the newly developed atomic bomb on August 6, 1945. Most of the city was destroyed.

Alger Hiss (1904–1996) During the second Red Scare he had served in several government departments and was accused of being a spy for the Soviet Union and was convicted of lying about espionage. The case was politically damaging to the Truman administration because the president called the charges against Hiss a "red herring."

Adolph Hitler (1889–1945) The leader of the Nazis who advocated a violent anti-Semitic, anti-Marxist, pan-German ideology. He started World War II in Europe and orchestrated the systematic murder of some 6 million Jews along with more than a million others.

HIV/AIDS Human immunodeficiency virus (HIV) transmitted via the bodily fluids of infected persons to cause acquired immunodeficiency syndrome (AIDS), an often-fatal disease of the immune system when it appeared in the 1980s.

holding company A corporation established to own and manage other companies' stock rather than to produce goods and services itself.

Holocaust Systematic racist attempt by the Nazis to exterminate all Jews in Europe, resulting in the murder of more than 6 million Jews and more than 5 million other "undesirables."

Homestead Act (1862) Legislation granting "homesteads" of 160 acres of government-owned land to settlers who agreed to work the land for at least five years.

Homestead Steel strike (1892) Labor conflict at the Homestead steel mill near Pittsburgh, Pennsylvania, culminating in a battle between strikers and private security agents hired by the factory's management.

Herbert Hoover (1874–1964) Prior to becoming president, Hoover served as the secretary of commerce in both the Harding and Coolidge administrations. As president during the Great Depression, he believed that the nation's business structure was sound and sought to revive the economy through boosting the nation's confidence. He also tried to restart the economy with government constructions projects, lower taxes and new federal loan programs, but nothing worked.

horizontal integration The process by which a corporation acquires or merges with its competitors.

horse A tall, four-legged mammal (*Equus caballus*), domesticated and bred since prehistoric times for carrying riders and pulling heavy loads. The Spanish introduced horses to the Americas, eventually transforming many Native American cultures.

House Committee on Un-American Activities (HUAC) Committee of the U.S. House of Representatives formed in 1938; it was originally tasked with investigating Nazi subversion during the Second World War and later shifted its focus to rooting out Communists in the government and the motion-picture industry.

Sam Houston (1793–1863) During Texas's fight for independence from Mexico, Sam Houston was the commander in chief of the Texas forces, and he led the attack that captured General Antonio López de Santa Anna. After Texas gained its independence, he was named its first president.

How the Other Half Lives In this book, early muckraking journalist Jacob Riis exposed the slum conditions in New York City.

General William Howe (1729–1814) As the commander of the British army in the Revolutionary War, he seized New York City from Washington's army, but failed to capture it. He missed several more opportunities to quickly end the rebellion, and he resigned his command after the British defeat at Saratoga.

Saddam Hussein (1937–2006) The former dictator of Iraq who became the head of state in 1979. In 1980, he invaded Iran and started the eight-year-long Iran-Iraq War. In 1990, he invaded Kuwait, which caused the Gulf War of 1991. In 2003, he was overthrown and captured when the United States invaded. He was sentenced to death by hanging in 2006.

Anne Hutchinson (1591–1643) The articulate, strong-willed, and intelligent wife of a prominent Boston merchant, who espoused her belief in direct divine revelation.

She quarreled with Puritan leaders over her beliefs; and they banished her from the colony.

Immigration Act of 1924 Federal legislation intended to favor northern and western European immigrants over those from southern and eastern Europe by restricting the number of immigrants from any one European country to 2 percent of the total number of immigrants per year, with an overall limit of slightly over 150,000 new arrivals per year.

Immigration and Nationality Services Act of 1965 (Hart-Cellar Act) Legislation that abolished discriminatory quotas based upon immigrants' national origin and treated all nationalities and races equally.

impeachment A formal misconduct charge made against a public official, usually the president, by the House of Representatives. The official's removal from office requires a separate process in the form of a trial facilitated by the Senate. A guilty verdict from two-thirds of the participating senators leads to a conviction.

imperialism The use of diplomatic or military force to extend a nation's power and enhance its economic interests, often by acquiring territory or colonies and justifying such behavior with assumptions of racial superiority.

indentured servants Settlers who consented to work for a defined period of labor (often four to seven years) in exchange for having their passage to the New World paid by their "master."

Independent Treasury Act (1840) System created by President Martin Van Buren and approved by Congress in 1840 whereby the federal government moved its funds from favored state banks to the U.S. Treasury, whose financial transactions could only be in gold or silver coins of paper currency backed by gold or silver.

"Indian New Deal" This phrase refers to the reforms implemented for Native Americans during the New Deal era. John Collier, the commissioner of the Bureau of Indian Affairs (BIA), increased the access Native Americans had to relief programs and employed more Native Americans at the BIA. He worked to pass the Indian Reorganization Act. However, the version of the act passed by Congress was a much-diluted version of Collier's original proposal and did not greatly improve the lives of Native Americans.

Indian Removal Act (1830) Law permitting the forced relocation of Indians to federal lands west of the Mississippi River in exchange for the land they occupied in the East and South.

Indian wars Bloody conflicts between U.S. soldiers and Native Americans that raged in the West from the early 1860s to the late 1870s, sparked by American settlers moving into ancestral Indian lands.

Indochina This area of Southeast Asia consists of Laos, Cambodia, and Vietnam and was once controlled by France as a colony. After the Viet Minh defeated the French, the Geneva Accords were signed, which ended French colonial rule. The agreement created the independent nations of Laos and Cambodia and divided Vietnam along the 17th parallel until an election would reunify the country. Fearing a Communist take over, the United States government began intervening in the region during the Truman administration, which led to President Johnson's full-scale military involvement in Vietnam.

industrialization Major shift in the nineteenth century from handmade manufacturing to mass production in mills and factories using water-, coal-, and steam-powered machinery.

Industrial Revolution Major shift in the nineteenth century from hand-made manufacturing to mass production in mills and factories using water-, coal-, and steam-powered machinery.

industrial war A new concept of war enabled by industrialization that developed from the early 1800s through the Atomic Age. New technologies, including automatic weaponry, forms of transportation like the railroad and airplane, and communication technologies such as the telegraph and telephone, enabled nations to equip large, mass-conscripted armies with chemical and automatic weapons to decimate opposing armies in a "total war."

Industrial Workers of the World (IWW) A radical union organized in Chicago in 1905, nicknamed the Wobblies; its opposition to World War I led to its destruction by the federal government under the Espionage Act.

infectious diseases Also called contagious diseases, illnesses that can pass from one person to another by way of invasive biological organisms able to reproduce in the bodily tissues of their hosts. Europeans unwittingly brought many such diseases to the Americas, devastating the Native American peoples.

The Influence of Sea Power upon History, 1660–1783 **(1890)** Historical work in which Rear Admiral Alfred Thayer Mahan argues that a nation's greatness and prosperity comes from the power of its navy; the book helped bolster imperialist sentiment in the United States in the late nineteenth century.

Intermediate-Range Nuclear Forces (INF) Treaty (1987) Agreement signed by U.S. president Ronald Reagan and Soviet premier Mikhail Gorbachev to eliminate the deployment of intermediate-range missiles with nuclear warheads.

internal improvements Construction of roads, bridges, canals, harbors, and other infrastructural projects intended to facilitate the flow of goods and people.

internationalists Prior to the United States' entry in World War II, internationalists believed that America's national security depended on aiding Britain in its struggle against Germany.

Interstate Commerce Commission (ICC) (1887) An independent federal agency established to oversee businesses engaged in interstate trade, especially railroads, but whose regulatory power was limited when tested in the courts.

interstate highway system In the late 1950s, construction began on a national network of interstate superhighways for the purpose of commerce and defense. The interstate highways would enable the rapid movement of military convoys and the evacuation of cities after a nuclear attack.

Iran-Contra affair (1987) Reagan administration scandal over the secret, unlawful U.S. sale of arms to Iran in partial exchange for the release of hostages in Lebanon; the arms money in turn was used illegally to aid Nicaraguan right-wing insurgents, the Contras.

Iranian hostage crisis (1979) Storming of the U.S. embassy in Tehran by Iranian revolutionaries, who held fifty-two Americans hostage for 444 days, despite President Carter's appeals for their release as well as a botched rescue attempt.

Irish Potato Famine In 1845, an epidemic of potato rot brought a famine to rural Ireland that killed over 1 million peasants and instigated a huge increase in the number of Irish immigrating to America. By 1850, the Irish made up 43 percent of the foreign-born population in the United States; and in the 1850s, they made up over half the population of New York City and Boston.

iron curtain Term coined by Winston Churchill to describe the cold war divide between western Europe and the Soviet Union's Eastern European satellites.

Iroquois League An alliance of the Iroquois tribes, originally formed sometime between 1450 and 1600, that used their combined strength to pressure Europeans to work with them in the fur trade and to wage war across what is today eastern North America.

Andrew Jackson (1767–1837) As a major general in the Tennessee militia, he had a number of military successes. As president, he worked to enable the "common man" to play a greater role in the political arena. He vetoed the re-chartering of the Second National Bank and reduced federal spending. When South Carolina nullified the Tariffs of 1828 and 1832, Jackson requested that Congress pass a "force bill" that would authorize him to use the army to compel the state to comply with the tariffs. He forced eastern Indians to move west of the Mississippi River so their lands could be used by white settlers. Groups of those who opposed Jackson come together to form a new political party called the Whigs.

Thomas "Stonewall" Jackson (1824–1863) A Confederate general who was known for his fearlessness in leading rapid marches, bold flanking movements, and furious assaults. He earned his nickname at the Battle of the First Bull Run for standing courageously against Union fire. During the battle of Chancellorsville, his own men accidentally mortally wounded him.

William James (1842–1910) He was the founder of Pragmatism and one of the fathers of modern psychology. He believed that ideas gained their validity not from their inherent truth, but from their social consequences and practical application.

Jay's Treaty (1794) Agreement between Britain and the United States, negotiated by Chief Justice John Jay, that settled disputes over trade, prewar debts owed to British merchants, British-occupied forts in American territory, and the seizure of American ships and cargo.

Jazz Age Term coined by writer F. Scott Fitzgerald to characterize the spirit of rebellion and spontaneity among young Americans in the 1920s, a spirit epitomized by the hugely popular jazz music of the era.

Thomas Jefferson (1743–1826) He was a plantation owner, author, the drafter of the Declaration Independence, ambassador to France, leader of the Republican party, secretary of state, and the third president of the United States. As president, he purchased the Louisiana territory from France, withheld appointments made by President Adams leading to *Marybury v. Madison*, outlawed foreign slave trade, and was committed to a "wise and frugal" government.

Jeffersonian Republicans Political party founded by Thomas Jefferson in opposition to the Federalist party led by Alexander Hamilton and John Adams; also known as the Democratic-Republican party.

Jesuits A religious order founded in 1540 by Ignatius Loyola. They sought to counter the spread of Protestantism during the Protestant Reformation and spread the Catholic faith through work as missionaries. Roughly 3,500 served in New Spain and New France.

"Jim Crow" laws In the New South, these laws mandated the separation of races in various public places that served as a way for the ruling whites to impose their will on all areas of black life.

Andrew Johnson (1808–1875) He was elevated to the presidency after Abraham Lincoln's assassination. In order to restore the Union after the Civil War, he issued an amnesty proclamation and required former Confederate states to ratify the Thirteenth Amendment. After disagreements over the power to restore states rights, the Radical Republicans attempted to impeach Johnson but fell short on the required number of votes needed to remove him from office.

Lyndon B. Johnson (1908–1973) Former member of the House of Representatives and the former Majority Leader of the Senate, Vice President Lyndon B. Johnson assumed the presidency after President Kennedy's assassination. During his presidency, he passed the Civil Rights Act of 1964, declared a "war on poverty" promoting his own social program called the Great Society, and signed the Immigration and Nationality Service Act of 1965. Johnson greatly increased America's role in Vietnam.

Johnson's Restoration Plan Plan to require southern states to ratify the Thirteenth Amendment, disqualify wealthy ex-Confederates from voting, and appoint a Unionist governor.

joint-stock companies Businesses owned by investors, who purchase shares of companies' stocks and share all the profits and losses.

Kansas-Nebraska Act (1854) Controversial legislation that created two new territories taken from Native Americans, Kansas and Nebraska, where residents would vote to decide whether slavery would be allowed (popular sovereignty).

Florence Kelley (1859–1932) As the head of the National Consumer's League, she led the crusade to promote state laws to regulate the number of working hours imposed on women who were wives and mothers.

George F. Kennan (1904–2005) While working as an American diplomat, he devised the strategy of containment, which called for the halting of Soviet expansion. It became America's choice strategy throughout the cold war.

John F. Kennedy (1917–1963) He was elected president in 1960. Despite the difficulties he had in getting his legislation through Congress, he established the Alliance for Progress programs to help Latin America, the Peace Corps, the Trade Expansion Act of 1962, and funding for urban renewal projects and the space program. His foreign political involvement included the failed Bay of Pigs invasion and the missile crisis in Cuba, as well as support of local governments in Indochina. In 1963, he was assassinated by Lee Harvey Oswald in Dallas, Texas.

Kent State During the spring of 1970, students on college campuses across the country protested the expansion of the Vietnam War into Cambodia. At Kent State University, the National Guard attempted to quell the rioting students. The guardsmen panicked and shot at rock-throwing demonstrators. Four student bystanders were killed.

Kentucky and Virginia Resolutions (1798–1799) Passed in response to the Alien and Sedition Acts, the resolutions advanced the state-compact theory that held states could nullify an act of Congress if they deemed it unconstitutional.

Francis Scott Key (1779–1843) During the War of 1812, he watched British forces bombard Fort McHenry, but fail to take it. Seeing the American flag still flying over the fort at dawn inspired him to write "The Star-Spangled Banner," which became the American national anthem.

Martin Luther King Jr. (1929–1968) A central leader of the civil rights movement, he urged people to use nonviolent civil disobedience to demand their rights and bring about change. He successfully led the Montgomery bus boycott. While in jail for his role in demonstrations, he wrote his famous "Letter from Birmingham City Jail," in which he defended his strategy of nonviolent protest. In 1963, he delivered his famous "I Have a Dream Speech" from the steps of the Lincoln Memorial as a part of the March on Washington. A year later, he was awarded the Nobel Peace Prize. In 1968, he was assassinated.

King Philip's War A bloody, three-year war in New England (1675–1676), resulting from the escalation of tensions between Indians and English settlers; the defeat of the Indians led to broadened freedoms for the settlers and their dispossessing the region's Indians of most of their land.

King William's War (War of the League of Augsburg) First (1689–1697) of four colonial wars between England and France.

Henry Kissinger (1923–) He served as the secretary of state and national security advisor in the Nixon administration. He negotiated with North Vietnam for an end to the Vietnam War, but the cease-fire did not last; South Vietnam fell to North Vietnam. He helped organize Nixon's historic trips to China and the Soviet Union. In the Middle East, he negotiated a cease-fire between Israel and its neighbors following the Yom

Kippur War and solidified Israel's promise to return to Egypt most of the land it had taken during the 1967 war.

Knights of Labor A national labor organization with a broad reform platform; reached peak membership in the 1880s.

Know-Nothings Nativist, anti-Catholic third party organized in 1854 in reaction to large-scale German and Irish immigration.

Ku Klux Klan Organized in Pulaski, Tennessee, in 1866 to terrorize former slaves who voted and held political offices during Reconstruction; a revived organization in the 1910s and 1920s stressed white, Anglo-Saxon, fundamentalist Protestant supremacy; the Klan revived a third time to fight the civil rights movement of the 1950s and 1960s in the South.

Marquis de Lafayette (1757–1834) A wealthy French idealist excited by the American cause, he offered to serve in Washington's army for free in exchange for being named a major general. He overcame Washington's initial skepticism to become one of his most trusted aides.

laissez-faire An economic doctrine holding that businesses and individuals should be able to pursue their economic interests without government interference.

Land Ordinance of 1785 Directed surveying of the Northwest Territory into townships of thirty-six sections (square miles) each, the sale of the sixteenth section of which was to be used to finance public education.

League of Nations Organization of nations formed in the aftermath of the First World War to mediate disputes and maintain international peace; despite President Wilson's intense lobbying for the League of Nations, Congress did not ratify the treaty and the United States failed to join.

Mary Elizabeth Lease (1850–1933) She was a leader of the farm protest movement who advocated violence if change could not be obtained at the ballot box. She believed that the urban-industrial East was the enemy of the working class.

Robert E. Lee (1807–1870) Even though he had served in the United States Army for thirty years, he chose to fight on the side of the Confederacy. Lee was excellent at using his field commanders and his soldiers respected him. However, General Ulysses S. Grant eventually wore down his army, and Lee surrendered to Grant at the Appomattox Court House on April 9, 1865.

Lend-Lease Act (1941) Legislation that allowed the president to lend or lease military equipment to any country whose own defense was deemed vital to the defense of the United States.

Levittown First low-cost, mass-produced development of suburban tract housing built by William Levitt on Long Island, New York, in 1947.

Lewis and Clark expedition (1804–1806) Led by Meriwether Lewis and William Clark, a mission to the Pacific coast commissioned for the purposes of scientific and geographical exploration

Battle of Lexington and Concord The first shots fired in the Revolutionary War, on April 19, 1775, near Boston; approximately 100 Minutemen and 250 British soldiers were killed.

Liberator William Lloyd Garrison started this anti-slavery newspaper in 1831 in which he renounced gradualism and called for abolition.

Queen Liliuokalani (1838–1917) In 1891, she ascended to the throne of the Hawaiian royal family and tried to eliminate white control of the Hawaiian government. Two years later, Hawaii's white population revolted and seized power with the support of American Marines.

Abraham Lincoln (1809–1865) Shortly after he was elected president in 1860, southern states began seceding from the Union, and in April of 1861 he declared war on the seceding states. On January 1, 1863, Lincoln signed the Emancipation Proclamation. At the end of the war, he favored a reconstruction strategy for the former Confederate states that did not radically alter southern social and economic life. He was assassinated by John Wilkes Booth at Ford's Theater on April 14, 1865.

Lincoln-Douglas debates (1858) During the Illinois race between Republican Abraham Lincoln and Democrat Stephen A. Douglas for a seat in the U.S. Senate, a series of seven dramatic debates focusing on the issue of slavery in the territories.

John Locke (1632–1704) An English philosopher whose ideas were influential during the Enlightenment. He argued in his *Essay on Human Understanding* (1690) that humanity is largely the product of the environment, the mind being a blank tablet, *tabula rasa*, on which experience is written.

Henry Cabot Lodge (1850–1924) He was the chairman of the Senate Foreign Relations Committee who favored limiting America's involvement in the League of Nations' covenant and sought to amend the Treaty of Versailles.

de Lôme letter (1898) Private correspondence written by the Spanish ambassador to the U.S., Depuy de Lôme, that described President McKinley as "weak"; the letter was stolen by Cuban revolutionaries and published in the *New York Journal*, deepening American resentment of Spain and moving the two countries closer to war in Cuba.

Lone Star Republic After winning independence from Mexico, Texas became its own nation that was called the Lone Star Republic. In 1836, Texans drafted a constitution, legalized slavery, banned free blacks, named Sam Houston president, and voted for the annexation to the United States. However, quarrels over adding a slave state and fears of instigating a war with Mexico delayed Texas's entrance into the Union until December 29, 1845.

Huey P. Long (1893–1935) He began his political career in Louisiana where he developed a reputation for being an unscrupulous reformer. As a U.S. senator, he became a critic of President Roosevelt's New Deal Plan and offered his alternative called the Share-the-Wealth program. He was assassinated in 1935.

Lost Cause narrative Southern whites' view of secession as a noble "lost cause." A revisionist version of history that glamorized plantation culture and insisted that the Civil War had little to do with slavery and everything to do with a defense of states' rights from the Republican party and the "War of Northern Aggression."

Lost Generation Label given to modernist writers and authors, such as F. Scott Fitzgerald and Ernest Hemingway, who had lost faith in the values and institutions of Western civilization in the aftermath of the Great War.

Louisiana Purchase (1803) President Thomas Jefferson's purchase of the Louisiana Territory from France for $15 million, doubling the size of U.S. territory.

Lowell system Model New England factory communities that during the first half of the nineteenth century provided employees, mostly young women, with meals, a boardinghouse, and moral discipline, as well as educational and cultural opportunities.

Loyalists Colonists who remained loyal to Great Britain before and during the Revolutionary War.

Lusitania British ocean liner torpedoed and sunk by a German U-boat in 1915; the deaths of nearly 1,200 of its civilian passengers, including many Americans, caused international outrage.

Martin Luther (1483–1546) A German monk who founded the Lutheran church. He protested abuses in the Catholic Church by posting his Ninety-five Theses, which began the Protestant Reformation.

General Douglas MacArthur (1880–1964) During World War II, he and Admiral Chester Nimitz dislodged the Japanese military from the Pacific Islands they had occupied. Following the war, he was in charge of the occupation of Japan. After North Korea invaded South Korea, Truman sent the U.S. military to defend South Korea under the command of MacArthur. Later in the war, Truman expressed his willingness to negotiate the restoration of prewar boundaries which MacArthur attempted to undermine. Truman fired MacArthur for his open insubordination.

James Madison (1751–1836) He participated in the Constitutional Convention during which he proposed the Virginia Plan. He believed in a strong federal government and was a leader of the Federalists. However, he also presented to Congress the Bill of Rights and drafted the Virginia Resolutions. As secretary of state, he withheld a commission for William Marbury, which led to the landmark *Marbury v. Madison* decision. During his presidency, he declared war on Britain in response to violations of American shipping rights, which started the War of 1812.

U.S. battleship *Maine* American warship that exploded in the Cuban port of Havana on January 25, 1898; though later discovered to be the result of an accident, the destruction of the *Maine* was attributed by war-hungry Americans to Spain, contributing to the onset of the War of 1898.

maize (corn) The primary grain crop in Mesoamerica yielding small kernels often ground into cornmeal. Easy to grow in a broad range of conditions, it enabled a global population explosion after being brought to Europe, Africa, and Asia.

Malcolm X (1925–1964) The most articulate spokesman for black power. Originally the chief disciple of Elijah Muhammad, the black Muslim leader in the United States, Malcolm X broke away and founded his own organization committed to establishing relations between African Americans and the nonwhite peoples of the world. Near the end of his life, he began to preach a biracial message of social change. In 1964, he was assassinated by members of a rival group of black Muslims.

Manchuria incident The northeast region of Manchuria was an area contested between China and Russia. In 1931, the Japanese claimed that they needed to protect their extensive investments in the area and moved their army into Manchuria. They quickly conquered the region and set up their own puppet empire. China asked both the United States and the League of Nations for help and neither responded.

manifest destiny The widespread belief that America was "destined" by God to expand westward across the continent into lands claimed by Native Americans as well as European nations.

Horace Mann (1796–1859) He believed the public school system was the best way to achieve social stability and equal opportunity. As a reformer of education, he sponsored a state board of education, the first state-supported "normal" school for training teachers, a state association for teachers, the minimum school year of six months, and led the drive for a statewide school system.

Marbury v. Madison **(1803)** First Supreme Court decision to declare a federal law—the Judiciary Act of 1801—unconstitutional.

March on Washington Civil rights demonstration on August 28, 1963, on the National Mall, where Martin Luther King Jr. gave his famous "I Have a Dream" speech.

March to the Sea (1864) The Union army's devastating march through Georgia from Atlanta to Savannah led by General William T. Sherman, intended to demoralize civilians and destroy the resources the Confederate army needed to fight.

market-based economy Large-scale manufacturing and commercial agriculture that emerged in America during the first half of the nineteenth century, displacing much of the premarket subsistence and barter-based economy and producing boom-and-bust cycles while raising the American standard of living.

marriage equality The legal right for gay and lesbian couples to marry; it became the most divisive issue in the culture wars of the early 2010s as more and more court rulings affirmed this right in states and municipalities across the United States. The 2015 Supreme Court case *Obergefell v. Hodges* affirmed the right to same-sex marriage, also known as marriage equality, nationally.

George C. Marshall (1880–1959) As the chairman of the Joint Chiefs of Staff, he orchestrated the Allied victories over Germany and Japan in the Second World War. In 1947, he became President Truman's secretary of state and proposed the massive reconstruction program for western Europe called the Marshall Plan.

Chief Justice John Marshall (1755–1835) During his long tenure as chief justice of the supreme court (1801–1835), he established the foundations for American jurisprudence, the authority of the Supreme Court, and the constitutional supremacy of the national government over states.

Marshall Plan (1948) Secretary of State George C. Marshall's post–World War II program providing massive U.S. financial and technical assistance to war-torn European countries.

Massachusetts Bay Colony English colony founded by English Puritans in 1630 as a haven for persecuted Congregationalists.

massive resistance White rallying cry disrupting federal efforts to enforce racial integration in the South.

massive retaliation Strategy that used the threat of nuclear warfare as a means of combating the global spread of communism.

Mayflower Compact A formal agreement signed by the Separatist colonists aboard the *Mayflower* in 1620 to abide by laws made by leaders of their own choosing.

Senator Joseph R. McCarthy (1908–1957) In 1950, this senator became the shrewdest and most ruthless exploiter of America's anxiety of communism. He claimed that the United States government was full of Communists and led a witch hunt to find them, but he was never able to uncover a single communist agent.

McCarthyism Anti-Communist hysteria led by Senator Joseph McCarthy's "witch hunts" attacking the loyalty of politicians, federal employees, and public figures, despite a lack of evidence.

George B. McClellan (1826–1885) In 1861, President Abraham Lincoln appointed him head of the Army of the Potomac and, later, general in chief of the U.S. Army. He built his army into well trained and powerful force. After failing to achieve a decisive victory against the Confederacy, he was removed from command in 1862.

Cyrus Hall McCormick (1809–1884) In 1831, he invented a mechanical reaper to harvest wheat, which transformed the scale of agriculture. By hand a farmer could only harvest a half an acre a day, while the McCormick reaper allowed two people to harvest twelve acres of wheat a day.

McCormick reaper Mechanical reaper invented by Cyrus Hall McCormick in 1831 that dramatically increased the production of wheat.

McCulloch v. Maryland (1819) Supreme Court ruling that prohibited states from taxing the Bank of the United States.

William McKinley (1843–1901) As a congressman, he was responsible for the McKinley Tariff of 1890, which raised the duties on manufactured products to their highest level ever. Voters disliked the tariff and McKinley, as well as other Republicans, lost his seat in Congress the next election. However, he won the presidential election of 1896 and raised the tariffs again. In 1898, he annexed Hawaii and declared war on Spain. The war concluded with the Treaty of Paris, which gave America control over Puerto Rico, Guam, and the Philippines. Soon America was fighting Filipinos, who were seeking independence for their country. In 1901, McKinley was assassinated.

Robert McNamara (1916–) He was the secretary of defense for both President Kennedy and President Johnson and a supporter of America's involvement in Vietnam.

Medicare and Medicaid Health-care programs designed to aid the elderly and disadvantaged, respectively, as part of President Johnson's Great Society initiative.

Andrew W. Mellon (1855–1937) As President Harding's secretary of the Treasury, he sought to generate economic growth through reducing government spending and lowering taxes. However, he insisted that the tax reductions mainly go to the rich because he believed the wealthy would reinvest their money. In order to bring greater efficiency and nonpartisanship to the government's budget process, he persuaded Congress to created a new Bureau of the Budget and a General Accounting Office.

mercantilism Policy of Great Britain and other imperial powers of regulating the economies of colonies to benefit the mother country.

James Meredith (1933–) In 1962, the governor of Mississippi defied a Supreme Court ruling and refused to allow James Meredith, an African American, to enroll at the University of Mississippi. Federal marshals were sent to enforce the law which led to clashes between a white mob and the marshals. Federal troops intervened and two people were killed and many others were injured. A few days later, Meredith was able to register at the university.

Merrimack* (ship renamed the *Virginia*) and the *Monitor First engagement between ironclad ships; fought at Hampton Roads, Virginia, on March 9, 1862.

Metacomet or King Philip (?–1676) The chief of the Wampanoages, who the colonists called King Philip. He resented English efforts to convert Indians to Christianity and waged a war against the English colonists in which he was killed.

Mexica Otherwise known as "Aztecs," a Mesoamerican people of northern Mexico who founded the vast Aztec Empire in the fourteenth century, later conquered by the Spanish under Hernán Cortés in 1521.

microprocessor An electronic circuit printed on a small silicon chip; a major technological breakthrough in 1971, it paved the way for the development of the personal computer.

Middle Passage The hellish and often deadly middle leg of the transatlantic "Triangular Trade" in which European ships carried manufactured goods to Africa, then transported enslaved Africans to the Americas and the Caribbean, and finally conveyed American agricultural products back to Europe; from the late sixteenth to the early nineteenth centuries, some 12 million Africans were transported via the Middle Passage, unknown millions more dying en route.

Battle of Midway A 1942 battle that proved to be a turning point in the Pacific front during World War II; it was the Japanese navy's first major defeat in 350 years.

militant nonviolence After the success of the Montgomery bus boycott, people were inspired by Martin Luther King Jr.'s use of this nonviolent form of protest. Throughout the civil rights movement, demonstrators used this method of protest to challenge racial segregation in the South.

Militia Act (1862) Congressional measure that permitted freed slaves to serve as laborers or soldiers in the United States Army.

Ho Chi Minh (1890–1969) He was the Vietnamese communist resistance leader who drove the French and the United States out of Vietnam. After the Geneva Accords divided the region into four countries, he controlled North Vietnam, and ultimately became the leader of all of Vietnam at the conclusion of the Vietnam War.

minstrelsy A form of entertainment that was popular from the 1830s to the 1870s. The performances featured white performers who were made up as African Americans or blackface. They performed banjo and fiddle music, "shuffle" dances and lowbrow humor that reinforced racial stereotypes.

Minutemen Special units organized by the militia to be ready for quick mobilization.

***Miranda v. Arizona* (1966)** U.S. Supreme Court decision required police to advise persons in custody of their rights to legal counsel and against self-incrimination.

Mississippi Plan (1890) Series of state constitutional amendments that sought to severely disenfranchise black voters and were quickly adopted by other southern states.

Missouri Compromise (1820) Legislative decision to admit Missouri as a slave state and abolish slavery in the area west of the Mississippi River and north of the parallel 36°30′.

Model T Ford Henry Ford developed this model of car so that it was affordable for everyone. Its success led to an increase in the production of automobiles which stimulated other related industries such steel, oil, and rubber. The mass use of automobiles increased the speed goods could be transported, encouraged urban sprawl, and sparked real estate booms in California and Florida.

moderate Republicanism Promise to curb federal government and restore state and local government authority, spearheaded by President Eisenhower.

modernism An early-twentieth-century intellectual and artistic movement that rejected traditional notions of reality and adopted radical new forms of artistic expression.

money problem Late-nineteenth-century national debate over the nature of U.S. currency; supporters of a fixed gold standard were generally money lenders, and thus preferred to keep the value of money high, while supporters of silver (and gold) coinage were debtors, they owed money, so they wanted to keep the value of money low by increasing the currency supply (inflation).

monopoly A corporation so large that it effectively controls the entire market for its products or services.

James Monroe (1758–1831) He served as secretary of state and war under President Madison and was elected president. As the latter, he signed the Transcontinental Treaty with Spain which gave the United States Florida and expanded the Louisiana territory's western border to the Pacific coast. In 1823, he established the Monroe Doctrine. This foreign policy proclaimed the American continents were no longer open to colonization and America would be neutral in European affairs.

Monroe Doctrine (1823) U.S. foreign policy that barred further colonization in the Western Hemisphere by European powers and pledged that there would be no American interference with any existing European colonies.

Montgomery bus boycott (1955–1956) Boycott of bus system in Montgomery, Alabama, organized by civil rights activists after the arrest of Rosa Parks.

Moral Majority Televangelist Jerry Falwell's political lobbying organization, the name of which became synonymous with the Religious Right—conservative evangelical Protestants who helped ensure President Ronald Reagan's 1980 victory.

J. Pierpont Morgan (1837–1913) As a powerful investment banker, he would acquire, reorganize, and consolidate companies into giant trusts. His biggest achievement was the consolidation of the steel industry into the United States Steel Corporation, which was the first billion-dollar corporation.

J. Pierpont Morgan and Company An investment bank under the leadership of J. Pierpont Morgan that bought or merged unrelated American companies, often using capital acquired from European investors.

Mormons Members of the Church of Jesus Christ of Latter-day Saints, which dismissed other Christian denominations, emphasizing universal salvation and a modest lifestyle; Mormons were often persecuted for their secrecy and clannishness.

Morrill Land Grant College Act (1862) Federal statute that allowed for the creation of land-grant colleges and universities, which were founded to provide technical education in agriculture, mining, and industry.

Samuel F. B. Morse (1791–1872) In 1832, he invented the telegraph and revolutionized the speed of communication.

mountain men Inspired by the fur trade, these men left civilization to work as trappers and reverted to a primitive existence in the wilderness. They were the first white people to find routes through the Rocky Mountains, and they pioneered trails that settlers later used to reach the Oregon country and California in the 1840s.

muckrakers Writers who exposed corruption and abuses in politics, business, consumer safety, working conditions, and more, spurring public interest in progressive reforms.

Mugwumps Reformers who bolted from the Republican party in 1884 to support Democratic Grover Cleveland for president over Republican James G. Blaine, whose secret dealings on behalf of railroad companies had brought charges of corruption.

mulattoes Mixed-race people who constituted most of the South's free black population.

Benito Mussolini (1883–1945) The Italian founder of the Fascist party who came to power in Italy in 1922 and allied himself with Adolf Hitler and the Axis powers during the Second World War.

National Association for the Advancement of Colored People (NAACP) Organization founded in 1910 by black activists and white progressives that promoted education as a means of combating social problems and focused on legal action to secure the civil rights supposedly guaranteed by the Fourteenth and Fifteenth Amendments.

National Banking Act (1863) The U.S. Congress created a national banking system to finance the enormous expense of the Civil War. It enabled loans to the government and established a single national currency, including the issuance of paper money ("greenbacks").

National Industrial Recovery Act (1933) Passed on the last of the Hundred Days; it created public-works jobs through the Federal Emergency Relief Administration and established a system of self-regulation for industry through the National Recovery Administration, which was ruled unconstitutional in 1935.

National Labor Union (NLU) A federation of labor and reform leaders established in 1866 to advocate for new state and local laws to improve working conditions.

National Recovery Administration (NRA) (1933) Controversial federal agency that brought together business and labor leaders to create "codes of fair competition" and "fair labor" policies, including a national minimum wage.

National Security Act (1947) Congressional legislation that created the Department of Defense, the National Security Council, and the Central Intelligence Agency.

National Socialist German Workers' Party (Nazi) Founded in the 1920s, this party gained control over Germany under the leadership of Adolf Hitler in 1933 and continued in power until Germany's defeat at the end of the Second World War. It advocated a violent anti-Semitic, anti-Marxist, pan-German ideology. The Nazi party perpetrated the Holocaust.

National Trades' Unions Formed in 1834 to organize all local trade unions into a stronger national association, only to be dissolved amid the economic depression during the late 1830s.

nativism Reactionary conservative movement characterized by heightened nationalism, anti-immigrant sentiment, and the enactment of laws setting stricter regulations on immigration.

nativists Members of a reactionary conservative movement characterized by heightened nationalism, anti-immigrant sentiment, and the enactment of laws setting stricter regulations on immigration.

natural rights An individual's basic rights that should not be violated by any government or community.

Navigation Acts (1650–1775) Restrictions passed by the British Parliament to control colonial trade and bolster the mercantile system.

Negrophobia A violent new wave of racism that spread in the late nineteenth century largely spurred by white resentment for African American financial success and growing political influence.

neutrality laws Series of laws passed by Congress aimed at avoiding entering a Second World War; these included the Neutrality Act of 1935, which banned loans to warring nations.

new conservatism The political philosophy of those who led the conservative insurgency of the early 1980s. This brand of conservatism was personified in Ronald Reagan who believed in less government, supply-side economics, and "family values."

New Democrats Centrist ("moderate") Democrats led by President Bill Clinton that emerged in the late 1980s and early 1990s to challenge the "liberal" direction of the party.

"new economy" Period of sustained economic prosperity during the nineties marked by budget surpluses, the explosion of dot.com industries, low inflation, and low unemployment.

New France The name used for the area of North America that was colonized by the French. Unlike Spanish or English colonies, New France had a small number of colonists, which forced them to initially seek good relations with the indigenous people they encountered.

New Freedom Program championed in 1912 by the Woodrow Wilson campaign that aimed to restore competition in the economy by eliminating all trusts rather than simply regulating them.

New Frontier Proposed domestic program championed by the incoming Kennedy administration in 1961 that aimed to jump-start the economy and trigger social progress.

new immigrants Wave of newcomers from southern and eastern Europe, including many Jews, who became a majority among immigrants to America after 1890.

New Jersey Plan The delegations to the Constitutional Convention were divided between two plans on how to structure the government: New Jersey wanted one legislative body with equal representation for each state.

New Left Term coined by the Students for a Democratic Society to distinguish their efforts at grassroots democracy from those of the 1930s Old Left, which had embraced orthodox Marxism.

New Mexico A U.S. territory and later a state in the American Southwest, originally established by the Spanish, who settled there in the sixteenth century, founded Catholic missions, and exploited the region's indigenous peoples.

New Nationalism Platform of the Progressive party and slogan of former President Theodore Roosevelt in the presidential campaign of 1912; stressed government activism, including regulation of trusts, conservation, and recall of state court decisions that had nullified progressive programs.

"New Negro" In the 1920s, a slow and steady growth of black political influence occurred in northern cities where African Americans were freer to speak and act. This political activity created a spirit of protest that expressed itself culturally in the Harlem Renaissance and politically in "new Negro" nationalism.

New Netherland Dutch colony conquered by the English in 1667 and out of which four new colonies were created—New York, New Jersey, Pennsylvania, and Delaware.

Battle of New Orleans (1815) Final major battle in the War of 1812, in which the Americans under General Andrew Jackson unexpectedly and decisively countered the British attempt to seize the port of New Orleans, Louisiana.

New South *Atlanta Constitution* editor Henry W. Grady's 1886 term for the prosperous post–Civil War South: democratic, industrial, urban, and free of nostalgia for the defeated plantation South.

New York Journal In the late 1890s, William Randolph Hearst's *New York Journal* and its rival, the *New York World*, printed sensationalism on the Cuban revolution as part of their heated competition for readership. The *New York Journal* printed a negative letter from the Spanish ambassador about President McKinley and inflammatory coverage of the sinking of the *Maine* in Havana Harbor. These two events roused the American public's outcry against Spain.

New York World In the late 1890s, Joseph Pulitzer's *New York World* and its rival, the *New York Journal*, printed sensationalism on the Cuban revolution as part of their heated competition for readership.

Admiral Chester Nimitz (1885–1966) During the Second World War, he was the commander of central Pacific. Along with General Douglas MacArthur, he dislodged the Japanese military from the Pacific Islands they had occupied.

Nineteenth Amendment (1920) Constitutional amendment that granted women the right to vote.

Richard M. Nixon (1913–1994) He first came to national prominence as a congress-man involved in the investigation of Alger Hiss, and later served as vice president during the Eisenhower administration. After being elected president in 1968, he slowed the federal enforcement of civil rights and appointed pro-Southern justices to the Supreme Court. He began a program of Vietnamization of the war. In 1973, America, North and South Vietnam, and the Viet Cong agreed to end the war and the United States withdrew. However, the cease-fire was broken, and the South Vietnam fell to North Vietnam. In 1970, Nixon declared that America was no longer the world's policeman and he would seek some partnerships with Communist countries, historically traveling to China and the Soviet Union. In 1972, he was reelected, but the Watergate scandal erupted shortly after his victory; he resigned the presidency under threat of impeachment.

No Child Left Behind President George W. Bush's education reform plan that required states to set and meet learning standards for students and make sure that all students were "proficient" in reading and writing by 2014. States had to submit annual reports of students' standardized test scores. Teachers were required to be "proficient" in their subject area. Schools who failed to show progress would face sanctions. States criticized the lack of funding for remedial programs and noted that poor school districts would find it very difficult to meet the new guidelines.

nonviolent civil disobedience Tactic of defying unjust laws through peaceful actions championed by Dr. Martin Luther King Jr.

Lord North (1732–1792) The first minister of King George III's cabinet whose efforts to subdue the colonies only brought them closer to revolution. He helped bring about the Tea Act of 1773, which led to the Boston Tea Party. In an effort to discipline Boston, he wrote, and Parliament passed, four acts that galvanized colonial resistance.

North American Free Trade Agreement (NAFTA) (1994) Agreement eliminating trade barriers that was signed by the United States, Canada, and Mexico, making North America the largest free-trade zone in the world.

North Atlantic Treaty Organization (NATO) Defensive alliance founded in 1949 by ten western European nations, the United States, and Canada to deter Soviet expansion in Europe.

Northwest Ordinance (1787) Land policy for new western territories in the Ohio Valley that established the terms and conditions for self-government and statehood while also banning slavery from the region.

NSC-68 (1950) Top-secret policy paper approved by President Truman that outlined a militaristic approach to combating the spread of global communism.

nullification The right claimed by some states to veto a federal law deemed unconstitutional.

Nuremberg trials At the site of the annual Nazi party rallies, twenty-one major German offenders faced an international military tribunal for Nazi atrocities. After a ten-month trial, the court acquitted three and sentenced eleven to death, three to life imprisonment, and four to shorter terms.

Barack Obama (1961–) In the 2008 presidential election, Senator Barack Obama mounted an innovative Internet based and grassroots orientated campaign. As the nation's economy nose-dived in the fall of 2008, Obama linked the Republican economic philosophy with the country's dismal financial state and promoted a message of "change" and "politics of hope," which resonated with voters. He decisively won the presidency and became America's first person of color to be elected president. In 2012, Obama successfully won re-election to serve as president for a second term.

Occupy Wall Street A grassroots movement protesting a capitalist system that fostered social and economic inequality. Begun in Zuccotti Park, New York City, during 2011, the movement spread rapidly across the nation, triggering a national conversation about income inequality and protests of the government's "bailouts" of the banks and corporations allegedly responsible for the Great Recession.

Sandra Day O'Connor (1930–) She was the first woman to serve on the Supreme Court of the United States and was appointed by President Reagan. Reagan's critics charged that her appointment was a token gesture and not a sign of any real commitment to gender equality.

Ohio gang In order to escape the pressures of the White House, President Harding met with a group of people, called the "Ohio gang," in a house on K Street in Washington D.C. Members of this gang were given low-level positions in the American government and they used their White House connection to "line their pockets" by granting government contracts without bidding, which led to a series of scandals, most notably the Teapot Dome Scandal.

Old Southwest Region covering western Georgia, Alabama, Mississippi, Louisiana, Arkansas, and Texas, where low land prices and fertile soil attracted hundreds of thousands of settlers after the American Revolution.

Frederick Law Olmsted (1822–1903) In 1858, he constructed New York's Central Park, which led to a growth in the movement to create urban parks. He went on to design parks for Boston, Brooklyn, Chicago, Philadelphia, San Francisco, and many other cities.

Open Door policy (1899) Official U.S. insistence that Chinese trade would be open to all nations; Secretary of State John Hay unilaterally announced the policy in hopes of protecting the Chinese market for U.S. exports.

open range Informal system of governing property on the frontier in which small ranchers could graze their cattle anywhere on unfenced lands; brought to an end by the introduction of barbed wire, a low-cost way to fence off one's land.

open shop Business policy of not requiring union membership as a condition of employment; such a policy, where legal, has the effect of weakening unions and diminishing workers' rights.

Operation Desert Shield After Saddam Hussein invaded Kuwait in 1990, President George H. W. Bush sent American military forces to Saudi Arabia on a strictly defensive mission. They were soon joined by a multinational coalition. When the coalition's mission changed to the retaking of Kuwait, the operation was renamed Desert Storm.

Operation Desert Storm (1991) Assault by American-led multinational forces that quickly defeated Iraqi forces under Saddam Hussein in the First Gulf War, ending the Iraqi occupation of Kuwait.

Operation Overlord The Allies' assault on Hitler's "Atlantic Wall," a seemingly impregnable series of fortifications and minefields along the French coastline that German forces had created using captive Europeans for laborers.

J. Robert Oppenheimer (1904–1967) He led the group of physicists at the laboratory in Los Alamos, New Mexico, who constructed the first atomic bomb.

Oregon Country The Convention of 1818 between Britain and the United States established the Oregon Country as being west of the crest of the Rocky Mountains and the two countries were to jointly occupy it. In 1824, the United States and Russia signed a treaty that established the line of 54°40′ as the southern boundary of Russia's territorial claim in North America. A similar agreement between Britain and Russia finally gave the Oregon Country clearly defined boarders, but it remained under joint British and American control.

Oregon fever The lure of fertile land and economic opportunities in the Oregon Country that drew thousands of settlers westward, beginning in the late 1830s.

Osceola (1804?–1838) He was the leader of the Seminole nation who resisted the federal Indian removal policy through a protracted guerilla war. In 1837, he was treacherously seized under a flag of truce and imprisoned at Fort Moultrie, where he was left to die.

Overland Trails Trail routes followed by wagon trains bearing settlers and trade goods from Missouri to the Oregon Country, California, and New Mexico, beginning in the 1840s.

Pacific Railway Act (1862) Congress provided funding for a transcontinental railroad from Nebraska west to California.

A. Mitchell Palmer (1872–1936) As the attorney general, he played an active role in the government's response to the Red Scare. After several bombings across America, including one at Palmer's home, he and other Americans became convinced that there was a well-organized Communist terror campaign at work. The federal government launched a campaign of raids, deportations, and collecting files on radical individuals.

Panic of 1819 A financial panic that began a three-year-long economic crisis triggered by a reduced demand of American imports, declining land values, and reckless practices by local and state banks.

Panic of 1837 A financial calamity in the United States brought on by a dramatic slowdown in the British economy and falling cotton prices, failed crops, high inflation, and reckless state banks.

Panic of 1873 A financial calamity in the United States brought on by a dramatic slowdown in the British economy and exacerbated by falling cotton prices, failed crops, high inflation, and reckless state banks.

Panic of 1893 A major collapse in the national economy after several major railroad companies declared bankruptcy, leading to a severe depression and several violent clashes between workers and management.

panning A method of mining that used a large metal pan to sift gold dust and nuggets from riverbeds during the California gold rush of 1849.

Rosa Parks (1913–2005) In 1955, she refused to give up her seat to a white man on a city bus in Montgomery, Alabama, which a local ordinance required of blacks. She was arrested for disobeying the ordinance. In response, black community leaders organized the Montgomery bus boycott.

Parliament Legislature of Great Britain, composed of the House of Commons, whose members are elected, and the House of Lords, whose members are either hereditary or appointed.

party "boss" A powerful political leader who controlled a "machine" of associates and operatives to promote both individual and party interests, often using informal tactics such as intimidation or the patronage system.

paternalism A moral position developed during the first half of the nineteenth century which claimed that slaves were deprived of liberty for their own "good." Such a rationalization was adopted by some slave owners to justify slavery.

Patriots Colonists who rebelled against British authority before and during the Revolutionary War.

patronage An informal system (sometimes called the "spoils system") used by politicians to reward their supporters with government appointments or contracts.

Alice Paul (1885–1977) She was a leader of the women's suffrage movement and head of the Congressional Committee of National Women Suffrage Association. She instructed female suffrage activists to use more militant tactics, such as picketing state legislatures, chaining themselves to public buildings, inciting police to arrest them, and undertaking hunger strikes.

Norman Vincent Peale (1898–1993) He was a champion of the upbeat and feel-good theology that was popular in the 1950s religious revival. He advocated getting rid of any depressing or negative thoughts and replacing them with "faith, enthusiasm and joy," which would make an individual popular and well liked.

Pearl Harbor (1941) Surprise Japanese attack on the U.S. fleet at Pearl Harbor on December 7, which prompted the immediate American entry into the war.

peculiar institution A phrase used by whites in the antebellum South to refer to slavery without using the word slavery.

Pentagon Papers Informal name for the Defense Department's secret history of the Vietnam conflict; leaked to the press by former official Daniel Ellsberg and published in the *New York Times* in 1971.

People's party (Populists) Political party largely made up of farmers from the South and West that struggled to gain political influence from the East. Populists advocated a variety of reforms, including free coinage of silver, a progressive income tax, postal savings banks, regulation of railroads, and direct election of U.S. senators.

Pequot War Massacre in 1637 and subsequent dissolution of the Pequot Nation by Puritan settlers, who seized the Indians' lands.

perestroika Russian term for "economic restructuring"; applied to Mikhail Gorbachev's series of political and economic reforms that included shifting a centrally planned Commmunist economy to a mixed economy allowing for capitalism.

Commodore Matthew Perry (1794–1858) In 1854, he negotiated the Treaty of Kanagawa, which was the first step in starting a political and commercial relationship between the United States and Japan.

John J. Pershing United States general sent by President Wilson to put down attacks on the Mexican border led by Francisco "Pancho" Villa.

Personal Responsibility and Work Opportunity Act of 1996 (PRWOA) Comprehensive welfare-reform measure, passed by a Republican Congress and signed by President Clinton, that aimed to decrease the size of the "welfare state" by limiting the amount of government aid provided the unemployed so as to encourage recipients to find jobs.

"pet banks" During President Andrew Jackson's fight with the national bank, Jackson resolved to remove all federal deposits from it. To comply with Jackson's demands, Secretary of the Treasury Taney continued to draw on government's accounts in the national bank, but deposit all new federal receipts in state banks. The state banks that received these deposits were called "pet banks."

Pilgrims Puritan Separatists who broke completely with the Church of England and sailed to the New World aboard the *Mayflower*, founding Plymouth Colony on Cape Cod in 1620.

Dien Bien Phu Cluster of Vietnamese villages and site of a major Vietnamese victory over the French in the First Indochina War.

Gifford Pinchot (1865–1946) As the head of the Division of Forestry, he implemented a conservation policy that entailed the scientific management of natural resources to serve the public interest. His work helped start the conservation movement.

Elizabeth Lucas Pinckney (1722? –1793) One of the most enterprising horticulturists in colonial America, she began managing her family's three plantations in South Carolina at the age of sixteen. She had tremendous success growing indigo, which led to many other plantations growing the crop as well.

Pinckney's Treaty Treaty with Spain negotiated by Thomas Pinckney in 1795; established United States boundaries at the Mississippi River and the 31st parallel and allowed open transportation on the Mississippi.

Francisco Pizarro (1478?–1541) In 1531, he lead his Spanish soldiers to Peru and conquered the Inca Empire.

plain white folk Yeoman farmers who lived and worked on their own small farms, growing a food and cash crops to trade for necessities.

plantation mistress Matriarch of a planter's household, responsible for supervising the domestic aspects of the estate.

planters Owners of large farms in the South that were worked by twenty or more slaves and supervised by overseers.

political "machine" A network of political activists and elected officials, usually controlled by a powerful "boss," that attempts to manipulate local politics

James Knox Polk "Young Hickory" (1795–1849) As president, his chief concern was the expansion of the United States. Shortly, after taking office, Mexico broke off relations with the United States over the annexation of Texas. Polk declared war on Mexico and sought to subvert Mexican authority in California. The United States defeated Mexico; and the two nations signed the Treaty of Guadalupe Hidalgo in which Mexico gave up any claims on Texas north of the Rio Grande River and ceded New Mexico and California to the United States.

Pontiac's Rebellion (1763) An Indian attack on British forts and settlements after France ceded to the British its territory east of the Mississippi River, as part of the Treaty of Paris, without consulting France's Indian allies.

popular sovereignty Legal concept by which the white male settlers in a new U.S. territory would vote to decide whether or not to permit slavery.

Populist/People's party Political success of Farmers' Alliance candidates encouraged the formation in 1892 of the People's party (later renamed the Populist party); active until 1912, it advocated a variety of reform issues, including free coinage of silver, income tax, postal savings, regulation of railroads, and direct election of U.S. senators.

Pottawatomie Massacre In retaliation for the "sack of Lawrence," John Brown and his abolitionist cohorts hacked five men to death in the pro-slavery settlement of Pottawatomie, Kansas, on May 24, 1856, triggering a guerrilla war in the Kansas Territory that cost 200 settler lives.

Powhatan Confederacy An alliance of several powerful Algonquian tribes under the leadership of Chief Powhatan, organized into thirty chiefdoms along much of the Atlantic coast in the late sixteenth and early seventeenth centuries.

Chief Powhatan Wahunsonacock He was called Powhatan by the English after the name of his tribe, and was the powerful, charismatic chief of numerous Algonquian-speaking towns in eastern Virginia representing over 10,000 Indians.

pragmatism William James founded this philosophy in the early 1900s. Pragmatists believed that ideas gained their validity not from their inherent truth, but from their social consequences and practical application.

professions Occupations requiring specialized knowledge of some field; the Industrial Revolution and its new organization of labor created an array of professions in the nineteenth century.

Progressive party In the 1912 election, Theodore Roosevelt was unable to secure the Republican nomination for president. He left the Republican party and formed his own party of progressive Republicans, called the "Bull Moose" party (later Progressive party). Roosevelt and Taft split the Republican vote, which allowed Democrat Woodrow Wilson to win.

progressivism A sometimes grassroots and sometimes elite-driven national movement for social and political reforms that called for more government regulation of business, supported by elements of both major political parties during the Progressive Era (1890–1920).

Prohibition National ban on the manufacture and sale of alcohol that lasted from 1920 to 1933, though the law was widely violated and proved too difficult to enforce effectively.

proprietary colonies A colony owned by an individual, rather than a joint-stock company.

Protestant Reformation Sixteenth-century religious movement initiated by Martin Luther, a German monk whose public criticism of corruption in the Roman Catholic Church, and whose teaching that Christians can communicate directly with God, gained a wide following.

pueblos The Spanish term for the adobe cliff dwellings of the indigenous people of the southwestern United States.

Pullman strike (1894) A national strike by the American Railway Union, whose members shut down major railways in sympathy with striking workers in Pullman, Illinois; ended with intervention of federal troops.

Puritans English religious dissenters who sought to "purify" the Church of England of its Catholic practices.

Quakers George Fox founded the Quaker religion in 1647. They rejected the use of formal sacraments and ministry, refused to take oaths and embraced pacifism. Fleeing persecution, they settled and established the colony of Pennsylvania.

race-based slavery Institution that uses racial characteristics and myths to justify enslaving a people.

Radical Republicans Senators and congressmen who, strictly identifying the Civil War with the abolitionist cause, sought swift emancipation of the slaves, punishment of the rebels, and tight controls over the former Confederate states after the war.

railroads Steam-powered vehicles that improved passenger transportation, quickened western settlement, and enabled commercial agriculture in the nineteenth century.

Raleigh's Roanoke Island Colony English expedition of 117 settlers, including Virginia Dare, the first English child born in the New World; colony disappeared from Roanoke Island in the Outer Banks sometime between 1587 and 1590.

A. Philip Randolph (1889–1979) He was the head of the Brotherhood of Sleeping Car Porters who planned a march on Washington D.C. to demand an end to racial discrimination in the defense industries. To stop the march, the Roosevelt administration negotiated an agreement with the Randolph group. The demonstration would be called off and an executive order would be issued that forbid discrimination in defense work and training programs and set up the Fair Employment Practices Committee.

range wars In the late 1800s, conflicting claims over land and water rights triggered violent disputes between farmers and ranchers in parts of the western United States.

Ronald Reagan (1911–2004) In 1980, the former actor and governor of California was elected president. In office, he reduced social spending, cut taxes, and increased defense spending. During his presidency, the federal debt tripled, the federal deficit rose, programs such as housing and school lunches were cut, and the HIV/AIDS crisis grew to prominence in the United States. He signed an arms-control treaty with the Soviet Union in 1987, authorized covert CIA operations in Central America, and in 1986 the Iran-Contra scandal was revealed.

Reaganomics President Reagan's "supply-side" economic philosophy combining tax cuts with the goals of decreased government spending, reduced regulation of business, and a balanced budget.

Reconstruction Finance Corporation (1932) Federal program established under President Hoover to loan money to banks and other corporations to help them avoid bankruptcy.

Red Power Activism by militant Native American groups to protest living conditions on Indian reservations through demonstrations, legal action, and, at times, violence.

First Red Scare Fear among many Americans after the First World War of Communists in particular and noncitizens in general, it was a reaction to the Russian Revolution, mail bombs, strikes, and riots.

redeemers Post–Civil War Democratic leaders who supposedly saved the South from Yankee domination and preserved the primarily rural economy.

Dr. Walter Reed (1851–1902) His work on yellow fever in Cuba led to the discovery that the fever was carried by mosquitoes. This understanding helped develop more effective controls of the worldwide disease.

reform Darwinism A social philosophy developed by Lester Frank War that challenged the ruthlessness of social Darwinism by asserting that humans were not passive pawns of evolutionary forces. Instead, people could actively shape the process of evolutionary social development through cooperation, innovation, and planning.

Reformation European religious movement that challenged the Catholic Church and resulted in the beginnings of Protestant Christianity. During this period, Catholics and Protestants persecuted, imprisoned, tortured, and killed each other in large numbers.

religious right Christian conservatives with a faith-based political agenda that includes prohibition of abortion and allowing prayer in public schools.

reparations As a part of the Treaty of Versailles, Germany was required to confess its responsibility for the First World War and make payments to the victors for the entire expense of the war. These two requirements created a deep bitterness among Germans.

Report on Manufactures First Secretary of the Treasury Alexander Hamilton's 1791 analysis that accurately foretold the future of American industry and proposed tariffs and subsidies to promote it.

republican ideology Political belief in representative democracy in which citizens govern themselves by electing representatives, or legislators, to make key decisions on the citizens' behalf.

republican simplicity Deliberate attitude of humility and frugality, as opposed to monarchical pomp and ceremony, adopted by Thomas Jefferson in his presidency.

Republicans First used during the early nineteenth century to describe supporters of a strict interpretation of the Constitution, which they believed would safeguard individual freedoms and states' rights from the threats posed by a strong central government. The idealist Republican vision of sustaining an agrarian-oriented union was developed largely by Thomas Jefferson.

return to normalcy Campaign promise of Republican presidential candidate Warren G. Harding in 1920, meant to contrast with Woodrow Wilson's progressivism and internationalism.

Paul Revere (1735–1818) On the night of April 18, 1775, British soldiers marched toward Concord to arrest American Revolutionary leaders and seize their depot of supplies. Paul Revere famously rode through the night and raised the alarm about the approaching British troops.

Roaring Twenties The 1920s, an era of social and intellectual revolution in which young people experimented with new forms of recreation and sexuality. The Eastern, urban cultural shift clashed with conservative and insular Midwestern America, which increased the tensions between the two regions.

Jackie Robinson (1919–1972) In 1947, he became the first African American to play major league baseball. He won over fans and players and stimulated the integration of other professional sports.

rock-and-roll music Alan Freed, a disc jockey, noticed white teenagers were buying rhythm and blues records that had been only purchased by African Americans and Hispanic Americans. Freed began playing these records, but called them rock-and-roll records as a way to overcome the racial barrier. As the popularity of the music genre increased, it helped bridge the gap between "white" and "black" music.

John D. Rockefeller (1839–1937) In 1870, he founded the Standard Oil Company of Ohio, which was his first step in creating his vast oil empire. He perfected the idea of a holding company.

Roe v. Wade **(1973)** Landmark Supreme Court decision striking down state laws that banned abortions during the first trimester of pregnancy.

Roman Catholicism The Christian faith and religious practices of the Roman Catholic Church, which exerted great political, economic, and social influence on much of Western Europe and, through the Spanish and Portuguese Empires, on the Americas.

Romanticism Philosophical, literary, and artistic movement of the nineteenth century that was largely a reaction to the rationalism of the previous century; Romantics valued emotion, mysticism, and individualism.

Eleanor Roosevelt (1884–1962) She redefined the role of the presidential spouse and was the first woman to address a national political convention, write a nationally syndicated column and hold regular press conferences. She travelled throughout the nation to promote the New Deal, women's causes, organized labor, and meet with African American leaders.

Franklin Delano Roosevelt (1882–1945) Elected during the Great Depression, Roosevelt sought to help struggling Americans through his New Deal programs that created employment and social programs, such as Social Security. After the bombing of Pearl Harbor, he declared war on Japan and Germany and led the country through most of the Second World War before dying of cerebral hemorrhage.

Theodore Roosevelt (1858–1919) As the assistant secretary of the navy, he supported expansionism, American imperialism, and war with Spain. He led the Rough Riders in Cuba during the war of 1898 and used the notoriety of this military campaign for political gain. As President McKinley's vice president, he succeeded McKinley after his assassination. His forceful foreign policy became known as "big stick diplomacy." Domestically, his policies on natural resources helped start the conservation movement. Unable to win the Republican nomination for president in 1912, he formed his own party of progressive Republicans called the "Bull Moose" party.

religious Right Christian conservatives with a faith-based political agenda that includes allowing prayer in public schools and prohibition of abortion.

Roosevelt Corollary (1904) President Theodore Roosevelt's revision of the Monroe Doctrine (1823) in which he argued that the United States could use military force in Central and South American nations to prevent European nations from intervening in the Western Hemisphere.

Rough Riders The First U.S. Volunteer Cavalry, led in the War of 1898 by Theodore Roosevelt; they were victorious in their only engagement, the Battle of San Juan Hill near Santiago, Cuba, and Roosevelt was celebrated as a national hero, bolstering his political career.

Royal Proclamation of 1763 Proclamation drawing a boundary along the Appalachian Mountains from Canada to Georgia in order to minimize occurrences of settler–Indian violence; colonists were forbidden to go west of the line.

Rust Belt Parts of the midwestern and northeastern United States marked by industrial decline and falling populations during the second half of the twentieth century, exemplified by steel-manufacturing cities in Ohio and Pennsylvania.

Nicola Sacco (1891–1927) In 1920, he and Bartolomeo Vanzetti were Italian immigrants who were arrested for stealing $16,000 and killing a paymaster and his guard. Their trial took place during a time of numerous bombings by anarchists and their judge was openly prejudicial; many liberals and radicals believe that their conviction was based on their political ideas and ethnic origin rather than the evidence against them.

Sacco and Vanzetti case (1921) Trial of two Italian immigrants that occurred at the height of Italian immigration and against the backdrop of numerous terror attacks by anarchists; despite a lack of clear evidence, the two defendants, both self-professed anarchists, were convicted of murder and were executed in 1927.

saloons Bars or taverns where mostly men would gather to drink, eat, relax, play games, and, often, to discuss politics.

salutary neglect Informal British policy during the first half of the eighteenth century that allowed the American colonies considerable freedom to pursue their economic and political interests in exchange for colonial obedience.

Sand Creek Massacre (1864) Colonel Chivington's unprovoked slaughter of the Cheyennes and Arapahos in Colorado, initially reported as a justified battle but soon exposed for the despicable massacre it was.

Sandinista Cuban-sponsored government that came to power in Nicaragua after toppling a corrupt dictator. The State Department believed that the Sandinistas were supplying the leftist Salvadoran rebels with Cuban and Soviet arms. In response, the Reagan administration ordered the CIA to train and supply guerrilla bands of anti-Communist Nicaraguans called Contras. A cease-fire agreement between the Contras and Sandinistas was signed in 1988.

Sandlot Incident Violence occurring during the Great Railroad Strike of 1877, when mobs of frustrated working-class whites in San Francisco attacked Chinese immigrants, blaming them for economic hardship.

General Antonio López de Santa Anna (1794–1876) In 1834, he seized political power in Mexico and became a dictator. In 1835, Texans rebelled against him and he led his army to Texas to crush their rebellion. He captured the mission called the Alamo and killed all of its defenders, which inspired Texans to continue resistance and Americans to volunteer to fight for Texas. The Texans captured Santa Anna during a surprise attack and he bought his freedom by signing a treaty recognizing Texas's independence.

Battles of Saratoga Decisive defeat of 5,000 British troops under General John Burgoyne in several battles near Saratoga, New York, in October 1777; the American victory helped convince France to enter the war on the side of the Patriots.

scalawags White southern Republicans—some former Unionists—who served in Reconstruction governments.

Phyllis Schlafly (1924–2016) A right-wing Republican activist who spearheaded the anti-feminism movement. She believed feminists were "anti-family, anti-children, and pro-abortion." She worked against the equal-rights amendment for women and civil rights protection for gays.

Scopes Trial Highly publicized 1925 trial of a high school teacher in Tennessee for violating a state law that prohibited the teaching of evolution; the trial was seen as the climax of the fundamentalist war on Darwinism.

Winfield Scott (1786–1866) During the Mexican War, he was the American general who captured Mexico City, which ended the war. Using his popularity from his military success, he ran as a Whig party candidate for President.

Sears, Roebuck and Company By the end of the nineteenth century, this company dominated the mail-order industry and helped create a truly national market. Its mail-order catalog and low prices allowed people living in rural areas and small towns to buy products that were previously too expensive or available only to city dwellers.

secession Shortly after President Abraham Lincoln was elected, southern states began dissolving their ties with the United States because they believed Lincoln and the Republican party were a threat to slavery.

Second Bank of the United States (B.U.S) Established in 1816 after the first national bank's charter expired; it stabilized the economy by creating a sound national currency, by making loans to farmers, small manufacturers, and entrepreneurs, and by regulating the ability of state banks to issue their own paper currency.

Second Great Awakening Religious revival movement that arose in reaction to the growth of secularism and rationalist religion; spurred the growth of the Baptist and Methodist churches.

Second Industrial Revolution Beginning in the late nineteenth century, a wave of technological innovations, especially in iron and steel production, steam and electrical power, and telegraphic communications, all of which spurred industrial development and urban growth.

Second New Deal (1935–1938) Expansive cluster of legislation proposed by President Roosevelt that established new regulatory agencies, strengthened the rights of workers to organize unions, and laid the foundation of a federal social welfare system through the creation of Social Security.

second two-party system The political party system in the United States between 1828 and 1854, consisting of Andrew Jackson's Democratic Party and Henry Clay's Whig Party. The first two party system consisted of the Federalist and Democratic-Republican Parties.

Securities and Exchange Commission (1934) Federal agency established to regulate the issuance and trading of stocks and bonds in an effort to avoid financial panics and stock market "crashes."

Seneca Falls Convention (1848) Convention organized by feminists Lucretia Mott and Elizabeth Cady Stanton to promote women's rights and issue the pathbreaking Declaration of Sentiments.

separate but equal Principle underlying legal racial segregation, which was upheld in *Plessy v. Ferguson* (1896) and struck down in *Brown v. Board of Education* (1954).

separation of powers Strict division of the powers of government among three separate branches (executive, legislative, and judicial) which, in turn, check and balance each other.

September 11 On September 11, 2001, Islamic terrorists, who were members of the al Qaeda terrorist organization, hijacked four commercial airliners. Two were flown into the World Trade Center, a third into the Pentagon, and a fourth plane was brought down in Pennsylvania. In response, President George W. Bush launched his "war on terrorism." His administration assembled an international coalition to fight terrorism, which invaded Afghanistan after the country's government would not turn over Osama bin Laden. Bush and Congress passed the U.S.A. Patriot Act, which allowed government agencies to try suspected terrorists in secret military courts and eavesdrop on confidential conversations.

settlement houses Product of the late nineteenth-century movement to offer a broad array of social services in urban immigrant neighborhoods; Chicago's Hull House was one of hundreds of settlement houses that operated by the early twentieth century.

Seventeenth Amendment (1913) Constitutional amendment that provided for the direct election of senators rather than the traditional practice allowing state legislatures to name them.

Shakers Founded by Mother Ann Lee Stanley in England, the United Society of Believers in Christ's Second Appearing settled in Watervliet, New York, in 1774 and subsequently established eighteen additional communes in the Northeast, Indiana, and Kentucky.

share tenants Poor farmers who rented land to farm in exchange for a substantial share of the crop, though they would often have their own horse or mule, tools, and line of credit with a nearby store.

sharecroppers Poor, mostly black farmers who would work an owner's land in return for shelter, seed, fertilizer, mules, supplies, and food, as well as a substantial share of the crop produced.

Share-the-Wealth program Huey Long offered this program as an alternative to the New Deal. The program proposed to confiscate large personal fortunes, which would be used to guarantee every poor family a cash grant of $5,000 and every worker an annual income of $2,500. This program promised to provide pensions, reduce working hours, pay veterans' bonuses, and ensures a college education to every qualified student.

Shays's Rebellion (1786–1787) Storming of the Massachusetts federal arsenal by Daniel Shays and 1,200 armed farmers seeking debt relief from the state legislature through issuance of paper currency and lower taxes.

silent majority Term popularized by President Richard Nixon to describe the great majority of American voters who did not express their political opinions publicly—"the non-demonstrators."

Sixteenth Amendment (1913) Constitutional amendment that authorized the federal income tax.

slave codes Ordinances passed by a colony or state to regulate the behavior of slaves, often including brutal punishments for infractions.

Alfred E. Smith (1873–1944) In the 1928 presidential election, he won the Democratic nomination, but failed to win the presidency. Rural voters distrusted him for being Catholic and the son of Irish immigrants as well as his anti-Prohibition stance.

Captain John Smith (1580–1631) A swashbuckling soldier of fortune with rare powers of leadership and self-promotion, he was appointed to the resident council to manage Jamestown.

Joseph Smith (1805–1844) In 1823, he claimed that the Angel Moroni showed him the location of several gold tablets on which the Book of Mormon was written. Using the Book of Mormon as his gospel, he founded the Church of Jesus Christ of Latter-day Saints, or Mormons. In 1839, they settled in Commerce, Illinois, to avoid persecution. In 1844, Joseph and his brother were arrested and jailed for ordering the destruction of a newspaper that opposed them. While in jail, an anti-Mormon mob stormed the jail and killed both of them.

social Darwinism The application of Charles Darwin's theory of evolutionary natural selection to human society; Social Darwinists used the concept of "survival of the fittest" to justify class distinctions, explain poverty, and oppose government intervention in the economy.

social gospel Protestant movement that stressed the Christian obligation to address the mounting social problems caused by urbanization and industrialization.

social justice An important part of the Progressive's agenda, social justice sought to solve social problems through reform and regulation. Methods used to bring about social justice ranged from the founding of charities to the legislation of a ban on child labor.

Social Security Act (1935) Legislation enacted to provide federal assistance to retired workers through tax-funded pension payments and benefit payments to the unemployed and disabled.

Sons of Liberty First organized by Samuel Adams in the 1770s, groups of colonists dedicated to militant resistance against British control of the colonies.

Hernando de Soto (1500?–1542) A conquistador who explored the west coast of Florida, western North Carolina, and along the Arkansas river from 1539 till his death in 1542.

Southern Christian Leadership Conference (SCLC) Civil rights organization formed by Dr. Martin Luther King Jr., that championed nonviolent direct action as a means of ending segregation.

"southern strategy" This strategy was a major reason for Richard Nixon's victory in the 1968 presidential election. To gain support in the South, Nixon assured southern conservatives that he would slow the federal enforcement of civil rights laws and appoint pro-southern justices to the Supreme Court. As president, Nixon fulfilled these promises.

Spanish Armada A massive Spanish fleet of 130 warships that was defeated at Plymouth in 1588 by the English navy during the reign of Queen Elizabeth I.

Spanish flu Unprecedentedly lethal influenza epidemic of 1918 that killed more than 22 million people worldwide.

Herbert Spencer (1820–1903) As the first major proponent of social Darwinism, he argued that human society and institutions are subject to the process of natural selection and that society naturally evolves for the better. He was against any form of government interference with the evolution of society, like business regulations, because it would help the "unfit" to survive.

spirituals Songs with religious messages sung by slaves to help ease the strain of field labor and to voice their suffering at the hands of their masters and overseers.

spoils system The term—meaning the filling of federal government jobs with persons loyal to the party of the president—originated in Andrew Jackson's first term; the system was replaced in the Progressive Era by civil service.

Square Deal Roosevelt's progressive agenda of the "Three C's": control of corporations, conservation of natural resources, and consumer protection.

stagflation Term coined by economists during the Nixon presidency to describe the unprecedented situation of stagnant economic growth and consumer price inflation occurring at the same time.

Joseph Stalin (1879–1953) The Bolshevik leader who succeeded Lenin as the leader of the Soviet Union in 1924 and ruled the country until his death. During his totalitarian rule of the Soviet Union, he used purges and a system of forced labor camps to maintain control over the country, and claimed vast areas of Eastern Europe for Soviet domination.

Stalwarts Conservative Republican party faction during the presidency of Rutherford B. Hayes, 1877–1881; led by Senator Roscoe B. Conkling of New York, Stalwarts opposed civil service reform and favored a third term for President Ulysses S. Grant.

Stamp Act (1765) Act of Parliament requiring that all printed materials (e.g., newspapers, bonds, and even playing cards) in the American colonies use paper with an official tax stamp in order to pay for British military protection of the colonies.

Stamp Act Congress Twenty-seven delegates from nine of the colonies met from October 7 to 25, 1765 and wrote a Declaration of the Rights and Grievances of the Colonies, a petition to the King and a petition to Parliament for the repeal of the Stamp Act.

Standard Oil Company Corporation under the leadership of John D. Rockefeller that attempted to dominate the entire oil industry through horizontal and vertical integration.

Elizabeth Cady Stanton (1815–1902) A prominent reformer and advocate for the rights of women, she helped organize the Seneca Falls Convention to discuss women's rights. The convention was the first of its kind and produced the Declaration of Sentiments, which proclaimed the equality of men and women.

staple crop A profitable market crop, such as cotton, tobacco, or rice that predominates in a given region.

state constitutions Charters that define the relationship between the state government and local governments and individuals, and also protects their rights from violation by the national government.

steamboats Ships and boats powered by wood-fired steam engines. First used in the early nineteenth century, they made two-way traffic possible in eastern river systems, creating a transcontinental market and an agricultural empire.

Thaddeus Stevens (1792–1868) As one of the leaders of the Radical Republicans, he argued that the former Confederate states should be viewed as conquered provinces, which were subject to the demands of the conquerors. He believed that all of Southern society needed to be changed, and he supported the abolition of slavery and racial equality.

Adlai E. Stevenson (1900–1965) In the 1952 and 1956 presidential elections, he was the Democratic nominee who lost to Dwight Eisenhower. He was also the U.S. Ambassador to the United Nations and is remembered for his famous speech in 1962 before the UN Security Council that unequivocally demonstrated that the Soviet Union had built nuclear missile bases in Cuba.

Stonewall riots (1969) Violent clashes between police and lesbian, gay, bisexual, transgender, and queer (LGBTQ) patrons of New York City's Stonewall Inn, seen as the starting point of the modern LGBTQ rights movement.

Stono Rebellion (1739) A slave uprising in South Carolina that was brutally quashed, leading to executions as well as a severe tightening of the slave code.

Strategic Arms Limitation Talks (SALT I) (1972) Agreement signed by President Nixon and Secretary Brezhnev prohibiting the development of missile defense systems in the United States and Soviet Union and limiting the quantity of nuclear warheads for both.

Strategic Defense Initiative (SDI) (1983) Ronald Reagan's proposed space-based antimissile defense system, dubbed "Star Wars" by the media, that aroused great controversy and escalated the arms race between the United States and the Soviet Union.

Levi Strauss (1829–1902) A Jewish tailor who followed miners to California during the gold rush and began making durable work pants that were later dubbed blue jeans or Levi's.

Student Nonviolent Coordinating Committee (SNCC) Interracial organization formed in 1960 with the goal of intensifying the effort to end racial segregation.

Students for a Democratic Society (SDS) Major organization of the New Left, founded at the University of Michigan in 1960 by Tom Hayden and Al Haber.

suburbia Communities formed from mass migration of middle-class whites from urban centers.

Suez crisis (1956) British, French, and Israeli attack on Egypt after Nasser's seizure of the Suez Canal; President Eisenhower interceded to demand the withdrawal of the British, French, and Israeli forces from the Sinai Peninsula and the canal.

Sun Belt The label for an arc that stretched from the Carolinas to California. During the postwar era, much of the urban population growth occurred in this area.

"surge" In early 2007, President Bush decided he would send a "surge" of new troops to Iraq and implement a new strategy. U.S. forces would shift their focus from offensive operations to the protection of Iraqi civilians from attacks by terrorist insurgents and sectarian militias. While the "surge" reduced the violence in Iraq, Iraqi leaders were still unable to develop a self-sustaining democracy.

Taft-Hartley Labor Act (1947) Congressional legislation that banned "unfair labor practices" by labor unions, required union leaders to sign anti-Communist "loyalty oaths," and prohibited federal employees from going on strike.

Taliban A coalition of ultraconservative Islamists who rose to power in Afghanistan after the Soviets withdrew. The Taliban leaders gave Osama bin Laden a safe haven in their country in exchange for aid in fighting the Northern Alliance, who were rebels opposed to the Taliban. After they refused to turn bin Laden over to the United States, America invaded Afghanistan.

Tammany Hall The "city machine" used by "Boss" Tweed to dominate politics in New York City until his arrest in 1871.

tariff A tax on goods imported from other nations, typically used to protect home industries from foreign competitors and to generate revenue for the federal government.

Tariff of 1816 A cluster of taxes on imports passed by Congress to protect America's emerging iron and textile industries from British competition.

Tariff of 1832 This tariff act reduced the duties on many items, but the tariffs on cloth and iron remained high. South Carolina nullified it along with the tariff of 1828. President Andrew Jackson sent federal troops to the state and asked Congress to grant him the authority to enforce the tariffs. Henry Clay presented a plan of gradually reducing the tariffs until 1842, which Congress passed and ended the crisis.

Tariff of Abominations (1828) Tax on imported goods, including British cloth and clothing, that strengthened New England textile companies but hurt southern consumers, who experienced a decrease in British demand for raw cotton grown in the South.

tariff reform (1887) Effort led by the Democratic party to reduce taxes on imported goods, which Republicans argued were needed to protect American industries from foreign competition.

Troubled Asset Relief Program (TARP) In 2008 President George W. Bush signed into law the bank bailout fund called Troubled Asset Relief Program (TARP), which required the Treasury Department to spend $700 billion to keep banks and other financial institutions from collapsing.

Zachary Taylor (1784–1850) During the Mexican War, he scored two quick victories against Mexico, which made him very popular in America. He used his popularity from his military victories to be elected president as a member of the Whig party, but died before he could complete his term.

Taylorism Labor system based on detailed study of work tasks, championed by Frederick Winslow Taylor, intended to maximize efficiency and profits for employers.

Tea Party Right-wing populist movement, largely made up of middle-class, white male conservatives, that emerged as a response to the expansion of the federal government under the Obama administration.

Teapot Dome Affair (1923) Harding administration scandal in which Secretary of the Interior Albert B. Fall profited from secret leasing of government oil reserves in Wyoming to private oil companies.

Tecumseh (1768–1813) He was a leader of the Shawnee tribe who tried to unite all Indians into a confederation that could defend their hunting grounds. He believed that no land cessions could be made without the consent of all the tribes since they held the land in common. His beliefs and leadership made him seem dangerous to the American government and they waged war on him and his tribe. He was killed at the Battle of the Thames.

Tecumseh's Indian Confederacy A group of Native Americans under leadership of Shawnee leader Tecumseh and his prophet brother Tenskwatawa; its mission of fighting off American expansion was thwarted in the Battle of Tippecanoe (1811), when the confederacy fell apart.

telegraph system System of electronic communication invented by Samuel F. B. Morse that could be transmitted instantaneously across great distances (first used in the 1840s).

Teller Amendment Addition to the congressional war resolution of April 20, 1898, which marked the U.S. entry into the war with Spain; the amendment declared that the United States' goal in entering the war was to ensure Cuba's independence, not to annex Cuba as a territory.

temperance A widespread reform movement, led by militant Christians, focused on reducing the use of alcoholic beverages.

tenements Shabby, low-cost inner-city apartment buildings that housed the urban poor in cramped, unventilated apartments.

Tenochtitlán The capital city of the Aztec Empire. The city was built on marshy islands on the western side of Lake Tetzcoco, which is the site of present-day Mexico City.

Tet offensive (1968) Surprise attack by Viet Cong guerrillas and the North Vietnamese army on U.S. and South Vietnamese forces that shocked the American public and led to widespread sentiment against the war.

Texas Revolution (1835–1836) Conflict between Texas colonists and the Mexican government that resulted in the creation of the separate Republic of Texas in 1836.

textile industry Commercial production of thread, fabric, and clothing from raw cotton in mills in New England during the first half of the nineteenth century, and later in the South in the late nineteenth century.

Thirteenth Amendment (1865) Amendment to the U. S. Constitution that freed all slaves in the United States.

Battle of Tippecanoe (1811) Battle in northern Indiana between U.S. troops and Native American warriors led by Tenskwatawa, the brother of Tecumseh, who had organized an anti-American Indian confederacy to fight American efforts to settle on Indian lands.

tobacco A cash crop grown in the Caribbean as well as the Virginia and Maryland colonies, made increasingly profitable by the rapidly growing popularity of smoking in Europe after the voyages of Columbus.

Gulf of Tonkin incident On August 2 and 4 of 1964, North Vietnamese vessels attacked two American destroyers in the Gulf of Tonkin off the coast of North Vietnam. President Johnson described the attacks as unprovoked. In reality, the U.S. ships were monitoring South Vietnamese attacks on North Vietnamese islands that America advisors had planned. The incident spurred the Tonkin Gulf resolution.

Tonkin Gulf Resolution Congressional action that granted the president unlimited authority to defend U.S. forces abroad, passed in August 1964 after an allegedly unprovoked attack on American warships off the coast of North Vietnam.

Tories Term used by Patriots to refer to Loyalists, or colonists who supported the Crown after the Declaration of Independence.

Townshend Acts Parliamentary measures to extract more revenue from the colonies; the Revenue Act of 1767, which taxed tea, paper, and other colonial imports, was one of the most notorious of these policies.

Trail of Tears (1832–1840) The Cherokees' 800-mile journey from the southern Appalachians to Indian Territory (in present-day Oklahoma); 4,000 people died along the way.

transcendentalism Philosophy of a small group of New England writers and thinkers who advocated personal spirituality, self-reliance, social reform, and harmony with nature.

Transcontinental railroad First line across the continent from Omaha, Nebraska, to Sacramento, California, established in 1869 with the linkage of the Union Pacific and Central Pacific railroads at Promontory, Utah.

Transcontinental Treaty (1819) (Adams-Onís Treaty) Treaty between Spain and the United States that clarified the boundaries of the Louisiana Purchase and arranged the transfer of Florida to the United States in exchange for cash.

Treaty of Ghent Agreement between Great Britain and the United States that ended the War of 1812, signed on December 24, 1814.

Treaty of Guadalupe Hidalgo (1848) Treaty between United States and Mexico that ended the Mexican-American War.

Treaty of Paris (1763) Settlement between Great Britain and France that ended the French and Indian War.

Treaty of Versailles Peace treaty that ended the First World War, forcing Germany to dismantle its military, pay immense war reparations, and give up its colonies around the world.

trench warfare A form of prolonged combat between the entrenched positions of opposing armies, often with little tactical movement.

Battle of Trenton A surprising and pivotal victory for General Washington and American forces in December 1776 that resulted in major British and Hessian losses.

triangular trade A network of trade in which exports from one region were sold to another region, which sent its exports to a third region, which exported its own goods back to the first country or colony.

Harry S. Truman (1884–1972) As President Roosevelt's vice president, he succeeded him after his death near the end of the Second World War. After the war, Truman wrestled with the inflation of both prices and wages, worked with Congress to pass the National Security Act, and banned racial discrimination in the hiring of federal employees and ended racial segregation in the armed forces. In foreign affairs, he established the Truman Doctrine to contain communism, developed the Marshall Plan to rebuild Europe, and sent the U.S. military to defend South Korea after North Korea invaded.

Truman Doctrine (1947) President Truman's program of "containing" communism in Eastern Europe and providing economic and military aid to any nations at risk of Communist takeover.

Donald J. Trump (1946–) The 45th President of the United States.

trust A business arrangement that gives a person or corporation (the "trustee") the legal power to manage another person's money or another company without owning those entities outright.

Sojourner Truth (1797?–1883) She was born into slavery, but New York State freed her in 1827. She spent the 1840s and 1850s travelling across the country and speaking to audiences about her experiences as slave and asking them to support abolition and women's rights.

Harriet Tubman (1820–1913) She was born a slave, but escaped to the North. She then returned to the South nineteen times and guided 300 slaves to freedom.

Frederick Jackson Turner An influential historian who authored the "Frontier Thesis" in 1893, arguing that the existence of an alluring frontier and the experience of persistent westward expansion informed the nation's democratic politics, unfettered economy, and rugged individualism.

Nat Turner (1800–1831) He was the leader of the only slave revolt to get past the planning stages. In August of 1831, the revolt began with the slaves killing the members of Turner's master's household. Then they attacked other neighboring farmhouses and recruited more slaves until the militia crushed the revolt. At least fifty-five whites were killed during the uprising and seventeen slaves were hanged afterwards.

Nat Turner's Rebellion (1831) Insurrection in rural Virginia led by black overseer Nat Turner, who killed slave owners and their families; in turn, federal troops indiscriminately killed hundreds of slaves in the process of putting down Turner and his rebels.

Tuskegee Airmen U.S. Army Air Corps unit of African American pilots whose combat success spurred military and civilian leaders to desegregate the armed forces after the war.

Mark Twain (1835–1910) Born Samuel Langhorne Clemens in Missouri, he became a popular humorous writer and lecturer and established himself as one of the great American satirists and authors. His two greatest books, *The Adventures of Tom Sawyer* and *The Adventures of Huckleberry Finn*, drew heavily on his childhood in Missouri.

"Boss" Tweed (1823–1878) An infamous political boss in New York City, Tweed used his "city machine," the Tammany Hall ring, to rule, plunder and sometimes improve the city's government. His political domination of New York City ended with his arrest in 1871 and conviction in 1873.

Twenty-first Amendment (1933) Repealed prohibition on the manufacture, sale, and transportation of alcoholic beverages, effectively nullifying the Eighteenth Amendment.

two-party system Domination of national politics by two major political parties, such as the Whigs and Democrats during the 1830s and 1840s.

U-boat German military submarine (*Unterseeboot*) used during the First World War to attack enemy naval vessels as well as merchant ships of enemy and neutral nations.

Underground Railroad A secret system of routes and safe houses through which runaway slaves were led to freedom in the North.

Unitarians Members of the liberal New England Congregationalist offshoot, often well-educated and wealthy, who profess the oneness of God and the goodness of rational man.

United Farm Workers (UFW) Organization formed in 1965 to represent the interests of Mexican American migrant workers.

United Nations Security Council A major agency within the United Nations which remains in permanent session and has the responsibility of maintaining international peace and security. Originally, it consisted of five permanent members, (United States, Soviet Union, Britain, France, and the Republic of China), and six members elected to two-year terms. After 1965, the number of rotating members was increased to ten. In 1971, the Republic of China was replaced with the People's Republic of China and the Soviet Union was replaced by the Russian Federation in 1991.

Universalists Members of a New England religious movement, often from the working class, who believed in a merciful God and universal salvation.

USA Patriot Act (2001) Wide-reaching Congressional legislation, triggered by the war on terror, which gave government agencies the right to eavesdrop on confidential conversations between prison inmates and their lawyers and permitted suspected terrorists to be tried in secret military courts.

utopian communities Ideal communities that offered innovative social and economic relationships to those who were interested in achieving salvation.

Valley Forge American military encampment near Philadelphia, where more than 3,500 soldiers deserted or died from cold and hunger in the winter of 1777–1778.

Cornelius Vanderbilt (1794–1877) In the 1860s, he consolidated several separate railroad companies into one vast entity, New York Central Railroad.

Bartolomeo Vanzetti (1888–1927) In 1920, he and Nicola Sacco were Italian immigrants who were arrested for stealing $16,000 and killing a paymaster and his guard. Their trial took place during a time of numerous bombings by anarchists and their judge was openly prejudicial. Many liberals and radicals believe that their conviction was based on their political ideas and ethnic origin rather than the evidence against them.

vertical integration The process by which a corporation gains control of all aspects of the resources and processes needed to produce and sell a product.

Amerigo Vespucci (1455–1512) Italian explorer who reached the New World in 1499 and was the first to suggest that South America was a new continent. Afterward, European mapmakers used a variant of his first name, America, to label the New World.

Battle of Vicksburg (1863) A protracted battle in northern Mississippi in which Union forces under Ulysses Grant besieged the last major Confederate fortress on the Mississippi River, forcing the inhabitants into starvation and then submission.

Viet Cong Communist guerrillas in Vietnam who launched attacks on the Diem government.

Vietnamization Nixon-era policy of equipping and training South Vietnamese forces to take over the burden of combat from U.S. troops.

Vikings Norse people from Scandinavia who sailed to Newfoundland about a.d. 1001.

Francisco Pancho Villa (1877–1923) While the leader of one of the competing factions in the Mexican civil war, he provoked the United States into intervening. He hoped attacking the United States would help him build a reputation as an opponent of the United States, which would increase his popularity and discredit Mexican President Carranza.

Virginia Company A joint stock enterprise that King James I chartered in 1606. The company was to spread Christianity in the New World as well as find ways to make a profit in it.

Virginia Plan The delegations to the Constitutional Convention were divided between two plans on how to structure the government: Virginia called for a strong central government and a two-house legislature apportioned by population.

Virginia Statute of Religious Freedom A Virginia law, drafted by Thomas Jefferson in 1777 and enacted in 1786, that guarantees freedom of, and from, religion.

virtual representation The idea that the American colonies, although they had no actual representative in Parliament, were "virtually" represented by all members of Parliament.

Voting Rights Act of 1965 Legislation ensuring that all Americans were able to vote; the law ended literacy tests and other means of restricting voting rights.

Wagner Act (1935) Legislation that guaranteed workers the right to organize unions, granted them direct bargaining power, and barred employers from interfering with union activities.

George Wallace (1919–1998) An outspoken defender of segregation. As the governor of Alabama, he once attempted to block African American students from enrolling at the University of Alabama. He ran as the presidential candidate for the American Independent party in 1968, appealing to voters who were concerned about rioting anti-war protestors, the welfare system, and the growth of the federal government.

war hawks In 1811, congressional members from the southern and western districts who clamored for a war to seize Canada and Florida were dubbed "war hawks."

War of 1812 (1812–1815) Conflict fought in North America and at sea between Great Britain and the United States over American shipping rights and British efforts to spur Indian attacks on American settlements. Canadians and Native Americans also fought in the war.

war on terror Global crusade to root out anti-American, anti-Western Islamist terrorist cells launched by President George W. Bush as a response to the 9/11 attacks.

War Powers Act (1973) Legislation requiring the president to inform Congress within 48 hours of the deployment of U.S. troops abroad and to withdraw them after 60 days unless Congress approves their continued deployment.

War Production Board Federal agency created by President Roosevelt in 1942 that converted America's industrial output to war production.

war relocation camps Detention camps housing thousands of Japanese Americans from the West Coast who were forcibly interned from 1942 until the end of the Second World War.

Warren Court The U.S. Supreme Court under Chief Justice Earl Warren, 1953–1969, decided such landmark cases as *Brown v. Board of Education* (school desegregation), *Baker v. Carr* (legislative redistricting), and *Gideon v. Wainwright* and *Miranda v. Arizona* (rights of criminal defendants).

Booker T. Washington (1856–1915) He founded a leading college for African Americans in Tuskegee, Alabama, and become the foremost black educator in America by the 1890s. He believed that the African American community should establish an economic base for its advancement before striving for social equality. His critics charged that his philosophy sacrificed educational and civil rights for dubious social acceptance and economic opportunities.

George Washington (1732–1799) In 1775, the Continental Congress named him the commander in chief of the Continental Army which defeated the British in the American Revolution. He had previously served as an officer in the French and Indian War. In 1787, he was the presiding officer over the Constitutional Convention, but participated little in the debates. In 1789, the Electoral College chose Washington to be the nation's first president. Washington faced the nation's first foreign and domestic crises, maintaining the United States' neutrality in foreign affairs. After two terms in office, Washington chose to step down; and the power of the presidency was peacefully passed to John Adams.

Watergate (1972–1974) Scandal that exposed the criminality and corruption of the Nixon administration and ultimately led to President Nixon's resignation in 1974.

weapons of mass destruction (WMDs) Radioactive, chemical, or biological weapons capable of unleashing mass death and damage. The Bush administration believed Saddam Hussein to possess such weapons, which it used to justify the second U.S invasion of Iraq during the War on Terror following the 9/11 terrorist bombings.

Daniel Webster (1782–1852) As a representative from New Hampshire, he led the New Federalists in opposition to the moving of the second national bank from Boston to Philadelphia. Later, he served as representative and a senator for Massachusetts and emerged as a champion of a stronger national government. He also switched from opposing to supporting tariffs because New England had built up its manufactures with the understanding tariffs would protect them from foreign competitors.

Webster-Ashburton Treaty Settlement in 1842 of U.S.–Canadian border disputes in Maine, New York, Vermont, and in the Wisconsin Territory (now northern Minnesota).

Webster-Hayne debate U.S. Senate debate of January 1830 between Daniel Webster of Massachusetts and Robert Hayne of South Carolina over nullification and states' rights.

Western Front The contested frontier between the Central and Allied Powers that ran along northern France and across Belgium.

Whig party Political party founded in 1834 in opposition to the Jacksonian Democrats; Whigs supported federal funding for internal improvements, a national bank, and high tariffs on imported goods.

Whigs Another name for revolutionary Patriots.

Whiskey Rebellion (1794) Violent protest by western Pennsylvania farmers against the federal excise tax on corn whiskey, put down by a federal army.

Eli Whitney (1765–1825) He invented the cotton gin which could separate cotton from its seeds. One machine operator could separate fifty times more cotton than worker could by hand, which led to an increase in cotton production and prices. These increases gave planters a new profitable use for slavery and a lucrative slave trade emerged from the coastal South to the Southwest.

Wilderness Road Originally an Indian path through the Cumberland Gap, it was used by over 300,000 settlers who migrated westward to Kentucky in the last quarter of the eighteenth century.

Roger Williams (1603–1683) Puritan who believed that the purity of the church required a complete separation between church and state and freedom from coercion in matters of faith. In 1636, he established the town of Providence, the first permanent settlement in Rhode Island and the first to allow religious freedom in America.

Wendell L. Willkie (1892–1944) In the 1940 presidential election, he was the Republican nominee who ran against President Roosevelt. He supported aid to the Allies and criticized the New Deal programs. Voters looked at the increasingly dangerous world situation and chose to keep President Roosevelt in office for a third term.

Wilmot Proviso (1846) Proposal by Congressman David Wilmot, a Pennsylvania Democrat, to prohibit slavery in any land acquired in the Mexican-American War.

Woodrow Wilson (1856–1924) In the 1912 presidential election, Woodrow Wilson ran under the slogan of New Freedom, which promised to improve of the banking system, lower tariffs, and break up monopolies. At the beginning of the First World War, Wilson kept America neutral, but provided the Allies with credit for purchases of supplies; however, the sinking of U.S. merchant ships and the Zimmerman telegram caused him to ask Congress to declare war on Germany. Wilson supported the entry of America into the League of Nations and the ratification of the Treaty of Versailles, but Congress would not approve the entry or ratification.

John Winthrop Puritan leader and Governor of the Massachusetts Bay Colony who resolved to use the colony as a refuge for persecuted Puritans and as an instrument of building a "wilderness Zion" in America.

women's suffrage Movement to give women the right to vote through a constitutional amendment, spearheaded by Susan B. Anthony and Elizabeth Cady Stanton's National Woman Suffrage Association.

Women Accepted for Voluntary Emergency Services (WAVES) During the Second World War, the increased demand for labor shook up old prejudices about gender roles in the workplace and in the military. Nearly 200,000 women served in the Women's Army Corps or its naval equivalent, Women Accepted for Volunteer Emergency Service (WAVES).

Women's Army Corps Women's branch of the United States Army; by the end of the Second World War nearly 150,000 women had served in the WAC.

women's movement Wave of activism sparked by Betty Friedan's *The Feminine Mystique* (1963); it argued for equal rights for women and fought against the cult of domesticity of the 1950s that limited women's roles to the home as wife, mother, and housewife.

women's work The traditional term referring to routine tasks in the house, garden, and fields performed by women. The sphere of women's occupations expanded in the colonies to include medicine, shopkeeping, upholstering, and the operation of inns and taverns.

Woodstock In 1969, roughly a half a million young people converged on a farm near Bethel, New York, for a three-day music festival that was an expression of the flower children's free spirit.

Works Progress Administration (1935) Government agency established to manage several federal job programs created under the New Deal; the WPA became the largest employer in the nation.

Battle of Wounded Knee Last incident of the Indians Wars took place in 1890 in the Dakota Territory, where the U.S. Cavalry killed over 200 Sioux men, women, and children who were in the process of surrender.

XYZ affair French foreign minister Tallyrand's three anonymous agents demanded payments to stop French plundering of American ships in 1797; refusal to pay the bribe led to two years of sea war with France (1798–1800).

Yalta Conference (1945) Meeting of the "Big Three" Allied leaders, Franklin D. Roosevelt, Winston Churchill, and Joseph Stalin, to discuss how to divide control of postwar Germany and Eastern Europe

yellow journalism A type of news reporting, epitomized in the 1890s by the newspaper empires of William Randolph Hearst and Joseph Pulitzer, that intentionally manipulates public opinion through sensational headlines, illustrations, and articles about both real and invented events.

yeomen Small landowners (the majority of white families in the South) who farmed their own land and usually did not own slaves.

Battle of Yorktown Last major battle of the Revolutionary War; General Cornwallis along with over 7,000 British troops surrendered to George Washington at Yorktown, Virginia, on October 17, 1781.

Brigham Young (1801–1877) Following Joseph Smith's death, he became the leader of the Mormons and promised Illinois officials that the Mormons would leave the state. In 1846, he led the Mormons to Utah and settled near the Salt Lake. After the United States gained Utah as part of the Treaty of Guadalupe Hidalgo, he became the governor of the territory and kept the Mormons virtually independent of federal authority.

youth culture The youth of the 1950s had more money and free time than any previous generation which allowed a distinct youth culture to emerge. A market emerged for products and activities that were specifically for young people such as transistor radios, rock records, *Seventeen* magazine, and Pat Boone movies.

Zimmermann telegram Message sent by a German official to the Mexican government in 1917 urging an invasion of the United States; the telegram was intercepted by British intelligence agents and angered Americans, many of whom called for war against Germany.

APPENDIX

THE DECLARATION OF INDEPENDENCE (1776)

When in the Course of human events, it becomes necessary for one people to dissolve the political bands which have connected them with another, and to assume among the powers of the earth, the separate and equal station to which the Laws of Nature and of Nature's God entitle them, a decent respect to the opinions of mankind requires that they should declare the causes which impel them to the separation.

We hold these truths to be self-evident, that all men are created equal, that they are endowed by their Creator with certain unalienable Rights, that among these are Life, Liberty and the pursuit of Happiness. —That to secure these rights, Governments are instituted among Men, deriving their just powers from the consent of the governed, —That whenever any Form of Government becomes destructive of these ends, it is the Right of the People to alter or to abolish it, and to institute new Government, laying its foundation on such principles and organizing its powers in such form, as to them shall seem most likely to effect their Safety and Happiness. Prudence, indeed, will dictate that Governments long established should not be changed for light and transient causes; and accordingly all experience hath shewn, that mankind are more disposed to suffer, while evils are sufferable, than to right themselves by abolishing the forms to which they are accustomed. But when a long train of abuses and usurpations, pursuing invariably the same Object evinces a design to reduce them under absolute Despotism, it is their right, it is their duty, to throw off such Government, and to provide new Guards for their future security.—Such has been the patient sufferance of these Colonies; and such is now the necessity which constrains them to alter their former Systems of Government. The history of the present King of Great Britain is a history of repeated injuries and usurpations, all having in direct object the establishment of an absolute Tyranny over these States. To prove this, let Facts be submitted to a candid world.

He has refused his Assent to Laws, the most wholesome and necessary for the public good.

He has forbidden his Governors to pass Laws of immediate and pressing importance, unless suspended in their operation till his Assent should be obtained; and when so suspended, he has utterly neglected to attend to them.

He has refused to pass other Laws for the accommodation of large districts of people, unless those people would relinquish the right of Representation in the Legislature, a right inestimable to them and formidable to tyrants only.

He has called together legislative bodies at places unusual, uncomfortable, and distant from the depository of their public Records, for the sole purpose of fatiguing them into compliance with his measures.

He has dissolved Representative Houses repeatedly, for opposing with manly firmness his invasions on the rights of the people.

He has refused for a long time, after such dissolutions, to cause others to be elected; whereby the Legislative powers, incapable of Annihilation, have returned to the People at large for their exercise; the State remaining in the mean time exposed to all the dangers of invasion from without, and convulsions within.

He has endeavoured to prevent the population of these States; for that purpose obstructing the Laws for Naturalization of Foreigners; refusing to pass others to encourage their migrations hither, and raising the conditions of new Appropriations of Lands.

He has obstructed the Administration of Justice, by refusing his Assent to Laws for establishing Judiciary powers.

He has made Judges dependent on his Will alone, for the tenure of their offices, and the amount and payment of their salaries.

He has erected a multitude of New Offices, and sent hither swarms of Officers to harrass our people, and eat out their substance.

He has kept among us, in times of peace, Standing Armies without the Consent of our legislatures.

He has affected to render the Military independent of and superior to the Civil power.

He has combined with others to subject us to a jurisdiction foreign to our constitution, and unacknowledged by our laws; giving his Assent to their Acts of pretended Legislation:

For quartering large bodies of armed troops among us:

For protecting them, by a mock Trial, from punishment for any Murders which they should commit on the Inhabitants of these States:

For cutting off our Trade with all parts of the world:

For imposing Taxes on us without our Consent:

For depriving us in many cases, of the benefits of Trial by Jury:

For transporting us beyond Seas to be tried for pretended offences

For abolishing the free System of English Laws in a neighbouring Province, establishing therein an Arbitrary government, and enlarging its Boundaries so as to render it at once an example and fit instrument for introducing the same absolute rule into these Colonies:

For taking away our Charters, abolishing our most valuable Laws, and altering fundamentally the Forms of our Governments:

For suspending our own Legislatures, and declaring themselves invested with power to legislate for us in all cases whatsoever.

He has abdicated Government here, by declaring us out of his Protection and waging War against us.

He has plundered our seas, ravaged our Coasts, burnt our towns, and destroyed the lives of our people.

He is at this time transporting large Armies of foreign Mercenaries to compleat the works of death, desolation and tyranny, already begun with circumstances of Cruelty & perfidy scarcely paralleled in the most barbarous ages, and totally unworthy the Head of a civilized nation.

He has constrained our fellow Citizens taken Captive on the high Seas to bear Arms against their Country, to become the executioners of their friends and Brethren, or to fall themselves by their Hands.

He has excited domestic insurrections amongst us, and has endeavoured to bring on the inhabitants of our frontiers, the merciless Indian Savages, whose known rule of warfare, is an undistinguished destruction of all ages, sexes and conditions.

In every stage of these Oppressions We have Petitioned for Redress in the most humble terms: Our repeated Petitions have been answered only by repeated injury. A Prince whose character is thus marked by every act which may define a Tyrant, is unfit to be the ruler of a free people.

Nor have We been wanting in attentions to our Brittish brethren. We have warned them from time to time of attempts by their legislature to extend an unwarrantable jurisdiction over us. We have reminded them of the circumstances of our emigration and settlement here. We have appealed to their native justice and magnanimity, and we have conjured them by the ties of our common kindred to disavow these usurpations, which, would inevitably interrupt our connections and correspondence. They too have been deaf to the voice of justice and of consanguinity. We must, therefore, acquiesce in the necessity, which denounces our Separation, and hold them, as we hold the rest of mankind, Enemies in War, in Peace Friends.

We, therefore, the Representatives of the united States of America, in General Congress, Assembled, appealing to the Supreme Judge of the world for the rectitude of our intentions, do, in the Name, and by Authority of the good People of these Colonies, solemnly publish and declare, That these United Colonies are, and of Right ought to be Free and Independent States; that they are Absolved from all Allegiance to the British Crown, and that all political connection between them and the State of Great Britain, is and ought to be totally dissolved; and that as Free and Independent States, they have full Power to levy War, conclude Peace, contract Alliances, establish Commerce, and to do all other Acts and Things which Independent States may of right do. And for the support of this Declaration, with a firm reliance on the protection of divine Providence, we mutually pledge to each other our Lives, our Fortunes and our sacred Honor.

Georgia
Button Gwinnett
Lyman Hall
George Walton

North Carolina
William Hooper
Joseph Hewes
John Penn

South Carolina
Edward Rutledge
Thomas Heyward, Jr.
Thomas Lynch, Jr.
Arthur Middleton

Massachusetts
John Hancock

Maryland
Samuel Chase
William Paca
Thomas Stone
Charles Carroll of
    Carrollton

Virginia
George Wythe
Richard Henry Lee
Thomas Jefferson
Benjamin Harrison
Thomas Nelson, Jr.
Francis Lightfoot Lee
Carter Braxton

Pennsylvania
Robert Morris
Benjamin Rush
Benjamin Franklin
John Morton
George Clymer
James Smith
George Taylor
James Wilson
George Ross

Delaware
Caesar Rodney
George Read
Thomas McKean

New York
William Floyd
Philip Livingston
Francis Lewis
Lewis Morris

New Jersey
Richard Stockton
John Witherspoon
Francis Hopkinson
John Hart
Abraham Clark

New Hampshire
Josiah Bartlett
William Whipple

Massachusetts
Samuel Adams
John Adams
Robert Treat Paine
Elbridge Gerry

Rhode Island
Stephen Hopkins
William Ellery

Connecticut
Roger Sherman
Samuel Huntington
William Williams
Oliver Wolcott

New Hampshire
Matthew Thornton

ARTICLES OF CONFEDERATION (1787)

To ALL TO WHOM these Presents shall come, we the undersigned Delegates of the States affixed to our Names send greeting.

Whereas the Delegates of the United States of America in Congress assembled did on the fifteenth day of November in the Year of our Lord One Thousand Seven Hundred and Seventy-seven, and in the Second Year of the Independence of America agree to certain articles of Confederation and perpetual Union between the States of Newhampshire, Massachusetts-bay, Rhodeisland and Providence Plantations, Connecticut, New York, New Jersey, Pennsylvania, Delaware, Maryland, Virginia, North-Carolina, South-Carolina and Georgia in the Words following, viz.

Articles of Confederation and perpetual Union between the States of Newhampshire, Massachusetts-bay, Rhodeisland and Providence Plantations, Connecticut, New-York, New-Jersey, Pennsylvania, Delaware, Maryland, Virginia, North-Carolina, South-Carolina and Georgia.

ARTICLE I. The stile of this confederacy shall be "The United States of America."

ARTICLE II. Each State retains its sovereignty, freedom and independence, and every power, jurisdiction and right, which is not by this confederation expressly delegated to the United States, in Congress assembled.

ARTICLE III. The said States hereby severally enter into a firm league of friendship with each other, for their common defence, the security of their liberties, and their mutual and general welfare, binding themselves to assist each other, against all force offered to, or attacks made upon them, or any of them, on account of religion, sovereignty, trade or any other pretence whatever.

ARTICLE IV. The better to secure and perpetuate mutual friendship and intercourse among the people of the different States in this Union, the free inhabitants of each of these States, paupers, vagabonds and fugitives from justice excepted, shall be entitled to all privileges and immunities of free citizens in the several States; and the people of each State shall have free ingress and regress to and from any other State, and shall enjoy therein all the privileges of trade and commerce, subject to the same duties, impositions and restrictions as the inhabitants thereof respectively, provided that such restrictions shall not extend so far as to prevent the removal of property imported into any State, to any other State of which the owner is an inhabitant; provided also that no imposition, duties or restriction shall be laid by any State, on the property of the United States, or either of them.

If any person guilty of, or charged with treason, felony, or other high misdemeanor in any State, shall flee from justice, and be found in any of the United States, he shall upon demand of the Governor or Executive power, of the State from which he fled, be delivered up and removed to the State having jurisdiction of his offence.

Full faith and credit shall be given in each of these States to the records, acts and judicial proceedings of the courts and magistrates of every other State.

ARTICLE V. For the more convenient management of the general interests of the United States, delegates shall be annually appointed in such manner as the legislature of each State shall direct, to meet in Congress on the first Monday in November, in every year, with a power reserved to each State, to recall its delegates, or any of them, at any time within the year, and to send others in their stead, for the remainder of the year.

No State shall be represented in Congress by less than two, nor by more than seven members; and no person shall be capable of being a delegate for more than three years in any term of six years; nor shall any person, being a delegate, be capable of holding any office under the United States, for which he, or another for his benefit receives any salary, fees or emolument of any kind.

Each State shall maintain its own delegates in a meeting of the States, and while they act as members of the committee of the States.

In determining questions in the United States, in Congress assembled, each State shall have one vote.

Freedom of speech and debate in Congress shall not be impeached or questioned in any court, or place out of Congress, and the members of Congress shall be protected in their persons from arrests and imprisonments, during the time of their going to and from, and attendance on Congress, except for treason, felony, or breach of the peace.

ARTICLE VI. No State without the consent of the United States in Congress assembled, shall send any embassy to, or receive any embassy from, or enter into any conference, agreement, alliance or treaty with any king, prince or state; nor shall any person holding any office of profit or trust under the United States, or any of them, accept of any present, emolument, office or title of any kind whatever from any king, prince or foreign state; nor shall the United States in Congress assembled, or any of them, grant any title of nobility.

No two or more States shall enter into any treaty, confederation or alliance whatever between them, without the consent of the United States in Congress assembled, specifying accurately the purposes for which the same is to be entered into, and how long it shall continue.

No State shall lay any imposts or duties, which may interfere with any stipulations in treaties, entered into by the United States in Congress assembled, with any king, prince or state, in pursuance of any treaties already proposed by Congress, to the courts of France and Spain.

No vessels of war shall be kept up in time of peace by any State, except such number only, as shall be deemed necessary by the United States in Congress assembled, for the defence of such State, or its trade; nor shall any body of forces be kept up by any State, in time of peace, except such number only, as in the judgment of the United States, in Congress assembled, shall be deemed requisite to garrison the forts necessary for the defence of such State; but every State shall always keep up a well regulated and disciplined militia, sufficiently armed and accoutred, and shall provide and constantly have ready for use, in public stores, a due number of field pieces and tents, and a proper quantity of arms, ammunition and camp equipage.

No State shall engage in any war without the consent of the United States in Congress assembled, unless such State be actually invaded by enemies, or shall have received certain advice of a resolution being formed by some nation of Indians to invade such State, and the danger is so imminent as not to admit of a delay, till the United States in Congress assembled can be consulted: nor shall any State grant commissions to any ships or vessels of war, nor letters of marque or reprisal, except it be after a declaration of war by the United States in Congress assembled, and then only against the kingdom or state and the subjects thereof, against which war has been so declared, and under such regulations as shall be established by the United States in Congress assembled, unless such State be infested by pirates, in which case vessels of war may be fitted out for that occasion, and kept so long as the danger shall continue, or until the United States in Congress assembled shall determine otherwise.

ARTICLE VII. When land-forces are raised by any State of the common defence, all officers of or under the rank of colonel, shall be appointed by the Legislature of each State respectively by whom such forces shall be raised, or in such manner as such State shall direct, and all vacancies shall be filled up by the State which first made the appointment.

ARTICLE VIII. All charges of war, and all other expenses that shall be incurred for the common defence or general welfare, and allowed by the United States in Congress assembled, shall be defrayed out of a common treasury, which shall be supplied by the several States, in proportion to the value of all land within each State, granted to or surveyed for any person, as such land and the buildings and improvements thereon shall be estimated according to such mode as the United States in Congress assembled, shall from time to time direct and appoint.

The taxes for paying that proportion shall be laid and levied by the authority and direction of the Legislatures of the several States within the time agreed upon by the United States in Congress assembled.

ARTICLE IX. The United States in Congress assembled, shall have the sole and exclusive right and power of determining on peace and war, except in the cases mentioned in the sixth article—of sending and receiving ambassadors— entering into treaties and alliances, provided that no treaty of commerce shall be made whereby the legislative power of the respective States shall be restrained from imposing such imposts and duties on foreigners, as their own people are subjected to, or from prohibiting the exportation or importation of and species of goods or commodities whatsoever—of establishing rules for deciding in all cases, what captures on land or water shall be legal, and in what manner prizes taken by land or naval forces in the service of the United States shall be divided or appropriated—of granting letters of marque and reprisal in times of peace—appointing courts for the trial of piracies and felonies committed on the high seas and establishing courts for receiving and determining finally appeals in all cases of captures, provided that no member of Congress shall be appointed a judge of any of the said courts.

The United States in Congress assembled shall also be the last resort on appeal in all disputes and differences now subsisting or that hereafter may arise between two or more States concerning boundary, jurisdiction or any other cause whatever; which authority shall always be exercised in the manner following. Whenever the legislative or executive authority or lawful agent of any State in controversy with another shall present a petition to Congress, stating the matter in question and praying for a hearing, notice thereof shall be given by order of Congress to the legislative or executive authority of the other State in controversy, and a day assigned for the appearance of the parties by their lawful agents, who shall then be directed to appoint by joint consent, commissioners or judges to constitute a court for hearing and determining the matter in question: but if they cannot agree, Congress shall name three persons out of each of the United States, and from the list of such persons each party shall alternately strike out one, the petitioners beginning, until the number shall be reduced to thirteen; and from that number not less than seven, nor more than nine names as Congress shall direct, shall in the presence of Congress be drawn out by lot, and the persons whose names shall be so drawn or any five of them, shall be commissioners or judges, to hear and finally determine the controversy, so always as a major part of the judges who shall hear the cause shall agree in the determination: and if either party shall neglect to attend at the day appointed, without reasons, which Congress shall judge sufficient, or being present shall refuse to strike, the Congress shall proceed to nominate three persons out of each State, and the Secretary of Congress shall strike in behalf of such party absent or refusing; and the judgment and sentence of the court to be appointed, in the manner before prescribed, shall be final and conclusive; and if any of the parties shall refuse to submit to the authority of such court, or to appear or defend their claim or cause, the court shall nevertheless proceed to pronounce sentence, or judgment, which shall in like manner be final and decisive, the judgment or sentence and other proceedings being in either case transmitted to Congress, and lodged among the acts of Congress for the security of the parties concerned: provided that every commissioner, before he sits in judgment, shall take an oath to be administered by one of the judges of the supreme or superior court of the State where the case shall be tried, "well and truly to hear and determine the matter in question, according to the best of his judgment, without favour, affection or hope of reward:" provided also that no State shall be deprived of territory for the benefit of the United States.

All controversies concerning the private right of soil claimed under different grants of two or more States, whose jurisdiction as they may respect such lands, and the states which passed such grants are adjusted, the said grants or either of them being at the same time claimed to have originated antecedent to such settlement of jurisdiction, shall on the petition of either party to the Congress of the United States, be finally determined as near as may be in the same manner as is before prescribed for deciding disputes respecting territorial jurisdiction between different States.

The United States in Congress assembled shall also have the sole and exclusive right and power of regulating the alloy and value of coin struck by their own authority, or by that of the respective States—fixing the standard of weights and measures throughout the United States—regulating the trade and managing all affairs with the Indians, not members of any of the States, provided that the legislative right of any State within its own limits be not infringed or violated—establishing and regulating post-offices from one State to another, throughout all of the United States, and exacting such postage on the papers passing thro' the same as may be requisite to defray the expenses of the said office—appointing all officers of the land forces, in the service of the United States, excepting regimental officers—appointing all the officers of the naval forces, and commissioning all officers whatever in the service of the United States—making rules for the government and regulation of the said land and naval forces, and directing their operations.

The United States in Congress assembled shall have authority to appoint a committee, to sit in the recess of Congress, to be denominated "a Committee of the States," and to consist of one delegate from each State; and to appoint such other committees and civil officers as may be necessary for managing the general affairs of the United States under their direction—to appoint one of their number to preside, provided that no person be allowed to serve in the office of president more than one year in any term of three years; to ascertain the necessary sums of money to be raised for the service of the United States, and to appropriate and apply the same for defraying the public expenses—to borrow money, or emit bills on the credit of the United States, transmitting every half year to the respective States an account of the sums of money so borrowed or emitted,—to build and equip a navy—to agree upon the number of land forces, and to make requisitions from each State for its quota, in proportion to the number of white inhabitants in such State; which requisition shall be binding, and thereupon the Legislature of each State shall appoint the regimental officers, raise the men and cloath, arm and equip them in a soldier like manner, at the expense of the United States; and the officers and men so cloathed, armed and equipped shall march to the place appointed, and within the time agreed on by the United States in Congress assembled: but if the United States in Congress assembled shall, on consideration of circumstances judge proper that any State should not raise men, or should raise a smaller number of men than the quota thereof, such extra number shall be raised, officered, cloathed, armed and equipped in the same manner as the quota of such State, unless the legislature of such State shall judge that such extra number cannot be safely spared out of the same, in which case they shall raise officer, cloath, arm and equip as many of such extra number as they judge can be safely spared. And the officers and men so cloathed, armed and equipped, shall march to the place appointed, and within the time agreed on by the United States in Congress assembled.

The United States in Congress assembled shall never engage in a war, nor grant letters of marque and reprisal in time of peace, nor enter into any treaties or alliances, nor coin money, nor regulate the value thereof, nor ascertain the sums and expenses necessary for the defence and welfare of the United States, or any of them, nor emit bills, nor borrow money on the credit of the United States, nor appropriate money, nor agree upon the number of vessels to be built or purchased, or the number of land or sea forces to be raised, nor appoint a commander in chief of the army or navy, unless nine States assent to the same: nor shall a question on any other point, except for adjourning from day to day be determined, unless by the votes of a majority of the United States in Congress assembled.

The Congress of the United States shall have power to adjourn to any time within the year, and to any place within the United States, so that no period of adjournment be for a longer duration than the space of six months, and shall publish the journal of their proceedings monthly, except such parts thereof relating to treaties, alliances or military operations, as in their judgment require secresy; and the yeas and nays of the delegates of each State on any question shall be entered on the Journal, when it is desired by any delegate; and the delegates of a State, or any of them, at his or their request shall be furnished with a transcript of the said journal, except such parts as are above excepted, to lay before the Legislatures of the several States.

ARTICLE X. The committee of the States, or any nine of them, shall be authorized to execute, in the recess of Congress, such of the powers of Congress as the United States in Congress assembled, by the consent of nine States, shall from time to time think expedient to vest them with; provided that no power be delegated to the said committee, for the exercise of which, by the articles of confederation, the voice of nine States in the Congress of the United States assembled is requisite.

ARTICLE XI. Canada acceding to this confederation, and joining in the measures of the United States, shall be admitted into, and entitled to all the advantages of this Union: but no other colony shall be admitted into the same, unless such admission be agreed to by nine States.

ARTICLE XII. All bills of credit emitted, monies borrowed and debts contracted by, or under the authority of Congress, before the assembling of the United States, in pursuance of the present confederation, shall be deemed and considered as a charge against the United States, for payment and satisfaction whereof the said United States, and the public faith are hereby solemnly pledged.

ARTICLE XIII. Every State shall abide by the determinations of the United States in Congress assembled, on all questions which by this confederation are submitted to them. And the articles of this confederation shall be inviolably observed by every State, and the Union shall be perpetual; nor shall any alteration at any time hereafter be made in any of them; unless such alteration be agreed to in a Congress of the United States, and be afterwards confirmed by the Legislatures of every State.

And whereas it has pleased the Great Governor of the world to incline the hearts of the Legislatures we respectively represent in Congress, to approve of, and to authorize us to ratify the said articles of confederation and perpetual union. Know ye that we the undersigned delegates, by virtue of the power and authority to us given for that purpose, do by these presents, in the name and in behalf of our respective constituents, fully and entirely ratify and confirm each and every of the said articles of confederation and perpetual union, and all and singular the matters and things therein contained: and we do further solemnly plight and engage the faith of our respective constituents, that they shall abide by the determinations of the United States in Congress assembled, on all questions, which by the said confederation are submitted to them. And that the articles thereof shall be inviolably observed by the States we respectively represent, and that the Union shall be perpetual.

In witness thereof we have hereunto set our hands in Congress. Done at Philadelphia in the State of Pennsylvania the ninth day of July in the year of our Lord one thousand seven hundred and seventy-eight, and in the third year of the independence of America.

THE CONSTITUTION OF THE UNITED STATES (1787)

We the People of the United States, in Order to form a more perfect Union, establish Justice, insure domestic Tranquility, provide for the common defence, promote the general Welfare, and secure the Blessings of Liberty to ourselves and our Posterity, do ordain and establish this Constitution for the United States of America.

ARTICLE. I.

SECTION. 1. All legislative Powers herein granted shall be vested in a Congress of the United States, which shall consist of a Senate and House of Representatives.

SECTION. 2. The House of Representatives shall be composed of Members chosen every second Year by the People of the several States, and the Electors in each State shall have the Qualifications requisite for Electors of the most numerous Branch of the State Legislature.

No Person shall be a Representative who shall not have attained to the Age of twenty five Years, and been seven Years a Citizen of the United States, and who shall not, when elected, be an Inhabitant of that State in which he shall be chosen.

Representatives and direct Taxes shall be apportioned among the several States which may be included within this Union, according to their respective Numbers, which shall be determined by adding to the whole Number of free Persons, including those bound to Service for a Term of Years, and excluding Indians not taxed, three fifths of all other Persons. The actual Enumeration shall be made within three Years after the first Meeting of the Congress of the United States, and within every subsequent Term of ten Years, in such Manner as they shall by Law direct. The Number of Representatives shall not exceed one for every thirty Thousand, but each State shall have at Least one Representative; and until such enumeration shall be made, the State of New Hampshire shall be entitled to chuse three, Massachusetts eight, Rhode-Island and Providence Plantations one, Connecticut five, New-York six, New Jersey four, Pennsylvania eight, Delaware one, Maryland six, Virginia ten, North Carolina five, South Carolina five, and Georgia three.

When vacancies happen in the Representation from any State, the Executive Authority thereof shall issue Writs of Election to fill such Vacancies.

The House of Representatives shall chuse their Speaker and other Officers; and shall have the sole Power of Impeachment.

SECTION. 3. The Senate of the United States shall be composed of two Senators from each State, chosen by the Legislature thereof for six Years; and each Senator shall have one Vote.

Immediately after they shall be assembled in Consequence of the first Election, they shall be divided as equally as may be into three Classes. The Seats of the Senators of the first Class shall be vacated at the Expiration of the second Year, of the second Class at the Expiration of the fourth Year, and of the third Class at the Expiration of the sixth Year, so that one third may be chosen every second Year; and if Vacancies happen by Resignation, or otherwise, during the Recess of the Legislature of any State, the Executive thereof may make temporary Appointments until the next Meeting of the Legislature, which shall then fill such Vacancies.

No Person shall be a Senator who shall not have attained to the Age of thirty Years, and been nine Years a Citizen of the United States, and who shall not, when elected, be an Inhabitant of that State for which he shall be chosen.

The Vice President of the United States shall be President of the Senate, but shall have no Vote, unless they be equally divided.

The Senate shall chuse their other Officers, and also a President pro tempore, in the Absence of the Vice President, or when he shall exercise the Office of President of the United States.

The Senate shall have the sole Power to try all Impeachments. When sitting for that Purpose, they shall be on Oath or Affirmation. When the President of the United States is tried, the Chief Justice shall preside: And no Person shall be convicted without the Concurrence of two thirds of the Members present.

Judgment in Cases of Impeachment shall not extend further than to removal from Office, and disqualification to hold and enjoy any Office of honor, Trust or Profit under the United States: but the Party convicted shall nevertheless be liable and subject to Indictment, Trial, Judgment and Punishment, according to Law.

SECTION. 4. The Times, Places and Manner of holding Elections for Senators and Representatives, shall be prescribed in each State by the Legislature thereof; but the Congress may at any time by Law make or alter such Regulations, except as to the Places of chusing Senators.

The Congress shall assemble at least once in every Year, and such Meeting shall be on the first Monday in December, unless they shall by Law appoint a different Day.

SECTION. 5. Each House shall be the Judge of the Elections, Returns and Qualifications of its own Members, and a Majority of each shall constitute a Quorum to do Business; but a smaller Number may adjourn from day to day, and may be authorized to compel the Attendance of absent Members, in such Manner, and under such Penalties as each House may provide.

Each House may determine the Rules of its Proceedings, punish its Members for disorderly Behaviour, and, with the Concurrence of two thirds, expel a Member.

Each House shall keep a Journal of its Proceedings, and from time to time publish the same, excepting such Parts as may in their Judgment require Secrecy; and the Yeas and Nays of the Members of either House on any question shall, at the Desire of one fifth of those Present, be entered on the Journal.

Neither House, during the Session of Congress, shall, without the Consent of the other, adjourn for more than three days, nor to any other Place than that in which the two Houses shall be sitting.

SECTION. 6. The Senators and Representatives shall receive a Compensation for their Services, to be ascertained by Law, and paid out of the Treasury of the United States. They shall in all Cases, except Treason, Felony and Breach of the Peace, be privileged from Arrest during their Attendance at the Session of their respective Houses, and in going to and returning from the same; and for any Speech or Debate in either House, they shall not be questioned in any other Place.

No Senator or Representative shall, during the Time for which he was elected, be appointed to any civil Office under the Authority of the United States, which shall have been created, or the Emoluments whereof shall have been encreased during such time; and no Person holding any Office under the United States, shall be a Member of either House during his Continuance in Office.

SECTION. 7. All Bills for raising Revenue shall originate in the House of Representatives; but the Senate may propose or concur with Amendments as on other Bills.

Every Bill which shall have passed the House of Representatives and the Senate shall, before it become a Law, be presented to the President of the United States; If he approve he shall sign it, but if not he shall return it, with his

Objections to that House in which it shall have originated, who shall enter the Objections at large on their Journal, and proceed to reconsider it. If after such Reconsideration two thirds of that House shall agree to pass the Bill, it shall be sent, together with the Objections, to the other House, by which it shall likewise be reconsidered, and if approved by two thirds of that House, it shall become a Law. But in all such Cases the Votes of both Houses shall be determined by yeas and Nays, and the Names of the Persons voting for and against the Bill shall be entered on the Journal of each House respectively. If any Bill shall not be returned by the President within ten Days (Sundays excepted) after it shall have been presented to him, the Same shall be a Law, in like Manner as if he had signed it, unless the Congress by their Adjournment prevent its Return, in which Case it shall not be a Law.

Every Order, Resolution, or Vote to which the Concurrence of the Senate and House of Representatives may be necessary (except on a question of Adjournment) shall be presented to the President of the United States; and before the Same shall take Effect, shall be approved by him, or being disapproved by him, shall be repassed by two thirds of the Senate and House of Representatives, according to the Rules and Limitations prescribed in the Case of a Bill.

SECTION. 8. The Congress shall have Power To lay and collect Taxes, Duties, Imposts and Excises, to pay the Debts and provide for the common Defence and general Welfare of the United States; but all Duties, Imposts and Excises shall be uniform throughout the United States;

To borrow Money on the credit of the United States;

To regulate Commerce with foreign Nations, and among the several States, and with the Indian Tribes;

To establish an uniform Rule of Naturalization, and uniform Laws on the subject of Bankruptcies throughout the United States;

To coin Money, regulate the Value thereof, and of foreign Coin, and fix the Standard of Weights and Measures;

To provide for the Punishment of counterfeiting the Securities and current Coin of the United States;

To establish Post Offices and post Roads;

To promote the Progress of Science and useful Arts, by securing for limited Times to Authors and Inventors the exclusive Right to their respective Writings and Discoveries;

To constitute Tribunals inferior to the supreme Court;

To define and punish Piracies and Felonies committed on the high Seas, and Offences against the Law of Nations;

To declare War, grant Letters of Marque and Reprisal, and make Rules concerning Captures on Land and Water;

To raise and support Armies, but no Appropriation of Money to that Use shall be for a longer Term than two Years;

To provide and maintain a Navy;

To make Rules for the Government and Regulation of the land and naval Forces;

To provide for calling forth the Militia to execute the Laws of the Union, suppress Insurrections and repel Invasions;

To provide for organizing, arming, and disciplining, the Militia, and for governing such Part of them as may be employed in the Service of the United States, reserving to the States respectively, the Appointment of the Officers, and the Authority of training the Militia according to the discipline prescribed by Congress;

To exercise exclusive Legislation in all Cases whatsoever, over such District (not exceeding ten Miles square) as may, by Cession of particular States, and the Acceptance of Congress, become the Seat of the Government of the United States, and to exercise like Authority over all Places purchased by the Consent of the Legislature of the State in which the Same shall be, for the Erection of Forts, Magazines, Arsenals, dock-Yards, and other needful Buildings;—And

To make all Laws which shall be necessary and proper for carrying into Execution the foregoing Powers, and all other Powers vested by this Constitution in the Government of the United States, or in any Department or Officer thereof.

SECTION. 9. The Migration or Importation of such Persons as any of the States now existing shall think proper to admit, shall not be prohibited by the Congress prior to the Year one thousand eight hundred and eight, but a Tax or duty may be imposed on such Importation, not exceeding ten dollars for each Person.

The Privilege of the Writ of Habeas Corpus shall not be suspended, unless when in Cases of Rebellion or Invasion the public Safety may require it.

No Bill of Attainder or ex post facto Law shall be passed.

No Capitation, or other direct, Tax shall be laid, unless in Proportion to the Census or enumeration herein before directed to be taken.

No Tax or Duty shall be laid on Articles exported from any State.

No Preference shall be given by any Regulation of Commerce or Revenue to the Ports of one State over those of another; nor shall Vessels bound to, or from, one State, be obliged to enter, clear, or pay Duties in another.

No Money shall be drawn from the Treasury, but in Consequence of Appropriations made by Law; and a regular Statement and Account of the Receipts and Expenditures of all public Money shall be published from time to time.

No Title of Nobility shall be granted by the United States: And no Person holding any Office of Profit or Trust under them, shall, without the Consent of the Congress, accept of any present, Emolument, Office, or Title, of any kind whatever, from any King, Prince, or foreign State.

SECTION. 10. No State shall enter into any Treaty, Alliance, or Confederation; grant Letters of Marque and Reprisal; coin Money; emit Bills of Credit; make any Thing but gold and silver Coin a Tender in Payment of Debts; pass any Bill of Attainder, ex post facto Law, or Law impairing the Obligation of Contracts, or grant any Title of Nobility.

No State shall, without the Consent of the Congress, lay any Imposts or Duties on Imports or Exports, except what may be absolutely necessary for executing it's inspection Laws: and the net Produce of all Duties and Imposts, laid by any State on Imports or Exports, shall be for the Use of the Treasury of the United States; and all such Laws shall be subject to the Revision and Controul of the Congress.

No State shall, without the Consent of Congress, lay any Duty of Tonnage, keep Troops, or Ships of War in time of Peace, enter into any Agreement or Compact with another State, or with a foreign Power, or engage in War, unless actually invaded, or in such imminent Danger as will not admit of delay.

ARTICLE. II.

SECTION. 1. The executive Power shall be vested in a President of the United States of America. He shall hold his Office during the Term of four Years, and, together with the Vice President, chosen for the same Term, be elected, as follows:

Each State shall appoint, in such Manner as the Legislature thereof may direct, a Number of Electors, equal to the whole Number of Senators and Representatives to which the State may be entitled in the Congress: but no Senator or Representative, or Person holding an Office of Trust or Profit under the United States, shall be appointed an Elector.

The Electors shall meet in their respective States, and vote by Ballot for two Persons, of whom one at least shall not be an Inhabitant of the same State with themselves. And they shall make a List of all the Persons voted for, and of the Number of Votes for each; which List they shall sign and certify, and transmit sealed to the Seat of the Government of the United States, directed to the President of the Senate. The President of the Senate shall, in the Presence of the Senate and House of Representatives, open all the Certificates, and the Votes shall then be counted. The Person having the greatest Number of Votes shall be the President, if such Number be a Majority of the whole Number of Electors appointed; and if there be more than one who have such Majority, and have an equal Number of Votes, then the House of Representatives shall immediately chuse by Ballot one of them for President; and if no Person have a Majority, then from the five highest on the List the said House shall in like Manner chuse the President. But in chusing the President, the Votes shall be taken by States, the Representation from each State having one Vote; A quorum for this purpose shall consist of a Member or Members from two thirds of the States, and a Majority of all the States shall be necessary to a Choice. In every Case, after the Choice of the President, the Person having the greatest Number of Votes of the Electors shall be the Vice President. But if there should remain two or more who have equal Votes, the Senate shall chuse from them by Ballot the Vice President.

The Congress may determine the Time of chusing the Electors, and the Day on which they shall give their Votes; which Day shall be the same throughout the United States.

No Person except a natural born Citizen, or a Citizen of the United States, at the time of the Adoption of this Constitution, shall be eligible to the Office of President; neither shall any Person be eligible to that Office who shall not have attained to the Age of thirty five Years, and been fourteen Years a Resident within the United States.

In Case of the Removal of the President from Office, or of his Death, Resignation, or Inability to discharge the Powers and Duties of the said Office, the Same shall devolve on the Vice President, and the Congress may by Law provide for the Case of Removal, Death, Resignation or Inability, both of the President and Vice President, declaring what Officer shall then act as President, and such Officer shall act accordingly, until the Disability be removed, or a President shall be elected.

The President shall, at stated Times, receive for his Services, a Compensation, which shall neither be increased nor diminished during the Period for which he shall have been elected, and he shall not receive within that Period any other Emolument from the United States, or any of them.

Before he enter on the Execution of his Office, he shall take the following Oath or Affirmation:—"I do solemnly swear (or affirm) that I will faithfully execute the Office of President of the United States, and will to the best of my Ability, preserve, protect and defend the Constitution of the United States."

SECTION. 2. The President shall be Commander in Chief of the Army and Navy of the United States, and of the Militia of the several States, when called into the actual Service of the United States; he may require the Opinion, in writing, of the principal Officer in each of the executive Departments, upon any Subject relating to the Duties of their respective Offices, and he shall have Power to grant Reprieves and Pardons for Offences against the United States, except in Cases of Impeachment.

He shall have Power, by and with the Advice and Consent of the Senate, to make Treaties, provided two thirds of the Senators present concur; and he shall nominate, and by and with the Advice and Consent of the Senate, shall appoint Ambassadors, other public Ministers and Consuls, Judges of the supreme Court, and all other Officers of the United States, whose Appointments are not herein otherwise provided for, and which shall be established by Law: but the Congress may by Law vest the Appointment of such inferior Officers, as they think proper, in the President alone, in the Courts of Law, or in the Heads of Departments.

The President shall have Power to fill up all Vacancies that may happen during the Recess of the Senate, by granting Commissions which shall expire at the End of their next Session.

SECTION. 3. He shall from time to time give to the Congress Information of the State of the Union, and recommend to their Consideration such Measures as he shall judge necessary and expedient; he may, on extraordinary Occasions, convene both Houses, or either of them, and in Case of Disagreement between them, with Respect to the Time of Adjournment, he may adjourn them to such Time as he shall think proper; he shall receive Ambassadors and other public Ministers; he shall take Care that the Laws be faithfully executed, and shall Commission all the Officers of the United States.

SECTION. 4. The President, Vice President and all civil Officers of the United States, shall be removed from Office on Impeachment for, and Conviction of, Treason, Bribery, or other high Crimes and Misdemeanors.

ARTICLE. III.

SECTION. 1. The judicial Power of the United States shall be vested in one supreme Court, and in such inferior Courts as the Congress may from time to time ordain and establish. The Judges, both of the supreme and inferior Courts, shall hold their Offices during good Behaviour, and shall, at stated Times, receive for their Services a Compensation, which shall not be diminished during their Continuance in Office.

SECTION. 2. The judicial Power shall extend to all Cases, in Law and Equity, arising under this Constitution, the Laws of the United States, and Treaties made, or which shall be made, under their Authority;—to all Cases affecting Ambassadors, other public Ministers and Consuls;—to all Cases of admiralty and maritime Jurisdiction;—to Controversies to which the United States shall be a Party;—to Controversies between two or more States;—between a State and Citizens of another State,—between Citizens of different States,—between Citizens of the same State claiming Lands under Grants of different States, and between a State, or the Citizens thereof, and foreign States, Citizens or Subjects.

In all Cases affecting Ambassadors, other public Ministers and Consuls, and those in which a State shall be Party, the supreme Court shall have original Jurisdiction. In all the other Cases before mentioned, the supreme Court shall have appellate Jurisdiction, both as to Law and Fact, with such Exceptions, and under such Regulations as the Congress shall make.

The Trial of all Crimes, except in Cases of Impeachment, shall be by Jury; and such Trial shall be held in the State where the said Crimes shall have been committed; but when not committed within any State, the Trial shall be at such Place or Places as the Congress may by Law have directed.

SECTION. 3. Treason against the United States, shall consist only in levying War against them, or in adhering to their Enemies, giving them Aid and Comfort. No Person shall be convicted of Treason unless on the Testimony of two Witnesses to the same overt Act, or on Confession in open Court.

The Congress shall have Power to declare the Punishment of Treason, but no Attainder of Treason shall work Corruption of Blood, or Forfeiture except during the Life of the Person attainted.

ARTICLE. IV.

SECTION. 1. Full Faith and Credit shall be given in each State to the public Acts, Records, and judicial Proceedings of every other State. And the Congress may by general Laws prescribe the Manner in which such Acts, Records and Proceedings shall be proved, and the Effect thereof.

SECTION. 2. The Citizens of each State shall be entitled to all Privileges and Immunities of Citizens in the several States.

A Person charged in any State with Treason, Felony, or other Crime, who shall flee from Justice, and be found in another State, shall on Demand of the executive Authority of the State from which he fled, be delivered up, to be removed to the State having Jurisdiction of the Crime.

No Person held to Service or Labour in one State, under the Laws thereof, escaping into another, shall, in Consequence of any Law or Regulation therein, be discharged from such Service or Labour, but shall be delivered up on Claim of the Party to whom such Service or Labour may be due.

SECTION. 3. New States may be admitted by the Congress into this Union; but no new State shall be formed or erected within the Jurisdiction of any other State; nor any State be formed by the Junction of two or more States, or Parts of States, without the Consent of the Legislatures of the States concerned as well as of the Congress.

The Congress shall have Power to dispose of and make all needful Rules and Regulations respecting the Territory or other Property belonging to the United States; and nothing in this Constitution shall be so construed as to Prejudice any Claims of the United States, or of any particular States.

SECTION. 4. The United States shall guarantee to every State in this Union a Republican Form of Government, and shall protect each of them against Invasion; and on Application of the Legislature, or of the Executive (when the Legislature cannot be convened), against domestic Violence.

ARTICLE. V.

The Congress, whenever two thirds of both Houses shall deem it necessary, shall propose Amendments to this Constitution, or, on the Application of the Legislatures of two thirds of the several States, shall call a Convention for proposing Amendments, which, in either Case, shall be valid to all Intents and Purposes, as Part of this Constitution, when ratified by the Legislatures of three fourths of the several States, or by Conventions in three fourths thereof, as the one or the other Mode of Ratification may be proposed by the Congress; Provided that no Amendment which may be made prior to the Year One thousand eight hundred and eight shall in any Manner affect the first and fourth Clauses in the Ninth Section of the first Article; and that no State, without its Consent, shall be deprived of its equal Suffrage in the Senate.

ARTICLE. VI.

All Debts contracted and Engagements entered into, before the Adoption of this Constitution, shall be as valid against the United States under this Constitution, as under the Confederation.

This Constitution, and the Laws of the United States which shall be made in Pursuance thereof; and all Treaties made, or which shall be made, under the Authority of the United States, shall be the supreme Law of the Land; and the Judges in every State shall be bound thereby, any Thing in the Constitution or Laws of any State to the Contrary notwithstanding.

The Senators and Representatives before mentioned, and the Members of the several State Legislatures, and all executive and judicial Officers, both of the United States and of the several States, shall be bound by Oath or Affirmation, to support this Constitution; but no religious Test shall ever be required as a Qualification to any Office or public Trust under the United States.

Article. VII.

The Ratification of the Conventions of nine States, shall be sufficient for the Establishment of this Constitution between the States so ratifying the Same.

The Word, "the," being interlined between the seventh and eighth Lines of the first Page, the Word "Thirty" being partly written on an Erazure in the fifteenth Line of the first Page, The Words "is tried" being interlined between the thirty second and thirty third Lines of the first Page and the Word "the" being interlined between the forty third and forty fourth Lines of the second Page.

Attest William Jackson Secretary

Done in Convention by the Unanimous Consent of the States present the Seventeenth Day of September in the Year of our Lord one thousand seven hundred and Eighty seven and of the Independance of the United States of America the Twelfth In witness whereof We have hereunto subscribed our Names,

G°. Washington
Presidt and deputy from Virginia

Delaware	Geo: Read Gunning Bedford jun John Dickinson Richard Bassett Jaco: Broom

New Hampshire	John Langdon Nicholas Gilman

Massachusetts	Nathaniel Gorham Rufus King

Maryland	James McHenry Dan of St Thos. Jenifer Danl. Carrol

Connecticut	Wm. Saml. Johnson Roger Sherman

Virginia	John Blair James Madison Jr.

New York	Alexander Hamilton

North Carolina	Wm. Blount Richd. Dobbs Spaight Hu Williamson

New Jersey	Wil: Livingston David Brearley Wm. Paterson Jona: Dayton

South Carolina	J. Rutledge Charles Cotesworth Pinckney Charles Pinckney Pierce Butler

Georgia	William Few Abr Baldwin

Pennsylvania	B Franklin Thomas Mifflin Robt. Morris Geo. Clymer Thos. FitzSimons Jared Ingersoll James Wilson Gouv Morris

Amendments to the Constitution

The Bill of Rights: A Transcription

THE PREAMBLE TO THE BILL OF RIGHTS Congress of the United States begun and held at the City of New-York, on Wednesday the fourth of March, one thousand seven hundred and eighty nine.

THE Conventions of a number of the States, having at the time of their adopting the Constitution, expressed a desire, in order to prevent misconstruction or abuse of its powers, that further declaratory and restrictive clauses should be added: And as extending the ground of public confidence in the Government, will best ensure the beneficent ends of its institution.

RESOLVED by the Senate and House of Representatives of the United States of America, in Congress assembled, two thirds of both Houses concurring, that the following Articles be proposed to the Legislatures of the several States, as amendments to the Constitution of the United States, all, or any of which Articles, when ratified by three fourths of the said Legislatures, to be valid to all intents and purposes, as part of the said Constitution; viz.

ARTICLES in addition to, and Amendment of the Constitution of the United States of America, proposed by Congress, and ratified by the Legislatures of the several States, pursuant to the fifth Article of the original Constitution.

Note: The first ten amendments to the Constitution were ratified December 15, 1791, and form what is known as the "Bill of Rights."

Amendment I

Congress shall make no law respecting an establishment of religion, or prohibiting the free exercise thereof; or abridging the freedom of speech, or of the press; or the right of the people peaceably to assemble, and to petition the Government for a redress of grievances.

Amendment II

A well regulated Militia, being necessary to the security of a free State, the right of the people to keep and bear Arms, shall not be infringed.

AMENDMENT III

No Soldier shall, in time of peace be quartered in any house, without the consent of the Owner, nor in time of war, but in a manner to be prescribed by law.

AMENDMENT IV

The right of the people to be secure in their persons, houses, papers, and effects, against unreasonable searches and seizures, shall not be violated, and no Warrants shall issue, but upon probable cause, supported by Oath or affirmation, and particularly describing the place to be searched, and the persons or things to be seized.

AMENDMENT V

No person shall be held to answer for a capital, or otherwise infamous crime, unless on a presentment or indictment of a Grand Jury, except in cases arising in the land or naval forces, or in the Militia, when in actual service in time of War or public danger; nor shall any person be subject for the same offence to be twice put in jeopardy of life or limb; nor shall be compelled in any criminal case to be a witness against himself, nor be deprived of life, liberty, or property, without due process of law; nor shall private property be taken for public use, without just compensation.

AMENDMENT VI

In all criminal prosecutions, the accused shall enjoy the right to a speedy and public trial, by an impartial jury of the State and district wherein the crime shall have been committed, which district shall have been previously ascertained by law, and to be informed of the nature and cause of the accusation; to be confronted with the witnesses against him; to have compulsory process for obtaining witnesses in his favor, and to have the Assistance of Counsel for his defence.

AMENDMENT VII

In Suits at common law, where the value in controversy shall exceed twenty dollars, the right of trial by jury shall be preserved, and no fact tried by a jury, shall be otherwise re-examined in any Court of the United States, than according to the rules of the common law.

AMENDMENT VIII

Excessive bail shall not be required, nor excessive fines imposed, nor cruel and unusual punishments inflicted.

AMENDMENT IX

The enumeration in the Constitution, of certain rights, shall not be construed to deny or disparage others retained by the people.

AMENDMENT X

The powers not delegated to the United States by the Constitution, nor prohibited by it to the States, are reserved to the States respectively, or to the people.

AMENDMENT XI

Passed by Congress March 4, 1794. Ratified February 7, 1795.

Note: Article III, section 2, of the Constitution was modified by amendment 11.

The Judicial power of the United States shall not be construed to extend to any suit in law or equity, commenced or prosecuted against one of the United States by Citizens of another State, or by Citizens or Subjects of any Foreign State.

AMENDMENT XII

Passed by Congress December 9, 1803. Ratified June 15, 1804.

Note: A portion of Article II, section 1 of the Constitution was superseded by the 12th amendment.

The Electors shall meet in their respective states and vote by ballot for President and Vice-President, one of whom, at least, shall not be an inhabitant of the same state with themselves; they shall name in their ballots the person voted for as President, and in distinct ballots the person voted for as Vice-President, and they shall make distinct lists of all persons voted for as President, and of all persons voted for as Vice-President, and of the number of votes for each, which lists they shall sign and certify, and transmit sealed to the seat of the government of the United States, directed to the President of the Senate; — the President of the Senate shall, in the presence of the Senate and House of Representatives, open all the certificates and the votes shall then be counted; — The person having the greatest number of votes for President, shall be the President, if such number be a majority of the whole number of Electors appointed; and if no person have such majority, then from the persons having the highest numbers not exceeding three on the list of those voted for as President, the House of Representatives shall choose immediately, by ballot, the President. But in choosing the President, the votes shall be taken by states, the representation from each state having one vote; a quorum for this purpose shall consist of a member or members from two-thirds of the states, and a majority of all the states shall be necessary to a choice. [And if the House of Representatives shall not choose a President whenever the right of choice shall devolve upon them, before the fourth day of March next following, then the Vice-President shall act as President, as in case of the death or other constitutional disability of the President. —]* The person having the greatest number of votes as Vice-President, shall be the Vice-President, if such number be a majority of the whole number of Electors appointed, and if no person have a majority, then from the two highest numbers on the list, the Senate shall choose the Vice-President; a quorum for the purpose shall consist of two-thirds of the whole number of Senators, and a majority of the whole number shall be necessary to a choice. But no person constitutionally ineligible to the office of President shall be eligible to that of Vice-President of the United States.

AMENDMENT XIII

Passed by Congress January 31, 1865. Ratified December 6, 1865.

Note: A portion of Article IV, section 2, of the Constitution was superseded by the 13th amendment.

SECTION 1. Neither slavery nor involuntary servitude, except as a punishment for crime whereof the party shall have been duly convicted, shall exist within the United States, or any place subject to their jurisdiction.

SECTION 2. Congress shall have power to enforce this article by appropriate legislation.

———————————

Superseded by section 3 of the 20th amendment.

AMENDMENT XIV

Passed by Congress June 13, 1866. Ratified July 9, 1868.

Note: Article I, section 2, of the Constitution was modified by section 2 of the 14th amendment.

SECTION 1. All persons born or naturalized in the United States, and subject to the jurisdiction thereof, are citizens of the United States and of the State wherein they reside. No State shall make or enforce any law which shall abridge the privileges or immunities of citizens of the United States; nor shall any State deprive any person of life, liberty, or property, without due process of law; nor deny to any person within its jurisdiction the equal protection of the laws.

SECTION 2. Representatives shall be apportioned among the several States according to their respective numbers, counting the whole number of persons in each State, excluding Indians not taxed. But when the right to vote at any election for the choice of electors for President and Vice-President of the United States, Representatives in Congress, the Executive and Judicial officers of a State, or the members of the Legislature thereof, is denied to any of the male inhabitants of such State, being twenty-one years of age,* and citizens of the United States, or in any way abridged, except for participation in rebellion, or other crime, the basis of representation therein shall be reduced in the proportion which the number of such male citizens shall bear to the whole number of male citizens twenty-one years of age in such State.

SECTION 3. No person shall be a Senator or Representative in Congress, or elector of President and Vice-President, or hold any office, civil or military, under the United States, or under any State, who, having previously taken an oath, as a member of Congress, or as an officer of the United States, or as a member of any State legislature, or as an executive or judicial officer of any State, to support the Constitution of the United States, shall have engaged in insurrection or rebellion against the same, or given aid or comfort to the enemies thereof. But Congress may by a vote of two-thirds of each House, remove such disability.

SECTION 4. The validity of the public debt of the United States, authorized by law, including debts incurred for payment of pensions and bounties for services in suppressing insurrection or rebellion, shall not be

---

Changed by section 1 of the 26th amendment.

questioned. But neither the United States nor any State shall assume or pay any debt or obligation incurred in aid of insurrection or rebellion against the United States, or any claim for the loss or emancipation of any slave; but all such debts, obligations and claims shall be held illegal and void.

SECTION 5. The Congress shall have the power to enforce, by appropriate legislation, the provisions of this article.

AMENDMENT XV

Passed by Congress February 26, 1869. Ratified February 3, 1870.

SECTION 1. The right of citizens of the United States to vote shall not be denied or abridged by the United States or by any State on account of race, color, or previous condition of servitude—

SECTION 2. The Congress shall have the power to enforce this article by appropriate legislation.

AMENDMENT XVI

Passed by Congress July 2, 1909. Ratified February 3, 1913.

Note: Article I, section 9, of the Constitution was modified by amendment 16.

The Congress shall have power to lay and collect taxes on incomes, from whatever source derived, without apportionment among the several States, and without regard to any census or enumeration.

AMENDMENT XVII

Passed by Congress May 13, 1912. Ratified April 8, 1913.

Note: Article I, section 3, of the Constitution was modified by the 17th amendment.

The Senate of the United States shall be composed of two Senators from each State, elected by the people thereof, for six years; and each Senator shall have one vote. The electors in each State shall have the qualifications requisite for electors of the most numerous branch of the State legislatures.

When vacancies happen in the representation of any State in the Senate, the executive authority of such State shall issue writs of election to fill such vacancies: *Provided*, That the legislature of any State may empower the executive thereof to make temporary appointments until the people fill the vacancies by election as the legislature may direct.

This amendment shall not be so construed as to affect the election or term of any Senator chosen before it becomes valid as part of the Constitution.

AMENDMENT XVIII

Passed by Congress December 18, 1917. Ratified January 16, 1919. Repealed by amendment 21.

SECTION 1. After one year from the ratification of this article the manufacture, sale, or transportation of intoxicating liquors within, the importation thereof into, or the exportation thereof from the United States and all territory subject to the jurisdiction thereof for beverage purposes is hereby prohibited.

SECTION 2. The Congress and the several States shall have concurrent power to enforce this article by appropriate legislation.

SECTION 3. This article shall be inoperative unless it shall have been ratified as an amendment to the Constitution by the legislatures of the several States, as provided in the Constitution, within seven years from the date of the submission hereof to the States by the Congress.

AMENDMENT XIX

Passed by Congress June 4, 1919. Ratified August 18, 1920.

The right of citizens of the United States to vote shall not be denied or abridged by the United States or by any State on account of sex.

Congress shall have power to enforce this article by appropriate legislation.

AMENDMENT XX

Passed by Congress March 2, 1932. Ratified January 23, 1933.

Note: Article I, section 4, of the Constitution was modified by section 2 of this amendment. In addition, a portion of the 12th amendment was superseded by section 3.

SECTION 1. The terms of the President and the Vice President shall end at noon on the 20th day of January, and the terms of Senators and Representatives at noon on the 3rd day of January, of the years in which such terms would have ended if this article had not been ratified; and the terms of their successors shall then begin.

SECTION 2. The Congress shall assemble at least once in every year, and such meeting shall begin at noon on the 3d day of January, unless they shall by law appoint a different day.

SECTION 3. If, at the time fixed for the beginning of the term of the President, the President elect shall have died, the Vice President elect shall become President. If a President shall not have been chosen before the time fixed for the beginning of his term, or if the President elect shall have failed to qualify, then the Vice President elect shall act as President until a President shall have qualified; and the Congress may by law provide for the case wherein neither a President elect nor a Vice President shall have qualified, declaring who shall then act as President, or the manner in which one who is to act shall be selected, and such person shall act accordingly until a President or Vice President shall have qualified.

SECTION 4. The Congress may by law provide for the case of the death of any of the persons from whom the House of Representatives may choose a President whenever the right of choice shall have devolved upon them, and for the case of the death of any of the persons from whom the Senate may choose a Vice President whenever the right of choice shall have devolved upon them.

SECTION 5. Sections 1 and 2 shall take effect on the 15th day of October following the ratification of this article.

SECTION 6. This article shall be inoperative unless it shall have been ratified as an amendment to the Constitution by the legislatures of three-fourths of the several States within seven years from the date of its submission.

AMENDMENT XXI

Passed by Congress February 20, 1933. Ratified December 5, 1933.

SECTION 1. The eighteenth article of amendment to the Constitution of the United States is hereby repealed.

SECTION 2. The transportation or importation into any State, Territory, or Possession of the United States for delivery or use therein of intoxicating liquors, in violation of the laws thereof, is hereby prohibited.

SECTION 3. This article shall be inoperative unless it shall have been ratified as an amendment to the Constitution by conventions in the several States, as provided in the Constitution, within seven years from the date of the submission hereof to the States by the Congress.

AMENDMENT XXII

Passed by Congress March 21, 1947. Ratified February 27, 1951.

SECTION 1. No person shall be elected to the office of the President more than twice, and no person who has held the office of President, or acted as President, for more than two years of a term to which some other person was elected President shall be elected to the office of President more than once. But this Article shall not apply to any person holding the office of President when this Article was proposed by Congress, and shall not prevent any person who may be holding the office of President, or acting as President, during the term within which this Article becomes operative from holding the office of President or acting as President during the remainder of such term.

SECTION 2. This article shall be inoperative unless it shall have been ratified as an amendment to the Constitution by the legislatures of three-fourths of the several States within seven years from the date of its submission to the States by the Congress.

AMENDMENT XXIII

Passed by Congress June 16, 1960. Ratified March 29, 1961.

SECTION 1. The District constituting the seat of Government of the United States shall appoint in such manner as Congress may direct:

A number of electors of President and Vice President equal to the whole number of Senators and Representatives in Congress to which the District would be entitled if it were a State, but in no event more than the least populous State; they shall be in addition to those appointed by the States, but they shall be considered, for the purposes of the election of President and Vice President, to be electors appointed by a State; and they shall meet in the District and perform such duties as provided by the twelfth article of amendment.

SECTION 2. The Congress shall have power to enforce this article by appropriate legislation.

AMENDMENT XXIV

Passed by Congress August 27, 1962. Ratified January 23, 1964.

SECTION 1. The right of citizens of the United States to vote in any primary or other election for President or Vice President, for electors for President or Vice President, or for Senator or Representative in Congress, shall not be denied or abridged by the United States or any State by reason of failure to pay poll tax or other tax.

SECTION 2. The Congress shall have power to enforce this article by appropriate legislation.

AMENDMENT XXV

Passed by Congress July 6, 1965. Ratified February 10, 1967.

Note: Article II, section 1, of the Constitution was affected by the 25th amendment.

SECTION 1. In case of the removal of the President from office or of his death or resignation, the Vice President shall become President.

SECTION 2. Whenever there is a vacancy in the office of the Vice President, the President shall nominate a Vice President who shall take office upon confirmation by a majority vote of both Houses of Congress.

SECTION 3. Whenever the President transmits to the President pro tempore of the Senate and the Speaker of the House of Representatives his written declaration that he is unable to discharge the powers and duties of his office, and until he transmits to them a written declaration to the contrary, such powers and duties shall be discharged by the Vice President as Acting President.

SECTION 4. Whenever the Vice President and a majority of either the principal officers of the executive departments or of such other body as Congress may by law provide, transmit to the President pro tempore of the Senate and the Speaker of the House of Representatives their written declaration that the President is unable to discharge the powers and duties of his office, the Vice President shall immediately assume the powers and duties of the office as Acting President.

Thereafter, when the President transmits to the President pro tempore of the Senate and the Speaker of the House of Representatives his written declaration that no inability exists, he shall resume the powers and duties of his office unless the Vice President and a majority of either the principal officers of the executive department or of such other body as Congress may by law provide, transmit within four days to the President pro tempore of the Senate and the Speaker of the House of Representatives their written declaration that the President is unable to discharge the powers and duties of his office. Thereupon Congress shall decide the issue, assembling within forty-eight hours for that purpose if not in session. If the Congress, within twenty-one days after receipt of the latter written declaration, or, if Congress is not in session, within twenty-one days after Congress is required to assemble, determines by two-thirds vote of both Houses that the President is unable to discharge the powers and duties of his office, the Vice President shall continue to discharge the same as Acting President; otherwise, the President shall resume the powers and duties of his office.

AMENDMENT XXVI

Passed by Congress March 23, 1971. Ratified July 1, 1971.

Note: Amendment 14, section 2, of the Constitution was modified by section 1 of the 26th amendment.

SECTION 1. The right of citizens of the United States, who are eighteen years of age or older, to vote shall not be denied or abridged by the United States or by any State on account of age.

SECTION 2. The Congress shall have power to enforce this article by appropriate legislation.

AMENDMENT XXVII

Originally proposed Sept. 25, 1789. Ratified May 7, 1992.

No law, varying the compensation for the services of the Senators and Representatives, shall take effect, until an election of representatives shall have intervened.

PRESIDENTIAL ELECTIONS

Year	Number of States	Candidates	Parties	Popular Vote	% of Popular Vote	Electoral Vote	% Voter Participation
1789	11	**GEORGE WASHINGTON**	No party			69	
		John Adams	designations			34	
		Other candidates				35	
1792	15	**GEORGE WASHINGTON**	No party			132	
		John Adams	designations			77	
		George Clinton				50	
		Other candidates				5	
1796	16	**JOHN ADAMS**	Federalist			71	
		Thomas Jefferson	Democratic-Republican			68	
		Thomas Pinckney	Federalist			59	
		Aaron Burr	Democratic-Republican			30	
		Other candidates				48	
1800	16	**THOMAS JEFFERSON**	Democratic-Republican			73	
		Aaron Burr	Democratic-Republican			73	
		John Adams	Federalist			65	
		Charles C. Pinckney	Federalist			64	
		John Jay	Federalist			1	
1804	17	**THOMAS JEFFERSON**	Democratic-Republican			162	
		Charles C. Pinckney	Federalist			14	

Year	Number of States	Candidates	Parties	Popular Vote	% of Popular Vote	Electoral Vote	% Voter Participation
1808	17	**JAMES MADISON**	Democratic-Republican			122	
		Charles C. Pinckney	Federalist			47	
		George Clinton	Democratic-Republican			6	
1812	18	**JAMES MADISON**	Democratic-Republican			128	
		DeWitt Clinton	Federalist			89	
1816	19	**JAMES MONROE**	Democratic-Republican			183	
		Rufus King	Federalist			34	
1820	24	**JAMES MONROE**	Democratic-Republican			231	
		John Quincy Adams	Independent			1	
1824	24	**JOHN QUINCY ADAMS**	Democratic-Republican	108,740	30.5	84	26.9
		Andrew Jackson	Democratic-Republican	153,544	43.1	99	
		Henry Clay	Democratic-Republican	47,136	13.2	37	
		William H. Crawford	Democratic-Republican	46,618	13.1	41	
1828	24	**ANDREW JACKSON**	Democratic	647,286	56.0	178	57.6
		John Quincy Adams	National-Republican	508,064	44.0	83	

Year	Number of States	Candidates	Parties	Popular Vote	% of Popular Vote	Electoral Vote	% Voter Participation
1832	24	**ANDREW JACKSON**	Democratic	688,242	54.5	219	55.4
		Henry Clay	National-Republican	473,462	37.5	49	
		William Wirt	Anti-Masonic }	101,051	8.0	7	
		John Floyd	Democratic }			11	
1836	26	**MARTIN VAN BUREN**	Democratic	765,483	50.9	170	57.8
		William H. Harrison	Whig }			73	
		Hugh L. White	Whig }	739,795	49.1	26	
		Daniel Webster	Whig }			14	
		W. P. Mangum	Whig }			11	
1840	26	**WILLIAM H. HARRISON**	Whig	1,274,624	53.1	234	80.2
		Martin Van Buren	Democratic	1,127,781	46.9	60	
1844	26	**JAMES K. POLK**	Democratic	1,338,464	49.6	170	78.9
		Henry Clay	Whig	1,300,097	48.1	105	
		James G. Birney	Liberty	62,300	2.3		
1848	30	**ZACHARY TAYLOR**	Whig	1,360,967	47.4	163	72.7
		Lewis Cass	Democratic	1,222,342	42.5	127	
		Martin Van Buren	Free Soil	291,263	10.1		
1852	31	**FRANKLIN PIERCE**	Democratic	1,601,117	50.9	254	69.6
		Winfield Scott	Whig	1,385,453	44.1	42	
		John P. Hale	Free Soil	155,825	5.0		
1856	31	**JAMES BUCHANAN**	Democratic	1,832,955	45.3	174	78.9
		John C. Frémont	Republican	1,339,932	33.1	114	
		Millard Fillmore	American	871,731	21.6	8	

Year	No.	Candidate	Party	Popular Vote	%	Electoral Vote	% Participation
1860	33	**ABRAHAM LINCOLN**	Republican	1,865,593	39.8	180	81.2
		Stephen A. Douglas	Democratic	1,382,713	29.5	12	
		John C. Breckinridge	Democratic	848,356	18.1	72	
		John Bell	Constitutional Union	592,906	12.6	39	
1864	36	**ABRAHAM LINCOLN**	Republican	2,206,938	55.0	212	73.8
		George B. McClellan	Democratic	1,803,787	45.0	21	
1868	37	**ULYSSES S. GRANT**	Republican	3,013,421	52.7	214	78.1
		Horatio Seymour	Democratic	2,706,829	47.3	80	
1872	37	**ULYSSES S. GRANT**	Republican	3,596,745	55.6	286	71.3
		Horace Greeley	Democratic	2,843,446	43.9	66	
1876	38	Rutherford B. Hayes	Republican	4,036,572	48.0	185	81.8
		Samuel J. Tilden	Democratic	4,284,020	51.0	184	
1880	38	**JAMES A. GARFIELD**	Republican	4,453,295	48.5	214	79.4
		Winfield S. Hancock	Democratic	4,414,082	48.1	155	
		James B. Weaver	Greenback-Labor	308,578	3.4		
1884	38	**GROVER CLEVELAND**	Democratic	4,879,507	48.5	219	77.5
		James G. Blaine	Republican	4,850,293	48.2	182	
		Benjamin F. Butler	Greenback-Labor	175,370	1.8		
		John P. St. John	Prohibition	150,369	1.5		
1888	38	**BENJAMIN HARRISON**	Republican	5,477,129	47.9	233	79.3
		Grover Cleveland	Democratic	5,537,857	48.6	168	
		Clinton B. Fisk	Prohibition	249,506	2.2		
		Anson J. Streeter	Union Labor	146,935	1.3		

Year	Number of States	Candidates	Parties	Popular Vote	% of Popular Vote	Electoral Vote	% Voter Participation
1892	44	**GROVER CLEVELAND**	Democratic	5,555,426	46.1	277	74.7
		Benjamin Harrison	Republican	5,182,690	43.0	145	
		James B. Weaver	People's	1,029,846	8.5	22	
		John Bidwell	Prohibition	264,133	2.2		
1896	45	**WILLIAM MCKINLEY**	Republican	7,102,246	51.1	271	79.3
		William J. Bryan	Democratic	6,492,559	47.7	176	
1900	45	**WILLIAM MCKINLEY**	Republican	7,218,491	51.7	292	73.2
		William J. Bryan	Democratic; Populist	6,356,734	45.5	155	
		John C. Wooley	Prohibition	208,914	1.5		
1904	45	**THEODORE ROOSEVELT**	Republican	7,628,461	57.4	336	65.2
		Alton B. Parker	Democratic	5,084,223	37.6	140	
		Eugene V. Debs	Socialist	402,283	3.0		
		Silas C. Swallow	Prohibition	258,536	1.9		
1908	46	**WILLIAM H. TAFT**	Republican	7,675,320	51.6	321	65.4
		William J. Bryan	Democratic	6,412,294	43.1	162	
		Eugene V. Debs	Socialist	420,793	2.8		
		Eugene W. Chafin	Prohibition	253,840	1.7		
1912	48	**WOODROW WILSON**	Democratic	6,296,547	41.9	435	58.8
		Theodore Roosevelt	Progressive	4,118,571	27.4	88	
		William H. Taft	Republican	3,486,720	23.2	8	
		Eugene V. Debs	Socialist	900,672	6.0		
		Eugene W. Chafin	Prohibition	206,275	1.4		

Year	Number of States	Candidates	Parties	Popular Vote	% of Popular Vote	Electoral Vote	% Voter Participation
1916	48	**WOODROW WILSON**	Democratic	9,127,695	49.4	277	61.6
		Charles E. Hughes	Republican	8,533,507	46.2	254	
		A. L. Benson	Socialist	585,113	3.2		
		J. Frank Hanly	Prohibition	220,506	1.2		
1920	48	**WARREN G. HARDING**	Republican	16,143,407	60.4	404	49.2
		James M. Cox	Democratic	9,130,328	34.2	127	
		Eugene V. Debs	Socialist	919,799	3.4		
		P. P. Christensen	Farmer-Labor	265,411	1.0		
1924	48	**CALVIN COOLIDGE**	Republican	15,718,211	54.0	382	48.9
		John W. Davis	Democratic	8,385,283	28.8	136	
		Robert M. La Follette	Progressive	4,831,289	16.6	13	
1928	48	**HERBERT C. HOOVER**	Republican	21,391,993	58.2	444	56.9
		Alfred E. Smith	Democratic	15,016,169	40.9	87	
1932	48	**FRANKLIN D. ROOSEVELT**	Democratic	22,809,638	57.4	472	56.9
		Herbert C. Hoover	Republican	15,758,901	39.7	59	
		Norman Thomas	Socialist	881,951	2.2		
1936	48	**FRANKLIN D. ROOSEVELT**	Democratic	27,752,869	60.8	523	61.0
		Alfred M. Landon	Republican	16,674,665	36.5	8	
		William Lemke	Union	882,479	1.9		
1940	48	**FRANKLIN D. ROOSEVELT**	Democratic	27,307,819	54.8	449	62.5
		Wendell L. Willkie	Republican	22,321,018	44.8	82	
1944	48	**FRANKLIN D. ROOSEVELT**	Democratic	25,606,585	53.5	432	55.9
		Thomas E. Dewey	Republican	22,014,745	46.0	99	

Year	Number of States	Candidates	Parties	Popular Vote	% of Popular Vote	Electoral Vote	% Voter Participation
1948	48	**HARRY S. TRUMAN**	Democratic	24,179,345	49.6	303	53.0
		Thomas E. Dewey	Republican	21,991,291	45.1	189	
		J. Strom Thurmond	States' Rights	1,176,125	2.4	39	
		Henry A. Wallace	Progressive	1,157,326	2.4		
1952	48	**DWIGHT D. EISENHOWER**	Republican	33,936,234	55.1	442	63.3
		Adlai E. Stevenson	Democratic	27,314,992	44.4	89	
1956	48	**DWIGHT D. EISENHOWER**	Republican	35,590,472	57.6	457	60.6
		Adlai E. Stevenson	Democratic	26,022,752	42.1	73	
1960	50	**JOHN F. KENNEDY**	Democratic	34,226,731	49.7	303	62.8
		Richard M. Nixon	Republican	34,108,157	49.5	219	
1964	50	**LYNDON B. JOHNSON**	Democratic	43,129,566	61.1	486	61.9
		Barry M. Goldwater	Republican	27,178,188	38.5	52	
1968	50	**RICHARD M. NIXON**	Republican	31,785,480	43.4	301	60.9
		Hubert H. Humphrey	Democratic	31,275,166	42.7	191	
		George C. Wallace	American Independent	9,906,473	13.5	46	
1972	50	**RICHARD M. NIXON**	Republican	47,169,911	60.7	520	55.2
		George S. McGovern	Democratic	29,170,383	37.5	17	
		John G. Schmitz	American	1,099,482	1.4		
1976	50	**JIMMY CARTER**	Democratic	40,830,763	50.1	297	53.5
		Gerald R. Ford	Republican	39,147,793	48.0	240	

Year		Candidate	Party	Popular Vote	% Popular Vote	Electoral Vote	% Voter Participation
1980	50	**RONALD REAGAN**	Republican	43,901,812	50.7	489	52.6
		Jimmy Carter	Democratic	35,483,820	41.0	49	
		John B. Anderson	Independent	5,719,437	6.6		
		Ed Clark	Libertarian	921,188	1.1		
1984	50	**RONALD REAGAN**	Republican	54,451,521	58.8	525	53.1
		Walter F. Mondale	Democratic	37,565,334	40.6	13	
1988	50	**GEORGE H. W. BUSH**	Republican	47,917,341	53.4	426	50.1
		Michael Dukakis	Democratic	41,013,030	45.6	111	
1992	50	**BILL CLINTON**	Democratic	44,908,254	43.0	370	55.0
		George H. W. Bush	Republican	39,102,343	37.4	168	
		H. Ross Perot	Independent	19,741,065	18.9		
1996	50	**BILL CLINTON**	Democratic	47,401,185	49.0	379	49.0
		Bob Dole	Republican	39,197,469	41.0	159	
		H. Ross Perot	Independent	8,085,295	8.0		
2000	50	**GEORGE W. BUSH**	Republican	50,455,156	47.9	271	50.4
		Al Gore	Democrat	50,997,335	48.4	266	
		Ralph Nader	Green	2,882,897	2.7		
2004	50	**GEORGE W. BUSH**	Republican	62,040,610	50.7	286	60.7
		John F. Kerry	Democrat	59,028,444	48.3	251	
2008	50	**BARACK OBAMA**	Democrat	69,456,897	52.9	365	63.0
		John McCain	Republican	59,934,814	45.7	173	
2012	50	**BARACK OBAMA**	Democrat	65,915,795	51.1	332	57.5
		Mitt Romney	Republican	60,933,504	47.2	206	
2016	50	**DONALD TRUMP**	Republican	62,979,636	46.1	304	60.2
		Hillary Rodham Clinton	Democrat	65,844,610	48.2	227	
		Gary Johnson	Libertarian	4,489,235	3.3		
		Jill Stein	Green	1,457,226	1.1		

Candidates receiving less than 1 percent of the popular vote have been omitted. Thus the percentage of popular vote given for any election year may not total 100 percent.

Before the passage of the Twelfth Amendment in 1804, the electoral college voted for two presidential candidates; the runner-up became vice president.

ADMISSION OF STATES

Order of Admission	State	Date of Admission	Order of Admission	State	Date of Admission
1	Delaware	December 7, 1787	26	Michigan	January 26, 1837
2	Pennsylvania	December 12, 1787	27	Florida	March 3, 1845
3	New Jersey	December 18, 1787	28	Texas	December 29, 1845
4	Georgia	January 2, 1788	29	Iowa	December 28, 1846
5	Connecticut	January 9, 1788	30	Wisconsin	May 29, 1848
6	Massachusetts	February 7, 1788	31	California	September 9, 1850
7	Maryland	April 28, 1788	32	Minnesota	May 11, 1858
8	South Carolina	May 23, 1788	33	Oregon	February 14, 1859
9	New Hampshire	June 21, 1788	34	Kansas	January 29, 1861
10	Virginia	June 25, 1788	35	West Virginia	June 30, 1863
11	New York	July 26, 1788	36	Nevada	October 31, 1864
12	North Carolina	November 21, 1789	37	Nebraska	March 1, 1867
13	Rhode Island	May 29, 1790	38	Colorado	August 1, 1876
14	Vermont	March 4, 1791	39	North Dakota	November 2, 1889
15	Kentucky	June 1, 1792	40	South Dakota	November 2, 1889
16	Tennessee	June 1, 1796	41	Montana	November 8, 1889
17	Ohio	March 1, 1803	42	Washington	November 11, 1889
18	Louisiana	April 30, 1812	43	Idaho	July 3, 1890
19	Indiana	December 11, 1816	44	Wyoming	July 10, 1890
20	Mississippi	December 10, 1817	45	Utah	January 4, 1896
21	Illinois	December 3, 1818	46	Oklahoma	November 16, 1907
22	Alabama	December 14, 1819	47	New Mexico	January 6, 1912
23	Maine	March 15, 1820	48	Arizona	February 14, 1912
24	Missouri	August 10, 1821	49	Alaska	January 3, 1959
25	Arkansas	June 15, 1836	50	Hawaii	August 21, 1959

POPULATION OF THE UNITED STATES

Year	Number of States	Population	% Increase	Population per Square Mile
1790	13	3,929,214		4.5
1800	16	5,308,483	35.1	6.1
1810	17	7,239,881	36.4	4.3
1820	23	9,638,453	33.1	5.5
1830	24	12,866,020	33.5	7.4
1840	26	17,069,453	32.7	9.8
1850	31	23,191,876	35.9	7.9
1860	33	31,443,321	35.6	10.6
1870	37	39,818,449	26.6	13.4
1880	38	50,155,783	26.0	16.9
1890	44	62,947,714	25.5	21.1
1900	45	75,994,575	20.7	25.6
1910	46	91,972,266	21.0	31.0
1920	48	105,710,620	14.9	35.6
1930	48	122,775,046	16.1	41.2
1940	48	131,669,275	7.2	44.2
1950	48	150,697,361	14.5	50.7
1960	50	179,323,175	19.0	50.6
1970	50	203,235,298	13.3	57.5
1980	50	226,504,825	11.4	64.0
1985	50	237,839,000	5.0	67.2
1990	50	250,122,000	5.2	70.6
1995	50	263,411,707	5.3	74.4
2000	50	281,421,906	6.8	77.0
2005	50	296,410,404	5.3	77.9
2010	50	308,745,538	9.7	87.4
2015	50	321,931,311	4.3	91.1

LEGAL IMMIGRATION TO THE UNITED STATES, FISCAL YEARS 1820–2016**

Year	Number	Year	Number	Year	Number	Year	Number
1820–1989	55,457,531	1871–80	2,812,191	1921–30	4,107,209	1971–80	4,493,314
1820	8,385	1871	321,350	1921	805,228	1971	370,478
1821–30	143,439	1872	404,806	1922	309,556	1972	384,685
1821	9,127	1873	459,803	1923	522,919	1973	400,063
1822	6,911	1874	313,339	1924	706,896	1974	394,861
1823	6,354	1875	227,498	1925	294,314	1975	386,914
1824	7,912	1876	169,986	1926	304,488	1976	398,613
1825	10,199	1877	141,857	1927	335,175	1976 TQ	103,676
1826	10,837	1878	138,469	1928	307,255	1977	462,315
1827	18,875	1879	177,826	1929	279,678	1978	601,442
1828	27,382	1880	457,257	1930	241,700	1979	460,348
1829	22,520	1881–90	5,246,613	1931–40	528,431	1980	530,639
1830	23,322	1881	669,431	1931	97,139	1981–90	7,338,062
1831–40	599,125	1882	788,992	1932	35,576	1981	596,600
1831	22,633	1883	603,322	1933	23,068	1982	594,131
1832	60,482	1884	518,592	1934	29,470	1983	559,763
1833	58,640	1885	395,346	1935	34,956	1984	543,903
1834	65,365	1886	334,203	1936	36,329	1985	570,009
1835	45,374	1887	490,109	1937	50,244	1986	601,708
1836	76,242	1888	546,889	1938	67,895	1987	601,516
1837	79,340	1889	444,427	1939	82,998	1988	643,025
1838	38,914	1890	455,302	1940	70,756	1989	1,090,924
1839	68,069	1891–1900	3,687,564	1941–50	1,035,039	1990	1,536,483
1840	84,066	1891	560,319	1941	51,776	1991–2000	9,090,857
1841–50	1,713,251	1892	579,663	1942	28,781	1991	1,827,167
1841	80,289	1893	439,730	1943	23,725	1992	973,977
1842	104,565	1894	285,631	1944	28,551	1993	904,292
		1895	258,536	1945	38,119	1994	804,416
		1896	343,267	1946	108,721		

Year	Number	Year	Number	Year	Number	Year	Number
1843	52,496	1897	230,832	1947	147,292	1995	720,461
1844	78,615	1898	229,299	1948	170,570	1996	915,900
1845	114,371	1899	311,715	1949	188,317	1997	798,378
1846	154,416	1900	448,572	1950	249,187	1998	660,477
1847	234,968					1999	644,787
1848	226,527	**1901–10**	**8,795,386**	**1951–60**	**2,515,479**	2000	841,002
1849	297,024	1901	487,918	1951	205,717		
1850	369,980	1902	648,743	1952	265,520	**2001–10**	**10,503,454**
		1903	857,046	1953	170,434	2001	1,058,902
1851–60	**2,598,214**	1904	812,870	1954	208,177	2002	1,059,356
1851	379,466	1905	1,026,499	1955	237,790	2003	705,827
1852	371,603	1906	1,100,735	1956	321,625	2004	957,883
1853	368,645	1907	1,285,349	1957	326,867	2005	1,122,373
1854	427,833	1908	782,870	1958	253,265	2006	1,266,129
1855	200,877	1909	751,786	1959	260,686	2007	1,052,415
1856	200,436	1910	1,041,570	1960	265,398	2008	1,107,126
1857	251,306					2009	1,130,818
1858	123,126	**1911–20**	**5,735,811**	**1961–70**	**3,321,677**	2010	1,042,625
1859	121,282	1911	878,587	1961	271,344		
1860	153,640	1912	838,172	1962	283,763	**2011–15**	**5,356,671**
		1913	1,197,892	1963	306,260	2011	1,062,040
1861–70	**2,314,824**	1914	1,218,480	1964	292,248	2012	1,031,631
1861	91,918	1915	326,700	1965	296,697	2013	523,000
1862	91,985	1916	298,826	1966	323,040	2014	1,360,000
1863	176,282	1917	295,403	1967	361,972	2015	1,380,000
1864	193,418	1918	110,618	1968	454,448		
1865	248,120	1919	141,132	1969	358,579		
1866	318,568	1920	430,001	1970	373,326		
1867	315,722						
1868	138,840						
1869	352,768						
1870	387,203						

Source: U.S. Department of Homeland Security.

IMMIGRATION BY REGION AND SELECTED COUNTRY OF LAST RESIDENCE, FISCAL YEARS 1820–2015

Region and country of last residence	1820 to 1829	1830 to 1839	1840 to 1849	1850 to 1859	1860 to 1869	1870 to 1879	1880 to 1889	1890 to 1899
Total	128,502	538,381	1,427,337	2,814,554	2,081,261	2,742,137	5,248,568	3,694,294
Europe	99,272	422,771	1,369,259	2,619,680	1,877,726	2,251,878	4,638,677	3,576,411
Austria-Hungary	—	—	—	—	3,375	60,127	314,787	534,059
Austria	—	—	—	—	2,700	54,529	204,805	268,218
Hungary	—	—	—	—	483	5,598	109,982	203,350
Belgium	28	20	3,996	5,765	5,785	6,991	18,738	19,642
Bulgaria	—	—	—	—	—	—	—	52
*Former Czechoslovakia	—	—	—	—	—	—	—	—
Denmark	173	927	671	3,227	13,553	29,278	85,342	56,671
Finland	—	—	—	—	—	—	—	—
France	7,694	39,330	75,300	81,778	35,938	71,901	48,193	35,616
Germany	5,753	124,726	385,434	976,072	723,734	751,769	1,445,181	579,072
Greece	17	49	17	32	51	209	1,807	12,732
Ireland	51,617	170,672	656,145	1,029,486	427,419	422,264	674,061	405,710
Italy	430	2,225	1,476	8,643	9,853	46,296	267,660	603,761
Netherlands	1,105	1,377	7,624	11,122	8,387	14,267	52,715	29,349
Norway-Sweden	91	1,149	12,389	22,202	82,937	178,823	586,441	334,058
Norway	—	—	—	—	16,068	88,644	185,111	96,810
Sweden	—	—	—	—	24,224	90,179	401,330	237,248
Poland	19	366	105	1,087	1,886	11,016	42,910	107,793
Portugal	177	820	196	1,299	2,083	13,971	15,186	25,874
Romania	—	—	—	—	—	—	5,842	6,808
Russia	86	280	520	423	1,670	35,177	182,698	450,101
Spain	2,595	2,010	1,916	8,795	6,966	5,540	3,995	9,189
Switzerland	3,148	4,430	4,819	24,423	21,124	25,212	81,151	37,020
United Kingdom	26,336	74,350	218,572	445,322	532,956	578,447	810,900	328,759
*Former Yugoslavia	—	—	—	—	—	—	—	—
Other Europe	3	40	79	4	9	590	1,070	145

Asia	34	55	121	36,080	54,408	134,128	71,151	61,285
China	3	8	32	35,933	54,028	133,139	65,797	15,268
Hong Kong	—	—	—	42	50	166	247	102
India	9	38	33	—	—	—	—	102
Iran	—	—	—	—	—	—	—	—
*Israel	—	—	—	—	—	—	—	—
Japan	—	8	45	94	138	193	1,583	13,998
Jordan	—	—	—	—	—	—	—	—
*Korea	—	—	—	—	—	—	—	—
Philippines	—	—	—	—	—	—	—	—
Syria	—	—	—	—	—	—	—	—
Taiwan	—	—	—	—	—	—	—	—
Turkey	19	1	11	11	129	382	2,478	27,510
Vietnam	—	—	—	—	—	—	—	—
Other Asia	3	—	—	—	63	248	1,046	4,407
North America	9,655	31,905	50,516	84,145	130,292	345,010	524,826	37,350
Canada and Newfoundland	2,297	11,875	34,285	64,171	117,978	324,310	492,865	3,098
Mexico	3,835	7,187	3,069	3,446	1,957	5,133	2,405	734
Caribbean	3,061	11,792	11,803	12,447	8,751	14,285	27,323	31,480
Cuba	—	—	—	—	—	—	—	—
Dominican Republic	—	—	—	—	—	—	—	—
Haiti	—	—	—	—	—	—	—	—
Jamaica	—	—	—	—	—	—	—	—
Other Caribbean	3,061	11,792	11,803	12,447	8,751	14,285	27,323	31,480
Central America	57	94	297	512	70	173	279	649
Belize	—	—	—	—	—	—	—	—
Costa Rica	—	—	—	—	—	—	—	—
El Salvador	—	—	—	—	—	—	—	—
Guatemala	—	—	—	—	—	—	—	—
Honduras	—	—	—	—	—	—	—	—
Nicaragua	—	—	—	—	—	—	—	—
Panama	—	—	—	—	—	—	—	—
Other Central America	57	94	297	512	70	173	279	649
South America	405	957	1,062	3,569	1,536	1,109	1,954	1,389
Argentina	—	—	—	—	—	—	—	—
Bolivia	—	—	—	—	—	—	—	—

Region and country of last residence	1820 to 1829	1830 to 1839	1840 to 1849	1850 to 1859	1860 to 1869	1870 to 1879	1880 to 1889	1890 to 1899
Brazil	—	—	—	—	—	—	—	—
Chile	—	—	—	—	—	—	—	—
Colombia	—	—	—	—	—	—	—	—
Ecuador	—	—	—	—	—	—	—	—
Guyana	—	—	—	—	—	—	—	—
Paraguay	—	—	—	—	—	—	—	—
Peru	—	—	—	—	—	—	—	—
Suriname	—	—	—	—	—	—	—	—
Uruguay	—	—	—	—	—	—	—	—
Venezuela	—	—	—	—	—	—	—	—
Other South America	405	957	1,062	3,569	1,536	1,109	1,954	1,389
Other America	—	—	—	—	—	—	—	—
Africa	15	50	61	84	407	371	763	432
Egypt	—	—	—	—	4	29	145	51
Ethiopia	—	—	—	—	—	—	—	—
Liberia	1	8	5	7	43	52	21	9
Morocco	—	—	—	—	—	—	—	—
South Africa	—	—	—	—	35	48	23	9
Other Africa	14	42	56	77	325	242	574	363
Oceania	3	7	14	166	187	9,996	12,361	4,704
Australia	2	1	2	15	—	8,930	7,250	3,098
New Zealand	—	—	—	—	—	39	21	12
Other Oceania	1	6	12	151	187	1,027	5,090	1,594
Not Specified	19,523	83,593	7,366	74,399	18,241	754	790	14,112

Region and country of last residence	1900 to 1909	1910 to 1919	1920 to 1929	1930 to 1939	1940 to 1949	1950 to 1959	1960 to 1969	1980 to 1989
Total	8,202,388	6,347,380	4,295,510	699,375	856,608	2,499,268	3,213,749	6,244,379
Europe	7,572,569	4,985,411	2,560,340	444,399	472,524	1,404,973	1,133,443	668,866
Austria-Hungary	2,001,376	1,154,727	60,891	12,531	13,574	113,015	27,590	20,437
Austria	532,416	589,174	31,392	5,307	8,393	81,354	17,571	15,374
Hungary	685,567	565,553	29,499	7,224	5,181	31,661	10,019	5,063
Belgium	37,429	32,574	21,511	4,013	12,473	18,885	9,647	7,028
Bulgaria	34,651	27,180	2,824	1,062	449	97	598	1,124
*Former Czechoslovakia	—	—	101,182	17,757	8,475	1,624	2,758	5,678
Denmark	61,227	45,830	34,406	3,470	4,549	10,918	9,797	4,847
Finland	—	—	16,922	2,438	2,230	4,923	4,310	2,569
France	67,735	60,335	54,842	13,761	36,954	50,113	46,975	32,066
Germany	328,722	174,227	386,634	119,107	119,506	576,905	209,616	85,752
Greece	145,402	198,108	60,774	10,599	8,605	45,153	74,173	37,729
Ireland	344,940	166,445	202,854	28,195	15,701	47,189	37,788	22,210
Italy	1,930,475	1,229,916	528,133	85,053	50,509	184,576	200,111	55,562
Netherlands	42,463	46,065	29,397	7,791	13,877	46,703	37,918	11,234
Norway-Sweden	426,981	192,445	170,329	13,452	17,326	44,224	36,150	13,941
Norway	182,542	79,488	70,327	6,901	8,326	22,806	17,371	3,835
Sweden	244,439	112,957	100,002	6,551	9,000	21,418	18,779	10,106
Poland	—	—	223,316	25,555	7,577	6,465	55,742	63,483
Portugal	65,154	82,489	44,829	3,518	6,765	13,928	70,568	42,685
Romania	57,322	13,566	67,810	5,264	1,254	914	2,339	24,753
Russia	1,501,301	1,106,998	61,604	2,463	605	453	2,329	33,311
Spain	24,818	53,262	47,109	3,669	2,774	6,880	40,793	22,783
Switzerland	32,541	22,839	31,772	5,990	9,904	17,577	19,193	8,316
United Kingdom	469,518	371,878	341,552	61,813	131,794	195,709	220,213	153,644
*Former Yugoslavia	—	—	49,215	6,920	2,039	6,966	17,990	16,267
Other Europe	514	6,527	22,434	9,978	5,584	11,756	6,845	3,447
Asia	299,836	269,736	126,740	19,231	34,532	135,844	358,605	2,391,356
China	19,884	20,916	30,648	5,874	16,072	8,836	14,060	170,897
Hong Kong	—	—	—	—	—	13,781	67,047	112,132
India	3,026	3,478	2,076	554	1,692	1,850	18,638	231,649
Iran	—	—	208	198	1,144	3,195	9,059	98,141
*Israel	—	—	—	—	98	21,376	30,911	43,669

Region and country of last residence	1900 to 1909	1910 to 1919	1920 to 1929	1930 to 1939	1940 to 1949	1950 to 1959	1960 to 1969	1980 to 1989
Japan	139,712	77,125	42,057	2,683	1,557	40,651	40,956	44,150
Jordan	—	—	—	—	—	4,899	9,230	28,928
*Korea	—	—	—	—	83	4,845	27,048	322,708
Philippines	—	—	—	391	4,099	17,245	70,660	502,056
Syria	—	—	5,307	2,188	1,179	1,091	2,432	14,534
Taiwan	—	—	—	—	—	721	15,657	119,051
Turkey	127,999	160,717	40,450	1,327	754	2,980	9,464	19,208
Vietnam	—	—	—	—	—	290	2,949	200,632
Other Asia	9,215	7,500	5,994	6,016	7,854	14,084	40,494	483,601
North America	277,809	1,070,539	1,591,278	230,319	328,435	921,610	1,674,172	2,695,329
Canada and Newfoundland	123,067	708,715	949,286	162,703	160,911	353,169	433,128	156,313
Mexico	31,188	185,334	498,945	32,709	56,158	273,847	441,824	1,009,586
Caribbean	100,960	120,860	83,482	18,052	46,194	115,661	427,235	790,109
Cuba	—	—	12,769	10,641	25,976	73,221	202,030	132,552
Dominican Republic	—	—	—	1,026	4,802	10,219	83,552	221,552
Haiti	—	—	—	156	823	3,787	28,992	121,406
Jamaica	—	—	—	—	—	7,397	62,218	193,874
Other Caribbean	100,960	120,860	70,713	6,229	14,593	21,037	50,443	120,725
Central America	7,341	15,692	16,511	6,840	20,135	40,201	98,560	339,376
Belize	77	40	285	193	433	1,133	4,185	14,964
Costa Rica	—	—	—	431	1,965	4,044	17,975	25,017
El Salvador	—	—	—	597	4,885	5,094	14,405	137,418
Guatemala	—	—	—	423	1,303	4,197	14,357	58,847
Honduras	—	—	—	679	1,874	5,320	15,078	39,071
Nicaragua	—	—	—	405	4,393	7,812	10,383	31,102
Panama	—	—	—	1,452	5,282	12,601	22,177	32,957
Other Central America	7,264	15,652	16,226	2,660	—	—	—	—

Region / Country								
South America	15,253	39,938	43,025	9,990	19,662	78,418	250,754	399,862
Argentina	—	—	—	1,067	3,108	16,346	49,384	23,442
Bolivia	—	—	—	50	893	2,759	6,205	9,798
Brazil	—	—	4,627	1,468	3,653	11,547	29,238	22,944
Chile	—	—	—	347	1,320	4,669	12,384	19,749
Colombia	—	—	—	1,027	3,454	15,567	68,371	105,494
Ecuador	—	—	—	244	2,207	8,574	34,107	48,015
Guyana	—	—	—	131	596	1,131	4,546	85,886
Paraguay	—	—	—	33	85	576	1,249	3,518
Peru	—	—	—	321	1,273	5,980	19,783	49,958
Suriname	—	—	—	25	130	299	612	1,357
Uruguay	—	—	—	112	754	1,026	4,089	7,235
Venezuela	—	—	—	1,155	2,182	9,927	20,758	22,405
Other South America	15,253	39,938	38,398	4,010	7	17	28	61
Other America	—	—	29	25	25,375	60,314	22,671	83
Africa	6,326	8,867	6,362	2,120	6,720	13,016	23,780	141,990
Egypt	—	—	1,063	781	1,613	1,996	5,581	26,744
Ethiopia	—	—	—	10	28	302	804	12,927
Liberia	—	—	—	35	37	289	841	6,420
Morocco	—	—	—	73	879	2,703	2,880	3,471
South Africa	6,326	8,867	5,299	312	1,022	2,278	4,360	15,505
Other Africa	—	—	—	909	3,141	5,448	9,314	76,923
Oceania	12,355	12,339	9,860	3,306	14,262	11,353	23,630	41,432
Australia	11,191	11,280	8,404	2,260	11,201	8,275	14,986	16,901
New Zealand	—	—	935	790	2,351	1,799	3,775	6,129
Other Oceania	1,164	1,059	521	256	710	1,279	4,869	18,402
Not Specified	33,493	488	930	—	135	12,472	119	305,406

Region and country of last residence	1990 to 1999	2000 to 2009	2010	2011	2012	2013	2014	2015	2016
Total	9,775,398	10,299,430	1,042,625	1,062,040	1,031,631	990,553	1,016,518	1,051,031	1,183,505
Europe	1,348,612	1,349,609	95,429	90,712	86,956	91,095	87,790	90,789	98,043
Austria-Hungary	27,529	33,929	4,325	4,703	3,208	2,061	2,058	2,965	2,620
Austria	18,234	21,151	3,319	3,654	2,199	1,053	1,088	1,928	1,621
Hungary	9,295	12,778	1,006	1,049	1,009	1,008	970	1,037	999
Belgium	7,077	8,157	732	700	698	803	775	809	821
Bulgaria	16,948	40,003	2,465	2,549	2,322	2,720	2,886	2,585	2,560
*Former Czechoslovakia	8,970	18,691	1,510	1,374	1,316	1,258	1,168	1,236	1,299
Denmark	6,189	6,049	545	473	492	546	533	634	562
Finland	3,970	3,970	414	398	373	360	368	397	512
France	35,945	45,637	4,339	3,967	4,201	4,668	4,544	5,034	5,473
Germany	92,207	122,373	7,929	7,072	6,732	6,880	6,387	5,965	5,895
Greece	25,403	16,841	966	1,196	1,264	1,526	1,388	1,330	1,664
Ireland	65,384	15,642	1,610	1,533	1,694	1,765	1,721	1,798	1,895
Italy	75,992	28,329	2,956	2,670	2,946	3,233	3,647	3,829	4,385
Netherlands	13,345	17,351	1,520	1,258	1,294	1,376	1,373	1,505	1,550
Norway-Sweden	17,825	19,382	1,662	1,530	1,441	1,665	1,479	1,551	1,729
Norway	5,211	4,599	363	405	314	389	332	357	404
Sweden	12,614	14,783	1,299	1,125	1,127	1,276	1,147	1,194	1,325
Poland	172,249	117,921	7,391	6,634	6,024	6,073	5,437	4,921	5,287
Portugal	25,497	11,479	759	878	837	917	920	869	1,017
Romania	48,136	52,154	3,735	3,679	3,477	3,475	3,022	3,160	3,322
Russia	433,427	167,152	7,502	8,548	10,114	10,154	9,455	9,030	9,280
Spain	18,443	17,695	2,040	2,319	2,316	2,970	3,341	3,707	4,018
Switzerland	11,768	12,173	868	861	916	1,040	888	1,007	1,090
United Kingdom	156,182	171,979	14,781	13,443	13,938	15,321	14,395	14,653	14,887
*Former Yugoslavia	57,039	131,831	4,772	4,611	4,488	4,445	4,321	4,721	5,392
Other Europe	29,087	290,871	22,608	20,316	16,865	17,839	17,684	19,083	22,785

Region								
Asia	2,859,899	3,470,835	410,209	438,580	389,301	419,382	405,854	442,854
China	342,058	591,711	67,634	83,603	68,410	72,492	70,977	77,658
Hong Kong	116,894	57,583	3,263	3,149	2,614	2,515	2,426	2,982
India	352,528	590,464	66,185	66,331	65,506	74,451	61,380	61,691
Iran	76,899	76,755	9,078	9,015	9,658	8,894	9,074	9,596
*Israel	41,340	54,081	5,172	4,389	4,555	4,251	4,324	4,652
Japan	66,582	84,552	7,100	6,751	6,383	5,980	5,808	5,709
Jordan	42,755	53,550	9,327	8,211	5,949	9,028	7,835	7,345
*Korea	179,770	209,758	22,022	22,748	22,937	20,313	16,976	21,329
Philippines	534,338	545,463	56,399	55,251	52,955	48,633	54,307	50,609
Syria	22,906	30,807	7,424	7,983	3,999	4,677	5,459	3,800
Taiwan	132,647	92,657	6,785	6,206	5,336	4,712	4,814	5,062
Turkey	38,687	48,394	7,435	9,040	7,189	7,248	8,762	8,635
Vietnam	275,379	289,616	30,065	33,486	26,578	29,825	30,332	40,412
Other Asia	637,116	745,444	112,320	122,417	107,232	126,363	123,380	143,374
North America	5,137,743	4,441,529	426,981	423,277	399,380	400,102	439,228	502,639
Canada and Newfoundland	194,788	236,349	19,491	19,506	20,489	17,670	19,309	19,349
Mexico	2,757,418	1,704,166	138,717	142,823	134,198	133,107	157,227	172,726
Caribbean	1,004,687	1,053,357	139,389	133,012	121,349	133,550	146,086	180,479
Cuba	159,037	271,742	33,372	36,261	31,343	46,505	54,178	66,120
Dominican Republic	359,818	291,492	53,890	46,036	41,487	44,550	50,382	60,613
Haiti	177,446	203,827	22,336	21,802	20,083	15,107	16,787	23,185
Jamaica	177,143	172,523	19,439	19,298	19,052	18,804	17,362	22,833
Other Caribbean	181,243	113,773	10,352	9,615	9,384	8,584	7,377	7,728
Central America	610,189	591,130	43,597	43,249	44,056	43,638	46,556	54,512
Belize	12,600	9,682	997	933	969	823	804	878
Costa Rica	17,054	21,571	2,306	2,230	2,232	2,018	2,121	2,295
El Salvador	273,017	251,237	18,547	18,477	18,015	18,964	18,699	21,268
Guatemala	126,043	156,992	10,263	10,795	9,829	9,871	11,466	12,548
Honduras	72,880	63,513	6,381	6,053	8,795	8,025	9,071	12,996

Region and country of last residence	1990 to 1999	2000 to 2009	2010	2011	2012	2013	2014	2015	2016
Nicaragua	80,446	70,015	3,476	3,314	2,943	2,940	2,773	3,262	3,397
Panama	28,149	18,120	1,627	1,447	1,363	1,276	1,164	1,133	1,130
Other Central America									
South America	570,624	856,508	85,783	84,687	77,748	79,287	72,135	70,049	75,571
Argentina	30,065	47,955	4,312	4,335	4,218	4,227	3,757	3,542	3,783
Bolivia	18,111	21,921	2,211	2,113	1,920	2,005	1,663	1,549	1,481
Brazil	50,744	115,404	12,057	11,643	11,248	10,772	10,246	11,247	13,528
Chile	18,200	19,792	1,940	1,854	1,628	1,751	1,591	1,620	1,711
Colombia	137,985	236,570	21,861	22,130	20,272	20,611	17,614	16,509	16,830
Ecuador	81,358	107,977	11,463	11,068	9,284	10,553	10,871	9,816	10,779
Guyana	74,407	70,373	6,441	6,288	5,282	5,564	6,031	5,313	4,909
Paraguay	6,082	4,623	449	501	454	437	363	353	400
Peru	110,117	137,614	14,063	13,836	12,414	12,370	10,450	9,973	10,519
Suriname	2,285	2,363	202	167	216	170	160	116	130
Uruguay	6,062	9,827	1,286	1,521	1,348	1,314	1,098	1,023	911
Venezuela	35,180	82,087	9,497	9,229	9,464	9,512	8,289	8,985	10,590
Other South America	28	2	1	2	-	1	2	3	-
Other America	37	19	4			1	2	1	2
Africa	346,416	759,734	98,246	97,429	103,685	94,589	94,834	98,677	110,754
Egypt	44,604	81,564	9,822	9,096	10,172	10,719	12,043	13,907	13,367
Ethiopia	40,097	87,207	13,853	13,985	15,400	13,484	12,926	12,566	13,699
Liberia	13,587	23,316	2,924	3,117	3,451	3,036	3,681	3,580	3,545
Morocco	15,768	40,844	4,847	4,249	3,534	3,202	3,495	3,569	4,447
South Africa	21,964	32,221	2,705	2,754	2,960	2,693	2,871	3,298	3,441
Other Africa	210,396	494,582	64,095	64,228	68,168	61,455	59,818	61,757	72,255
Oceania	56,800	65,793	5,946	5,825	5,573	6,061	5,980	6,227	6,489
Australia	24,288	32,728	3,077	3,062	3,146	3,529	3,582	3,795	4,173
New Zealand	8,600	12,495	1,046	1,006	980	1,027	941	978	939
Other Oceania	23,912	20,570	1,823	1,757	1,447	1,505	1,457	1,454	1,377
Not Specified	25,928	211,930	5,814	6,217	9,265	10,127	8,430	10,256	22,726

—Represents zero or not available. *Note that a) Korea split into North Korea and South Korea in 1945; b) Czechoslovakia separated into the Czech Republic and the Slovak Republic in 1993; c) Former Yugoslavia, beginning in the 1990s, broke into the six nations of Serbia, Montenegro, Slovenia, Croatia, Macedonia, and Kosovo; d) and due to the way United States immigration statistics are recognized and collected, immigrants from the Occupied Palestinian Territories are grouped together with immigrants from Israel. **This data tracks the number of people who are annually granted legal permanent residence.

PRESIDENTS, VICE PRESIDENTS, AND SECRETARIES OF STATE

President	Vice President	Secretary of State
1. George Washington, Federalist 1789	John Adams, Federalist 1789	Thomas Jefferson 1789 Edmund Randolph 1794 Timothy Pickering 1795
2. John Adams, Federalist 1797	Thomas Jefferson, Dem.-Rep. 1797	Timothy Pickering 1797 John Marshall 1800
3. Thomas Jefferson, Dem.-Rep. 1801	Aaron Burr, Dem.-Rep. 1801 George Clinton, Dem.-Rep. 1805	James Madison 1801
4. James Madison, Dem.-Rep. 1809	George Clinton, Dem.-Rep. 1809 Elbridge Gerry, Dem.-Rep. 1813	Robert Smith 1809 James Monroe 1811
5. James Monroe, Dem.-Rep. 1817	Daniel D. Tompkins, Dem.-Rep. 1817	John Q. Adams 1817
6. John Quincy Adams, Dem.-Rep. 1825	John C. Calhoun, Dem.-Rep. 1825	Henry Clay 1825
7. Andrew Jackson, Democratic 1829	John C. Calhoun, Democratic 1829 Martin Van Buren, Democratic 1833	Martin Van Buren 1829 Edward Livingston 1831 Louis McLane 1833 John Forsyth 1834
8. Martin Van Buren, Democratic 1837	Richard M. Johnson, Democratic 1837	John Forsyth 1837
9. William H. Harrison, Whig 1841	John Tyler, Whig 1841	Daniel Webster 1841

	President	Vice President	Secretary of State
10.	John Tyler, Whig and Democratic 1841	None	Daniel Webster 1841 Hugh S. Legaré 1843 Abel P. Upshur 1843 John C. Calhoun 1844
11.	James K. Polk, Democratic 1845	George M. Dallas, Democratic 1845	James Buchanan 1845
12.	Zachary Taylor, Whig 1849	Millard Fillmore, Whig 1848	John M. Clayton 1849
13.	Millard Fillmore, Whig 1850	None	Daniel Webster 1850 Edward Everett 1852
14.	Franklin Pierce, Democratic 1853	William R. King, Democratic 1853	William L. Marcy 1853
15.	James Buchanan, Democratic 1857	John C. Breckinridge, Democratic 1857	Lewis Cass 1857 Jeremiah S. Black 1860
16.	Abraham Lincoln, Republican 1861	Hannibal Hamlin, Republican 1861 Andrew Johnson, Unionist 1865	William H. Seward 1861
17.	Andrew Johnson, Unionist 1865	None	William H. Seward 1865
18.	Ulysses S. Grant, Republican 1869	Schuyler Colfax, Republican 1869 Henry Wilson, Republican 1873	Elihu B. Washburne 1869 Hamilton Fish 1869
19.	Rutherford B. Hayes, Republican 1877	William A. Wheeler, Republican 1877	William M. Evarts 1877

	President	Vice President	Secretary of State
20.	James A. Garfield, Republican 1881	Chester A. Arthur, Republican 1881	James G. Blaine 1881
21.	Chester A. Arthur, Republican 1881	None	Frederick T. Frelinghuysen 1881
22.	Grover Cleveland, Democratic 1885	Thomas A. Hendricks, Democratic 1885	Thomas F. Bayard 1885
23.	Benjamin Harrison, Republican 1889	Levi P. Morton, Republican 1889	James G. Blaine 1889 John W. Foster 1892
24.	Grover Cleveland, Democratic 1893	Adlai E. Stevenson, Democratic 1893	Walter Q. Gresham 1893 Richard Olney 1895
25.	William McKinley, Republican 1897	Garret A. Hobart, Republican 1897 Theodore Roosevelt, Republican 1901	John Sherman 1897 William R. Day 1898 John Hay 1898
26.	Theodore Roosevelt, Republican 1901	Charles Fairbanks, Republican 1905	John Hay 1901 Elihu Root 1905 Robert Bacon 1909
27.	William H. Taft, Republican 1909	James S. Sherman, Republican 1909	Philander C. Knox 1909
28.	Woodrow Wilson, Democratic 1913	Thomas R. Marshall, Democratic 1913	William J. Bryan 1913 Robert Lansing 1915 Bainbridge Colby 1920
29.	Warren G. Harding, Republican 1921	Calvin Coolidge, Republican 1921	Charles E. Hughes 1921
30.	Calvin Coolidge, Republican 1923	Charles G. Dawes, Republican 1925	Charles E. Hughes 1923 Frank B. Kellogg 1925

	President	Vice President	Secretary of State
31.	Herbert Hoover, Republican 1929	Charles Curtis, Republican 1929	Henry L. Stimson 1929
32.	Franklin D. Roosevelt, Democratic 1933	John Nance Garner, Democratic 1933 Henry A. Wallace, Democratic 1941 Harry S. Truman, Democratic 1945	Cordell Hull 1933 Edward R. Stettinius, Jr. 1944
33.	Harry S. Truman, Democratic 1945	Alben W. Barkley, Democratic 1949	Edward R. Stettinius, Jr. 1945 James F. Byrnes 1945 George C. Marshall 1947 Dean G. Acheson 1949
34.	Dwight D. Eisenhower, Republican 1953	Richard M. Nixon, Republican 1953	John F. Dulles 1953 Christian A. Herter 1959
35.	John F. Kennedy, Democratic 1961	Lyndon B. Johnson, Democratic 1961	Dean Rusk 1961
36.	Lyndon B. Johnson, Democratic 1963	Hubert H. Humphrey, Democratic 1965	Dean Rusk 1963
37.	Richard M. Nixon, Republican 1969	Spiro T. Agnew, Republican 1969 Gerald R. Ford, Republican 1973	William P. Rogers 1969 Henry Kissinger 1973
38.	Gerald R. Ford, Republican 1974	Nelson Rockefeller, Republican 1974	Henry Kissinger 1974
39.	Jimmy Carter, Democratic 1977	Walter Mondale, Democratic 1977	Cyrus Vance 1977 Edmund Muskie 1980

	President	Vice President	Secretary of State
40.	Ronald Reagan, Republican 1981	George H. W. Bush, Republican 1981	Alexander Haig 1981 George Schultz 1982
41.	George H. W. Bush, Republican 1989	J. Danforth Quayle, Republican 1989	James A. Baker 1989 Lawrence Eagleburger 1992
42.	William J. Clinton, Democratic 1993	Albert Gore, Jr., Democratic 1993	Warren Christopher 1993 Madeleine Albright 1997
43.	George W. Bush, Republican 2001	Richard B. Cheney, Republican 2001	Colin L. Powell 2001 Condoleezza Rice 2005
44.	Barack Obama, Democratic 2009	Joseph R. Biden, Democratic 2009	Hillary Rodham Clinton 2009 John Kerry 2013
45.	Donald J. Trump, Republican 2017	Michael R. Pence, Republican 2017	Rex W. Tillerson 2017 Michael R. Pompeo 2018

FURTHER READINGS

CHAPTER 1

A fascinating study of pre-Columbian migration is Gavin Menzes and Ian Hudson, *Who Discovered America?: The Untold Story of the Peopling of the Americas* (2014). Clarissa Confer's *Daily Life in Pre-Columbian Native America* (2007) reveals what life was like before the arrival of Europeans. Erik Wahlgren describes the Norse settlements in the north Atlantic in *The Vikings and America* (2000). Alice B. Kehoe's *North American Indians: A Comprehensive Account*, 3rd ed. (2005), provides an encyclopedic treatment of Native Americans. Equally valuable is Anton Truer's *Atlas of Indian Nations* (2014). See also Charles Mann's *1491: New Revelations of the Americas before Columbus* (2005) and *1493: Uncovering the New World that Columbus Created* (2011), Colin G. Calloway's *One Vast Winter Count: The Native American West* (2006), Daniel K. Richter, *Before the Revolution: America's Ancient Pasts* (2011), and Peter Silver's *Our Savage Neighbors: How Indian War Transformed Early America* (2008). On North America's largest Native American city, see Timothy R. Pauketat, *Cahokia* (2010).

The conflict between Native Americans and Europeans is in the focus of James Axtell's *The Invasion Within: The Contest of Cultures in Colonial North America* (1986) and *Beyond 1492: Encounters in Colonial North America* (1992). Colin G. Calloway's *New Worlds for All: Indians, Europeans, and the Remaking of Early America* (1997) explores the ecological effects of European settlement while Peter Mitchell's *Horse Nations* explains the transformational impact of horses on Native Americans.

On the religious turmoil of the era, see and Matthew Carr's *Blood and Faith: The Purging of Muslim Spain* (2010), Carlos M.N. Eire's *Reformations: The Early Modern World, 1450–1650* (2016), Alec Ryrie's *Protestants: The Faith That Made the Modern World* (2017), Lyndal Roper's *Martin Luther: Renegade and Prophet* (2017), John M. Todd's *Luther: A Life* (2008), and Peter H. Wilson's *Europe's Tragedy: A History of the Thirty Years' War* (2009).

For changes in science and technology, see David Wooton's *The Invention of Science* (2015).

Laurence Bergreen examines the voyages of Columbus in *Columbus: The Four Voyages* (2011). To learn about the queen who sent Columbus to the New World, see Kristin Downey's *Isabella: The Warrior Queen* (2014). For sweeping overviews of Spain's creation of a global empire, see Hugh Thomas's *Rivers of Gold: The Rise of the Spanish Empire, from Columbus to Magellan* (2004) and *World without End: Spain, Philip II, and the First Global Empire* (2016), Robert Goodwin, *Spain: The Center of the World, 1519–1682* (2015). David J. Weber examines Spanish colonization in *The Spanish Frontier in North America* (1992). On Portugal, see Roger Crowley's *Conquerors: How Portugal Forged the First Global Empire* (2016). For the French experience, see William J. Eccles's *France in America*, rev. ed. (1990). For an insightful comparison of Spanish and English modes of settlement, see J. H. Elliott, *Empires of the Atlantic World: Britain and Spain in America, 1492–1830* (2006).

CHAPTER 2

Two excellent surveys of early American history are Peter C. Hoffer's *The Brave New World: A History of Early America*, 2nd ed. (2006), and William R. Polk's *The Birth of America: From before Columbus to the Revolution* (2006).

Bernard Bailyn's *The Barbarous Years: The Peopling of British North America: The Conflict of Civilizations, 1600–1675* (2013) tells the often brutal story of British settlement in America during the seventeenth century. On the impact of the American environment on colonial settlement, see Malcolm Gaskill's *Between Two Worlds: How the English Became Americans* (2015). The best overview of the colonization of North America is Alan Taylor's *American Colonies: The Settling of North America* (2001). On the interactions among Indian, European, and African cultures, see Andrew Lipman's *The Saltwater Frontier: Indians and the Contest for the American Coast* (2015) and Gary B. Nash's *Red, White, and Black: The Peoples of Early North America*, 5th ed. (2005).

A good overview of the founding of Virginia and Maryland is Jean and Elliott Russo's *The Early Chesapeake in British North America* (2012). For information regarding the Puritan settlement of New England, see David D. Hall's *A Reforming People: Puritanism and the Transformation of Public Life in New England* (2013). The best biography of John Winthrop is Francis J. Bremer's *John Winthrop: America's Forgotten Founding Father* (2003). On Roger Williams, see John M. Barry's *Roger Williams and the*

Creation of the American Soul (2012) and James A. Warren's *God, War, and Providence* (2018).

The pattern of settlement in the middle colonies is explained in Barry Levy's *Quakers and the American Family: British Settlement in the Delaware Valley* (1988). On the early history of New York, see Russell Shorto's *The Island at the Center of the World: The Epic Story of Dutch Manhattan and the Forgotten Colony That Shaped America* (2004). Settlement of the Chesapeake Bay region is traced in James Horn's *Adapting to a New World: English Society in the Seventeenth-Century Chesapeake* (1994). On North Carolina, see Noeleen McIlvenna's *A Very Mutinous People: The Struggle for North Carolina, 1660-1713* (2009).

On shifting political life in England, see Peter Ackroyd, *The History of England from James I to the Glorious Revolution* (2015) and Steve Pincus, *1688: The First Modern Revolution* (2009). For a study of race and the settlement of South Carolina, see Peter H. Wood's *Black Majority: Negroes in Colonial South Carolina from 1670 through the Stono Rebellion* (1974). On the flourishing trade in captive Indians, see Alan Gallay's *The Indian Slave Trade: The Rise of the English Empire in the American South, 1670–1717* (2002) and Andres Resendez's *The Other Slavery* (2016). On the Yamasee War, see Steven J. Oatis's *A Colonial Complex: South Carolina's Frontiers in the Era of the Yamasee War, 1680–1730* (2004) and William L. Ramsey's *The Yamasee War* (2010).

CHAPTER 3

The diversity of colonial societies may be seen in David Hackett Fischer's *Albion's Seed: Four British Folkways in America* (1989). John Frederick Martin's *Profits in the Wilderness: Entrepreneurship and the Founding of New England Towns in the Seventeenth Century* (1991) indicates that economic concerns rather than spiritual motives were driving forces in many New England towns.

Bernard Rosenthal challenges many myths concerning the Salem witch trials in *Salem Story: Reading the Witch Trials of 1692* (1993). Mary Beth Norton's *In the Devil's Snare: The Salem Witchcraft Crisis of 1692* (2002) emphasizes the role of Indian violence, while Stacy Schiff's *The Witches* (2016) provides a riveting analysis of the many factors influencing the outbreak of anti-witch hysteria. See also Benjamin C. Ray's *Satan and Salem: The Witch-Hunt Crisis of 1692* (2015).

Discussions of women in the New England colonies can be found in Laurel Thatcher Ulrich's *Good Wives: Image and Reality in the Lives of Women in Northern New England, 1650–1750* (1980), and Mary Beth Norton, *Separated by Their Sex: Women in Public and Private in the Colonial Atlantic World* (2011). On women and religion, see Susan Juster's *Disorderly Women: Sexual Politics and Evangelicalism in Revolutionary New England* (1994). John Demos describes family life in *A Little Commonwealth: Family Life in Plymouth Colony*, new ed. (2000).

For an excellent overview of Indian relations with Europeans, see Colin G. Calloway's *New Worlds for All: Indians, Europeans, and the Remaking of Early America* (1997). For analyses of Indian wars, see Alfred A. Cave's *The Pequot War* (1996), James D. Drake's *King Philip's War: Civil War in New England* (2000), and Jill Lepore's *The Name of War: King Philip's War and the Origins of American Identity* (1998). The story of the Iroquois is told well in Daniel K. Richter's *The Ordeal of the Longhouse: The Peoples of the Iroquois League in the Era of European Colonization* (1992). Indians in the southern colonies are the focus of James Axtell's *The Indians' New South: Cultural Change in the Colonial Southeast* (1997). On the fur trade, see Eric Jay Dolan, *Fur, Fortune, and Empire: The Epic Story of the Fur Trade in America* (2010). For the Glorious Revolution, see Steve Pincus's *1688: The First Modern Revolution* (2009).

For the social history of the southern colonies, see Allan Kulikoff's *Tobacco and Slaves: The Development of Southern Cultures in the Chesapeake, 1680–1800* (1986). On the interaction of the cultures of blacks and whites, see Mechal Sobel's *The World They Made Together: Black and White Values in Eighteenth-Century Virginia* (1987). On the slave trade, see William St. Clair's *The Door of No Return* (2007). African Americans during colonial settlement are the focus of Timothy H. Breen and Stephen Innes's *"Myne Owne Ground": Race and Freedom on Virginia's Eastern Shore, 1640–1676*, new ed. (2004). David W. Galenson's *White Servitude in Colonial America: An Economic Analysis* (1981) looks at the indentured labor force.

Henry F. May's *The Enlightenment in America* (1976) and Donald H. Meyer's *The Democratic Enlightenment* (1976) examine intellectual trends in eighteenth-century America while Jonathan Israel does the same for Europe in *Enlightenment Contested: Philosophy, Modernity, and the Emancipation of Man, 1670–1752* (2006). See also Dorinda Outram's *Panorama of the Enlightenment* (2006). On the Great Awakening, see Frank Lambert's *Inventing the "Great Awakening"* (1999), and Thomas S. Kidd's *The Great Awakening: The Roots of Evangelical Christianity in Colonial America* (2007). Excellent biographies of the key revivalists are Phillip F. Gura's *Jonathan Edwards: A Life* (2003) and Thomas S. Kidd's *George Whitefield* (2015).

CHAPTER 4

A good introduction to the imperial phase of the colonial conflicts is Douglas Edward Leach's *Arms for Empire: A Military History of the British Colonies in North America, 1607–1763* (1973). Also useful is Brendan Simms's *Three Victories and a Defeat: The Rise and Fall of the First British Empire* (2008). Fred Anderson's *Crucible of War: The Seven Years' War and the Fate of Empire in British North America, 1754–1766* (2000) is the best history of the Seven Years' War along with D. Peter MacLeod's *Northern Armageddon* (2016). For the implications of the British victory in 1763, see Colin G. Calloway's *The Scratch of a Pen: 1763 and the Transformation of North America* (2006). On the French colonies in North America, see David Hackett Fisher's *Champlain's Dream* (2008) and Allan Greer's *The People of New France* (1997).

For a narrative survey of the events leading to the Revolution, see Edward Countryman's *The American Revolution,* rev. ed. (2003) and Eric Hinderaker's *Boston's Massacre* (2017). For Great Britain's perspective on the imperial conflict, see Ian R. Christie's *Crisis of Empire: Great Britain and the American Colonies, 1754–1783* (1966). Also see Jeremy Black's *George III: America's Last King* (2007) and David Preston's *Braddock's Defeat* (2015). For the British perspective, see Nick Bunker's *An Empire on the Edge: How Britain Came to Fight America* (2015). For a social history of the Revolution, see Gary Nash's *The Unknown American Revolution* (2006).

The intellectual foundations of revolt are explored in Bernard Bailyn's *The Ideological Origins of the American Revolution* (1992). To understand how these views were connected to organized protest, see Jon Butler's *Becoming America: The Revolution before 1776* (2000) and Kevin Phillips's *1775: A Good Year for a Revolution* (2012). On the first major battle, see Nathaniel Philbrick's *Bunker Hill: A City, A Siege, A Revolution* (2013).

On the efforts of colonists to boycott the purchase of British goods, see T. H. Breen's *The Marketplace of Revolution: How Consumer Politics Shaped American Independence* (2004). For the events during the summer of 1776, see Joseph J. Ellis's *Revolutionary Summer: The Birth of American Independence.* Pauline Maier's *American Scripture: Making the Declaration of*

Independence (1997) remains the best analysis of the framing of that document. The best analysis of why Americans supported independence is Thomas Slaughter's *Independence: The Tangled Roots of the American Revolution* (2014).

CHAPTER 5

Military affairs in the early phases of the Revolutionary War are the focus of John Ferling's *Almost a Miracle: The American Victory in the War for Independence* (2009). The Revolutionary War is the subject of Gordon S. Wood's *The Radicalism of the American Revolution* (1991), Holger Hoock's *Scars of Independence: America's Violent Birth* (2017) and Jeremy Black's *War for America: The Fight for Independence, 1775–1783* (1991). John Ferling's *Setting the World Ablaze: Washington, Adams, Jefferson, and the American Revolution* (2000) highlights the roles played by key leaders. For a splendid account of Washington's generalship, see Robert Middlekauf's *Washington's Revolution: The Making of America's First Great Leader* (2015).

On the social history of the Revolutionary War, see John W. Shy's *A People Numerous and Armed: Reflections on the Military Struggle for American Independence*, rev. ed. (1990). Colin G. Calloway tells the neglected story of the Indian experiences in the Revolution in *The American Revolution in Indian Country: Crisis and Diversity in Native American Communities* (1995). For a broader assessment of the Revolution, see Alan Taylor's *American Revolutions: A Continental History* (2016).

Why some Americans remained loyal to the Crown is the subject of Thomas B. Allen's *Tories: Fighting for the King in America's First Civil War* (2010) and Maya Jasanoff's *Liberty's Exiles: American Loyalists in the Revolutionary War* (2011). A superb study of African Americans during the Revolutionary era is Douglas R. Egerton's *Death or Liberty: African Americans and Revolutionary America* (2009). For insights into the role of Native Americans in the war, see Colin Calloway's *The American Revolution in Indian Country* (1995), and Joseph Glatthaar and James Kirby Martin's *Forgotten Allies: The Oneida Indians and the American Revolution* (2007). The strategic American victory at Saratoga is the focus of Richard M. Ketchum's *Saratoga: Turning Point of America's Revolutionary War* (1999).

Carol Berkin's *Revolutionary Mothers: Women in the Struggle for America's Independence* (2005) documents the role that women played in securing independence. A superb biography of Revolutionary America's most prominent woman is Woody Holton's *Abigail Adams* (2010). A fine new biography of America's commander in chief is Ron Chernow's *Washington: A Life* (2010). The best analysis of the British side of the war is Andrew Jackson O'Shaughnessy's *The Men Who Lost America: British Leadership, the American Revolution, and the Fate of Empire* (2013).

CHAPTER 6

A good overview of the Confederation period is Richard B. Morris's *The Forging of the Union, 1781–1789* (1987). Another useful analysis of this period is Richard Buel Jr's *Securing the Revolution: Ideology in American Politics, 1789–1815* (1972). For the role played by key leaders, see Joseph J. Ellis's *The Quartet: Orchestrating the Second American Revolution, 1783-1789* (2016). David P. Szatmary's *Shays's Rebellion: The Making of an Agrarian Insurrection* (1980) covers that fateful incident. For a fine account of cultural change during the period, see Joseph J. Ellis's *After the Revolution: Profiles of Early American Culture* (1979).

An excellent overview of post-Revolutionary life is Joyce Appleby's *Inheriting the Revolution: The First Generation of Americans* (2000). On the political philosophies contributing to the drafting of the Constitution, see Ralph Lerner's *The Thinking Revolutionary: Principle and Practice in the New Republic* (1987). For the dramatic story of the framers of the Constitution, see Richard Beeman's *Plain, Honest Men: The Making of the American Constitution* (2009). Woody Holton's *Unruly Americans and the Origins of the Constitution* (2007) emphasizes the role of taxes and monetary policies in the crafting of the Constitution. The complex story of ratification is well told in Pauline Maier's *Ratification: The People Debate the Constitution, 1787–1788* (2010). An excellent study of James Madison's development as a political theorist is Michael Signer's *Becoming Madison* (2015).

On attitudes toward religion in the new United States, see Mark Lilla's *The Stillborn God: Religion, Politics, and the Modern West* (2007) and John Meacham's *American Gospel: God, the Founding Fathers and the Making of a Nation* (2006).

The best introduction to the early Federalists remains John C. Miller's *The Federalist Era, 1789–1801* (2011). Other works analyze the ideological debates among the nation's first leaders. Richard Buel Jr's *Securing the Revolution: Ideology in American Politics, 1789–1815* (1972), Joyce Appleby's *Capitalism and a New Social Order: The Republican Vision of the 1790s* (1984), and Stanley Elkins and Eric McKitrick's *The Age of Federalism: The Early American Republic, 1788–1800*

(1993) trace the persistence and transformation of ideas first fostered during the Revolutionary crisis. The best studies of Washington's political career are John Ferling's *The Ascent of George Washington: The Hidden Political Genius of an American Icon* (2009) and Edward Larson's *The Return of George Washington: Uniting the States, 1783–1789* (2015). For compelling portraits of four key leaders, see Joseph J. Ellis's *The Quartet: Orchestrating the Second American Revolution, 1783–1789* (2015).

The 1790s may also be understood through the views and behavior of national leaders. See the following biographies: Richard Brookhiser's *Founding Father: Rediscovering George Washington* (1996), *Alexander Hamilton, American* (1999), and *James Madison* (2013), and Joseph J. Ellis's *Passionate Sage: The Character and Legacy of John Adams* (1993). On social life, see Jack Larkin's *Everyday Life in America, 1790–1840* (1989).

On the formation of the federal government and its economic policies, see Thomas K. McCraw's *The Founders and Finance* (2012). Federalist foreign policy is explored in Jerald A. Comb's *The Jay Treaty: Political Battleground of the Founding Fathers* (1970) and William Stinchcombe's *The XYZ Affair* (1980).

CHAPTER 7

Marshall Smelser's *The Democratic Republic, 1801–1815* (1968) presents an overview of the Republican administrations. Even more comprehensive is Gordon S. Wood's *Empire of Liberty: A History of the Early Republic, 1789–1815* (2010). The best treatment of the election of 1800 is Edward J. Larson's *A Magnificent Catastrophe: The Tumultuous Election of 1800* (2008).

The standard biography of Jefferson is Joseph J. Ellis's *American Sphinx: The Character of Thomas Jefferson* (1996). More recent analyses include John Boles's *Jefferson* (2017) and Andrew Burstein's *Democracy's Muse* (2015). On the life of Jefferson's friend and successor, see Drew R. McCoy's *The Last of the Fathers: James Madison and the Republican Legacy* (1989). Joyce Appleby's *Capitalism and a New Social Order: The Republican Vision of the 1790s* (1984) minimizes the impact of Republican ideology.

Linda K. Kerber's *Federalists in Dissent: Imagery and Ideology in Jeffersonian American* (1970) explores the Federalists while out of power. The concept of judicial review and the courts can be studied in Cliff Sloan and David McKean's *The Great Decision: Jefferson, Adams, Marshall, and the Battle for the Supreme Court* (2009). Milton Lomask's two volumes, *Aaron Burr: The Years from Princeton to Vice President, 1756–1805* (1979) and *The Conspiracy and the Years of Exile, 1805–1836* (1982), trace the career of that remarkable American. A more recent biography is Nancy Isenberg's *Fallen Founder: The Life of Aaron Burr* (2008).

For the Louisiana Purchase, consult Jon Kukla's *A Wilderness So Immense: The Louisiana Purchase and the Destiny of America* (2003). The development of the states bordering the Gulf of Mexico is told well in Jack E. Davis's *The Gulf: The Making of an American Sea* (2017). For a captivating account of the Lewis and Clark expedition, see Stephen Ambrose's *Undaunted Courage: Meriwether Lewis, Thomas Jefferson, and the Opening of the American West* (1996).

Burton Spivak's *Jefferson's English Crisis: Commerce, Embargo, and the Republican Revolution* (1979) discusses Anglo-American relations during Jefferson's administration; Clifford L. Egan's *Neither Peace Nor War: Franco-American Relations, 1803–1812* (1983) covers America's relations with France. An excellent revisionist treatment of the events that brought on war in 1812 is J. C. A. Stagg's *Mr. Madison's War: Politics, Diplomacy, and Warfare in the Early American Republic, 1783–1830* (1983). See also Paul A. Gilje's *Free Trade and Sailors' Rights in the War of 1812* (2013). The war itself is the focus of Donald R. Hickey's *The War of 1812: A Forgotten Conflict* (1989). For the perspective of those who fought in the war, see A. J. Langguth's *Union 1812: The Americans Who Fought the Second War of Independence* (2007). See also Alan Taylor's award-winning *The Civil War of 1812: American Citizens, British Subjects, Irish Rebels, and Indian Allies* (2011).

CHAPTER 8

The best overview of the second quarter of the nineteenth century is Daniel Walker Howe, *What Hath God Wrought: The Transformation of America, 1815–1845* (2007). The classic study of transportation and economic growth is George Rogers Taylor's *The Transportation Revolution, 1815–1860* (1951). A more recent treatment is Sarah H. Gordon's *Passage to Union: How the Railroads Transformed American Life, 1829–1929* (1996). On the Erie Canal, see Carol Sheriff's *The Artificial River: The Erie Canal and the Paradox of Progress, 1817–1862* (1996). See also John Lauritz Larson's *Internal Improvement: National Public Works and the Promise of Popular Government in the Early United States* (2001). On the development of clipper ships, see Stephen Ujifusa's *Barons of the Sea: The Race to Build Clipper Ships* (2018).

Several books focus on social issues of the post-Revolutionary period, including *Keepers of the Revolution: New Yorkers at Work in the Early Republic*

(1992), edited by Paul A. Gilje and Howard B. Rock; Ronald Schultz's *The Republic of Labor: Philadelphia Artisans and the Politics of Class, 1720–1830* (1993); and Peter Way's *Common Labor: Workers and the Digging of North American Canals, 1780–1860* (1993).

On the industrial revolution, see Charles R. Morris's *The Dawn of Innovation: The First American Industrial Revolution* (2013). The impact of technology is examined in David J. Jeremy's *Transatlantic Industrial Revolution: The Diffusion of Textile Technologies between Britain and America, 1790–1830s* (1981). On the invention of the telegraph, see Kenneth Silverman's *Lightning Man: The Accursed Life of Samuel F. B. Morse* (2003). For the story of steamboats, see Andrea Sutcliffe's *Steam: The Untold Story of America's First Great Invention* (2004).

The outlook of the working class during this time of transition is surveyed in Edward E. Pessen's *Most Uncommon Jacksonians: The Radical Leaders of the Early Labor Movement* (1967). See also James R. Barrett's *History from the Bottom Up and Inside Out: Ethnicity, Race, and Identity in Working-Class History* (2017). Detailed case studies of working communities include Anthony F. C. Wallace's *Rockdale: The Growth of an American Village in the Early Industrial Revolution* (1978), Thomas Dublin's *Women at Work: The Transformation of Work and Community in Lowell, Massachusetts, 1826–1860* (1979), and Sean Wilentz's *Chants Democratic: New York and the Rise of the American Working Class, 1788–1850* (1984).

For a fine treatment of urbanization, see Charles N. Glaab and A. Theodore Brown's *A History of Urban America* (1967). On immigration, see John Bodnar's *The Transplanted: A History of Immigrants in Urban America* (1987), Roger Daniels's *Coming to America: A History of Immigration and Ethnicity in American Life* (2002), Leonard Dinnerstein's *Ethnic Americans: A History of Immigration* (2009), Jay P. Dolan's *The Irish Americans* (2008), and John Kelly's *The Graves Are Walking: The Great Famine and the Saga of the Irish People* (2012).

CHAPTER 9

The standard overview of the Era of Good Feelings remains George Dangerfield's *The Awakening of American Nationalism, 1815–1828* (1965). A classic summary of the economic trends of the period is Douglass C. North's *The Economic Growth of the United States, 1790–1860* (1961). An excellent synthesis of the era is Charles Sellers's *The Market Revolution: Jacksonian America, 1815–1846* (1991).

On Monroe, see Harlow Giles Unger's *The Last Founding Father* (2010). On John Quincy Adams, see William J. Cooper's *The Lost Founding Father* (2017) and Charles N. Edel's *John Quincy Adams and the Grand Strategy of the Republic* (2014). For diplomatic relations during James Monroe's presidency, see William Earl Weeks's *John Quincy Adams and American Global Empire* (1992). For relations after 1812, see Ernest R. May's *The Making of the Monroe Doctrine* (1975). The campaign that brought Andrew Jackson to the White House is analyzed in Robert Vincent Remini's *The Election of Andrew Jackson* (1963).

CHAPTER 10

The best comprehensive surveys of politics and culture during the Jacksonian era are Daniel Walker Howe's *What Hath God Wrought: The Transformation of America, 1815–1848* (2007) and David S. Reynolds's *Waking Giant: America in the Age of Jackson* (2008). A more political focus can be found in Harry L. Watson's *Liberty and Power: The Politics of Jacksonian America* (1990). On the rise of urban political machines, see Terry Golway's *Machine Made: Tammany Hall and the Creation of Modern American Politics* (2014).

For an outstanding analysis of women in New York City during the Jacksonian period, see Christine Stansell's *City of Women: Sex and Class in New York, 1789–1860* (1986). In *Chants Democratic: New York City and the Rise of the American Working-Class, 1788–1850* (1984), Sean Wilentz analyzes the social basis of working-class politics. More recently, Wilentz has traced the democratization of politics in *The Rise of American Democracy: Jefferson to Lincoln* (2009).

The best biography of Jackson remains Robert Vincent Remini's three-volume work: *Andrew Jackson: The Course of American Empire, 1767–1821* (1977), *Andrew Jackson: The Course of American Freedom, 1822–1832* (1981), and *Andrew Jackson: The Course of American Democracy, 1833–1845* (1984). A more critical study of the seventh president is Andrew Burstein's *The Passions of Andrew Jackson* (2003). See also Jon Meachem's *American Lion: Andrew Jackson in the White House* (2009). On Jackson and the Indians see Robert Remini's *Andrew Jackson and His Indian Wars* (2001). The story of the Trail of Tears is told in A. J. Langguth's *Driven West: Andrew Jackson and the Trail of Tears* (2011).

On Jackson's successor, consult Ted Widmer's *Martin Van Buren* (2005). Studies of other major figures of the period include John Niven's *John C. Calhoun and the Price of Union: A Biography* (1988), Merrill D. Peterson's *The Great*

Triumvirate: Webster, Clay, and Calhoun (1987), James C. Klotter's *Henry Clay: The Man Who Would be President* (2018), and *Daniel Webster: The Man and His Time* (1997).

The political philosophies of Jackson's opponents are treated in Michael F. Holt's *The Rise and Fall of the American Whig Party: Jacksonian Politics and the Onset of the Civil War* (1999) and Harry L. Watson's *Andrew Jackson vs. Henry Clay: Democracy and Development in Antebellum America* (1998). The outstanding book on the nullification issue remains William W. Freehling's *Prelude to Civil War: The Nullification Controversy in South Carolina, 1816–1836* (1965). John M. Belohlavek's *"Let the Eagle Soar!": The Foreign Policy of Andrew Jackson* (1985) is a thorough study of Jacksonian diplomacy.

CHAPTER 11

Three efforts to understand the mind of the Old South and its defense of slavery are Eugene D. Genovese's *The Slaveholders' Dilemma: Freedom and Progress in Southern Conservative Thought, 1820–1860* (1992), William W. Freehling's *The Road to Disunion: Secessionists Triumphant, 1854–1861* (2007), and Walter Johnson's *River of Dark Dreams: Slavery and Empire in the Cotton Kingdom* (2013). Stephanie McCurry's *Masters of Small Worlds: Yeoman Households, Gender Relations, and the Political Culture of the Antebellum South Carolina Low Country* (1995) describes southern households, religion, and political culture. The best recent book on the role of slavery in creating the cotton culture is Edward E. Baptist's *The Half Has Never Been Told: Slavery and the Making of American Capitalism* (2014).

Other essential works on southern culture and society include Bertram Wyatt-Brown's *Honor and Violence in the Old South* (1986), Elizabeth Fox-Genovese's *Within the Plantation Household: Black and White Women of the Old South* (1988), Catherine Clinton's *The Plantation Mistress: Woman's World in the Old South* (1982), Joan E. Cashin's *A Family Venture: Men and Women on the Southern Frontier* (1991), and Theodore Rosengarten's *Tombee: Portrait of a Cotton Planter* (1986).

John W. Blassingame's *The Slave Community: Plantation Life in the Antebellum South,* rev. and enlarged ed. (1979), Eugene D. Genovese's *Roll, Jordan, Roll: The World the Slaves Made* (1974), and Herbert G. Gutman's *The Black Family in Slavery and Freedom, 1750–1925* (1976) all stress the theme of a persisting and identifiable slave culture.

On the question of slavery's profitability, see Sven Beckert's *Empire of Cotton: A Global History* (2014), Robert William Fogel and Stanley L. Engerman's *Time on the Cross: The Economics of American Negro Slavery* (1974), Robert Johnson's *River of Dark Dreams: Slavery and Empire in the Cotton Kingdom* (2017), and Edward E. Baptist's *The Half Has Never Been Told* (2014). Charles Joyner's *Down by the Riverside: A South Carolina Slave Community* (1984) offers a vivid reconstruction of one community.

CHAPTER 12

Russel Blaine Nye's *Society and Culture in America, 1830–1860* (1974) provides a wide-ranging survey of the Romantic movement. On the reform impulse, consult Ronald G. Walter's *American Reformers, 1815–1860*, rev. ed. (1997). Revivalist religion is treated in Nathan O. Hatch's *The Democratization of American Christianity* (1989), Christine Leigh Heyrman's *Southern Cross: The Beginnings of the Bible Belt* (1997), and Ellen Eslinger's *Citizens of Zion: The Social Origins of Camp Meeting Revivalism* (1999). On the Mormons, see Alex Beam's *American Crucifixion: The Murder of Joseph Smith and the Fate of the Mormon Church* (2014).

The best treatments of transcendentalist thought are Paul F. Boller's *American Transcendentalism, 1830–1860: An Intellectual Inquiry* (1974) and Philip F. Gura's *American Transcendentalism: A History* (2007). On Henry D. Thoreau, see Michael Sims's *The Adventures of Henry Thoreau* (2014). Edgar Allan Poe is the subject of Jerome McGann's *The Poet Edgar Allan Poe: Alien Angel* (2015). For the war against alcohol, see W. J. Rorabaugh's *The Alcoholic Republic: An American Tradition* (1979) and Barbara Leslie Epstein's *The Politics of Domesticity: Women, Evangelism, and Temperance in Nineteenth-Century America* (1981). On prison reform and other humanitarian projects, see David J. Rothman's *The Discovery of the Asylum: Social Order and Disorder in the New Republic*, rev. ed. (2002), and Thomas J. Brown's biography *Dorothea Dix: New England Reformer* (1998).

Useful surveys of abolitionism include Manisha Sinha's *The Slave's Cause: A History of Abolition*(2017), James Brewer Stewart's *Holy Warriors: The Abolitionists and American Slavery*, rev. ed. (1997), and Julie Roy Jeffrey's *The Great Silent Army of Abolitionism: Ordinary Women in the Antislavery Movement* (1998). For the pro-slavery argument as it developed in the South, see Larry E. Tise's *Proslavery: A History of the Defense of Slavery in America, 1701–1840* (1987) and James Oakes's *The Ruling Race: A History of American*

Slaveholders (1982). The problems southerners had in justifying slavery are explored in Kenneth S. Greenberg's *Masters and Statesmen: The Political Culture of American Slavery* (1985). For the dramatic story of the role of the Underground Railroad in freeing slaves, see Eric Foner's *Gateway to Freedom: The Hidden History of the Underground Railroad* (2015).

CHAPTER 13

For background on Whig programs and ideas, see Michael F. Holt's *The Rise and Fall of the American Whig Party: Jacksonian Politics and the Onset of the Civil War* (1999). On John Tyler, see Edward P. Crapol's *John Tyler: The Accidental President* (2006). On the expansionist impulse westward, see Walter Nugent's *Habits of Empire: A History of American Expansionism* (2008) and Richard White's *"It's Your Misfortune and None of My Own": A New History of the American West* (1991). On the creation of the California missions, see Steven W. Hackel's *Junipero Serra: California's Founding Father* (2013) and Gregory Orfalea's *Journey to the Sun: Junipero Serra's Dream and the Founding of California* (2014).

For the expansionism of the 1840s, see Steven E. Woodworth's *Manifest DwnbExpansion and the Road to the Civil War* (2010). The movement of settlers to the West is ably documented in John Mack Faragher's *Women and Men on the Overland Trail*, 2nd ed. (2001), David Dary's *The Santa Fe Trail: Its History, Legends, and Lore* (2000), and Rinker Buck's *The Oregon Trail* (2015). For first-hand accounts of life on the Overland Trails, see Michael L. Tate, ed., *The Great Medicine Road: Narratives of the Oregon, California, and Mormon Trails* (2014). On the Donner Party tragedy, see Michael Wallis's *The Best Land under Heaven: The Donner Party in the Age of Manifest Destiny* (2017).

Gene M. Brack's *Mexico Views Manifest Destiny, 1821–1846: An Essay on the Origins of the Mexican War* (1975) takes Mexico's viewpoint on U.S. designs on the West. For the American perspective on Texas, see Joel H. Silbey's *Storm over Texas: The Annexation Controversy and the Road to Civil War* (2005). On the siege of the Alamo, see William C. Davis's *Three Roads to the Alamo: The Lives and Fortunes of David Crockett, James Bowie, and William Barret Travis* (1998) and James Donovan's *The Blood of Heroes* (2012). An excellent biography related to the emergence of Texas is Gregg Cantrell's *Stephen F. Austin: Empresario of Texas* (1999).

On James K. Polk, see Robert W. Merry's *A Country of Vast Designs: James K. Polk, the Mexican War, and the Conquest of the American Continent* (2009). The best survey of the military conflict is John S. D. Eisenhower's *So Far from God: The U.S. War with Mexico, 1846–1848* (1989). The Mexican

War as viewed from the perspective of the soldiers is described in Richard Bruce Winders's *Mr. Polk's Army: American Military Experience in the Mexican War* (1997). On the diplomatic aspects of Mexican-American relations, see David M. Pletcher's *The Diplomacy of Annexation: Texas, Oregon, and the Mexican War* (1973).

CHAPTER 14

The best surveys of the forces and events leading to the Civil War include James M. McPherson's *Battle Cry of Freedom: The Civil War Era* (1988) and *The War That Forged a Nation: Why the Civil War Still Matters* (2017), Stephen B. Oates's *The Approaching Fury: Voices of the Storm, 1820–1861* (1997), James Oakes's *The Scorpion's Sting: Antislavery and the Coming of the Civil War* (2015), and Bruce Levine's *Half Slave and Half Free: The Roots of Civil War* (1992). The most recent narrative of the political debate leading to secession is Michael A. Morrison's *Slavery and the American West: The Eclipse of Manifest Destiny and the Coming of the Civil War* (1997). The best brief history of the Civil War, at less than a hundred pages, is Louis Masur's *The Civil War: A Concise History* (2011).

Mark J. Stegmaier's *Texas, New Mexico, and the Compromise of 1850: Boundary Dispute and Sectional Crisis* (1996) probes that crucial dispute, while Michael F. Holt's *The Political Crisis of the 1850s* (1978) traces the demise of the Whigs. See also Fergus M. Bordewich's *America's Great Debate: Henry Clay, Stephen A. Douglas, and the Compromise That Preserved the Union* (2012). Eric Foner, in *Free Soil, Free Labor, Free Men: The Ideology of the Republican Party before the Civil War* (1970), shows how events and ideas combined in the formation of a new political party. The pivotal *Dred Scott* case is assessed in Earl M. Maltz's *Dred Scott and the Politics of Slavery* (2007).

On the role of John Brown in the sectional crisis, see Robert E. McGlone's *John Brown's War Against Slavery* (2009). A detailed study of the South's journey to secession is William W. Freehling's *The Road to Disunion*, vol. 1, *Secessionists at Bay, 1776–1854* (1990), and *The Road to Disunion*, vol. 2, *Secessionists Triumphant, 1854–1861* (2007). Robert E. Bonner traces the emergence of southern nationalism in *Mastering America: Southern Slaveholders and the Crisis of American Nationhood* (2009).

On the Buchanan presidency, see Jean H. Baker's *James Buchanan* (2004). Maury Klein's *Days of Defiance: Sumter, Secession, and the Coming of the Civil War* (1997) treats the Fort Sumter controversy. An excellent collection of interpretive essays is *Why the Civil War Came* (1996), edited by Gabor S. Boritt.

CHAPTER 15

On the start of the Civil War, see Adam Goodheart's *1861: The Civil War Awakening* (2011). The best one-volume overview of the Civil War period is James M. McPherson's *Battle Cry of Freedom: The Civil War Era* (1988). A more recent synthesis of the war and its effects is David Goldfield's *America Aflame: How the Civil War Created a Nation* (2011). The best brief history is Louis Masur's *The Civil War: A Concise History* (2011). A good introduction to the military events is Herman Hattaway's *Shades of Blue and Gray: An Introductory Military History of the Civil War* (1997). The outlook and experiences of the common soldier are explored in James M. McPherson's *For Cause and Comrades: Why Men Fought in the Civil War* (1997. For the global dimensions of the conflict, see Don H. Doyle's *The Cause of All Nations: An International History of the American Civil War* (2015).

The northern war effort is highlighted in Gary W. Gallagher's *The Union War* (2011). For emphasis on the South, see Gallagher's *The Confederate War* (1997). A sparkling account of the birth of the Rebel nation is William C. Davis's *"A Government of Our Own": The Making of the Confederacy* (1994). On the president of the Confederacy, see James M. McPherson's *Embattled Rebel: Jefferson Davis as Commander in Chief* (2014). . On two of the leading Confederate commanders, see Michael Korda's *Clouds of Glory: The Life and Legend of Robert E. Lee* (2014) and S. C. Gwynne's *Rebel Yell: Stonewall Jackson* (2014). On the key Union generals, see Lee Kennett's *Sherman: A Soldier's Life* (2001) and Josiah Bunting III's *Ulysses S. Grant* (2004). The controversy over Sherman's March to the Sea is the focus of Matthew Carr's *Sherman's Ghosts: Soldiers, Civilians, and the American Way of War* (2015). For a lively account of the Confederacy's leader, see James M. McPherson's *Embattled Rebel: Jefferson Davis and the Confederate Civil War* (2014).

The history of the North during the war is surveyed in Philip Shaw Paludan's *A People's Contest: The Union and Civil War, 1861–1865*, 2nd ed. (1996), and J. Matthew Gallman's *The North Fights the Civil War: The Home Front* (1994). See also Jennifer L. Weber's *Copperheads: The Rise and Fall of Lincoln's Opponents in the North* (2006). The central northern political figure, Abraham Lincoln, is the subject of many books. See James McPherson's *Abraham Lincoln* (2009) and Ronald C. White Jr., *A. Lincoln: A Biography* (2009).

The experience of the African American soldier is surveyed in Joseph T. Glatthaar's *Forged in Battle: The Civil War Alliance of Black Soldiers and White Officers* (1990) and Ira Berlin, Joseph P. Reidy, and Leslie S. Rowland's *Freedom's Soldiers: The Black Military Experience in the Civil War* (1998). For the

African American woman's experience, see Jacqueline Jones's *Labor of Love, Labor of Sorrow: Black Women, Work and the Family, from Slavery to the Present* (1985). On Lincoln's evolving racial views, see Eric Foner's *The Fiery Trial: Abraham Lincoln and American Slavery* (2010). The war's impact on slavery is the focus of James Oakes's *Freedom National: The Destruction of Slavery in the United States, 1861–1865* (2013) and Bruce Levine's *The Fall of the House of Dixie* (2013). On the emancipation proclamation, see Louis P. Masur's *Lincoln's Hundred Days: The Emancipation Proclamation and the War for the Union* (2012). For a sensory perspective on the fighting, see Mark M. Smith's *The Smell of Battle, the Taste of Siege: A Sensory History of the Civil War* (2014).

Recent gender and ethnic studies include Nina Silber's *Gender and the Sectional Conflict* (2008), Drew Gilpin Faust's *Mothers of Invention: Women of the Slaveholding South in the American Civil War* (1996), Judith Giesberger and Randall Miller's *Women and the American Civil War* (2018), George C. Rable's *Civil Wars: Women and the Crisis of Southern Nationalism* (1989), and William L. Burton's *Melting Pot Soldiers: The Union's Ethnic Regiments*, 2nd ed. (1998). What Civil War veterans experienced after the conflict ended is the subject of Brian Matthew Jordan's *Marching Home* (2015) and Gregory P. Downs's *After Appomattox: Military Occupation and the Ends of War* (2015).

CHAPTER 16

The most comprehensive treatment of Reconstruction is Eric Foner's *Reconstruction: America's Unfinished Revolution, 1863–1877* (1988). A good brief history is Alan Guelzo's *Reconstruction: A Concise History* (2018). On Andrew Johnson, see Hans L. Trefousse's *Andrew Johnson: A Biography* (1989) and David D. Stewart's *Impeached: The Trial of Andrew Johnson and the Fight for Lincoln's Legacy* (2009).

Scholars have been sympathetic to the aims and motives of the Radical Republicans. See, for instance, Herman Belz's *Reconstructing the Union: Theory and Policy during the Civil War* (1969) and Richard Nelson Current's *Those Terrible Carpetbaggers: A Reinterpretation* (1988). The ideology of the Radicals is explored in Michael Les Benedict's *A Compromise of Principle: Congressional Republicans and Reconstruction, 1863–1869* (1974). On the black political leaders, see Phillip Dray's *Capitol Men: The Epic Story of Reconstruction through the Lives of the First Black Congressmen* (2008).

The intransigence of southern white attitudes is examined in Michael Perman's *Reunion without Compromise: The South and Reconstruction, 1865–1868* (1973) and Dan T. Carter's *When the War Was Over: The Failure of*

Self-Reconstruction in the South, 1865–1867 (1985). Allen W. Trelease's *White Terror: The Ku Klux Klan Conspiracy and Southern Reconstruction* (1971) covers the various organizations that practiced vigilante tactics. On the massacre of African Americans, see Charles Lane's *The Day Freedom Died: The Colfax Massacre, the Supreme Court, and the Betrayal of Reconstruction* (2008).

The difficulties former slaves had in adjusting to the new labor system are documented in James L. Roark's *Masters without Slaves: Southern Planters in the Civil War and Reconstruction* (1977). Books on southern politics during Reconstruction include Michael Perman's *The Road to Redemption: Southern Politics, 1869–1879* (1984), Terry L. Seip's *The South Returns to Congress: Men, Economic Measures, and Intersectional Relationships, 1868–1879* (1983), and Mark W. Summers's *Railroads, Reconstruction, and the Gospel of Prosperity: Aid under the Radical Republicans, 1865–1877* (1984).

Numerous works study the freed blacks' experience in the South. Start with Leon F. Litwack's *Been in the Storm So Long: The Aftermath of Slavery* (1979). The Freedmen's Bureau is explored in William S. McFeely's *Yankee Stepfather: General O. O. Howard and the Freedmen* (1968). The situation of freed slave women is in the focus of Jacqueline Jones's *Labor of Love, Labor of Sorrow: Black Women, Work and the Family, from Slavery to the Present* (1985).

The politics of corruption outside the South is depicted in William S. McFeely's *Grant: A Biography* (1981). The best recent biography of the 18th president is Ron Chernow's *Grant* (2017). The political maneuvers of the election of 1876 and the resultant crisis and compromise are explained in Michael Holt's *By One Vote: The Disputed Presidential Election of 1876* (2008).

PHOTO CREDITS

CHAPTER 7: p. 274: Photography by Erik Arnesen © Nicholas S. West; **p. 279:** Library of Congress; **p. 282:** Collection of the New-York Historical Society, USA/Bridgeman Images; **p. 287:** Greg Vaughn/ Alamy Stock Photo; **p. 291:** Library of Congress; **p. 295:** Library of Congress; **p. 305:** Sarin Images/ GRANGER — All rights reserved.

PART III: p. 315: George Caleb Bingham, American, 1811–1879; The Verdict of the People, 1854–55; oil on canvas; 46 x 55 inches; Saint Louis Art Museum, Gift of Bank of America 45:2001; **p. 316:** Yale University Art Gallery/Wikimedia, pd; **p. 317:** The Walters Art Museum, Baltimore.

CHAPTER 8: p. 318: GRANGER — All rights reserved; **p. 325:** © Collection of the New-York Historical Society/Bridgeman Images; **p. 329:** Fenimore Art Museum, Cooperstown, New York, Gift of Stephen C. Clark, N0394.1955. Photograph by Richard Walker; **p. 332:** GRANGER — All rights reserved; **p. 335:** GRANGER — All rights reserved; **p. 340:** Board of Trustees, National Gallery of Art, Washington 1980.62.9.(2794) PA; **p. 341:** Library of Congress; **p. 344:** Library of Congress; **p. 345:** The New York Public Library/Art Resource, NY; **p. 346:** John W. Bennett Labor Collection, Special Collections and University Archives, W.E.B. Du Bois Library, University of Massachusetts Amherst; **p. 347:** GRANGER — All rights reserved.

CHAPTER 9: p. 352: Photo © Christie's Images/Bridgeman Images; **p. 357:** The Metropolitan Museum of Art, New York/Rogers Fund, 1942; **p. 359:** GRANGER — All rights reserved; **p. 365:** GRANGER — All rights reserved; **p. 366:** The Metropolitan Museum of Art, New York/Gift of I. N. Phelps Stokes, Edward S. Hawes, Alice Mary Hawes, and Marion Augusta Hawes, 1937; **p. 370:** Courtesy of Historical Society of Pennsylvania Collection,/Bridgeman Images; **p. 373:** Yale University Art Gallery/Wikimedia, pd.

CHAPTER 10: p. 378: The Museum of the City of New York/Art Resource, NY; **p. 382:** Library of Congress; **p. 384:** Library of Congress; **p. 387:** National Archives; **p. 390:** GRANGER — All rights reserved; **p. 392:** Library of Congress; **p. 394:** Courtesy Boston Art Commission 2018; **p. 397:** George Caleb Bingham, American, 1811–1879; The Verdict of the People, 1854–55; oil on canvas; 46 x 55 inches; Saint Louis Art Museum, Gift of Bank of America 45:2001; **p. 405:** © CORBIS/Corbis via Getty Images; **p. 406:** Library of Congress.

CHAPTER 11: p. 414: Universal History Archive/UIG/Bridgeman Images; **p. 417:** Eron Johnson Antiques; **p. 420:** GRANGER — All rights reserved; **p. 427:** Fotosearch/Getty Images; **p. 431:** © Atwater Kent Museum of Philadelphia/Courtesy of Historical Society of Pennsylvania Collection/Bridgeman Images; **p. 432:** The New York Historical Society/Getty Images; **p. 437:** Courtesy of the Peabody Museum of Archaeology and Ethnology, Harvard University, PM 35-5-10/53044; **p. 441:** Private Collection/Peter Newark American Pictures/Bridgeman Images; **p. 442:** The Historic New Orleans Collection/Bridgeman Images.

CHAPTER 12: p. 450: Munson-Williams-Proctor Arts Institute/Art Resource, NY; **p. 454:** GRANGER — All rights reserved; **p. 457:** The Metropolitan Museum of Art, New York/Rogers Fund, 1942; **p. 461:** Lordprice Collection/Alamy Stock Photo; **p. 464:** FineArt/Alamy Stock Photo; **p. 467:** National Portrait Gallery, Smithsonian Institution; gift of anonymous donor; **p. 469:** GRANGER — All rights reserved; **p. 471:** Library of Congress; **p. 472:** The Walters Art Museum, Baltimore; **p. 477 (left):** Library of Congress; **(right):** Private Collection/J. T. Vintage/Bridgeman Images; **p. 479:** GRANGER — All rights reserved; **p. 484:** GRANGER — All rights reserved; **p. 487:** GRANGER — All rights reserved; **p. 489 (both):** Library of Congress; **p. 492 (left):** GRANGER — All rights reserved; **(right):** Library of Congress.

PART IV: p. 499: Private Collection/The Stapleton Collection/Bridgeman Images; **p. 500:** Photo © Civil War Archive/Bridgeman Images.

CHAPTER 13: p. 502: Butler Institute of American Art, Youngstown, OH, USA/Gift of Joseph G. Butler III 1946/Bridgeman Images; **p. 506:** Library of Congress; **p. 508:** The Metropolitan Museum of Art, New York/Morris K. Jesup Fund, 1933; **p. 511:** Private Collection/Peter Newark American Pictures/Bridgeman Images; **p. 513:** © North Wind Picture Archives; **p. 517:** MPI/Getty Images; **p. 521:** Sarin Images/GRANGER — All rights reserved; **p. 528:** American Antiquarian Society, Worcester, Massachusetts, USA/Bridgeman Images; **p. 534:** Library of Congress.

CHAPTER 14: p. 540: Sarin Images/GRANGER — All rights reserved; **p. 542:** American Antiquarian Society, Worcester, Massachusetts, USA/Bridgeman Images; **p. 544:** Art Resource; **p. 547:** Sarin Images/GRANGER — All rights reserved; **p. 552:** Sarin Images/GRANGER — All rights reserved; **p. 554:** GRANGER — All rights reserved; **p. 557:** ©akg-images/The Image Works; **p. 562:** Pictorial Press Ltd/Alamy Stock Photo; **p. 567:** Hi-Story/Alamy Stock Photo; **p. 569:** Private Collection/Peter Newark American Pictures/Bridgeman Images; **p. 572:** Sarin Images/GRANGER — All rights reserved.

CHAPTER 15: p. 578: Chicago History Museum, ICHi-052424; Dennis Malone Carter, artist; **p. 586:** Bettmann/Corbis/Getty Images; **p. 587:** Public Domain; **p. 591:** Private Collection/The Stapleton Collection/Bridgeman Images; **p. 597:** Library of Congress; **p. 599:** Library of Congress; **p. 601:** Library of Congress; **p. 602:** Library of Congress; **p. 607:** Beinecke Rare Book and Manuscript Library, Yale University/Wikimedia Commons; **p. 609:** Library of Congress; **p. 610:** Boston Athenaeum, USA/Bridgeman Images; **p. 613:** Library of Congress; **p. 614:** Library of Congress; **p. 617:** Library of Congress; **p. 621:** Library of Congress; **p. 622:** National Archives.

CHAPTER 16: p. 638: Smithsonian American Art Museum, Washington, DC/Art Resource; **p. 641:** GRANGER — All rights reserved; **p. 645:** © Maryann Groves/North Wind Picture Archives; **p. 649:** Library of Congress; **p. 651:** Library of Congress; **p. 656:** Library of Congress; **p. 658:** Bettmann/Corbis/Getty Images; **p. 659:** GRANGER — All rights reserved; **p. 662:** Library of Congress.

INDEX

Page numbers in *italics* refer to illustrations.